BLACKS IN THE NEW WORLD

August Meier, Series Editor

Black Ohio
and the Color Line
1860–1915

David A. Gerber

Black Ohio and the Color Line 1860–1915

UNIVERSITY OF ILLINOIS PRESS

Urbana Chicago London

FOR C. W. K.

GN

Publication of this work was supported in part by a grant
from the Ford Foundation under its Ethnic Studies Program.

Library of Congress Cataloging in Publication Data

Gerber, David A   1944–
    Black Ohio and the color line, 1860–1915.

    (Blacks in the New World)
    Bibliography: p.
    Includes index.
    1. Afro-Americans—Ohio—History.   2. Ohio—
Race question.   I. Title.   II. Series.
E185.93.02G47   977.1′004′96073   76-27285
ISBN 0-252-00534-1

Contents

Key to Footnote Abbreviations

CHS	Cincinnati Historical Society
CCHS	Chautauqua County Historical Society
FU	Fisk University Library
HL	Rutherford B. Hayes Library
HU	Moorland-Spingarn Collection, Howard University
LC	Library of Congress, Manuscripts Division
OHS	Ohio Historical Society
UC	Joseph Regenstein Library, University of Chicago
WRHS	Western Reserve Historical Society
WU	Carnegie Library, Wilberforce University

Preface

The late Malcolm X once said something to the effect that the states of the Union have been so permeated by racism that, for black Americans, the "South" has been any place below the Canadian border. However great a truth his words might express for us, from the perspective of the northern urban upheavals in the late 1960s and the concurrent "discovery" of a profound northern racial pathology, historically black Americans have tended to proceed on different premises. At some time early in the history of racial oppression in colonial North America, generations of slaves came to understand that by following the North Star, traveling only at night and lying low during the dangerous daylight hours, they might find freedom from bondage. Ever since those early adventures in flight and freedom, the North has been the destination of blacks in quest of self-determination, dignity, and opportunity. Though the early slaves who discovered the mysteries of the North Star might well have been more African than American in their perspectives, they shared with their more Westernized descendants the hope that life might somehow be better above the Mason-Dixon Line. Thus, fed by migration from the plantations, farms, and villages of the South, the black population outside southern states has grown dramatically over the last two centuries. From just below 70,000 at the time of the nation's first census in 1790, the black population outside the South had reached some 345,000 on the eve of the Civil War, and it climbed to about a million by 1910. Since 1910, spurred by wartime prosperity and industrial growth, changes in the southern agriculture economy, and rising black expectations, this internal migration has reached epic proportions; while never more than 10 percent of Afro-Americans resided outside the South between 1790 and 1910, as many as half of the nation's 23,000,000 blacks now do, generally huddled together in the congested, deteriorating ghettoes of our northern and western cities. The consequences of this resettlement are everywhere around us and have entered our national life, inextricably intertwined with other social, economic, and political crises, to become a primary challenge to any serious agenda for domestic reconstruction.

Yet the recognition that this ever-expanding northern black minority has a long, complex, and retrievable past has been slow to emerge. We have ignored particularly the years between the Civil War and World War I, a time when the seeds of our contemporary racial situation were sown. While much (though only enough upon which to base a preliminary understanding) has been written about southern blacks between Emancipation and the Great Migration of 1916–20, and about the long-term reaction against black freedom and citizenship after the collapse of Reconstruction, we have known considerably less about northern black life following Reconstruction. Slowly, however, with impetus provided during the last two decades by dramatic developments in race relations, historians have begun to investigate the origins of the northern black ghetto, the development of black civil, political, social, and economic status in the North, and the racial attitudes of northern whites, with special concentration on the late nineteenth and early twentieth centuries. Less has been written on the internal development of northern black communities, but we are also now beginning to gain insight into their social structures and institutional life, the development of black folk culture in northern cities, and the racial attitudes, strategies, and ideologies of northern black leadership.

Through a study of Ohio's race relations and black communities in the late nineteenth and early twentieth centuries, I hope to provide perspectives on some of these problems. While I have concentrated primarily on the evolution of black citizenship and the struggle of black leadership to speed the pace of racial advancement, I have attempted to relate the ongoing development of race relations, national and local, and the internal development of black communities to the study of both. Ohio can provide us with an interesting and important case study of the patterns of northern race relations and black community development. In addition to the fact that Ohio had one of the largest black populations in the North throughout the nineteenth century, the state witnessed a constant stream of intrastate and interstate black migration, the former from the rural areas and villages where early generations of black settlers tended to reside, and the latter from the surrounding border states of the Upper South to the large cities. Growing and shifting black populations posed an important threat to the existing racial status quo, challenging both black and white attitudes toward racial advancement, accelerating the pace of black community development in the cities, and complementing national and

regional forces in setting the pattern of race relations and racial progress. Furthermore, Ohio's own intrastate regionalism, particularly evident in the development of its race relations, provides an excellent
cross-section of the people and attitudes found throughout the Midwest, thus permitting a comparative perspective. Finally, during the
late nineteenth century the Ohio state legislature, influenced greatly
by the power of blacks in state and local politics, served as an important forum for the discussion and legal resolution of significant racial
issues, providing us with a particularly clear insight into the dynamics
of racial advancement in a northern state in that period.

Along the way, I have come to owe thanks to many individuals and
institutions. Of the latter, I would offer special thanks to the American
Institute for Marxist Studies, the American Baptist Historical Society,
the Amistad Research Center, the Akron Public Library, the Allen
County Historical Society, the Olive Kettering Library of Antioch Col-
lege, the Joseph Regenstein Library of the University of Chicago, the
Chicago Historical Society, the University of Cincinnati Library, the
Cincinnati Historical Society, the Chautauqua County Historical So-
ciety, the Public Library of Cincinnati and Hamilton County, the Cin-
cinnati Board of Education, the Columbus Board of Education, the
Carnegie Public Library of Washington Court House (Ohio), the
Cleveland Public Library, the Dayton Board of Education, the William
Perkins Library of Duke University, the Darke County Historical So-
ciety, the Green County District Library of Xenia (Ohio), the Ruther-
ford B. Hayes Library, the Moorland-Spingarn Collection of Howard
University, and the Houghton Library of Harvard University. In addi-
tion, thanks must also go to Fisk University Library, the Manuscripts
Division of the Library of Congress, the Oberlin College Library, the
Ohio University Library, the Ohio State University Library, the Ohio
State University Archives, the Mahoning Valley Historical Society, the
Cartographic Division of the National Archives, the Steubenville Public Library, the Western Reserve Historical Society, the Warden Public
Library of Springfield (Ohio), the Warren County Historical Society,
the State Historical Society of Wisconsin, and the John McIntire Public Library of Zanesville, Ohio. A very profound and special debt of
gratitude is owed the Ohio Historical Society at Columbus and its
very helpful and considerate staff.

A number of archivists, librarians, and others were of great help. I
thank Marion Bates, Doris Berger, Julie and David Berkowitz, Charles
Cooney, Russell H. Davis, Mrs. G. F. Dalavie, Sara Fuller, Frances
Forman, Dennis Harrison, Virginia Hawley, Ruth Helmuth, David

Larson, Frank Levstick, George Kirk, Kermit Pike, Dorothy Porter, Russell Jelliffe, Clifton Johnson, Joyce Merritt, Melwood Stanhope, Myron Siefert, the Reverend Edward C. Starr, Ann Lowry Weir, and Conrad Weitzel. I thank as well my various research assistants and helpers, Judith Arnold, Julie Brocklehurst, David Miller, and Jerel Zoltick. Finally, a number of historians offered important advice and criticism. C. Vann Woodward, Lewis Perry, David Katzman, and James McPherson read and deeply influenced the manuscript at various stages, while Herbert Aptheker, Brewton Berry, Herbert Gutman, and Christopher Wye provided me with important leads to helpful data. My greatest debt is to August Meier, a diligent, exacting, and dedicated scholar and editor, who helped me at every stage of my work.

I have also depended upon the very generous financial support of the Ford Foundation's program of fellowships in ethnic studies, the Research Foundation of the State University of New York, and lastly and most profoundly the Shelby Cullom Davis Center of the department of history at Princeton University, which provided me with the much-needed free time to finish this manuscript.

—D. A. G.

Part I

Black Ohio: Origins and Development in the Late Nineteenth Century

1

Ante-Bellum: Race Relations
and Black Life before 1860

I

For the newly organized territories of the old northwestern frontier, there was from the beginning a problem of black-white relations. On the fringes of the slave South, areas in the probable path of southern black migration were likely to have among their early settlers southern partisans of slavery or repression of the free Negro. The future states of Illinois, Indiana, and Ohio particularly could not long avoid conflict and tension over their relation to slavery and to black America. The federal government, which was then in the throes of an agonizing and ultimately limited attempt to reconcile the democratic ethos of the American Revolution with slavery and racism, had decided that slavery would not exist within the Northwest Territory's boundaries. The Northwest Ordinance of 1787 barred the transplanting of the slave system into the region east of the Mississippi and north of the Ohio. Though pro-slavery partisans made spirited attempts to overturn this decision, they were unsuccessful.[1]

Ohio's first constitutional convention, meeting in 1802, showed a strong desire to keep slavery from the state. Indeed, most delegates were so adamant on the exclusion of slavery that they took special pains to insure that the state constitution protected black apprentices and servants from a lapse into involuntary servitude. The convention showed greater ambiguity, however, on the question of Negro rights. While refusing to restrict a broad range of civil rights, such as the rights of settlement, jury service, eligibility for the state militia, and giving testimony in court, it choose to deny blacks the vote. For the most part, Ohio's founding fathers intended to permit blacks to reside

[1] Charles T. Hickok, *The Negro in Ohio, 1802–1870* (Cleveland, 1896), ch. 1.

in the state and enjoy the protection of its laws, but to have no part in governing.[2]

The state legislature was more directly representative of and responsive to the racial views of the white majority than the constitutional convention, and in the following years it created harshly proscriptive "black laws" which rigidly defined the civil status of blacks.[3] Though Ohio's founding fathers had refused to restrict black settlement, and though in 1800 there were only 337 blacks (less than 1 percent of the total population) among Ohio's pioneers, the legislature acted in 1804 and 1807 to make black settlement difficult. Blacks entering the state were required to register themselves and their families with county clerks, to carry certificates attesting to their freedom, and to post $500 bond within twenty days of arrival in Ohio. Whites employing unregistered blacks or harboring fugitives from slavery were subject to criminal prosecution. While unwieldy and generally unsuccessful in limiting black population growth, these laws provided an excellent weapon in the periodic harassment of black residents.[4]

In addition, the legislature acted to curb or remove civil protection and security. After 1802, black testimony in cases involving whites was prohibited, and the legislature acted in 1824, 1828, and 1831 to exclude blacks from jury service. Laws limiting their status as legal residents also made it impossible for blacks to obtain public charity. After 1803, the race was denied service in the state militia.[5] Nor was Ohio an exception to the almost universal denial of public education to blacks during the early nineteenth century. Though the first Ohio public school law was passed in 1821 and blacks were taxed locally to support the public schools, they were universally excluded from the state's new school system. No provision was made for their education until 1829, and even then a general refusal of many local officials to create black schools under the law caused its repeal two years later. In the next years, only a very few black children attended the regular public schools with their white peers. Thus during Ohio's first decades most black children were educated in private academies, financed by black and white contributions and often held in the back of churches or in crude shacks, or by individual private tutors.[6]

    [2] Helen M. Thurston, "The 1802 Ohio Constitutional Convention and the Status of the Negro," *Ohio History,* LXXXI (Winter, 1972), 21–35.
    [3] Betty Culpepper, "The Negro and the Black Laws of Ohio, 1803–1860" (Master's thesis, Kent State University, 1965), pp. 6–17; this thesis and "Race Hate in Early Ohio," *Negro History Bulletin,* X (June, 1947), 203–210, both list all the individual "black laws."
    [4] Thurston, "1802 Ohio Constitutional Convention," 35–37.
    [5] Culpepper, "Negro and Black Laws," pp. 9, 15–16.
    [6] Leonard Erickson, "The Color Line in Ohio Public Schools, 1829–1890"

By the early 1830s the repressive black laws were complete. Only gradually, and then not always successfully, would the legal proscription of black rights be challenged. As sectional hostility over slavery intensified throughout the nation in the next twenty years, the political forces of anti-slavery and abolition began to acquire power in Ohio and to work for recognition of black citizenship. In 1849 and 1850 the Free Soil party used its balance of power in the legislature, in which pro-slavery Democrats held a plurality, to win repeal of laws prohibiting black testimony and requiring blacks to post bond when entering Ohio. At the same time, the legislature began to provide for public black education. Legislation passed in 1849 obliged township trustees to use a prorated share of the common school fund for support of black schools, and it was supplemented in 1853 with a law providing guidelines for the creation of black school districts. The laws did not specifically bar integration by local initiative, but this option was not likely to be considered in the vast majority of communities. Implementation of the black school laws left much to be desired. The hostility of local white school officials often combined with meager funding to produce educational opportunities which were far from equal to white ones. Black schools were often poorly located and widely scattered. Some schools still were held in shacks, or occasionally blacks inherited white school buildings which had been abandoned because of age, size, or dilapidation. The curriculum was weak, the school year short, and teachers few; seldom was provision made for black schooling beyond training in basic literacy skills. This situation was never corrected during the ante-bellum period. The repeal of the testimony and bond laws marked the end of the ameliorative trend in the legislature, leaving black education inadequate and the laws barring black jury and militia service, voting, and public relief intact.[7]

As the black legal position evolved, so did racial custom, which worked informally to separate the races and limit black opportunity. Most blacks were poor and suffered sharply proscribed employment possibilities. While a few were able to acquire farms, most rural blacks were farm laborers or tenant farmers. Black artisans met with fierce competition and discrimination in attempts to practice their trades. Only where white competition was not considerable, where white mechanics' associations did not attempt to stop skilled blacks from get-

(Ph.D. dissertation, Ohio State University, 1959), pp. 54–71, 120–140, 174–177; Hickok, *Negro in Ohio*, pp. 103–105.

[7] Leonard Erickson, "Politics and the Repeal of Ohio's Black Laws, 1837–1849," *Ohio History*, LXXXII (Summer–Autumn, 1973), 154–175; Hickok, *Negro in Ohio*, pp. 50–52; Erickson, "Color Line in Ohio Public Schools," pp. 210–250.

ting work, and where black artisans (often through hard work at low wages) established reputations for very high quality work did blacks find a niche in the trades. Only in providing domestic and personal service for whites as barbers, servants, or laundresses did blacks have relatively unblocked opportunity. Though there were a handful of black retailers in the cities and towns, it was largely through service work that a few entrepreneurs emerged—for example, as barbershop owners or caterers. The vast majority, kept from the burgeoning factories and mills and from skilled work, labored as menials (porters, hostlers, janitors, clean-up workers, etc.) and as common day laborers on farms, in construction, on boats and docks. While work was plentiful in an expanding economy, this type of employment was often irregular and seasonal, and, in the case of common labor, adversely and immediately affected by the economic slumps.[8]

Whites shunned personal contact with blacks and kept them from hotels, restaurants, theaters (or at least the better seats), railroads (or at least the first-class cars), streetcars, and private hospitals and orphanages. Though blacks paid taxes for the support of local and county asylums and infirmaries, the mores of most communities barred them from using these facilities. Unless they received support or residence within the racial community, blacks who were poor, orphaned, insane, feeble, and elderly found their home and aid in jails, the only public institutions to which they were admitted. Nor did the universalistic doctrines of Christianity break the color line. Few blacks attended churches with whites; when they did, they were often confined to separate pews.[9]

[8] Richard C. Wade, "The Negro in Cincinnati, 1800–1830," *Journal of Negro History*, XXXIX (Jan., 1954), 45–56; Carter Woodson and Lorenzo Green, *The Negro Wage Earner* (Washington, 1930), p. 5; Ohio Anti-Slavery Convention, *Report on the Condition of the People of Color in the State of Ohio* (n.p., 1835), pp. 3, 8–12; "Race Hate in Early Ohio," p. 210; Richard W. Pih, "Negro Self-Improvement Efforts in Ante-Bellum Cincinnati, 1836–1850," *Ohio History*, LXXVIII (Summer, 1969), 181–182; Leonard Harding, "The Negro in Cincinnati, 1860–1870: A Demographic Study of a Transitional Decade" (Master's thesis, University of Cincinnati, 1967), pp. 2–17; Martin R. Delany, *The Condition, Elevation, Emigration, and Destiny of the Colored People* (Philadelphia, 1852), pp. 97–99, 145; J. F. Clarke, *The Present Condition of the Free People of Color of the United States* (Worcester, 1859), pp. 11–12.
[9] Leon Litwack, *North of Slavery: The Negro in the United States, 1790–1860* (Chicago, 1961), pp. 97–100; Hickok, *Negro in Ohio*; Benjamin Arnett, ed., *Proceedings of the Semi-Centenary Celebration of the African Methodist Episcopal Church of Cincinnati* (Cincinnati, 1874), p. 41; Calvary United Methodist Church, Cincinnati, *100th Anniversary, 1870–1970, Souvenir Centennial Edition* (Cincinnati, 1970), p. 1; Allen Temple, Centennial Commission, *Centennial Guide Allen Temple, A.M.E. Church . . . 1924* (Cincinnati, 1924), p. 10; Ohio Anti-Slavery Society, *Proceedings of a Convention of the Colored Men of Ohio . . . Cincinnati . . . November, 1858* (Cincinnati, 1858), p. 6.

Interracial intimacy was sanctioned when blacks served whites. Those who could afford the services of the coachman, butler, waiter, or bootblack had close contact with blacks, set in a context which did not disturb caste relations and governed by an attitude among whites that was paternalistic rather than egalitarian. Contacts between black domestics and the whites they served might occasionally be extended to include the blacks attending their employer's church. On the other hand, for those whites who could not regularly, if ever, afford the luxury of such services, yet wished at the same time to think of themselves as upwardly mobile, their ability to separate themselves from blacks and to check black economic competition helped to provide assurance, however dubious, of their own higher social status. There was then a tendency for racial asperities to increase as blacks came into economic competition and social contact with whites of equivalent socioeconomic status. This was particularly the case in the relations between blacks and the poverty-stricken Irish immigrants who began to enter Ohio cities and towns in the 1840s. The masses of unskilled, untutored, and scorned Irish who lived in the slums and worked on the docks alongside blacks at Cincinnati, Cleveland, and Toledo had an especially strong desire to raise their own status while leaving blacks behind them at the bottom of the social order. Frustrated in such efforts, they might channel their energies into hatred.[10] Thus few whites were unburdened enough by racial conventions to associate with blacks on an egalitarian basis. Indeed, probably only within the ranks of the most militant abolitionists or within the integrated urban demimonde of gamblers, thieves, and prostitutes did the races mingle freely, for each of these worlds defied society and its racial concerns.[11]

The white community's unwritten racial code also checked the attempt of Ohio's courts to recognize the citizenship and equality of at least one segment of the black population—the light-skinned. Unlike other New World societies which have faced the problem of black-white relations, the United States has failed to allow lighter Negroes to emerge as a separate caste with greater status and privilege.[12] Yet

[10] Pih, "Negro Self-Improvement," 180; Carter Woodson, "The Negroes of Cincinnati prior to the Civil War," *Journal of Negro History*, I (Jan., 1916), 5, 13; Carl Wittke, *The Irish in America* (Baton Rouge, 1956), pp. 29, 40–52.

[11] Intermingling in the demimonde was common in ante-bellum southern cities; Richard C. Wade, *Slavery in the Cities* (New York, 1964), pp. 156–157, 258–262. Lafcadio Hearn's Cincinnati reportage during the 1870s evocatively illustrates the ease of interracial mingling among the deviant poor in the dock and warehouse district of that city's notorious waterfront; see O. W. Frost, ed., *Children of the Levee* (Lexington, 1957). For social contacts between blacks and Ohio abolitionists, see Litwack, *North of Slavery*, pp. 220, 222–223.

[12] Explanations of the status differences of lighter-skinned Negroes in the United States and elsewhere are found in Winthrop Jordan, *White over Black:*

in ante-bellum Ohio the light-skinned were given a degree of special consideration, at least in law. In limiting the application of the suffrage, jury, militia, testimony, and education clauses of the state constitution and statutes to whites during the first decades of statehood, Ohio's lawmakers had left to the state supreme court the knotty problem of defining the word "white." In cases brought before the court by light-skinned Negroes during the 1830s and 1840s, the justices ruled that persons with more than 50 percent white ancestry must be considered "white" in their civil and political relations with society.[13]

To the extent that the court's decisions encouraged interracial contacts and civil equality, they were far from popular. The ever-narrowing majorities by which they were decided revealed that the judges themselves were becoming aware that they were in advance of public opinion. Before the Civil War, a judicial reaction had in fact begun. In 1859, in a case in which the court was asked to allow children with a preponderance of white ancestry to attend the regular public schools, the court overturned its own precedent and decided against admitting very light-skinned children into the schools.[14]

Doubtless the new ruling reflected social practice. While a very few light-skinned children occasionally attended integrated schools in cities where the dual school system was the rule (as, for example, at Cincinnati),[15] the tendency of custom was for anyone with a perceptible trace of African ancestry to be separated from society in the areas of potential interracial contact in which whites drew the color line on darker-skinned Negroes. In order for mulattoes to mingle freely and equally with whites in ante-bellum Ohio, it was more than likely that they had to "pass" for white.

Custom and political expediency helped define the voting opportunities of the light-skinned. While the ante-bellum courts continued to protect mulatto voting, the attitudes of local election officials varied according to local race relations and political alignments. Where they controlled the process of elections, Ohio's ante-bellum Democrats

American Attitudes toward the Negro, 1550–1812 (Chapel Hill, 1968), pp. 136–178; Marvin Harris, *Patterns of Race in the Americas* (New York, 1964), pp. 79–94; and Carl N. Degler, *Neither Black nor White: Slavery and Race Relations in Brazil and the United States* (New York, 1971), pp. 205–264.

[13] Polly Grey v. State of Ohio, 4 Ohio State Reports 353 (1831); Williams v. School Directors, 6 Ohio State Reports 570 (1834); Parker Jeffries v. John Ankeny et al., 11 Ohio State Reports 372 (1842); Edwin Thacker v. John Hawk et al., 11 Ohio State Reports 376 (1842).

[14] Van Camp v. Board of Education, 9 Ohio State Reports 407 (1859); Frank U. Quillin, *The Color Line in Ohio* (Ann Arbor, 1913), p. 18.

[15] Woodson, "Negroes of Cincinnati before Civil War," 18.

showed little desire to allow the antislavery Whig (and, later, Republican) mulattoes to vote.[16]

II

Ante-bellum Ohio was by no means unique among northern states in its development of comprehensive racial proscription, but its anti-black laws were certainly among the most severe. The state's location and the origins of many of its early white settlers help explain the development of this harsh legal repression. It was generally feared, particularly in the southern and central counties, that Ohio's common border with Kentucky and Virginia would make it a haven for free blacks and recently manumitted or fugitive slaves—a prospect unappealing to most early settlers. Accentuating anxieties over black in-migration were the class and geographical origins of many early Ohioans. Southerners and their descendants were found in considerable numbers in the southern and central regions. In the Virginia Military District of southwestern Ohio, a fifteen-county area between the Scioto and Little Miami rivers which was established after the American Revolution for the settlement of veterans from Virginia, Southerners formed a majority of the early white population. Immediately to the east, in the Symmes Purchase area between the Little and Great Miami rivers, Southerners also constituted a substantial percentage of the population. Most often representatives of the non-slave-holding, small farmer South rather than the plantation aristocracy, Ohio's Southerners had often migrated north to escape the economic and social effects upon their class of the slave system, which limited their socioeconomic mobility and access to political power. Yet they brought with them the anti-slavery, anti-black attitudes they had developed in their frustrating economic and political competition with slave labor and powerful white slave-holding interests. They wanted to limit black migration, and their political representatives were particularly outspoken among those calling for comprehensive legal proscription of blacks.[17]

[16] Alfred J. Anderson v. Thomas Milliken et al., 9 Ohio State Reports 596 (1859); Eugene H. Roseboom, *The Civil War Era, 1850–1873* (Columbus, 1944), pp. 341–342.

[17] Robert E. Chaddock, *Ohio before 1850: A Study of the Early Influence of Pennsylvania and Southern Populations in Ohio* (New York, 1908), p. 31–46; John D. Barnhart, "Sources of Southern Migration into the Old Northwest," *Mississippi Valley Historical Review*, XXII (June, 1935), 49–62, and Barnhart, "The Southern Influence in the Formation of Ohio," *Journal of Southern History*, III (Feb., 1937), 28–42. In 1850, 27% of Ohio's population was composed of persons born in the South; by 1860, after a decade of considerable migration from Europe and from other states into Ohio, a high rate of natural increase, and a de-

It was to be expected that the mood and practice of race relations in the areas in which these Southerners settled and influenced the creation of regional cultural patterns would be characterized by great intolerance. Indeed, the further one moved toward the banks of the Ohio, the more strictly were law and custom invoked to depress the Negro's status. But the nativity and heritage of white southern settlers was not the only factor which determined the evolving pattern of ante-bellum race relations. The intrastate variants in the patterning of race relations which came to characterize Ohio resulted from a complex interplay of factors. Unfortunately for those southern whites who came to Ohio to escape contact with blacks, it was in the river border and surrounding counties (particularly of south-central and southwestern Ohio), shading off into central Ohio's especially fertile farmlands, that the majority of the state's blacks would settle. In the counties along the Ohio, Scioto, and Little and Great Miami rivers, the percentage of blacks often grew quite large, for a northern state, ranging up to 8 percent by 1860 (as high in absolute terms as several thousand), with percentages in local communities as high as 17 percent (802 blacks in a population of 4,658) in 1860 at Xenia.[18] In and of themselves, large black populations in southern and central Ohio were enough to increase the possibility of racial tension considerably; but the mix of large black and southern white populations in southerly counties particularly lent itself to a rigidly proscribed pattern of interracial contacts.

Southern Ohio in the ante-bellum period maintained close economic and social ties with the slave South; these also lent a bit of southern flavor to lower Ohio communities. Connected to the South by steamboats which plied the Mississippi and Ohio, Cincinnati served as a commercial and financial center for southern planters. A string of lesser but bustling ports, including Marietta, Ironton, Portsmouth, Gallipolis, and Middleport, also had close economic ties with Virginia and Kentucky. Planters annually took the waters at noted spas in southwestern Ohio, particularly patronizing Tawawa Springs near Xenia. Even bondage found its way into Ohio. While slavery had no legal status in Ohio,

cline in the number of southern-born, the percentage fell to 5.8. Cincinnati is the only city for which ante-bellum census data on nativity of inhabitants exists; the southern-born constituted 5% (8,183 persons) of its population in 1860. Unfortunately, the census does not tell us how many persons *descended* from southern-born Ohioans resided in the state. U.S. Census Office, *The Seventh Census of the United States, 1850* (Washington, 1853), p. xxxvi, and *Population of the United States in 1860 . . . Eighth Census* (Washington, 1864), I, 398, 612.

[18] U.S. Census Office, *Ninth Census of the United States . . . 1870* (Washington, 1872), I, 226–241.

slaves trained in the arduous work of tobacco cultivation were hired from Kentucky masters by Ohio growers, and during the early decades of the nineteenth century bands of slaves could be seen crossing the Ohio at daybreak to work in the tobacco fields.[19]

In light of the pattern of black and white settlement and the ties of many whites with the slave states, it is not surprising that in the southern counties and in the river valleys of the Scioto and Miami in the central counties the color line in institutions and accommodations was rigid. From here most memorials against black settlement were sent to the legislature, and here most ante-bellum mob demonstrations against black settlers took place. Here, too, were communities which for many decades, even into the twentieth century, refused to allow blacks to reside within their borders. And here the American Colonization Society, founded in 1817 to foster the transplanting of free Negroes from American to African soil, found some of its most enthusiastic support.[20]

Southern and central Ohio were not monolithic, however, in either racial attitudes or practices. Particularly in the easterly counties but also in some southwestern ones, there resided New Englanders and Pennsylvanians who held more tolerant racial views. Along with renegade Southerners, Quakers, and blacks, they filled the ranks of the active antislavery and abolitionist movements, occasionally braving harassment to express their views; they also served as conductors on Ohio's Underground Railroad, aiding fugitives to safety and freedom.[21] Unusual education opportunities for blacks also existed in some areas, particularly in Greene County. While serving as president of Antioch College in Yellow Springs in 1856 and 1857, New Englander Horace Mann defied his board of trustees and faced the loss of several white students when he accepted blacks at the college. Nearby at Tawawa

[19] David Carl Shilling, "The Relation of Southern Ohio to the South during the Decade Preceding the Civil War," *Historical and Philosophical Society of Ohio Quarterly*, VIII, 1 (1913), 6–15, 27; "Concerning the Origins of Wilberforce," *Journal of Negro History*, VIII (July, 1923), 335–337; Chaddock, *Ohio before 1850*.

[20] Hickok, *Negro in Ohio*, ch. 4; Woodson, "Negroes of Cincinnati before Civil War," 1–16; Carter Woodson, *A Century of Negro Migration* (Washington, 1918), p. 57; Edward Wesley Shunk, "Ohio in Africa," *Ohio Archeological and Historical Quarterly*, LI, 1 (1942), 79–88; Francis Weisenburger, *The Passing of the Frontier, 1825–1850* (Columbus, 1841), p. 366; Quillin, *Color Line in Ohio*, pp. 32, 36–43; Gerald N. Grob, *Mental Institutions in America: Social Policy to 1875* (New York, 1973), p. 245.

[21] Weisenburger, *Passing of Frontier*, pp. 363–386; Eugene Roseboom, "Southern Ohio and the Union in 1863," *Mississippi Valley Historical Review*, XXXIX (June, 1952), 31–35; Wilbur H. Siebert, *The Mysteries of Ohio's Underground Railroads* (Columbus, 1951); Chaddock, *Ohio before 1850*, pp. 31–46.

Springs in 1856, the Cincinnati Conference of the Methodist Episcopal
Church, North, opened Wilberforce University for the education of
blacks.[22] Also, where antislavery forces were strong, again as at Greene
County, lighter-skinned Negroes are known to have voted.[23]

While the forces of tolerance were on the defensive near the Ohio
River, the opposite was true in northeastern Ohio, along the lakeshore
and the Pennsylvania border, shading off toward the east-central towns
of Lisbon, East Liverpool, Massilon, Canton, and Steubenville. Particularly noteworthy for racial liberalism was the Western Reserve, a nine-
county area in Ohio's extreme northeastern corner. Patterns of nativity
and population development help to account for the difference. Southerners were absent among the northeast's white settler population,
whose origins lay in Pennsylvania and New England. Reserve settlers
were almost exclusively New Englanders. At the same time, there were
few blacks; although both Cleveland and Oberlin had several hundred
blacks in 1860, this number was small in comparison to that found in
more southerly areas. As a result, there was less opportunity for racial
friction.[24]

Yet the region's uniqueness lay not simply in the relative lack of
racial conflict. Tolerance was often valued for its own sake, and much
of the early history of Ohio's northeast was involved with the struggle
against slavery and for the advancement of black America. The Reserve was a hotbed of abolitionist activity; its ports, at which fugitive
slaves are known to have been placed on boats bound for Canada,
were vital links on the Underground Railroad. In 1834, young abolitionists from the race-conscious border city of Cincinnati came to recently opened Oberlin College in Lorain County in search of a freer
environment in which to express and develop their antislavery commitment. While the emergence of the college as a bastion of abolitionism
marked an important step in the development of American antislavery
activism, it also laid the foundation for a uniquely tolerant community.
One of the conditions on which the young radical seminarians had
agreed to come to Oberlin was that the school begin admitting blacks.
After the reluctant trustees consented, from 5 to 8 percent of the student body throughout the nineteenth century would be black, and the
town of Oberlin itself would become a haven for blacks in search of
education and greater freedom. Under the influence of abolitionist

[22] Wilhelmina Robinson, "The Negro in the Village of Yellow Springs, Ohio,"
Negro History Bulletin, XXIX (Feb., 1966), 103–104; Frederick A. McGinnis,
A History and Interpretation of Wilberforce University (Blanchester, Ohio, 1941),
pp. 28–37.
[23] Columbus Statesman, Oct. 25, 1856; Cleveland Leader, Oct. 17, 1867.
[24] Weisenburger, Passing of Frontier, p. 10; Chaddock, Ohio before 1850,
pp. 31–46; U.S. Census Office, Ninth Census, I, 226–241.

radicalism, the races mingled in town and college with an ease rare in ante-bellum America.[25]

The racial liberalism of the Reserve extended into other realms as well. Although Ohio's public school system rarely placed black and white children together, in some reserve towns blacks were actually welcomed into the schools. At Cleveland, a firmly integrationist board of education began to admit blacks to the schools in the late 1840s, resisting all segregationist efforts to create a dual school system. Within the next decades the board began the almost unheard-of practice of hiring black teachers for the city's integrated classrooms.[26] Ante-bellum blacks also took part in the political life of the Reserve. At Oberlin, Negroes light and dark voted during the 1850s; John Mercer Langston, the slave-born black abolitionist and attorney who had been educated at Oberlin, was elected township clerk in 1855, making him one of the first black elected officials in the nation.[27] And, much to the dismay of Cleveland's substantial Democratic minority, Negroes, especially the lighter-skinned, voted occasionally in the 1850s.[28]

To be sure, there were contrary trends in the northeast. Cleveland and a few smaller towns in the Reserve had their own local branches of the American Colonization Society; these groups were weaker than local abolitionist organizations, but vocal nonetheless. In contrast to the militantly abolitionist *Leader*, Cleveland's *Plain Dealer* was as violently anti-black a newspaper as existed in the North. Public institutions might be open to Cleveland blacks, but the city's public accommodations were not always liberal in their policies; theaters and hotels at Cleveland often refused black travelers rooms and seated black theater patrons in a separate gallery.[29] Yet Ohio's northeast remained in stark contrast to much of the central and southern parts of the state

[25] Karl Geiser, "The Western Reserve in the Antislavery Movement, 1840–1860," Mississippi Valley Historical Association *Proceedings*, V (1911–12), 73–98; Robert Samuel Fletcher, *A History of Oberlin College from Its Founding through the Civil War* (Oberlin, 1943), esp. pp. 150–178; Wilbur G. Burroughs, "Oberlin's Part in the Slavery Conflict," *Ohio Archeological and Historical Quarterly*, XX, 2 (1911), 269–334; W. E. Bigglestone, "Oberlin College and the Negro Student, 1865–1940," *Journal of Negro History*, LVI (July, 1971), 198–199; Russell H. Davis, *Black Americans in Cleveland from George Peake to Carl B. Stokes, 1796–1969* (Washington, 1972), pp. 12–34.

[26] Erickson, "Color Line in Ohio Public Schools," pp. 225–227; Cleveland *Leader*, Mar. 21, 1860, Mar. 27, 1863, Aug. 9, 1876.

[27] John Mercer Langston, *From Virginia Plantation to the National Capitol* (Hartford, 1894), pp. 168–169; Cleveland *Aliened American*, Apr. 9, 1853; Cleveland *Plain Dealer*, Oct. 17, 1857.

[28] Cleveland *Leader*, Oct. 18, 1867; Russell H. Davis, "Negro Political Life Begins," Cleveland *Call and Post*, Sept. 10, 1966.

[29] Davis, *Black Americans in Cleveland*, pp. 8–10, 70–72; Culpepper, "Negro and Black Laws," p. 69; Weisenburger, *Passing of Frontier*, p. 336; Julian Krawcheck, "The Negro in Cleveland," 1, Cleveland *Press*, May 29, 1963.

where the large majority of Ohio blacks resided, and where blacks suffered harsh prejudice and comprehensive discrimination.

III

Despite discrimination, Ohio's black population grew steadily. The cumbersome legal machinery intended to impede black settlement could only be effective if county officials stalked the countryside and the city streets in search of unregistered blacks; few officials appear to have taken the trouble. In addition, even where blacks were registered by county clerks upon in-migration, as the law demanded, rarely was the $500 bond required before the repeal of the settlement law in 1850. Instead, the word of an established white resident or a respected black minister might suffice as a guarantee of good behavior.[30] Under the circumstances, it is not likely that the threat of enforcement deterred many who wished to leave the South for Ohio. Thus, from 337 blacks (generally servants, farmers, and trappers and their families) in 1800, the black population climbed slowly to 9,568 (1 percent of the total population) by 1830 and more rapidly thereafter, reaching 36,673 (1.6 percent) by 1860.[31]

While the use of threat of violence kept blacks from settling in a few isolated southern Ohio communities, it did not eliminate settlement at the more desirable and accessible locations. Cincinnati's periodic (1829, 1839, and 1841) anti-black violence is thought to have driven some 1,200 blacks from the city in the first year alone, many to exile in Canada; nevertheless, the black population there continued to grow, attracted by convenient location and by work made available by the city's booming economy. Numbering 690 in 1826, the black population of the city had reached 2,255 by 1840 and 3,731 by 1860; this last figure was more than twice that of Chillicothe, the urban center with the second-largest black population.[32]

[30] Erickson, "Color Line in Ohio Public Schools," pp. 25–26; Woodson, "Negroes of Cincinnati before Civil War," 6; Harvey Elam, "Record of Free Negroes Found Here," Xenia *Gazette*, Feb. 3, 4, 6, 13, 16, 21, 27, 1936.

[31] U.S. Bureau of the Census, *Negro Population, 1790–1915* (Washington, 1918), p. 45; Russell H. Davis, *Memorable Negroes of Cleveland's Past* (Cleveland, 1969), pp. 2–7; "More about Richard Stanup: George Washington's Chief of Servants," *Negro History Bulletin*, XXXII (May, 1969), 16–18; Ben Hayes, "Negro—No. 2," Columbus *Citizen Journal*, undated clippings, OHS.

[32] Quillin, *Color Line in Ohio*, pp. 32, 36–43; Woodson, "Negroes of Cincinnati before Civil War," 6–9; "The Banishment of the People of Color from Cincinnati," *Journal of Negro History*, VIII (July, 1923), 331–332; Marilyn Bailey, "From Cincinnati, Ohio to Wilberforce, Canada," *Journal of Negro History*, LXVIII (Oct., 1973), 427–440.

Violence, however, was the exception. Largely because it did not disturb the repressive patterning of race relations, black settlement met with little white resistance. An overwhelmingly rural people, often clustered together in the southern and central Ohio countryside in small, scattered enclaves composed of several families, and working as farm laborers or as independent farmers on small plots of their own, Ohio's blacks probably came into little contact and competition with whites. Cities and towns offered opportunities for greater racial contact and conflict, yet the less than 30 percent of the black population living in urban centers before 1860 were generally confined to menial occupations and bound strictly by racial custom and restrictive law. Though low-status whites continued to see blacks as a social and economic threat, in neither rural nor urban settings were blacks much able to threaten white interests. Also significant in checking the violent racial conflict which might have accompanied black population growth was the fact that the black increase was by no means sudden or locally concentrated.[33]

Far more important than the attitudes and actions of Ohio's whites in shaping the extent of black settlement were events in the slave South, where an unlikely combination of repression, white guilt, and paternalistic benevolence were prodding free and slave blacks northward. Though Ohio lore is rich in tales of the Underground Railroad, little is actually known of the runaway slaves who settled in the state. There probably were a significant number, though many no doubt passed through on the way to safer environs in Canada and elsewhere. For the most part, however, the origins of Ohio's ante-bellum black population are to be found in the Upper South (particularly Virginia, with a substantial minority from North Carolina and Kentucky), among recently emancipated slaves and the more established, older group of free people of color.[34]

Toward the end of the eighteenth century both groups were growing considerably in the Upper South, in response to complementary economic and ideological developments. Antislavery idealism, which had flowered during and just after the Revolution and would again

[33] U.S. Census Office, *Ninth Census*, I, 226–241; Carter Woodson, *Free Negro Heads of Households in the United States in 1830* (Washington, 1925), pp. 123–130. To illustrate this more or less scattered black population, by 1860 the census found blacks residing in all 88 counties; in only seven counties were there more than 1,000, and only in Cincinnati's Hamilton County were there more than 2,000. Another 19 counties had from 500 to 1,000.

[34] Larry Gara, *The Liberty Line: The Legend of the Underground Railroad* (Lexington, Ky., 1961), 6–7, 36–37, 94–96, 152–154; Wilbur Zelinsky, "The Population Geography of the Free Negro in Ante-Bellum America," *Population Studies,* III (Mar., 1950), 386–401.

rise in the 1830s with the emergence of militant abolitionism, led to
increased manumission by individual slaveholders, and to the passage
of laws facilitating manumission by state legislatures. At the same time,
the transition in some states from the exclusive cultivation of staple
crops which had exhausted the soil to less labor-intensive general farming decreased the need for large numbers of slaves and lessened the
economic impact of manumission. However, Kentucky was more recently developed; since the slave system there was reaping considerable profit for slave-holding planters and farmers, the state developed
a smaller population of free blacks. Thus, in spite of the equal proximity of both Virginia and Kentucky to Ohio, most black migrants were
Virginians.[35]

Though emancipated, free blacks in the ante-bellum Upper South
were socially insecure and of marginal means. Lacking solid ties with
white capital, they often found their labor unneeded where there were
sufficient numbers of slaves. Their civil and political rights were rigidly
proscribed everywhere, and throughout the ante-bellum decades their
status declined. The increasing political democratization of the white
South in the early nineteenth century gave more power to low-status
whites, who were eager to check black social and economic competition. At the same time the South was preoccupied to the point of occasional hysteria with the security of the slave system, and southern
whites increasingly tended to see free blacks, who might by design or
example foment slave rebellion, as a subversive force. The slave con-
spiracies and the Nat Turner revolt, the increasingly strident abolitionist criticism of the South, and the intensification of sectional conflict
over the spread of slavery into the West all led to repressive legislation
and informal harassment. The possibility of greater freedom in the
North spurred migration.[36] Free black migrants often sought out districts in Ohio and other northern states where kin, friends, and former
neighbors and townspeople from the South now lived.[37]

[35] Jordan, *White over Black,* pp. 316–321, 346–348, 406. In Kentucky between
1800 and 1860, free blacks as a percentage of the total black population ranged
between 2% and 4.5%; the range was between 5.4 and 10.5% in Virginia.
Bureau of the Census, *Negro Population, 1790–1915,* p. 57.

[36] Jordan, *White over Black,* pp. 406–414, 560–565, 575–581; John Hope
Franklin, *The Free Negro in North Carolina, 1790–1860* (Chapel Hill, 1943),
pp. 58–162, 192–225; Luther Porter Jackson, "The Virginia Free Negro Farmer
and Property Owner, 1830–1860," *Journal of Negro History,* XXIV (Oct., 1939),
390–439; Ira Berlin, *Slaves without Masters* (New York, 1975).

[37] An interesting coincidence of surnames between certain Ohio and Virginia
and North Carolina communities has been noted among blacks listed in the 1830
census. See Woodson, *Free Negro Heads of Households,* esp. pp. 123–130. The
same phenomenon has also been observed by one scholar investigating ante-bellum

The migrants in southeast and east-central Ohio, from Steubenville and Columbus on the north to Marietta, Gallipolis, and Portsmouth on the south, an area conveniently in the path of migration from the southeastern coastal states, tended to be from Virginia and North Carolina.[38] Muskingum County, for example, was a center of black settlement in southeastern Ohio; Zanesville and the nearby small village of Putnam were particularly important centers for black migrants. Both town and village attracted a significant number of large, clan-like families (among them the Guys, Gants, Weekses, Hunnicutts, Gazaways, and McSimpsons) whose descendants would be prominent in area and statewide black affairs for many years.[39] The many conveniently located ports of east-central and southeastern Ohio also attracted many Virginians and Carolinians, for work was plentiful on the docks and aboard steamboats.

The Western Reserve also experienced significant black in-migration from North Carolina in the 1850s. John P. Green, later a prominent Cleveland attorney and politician, recalled that during his boyhood North Carolina's free blacks lived under a "reign of terror," threatened with violence, forced removal, and daily harassment. In response, a number of free blacks from the Newberne-Fayetteville area set out for the North. The families of Green and of Charles Chesnutt (later a prominent Cleveland novelist) settled at Cleveland and Oberlin, to which other North Carolinians of their acquaintance had previously migrated.[40]

Southwestern and west-central Ohio, from Columbus and Springfield on the north to Ironton and Cincinnati on the south, also attracted migrants from throughout the Upper South, including a substantial number from nearby Kentucky. Here also black rural settlements de-

Indiana; see Emma Lou Thornborough, *The Negro in Indiana before 1900* (Indianapolis, 1957), p. 33.

[38] Harvey Scott, *A Complete History of Fairfield County, Ohio* (n.p., 1877), pp. 281–282; Francis Charles Hubbard, "A Short History of the Colored People of Barnesville" (1942, typescript filed at OHS); Ivan Tribe, "The Development of a Rural Community: Albany, Ohio, 1840–1880" (Master's thesis, Ohio University, 1967), pp. 2, 11; Columbus *Crisis,* Feb. 7, 1861; Jackson, "Virginia Free Negro Farmer," 409.

[39] Woodson, *Free Negro Heads of Households,* p. 128; Zanesville *Aurora,* Feb. 7, 1861; *Columbus Crisis,* Feb. 7, 1861; Cleveland *Journal,* June 15, 1907, Aug. 15, 1908.

[40] Woodson, *Century of Negro Migration,* pp. 37–38; John P. Green, *Fact Stranger Than Fiction: 75 Years of a Busy Life* (Cleveland, 1920), pp. 44–62; Helen M. Chesnutt, *Charles W. Chesnutt: Pioneer of the Color Line* (Chapel Hill, 1952), pp. 1–34; Alfred Vance Churchill, "Midwestern: The Colored People," *Northwest Ohio Quarterly,* XXV (Autumn, 1953), 166; Census Bureau, *Ninth Census,* I, 234.

veloped. The Darke County community of Long, for example, was founded in 1808 by people of mixed Negro, Indian, and German ancestry who had come to Ohio from Virginia. The settlement and the rich farmland around it subsequently attracted others of complex ancestry from the South; in an era which scorned interracial marriage, it offered a haven to interracial couples.[41] At the same time, the many prosperous cities and towns in southwestern Ohio also attracted blacks; in addition to Cincinnati, therefore, Hamilton, Dayton, Springfield, Xenia, and Washington Court House had all developed black populations of size (usually several hundred) by 1860.[42]

A significant stream of migration resulted from newly emancipated slaves, largely Virginians, settling on Ohio lands bought for them by former masters. Indeed, southern and central Ohio county histories and oral tradition tell many tales of grateful or conscience-stricken southern planters establishing faithful retainers on substantial agricultural holdings. In 1818, in what was probably the largest migration of this type, about nine hundred former slaves of Samuel Gist, an Englishman with plantations in Virginia, were settled under the terms of Gist's will on some 2,300 acres at two sites in Brown County. But as was the case with the four hundred ex-slaves of Virginian John Randolph who were settled on farmlands to the northwest of Mercer County, the Gist slaves had little capital other than land, and no control over that under the provisions of their paternalistic master's will. Both groups of ex-slaves were soon cheated out of considerable portions of land by agents of their masters' estates and local land speculators. The Randolph slaves were also victims of violence at the hands of their white neighbors, and were forced to flee to surrounding counties. Poor and practically landless, the ex-slaves and their descendants remained throughout the century near the areas where they had been settled, working as farm laborers or small holders engaged in a largely subsistence agriculture.[43]

However, most blacks who were settled in Ohio by masters came in

[41] W. E. B. Du Bois, "Long in Darke," *Colored American Magazine*, XVII (Nov., 1909), 353–355; Cleveland *Gazette*, Jan. 12, 1895; Jackson, "Virginia Free Negro Farmer," 410.

[42] Zelinsky, "Population Geography of Free Negro," 398; Sarah Grace Rider, "The Negro in Ohio with Special Reference to the Influence of the Civil War" (Master's thesis, Ohio State University, 1931), pp. 5–10; Census Office, *Eighth Census*, p. 612; Harvey Elam, "Record of Free Negroes," Xenia *Gazette*, Feb. 3, 4, 13, 16, 21, 27, 1936.

[43] William B. McGroarty, "Exploration in Mass Emancipation," *William and Mary Quarterly*, 2nd ser., XXI (July, 1941), 208–226; Leonard U. Hill, "John Randolph's Slaves Settle in Western Ohio," *Cincinnati Historical Society Bulletin*, XXII, 3 (1965), 179–187; Alma May, "The Negro and Mercer County" (Master's thesis, University of Dayton, 1968), pp. 55–56; Cleveland *Gazette*, Aug. 20, 1887, June 18, 1904.

smaller numbers, often in parties of small families, and were more securely provided for. The thirty-seven slaves of a Madison County, Virginia, planter who were settled at Burlington in Lawrence County in 1849 were supplied with funds adequate for the purchase of land and homes and for one year's maintenance.[44] Occasionally, too, black settlers were blood relatives of their masters, usually the natural children of liaisons between masters and slave mistresses. As the resort of Tawawa Springs declined before the Civil War because of the growing unwillingness of Southerners to spend their money and vacations in the North, it became the focus of settlement for emancipated women and their light-skinned children. The establishment of Wilberforce University, which for its first decades was more a preparatory school than a college, made Tawawa especially attractive to those eager to have their children be educated. Until the Civil War checked southern settlement and enrollment, the university catered almost exclusively to the natural children of southern planters.[45]

Not all masters were as benevolent in deciding the terms under which their slaves were to be freed. A significant minority of the antebellum black population was composed of persons who had worked, sometimes for years, to buy freedom for themselves and their loved ones. A census of two southern Ohio communities in the early 1830s revealed that almost 20 percent of the local black population had been freed through self-purchase or had been purchased by friends or, more often, kin. Usually in their thirties at the time of self-purchase, such individuals tended to be male artisans, cooks, dining room waiters, and barbers who had been allowed to save a small percentage of their earnings as hired-out slave workers. Others who had no special skills to market saved only through arduous menial labor; a number of young women purchased their freedom with money saved from laundering. After raising what in the 1830s was usually between $400 and $1,200 to buy their freedom, the self-purchased often then began to raise money to buy wives, children, aged parents, brothers and sisters, and friends. Decades and lifetimes were spent in this patient labor of love.[46]

[44] J. Earl Pratt, *The Promised Land* (New York, 1964), pp. 1–29.

[45] McGinnis, *History of Wilberforce*, pp. 36–37; "Concerning Origins of Wilberforce," 335–337; Cleveland *Leader*, June 23, 1860; Hallie Q. Brown, ed., *Pen Pictures of Pioneers of Wilberforce* (Xenia, 1937), pp. 34–44.

[46] Ohio Anti-Slavery Convention, *Report on the Condition of the Colored People in the State of Ohio . . . 1835* (n.p., 1835), pp. 8–9, 12; Robinson, "Negro in Yellow Springs," 104. A Virginia black who settled in Columbus was reported to have purchased his wife and baby for $650 and then an eleven-year-old son for $1,109. On the eve of the Civil War, he had plans to buy the freedom of three more children still in bondage. Columbus *Ohio State Journal*, July 17, 1860.

Doubtless some black migrants pressed on from Ohio in search of greater safety and opportunity. Yet many remained, and by 1860 centers of black settlement existed throughout the state. In time, particularly in the urban areas, the various migrant subcommunities based on family and point of origin began to coalesce and form new communities of northern black people. Proof of the increasing permanence of black Ohioans was the development of the mechanisms of black solidarity and self-help. Everywhere churches came first. During the 1820s and 1830s black missionaries like the Reverend Wallace Shelton, a Cincinnati Baptist who organized dozens of congregations, were spreading word of the independent black church movement in the East and helping local blacks to organize congregations of the Baptist and African Methodist Episcopal faiths. One church of each denomination was present in most cities and towns by 1860. Affiliated with the churches were Sunday schools, missionary societies, fund-raising communities to aid in the building and improvement of church structures, and occasionally temperance and moral uplift societies. Church governance and cooperation on a statewide basis had also begun. Two regional connections of the black Baptist church, which claimed the majority of Ohio black congregants, were established; one of these was the nation's first black Baptist regional connection. In addition, as the result of relentless missionary activity, Ohio had more A.M.E. church members than most northern states with comparable black populations, and it was established as an episcopal seat of the church.[47]

In larger urban centers one or several mutual aid societies soon arose, organized across denominational lines by the artisans, servants, shopkeepers, teachers, ministers, and service entrepreneurs (particularly barbershop owners) who made up the small black higher-status group. Typically, male associations like Xenia's Colored United Association, Columbus's Sons of Protection, and Cincinnati's Sons of Liberty and United Colored Association provided sickness and death benefits, good fellowship, and recreation opportunities, such as the annual picnics celebrating the 1833 emancipation of slaves in the British West

[47] Daniel Payne, *History of the A.M.E. Church*, ed. C. S. Smith (Nashville, 1891), pp. 44, 97, 118, 180, 205; Lewis G. Jordan, *Negro Baptist History* (Nashville, 1930), pp. 61, 193; Marie Lee, "History of the Second Baptist Church" (typescript at Carnegie Public Library, Washington Court House, Ohio); "History of the Zion Baptist Church—Xenia, Ohio" (typescript appended to Jennie Braddock, "The Colored People and Greene County, Ohio, 1800–1865" [Senior thesis, Antioch College, 1953, rev. 1962]); Allen Temple, Centennial Commission, *Centennial Guide* (1924), pp. 8–18; Randolph C. Downes, *Lakeport* (Toledo, 1951), pp. 378–380; Benjamin F. Prince, ed., *The Centennial Celebration of Springfield, Ohio* (Springfield, 1901), pp. 45–47; Davis, *Black Americans in Cleveland*, pp. 104–107.

Indies. A few either maintained burial plots within white-owned cemeteries, or (as in Cincinnati, where blacks were barred from white cemeteries) operated their own burial plots. Although they lacked insurance features, the women's organizations occasionally affiliated with male societies stressed moral uplift, temperance, and the sanctity of family life.[48] By 1860, however, the growing national black fraternals which promised more comprehensive, systematized benefits and compelling rituals, and their sororal affiliates composed of wives, daughters, and relatives of male members, made in-roads into Ohio. Seven lodges of the Prince Hall Order of Masons were present in 1860 (three at Cincinnati and one each at Cleveland, Columbus, Xenia, and Zanesville), while the first black Odd Fellows lodge west of New York City had recently been established at Cleveland.[49] Complementing the fraternal and sororal organizations were literary societies and various formal and informal social circles among the urban elite.[50]

Nowhere was the pace of community development as rapid as at Cincinnati, where the state's largest and one of its oldest black communities was located. Here blacks faced a combination of deep hostility and relatively great economic opportunity in a prosperous locale. Sustained particularly by service enterprise, a few retail stores, and many service and common labor jobs aboard steamboats and on the docks, by 1860 blacks in the Queen City had established five churches of four denominations and eleven fraternal and uplift societies, and for a time had conducted a building and investment association. In addition, in the face of discrimination in public institutions, a race-operated orphanage for black children was opened in 1844 with the financial assistance of Nicholas Longworth, a wealthy white citizen.[51] Doubtless other black communities in southern and central Ohio were as self-contained, but few had as active and varied an associational life.

Furthermore, while other black communities in Ohio had to struggle mightily before the establishment of black public education to finance

[48] Xenia *Torchlight*, Apr. 9, 1862; Xenia *Gazette*, July 17, 1864; Cincinnati *Gazette*, Sept. 18, 1865; Cleveland *Gazette*, Dec. 13, 1884; Arnett, ed., *Proceedings of the Semi-Centenary*, pp. 117–123; Wendell Phillips Dabney, *Cincinnati's Colored Citizens: Historical, Sociological, and Biographical* (Cincinnati, 1926), p. 193.

[49] Davis, *Black Americans in Cleveland*, p. 74; Charles Wesley, *The History of the Prince Hall Grand Lodge of Free and Accepted Masons of the State of Ohio, 1849–1960: An Epoch in American Fraternalism* (Wilberforce, 1961), pp. 1–69.

[50] Davis, *Black Americans in Cleveland*, pp. 121–122; Ben Hayes, "Negro—No. 8," Columbus *Citizen Journal*, undated clippings, OHS.

[51] Dabney, *Cincinnati's Colored Citizens*, pp. 45, 72–73; Woodson, "Negroes of Cincinnati before Civil War," 4–10; Arnett, ed., *Proceedings of the Semi-Centenary*, pp. 117–123.

small schools, the Cincinnatians were particularly successful in the development of a black school system. Prior to the passage of the 1849
school law, after unsuccessful attempts to gain public funding for black
education from the city council, blacks had founded five small, conveniently located elementary schools. In 1844, with the aid of a white
clergyman, the state's only black high school was established. Black
students helped to fund this school by giving choral concerts throughout the North. These schools became public in 1850, but, because of
the effort which had gone into their creation and administration, Cincinnati blacks desired to retain some control over them. After several
years of indifference to black requests, the legislature established a
black board of directors, composed of three persons to be elected by
the adult black males of the city. This board was charged with sub-
mitting yearly financial reports and budgets to the regular board of
education and to the city council, which controlled the allocation of
school funds. Under black directors and school administrators, with increased cooperation from white school officials as the years passed,
these schools were run efficiently and professionally; though their physical plants did not the equal those of the white schools, an effort was
made to provide similar curricula. The excellence of these schools as
compared to the usual one-room, ungraded ones available to blacks in
ante-bellum Ohio and elsewhere sometimes led black parents who
were particularly eager to have their children receive education to mi-
grate to Cincinnati. Until this arrangement ended almost two decades
later, when special laws governing schools in individual Ohio cities
were repealed in favor of uniform statutes, black Cincinnatians had a
unique opportunity to administer the affairs of a public institution
vital to their daily lives.[52]

While blacks sought to develop the mechanisms of solidarity and
self-help in their local communities, they also tried to do so at the
state level. Like other northern blacks, the Ohioans had met periodically in conventions to discuss their common problems—the hated
black laws, and the racial mores which sustained them—and had
planned tactics for obtaining relief. Occasionally the delegates appointed lobbyists to take their cause to the state legislature which had
done so much to limit their status as citizens. The conventions had also
discussed putting black self-help to work in the cause of racial advancement; in the 1830s they had taken an interest in helping local
black communities create their own schools, and they had urged moral
uplift through temperance, hard work, and religiosity.[53]

[52] Erickson, "Color Line in Ohio Public Schools," pp. 92–94, 115, 208–209.
[53] Howard Bell, "A Survey of the Negro Convention Movement, 1830–1861"
(Ph.D. dissertation, Northwestern University, 1953); Culpepper, "Negro and

From the convention movement there emerged a small but tireless and courageous group of racial leaders. Most were men who had risen as far as society would allow—artisans such as David Jenkins of Columbus, barbers and barbershop proprietors like Alfred Anderson of Hamilton, ministers like James Poindexter of Columbus, and a smattering of professionals including Cincinnati teacher Peter Clark and Cleveland newspaper editor William Howard Day. Such men had themselves known the frustrations of life in a hostile world. Peter Clark remembered many years later how, when young and jobless, he had been unable to feed his wife and infant; he had wanted to throw himself in the river and thus "end all my misery." Disgusted by American racism, Clark had once set off for Africa—only to turn back at New Orleans and return to Cincinnati to continue the fight.[54] These men had also borne the gratuitous insults of that world. While covering the state legislature for his paper, the Cleveland *Aliened American,* in 1854, Day had been excluded from the senate press gallery because of his race.[55] Yet, like David Jenkins, they persevered. John Ward of Columbus said that his friend Jenkins had for years conducted an almost single-handed lobby against the black laws in the halls and galleries of the legislature. "Every session," said Ward, "saw Jenkins in his place and old and new members learned to know and respect him." [56]

Others less steadfast felt their patience wearing thin by the late 1850s. Like other northern blacks, some Ohioans began to search for ultimate solutions. Before the 1850s black advocacy of settlement outside the United States had been seen as capitulation to prejudice; now a vocal minority of respected leaders began to favor emigration.[57] The emigrationists shared the belief, as one of them, the Reverend Thomas Dillon of Toledo's Warren Chapel A.M.E. Church, said, "in the impossibility of African elevation here in degree equal to white men." [58] And without hope in the future of America, they saw no reason to remain on American soil.

Such pessimism was not unwarranted. The late 1850s found most Ohio blacks pariahs, restricted and scorned, living in the state but in

Black Laws," pp. 32–34, 46–56, 62–63, 77; Erickson, "Color Line in Ohio Public Schools," pp. 61–71. Bell's dissertation has been published with the same title (New York, 1969).

[54] Cincinnati *Commercial,* Mar. 27, 1877; William J. Simmons, *Men of Mark: Eminent, Progressive, and Rising* (Cleveland, 1887), p. 245.

[55] W. E. B. Du Bois, "The World of William Howard Day," pp. 3–4 (n.d.), photostat, WRHS.

[56] Columbus *Ohio State Journal,* Feb. 25, 1870.

[57] Bell, "Negro Convention Movement," pp. 140–141; Culpepper, "Negro and Black Laws," pp. 82–84.

[58] Downes, *Lakeport,* p. 376.

no accurate sense citizens. Moreover, national events of the decade had made the black position even less secure. Congressional and judicial concessions to the slaveholder, in the form of the Fugitive Slave Law of 1850 and the *Dred Scott* decision of 1857, threatened northern blacks with kidnapping and Star Chamber justice. Cogently summarizing their position in Ohio in 1860, Ohio's black abolitionists stated despairingly:

> We, the colored people of Ohio are not only exposed to all the outrages of the Fugitive Slave Law and the Dred Scott decision and [suffer from] the want of an effective . . . law for the protection of our wives, children, and ourselves against the mansteraler and the kidnapper, but we are taxed without representation. We are excluded from any office of profit or honor in the state; we are constitutionally barred from the state militia; we are by law or prejudice shut out from all the benevolent institutions, which . . . are supported in part by the $65,000 taxes which we annually pay into the state treasury. Young colored offenders are excluded from the state Reform School and Farm. The county infirmaries are closed to our poor. We cannot in any courts have an impartial trial by a jury of our peers. In short, this state of our nativity or adoption affords us no protection for our personal liberty, and denies us almost every civil and political right.[59]

[59] Ohio Anti-Slavery Society, *Proceedings of the First Annual Meeting . . . 1860* (n.p., 1860), p. 1.

2

Civil War and Reconstruction

In the days after the outbreak of hostilities, the Lincoln administration and the people of the North hoped for a short war and fought for a limited aim: the restoration of the Union as it had been, a union of slave South and free North. At the start, therefore, the war did not offer the prospect of improved status for blacks. Yet the war became a protracted struggle with terrible carnage; as a result, it produced exigencies which forced a revolution in the nation's racial affairs. Disheartened by great losses among northern troops and frustrated by an inability to strike a quick death-blow at the rebellion, the North began in 1862 to reassess the relation between slavery and the war effort. Urged on by those who wished to marshal all available resources to crush the Confederacy, and by abolitionists seeking steps in the direction of an emancipation policy, the Lincoln administration moved to arm masses of runaway slaves in the South and to guarantee their freedom.

Making the wholesale freeing of millions of slaves in the Confederacy one of the northern war aims was much more difficult for Lincoln, his party, and the northern electorate to contemplate. Like most Northerners, Lincoln did not believe blacks to be equal to whites, and he had great doubts that millions of freed blacks could live in harmony with their white neighbors. But gradually, for lack of alternatives, emancipation became the administration's policy. As it was, of course, the Emancipation Proclamation freed only those slaves in areas where the Confederacy retained firm control, for the administration did not desire to alienate the Unionist slave states. Yet as more and more of the Confederacy fell before the progress of northern arms, greater numbers of slaves were freed, until by the end of the war a two-hundred-year-old system of bondage lay in ruins. The work of emancipation was completed in 1865 with the passage and ratification of the Thirteenth Amendment.

Events had greatly exceeded the expectations of men, and they continued to do so after the war. In the struggle for a restored Union and a reconstructed South, the ex-slaves would become the bulwark of northern efforts to check the resurgence of southern disloyalty. Brick by brick within the years following the war, a structure of federal legal guarantees was created to protect them from the vengeance of unreconstructed whites and to arm them to fight for the cause of Union in the South; these laws had important consequences for northern blacks. The 1866 federal Civil Rights Act and the Fourteenth and Fifteenth Amendments accorded blacks everywhere basic civil rights and the right to vote. Thus, by 1870, blacks came to appear at polling places and in jury boxes in both sections, and southern blacks, their political power backed by numbers and by the civil disabilities of their former masters, entered state assemblies and Congress. To be sure, the reconstruction of the nation's race relations was limited. Lacking capital and opportunity, blacks remained poor and without much likelihood of economic improvement. Furthermore, the federal legal guarantees were not won without bitter opposition in Congress from opponents of racial equality; the language of compromise and evasion, which future generations would interpret against the Negro's welfare, was present in each of the new constitutional amendments which were the pillars of black citizenship. Yet great strides had been made in less than a decade. Blacks had been transformed from slaves in the South and pariahs in the North to citizens and members of the political community.[1]

I

Throughout the 1860s, dramatic developments in Ohio's black-white relations would be closely tied to events in the South. This became evident first in the sharp increase in black population which resulted from migrations out of the South during and just after the war. Though blacks still composed less than 3 percent of Ohio's people, in the 1860s they increased by 72 percent (from 36,673 to 63,213), an unprecedented gain of 25,540 blacks in one decade. Nowhere else in the North were the increases as large. In 1860 Ohio had been fifth among northern states in the size of its black population and third in the per-

[1] For general treatments of slavery and race during the Civil War and Reconstruction, see W. R. Brock, *An American Crisis: Congress and Reconstruction, 1865–1867* (New York, 1963); James McPherson, *The Struggle for Equality: Abolitionists and the Negro in the Civil War and Reconstruction* (Princeton, 1964), and McPherson, *The Negro's Civil War* (New York, 1965); Benjamin Quarles, *The Negro in the Civil War* (Boston, 1953); Kenneth M. Stampp, *The Era of Reconstruction, 1865–1877* (New York, 1965).

centage of blacks in its total population. By 1870 the state had become second only to Pennsylvania in the former and to New Jersey in the latter. Though increasing numbers of blacks were found throughout the state, migrants tended to settle in the traditional centers of black population in the southern and central counties. Most counties west of the Scioto experienced black population gains of 50 and 100 percent, while a number of rural townships and such towns as Ironton, Portsmouth, Wilmington, and Springfield had growth rates of up to 150 percent.[2]

The early wartime migration consisted primarily of small bands of free blacks fleeing the progress of the war into areas of the South, such as the hill country of western Virginia and the mountains of eastern Tennessee and Kentucky, where slavery had never really taken root. In addition, small numbers of fugitive slaves from farther east, who took advantage of the intense fighting in Maryland and eastern and central Virginia in 1861–62 to break with their masters, had also begun to enter Ohio. During 1862 small bands of black refugees were reported roaming the southeastern Ohio countryside in search of food, shelter, and black settlements. By September large parties of western Virginians were reported making their way down the Ohio on flatboats. The immediate response of many whites was hysterical. Wild rumors of rape, pillage, and mayhem spread from county to county. Whites bolted their doors, and farmers carried guns when going to town.[3]

Democratic politicians and newspapers greatly reinforced this emotional reaction by responding with obstruction and racial abuse to every threat of the racial status quo. Illustrative of the conceptual and rhetorical level on which Democrats approached the race issue had been the decision of the Democratic minority in the legislature in April, 1861, to respond to the threat of civil war by introducing the question of miscegenation. There followed the passage, with the cooperation of a handful of Republicans, of Ohio's first law banning interracial marriage and sexual relations. The question had nothing to do with the grave national crisis at hand, nor was there need to outlaw that against which custom so effectively militated. Instead, Democratic agitation was intended to place Republican legislators in a position

[2] U.S. Census Office, *Ninth Census of the United States . . . 1870* (Washington, 1872), I, 226–241; U.S. Bureau of the Census, *Negro Population, 1790–1915* (Washington, 1918), pp. 45, 51.

[3] Gallipolis *Journal*, Sept. 16, 1862, Apr. 23, Oct. 22, Nov. 12, 19, 1863; Columbus *Crisis*, Jan. 29, Apr. 9, 23, 1862; Lancaster *Ohio Eagle*, May 22, 29, Aug. 3, 10, 17, 26, 1862; Athens *Messenger*, Feb. 20, 1862; Hillsboro *Highland Gazette*, Oct. 16, 1862; Portsmouth *Tribune*, Apr. 5, 1862.

where their possible opposition, whatever its basis, might be explained
to a highly suggestible electorate as a manifestation of pro-Negro sentiment.[4]

Democratic strategy changed in 1862. Hoping to embarrass the Lincoln administration and lessen public support for a war which was
now increasingly precipitating emancipation, rather than simply attempting to restore the Union as it had once been, the Ohio Democracy began to warn against the specter of a black horde rising in the
South to invade the North. Led by two of the North's most prominent
political racists, Columbus Congressman Samuel Sullivan "Sunset" Cox
and Dayton's Clement Vallandigham, the Democrats told white workingmen that the North would soon be inundated with cheap black
labor which would depress the living standard of the white masses.
Cox's well-circulated congressional address of June, 1862, "Emancipation and Its Results—Is Ohio to Be Africanized?," warned Ohio's
100,000 soldiers in the field that they would come home to find "these
negroes . . . filling their places, felling timber, ploughing ground
[and] gathering crops. . . ." He predicted that "labor that now goes
for $1 or $2 a day will fall to half that." [5] Attempting to prepare the
electorate for the fall elections, the Democratic press harped on these
themes during the summer.[6] In addition, throughout that year and the
next, numerous petitions to the now Republican-controlled legislature,
mainly from Democratic constituencies (many of which had very few
blacks and had experienced little, if any, recent black settlement), demanded immediate cessation of all black migration and occasionally
called for forced removal of already resident blacks.[7]

The Democrats' agitation on the wage and standard of living issue
no doubt exacerbated tensions between black and white stevedores on
the Lake Erie and Ohio River docks, and serious rioting occurred at

---

[4] Columbus *Gazette*, May 10, 1861; David Fowler, "Northern Attitudes toward
Interracial Marriage: A Study of Legislation and Public Opinion in the Middle
Atlantic States and the States of the Old Northwest" (Ph.D. dissertation, Yale
University, 1963), pp. 191–203, 208–209.

[5] Samuel Sullivan Cox, *Emancipation and Its Results—Is Ohio to Be African-
ized?* (Washington, 1862), p. 15; William Zornow, "Ohio Democrats and the
Africanization Issue in 1862," *Negro History Bulletin*, XI (June, 1948), 211–214;
V. Jacque Voegeli, "The Northwest and the Race Issue, 1861–1862," *Mississippi
Valley Historical Review*, L (Sept., 1963), 237–239.

[6] E.g., Cincinnati *Enquirer*, July 15, 1862; see Cincinnati *Enquirer*, Columbus
Crisis, and Lancaster *Ohio Eagle* for July, Aug., and Sept., 1862.

[7] Cleveland *Leader*, Jan. 16, Mar. 22, May 2, 1862, Jan. 23, 31, 1863; Columbus *Crisis*, Feb. 12, 26, 1862; Ohio General Assembly, *House Journal, 1863*,
Appendix, pp. 123–127; Sarah Grace Rider, "The Negro in Ohio with Special
Reference to the Influence of the Civil War" (Master's thesis, Ohio State University, 1931), p. 23 (map of origin of anti-migration petitions).

both Toledo and Cincinnati during the summer. Blacks had worked at both ports before, but in response to the wartime labor shortage there were even greater numbers in the early 1860s. Moreover, in the midst of the wartime boom, wages lagged behind prices. Fearing that the arrival of more blacks would depress the wage scale and ultimately cost them their jobs, the white (largely immigrant Irish) dock workers lashed out violently. At both cities, black workers were beaten and black property destroyed in Negro areas near the docks.[8]

The riots actually marked the end of large-scale anti-black violence during the war. Prior to the Confederate surrender, the fears of a black tidal wave were unfounded, so the political uses of migration lost force; after the overwhelming defeat of Vallandigham in the 1863 gubernatorial race, the Democrats dropped the issue. Yet many more blacks, particularly the Kentuckians, were still to come. Migration from Kentucky during the war had not been large because most Kentucky blacks had little opportunity to leave bondage. Emancipation had been blocked by the exclusion of Kentucky and other Unionist border slave states from the Emancipation Proclamation, and many of Kentucky's 225,000 slaves had been used by the army as laborers on roads and fortifications and camps.[9]

But as the need for black labor declined in the last years of the war, and because of a desire to speed emancipation, the army in Kentucky began to take steps to ensure freedom for slaves. The northern Kentucky commander, General John M. Palmer, ordered the enlistment of blacks; many of the first enlistees were runaways. Efforts to recruit blacks were greatly stepped up in the final months of the war in an effort to counter the Kentucky legislature's efforts to stall ratification of the Thirteenth Amendment. By war's end, some 29,000 blacks had been enlisted, and their freedom and that of their 70,000 dependents thus ensured. In May, 1865, in another effort to speed emancipation, Palmer issued thousands of passes, at first to free blacks only but then increasingly to all, allowing them to travel—gratis, if rail or steamboat transportation was necessary—to search for work. But because of Kentucky's restrictive laws on the employment of black labor, and a gen-

[8] Leonard Harding, "The Cincinnati Riots of 1862," *Cincinnati Historical Society Bulletin*, XXV (Oct., 1967), 229–239; Willis Lofton, "Northern Labor and the Negro during the Civil War," *Journal of Negro History*, XXXIV (July, 1949), 252–253; Toledo *Blade*, July 8, 9, 10, 11, 1862; Cincinnati *Gazette*, July 15, 17, 21, Aug. 26, Nov. 6, 1862.

[9] Eugene H. Roseboom, *The Civil War Era, 1850–1873* (Columbus, 1944), pp. 420–421; Ellis Merton Coulter, *Civil War and Readjustment in Kentucky* (Lexington, Ky., 1926), pp. 156–157, 163–164; Xenia *Torchlight*, Apr. 29, 1862; Springfield *Republic*, Jan. 7, 8, Sept. 10, 1862, Jan. 16, 1863; Cincinnati *Gazette*, July 19, 1864, Mar. 2, Oct. 17, 25, 1865.

eral hostility to freed black workers there just after the war's end, work
was especially difficult to find. When combined with the former slaves'
understandable desire to see the world—and at no cost to themselves—
the difficulty in getting work led many to leave Kentucky. By mid-
October, 1865, the Cincinnati *Gazette* guessed (probably with some
exaggeration) that some 10,000 blacks had left Kentucky for the North.
The paper noted that a sizable number of them had army-issued travel
passes marked "To Go to Cincinnati, Ohio." Complementing the Kentuckians were smaller numbers of blacks from Virginia and North Carolina and occasionally from the Deep South, who were also in search of
friends, relatives, and work.[10]

This migration did not have disastrous consequences for white labor,
nor did it heighten racial conflict or even (with the possible exception
of some Democratic newspapers) attract the amount of attention which
might have been expected in light of the state's past. The relative ease
with which Ohio absorbed her migrant blacks may be explained partly
by the character of the migrants themselves, their destinations in Ohio,
and the forces which aided their settlement. Like the migrants of previous decades, many appear to have come with their families, refugees
from the devastation of war. An 1862–63 census of the initial migrants
taken in southern and central Ohio by county auditors is suggestive:
of 831 migrants polled, 520 (63 percent) were enumerated in recog-
nizable family groups composed of one, or more often two, parents and
a number of children, and sometimes including cousins, grandparents,
and various generations of aunts and uncles.[11] Though General Palmer's order was intended to allow families to travel together, it is not
possible to estimate the extent to which this trend continued after the
war, when most black migrants entered Ohio. The fact that there were
211 more males than females among blacks in 1860 and 967 more in
1870 [12] suggests that males exceeded females among the migrants. Yet
the imbalance did not preclude the possibility of a considerable migra-

---

[10] Coulter, *Civil War and Readjustment*, pp. 258–270; Cincinnati *Gazette*,
July 29, Aug. 3, 17, Oct. 14, 26, 1865.

[11] The census was commissioned in 1862 in response to Democratic legislators'
demands for an investigation of black migration. The House's Republican majority commissioned the state auditor to ask county auditors to conduct a census
of migrants in local communities. Reports were obtained from 57 of the state's
88 counties by the beginning of 1864; these revealed that some 1,384 blacks had
recently come into Ohio. I examined the returns of 16 counties, all major black
population centers, which polled about 60% of the total migrants enumerated.
Nothing is known, however, of the polling methods employed by the county
auditors. The manuscript returns are on file at OHS. For the printed report and
statistical summary see Ohio, *House Journal, 1864,* p. 476, and Appendix, pp. 52–
62.

[12] Census Office, *Ninth Census,* II, 536–541.

tion of families. Also, like the earlier migrants, those of the war era had as their primary destination the countryside where blacks already lived, and doubtless many sought out the existing black settlements. Fully half of the black population increase during the 1860s was experienced by rural townships, with the remainder split evenly between the villages and the small towns and cities.[13] To the extent that the migrants came to Ohio in family groups, there was a strong incentive for them to settle down quickly. To the extent that the migrants had been rural people in the South, they had an opportunity to blend into a familiar agrarian way of life. All that was needed to complete a relatively easy transition was work for the migrants. Fortunately, during and immediately after the war the need for seasonal farm labor was great because so many young whites were in the army. In fact, as the Columbus *Ohio State Journal* reflected in 1870, the need for farm labor in southern Ohio remained unusually high well into the late 1860s.[14]

Many of those who did not become farm laborers apparently found work in menial and domestic fields where they rarely came into competition with whites. A brisk traffic of black servants and domestics from the South into the homes of Ohio whites began as early as 1861 when Rutherford B. Hayes, then a Union officer, dispatched several families of Virginia runaways to work in the homes of his relatives and friends at Fremont.[15] The importation of black domestics reached its peak after the war. A Miss Hager of Springfield, who was an agent of the philanthropic Christian Commission and a teacher among the freedmen at Camp Nelson, Kentucky, was alone responsible for bringing a large number of black Kentuckians to work as servants in the Springfield area in 1865. Late in December the depot at Springfield was reported filled with "ladies waiting to conduct their unseen and untried servants to their homes," and at about the same time the Cincinnati *Gazette* spoke of a general "ingress of colored servants" into the Queen City.[16]

The Christian Commission was only one of many black and white agencies working to aid freedmen in the South and black migrants in the North during and after the war. The abolitionist and humanitarian organizations took a hand in helping them, as did the black churches, which organized Freedmen's Aid Societies. Moreover, many affluent

[13] Ibid., I, 226–241.

[14] Auditor, Athens County, to Ohio State Auditor, Mar. 24, 1863; Columbus *Ohio State Journal*, May 18, 1870.

[15] Rutherford B. Hayes to Sardis Birchard, Dec. 19, 1861, Rutherford B. Hayes Papers, HL.

[16] Cincinnati *Gazette*, Oct. 13, Dec. 8, 1865; Columbus *Ohio Statesman*, Dec. 9, 1865.

and respectable whites who had kept aloof from the struggle against slavery and racism became interested in aiding blacks. An apocalyptic national crisis had evoked a spirit of sacrifice and charity in them, and slavery's death in the midst of a tragic war helped quicken sympathies for the long-suffering blacks. Thus at the end of the war some whites turned their efforts from rolling bandages and disseminating morale-boosting propaganda for the Union to helping blacks. With the cooperation of the federal Freedmen's Bureau, all of these efforts, black and white, produced an organization of hospitals and schools and distribution of food and clothing; temporary and permanent lodgings were found, and jobs were obtained for Ohio migrants. The agencies also provided transportation to locations where labor was needed. Finally, some migrants took an active role in speeding their own adjustment to new circumstances, usually by organizing churches. At Washington Court House, for example, migrants of the Methodist faith founded a church soon after settling in the town.[17]

II

Dramatic changes in the race's civil status occurred in Ohio during the war years, although they came grudgingly. At first few whites envisioned the war improving the status of Ohio blacks. Most whites would certainly have agreed with the remarks of a legislative committee which had been called upon in 1862 to investigate the first wave of black migration:

> The Negro race is looked upon by the people of Ohio as a class to be kept by themselves; to be barred of social intercourse with whites; to be deprived of all advantages which they cannot enjoy in common with their own class. . . . The colored man will not in all future time that he may remain an inhabitant . . . attain any material improvement in the social and political rights over that which he now enjoys.[18]

During the early war years some Ohio blacks also felt that the war was unlikely to change much for them. Pointing out that blacks had served in both the Revolution and the War of 1812, "A.R." stated in

[17] Joseph Holliday, "Freedmen's Aid Societies in Cincinnati," *Cincinnati Historical Society Bulletin*, XXII (May, 1964), 169–185; Levi Coffin, *Reminiscences* (Cincinnati, 1876), pp. 619–620; Benjamin Arnett, ed., *Proceedings of the Semi-Centenary Celebration of the African Methodist Episcopal Church of Cincinnati* (Cincinnati, 1874), pp. 26–27; Francis Weisenburger, *Columbus during the Civil War* (Columbus, 1963); Cincinnati *Gazette*, July 19, 1864, Oct. 28, 1865; Cleveland *Gazette*, June 17, 1899; Naomi Terry, "An Historical Sketch of Rogers A.M.E. Church" (undated typescript at Carnegie Public Library, Washington Court House, Ohio).

[18] Ohio, *House Journal, 1864*, p. 57.

an April, 1861, letter to the Toledo *Blade* that even their deaths on the battlefield had not served to ameliorate the race's plight. "Upon all occasions," "A.R." said, "the colored man has proved his loyalty and bravery to this government, and yet after doing all they could or were permitted to do, their rights have been ignored." [19] Other Toledo blacks seem to have agreed emphatically, for after attending a lecture given by a black emigrationist in September, a small party actually left for Haiti. By June, 1862, they were writing to urge other Toledo residents to join them.[20]

For those Ohio blacks who might have chosen to see other possibilities early in the war, hoping that by aiding the Union in its hour of need they would create a moral obligation to grant civil equality in Ohio, even if slavery in the South remained untouched, there was quick disappointment. In the first months of the war blacks at Cleveland, Columbus, and Cincinnati were refused when they offered themselves to recruiters; and when several Cleveland blacks offered to get up a regiment of black troops gathered from throughout the North but flying Ohio's colors, they were turned down by both Governor William Dennison and the secretary of war. Cincinnati blacks were even prohibited from holding a mass meeting in support of the Union.[21]

However reluctantly, wartime necessity eventually forced whites in Ohio and throughout the North to utilize black labor and troops. Just six weeks after the Cincinnati riots, when the city appeared threatened by Rebel General Kirby Smith's army in Kentucky, the panic-stricken city called upon the services of almost a thousand local blacks, known as the "Black Brigade," to work on fortifications on the Kentucky side of the river. While the brigade had been organized by a good friend of the race, antislavery Judge William Dickson, the individual blacks who comprised it were often recruited by intimidation. Yet the men labored mightly for three weeks, putting up defenses for the city.[22]

Similar manpower needs helped change the state's decision to oppose recruitment of black troops. Early 1862 had seen no change in white Ohioans' belief that the war was a white man's fight. Indeed, when John Mercer Langston urged Governor David Todd to enlist blacks in order to help fill the state's draft quotas, Todd had replied

[19] Toledo *Blade*, Apr. 22, 1861.

[20] Ibid., Sept. 14, 1861, June 26, 1862; Randolph C. Downes, *Lakeport* (Toledo, 1951), pp. 376–377.

[21] Quarles, *Negro in Civil War*, p. 29; Russell H. Davis, *Black Americans in Cleveland from George Peake to Carl B. Stokes, 1796–1969* (Washington, 1972), pp. 77; Cincinnati *Colored Citizen*, Nov. 7, 1863.

[22] Edgar A. Toppin, "Humbly They Served: The Black Brigade in the Defense of Cincinnati," *Journal of Negro History*, XXXVIII (Apr., 1963), 75–97.

peevishly, "Do you not know Mr. Langston that this is a white man's government; that white men are able to defend and protect it . . . ?"[23] But with the Lincoln administration's decision to arm southern blacks and the beginnings of a federal emancipation policy, the idea of organizing black regiments gained ground in the North. It was said that blacks could prove themselves worthy of freedom by fighting for it. At the same time, in light of the increasing northern criticism of the draft as the war dragged on, blacks would help fill quotas while helping to lessen dissension at home. Regiments of blacks were organized in Massachusetts and Kansas in January, 1863, and Langston and O. S. B. Wall, a black Oberlin shoe store proprietor, raised about nine hundred Ohioans for the Massachusetts 54th Volunteers. Not until six months later, however, did Todd begin to organize an Ohio regiment. In the midst of bitter and occasionally violent opposition to the war and the draft in southern and central counties, the governor in late June established the 127th Ohio Volunteers.[24]

Armed now with a federal commitment to emancipation and doubtless hoping that the war would precipitate important changes in Ohio's race relations, blacks responded enthusiastically. Money was raised at meetings to support recruiters, and a state convention was held at Xenia to coordinate fund-raising and enlistment activities. By November the regiment's quota was filled; during the war the men saw action in Virginia and North Carolina. Before the conflict ended, 5,092 blacks served as soldiers in the cause of Union and freedom.[25]

The acceptance of a black role in the war effort had been slow in coming, and ultimately it was dictated by expediency. Yet the organization of the "Black Brigade" and the enlistment of black soldiers marked the first occasion in which large numbers of Ohio blacks had been called upon to offer their services in the efforts of the larger community. From these slight but hopeful signs, and from the dramatic developments in the South, black Ohioans began again to believe in the possibility of equality and full citizenship. Symbolic of revived hopes were patriotic ceremonial dinners held for black Ohio soldiers returning from the field, and the decision of many black communities to celebrate September 22, the day of the issuance of Lincoln's Preliminary Emancipation Proclamation in 1862, as well as August 1, the anniversary of emancipation in the British West Indies in 1833. But

[23] Quoted in McPherson, *Negro's Civil War,* p. 180.
[24] Quarles, *Negro in Civil War,* pp. 192–193; Roseboom, *Civil War Era,* pp. 409–411.
[25] Charles Wesley, *Ohio Negroes in the Civil War* (Columbus, 1962), pp. 25–46.

the mood among blacks was neither sentimental nor unrealistic, for they were aware of the intensity of racial prejudice in many whites. "For the first time . . . our eyes have beheld the dawning prospect of a better day," said the resolutions of a Springfield meeting in January, 1865—but at the same time the resolutions warned of the continued existence of "burning misanthropy," "devilish prejudice," and "wicked oppression." [26]

Staking their claims upon the undeniable sacrifices of black soldiers, blacks leaders throughout the nation placed primary emphasis on obtaining the vote, which was seen as the vehicle by which they might obtain elevation to a fuller and more secure citizenship. As early as mid-1864 blacks throughout the North and in the conquered states of the South called for racial unity in pursuit of enfranchisement. Delegates from eighteen states met at Syracuse in October to establish a National Equal Rights League, which was to be the main vehicle for carrying forth the struggle for the vote, and they issued appeals for the creation of state and local leagues.[27] Ohio blacks met at Xenia in January, 1865, to establish a state league. Peter Clark was elected president, and David Jenkins, who had already begun lobbying efforts in the legislature, was chosen vice-president.[28] In the following two years local organizations were created throughout Ohio, but less formal local activities had already begun: in late January a petition calling for removal of the word "white" from the suffrage provision of the state constitution, bearing the signatures of 1,000 blacks from Pickaway and surrounding counties, reached the legislature.[29]

Yet in 1865 Ohio blacks could not be sanguine about the prospects for obtaining the vote. Though some whites were sympathetic toward the recently emancipated slave or the black refugee in the North at war's end, few signs indicated that whites were ready for black citizenship. While the political forces of Ohio's anti-war, Copperhead Democracy had been dealt a fatal blow by the defeat of Vallandigham in 1863, the Democracy remained strong, and the Democratic press continued to inveigh against emancipation and to equate any change in the status of blacks with an imminent, wholesale amalgamation of

[26] Springfield *News*, Jan. 11, Sept. 28, 29, 1865; Xenia *Sentinel*, Feb. 17, Mar. 17, 1865; Hillsboro *Highland News*, Sept. 28, 1865; Cincinnati *Gazette*, Aug. 9, Oct. 6, 1865.

[27] McPherson, *Negro's Civil War*, pp. 287–288.

[28] Springfield *News*, Jan. 11, 1865; Xenia *Sentinel*, Jan. 20, 1865; Ohio Equal Rights League, *Proceedings of the Convention of Colored Men of Ohio . . . Xenia . . . January, 1865 with the Convention of the Ohio Equal Rights League* (Cincinnati, 1865).

[29] Columbus *Ohio State Journal*, Jan. 19, 1865; Toledo *Blade*, May 24, 1865; Cleveland *Leader*, Aug. 29, 1866.

the races. The Democratic legislative minority voted in unison against ratification of the Thirteenth Amendment in 1865.[30]

The Unionist majority, a jerry-built coalition of Republicans and War Democrats, seemed no more willing to envision a different future for race relations in Ohio in 1865. Throughout the war, the need to maintain the coalition had led to avoidance of the race issue. The Republican segment was divided on the federal emancipation policy, with the abolitionist minority and the Western Reserve more adamant in support than the party generally. Moreover, downstate Republicans had shown considerable fear that emancipation would precipitate northward migration, and they had generated some of the anti-migration petitions which flooded the legislature in 1862–63. Then, too, all Republicans faced the important task of keeping the War Democrats solidly behind the administration's efforts to put down the rebellion, and the War Democrats showed little enthusiasm for emancipation. Thus, in February, 1865, the Unionist majority in the legislature ratified the Thirteenth Amendment quietly and without fanfare. Resolutions voicing approval of emancipation were not even allowed to reach a vote; to the extent that the matter was ever discussed publicly by Unionist politicians, emancipation was justified only in terms of military necessity.[31]

Fundamental, therefore, to the Unionist coalition was a refusal to look beyond the defeat of the rebellion and an avoidance of any discussion of the larger problems of black citizenship. As a result, the party emerged after Appomattox ill prepared to deal with enfranchisement. By the spring of 1865, some congressional Republicans had already begun to discuss enfranchising southern blacks in order to create a large loyal voting bloc in the South. In Ohio, Western Reserve Republicans called for enfranchisement in the state, but such views were much in advance of where most Ohio Unionists stood. While in 1864 and 1865 the Unionist majority in the legislature had been willing to lighten the individual hardships posed by discrimination, passing legislation facilitating the creation of more and better-located black schools and allowing blacks access to public relief funds, most seemed unable to imagine going further.[32]

[30] Roseboom, *Civil War Era*, pp. 421–435; George Porter, *Ohio Politics during the Civil War* (New York, 1911), p. 202; Circleville *Democrat*, July 7, 21, Aug. 11, 1865; Chillicothe *Advertiser*, Aug. 4, 1865.

[31] Porter, *Ohio Politics during Civil War*, pp. 110–119; Felice A. Bonadio, *North of Reconstruction: Ohio Politics, 1865–70* (New York, 1970), pp. 25–60.

[32] Ohio, *Laws, 1864*, pp. 32–33, and *1865*, p. 42; Porter, *Ohio Politics during Civil War*, pp. 202, 208–219; Edgar A. Toppin, "Negro Emancipation in Historic Retrospect. Ohio: The Negro Suffrage Issues in Post-bellum Ohio Politics," *Journal of Human Relations*, XI (1962–63), 235.

This became evident in June, 1865, at the party's state convention. The delegates nominated war hero General Jacob Cox for governor; he had only consented to the nomination on the condition that the party would agree to take no affirmative stand on black voting. The convention refused to accept a proposed platform put forward by Reserve Republicans which called for national enfranchisement by constitutional amendment; instead, it approved a lame statement affirming "the great principles of our government, as set forth in the Declaration of Independence." To heighten the evasion, in July Cox offered a plan for settling all blacks in a federally supported Negro dependency to be located along the south Atlantic coast. Moderating his position less than a month later, Cox actually declared for Negro suffrage, but even then he hedged on whether he favored state or federal action. Unionists retained control of the legislature, and Cox defeated Democratic General George Morgan, who ran on a platform which called Negro suffrage "a disgrace" and affirmed "government by white men." However, Cox received 65,000 fewer votes than the Unionist gubernatorial candidate had received two years earlier, with especially large losses in northeastern counties, where his inconsistency on black citizenship was particularly unpopular.[33] Yet while the suffrage question might have been faced more directly elsewhere in the North, it fared little better. Connecticut, Wisconsin, and Minnesota had referenda on black voting in the fall of 1865; all were defeats for blacks.[34]

Hesitancy in 1865 destined the question to become tied to the development of congressional plans for Reconstruction. As black voting came to be a key factor in the congressional program, it was apparent that northern Unionists could not escape the contradiction of refusing to live with black voting in their home states while forcing it upon southern whites, a position which Democrats were quick to exploit. For this reason, many northern Unionists, who had once been reluctant to take a stand because of the intense prejudice of their constituents, had felt the need to do so by early 1867, and they urged the party to place the issue before voters in the fall state elections throughout the North.[35]

[33] *The Ohio Platforms of the Republican and Democratic Parties from 1855 to 1881* (Columbus, 1881), p. 25; Porter, *Ohio Politics during Civil War*, pp. 206–219; Columbus *Ohio State Journal*, July 21, 22, 1865; Cincinnati *Commercial*, Aug. 22, 1865; Cleveland *Leader*, Aug. 23, 25, 1865; Circleville *Democrat*, Sept. 1, 15, 29, 1865.

[34] Leslie Fishel, Jr., "Northern Prejudice and Negro Suffrage, 1865–1870," *Mississippi Valley Historical Review*, XXXIX (Jan., 1954), 12–14.

[35] Ibid., 18–25. Cf. LaWanda and John H. Cox, "Negro Suffrage and Republican Politics: The Problem of Motivation in Reconstruction Historiography," *Jour-*

Division continued to exist, however, among Ohio Unionists. Unionist legislators would not support a bill to place the suffrage issue before voters that fall, in the form of a referendum on striking the word "white" from the constitution's suffrage clause, until it was paired with a proposal for a referendum on disfranchising up to 27,000 Ohio army deserters, some of them conscripted anti-war Democrats. Moreover, though the state convention approved a platform supporting Negro suffrage, county conventions in the southern and central regions, where Republican candidates might actually gain the most from black voting, refused to support the plank, feeling that it would cause a wholesale defection among downstate Unionists. Thus the battle for black voting fell squarely on the shoulders of Western Reserve Republicans and the small contingent of Radicals in other areas. The latter, along with gubernatorial nominee Rutherford B. Hayes, made a forthright, high-minded appeal for Negro suffrage. Affirming the principle of political equality and hoping to counter Democratic charges that blacks were unfit for citizenship, Unionist campaign officials that fall placed black spokesmen such as David Jenkins on the campaign circuit. For the first time blacks, who had anxiously awaited an opportunity to take their case to the people but had appreciated the extreme sensitivity of the suffrage question, were allowed to participate.[36]

However, a mood of despair characterized the Unionist campaign of 1867 almost from the beginning. In early September, a month before the polling, the Columbus *Ohio State Journal* acknowledged that appeals to conscience and ideals were having no effect; the paper apologetically pointed out that "a selfish appeal . . . [might] reach many men on whom any argument as to the abstract justice of manhood suffrage would be lost." The newspaper then promised reluctant Republicans in central and southern Ohio that black voting would insure Republican ascendancy in many political borderline counties, particularly in those counties which had seen the greatest recent black influx, and lessen Democratic majorities in others. Such arguments did little to counter Democratic claims that political opportunism motivated the campaign for black voting. And since Democrats insisted that black voting would inevitably lead to the breakdown of all barriers to interracial intimacy—Democratic women carried banners with the inscription, "Fathers! Husbands! Save Us From Negro Equality! White Husbands or None!" in that fall's elections parades—such arguments also

nal of Southern History, XXXIII (Aug., 1967), 303–330, esp., 317–319; William Gillette, *The Right to Vote: Politics and the Passage of the Fifteenth Amendment* (Baltimore, 1965).

[36] Porter, *Ohio Politics during Civil War*, pp. 241–248; Toppin, "Emancipation in Retrospect," 241–242; Columbus *Ohio State Journal*, Aug. 26, Sept. 2, 5, 17, 1867.

did little to educate an electorate conditioned for decades by such justifications of racial discrimination.[37]

The election was a debacle for both Unionists and Negro suffrage. The suffrage proposal alienated downstate Republicans and, along with dislike for the proposal to take the vote from deserters and for Republican policy in the South, sped the return of the War Democrats to the Democracy. Democrats won control of both houses and came within 3,000 votes of capturing the governorship. Negro suffrage was defeated in referenda at New York, Connecticut, and Minnesota, and it failed in Ohio by 38,353 votes. Except in and around the Reserve and in several Republican strongholds like Greene and Athens counties, it suffered emphatic rejection. While Hayes carried Hamilton County (Cincinnati) by 1,532 votes, the enfranchising proposal lost there by 4,677. Even in counties carried by Hayes *and* the proposal, including all but one in the Reserve, enfranchisement carried by margins considerably less than Hayes's.[38]

During the 1868–69 legislative session, the Democratic majority attempted to turn back the clock on racial advancement. Claiming that Hayes's victory was the result of mulatto voting in Republican constituencies, Democrats passed legislation disfranchising mulattoes and allowing election judges to issue sharp, humiliating challenges to any voter whose appearance bespoke African ancestry. They also rescinded the ratification of the Fourteenth Amendment by the previous legislature, and in 1869 rejected the Fifteenth Amendment. However, Republican executive action kept both resolutions from reaching Congress.[39]

When black enfranchisement came to Ohio, it was hardly an unqualified triumph for the forces of democracy and tolerance. The state campaign in the fall of 1869 witnessed a much greater emphasis on economic issues and political corruption than in other elections since the war. Republican candidates conceded that white voters simply were not interested in the suffrage issue. Perhaps with blacks now regularly voting in large numbers and holding office in the South, white Ohioans had come to accept the likelihood of black voting. At

[37] Columbus *Ohio State Journal*, Sept. 11, Oct. 10, 1867; Roseboom, *Civil War Era*, pp. 458–563; Porter, *Ohio Politics during Civil War*, p. 244.

[38] Cincinnati *Commercial*, Oct. 12, 1867; Frank U. Quillin, *The Color Line in Ohio* (Ann Arbor, 1913), p. 100. Negro suffrage was approved that fall by the voters of Iowa; Fishel, "Northern Prejudice," 20.

[39] Bucyrus *Journal*, Oct. 11, 1867; Columbus *Ohio Statesman*, n.d., quoted in Cleveland *Leader*, Oct. 18, 1867; Porter, *Ohio Politics during Civil War*, pp. 253–254; Ohio, *Laws, 1868*, pp. 95–100. Resistance to the mulatto disfranchisement law was present throughout the Republican counties; Xenia *Torchlight*, Apr. 15, 29, May 20, June 3, 1868; Columbus *Ohio State Journal*, May 29, 30, June 6, Aug. 15, Dec. 14, 1868.

any rate, they seemed willing to leave the matter up to the next legislature. Early in 1870, a coalition of Cincinnati's anti-corruption Independent Reformers and the Republicans united to ratify the Fifteenth
Amendment. Democrats to a man in both houses voted against ratification. The amendment was approved by paper-thin margins: 19 to 18
in the Senate, and 57 to 55 in the House.[40]

Yet while the issue was decided along strictly partisan lines, Democratic arguments against the amendment centered almost exclusively
on criticisms of centralized despotism in Republican Washington.
Abusive invective against blacks was conspicuously absent. Indeed,
the Cincinnati *Commercial's* correspondent noted that Democrats
showed "a discreet appreciation of the fact that the Democracy might
stand in need of colored votes before another election," and had thus
tempered its rhetoric in deference to the many black spectators in the
galleries. With blacks about to vote in sizable numbers in southern
and central Ohio, the Democrats were aware that blacks might wield
the balance of power in future elections. In spite of its own long record of hostility to black aspirations, and in the face of black pledges to
vote Republican, the Democracy was not above appeals to black
voters. In the upcoming spring municipal elections, blacks would cast
their first ballots under peaceful circumstances even in many Democratic constituencies, and some Democratic politicians actually attempted to court black support. Within a year and a half, under the
aegis of Vallandigham himself, the Democracy would come to accept
the race's new status as embodied in the Fourteenth and Fifteenth
amendments.[41]

Nothing could have been greater testimony to the power of the vote
or the emergence of a new status quo in race relations. But, in addition, as an indirect result of enfranchisement, blacks began in 1870 to
sit on Ohio juries. Though their right to do so had been guaranteed by
the 1866 federal Civil Rights Act and the Fourteenth Amendment,
efforts to empanel black jurors had failed because of local opposition.
Only after their admission to the political community were black successfully called to sit in judgment of their peers, white and black
alike.[42]

[40] Columbus *Ohio State Journal,* Sept. 7, 8, 13, 30, Oct. 2, 11, 1869, Jan. 14,
15, 19, 20, 21, 1870; Cincinnati *Commercial,* Aug. 6, Sept. 3, 4, Oct. 8, 9, 12,
1869.

[41] Cincinnati *Commercial,* Jan. 21, 1870, Feb. 9, 10, Apr. 2, 4, 5, 1870;
Cleveland *Leader,* Apr. 8, 1870; Clinton *Republican,* Apr. 7, 1870; Xenia
Torchlight, Apr. 13, 1870; Roseboom, *Civil War Era,* pp. 475–478; Rutherford B.
Hayes to Sardis Birchard, Apr. 5, 1870, Hayes Papers.

[42] Circleville *Democrat,* Nov. 3, 1865; Cleveland *Leader,* Aug. 8, 1871;
Xenia *Torchlight,* May 29, 1872; Ironton *Register,* Apr. 8, 1870; Columbus *Ohio
State Journal,* Apr. 8, 1870.

III

In two related ways the five years after the war marked an important turning point in the history of black Ohio. First, armed at last with civil and political guarantees, blacks could pursue the quest for true equality. Too, there was a new period in black population development, characterized by slow growth and a decline in southern in-migration, both of which helped to reinforce new civil and political opportunities. After decades of rapid population increase based on migration from the South, the rate of black growth would now fall from 72 percent in the 1860s to 26 percent in the 1870s and 9 percent in the 1880s. The percentage of Ohio blacks born in the South would fall markedly, from 50 in 1870 to 36 in 1900. Not until the 1890s, and particularly after the turn of the century, would the rate of growth once more climb and a large migration of Southerners begin. Like many rural Ohio blacks who were then leaving the countryside and villages, these Southerners would be bound for the large cities; by 1890, for the first time, over half of the state's blacks would live in urban areas.[43] But in the late nineteenth century, without the burden of continued adjustment to constant migration from the South and ever-growing black populations, race relations were able to settle into promising patterns, guided by the benign influences of civil and political equality, and blacks could seek participation and acceptance in the larger community.

Blacks reached out for their new opportunities. As ratification of the Fifteenth Amendment was celebrated throughout Ohio, black meetings passed resolutions affirming their faith in American democracy and expressing a desire to be responsible citizens. While acknowledging hope for friendship with whites, they disavowed any desire for "social equality" (the contemporary term for interracial contacts in more intimate settings), asking only for fair treatment and consideration as citizens of a common country. They recognized their obligation to apply their energies to the cause of racial uplift.[44]

Yet public demonstrations and pronouncements inadequately describe the transformation from pessimism to hope which many must have experienced during the war era. The case of William Parham of Cincinnati provides but one example. Born in Virginia in 1839 of free parents, Parham was taken to Philadelphia as a child in order to obtain

[43] Bureau of the Census, *Negro Population, 1790–1915*, pp. 44, 68, 92.

[44] Cincinnati *Commercial*, Feb. 8, Apr. 7, 1870; Columbus *Ohio State Journal*, Apr. 14, 30, May 14, 1870; Rutherford B. Hayes to Charles Frost, Feb. 17, 1870, Hayes to W. M. Garvey, Mar. 7, 1870, Hayes to R. H. Folger, Apr. 15, 1870, Hayes Papers.

a public school education. At nineteen, with neither trade nor profession, he went to Cincinnati in search of opportunity, and within a short time he earned a teaching certificate and found employment in the black schools.[45] But Parham's relatively elevated position as a teacher did not change his growing pessimism about the future of American blacks. Like many others, by 1860 he was giving serious consideration to emigrating. In September, 1862, only two weeks before the Preliminary Emancipation Proclamation was issued, he told his friend Jacob White of his hopes to leave for Jamaica. "Unless my mind should undergo a very sudden change," wrote Parham, "[I shall] make an effort to get out of this slave-ridden and Negro-hating country as soon as I can make it expedient to do so. My friend, you do not know how much I yearn to be a *man,* and having found that I can only do so by leaving the country, I am willing to accept the condition." [46]

Within a year, however, Parham had given up the thought of emigration, "at least for the present." It was not only that he had discovered the very substantial cost of resettlement, or that his position in the Cincinnati schools had become more promising since his recent appointment as a principal. As he told White with guarded optimism in August, 1863, he had begun to sense an important change. "The present aspect of things in this country," he wrote, "the injustice and outrage to which we are still subject notwithstanding, gives evidence of coming of a brighter and better day." In fact, Parham's faith in the race's future, and his own sense of the role which he, as an educated, articulate man, might play in the shaping of that future, had begun to develop considerably after the Emancipation Proclamation and with northern victories in the field. He concluded his August remarks to White with a call to action: "When this war is over the next war will be against prejudice which is conquered by intellect, and we shall need all the talent that we have among us or can possibly command." [47]

Parham would not leave the United States, and, with the coming of political and civil equality and the growth of southern blacks' power after the war, his path from despair to hope was completed. He certainly did not believe that racism was dead or that his race's victory was complete. But, like others, he had faith that blacks armed with the vote might protect themselves, while at the same time contending for broader rights. Thus, in 1874, in terms reminiscent of classic perorations on American democracy, Parham went before an audience of Cincinnati blacks to state his faith in the possibilities afforded by political equality:

[45] For a biographical sketch see Cleveland *Gazette,* Dec. 7, 1895.
[46] William Parham to Jacob White, Sept. 7, 1862, Jacob White Papers, HU.
[47] William Parham to Jacob White, Aug. 7, 1863, ibid.

In our country above all others the people bear rule. No royal prerogatives, no absolutism, no oligarchical or aristocratic control, but in the most emphatic and popular sense, a government of the people, by the people, and for the people. The people not only say who will bear rule, but from out of the ranks of the people come the rulers. . . . The degraded bondsmen of yesterday stands erect in the pride of his manhood today, and proudly treads the halls of legislation, a peer among the nation's proudest. The humblest citizen of the commonwealth may, by his ballot, decide the policy of this whole country, on the weightiest matters of public concern. Life and death, social standing, and the pursuits of happiness, are decided by the verdict of men chosen from the masses.[48]

[48] Quoted in Arnett, ed., *Proceedings of the Semi-Centenary*, p. 103.

3

The Color Line

The changes in the race's status were no less dramatic for Ohio's whites than they were for blacks like William Parham. Such changes demanded a considerable altering of perspectives on race relations—by no means an easy task for whites, even for many of the race's allies within and outside the Republican party. A decade of sudden, violent, and radical transformation had overthrown long-standing patterns of thought and of human relations. However reluctant the majority of white Ohioans had shown themselves to be in granting civil and political equality, and however much political necessity rather than humane ideals had pointed them in that direction, they were forced in 1870 to face the fact that blacks were no longer slaves and outcasts, but instead citizens and voters. As even the Democracy had begun to realize, it was necessary to begin to think of them for the first time in a manner which, for most whites, would have been unthinkable but a short time ago: as equals among equals, at least in their civil and political relations to society.

If the sudden and basic nature of the changes in race relations brought about by the 1860s was troubling for whites, so, too, was the relationship of government to the process by which the changes had come about. The new status of blacks was the product of a veritable constitutional revolution in which the central government, its authority already greatly expanded by the war, had intervened to an unprecedented extent in defining and securing the rights of a particular group. True, that group was weak, and the federal government had been its only ally against white resistance to emancipation and to legal guarantees establishing black citizenship. Yet Americans were deeply suspicious of strong central government, and they were wary lest the freedmen and their northern brethren become permanent wards of government. For these reasons especially, many white allies of the cause of racial equality believed that the Fifteenth Amendment, while representing the happy climax of efforts to build a solid foundation for black citizenship, had to mark the end of all special legislation which would depend on the positive intervention of government on behalf of blacks. The Cincinnati *Commercial*, a staunch ally of blacks, sounded a note common to those who saw the only future role of government in race relations as one of enforcing existing laws: ". . . Beyond this government cannot go. The negro must take care of himself or the white man will be obliged to do it . . . and we shall protest as earnestly against special legislation for the blacks as we have against laws discriminating against them. Left to themselves, under impartial laws, both whites and blacks, natives and adopted citizens, must work out their own salvation." [1] Thus, for the *Commercial* and others, blacks would have to prove themselves worthy of changes in social, economic, and cultural life, normally outside the sphere of government regulation, which would be necessary for custom to complement law in pursuit of an egalitarian society.

Yet the ability of blacks to make themselves acceptable to whites was only part of the new equation of social relations. After all, whites controlled the hotels, restaurants, theaters, and places of recreation and enlightenment to which blacks desiring interaction with the larger community might seek entrance. They controlled the economy in which blacks must seek work and training for advancement into better paying and more prestigious jobs. They controlled the appropriations for the black public schools, and thus shaped the quality of the preparation of black children for entrance into a competitive, achievement-oriented society. A number of black institutions of higher education were just then emerging in the South; however, in Ohio, especially to the extent that Wilberforce University would remain small, poor, and as much a preparatory school as a college during the late nineteenth century, whites controlled the colleges, universities, and professional schools into which blacks might seek entrance. Whites would have to change their time-honored habits or black opportunity would not increase appreciably. Much depended especially on changes in attitude, for the color line existed as much within the mind as a time-honored way of conceptualizing human relations as it did in a thousand different everyday settings. While the 1860s had done much to provide a basis for change in racial mores, customary attitudes died hard.

In pursuit of an egalitarian, color-blind society, blacks had what would prove to be an effective weapon: the vote. When, as we shall

[1] Cincinnati *Commercial*, Apr. 15, 1870.

later see, continual protests against inequities in black public education produced few, if any, changes in the quality of black public
schools, and conscientious white school officials themselves were forced
to admit that equality could not be achieved in the context of a dual
school system, black political power was eventually instrumental in
obtaining the passage of an 1887 school desegregation law. In addition, black political muscle in Ohio was flexed in the early 1870s to let
Ohio's federal legislators know that blacks desired passage of egalitarian Republican Senator Charles Sumner's bill to prohibit racial discrimination in a wide variety of public institutions and accommodations. In Ohio itself, discrimination in public accommodations would
be legislated against in 1884 and 1894, largely in deference to black
political power. That power would also be used to gain repeal in 1887
of the state's anti-miscegenation law, which had been used on occasion
to harass the relatively few interracial couples in some localities.[2]

Yet changes in white attitudes were not necessarily best gauged by
behavior forced by political calculation or the threat of a lawsuit. Indeed, in the areas where changes in white attitudes might be most
dramatically demonstrated—their willingness to mingle freely with
blacks in public and semi-public settings—neither law nor political
opportunism nor black threats and demands had much success in promoting daily interracial contacts.

In fact, whites responded to the earliest challenges by indicating
that they would readily accept some changes, but that there were limits beyond which they would not be pushed into an undesired intimacy
with blacks. During the war and Reconstruction years blacks, influenced by the progressive trend of local and national events, began to
seek relief from forms of discrimination that posed the greatest inconvenience or hazard to practical welfare, and whites tended to respond
by eventually accepting integration. Blacks first challenged exclusion
from streetcars and separate seating arrangements aboard railroad
trains, where they were forced to ride in smoking cars and ill-kept, uncomfortable second-class accommodations. During the war, with the
support of Republican newspapers and white allies, exclusion from
streetcars was successfully challenged in the courts of Cleveland and
Cincinnati, leading to permanent changes in policy by streetcar companies in the face of judicial reprimands and heavy damages based
upon the application of the common law. In the late 1860s blacks also
began to claim, under both the common law and the 1866 federal
Civil Rights Act, the right to ride in the better cars of trains if they

2 See below, ch. 8.

could afford a first-class ticket; here, too, they won damages in court.[3] By the 1870s discrimination on trains and streetcars was a thing of the past in Ohio. The general white public showed not a trace of resistance to this new situation; doubtless the fleeting nature of such contact and the lack of alternative transportation helped to facilitate integration. Nor was there white opposition in the late 1860s and early 1870s to the first entrance of Ohio's blacks into state custodial institutions, such as hospitals, asylums, orphanages, and reform schools, which had long been supported in part by black taxes. Integration in these settings did not involve close, prolonged contacts between blacks and large numbers of whites.[4]

But whites did not respond with either apathy or equanimity to attempts to force more intimate and prolonged interracial contacts, especially when those contacts would come in the context of leisure or recreation. Blacks continued to be subject to discrimination in hotels, restaurants, and theaters and other places of amusement and culture, usually by complete exclusion from the former and special seating or limited access arrangements in the latter. Thus, while they were beginning to accept the presence of blacks in state institutions and as fellow passengers on common carriers, whites were resisting the efforts of the federal Civil Rights Act of 1875 to bring about equality in public accommodations. The act as passed was a greatly weakened version of the original proposal offered to the Senate some years before by Charles Sumner and rejected by successive Republican Congresses. Many Congressmen voted for the law less in the belief that it would affect patterns of racial contact than in recognition of pledges to Negro voters and of the long, distinguished public career of Sumner, who had died the year before and whose last request was that civil rights legislation be passed.[5] As a means for changing the course of race relations, the law was met with as little enthusiasm in Ohio as it had been in Congress. Most newspapers did not even comment on its passage,

[3] Frank U. Quillin, *The Color Line in Ohio* (Ann Arbor, 1913), pp. 106–107; Cleveland *Leader*, July 1, 1864; Cincinnati *Gazette*, Nov. 25, 1865; Cleveland *Gazette*, June 7, 1899; Forrest Wood, *Black Scare: The Racist Response to Emancipation and Reconstruction* (Berkeley, 1968), p. 135; Benjamin Arnett, ed., *The Centennial Jubilee of Freedom* (Xenia, 1888), p. 79.

[4] Ohio, Board of Commissioners of Reform Schools, *12th Annual Report . . . 1867* (Columbus, 1868), p. 17; Ohio, Trustees and Superintendent, Girl's Industrial Home, *5th Annual Report . . . 1873* (Columbus, 1874), p. 15; Ohio *House Journal, 1866*, pp. 392, 401; Gerald N. Grob, *Mental Institutions in America: Social Policy to 1875* (New York, 1973), pp. 254–255.

[5] James McPherson, "The Abolitionists and the Civil Rights Act of 1875," *Journal of American History*, LII (Dec., 1865), 493–510; Bertram Wyatt-Brown, "A Cenotaph for Charles Sumner: The Civil Rights Law of 1875" (unpublished paper in the possession of James McPherson).

doubtless in the belief that it would never be enforced. However, a
few interested Democratic papers saw the act as the culmination of
Republican attempts to force complete social equality upon the races,
and they vowed resistance. "The Negro Equality Monstrosity Bill,"
said the Cincinnati *Enquirer*, represented "tyranny of the worst kind,"
taking away "the liberty of social choice in public places." The *Enquirer* demanded that Democratic state legislators introduce legislation
to nullify the act in Ohio.[6] Those Republican papers which offered
comment showed little approval and much embarrassment at the time
of passage, spending most of their commentary attempting to placate
white fears that the law would be enforced and suggesting that eventually it would be declared unconstitutional by the Supreme Court.
Even the Cleveland *Leader*, one of Ohio's most consistently militant
egalitarian newspapers, predicted that the law would prove no substitute for the forces of "time, association, and an advanced social and
political standard" by which other groups had been able to obtain
social acceptance. The *Leader* offered the view that a "general feeling
of strong opposition to the semi-social equalization" of the races destined the new law to very moderate success.[7] Most upset of all were
the proprietors of accommodations covered under the law, for they
feared that having to accept black patrons would drive away their
regular white customers. Then too, the businessmen generally shared
the racial views of their white patrons, and they were not always
eager to do business with blacks even if it were possible for them to
profit from it.[8]

For their part, blacks understood white opposition to interracial
mingling in certain settings. Though blacks deeply desired the passage
of the Sumner law, just as they would desire all legislation protecting
their rights, they were not eager to be insulted and abused for forcing
themselves in places where they were not welcome. Thus in the days
following passage of the federal law only a handful came forward to
press for their rights, usually without success, at hotels, saloons, restaurants, and elsewhere.[9] At the same time, blacks also feared that pub-

[6] Cincinnati *Enquirer*, Mar. 2, 9, 11, 12, 13, 26, 1875; Ironton *Democrat*,
Mar. 18, 1875; Lancaster *Ohio Eagle*, Mar 18, 1875.

[7] Cleveland *Leader*, Mar. 2, 3, 1875; Cincinnati *Commercial*, Mar. 5, 9, 1875.
The Xenia *Torchlight*, which had supported the Sumner bill as it struggled
through Congress in 1874, appears to have been the only Republican paper to
voice approval at the time of passage, though it admitted at the same time that
the new law would most likely not succeed in breaking down color barriers. Ibid.,
Sept. 30, Oct. 7, 21, 1874, Mar. 24, Apr. 14, 1875.

[8] Cincinnati *Enquirer*, Mar. 4, 5, 1875.

[9] Ibid., Mar. 9, 15, 24, 29, Apr. 2, 1875; Cleveland *Leader*, Mar. 8, 1875;
Jackson *Standard*, Apr. 8, 1875.

lic confrontations over equal access to public accommodations might produce violence or lead whites to seek repeal of laws expanding the race's rights. At Cleveland and Columbus racial spokesmen, wary of conflict eventuating from a wholesale assault on local color lines, warned their people not to seek admittance to places where they had yet to gain general acceptance.[10]

Unwilling to provoke confrontations with proprietors, blacks were no more willing to go to court to seek damages against them. Court fights were expensive, and, the procedures mandated by the 1875 law were inconvenient because federal courts were located only at Cincinnati and Columbus; such facts help to explain why only two lawsuits were filed by black Ohioans under the law before 1883, when the Supreme Court declared it unconstitutional.[11] Most blacks likewise failed to utilize state civil rights laws in court battles in more convenient local courts. Whatever their feelings about their abstract rights, the desire to forget the humiliation of public rebuffs at the color line often stopped all but a few from pressing legitimate claims in court. Besides, court fights were no guarantee of justice.[12] Often influenced by local racial mores, Ohio's courts erratically enforced state public accommodations legislation, and many blacks were rightly cynical about the value of filing lawsuits in prejudiced courts.[13]

Thus, in late nineteenth century Ohio custom continued to govern the more intimate forms of human association; through custom whites continued to insist upon the right to define and limit interracial contacts. Yet even in more intimate social settings discrimination was in-

[10] Columbus *Ohio State Journal*, Feb. 25, Mar 10, 1875; Cleveland *Leader*, Mar. 4, 1875.

[11] Neither case involved the usual public accommodations, however. United States v. Buntin, 10 F.730 (USCC, Ohio Southern District, 1882) was an attempt to use the law to force equal school facilities for blacks from local school officials in a southern Ohio township. Gray v. Cincinnati Southern Railroad Co., 11 F.683 (USCC, Ohio Southern District, 1882) was a suit in which the plaintiff contended that she had been denied a first-class accommodation on a train going from Cincinnati to the South, even though she held a first-class ticket. The 1875 law was hardly more effective elsewhere in the nation, according to one scholar who has studied its application and enforcement: John Hope Franklin, "The Enforcement of the Civil Rights Act of 1875" (paper presented at the meeting of the American Historical Association, Washington, Dec. 29, 1964).

[12] The refusal to sue under civil rights laws was a point of considerable intraracial contention; see Cleveland *Gazette*, Sept. 6, 1890, Sept. 12, 26, 1891, July 9, Aug. 20, 1892, July 11, 1896.

[13] Outright refusal of local courts to enforce civil rights legislation, usually through legal technicalities, and the unwillingness of judges and juries to award maximum damages available under the laws combined to weaken civil rights laws throughout the state, independent of region. Damages of as little as one cent were awarded occasionally; Cleveland *Gazette*, Apr. 18, 1885, May 29, 1886, Apr. 16, 30, 1887, Jan. 31, Apr. 4, 1891; Chillicothe *Advertiser*, June 25, 1892.

formal and often random in its application, and important regional and social factors caused variation in the extent of racal proscription. As before, the reputation of the northeastern counties for tolerance and openness and that of the southern counties for the greatest rigidity carried into the new era. In addition, the upper classes of black society —the relatively affluent and conventionally refined artisans, proprietors of small businesses, professionals, and those in the upper levels of domestic service—received more considerate treatment in public accommodations than did other blacks. To a large extent, of course, the problem of access to such accommodations was their problem to begin with; it is doubtful that the poor and those not conforming to white social and cultural norms could afford or desired to patronize expensive restaurants, hotels, and theaters.

The new patterning of race relations favored the light-skinned to some extent, but more as the result of class than of color per se. In the ante-bellum period, the better treatment accorded the light-skinned had been almost exclusively the result of judicial and legislative attempts to define "black" and "white" for the sake of better ordering proscriptive relations. The ultimate effect, therefore, was to reinforce the separation of the races by placing definite legal limits, already recognized by custom, on the social and political status of the darker-skinned. In the late nineteenth century the lighter-skinned, because they were often prominently represented in the black upper class, profited proportionately from the general increase in tolerance of higher-status blacks. Yet efforts to favor the lighter-skinned *as a group*, by reason of color alone, were usually not successful where white opinion was against interracial mixing. At Columbus in 1873, for example, the attempt of one theater owner to begin seating light-complected Negroes on the main floor, rather than in the balcony where Columbus blacks had traditionally been made to sit, created substantial white resistance. "So many people spoke about it, and their tone was so unfavorable," the proprietor told the Columbus *Dispatch*, explaining his decision to go back to the older seating policy, "that [I] was compelled to manage my business more discreetly." Under such circumstances, it was probably only to the extent that light-skinned Negroes might "pass" unnoticed for white that they were decidedly at an advantage.[14]

Whether light or dark, higher-status blacks enjoyed unprecedented opportunity for contact with whites of equivalent social rank as the result of the new patterning of race relations. With black citizenship now firmly established in law, the restraints which had kept higher-status

14 Columbus *Dispatch*, Dec. 2, 6, 1873.

whites from recognizing a basis for solidarity with their black counterparts had somewhat lessened. After all, as we shall see, these blacks and whites shared social and moral values, and while the blacks lacked the firm economic base and wealth of their white counterparts, they still aspired to the same lifestyle. The result was the social and cultural basis for an informal, sympathetic understanding across racial lines. Reinforcing other similarities of attitude and belief was a spiritual heritage in Protestantism which blacks possessed, unlike the Catholic and Jewish immigrants who would stream into America in the late nineteenth century. Indeed, to the extent that the universality of Christianity had been able to erode the color line before 1860, it had been among small numbers of the upper classes of both races, often servants and employers, who had worshipped together at the same churches. Where such interracial worship continued at all outside the very small villages in post-bellum Ohio, it occurred between the upper classes in higher-status denominations, particularly among Episcopalians, Congregationalists, and Presbyterians.[15] Furthermore, higher-status whites who felt secure in their wealth and status and anxious to hold on to their power were relatively unthreatened by the possible socioeconomic advancement and increasing social acceptance of a few blacks with whom they shared basic conservative visions of the good society. The Cincinnati *Evangelist,* the organ of local white Protestant philanthropic and missionary activities, revealed such an orientation early in the new era when it compared the claims of the city's blacks and immigrant Irish to moral support and practical assistance from philanthropic interests. "Of the colored people in this city," said the *Evangelist,* "we believe a larger proportion than of the Irish are worthy, inoffensive, and industrious, and they have a stronger claim to protection." [16]

Feeling greater sympathy for the aspirations of their black counterparts to a fuller citizenship, higher-status whites were at the same time somewhat less squeamish about public interracial mixing between persons of roughly equivalent social rank than whites generally were, and they tended to accept blacks more easily in relatively intimate social settings. It was often the case that, though smaller restaurants of lesser

[15] Usually only from the late 1890s on were separate black churches, affiliated with these denominations, founded. See Cleveland *Gazette,* Feb. 2, 1889, July 8, 1893, Mar. 19, 1898; Cincinnati *Commercial Tribune,* July 1, 1901; Indianapolis *Freeman,* June 12, 1909, June 5, Aug. 11, 14, 1915; Cleveland *Leader,* Jan. 13, 1868, June 17, 1901; Ivan Tribe, "The Development of a Rural Community: Albany, Ohio, 1840–1880" (Master's thesis, Ohio University, 1967), pp. 101–102. See below, pp. 132, 143.

[16] Cincinnati *Evangelist,* n.d., quoted in Cincinnati *Colored Citizen,* Nov. 7, 1863.

quality or expense refused service to blacks, the more expensive, high-quality ones, such as the dining rooms of the better hotels, did serve well-dressed, well-mannered Negroes. Harry Smith, the young editor of the black Cleveland *Gazette*, reported indignantly that while traveling through Springfield in 1883 he had been refused service by white "trash in an ill-smelling hole," "a one-horse restaurant," but that later the same night he got dinner in "Springfield's best hotel." Much to the surprise of the staunchly Republican Smith, the dining room and hotel were kept by a courteous and pleasant Democrat.[17]

Once more intimate interracial contacts between higher-status blacks and whites had been largely restricted to contexts in which blacks served whites, who responded in a spirit of condescension and paternalism, but now contacts were occasionally more egalitarian in spirit. It was not that the older servile relations had by any means disappeared, for some blacks of the upper class continued to depend upon work as servants, cooks, and carriage drivers for wealthy whites for their livelihood. Nor was it that white paternalism was dead; as the Cincinnati *Evangelist*'s use of the work "protection" in relation to the race's needs would suggest, the social disabilities and poverty which blacks suffered continued to make them objects of charity, pity, and moral homilies. Instead, the new era made more equal contacts possible in certain limited but nevertheless meaningful contexts—the jury box, the polling place, and occasionally the more intimate settings of hotels, restaurants, theaters, and the like.

While bringing "the gentlemen," in Harry Smith's oft-used phrase, of both races together in greater equality than ever before, the new era of race relations also provided blacks with important allies in the struggle for equality and fair treatment. In the practical context of daily relations between the races, this alliance frequently manifested itself in the informal efforts of individual whites to aid blacks in fighting the color line. Often whites acted as surrogates for blacks in situations where blacks would have been victims of discrimination had they acted alone. For example, for many years John Green of Cleveland had difficulty renting business suites in the better downtown office buildings, and thus he had white colleagues in the legal practice rent for him.[18] In similar fashion, white friends sometimes acted as intermediaries for blacks who wished to buy property or homes in neighborhoods where blacks were not welcome.[19] On the other occasions,

17 Cleveland *Gazette*, Oct. 6, 1883.
18 John P. Green, *Fact Stranger Than Fiction: 75 Years of a Busy Life* (Cleveland, 1920), pp. 350–351.
19 Mary Louise Mark, *Negroes in Columbus* (Columbus, 1928), p. 22.

whites indignant about the racial discrimination faced by upper-class black acquaintances challenged prejudiced whites directly. When Green was denied an inner table at a Cleveland restaurant in the 1880s and the owner attempted to seat him away from the rest of the patrons, he left—to return the next day with a number of prominent white friends, including a local Democratic judge, all of whom successfully persuaded the owner to seat Green with other customers.[20] Similar was the example of Mrs. Nicholas Alexander, one of the city's leading black socialites and the proprietor of a beauty salon frequented by Cincinnati's wealthiest white women. In 1894, with the aid of a wealthy white friend, she conducted a one-woman crusade against discrimination in local public accommodations.[21]

Such white support might be especially important in shaping race relations in those areas of the state, such as the centrally located urban centers of Dayton, Springfield, and Columbus, where the pattern of race relations was less certain than in the northeastern and southern counties. At Columbus, for example, blacks were admitted to county and municipal public custodial institutions and to the semi-public Home for The Friendless, an orphanage supported by white churches; high schools there were integrated in 1872 and elementary schools in 1882, and the situation in public accommodations was fluid. No definite pattern of discrimination had emerged in theaters, restaurants, or hotels by 1880, though there was a tendency for affluent, prominent blacks to be favored where facilities were generally closed to Negroes.[22] In 1880 the state legislature played an unusual role in fighting local discrimination; early in that year's legislative session, a scandal over the treatment of blacks in local accommodations rocked the General Assembly. Cincinnati Representative George Washington Williams,[23] the first black elected to the General Assembly, had been told by the headwaiter of a popular downtown restaurant frequented by legislators that he would be denied service unless he agreed to eat in the kitchen by himself or take his food outside, both common ploys for ridding restaurants of Negro patrons. An aristocratic mulatto with careers in both the ministry and law though he was not yet much over thirty, Williams had been entertained without incident in the finest hotels and

[20] Green, *Fact Stranger Than Fiction*, pp. 161–162.

[21] Cleveland *Gazette*, Apr. 29, 1894.

[22] Columbus *Dispatch*, Dec. 2, 1873; Columbus *Ohio State Journal*, Mar. 10, 1875, Feb. 25, 1878; Quillin, *Color Line in Ohio*, pp. 109–111; Richard Clyde Minor, "Negroes in Columbus" (Ph.D. dissertation, Ohio State University, 1936), pp. 239–241.

[23] William W. Simmons, *Men of Mark: Eminent, Progressive, and Rising* (Cleveland, 1887), pp. 371–383.

dining rooms of the city and was not about to consent to such a humiliating proposition. He left immediately, but the incident was observed by several legislators who spread word of the insult around the legislature, though they failed to intervene at the time. Within several days the legislature had established a special bipartisan committee to investigate the affair; it requested (and immediately received) a public apology from the owner, and demanded that he cease to discriminate against Negroes. When he proved intransigent in regard to the latter demand, informal pressure was placed on him, and his business was said to have declined considerably in the next years.[24] Several years after the Williams incident Democratic Governor George Hoadley, a long-time defender of Negro rights, was himself responsible for the closing of a Columbus skating rink when several prominent blacks complained to him that it was discriminating against them.[25] To the extent that other Columbus proprietors might wish to avoid public censure or diminished patronage, such allies could be very useful to Columbus blacks in their struggle for open facilities.

While they also profited from the intervention of white allies, blacks in the northeastern counties had a less difficult struggle for access to the better accommodations. Cleveland's reputation for racial liberalism was grounded in public schools which integrated both pupils and teaching staffs, and in relatively open accommodations. As in the antebellum period, there was discrimination in seating in some Cleveland theaters, but blacks were rarely, if ever, denied admission. In places of amusement (like skating rinks) they were generally accorded equal treatment, backed when occasionally necessary by courts which more consistently gave a positive interpretation of civil rights laws than those elsewhere in the state.[26] Restaurants of higher quality also welcomed refined, affluent black guests. George Myers, a local political leader and the owner of a popular barbershop catering to the city's most influential businessmen and professionals, spoke in the 1890s of having had dinner with his wife and another black couple at the exclusive Cleveland Yacht Club, followed by cocktails and then tea at two other prominent restaurants. The dining rooms of the better department stores also served those blacks affluent enough to shop in them.[27]

24 Ohio *House Journal, 1880,* p. 47, and Appendix, pp. 982–983; Cleveland *Gazette,* Apr. 14, 1896.

25 Cleveland *Gazette,* Feb. 14, 1885; Philip D. Jordan, *Ohio Comes of Age, 1873–1900* (Columbus, 1943), pp. 285–286.

26 Cleveland *Leader,* Jan. 5, Apr. 6, 1866, Dec. 25, 1868, Aug. 28, 1873, Nov. 30, 1874; Cleveland *Gazette,* Dec. 27, 1884, Jan 3, May 3, 1885, May 29, 1886, Feb. 7, 1891.

27 Cleveland *Leader,* Mar. 7, 1865; George Myers to John Green, Apr. 1, 1898, John P. Green Papers, WHRS; Cleveland *Gazette,* July 16, 1892.

Hotels, too, were generally open. As early as the 1850s the better ones had begun to serve an occasional Negro notable, and their dining rooms were serving blacks at least as early as 1865. The Cleveland *Gazette* boasted that all the better hotels served "colored gentlemen." Yet there were exceptions: the fashionable Hollenden House, where Myers kept his barbershop, limited itself to serving only an occasional prominent black, and the exclusive American House was known to refuse black patrons.[28]

At Oberlin, the pattern of race relations in both town and college was open in the late nineteenth century. Of his experience at Oberlin in the late 1860s William Sanders Scarborough, later a president of Wilberforce University, wrote, "I forgot I was a colored boy in the lack of prejudice and genial atmosphere that surrounded me, and enjoyed such life and amusements with others as they presented themselves to me."[29] Mary Church Terrell's memories of Oberlin a decade later were similar. For many years a fighter for racial equality, Mrs. Terrell remembered, "As a colored girl at Oberlin, I was accorded the same treatment . . . at that time as a white girl under similar circumstances. . . . Outward manifestations of prejudice against colored students would not have been permitted for one moment at that time by those in authority. . . . It would be difficult for a colored girl to go through a white school with fewer unpleasant experiences occasioned by race prejudice than I had." Mrs. Terrell recalled that she boarded with other women of both races at Ladies Hall, belonged to the women's literary societies, and served as an editor of the *Oberlin Review*.[30] Occasionally, however, private dining facilities and boarding houses serving both black and white students attempted to discriminate against blacks by having them sit at separate tables or refusing to rent them rooms; these establishments compromised Oberlin's reputation for tolerance. Though the college was known to intervene on behalf of black students experiencing such discrimination, some black alumni would remain embittered for years because of these practices.[31] In the town of Oberlin, the racial climate was open. Indeed, when a roller-skating rink proprietor attempted to break precedent by excluding

[28] Betty Culpepper, "The Negro and the Black Laws of Ohio, 1803–1860" (Master's thesis, Kent State University, 1965), p. 69; Cleveland *Leader*, Mar. 7, 1865; Cleveland *Gazette*, Apr. 30, July 12, Sept. 3, 1892.

[29] Sarah C. B. Scarborough and Bernice Sanders, eds., "Autobiography of the Life of William Sanders Scarborough" (undated typescript in the possession of T. K. Gibson), p. 5.

[30] Mary Church Terrell, *A Colored Woman in a White World* (Washington, 1940), pp. 33, 39–45.

[31] New York *Globe*, Aug. 11, 1883; Cleveland *Gazette*, Mar. 28, Apr. 25, 1891, June 25, 1892.

several black youths from his newly opened rink in 1884, the same youths "made it so hot for the owner" that he was forced to leave town for a time, a punishment which local public opinion sanctioned.[32]

Elsewhere in the Western Reserve and its immediate environs a relatively open situation prevailed in the late nineteenth century. Though occasional reports of discrimination found their way into the Negro press,[33] an unusual degree of racial contact was also present. At Massilon in Stark County, for example, the races dined together in 1886 at a dinner dance sponsored by a local black organization. Over two hundred whites came upon invitation. "There was no distinction shown on account of color," said the Cleveland Gazette's Massilon correspondent, adding casually, "Whites and blacks danced together." [34] Most schools of the northeastern regions towns were integrated well before the school desegregation law of 1887 or had never known segregation at all. Thus, when school integration brought chaos to some central and southern Ohio communities in the fall of 1887, the Steubenville Herald was moved to "inquire what all the racket is about." At Steubenville, said the paper, "the color line in the schools and other public places . . . has long been a thing of the past. Our schools are mixed and a colored couple in the most fashionable part of the Opera House does not excite any comment." [35]

Finally, it was only in the northeast that integration was found in social and recreational voluntary associations, such as lodges and YMCAs. Except for one post established by choice by some Cleveland blacks in 1886, black Civil War veterans in this region mingled freely with white veterans in integrated posts of the Grand Army of the Republic; at least six integrated posts were found at Cleveland itself. The Massilon post was not only integrated, but its commander was Robert Pinn, a black attorney. To the south—at Xenia, Cincinnati, Middleport, and Springfield—separate posts existed.[36] In addition, at a time when white fraternals barely recognized the existence of their black brethren, Cleveland and Youngstown boasted integrated Masonic lodges; they were usually white lodges with a handful of black members, but at Youngstown there was a black lodge with a white member.[37] While

[32] Cleveland Gazette, Dec. 20, 1884.

[33] Ibid., Dec. 20, 1884, Apr. 18, 1885, Apr. 2, June 25, 1892.

[34] Ibid., Jan. 1, 1887.

[35] Steubenville Herald, n.d., quoted in Belmont Chronicle, Sept. 22, 1887; Leonard Erickson, "The Color Line in Ohio Public Schools, 1829–1890" (Ph.D. dissertation, Ohio State University, 1959), pp. 223–227.

[36] Cleveland Gazette, Dec. 4, 1886, Feb. 25, 1888; Frank Levstik, "Robert A. Pinn," Negro History Bulletin, XXXVII (Nov., 1974), 305.

[37] Harry E. Davis, A History of Free Masonry among Negroes in America (n.p., 1946), pp. 178–179.

elsewhere in Ohio they discouraged Negro membership, the YMCA at Canton and Cleveland and the YWCA at Cleveland admitted small numbers of respected and conventionally respectable blacks.[38]

Conditions were far less open as one moved into southern Ohio, where relatively large numbers of blacks and local racial custom combined to produce greater separation of the races. Here the public schools often remained segregated until 1887; in a few towns, like Xenia, Gallipolis, and Hillsboro, they would continue to be segregated in defiance of law until well into the twentieth century.[39] Here, too, separate public custodial institutions often existed, or blacks were restricted to certain sections of existing facilities—in either case, in contrast to the integrated facilities of northeastern Ohio. During the 1880s, for example, the Colored House of Cincinnati served as both a hospital and a house of refuge, catering to the needs of persons of all ages and maladies. So decrepit was Colored House that it had been condemned by several grand juries. Black orphans at Cincinnati continued to live in the black orphan asylum and could not spend more than a day or so at the public orphanage. However, the lack of general facilities for young black indigents or delinquents who were not orphans often led to their admission to the regular House of Refuge, where a policy of dividing the races had unfortunate consequences. While whites were divided into groups according to their reason for being in the institution, all blacks, whether young orphans or teenage delinquents, were placed together. At other locations where there were neither separate facilities nor support for integration, black indigents, orphans, and the sickly might simply be allowed to drift without public support.[40]

Public accommodations at Cincinnati were less open than in Cleveland and Columbus, and blacks were more subject to abusive treatment there. Theaters were not consistent in their policies, often restricting blacks to certain sections, but sometimes admitting them on an equal basis. Private amusement parks, restaurants, and hotels often showed a cavalier disregard for civil rights laws, and they were notorious for turning away black diners and travelers regardless of class or

[38] Russell H. Davis, *Black Americans in Cleveland from George Peake to Carl B. Stokes* (Washington, 1972), pp. 262–263; Cleveland *Gazette*, Jan. 2, 1897, Jan. 31, 1903.

[39] Erickson, "Color Line in Ohio Public Schools," pp. 191–226.

[40] Columbus *Ohio State Journal*, Feb. 25, 1867; Xenia *Torchlight*, Dec. 15, 1869; Cleveland *Gazette*, Jan. 31, 1885; Quillin, *Color Line in Ohio*, p. 127; Wendell Phillips Dabney, *Cincinnati's Colored Citizens: Historical, Sociological, and Biographical* (Cincinnati, 1926), p. 400; Zane Miller, *Boss Cox's Cincinnati: Urban Politics in the Progressive Era* (New York, 1968), p. 68; Cincinnati, Bureau of Municipal Research, *The House of Refuge* (Cincinnati, 1912), p. 14.

fame.[41] When the Cincinnati *Enquirer* polled the city's leading inn-keepers after the passage of the 1875 Civil Rights Law, only one was willing to abide by the law. On the other hand, the owner of the city's highly reputed Burnet House explained that he would attempt to cir-cumvent the law by setting apart a section of the hotel for a black sleeping quarters and one of the three dining rooms for black diners. The owner of the St. James stated that opinion in the city and among its visitors, many of them Southerners, would never support integrated hotels; he stated frankly, "When I have to take Negroes into my hotel, I will shut down entirely . . . not because of any hatred for the race, but because it would ruin my business." He recalled sorrowfully that he had been threatened with violence in 1873 when he had given a room to P. B. S. Pinchback, the prominent Louisiana black politician who had served for a time as both lieutenant governor and governor of that state. He had since become more cautious, to the extent that he had once refused accommodations to a party of sixty trade union-ists, two of whom were black, when the whites insisted that their black comrades be given rooms. The matter was resolved when the blacks agreed to accept accommodations elsewhere.[42] Cincinnati's restaurants, including those of highest quality, drew the color line, denying blacks service or having them sit in remote corners. Politically prominent local blacks as well as a black minister visiting the city were known to have been forcibly ejected from one restaurant on two separate occasions in the early 1890s.[43] In the face of such treatment and widespread dis-crimination, Cincinnati blacks organized a Civil Rights League in the 1880s to contend for their rights in public accommodations, but they also tended to withdraw from white-owned facilities where they con-tinually encountered insult and humiliation.[44] By the early 1890s, therefore, they had established "four first class colored eating halls" which were said to cater to "the most cultured colored people"; black visitors to Cincinnati were referred to these dining rooms.[45] Similarly, black Cincinnatians continued to maintain two cemeteries, for racial discrimination did not stop at the grave in the Queen City; the city's larger cemeteries continued to refuse to bury the Negro dead.[46]

Unlike Cleveland and Columbus, nationally known blacks often re-ceived poor treatment at Cincinnati. Cleveland's John Green, a state

[41] Cleveland *Gazette*, Feb. 21, 1885, Mar. 27, 1886, Jan. 31, Feb. 7, Apr. 4, 1891, Oct. 8, 1892; Cincinnati *Gazette*, Jan. 14, 1887; Cincinnati *Commercial*, Mar. 9, 1875.

[42] Cincinnati *Enquirer*, Mar. 4, 5, 1875.

[43] Cleveland *Gazette*, Mar. 12, Apr. 16, 1887, Sept. 22, 1888, Jan. 4, 1890, Feb. 7, 1891, Jan. 2, 1894.

[44] Ibid., May 6, 1886, Apr. 7, 1887, Feb. 7, 1891.

[45] Ibid., Jan. 9, 1892.

[46] New York *Age*, June 14, 1890; Dabney, *Cincinnati's Colored Citizens*, p. 193.

representative who had recently won the gratitude of labor by sponsoring a bill to establish an annual Ohio Labor Day, was asked to address a Labor Day gathering at Cincinnati in 1890. He was refused rooms at several hotels before finally finding accommodations. The next year Green, now a member of the state senate, returned to address the same labor gathering. Though he registered without incident at the city's fashionable Gibson House, he found that he was expected to take his meals in the hotel's kitchen. When his protest failed to change the owner's attitude, he left immediately to find other lodging. The discriminatory policy of the Gibson House remained, however, and in the future traveling black notables continued to receive similar insult there.[47]

Yet it was testimony to the progressive spirit of the times that discrimination in public accommodations was regarded by some whites as wrong when its objects were men like Green. When they received word in 1891 of the treatment Green had received, the committee of Cincinnati labor leaders which had invited him to speak was reportedly bitter and indignant. And when the committee reported news of the incident to the local Republican campaign committee, under whose auspices gubernatorial candidate William McKinley had come to address the same Labor Day ceremony, the Republicans canceled McKinley's reservations at the same hotel in a show of solidarity. Then both the trade unionists and the Republicans visited Green to report their anger and apologies.[48]

As long as treatment like that given Green was a daily occurrence in Ohio, the last decades of the nineteenth century could hardly be described as a golden age in the state's race relations. Yet, as the response to the insult suffered by Green indicates, there were whites who were sincere enough in their egalitarian ideals to act against the color line, whether through direct confrontation or simply through the exercise of tolerance in daily life. Some were respected enough to call into question the morality of racial discrimination, and on occasion they might be powerful enough to force limited changes in the structure of discrimination. They believed that society should aspire to be more open to educated, accomplished, and conventionally refined Negroes like Green. Though limited by class and cultural factors, the ethos of the new era in race relations had important resonance, creating a receptive atmosphere which inspired and would be inspired by the efforts of black leaders to seek a society color blind in fact as well as in law.

[47] Cleveland *Gazette,* Sept. 6, 13, 1890, Sept. 12, 26, 1891, July 9, Aug. 20, 1892.
[48] Cincinnati *Post,* Sept. 7, 1891.

4

Employment and Economic Opportunity

Perhaps the most pressing daily problem facing the masses of Ohio blacks was earning a living. Here the new era revealed its greatest limitations, for it was unable to transcend the traditionally narrow boundaries of black employment in the state. While important changes were taking place in black civil status, the large majority of working black men and women throughout Ohio continued to be confined to low-paying, less prestigious jobs requiring few skills and offering only minimal opportunity for advancement. The leading preserve of black opportunity continued to lie in domestic and personal service; blacks were overrepresented in Ohio's service work force, and such work remained the most important route by which a very few became entrepreneurs. For working black women, domestic and personal service was for all practical purposes the only employment opportunity. The number of black skilled workers was limited to a corps of artisans in the building trades and a few assorted crafts and those, such as cooks and barbers, in the upper reaches of service work.

As had been the case before 1860, black workers continued to be greatly hindered by the indifference and hostility of many white workers and white employers to their aspirations for better employment. The lack of opportunity afforded by whites only reinforced the lack of mechanical, technical, and commercial skills with which most blacks had left slavery. Moreover, since they formed no more than 3 percent of Ohio's work force in the late nineteenth century, and rarely more than 15 percent of the total population even in those areas where they were most concentrated, Ohio blacks usually lacked the large numbers in any one occupation in a particular location which made black workers indispensable to white capital in many areas of the South and gave southern blacks the strength to compete successfully with whites. This lack of strength in numbers often hindered Ohio's black workers as they faced the challenge of an increasingly powerful and often hostile labor movement, and of a continuing but ever-growing influx of European immigrants, particularly in large cities. In the face of the racial bond between white workers and employers, and their own numerical weakness, black workers did not usually have a significant competitive advantage in their struggle to expand their economic opportunity and to best immigrants and their children.

Yet blacks continued to use what small weapons they had to contend for a firmer economic base, founded upon steady if usually unskilled or servile employment. In the late nineteenth century they held onto those opportunities which they had long enjoyed in domestic and personal service. In addition, in a few industrial fields, in those few locations where their numbers were relatively large or where white competition was particularly weak, they had the chance to grasp at whatever new opportunities presented themselves; slowly, in small numbers, they began to enter Ohio's mines, foundries, and factories. For a small, ambitious minority, there were also unprecedented opportunities opening up in professional life. Yet the pace of progressive change in economic opportunity was slow and erratic, and at the turn of the century most had been left untouched by those positive developments which did occur.

I

The 1890 census is the first for which there is aggregate data on black employment in Ohio. In that year, of Ohio's slightly more than 28,000 black working men, approximately three-quarters were employed as laborers and service workers.[1] The large majority of these men worked as common, unskilled, often outdoor labor in mechanical, transportation, and agricultural fields. In the rural areas of the river-border counties and in southwestern and west-central Ohio where most rural blacks lived, many lacked farmsteads of their own and continued to work as agricultural laborers. In the cities and towns black common laborers still worked in large numbers as hod carriers and general laborers on building and construction projects and as teamsters and draymen for retail and wholesale businesses. Others worked as stationary firemen, stoking furnaces where heat was used in generating power; as laborers in laying, grading, and caring for roads, streets, and railroad and streetcar tracks; and as general labor in warehouses, on loading

[1] U.S. Census Office, *Report on the Population of the United States, Eleventh Census . . . 1890* (Washington, 1897), I, pt. 2, pp. 596–597, 652–659.

platforms, on the docks of the lakes, rivers, and canals, and in lumber-yards and railroad yards.[2] In addition, mining emerged as a major Ohio industry in the 1870s and 1880s with the opening of the rich bituminous coal fields of the Mahoning, Tuscarawas, and Hocking valleys in east-central and southeastern Ohio, and blacks were employed as miners and mine laborers. Often up from southern coal fields and entering the mines in their very first years of operation, occasionally acting as strikebreakers in early labor disputes, the blacks won a firm place for themselves in Ohio mining; by 1890 there were some five hundred black miners and mine laborers in the state. Yet while they constituted a significant number of miners in individual coal districts, such as the Sunday Creek section of Perry County, blacks were no more than 2.5 percent of Ohio's coal mining force in that year.[3]

In urban areas blacks often met stiff competition, particularly from immigrants, in attempts to hold onto and expand employment in the common labor fields in which they had worked before 1860. They tended to do better where the European immigrant influx was less— often where immigrants settling locally had come in mid-century and were experiencing an upgrading of their employment in its closing decades. Under these circumstances, especially when their own numbers were relatively large, blacks might qualify as an important part of the labor force in a rapidly developing local economy. At Columbus blacks in 1890 were 7 percent and first- and second-generation foreign stock 44 percent of the work force; black opportunities were somewhat greater there than at Cincinnati and Cleveland, where blacks were respectively 4.5 and 1.5 percent, and immigrant stock about 75 percent at each. Smaller cities and towns approximating this demographic pattern also seem to have offered greater opportunities. For example, though blacks were found in relatively significant numbers as teamsters, draymen, and hacks in all three major cities, at Columbus they were 18 percent of those in the carrying trades (well over four times the figure for Cleveland and Cincinnati). At Xenia they were about a

[2] Ibid.; Columbus *Ohio State Journal*, Sept. 17, 1867, Nov. 12, 1879; Cincinnati *Enquirer*, Oct. 21, 1887; R. R. Wright, Jr., "The Negroes of Xenia, Ohio: A Social Study," U.S. Department of Labor *Bullentin* no. 48 (Sept., 1903), 1023–24, 1028; Xenia *Gazette*, July 31, 1885.

[3] Herbert Gutman, "Reconstruction in Ohio: Negroes in the Hocking Valley Coal Mines in 1873 and 1874," *Labor History*, III (Fall, 1962), 243–264, and "The Negro and the United Mine Workers of America: The Career and Letters of Richard L. Davis and Something of Their Meaning, 1890–1900," in Julius Jacobson, ed., *The Negro and the American Labor Movement* (New York, 1968), pp. 49–70; Stark County *Democrat*, May 28, 1874; Cincinnati *Commercial*, May 21, 1875; New Lexington *Tribune*, Sept. 16, 1880; Athens *Messenger*, Sept. 17, 1884; Cleveland *Gazette*, Jan. 10, 1885.

quarter of the total population during the late nineteenth century, easily outnumbering the town's largest white ethnic group (the Irish); there they controlled a large share of hacking, teaming, and draying. Similarly, though blacks were often found as helpers in the building trades, only at Columbus and Steubenville, where there were small immigrant populations, did they control a share of the hod-carrying work.[4]

Not surprisingly, it was in fields like hod-carrying that Ohio blacks were winning their greatest acceptance and power within labor unions, for their large numbers in some localities doomed any attempt at unionization without their support. Black unskilled workers were found in significant numbers in the expanding hod carriers' unions and in locals of the weaker stationary firemen's unions. Eventually, when it entered Ohio, they became important in the teamsters' union at a time when they were generally barred from, or admitted only in token numbers to, craft unions. At Columbus and in smaller cities like Steubenville, enough blacks were engaged in hod-carrying that they controlled black locals themselves or helped to run integrated locals.[5] The occasional entrance of blacks as strikebreakers in Ohio mines would appear to have made the chances for cooperation between black and white miners slim; however, once large numbers of blacks had established themselves in various coal districts and whites resigned themselves to their presence, organization across the color line was possible. Unionization came haltingly at first with the efforts of the Knights of Labor in the mid-1880s, but activity increased after the founding in 1890 of the firmly integrationist United Mine Workers. The UMW's white founders were keenly aware of the important representation of blacks in mining, not only in Ohio, but especially in the South.[6]

Yet during and after the late nineteenth century unions were able to do little to advance the conditions of unskilled workers, and the worker's position was often precarious. Coal miners and mine laborers faced long layoffs, wages which barely provided subsistence, infrequent wage payments, unsafe working conditions, iron-clad contracts barring union membership, and exploitative company stores and shabby

---

[4] Census Office, *Eleventh Census,* I, pt. 1, pp. 473–476, and pt. 2, pp. 596–597, 652–659; Richard Clyde Minor, "Negroes in Columbus" (Ph.D. dissertation, Ohio State University, 1936), pp. 40, 54, 55; Helen Hooven Santemyer, *Ohio Town* (Columbus, 1962), p. 98; Cleveland *Gazette,* Mar. 16, 1902.

[5] Cleveland *Gazette,* Sept. 26, 1891, Mar. 16, 1902; Cincinnati *Enquirer,* June 13, 1901; Columbus *Standard,* July 27, 1901.

[6] Gutman, "Negro and UMWA," pp. 49–127; Delmer John Truster, "Unionism among Ohio Miners in the Nineteenth Century" (Master's thesis, Ohio State University, 1947).

company housing in isolated rural villages.[7] Hod carriers and common laborers in construction were poorly paid and had little job security. They generally contracted for work by the day, but occasionally by the hour as well; the responsibility of employers to laborers rarely went beyond the short period of contracts or specific projects. In addition, because of the large capitalization of building projects, which made them dependent on bank loans and hence on the vicissitudes of the national economy, common labor in construction was particularly subject to unpredictable and long layoffs.[8]

Nor were unskilled laborers, rural and urban, immune to displacement as the result of technological change. An increasing mechanization of agriculture during the late nineteenth century undercut the position of farm workers, sending many of them migrating to cities and towns.[9] A similar change was occurring in dock and boat employment on the Ohio River. Large numbers of blacks worked as stevedores on the docks of Ohio River ports from Cincinnati to East Liverpool and as deckhands and firemen on the boat which plied the river in the immediate post-bellum years. Yet after the war steamboats became the victims of the proliferating railroads, and by 1880 black employment on the docks and aboard the boats was declining rapidly. At Cincinnati, one-third fewer blacks were at work in river transportation in 1880 than in 1870. The lake trade did not decline as greatly because of the growing traffic in iron ore from the mines of Minnesota and Michigan, and blacks continued to work on the docks of some lake ports like Lorain and as sailors. However, they had never worked here in anywhere near the same numbers as on the river. European immigrants did most of the work at bigger ports such as Cleveland, and the lakes generally offered little promise for black employment.[10]

[7] Edward Bemis, "Mine Labor in the Hocking Valley," American Economic Association *Proceedings*, III (July, 1888), 27–42; Truster, "Unionism among Ohio Miners," pp. 33–45; *United Mine Workers Journal*, Feb. 28, Apr. 18, July 18, 1895, Feb. 20, Apr. 30, Dec. 17, 1896; Sterling Spero and Abram L. Harris, *The Black Worker: The Negro and the American Labor Movement* (New York, 1931), pp. 353–354; Herbert Northrup, *Organized Labor and the Negro* (New York, 1944), pp. 154–155.

[8] Wright, "Negroes of Xenia," 1028–29; Arch Mersey, *The Laborers' Story, 1903–1953; The First Fifty Years of the International Carriers', Building and Common Laborers' Union (AFL)* (Washington, 1953), p. 38.

[9] Philip D. Jordan, *Ohio Comes of Age, 1873–1900* (Columbus, 1943), pp. 93–95, 106.

[10] Louis Hunter, *Steamboats on Western Rivers: An Economic and Technological History* (Cambridge, Mass., 1949), pp. 448–478; Paul Lammermeier, "Cincinnati's Black Community: The Origins of a Ghetto, 1870–1880," in John Bracey, August Meier, and Elliot Rudwick, eds., *The Rise of the Ghetto* (Belmont, Calif., 1971), p. 25; Cincinnati *Enquirer*, June 14, 1864; Columbus *Ohio State Journal*, Apr. 28, 1868; Cincinnati *Gazette*, June 20, 1866; Cleveland *Gazette*,

Factory work would have constituted a more stable form of employment for blacks than common outdoor labor, even if it need not have necessitated an upgrading of black technical and mechanical skills. But factory work for blacks had been scarce during the ante-bellum era, and they emerged from the 1860s without a greatly increased share of the factory labor force. At Cincinnati their most important such opportunity had been in the tobacco factories, where from 50 to 100 blacks worked as laborers on the eve of the Civil War. But factory work constituted only 2 percent of Cincinnati black employment in 1870,[11] and there is little evidence that blacks had been able to find their way into factories at other locations by then.

Yet in the midst of the rapid industrialization of Ohio cities in the late nineteenth century, black opportunity for steady factory work did begin to improve. Though their numbers were still not large, by the turn of the century black workers were gaining a firmer hold on factory employment in Ohio. From the late 1870s their major opportunity lay in the metal industries, which had a considerable need for unskilled and semi-skilled labor. The first significant entrance of blacks into iron foundries came at Springfield in the late 1870s. They began to work in small numbers in the mills serving the city's vast and rapidly expanding farm machinery industry, then the largest in the nation. At first their appearance in Springfield foundries was a consequence of a deliberate but informal benevolent effort by Asa Bushnell; a wealthy local manufacturer with liberal racial views, Bushnell wanted to help expand the industrial opportunity of local blacks. A few blacks were admitted to Bushnell's shops, and, much to the dismay of the all-white iron molders' union, it was Bushnell's desire that unskilled black workers might eventually learn the iron molder's trade.[12] Though Bushnell protected the blacks he brought into his shops in the face of union opposition, few more blacks were able to obtain work in Springfield's foundries until early in 1886. At that time both local and imported Tennessee blacks were brought in during conflict between management and local affiliates of the Knights of Labor concerning recognition of unionism and of the eight-hour day. Few strikebreakers appear to have stayed on in the foundries after the strike ended, but the power of the metal unions in Springfield was broken for many years to come, and blacks were able to find work, skilled and otherwise, in the iron shops

Nov. 16, 1889; Leslie Fishel, Jr., "The Negro's Welcome to the Western Reserve, 1900–1930," *Midwest Journal*, II, 1 (1949), 53.

[11] Lammermeier, "Cincinnati's Black Community," p. 25; J. F. Clarke, *The Present Condition of the Free Colored People of the United States* (New York, 1859), p. 11.

[12] Indianapolis *Freeman*, Aug. 21, 1897; Springfield *Republic*, Sept. 23, 1897.

without strong opposition. Further enhancing the possibility of black factory employment was Springfield's failure to attract immigrants after the initial entrance of a few thousand Irish and Germans before 1880. By 1900 only a quarter of the city's population was of first- and second-generation foreign stock; blacks were about 11 percent.[13]

The use of black strikebreakers was rare, however, confined for the most part to the coal mines in the 1870s and 1880s, and very seldom occurring in factories and mills. Rarer still was the strikebreaker who found permanent employment in a plant beset by conflict, or the strike that produced greatly expanded opportunity for large numbers of blacks.[14] Furthermore, white workers and their unions were often indifferent to expanded opportunity for black *unskilled* workers. This was particularly true in the metal industries. While unionism in iron, and particularly in steel, was generally weak in the state, even where unions had a foothold, unions did not object to the employment of small numbers of unskilled blacks. Therefore, those blacks entering iron and steel mills usually did so under peaceful circumstances. Their opportunities were greatest where there was no large pool of cheap immigrant labor, which was heavily represented in iron and steel at some locations. Cleveland was one of the nation's major steel producers, but very few blacks found employment in the mills. Indeed, in 1890 there were only three blacks in all the metal industries of the city,

13 Dayton *Journal*, Mar. 4, 5, 10, 1886; Cleveland *Gazette*, Mar. 13, May 22, 1886; Works Progress Administration, Writers' Project, typescript files of materials on Springfield and Clark County [on the strikes of 1886] (undated), OHS; Mahavira Prasada Shreevastava, "The Industrial Development of Springfield, Ohio: A Study of Economic Geography" (Ph.D. dissertation, Ohio State University, 1959), p. 51; E. S. Todd, *A Sociological Study of Springfield and Clark County, Ohio* (New York, 1904), pp. 33–35, 67.

14 Outside the coal mines, I have found but four instances of Negro strikebreaking, including the 1886 strikes at Springfield, in Ohio during the entire period from 1860 to World War I. The following are the instances which I have found: in addition to Springfield's iron mills in 1886, blacks were used at the steel and iron mills at Cleveland in 1901 (Cleveland *Gazette*, June 29, Aug. 17, 1901, and Cleveland *Leader*, Aug. 9, 10, 13, 15, 1901); in 1903 at the Clauss Shear Works at Fremont (Norwalk *Reflector*, May 11, 12, 13, 1903); in 1904 at the iron mill at Hanging Rock in Lawrence County (Cincinnati *Enquirer*, May 31, June 1, 2, 3, 4, 8, 1904). Blacks unwittingly brought to Cleveland to break a strike on the city's ore docks in 1887 refused to work when strikers explained the situation to them; see Cleveland *Gazette*, June 18, 1887. Instances of black strikebreaking in the coal fields occurred too widely to document with as much exactitude; however, after the 1880s, blacks were only rarely employed as strikebreakers in Ohio coal fields. For evidence on black strike-breaking in the mines, in addition to that cited above in note 3, see, for the 1890s, *United Mine Workers Journal*, April 30, 1891; Cleveland *Gazette*, Sept. 6, 1894; for after 1900, Pomeroy *Tribune-Telegram*, Jan. 9, Feb. 6, 13, 20, 27, Mar. 6, Apr. 3, 10, 1907. It should also be noted that in some of these incidents whites outnumbered blacks in the strike-breaking force.

while at Cincinnati, a much less significant foundry center, there were only thirteen black metal workers during that same year. At both cities first- and second-generation foreign stock then made up 80 to 90 percent of the work force in iron and steel.[15]

Columbus had a smaller foreign population, so blacks were coming to work in its foundries in considerably larger numbers. Columbus was not a major metal producer in 1890 and but sixteen blacks were employed as iron and steel workers in the city. They constituted only 2.4 percent of the city's metal workers, but blacks comprised less than 1 percent of such workers in Cincinnati and Cleveland. Beginning in the 1890s the management of Columbus's Ohio Malleable Iron began an aggressive campaign to recruit black workers, doubtless in the belief that they would be so grateful for any opportunity to break out of their dismal employment situation that they would not be prone to strike and join unions. The company also lured blacks with promises (which it kept) of building low-cost homes for its black workers near the foundry, in the newly developing northern section of the city.[16] While such inducements were not present in the smaller foundry centers, some blacks were also coming to work in the foundries and mills of northeastern and eastern Ohio. At the turn of the century, a few black workers could be found in the steel mills at Steubenville and Youngstown and in the iron and tin works at Salem, Canton, and Lisbon.[17]

Black factory employment was sparse outside the metal industries, but there was a trend toward some increase, particularly where white competition was weak and the immigrant labor force small. In the 1870s and 1880s Columbus blacks began to enter the shops of the Pennsylvania Railroad, where they worked as laborers and mechanics' helpers. At Xenia, with its relatively large black and smaller foreign population, approximately seventy-five blacks worked as laborers in the town's cordage factories around 1900, while a few did unskilled work in a distillery. Blacks were barred, however, from employment at the town's largest shoe factory, which depended on native white and Irish labor. In smaller towns, such as the centrally located com-

[15] Census Office, *Eleventh Census*, I, pt. 2, pp. 652–659; Jesse Robinson, *The Amalgamated Association of Iron, Steel, and Tin Workers* (Baltimore, 1920), pp. 46–47; David Brody, *Steelworkers in America: The Nonunion Era* (Cambridge, 1960), pp. 50–79.

[16] Census Office, *Eleventh Census*, I, pt. 2, pp. 657–658; Minor, "Negroes in Columbus," p. 172; Mary Louise Mark, *Negroes in Columbus* (Columbus, 1928), pp. 21–22.

[17] Cleveland *Gazette*, Aug. 9, Nov. 15, 1902; E. T. Heald, *Stark County Story: A Free People at Work* (Canton, 1959), p. 453. City directories: Salem, 1887; Steubenville, 1891, 1902; Youngstown, 1895, 1902.

munities of Mt. Vernon and Ulrichsville, factory employment might come to provide an important economic base for two hundred or so local blacks. Ulrichsville blacks comprised the majority of workers at the local sewer pipe plant, while at Mt. Vernon they worked at a small steel mill and an engine factory. There is no information to provide definite confirmation, but it is doubtful that industrial opportunity was very secure in such towns, since the increasing centralization of industrial production tended to undercut the position of small, independent producers outside the major urban centers. The declining black populations of towns like Ulrichsville in the late nineteenth century would tend to substantiate this view.[18]

II

No field of employment was as much associated with blacks as domestic and personal service. Many whites only came in contact with blacks when they needed their shoes shined, their hair cut, their homes cleaned, or their clothes washed. Moreover, blacks were highly visible in such occupations, for while they were overwhelmingly outnumbered in common labor by whites, they were particularly over-represented in Ohio's service work force. The 1890 census revealed that while blacks were about 3 percent of the Ohio working population, they constituted almost 12 percent of its service workers. While only 9 percent of the white work force was engaged in domestic and personal service, 40 percent of blacks were. Fully 28 percent (8,067 of 28,331 persons) of black working men and, because of the more limited opportunities of women generally, 89 percent (6,965 of 7,796 persons) of black working women were service workers. The blacks' leading competitors in domestic and personal service fields were first- and second-generation foreign workers, yet even they were nowhere near as concentrated in service work as were blacks. Ohio blacks constituted a much greater percentage of workers in individual service fields: 24 percent (1,372) of Ohio's barbers, 10 percent (7,648) of its domestics, servants, waiters, and waitresses, and 32 percent of its laundresses. But while those of first- and second-generation foreign stock in the work force might have been more numerous in individual service fields, their proportional representation in any field was not greater than their presence in the work force. Thus, while first- and second-generation foreign stock constituted 40 percent of Ohio's work force, they were 40 percent (2,286) of its

[18] Mark, *Negroes in Columbus*, p. 18; Wright, "Negroes of Xenia," 1028–29; Cleveland *Gazette*, Nov. 15, 1902; letter from G. Dunn, Ulrichsville Public Library, to author, Aug. 13, 1969.

barbers, 30 percent (22,149) of its domestics, servants, waiters, and waitresses, and 27 percent (3,497) of its laundresses.[19]

Blacks had a considerable range of opportunities in domestic and personal service. Most worked in the lower reaches of the services, where work was tedious, very low in prestige, and rarely promised upward mobility. Hostlers in stables would rarely, if ever, own their own horses; likewise porters, helpers, and clean-up men in retail stores would only very rarely, because of their race, rise to the more respectable position of clerk. The people who swept up and washed the floors of factories would never be given the opportunity to learn to work their machines. Then there were train, station, and sleeping car porters, barbers in small shops of lesser quality, cooks, dishwashers, and waiters in the small diners and luncheonettes (the "greasy spoons" of the day), and messengers, bootblacks, janitors, and odd-job men who cleaned privies, swept chimneys, did lawn work, and white-washed homes and fences.[20]

Though the opportunities for the average male service worker were limited, the alternatives for black women were far fewer. For the large majority of black women service workers, and thus for the overwhelming majority of working black women generally, service work meant almost exclusively laundering clothes, cleaning house (perhaps several houses a week), scrubbing floors in office buildings, making beds in hotels and hospitals, and waiting on tables in small restaurants of lesser quality. Contemporary attitudes toward the role of women barred both black and white women from the path by which the male waiter might hope to go from a small diner to a fashionable restaurant where the tips might be larger, or the cleaning man might become the head janitor of a large office building.[21]

In its upper reaches, however, service work might be relatively dignified, though still servile and often as tedious. For certain jobs considerable training and skill might be required, and the work might take place amidst surroundings which themselves lent some prestige to the worker. Blacks were found working as live-in cooks, coachmen, butlers, valets, governesses, and assorted household servants in the homes of wealthy whites. They also worked as chefs, stewards, and waiters in private clubs and finer restaurants, and in the luxurious dining rooms

[19] Census Office, *Eleventh Census,* I, pt. 2, pp. 596–597.

[20] Ibid.; Cincinnati *Commercial,* Apr. 15, 1870; Cleveland *Gazette,* Dec. 6, 1884, Dec. 21, 1901; Columbus *Dispatch,* June 11, 1897; Alfred Vance Churchill, "Midwestern: The Colored People," *Northwest Ohio Quarterly,* XXV (Autumn, 1953), 166; Wright, "Negroes of Xenia," 1028–29.

[21] Census Office, *Eleventh Census,* I, pt. 2, pp. 596–597; Wright, "Negroes of Xenia," 1028–29.

aboard passenger boats on the Great Lakes and the Ohio or in railroad dining cars or the private railroad cars of prominent businessmen. In big cities and small towns alike, they worked as barbers and hairdressers in the well-equipped, often black-owned and -managed beauty salons and barbershops located in office buildings, department stores, and quality hotels. Though they might not always welcome black guests, the same fine hotels, such as Cincinnati's Burnet House, Columbus's Neil House, Cleveland's Weddell and American houses, and a number of Lake Erie summer resorts all had dining rooms which were managed for many years (sometimes well before 1860, in the case of the old hotels) by black headwaiters, who were directing a carefully, often personally recruited staff of black waiters, kitchen workers, cooks, bartenders, and barboys. The better hotels also often had black bellboys, valets, and butlers, all directed (as at Cleveland's Hollenden House) by a black superintendent of service.[22]

The position of blacks in the service sector remained secure in the late nineteenth century. Whites seemed to actually prefer blacks for domestic and personal service, especially in and about the home, but also in restaurants and hotels. Contemporary racial stereotypes held that blacks, thought to be a docile, tractable, and loyal people, especially when firmly and properly trained, were perfectly fitted for domestic service. In addition, whatever their professions of social democracy, many whites doubtless found something alluring in the service of the black domestic or servant trained in the genteel traditions of the Old South. Labor of blacks in hotel work had been regarded so highly and considered such an assurance of quality that post-bellum advertisements for hotels sometimes stressed the fact that the hotel's staff was black as a guarantee of excellent service and luxury.[23]

Whites also recognized that the lack of employment alternatives for blacks often made them value such jobs more, and work at them longer and more dependably than would their immigrant and ethnic competitors. While the latter might need such employment in the earliest stage of their economic development in the United States, they eventually

[22] Russell H. Davis, Black Americans in Cleveland from George Peake to Carl B. Stokes, 1796–1969 (Washington, 1972), p. 97; Santemyer, Ohio Town, p. 105; Mark, Negroes in Columbus, p. 18; Minor, "Negroes in Columbus," p. 40; Wendell Phillips Dabney, Cincinnati's Colored Citizens: Historical, Sociological, and Biographical (Cincinnati, 1928), pp. 183–187; Francis Charles Hubbard, "A Short History of the Colored People of Barnesville, Ohio" (1942), typescript, OHS, pp. 4–5; City directories: Xenia, 1868, 1888; Columbus, 1871; Cincinnati, 1870, 1883; Cleveland, 1870, 1892; Sandusky, 1902; Indianapolis Freeman, June 26, 1897.

[23] E.g., Cincinnati Commercial, Sept. 6, 1872, advertisement for the recently opened European Hotel.

hoped to find less servile and more dignified, if unskilled, work. One observer recalled the competition for private domestic work between Xenia's blacks and Irish during the late nineteenth century, and its predictable resolution. Said Helen Santemyer, ". . . If for a while Irish Norahs and Katies threatened the livelihood of colored women by going out to service as hired girls, that did not last long, for the Irish were as quick as any other immigrant group to lift themselves to social equality, to scorn any labor that seemed to them, in a democracy, demeaning—and particularly demeaning when there must be competition with Negroes." [24] Whatever *their* feelings about the indignities of service, the blacks, especially women, had little choice. When the Norahs and Katies eventually went off to work in the factories and shops, black women continued to scrub floors and take in laundry. Because whites understood the rhythms and continuities of domestic service, some of them, like the editor of the Cincinnati *Gazette,* had taken heart during the large black influx at the end of the war. They saw that replacement might soon be on the way for those who suffered the employment of Irish and German domestics, whom the *Gazette* claimed to be "so unsteady and generally so worthless" as servants.[25]

Employment in the services brought a degree of personal security for black workers. Since these fields were less immediately subject to the downturns of economic life than common labor, they provided a relatively stable livelihood even in worsening times. However, working conditions were often poor. It was not simply that service was low in prestige, or that it increased the black service worker's dependence on the whims of white people. Working conditions and wages left something to be desired. Journeymen barbers worked long, irregular hours; until the passage of an Ohio Sunday closing law for barbershops in 1892, they often worked on Sundays in order to cater to the convenience of working men. Their wages were low, especially in smaller shops.[26] The plight of food service workers employed in hotels, restaurants, and attached to caterers was particularly bad, for while they might get board as well as pay, wages were low and employees lacked firm guarantees on overtime pay. Moreover, the alternating pattern of endlessly busy peak hours in sweltering kitchens followed by long periods of calm between meals made work in dining rooms at once monotonous and nerve-wracking. Waiters had special problems because they were heavily dependent upon the vagaries of tipping; so

[24] Santemyer, *Ohio Town,* p. 95.
[25] Cincinnati *Gazette,* Oct. 13, 1865.
[26] W. Scott Hall, *The Journeyman Barber's International Union of America* (Baltimore, 1936), pp. 39, 89; Cleveland *Plain Dealer,* Sept. 20, 1889.

black waiters and their champions were especially sensitive to the suggestion that waiters made large enough wages to get along without
large tips. When the Cleveland *Leader* contended in 1883 that the
city's hotel waiters drew large salaries, and with tips made as much as
$45 a month, the Cleveland *Gazette* was quick to take exception. Not
only were wages well below the $30 a month quoted by the *Leader,*
said the *Gazette,* but there was no accurate way to predict the tips a
waiter might make. "The *Leader,*" charged the *Gazette,* "is simply trying to create a sentiment against tipping, but until hotels pay living
wages, waiters will depend on tips." Adding to the waiters' troubles
and heightening their reliance on tips was the fact that where black
and white waiters worked together in the same dining rooms, blacks
sometimes drew smaller wages. Such was the case at Cincinnati in the
1880s.[27]

Unionism might have helped to deal with these problems, but unions
in service fields were either slow to develop or unconcerned with organizing blacks. The leading barbers' union, the Journeymen Barbers
International Union, was organized in the 1880s. It had little effect on
the status of black barbers, because it failed to organize any but the
small number of blacks working in integrated shops or in black-owned
shops in a few small towns.[28] Such towns may well have been ones in
which there were just enough black shops competing effectively with
white ones for whites to extend offers of union membership in the hope
of regulating black competition. Unionism in the food services was
quite weak in spite of low wages and poor working conditions. The
Knights of Labor did little of lasting value in these fields during its
most active period in the 1880s. What eventually became the largest
union in the field, the Hotel and Restaurant Employees International
League, began gaining ground in the 1890s. The union had black members from its earliest days, especially at Cleveland, where it did some
of its most effective organizing in Ohio. But with the exception of bar-
tending it had little success in organizing efforts. Attempts among hotel
waiters were especially ineffectual: their strikes were easily broken by
impressing chambermaids and laundry and kitchen workers into service in hotel dining rooms. In addition, a significant number of waiters
floated between summer and winter resorts. Not only were they difficult to organize, but during their off season they also provided a corps

[27] Cleveland *Leader,* Dec. 27, 1883; Cleveland *Gazette,* Dec. 29, 1883, July 18,
1885, May 21, 1892; Cincinnati *Commercial Tribune,* Sept. 25, 1887.
[28] Hall, *Journeymen Barber's International Union,* pp. 43–44; [rosters of membership of Ohio], *The Barbers' Journal,* XII (Sept., 1901), 208–257.

of itinerants who might be brought in to replace striking workers during prolonged conflicts.[29]

Still, with its inequities and indignities, domestic and personal service was a tried and proven path of black opportunity. It provided ambitious men with dreams: the waiter might become a steward; the barber, a shop proprietor. Practically speaking, it was a shelter against the less secure forms of employment available to blacks. Waiting table for whites and cutting their hair had drawbacks, but digging ditches and loading freight, when such work was available at all, were certainly no more appealing.

III

Before 1860 only a few blacks had been employed in industrial fields requiring advanced training. A significant number of black artisans had left slavery with skills adequate to practice crafts, but the competition of white artisans, aided by their color, their large numbers, and occasionally (as at Cincinnati) the ability of the ante-bellum mechanics' associations to curb black competition, had made it difficult for blacks to use their skills.[30] No more than 5 or 10 percent of black working men had been able to carve out places for themselves in skilled fields; they were to be found particularly in the building and decorating trades (plastering, bricklaying, carpentry, and painting in particular), iron molding, and blacksmithing, with a smaller number in tailoring, shoemaking, and a few other crafts. In the 1870s the scope of black skilled employment had been broadened by the addition of skilled and occasionally semi-managerial railroad positions, such as conductor, engineer, brakeman, flagman, switchman, and baggagemen. In the large majority of skilled fields, however, few if any blacks were to be found in late nineteenth-century Ohio. Blacks were largely absent, for example, from the ranks of coopers, printers, lithographers, upholsterers, cabinetmakers, draftsmen, toolmakers, machinists, lathe operators, wheelwrights, millwrights, and skilled urban streetcar workers.[31]

[29] Matthew Josephson, *Union House, Union Bar: The History of the Hotel and Restaurant Employees and Bartenders International Union*, AFL-CIO (New York, 1956), pp. 36, 84, 93–95; Jay Rubin and M. J. Obermeir, *Growth of a Union: The Life and Times of Edward Flore* (New York, 1943), p. 122; Cincinnati *Commercial Gazette*, Sept. 25, 27, 1887.

[30] Carter Woodson, "The Negroes of Cincinnati prior to the Civil War," *Journal of Negro History*, I (Jan., 1916), 5–6.

[31] Census Office, *Eleventh Census*, I, pt. 2, pp. 596–597; Cleveland *Gazette*, May 28, 1887, Jan. 7, 1899.

Their large numbers gave blacks some power in certain service trades and unskilled occupations. In contrast, the small numbers of Ohio blacks in skilled industrial fields, probably no more than about 1,800 in 1890, were of marginal importance in many local economies. In the trades in which blacks had their largest representation, they seldom had a share equal to their percentage of the work force. In 1890, when they were about 3 percent of the work force, they constituted only 1.5 percent (256) of Ohio's blacksmiths, 0.7 percent (277) of its carpenters, and 2 percent of its bricklayers. Plastering required close work in a stooped position for long periods of time and was, therefore, particularly unattractive as a trade; only there did blacks have a share of a skilled trade larger than their percentage in the work force. Ohio's 285 black plasterers in 1890 were just over 8 percent of the state's total.[32]

During the late nineteenth century there were great obstacles blocking the development of a large black skilled work force. While blacks had always found the terms of competition particularly severe in the skilled trades, the growth of powerful and often hostile craft unions which desired to guarantee their members job security by controlling the size of the job market made the position of black artisans and skilled workers even less secure. Nowhere was this more apparent than in the plight of the skilled train workers after the rise of the railroad unions in the 1880s. Blacks would have fewer opportunities to enter skilled railroad service because of the ascendance and management recognition of the powerful, racially exclusionist railroad workers' brotherhood of conductors, engineers, firemen, and trainmen (brakemen, flagmen, and switchmen). Though all of the brotherhoods wished to exclude black workers, the conductors and engineers were more successful in doing so, both nationally and in Ohio. In all four fields, however, there were very few northern blacks at work. Especially in the North, the recruitment of conductors and engineers was generally done out of the ranks of trainmen and firemen; thus the barring of even a few blacks from the latter was an added guarantee that the former would escape black competition. Beginning in the 1880s, the few Ohio blacks who occasionally obtained promotion to the rank of conductor, after years of service in subordinate skilled fields, met with tremendous difficulty in getting experienced, skilled train crews to work under them; usually they had to go to the trouble of training inexperienced crews, recruited from the ranks of the unskilled and semi-skilled, in order to get men to operate their trains. After the mid-1880s, blacks

[32] Census Office, *Eleventh Census*, I, pt. 2, pp. 596–597.

hired for skilled train work were usually taken on only because of sudden, acute local and regional labor shortages. As these older, skilled train workers retired, they were not replaced by younger black men.[33]

While the trends in other branches of skilled work were not as dramatic or as sudden as in the railroad trades, blacks in both iron molding and the building and decorating trades were also facing the challenge of growing union movements. These unions were often at odds with black workers. Iron molding was practiced by perhaps 100 to 150 blacks in late nineteenth century Ohio; locals of the International Iron Molders' Union excluded blacks from membership. The union was not strong in Ohio, but where it did exist (such as in some plants at Columbus and at Springfield before the strikes of the mid-1880s) it proscribed black opportunity. Only after the power of Springfield iron molders' locals had been broken by the failure of strikes were blacks able to enter iron molding in the city in any but very small numbers. Though founded in 1859, the union's national convention did not take a stand in favor of organizing black workers until 1896. In response to the growing number of southern blacks learning the trade while doing unskilled and semi-skilled work in southern foundries, it then decided to bring them into the union. This decision, however, had no effect upon local practices in Ohio.[34]

The situation in the building and decorating trades was somewhat different. Early in their history of unionism southern whites in carpentry, plastering, and bricklaying were forced to come to terms with the fact that they were competing with large numbers of southern blacks who had emerged from slavery with knowledge of their crafts. Relatively soon after the organization of national unions in bricklaying (1865),[35] carpentry (1881),[36] and plastering and cement finishing (1864) [37] it was decided that the self-interests of the white craftsmen and of trade unionism dictated that blacks be organized so that their competition could be regulated. Yet in the North, where the number

[33] Spero and Harris, *Black Worker*, pp. 284–287; Cleveland *Gazette*, May 24, 1884, Mar. 22, 1890, Feb. 28, Mar. 7, 1891, Sept. 26, 1903; Xenia *Gazette*, Sept. 9, 1902.

[34] Frank T. Stockten, *The International Molders Union of North America* (Baltimore, 1921), pp. 59–61; Minor, "Negroes in Columbus," p. 55; W. E. B. Du Bois, *The Negro American Artisan* (Atlanta, 1912), pp. 72, 111.

[35] Harry C. Bates, *Bricklayers' Century of Craftsmanship: A History of the Bricklayers, Masons, and Plasterers' International Union* (Washington, 1955), pp. 36, 52, 103, 122; Spero and Harris, *Black Worker*, pp. 18, 69.

[36] Maxwell C. Raddock, *Portrait of an American Labor Leader: William L. Hutcheson; Saga of the Union of the Brotherhood of Carpenters and Joiners of America, 1881–1954* (New York, 1955), pp. 373–374; Spero and Harris, *Black Worker*, p. 66.

[37] Spero and Harris, *Black Worker*, p. 69.

of black skilled workers was small, there often was little reason for the building trade unions to act upon the policies of their national offices. For their part, the nationals could do little (and sometimes failed to do anything) to force the locals to organize blacks.[38] Even during the mid-1880s, when the idealistic spirit of interracial solidarity was displayed so prominently in the confederation of unions, the Knights of Labor, it was rare for Ohio blacks to be represented in any but token numbers in the building trade unions, even when the unions were affiliates of the Knights. The craft unions remained largely practical-minded business unions, concerned more with protecting the wage scale and job security. Experiments in interracial cooperation would yield little of practical benefit, as long as Ohio blacks were found in such small numbers in the skilled labor force.

Policies of Ohio building and decorating locals ranged from outright exclusion to token admission. By the turn of the century only eight Cincinnati blacks were found in craft unions in the building trades; the majority were older men, most bricklayers, and of the latter all were said to be so light in color "as not to be noticed among the sun-burned and brick-dust covered men." At the same time, Cincinnati's bricklayers' locals refused to honor the traveling cards of visiting, union-affiliated black bricklayers, leaving traveling artisans without special connections outside the union virtually barred from practicing their trade in the city. Blacks in the city were generally barred from locals of the plasterers and carpenters, and from the weaker painters' unions.[39] Outside Cincinnati the picture was little different. At Cleveland in the 1870s and after, token blacks were found in carpenters', plasterers', and bricklayers' unions. In 1896 only five of the five hundred members of Cleveland's Local #5 of bricklayers were blacks, though at the time there were twenty or thirty black bricklayers and masons in Cleveland.[40] At Columbus, Dayton, Springfield, and Steubenville blacks appear to have been virtually excluded from most of the craft unions. At Dayton the bricklayers' union brought in a large number of the local black bricklayers in 1886, when it was feared that the blacks would be used to help break a strike. After the strike was won, the blacks were soon forced out of the union.[41]

Only at Youngstown, where about twenty black bricklayers (about

[38] Ibid., pp. 21–22, 69–70; Bates, *Bricklayers' Century,* p. 103; Northrup, *Organized Labor and the Negro,* pp. 23–27, 38–39, 42.

[39] W. E. B. Du Bois, *The Negro Artisan* (Atlanta, 1902), pp. 139, 163.

[40] Cleveland *Gazette,* Feb. 20, 1886, Jan. 18, 1896.

[41] Todd, *Springfield and Clark County* p. 67; Minor, "Negroes in Columbus," pp. 54–55; Frank U. Quillin, *The Color Line in Ohio* (Ann Arbor, 1913), pp. 137–138; Cleveland *Gazette,* Jan. 18, 1902.

15 percent of local union membership in that trade) were union-affiliated around the turn of the century, did blacks seem to have been present in any but token numbers. But there union membership resulted from the fact that among the pioneers of the city's bricklaying trade were the black Berry and Steward families; they had worked independently for many years but eventually formed a business partnership and intermarried. As contractors, the two families and their workers handled an impressive share of local bricklaying and masonry. Both families maintained an important presence in the local bricklayers' union, and individual members had even risen to local and regional office.[42] The life histories of other black union members around the state in the late nineteenth century are not known, but if the example of the Berrys and Stewards is representative, it may tell us something of these obscure men. The blacks who made up the race's token representation in Ohio's union locals might have been those few unusually well-respected artisans who had practiced their trades locally for many years, been present in locals since their formative period, and shown particularly great staying power in their crafts. With them perhaps came their associates and their children, trained by them in the same crafts. All of these were difficult qualifications for the average black artisan to meet.

Union exclusion in these trades did not in itself create discrimination against black craftsmen. Even before the rise of powerful unions in the building and decorating trades, black artisans in Ohio had faced difficult conditions involving the practice of their crafts. In the words of an Ironton plasterer reflecting on his career, they had traditionally been forced "to bid a little cheaper or be very superior in craftsmanship" [43] in order to counter the predilection of whites for white labor. Furthermore, to the extent that white artisans refused to work with them, black craftsmen had also found it difficult to obtain jobs on larger building projects which promised the most steady work and regular wages. Thus they had been forced to fall back on small jobs found here and there, or to do menial, unskilled work in order to make a living. Then, too, union membership carried no guarantee that blacks would do any better on the labor market. As the rejection of the traveling cards of black artisans at Cincinnati suggests, white unionists were not always willing to work with their black colleagues.

[42] Cleveland *Gazette*, Jan. 18, 1896, Feb. 23, 1901; "Berry and Steward Descendants Plan Annual Reunion Sunday," Youngstown *Vindicator*, July 30, 1953; "P. Ross Berry, 1835–1917" (no date), typescript at Mahoning Valley Historical Society, Youngstown.

[43] Du Bois, *Negro American Artisan*, p. 72.

Yet the unions did make a difference. By organizing the trades and creating greater solidarity among white artisans, while at the same time winning greater acceptance among employers, contractors, and the general public, the craft unions further altered the terms of competition in favor of whites. Moreover, by all but barring blacks from apprenticeship programs, they increased the probability that few blacks would find it possible to learn trades. Not many black artisans could afford to take on younger men and train them, while at the same time offering them a living wage—and few were the young black men who could afford anything less than a living wage.

Knowledge of all the difficulties facing black artisans dissuaded many young men from learning and practicing a trade. In 1886 Clevelander Jere Brown, a black state legislator and himself a carpenter and trade unionist, admitted reluctantly that discrimination by white artisans, unions, and employers was the most important reason why "our boys or at least the majority of them have no tendencies to enter mechanical pursuits." They preferred instead, said Brown, to try to enter professions where they believed they would encounter less prejudice. Due to a combination of union hostility and the attitudes of such young men, there were, by Brown's count, only three black apprentices at Cleveland in 1886; according to the 1890 census, there were but twenty-eight in the entire state.[44]

Although a number of forces limited the expansion of the black artisans in the building and decorating trades, some artisans continued to prosper. Particularly where unions were weak, and in certain fields like painting and (to some extent) plastering, and when they were able to establish excellent reputations through hard work, fine craftsmanship, and a keen competitive sense, individual black artisans might continue to vie for an important share of the market. They did just that at Xenia, Zanesville, and Chillicothe, for example.[45]

Then, too, strength lay in bringing skilled blacks together through the organization of contracting firms. Generally offshoots of work in a particular craft by individual artisans, the black contracting efforts were by no means new. Black artisans had faced tough competitive conditions prior to 1860 and had responded by drawing together and bidding for work on larger projects. At Columbus, David Jenkins was skilled in painting, glazing, and plastering; he had contracted for large

[44] Cleveland *Gazette,* Feb. 20, 1886; Census Office, *Eleventh Census,* I, pt. 2, pp. 596–597.
[45] Wright, "Negroes of Xenia," 1023–26; Cleveland *Gazette,* July 16, 1892; Helen M. Rainey, Chillicothe Public Library, to author, Aug. 4, 1969; City directories: Chillicothe, 1873, 1890; Zanesville, 1892.

projects and employed black artisans. He and his men had worked on the state capitol building several times, as well as on the exclusive Neil House and on the homes of Columbus's most prominent businessmen. Similarly, at Cincinnati the plasterers Bell and Knight had formed a partnership and had gotten contracts in 1851 to work in the public buildings of Hamilton County. They, too, worked on the expensive homes of prominent local whites.[46]

Black artisans responded to the tough competitive conditions of the late nineteenth century in the same way. The period saw increasing organization of black contracting endeavors, particularly in the larger cities and towns, where rapid population and economic growth created opportunities for work on lucrative projects, such as public buildings, homes, and factories. The scope of black contracting operations was wide-ranging. Some contractors were engaged in full-time work at large projects and employed a number of regular employees. Like the Berry and Steward contracting firm at Youngstown, the larger black endeavors were occasionally the product of a merger between two families, in each of which skills in a particular craft were passed down from generation to generation. This was the case, for example, with Columbus's Roney and Mitchell families, both of which were involved in plastering and painting and had developed a reputation for decorative ability in mid-nineteenth century Columbus. Like the Berrys and Stewards, both the Roneys and Mitchells had generally worked as independent families for many years, probably often in competition with one another, before forming a partnership in the post-war years.[47] However, most of the larger endeavors were like the firm of Robert Gratton Walker of Springfield, a product of efforts of ambitious individual artisans. Between the 1870s, when he entered the carpenter's trade at Springfield, and the turn of the century, Walker gradually created one of the most successful firms in Springfield; he and his associated artisans built hundreds of homes for Springfield's more affluent whites.[48] Such men did not always employ black craftsmen exclusively; particularly in smaller towns, where there were not always enough black artisans to take on large projects, whites were hired. Urbana's John Anderson, for example, did bricklaying and masonry on contract throughout the central Miami valley. He consistently took on large projects, such as a $100,000 factory at Urbana and the railroad

[46] Martin R. Delany, *The Condition, Elevation, Emigration, and Destiny of the Colored People* (Philadelphia, 1852), pp. 97–99.

[47] Cleveland *Gazette,* May 12, Aug. 11, 1888, July 16, 1892; City Directories: Columbus, 1865, 1872, 1888.

[48] G. F. Richings, *Evidences of Progress among Colored People* (Philadelphia, 1903), pp. 398–499; Indianapolis *Freeman,* Sept. 11, 1911.

station at Piqua, and he employed whites.[49] But most black contractors were not Walkers and Andersons. For the majority, contracting consisted of occasionally hiring a few individuals for work on projects too large to be done by one man. These contractors were only part-time heads of business firms, and contracting served as the means by which they might occasionally grasp at the sort of building and decorating opportunities which regularly came to white craftsmen.

IV

The major black business opportunity continued to lie in providing domestic and personal services for whites. The journeyman barber might become the barbershop proprietor, the cook a caterer, and the cab driver the owner of a fleet of cabs—a path which required patient saving, hard work, ambition, and a little luck.

Barbershops were an especially prominent form of black enterprise, largely because of the small amount of capital required. One needed only the skills of a barber or two, and a few fixtures such as chairs, mirrors, scissors, and razors, all of which could easily be purchased second hand for little money; even if bought new, they cost no more than a few hundred dollars.[50] The only space required was a room, perhaps rented for several dollars a month in a neighborhood office or commercial building whose location afforded convenient access to the trade of working men living and laboring in the area. The same opportunity lay open to black women, who might open small neighborhood beauty shops with just as little capital. Yet much more than the barbershop for the average man, the beauty salon was a luxury for the average woman; and at any rate, most women's pressing, constant responsibilities in the home checked the possibility of the beauty shop emerging, like the barbershop, as an informal social center. Both facts placed definite limits on the possibility of entrepreneurship among black women.

The ease of establishing such enterprises must not be confused with the likelihood of success. Indeed, because it was not difficult to open a beauty salon or barbershop, the neighborhood proprietor was likely to face the possibility of stiff competition. This was an especially important consideration for the black barbershop owner, to the extent that his shop attempted to tap a white market for service and to compete with white shops. Some black barbers resolved this difficulty by seeking the patronage of their own people. Once they made this deci-

---

[49] Richings, *Evidences of Progress*, pp. 499–500.
[50] Hall, *Journeyman Barber's International Union*, pp. 9–10.

sion, however, they committed themselves to dependence solely on the Negro market. Few were barbershops in late nineteenth century Ohio which served both blacks and whites, and black-owned shops were often placed in the position of having to close their doors to black customers. From time to time blacks attempted to open what were referred to as "equal rights shops," intended to serve both black and white, but the idea flew too much in the face of white Ohio's sense of interracial boundaries.[51] Under any circumstance, the Negro market in most Ohio cities, towns, and villages was neither large enough nor affluent enough to accommodate all of those blacks who wished to begin an enterprise and had no means for doing so other than a bit of savings and talent for trimming, cutting, and shaving hair. Thus, the average black shop fought for its life and was forced to keep late, irregular hours in order to be competitive.

If the small neighborhood barbershop was the bottom rung of black entrepreneurship, the luxurious, heavily capitalized shops paying high rent in the five or six most exclusive hotels and in the most distinguished business, office, and bank buildings, catering to a dependable market among affluent white businessmen and professionals, certainly represented the top. Indeed, they were the pinnacle of black business achievement in late nineteenth century Ohio, and they were the one profitable segment of enterprise in which blacks controlled a large share of the market.[52] Such a shop presented an impressive sight to the customer entering and taking a seat, there to await his turn upon the barber's chair. Under the overhead fans of the spacious, high-ceilinged room, the marble walls were lined with porcelain sinks, mirrors, and shelves with a multicolored array of hair tonic and cologne bottles. A dozen or more black barbers stood in starched white coats, their gleaming scissors and razors at work on the beards and pates of judges, bank presidents, executives, and congressmen. While the barbers worked the bootblacks shined shoes to a high gloss, and manicurists trimmed, filed, and polished fingernails. Here the barber was required to be an artist with his tools, but his talents were expected to go further. He gave hot towels without burning a face; he administered soporific facial and scalp massages; and he worked a hand broom with such facility that no particle of lint would be likely to return to

51 Cleveland *Leader*, July 1, 1864; Cincinnati *Commercial*, Sept. 23, 1873; Xenia *Gazette*, Oct. 28, 1873; Cleveland *Gazette*, Oct. 27, Dec. 8, 1883, June 14, 1884, Apr. 10, 17, 1886, June 6, 1891, Jan. 7, 21, July 29, 1893.
52 Minor, "Negroes in Columbus," p. 40; Ben Hayes, "Negro—No. 3," undated clipping, Columbus *Citizen-Journal*, on file OHS; Dabney, *Cincinnati's Colored Citizens*, pp. 183–185; Davis, *Black Americans in Cleveland*, pp. 160–162; Cincinnati *Colored Citizen*, May 19, 1866.

the outside world on the customer's lapel. Directing this operation in the larger shops was the foreman, whose job it was to see that customers were dealt with quickly and efficiently and that the morale of the barbers was high and the quality of their work consistently excellent.[53]

Over the foreman, barbers, manicurists, and bootblacks was the owner. He was usually preoccupied with keeping accounts, ordering supplies, pricing the latest in chairs, tools, and tonics, but often he might shave and cut the hair of a preferred customer. Bosses came to their positions in various ways. By the late nineteenth century, some of these quality shops had been owned by individual families for decades. Fountain Lewis had come to Cincinnati in the 1840s; he obtained work as a barber in the downtown shop of a Frenchman named Ferrée. Not long after that, Ferrée retired, and Lewis used his savings to purchase the shop. In subsequent decades, under Fountain and Fountain, Jr., the shop became a local landmark. In the words of Wendell Phillips Dabney, a black Cincinnatian who lived during the late nineteenth and early twentieth centuries and chronicled the history of blacks in the city, the senior Fountain made his shop "the great resort of bankers and aristocrats. Grant, Lincoln, and other famous dignitaries were soothed into slumber by the rhythmic music of his scissors or the magic touch of his razor." The shop remained in business through three generations of Lewises.[54]

Equally famous was George Myers's shop, located in Cleveland's Hollenden Hotel and described by the writer Elbert Hubbard as "the best barbershop in America." Myers's path to enterprise had been different from that of Fountain Lewis, Sr., for it had been greatly aided by substantial financial assistance from white patrons. Born at Baltimore in 1859, Myers was the son of Isaac Myers, a leader of the Baltimore free black community and an early champion of the cause of black workers. In 1879 George had come to Cleveland with knowledge of the barber's trade; he soon obtained a position as foreman of the black-owned barbershop at Cleveland's Weddell House. While employed there, the personable Myers had served and formed acquaintances with some of Cleveland's most prominent citizens, including the editor of the Cleveland *Plain Dealer*, Liberty Holden, whose views of race were considerably more tolerant than those of that paper's previous editors. When Holden opened the Hollenden House in 1888, he

[53] John A. Garraty, ed., *The Barber and the Historian: The Correspondence of George A. Myers and James Ford Rhodes, 1910–1923* (Columbus, 1956), pp. xvi–xvii; Cleveland *Gazette*, Jan. 20, 1885; Cleveland *Journal*, Sept. 19, 1908.
[54] Dabney, *Cincinnati's Colored Citizens*, p. 183; Cleveland *Gazette*, Aug. 9, 1902.

asked Myers to develop the new hotel's barbershop; the editor and a
number of Myers's Weddell House customers gave him a $2,000 loan
for the purchase of basic supplies. Much of Myers's Weddell House
clientele followed him to the Hollenden; during the next decades,
through his keen business ability and innovations in sanitation and customer convenience, Myers's shop established a national reputation.[55]

Catering was second only to barbering as a field of service enterprise in which blacks had developed an important presence. There
were considerably fewer caterers than barbershop proprietors, however, for catering was by no means an easy business to enter. While
the barber might be aided by the convenience of his location, and the
cost of his services was by no means prohibitive, the development of
the caterer's trade depended on the gradual growth of a reputation for
excellence among the very demanding and relatively few people who
could afford his services. As in barbering, there was a hierarchy among
caterers. Most traveled from house to house, cooking in their employers' kitchens on occasions such as dinner parties, birthdays, and
anniversaries. This was by no means an unprofitable business for those
who succeeded, but the most prestige and profit went to the few caterers who prepared banquets in rented halls for large wedding parties,
dances, meetings, and conventions in the days before hotels monopolized such work. Caterers almost always shared the same background.
Just as barbershop proprietors had once been journeymen barbers
working in someone else's shop, caterers were invariably former cooks
or servants in the homes of white families or cooks and head waiters
in restaurants, hotels, and private clubs. They were like Cincinnati's
Washington Simms, who had for many years been the steward at the
exclusive Avondale Club, or Cleveland's William N. Alexander, long a
head butler for wealthy whites; such people were amply prepared for
the catering business by years of practical experience in organizing
kitchen help and serving food. Like quality barbershops, catering enterprises tended to be passed down from generation to generation
within individual families. Cincinnati's Fossett family was the most
outstanding late nineteenth century example. Peter and William Fossett were the sons of "Jos" Fossett, a domestic slave on the estate of
Thomas Jefferson; the two brothers developed a very lucrative catering
firm in mid-nineteenth-century Cincinnati, preparing the city's most
lavish banquets. As he grew more successful, however, Peter Fossett
began to devote more and more of his time to the Baptist ministry,
leaving the business to his daughter Mattie and to brother William.

[55] Garraty, ed., *Barber and Historian,* pp. xvi–xviii, 126–127; Cleveland
Gazette, June 1, 1895.

When William died, the firm was left completely in the hands of Mattie and her husband John Miller, himself a prominent caterer. The Millers would head the firm for decades, strengthening its reputation.[56]

Cabbing and carrying was the last service field in which blacks enjoyed an important share of the total market. Every Ohio city and town had its Negro-owned and -operated cab and carrying businesses, ranging in the size from the lone driver with his team, working the theaters, hotels, and rialroad stations independently, to the more substantial operator with his his own livery stable and fleet of cabs. The latter were particularly successful when they were able to win a concession at a large hotel. Springfield's enterprising Henry Young, for example, for many years combined his duties as head baggage clerk of the city's largest hotel, the Arcade, with ownership of a transfer and cab service which brought guests to and from the Arcade and several other hotels. Young had the good fortune to know that whenever he placed guests and baggage on his vehicles, driven by his own employees, he was adding to his wealth.[57]

While those like Young labored tirelessly but profitably at providing respectable services to whites, other blacks in the urban centers made their livings at the often more lucrative enterprise of supplying whites with the entertainments which society at once desired and abhorred. These were the so-called shadies, the shady characters of notorious reputation who kept brothels, gambling dens, and saloons. The saloonkeepers were in the majority; their businesses were often fronts for various sorts of vice operations or for the sale of stolen goods. The shady saloonkeeper was not scrupulous about the ages of the young white men and women to whom he served liquor. No urban "red light" zone of the time was without its black-owned gambling dens, saloons, and brothels, staffed on occasion by both white and black women. Columbus's notorious "Bad Lands" section even boasted an opium den; frequented by affluent whites, it was owned by Alexander "Smoky" Hobbs, a black gangster born and bred in Columbus whose training gymnasium for prizefighters served as a legitimate front for his vice operations. Constantly surrounded by a retinue of retired fighters, the cigar-chewing, derby-wearing Hobbs was well known to both black and white Columbus, and few wordly people reached adulthood without at least hearing rumors about his business interests. Yet like the enterprises of other notorious shadies, Hobbs's resort was allowed to

[56] Dabney, *Cincinnati's Colored Citizens,* pp. 180–182; Cleveland *Gazette,* July 18, 1885, Feb. 20, 1904.

[57] Cincinnati *Colored Citizen,* May 19, 1886; Indianapolis *Freeman,* Sept. 9, 1911; Minor, "Negroes in Columbus," p. 40.

prosper because of his political connections and the apathy of the police.[58]

Hobbs made no effort to conceal his activities or to appear respectable in conventional terms; his lifestyle was every bit as flamboyant as that of the Runyonesque gangster of fiction. However, there were other shadies who attempted to separate their lifestyle from their enterprise; sometimes their businesses, while not particularly seemly, were in fact shortcuts to respectability. Such a person was Columbus's John Alexander, known far and wide to gamblers as the Black Prince. A handsome, well-groomed man with a home in one of the city's finest neighborhoods, Alexander for many years kept a gambling room at various Columbus locations. Free of the ambience of a bawdy house, Alexander's tastefully decorated gambling room was frequented by wealthy white gamblers from throughout the nation. Also attempting to maintain a respectable image while doing shady work was Cleveland's Moses Simmons. He put money made in saloonkeeping and race horse training to work by providing two important services for the black and white poor—moneylending and bailbonding—both of which had their purveyors at other locations.[59]

Outside of these service fields, legitimate and illegitimate, black businesses were scattered in many different realms, and they tended to decline dramatically in number. Rounding out the scope of service enterprise were a small number of black-owned tailor shops and janitorial services. There were also a few beauty salons and restaurants which usually catered to whites, but in a few cases (as in Cincinnati, where the color line proscribed black opportunity to eat in most white-owned establishments) catering to affluent blacks.[60] Black retailers and wholesalers numbered only approximately 73 in 1890. While here and there one found a black clothing or furniture store, most black retailers and wholesalers were grocers and bulk food suppliers, or combined teaming and hauling with the sale and delivery of coal and ice. They,

[58] Todd, *Springfield and Clark County*, pp. 106–107, 112–113; Minor, "Negroes in Columbus," pp. 116–118; Mark, *Negroes in Columbus*, pp. 20–21; Columbus *Dispatch*, Sept. 9, 1907, Sept. 11, 12, 1908 (on Hobbs's long-standing political influence); Dabney, *Cincinnati's Colored Citizens*, pp. 153–167; Cincinnati *Commercial*, Oct. 11, 1871; Cleveland *Gazette*, Oct. 9, Nov. 2, 1897, Jan. 14, May 20, 1899. The term "shadies" was used by Drake and Cayton in their classic study of Chicago blacks; St. Clair Drake and Horace R. Cayton, *Black Metropolis: A Study of Negro Life in a Northern City* (New York, 1945), pp. 524–525.
[59] Cleveland *Gazette*, Sept. 26, 1891; Cleveland *Leader*, Jan. 29, 1900.
[60] Cleveland *Gazette*, Jan. 9, July 16, 1892; Indianapolis *Freeman*, Sept. 9, 1911, Aug. 3, 1912, Aug. 24, 1914; Xenia *Torchlight*, Nov. 4, 1868; Census Office, *Eleventh Census*, I, pt. 2, pp. 596–597; City directories: Xenia, 1868, 1875–76; Chillicothe, 1897.

too, depended greatly upon white trade.[61] Outside of a few service businesses like barbershops, and a few saloons and restaurants, there was little effort to tap the small Negro market for goods and services. The one outstanding attempt was the black newspaper, an important source of enlightenment for the racial community. But because of the amount of capital required and the limited size of the readership in most localities, this was a very precarious investment. Most Ohio black papers were short lived, sometimes lasting no more than a month or two. Editors usually attempted to combine newspaper publishing with job printing—as did Harry Smith, whose Cleveland *Gazette* was the most successful black paper in late nineteenth century Ohio. But the competition of well-established white job printers, and the small demand of local blacks for printing, made this effort likely to fail.[62]

In an age when popular heroes were captains of industry and commerce, the lack of a black business presence outside service enterprise was a source of embarrassment for some blacks. A Cincinnati correspondent of the Cleveland *Gazette* wondered in 1888 whether the lack of black commercial activity did not somehow lend validity to the contention of Robert Toombs, a leading ante-bellum southern politician who based a defense of slavery upon the belief in Negro inferiority, that Negroes were a "scrub race of born servants." A walk through one of Cincinnati's outdoor markets on one summer evening had prompted this rush of doubt. The *Gazette*'s correspondent had seen some three thousand vendors, none of them, he estimated, with more than fifty dollars' worth of goods, plying their simple wares. Among them were only three or four blacks. Sharing with others a belief that service work was demeaning, he stated bitterly, "Our boys think it no disgrace to shine shoes, but an everlasting disgrace to sell shoestrings and matches." "Think of it," he concluded, reflecting on the growing number of blacks obtaining education, "hundreds of Pullman porters and barbers well-versed in Greek and Latin and the high mathematics." [63]

Such bitterness reflected a fear that blacks were not rising to contemporary standards of economic achievement. At the same time, it was also prompted by a desire to expand black employment oppor-

[61] Cleveland *Gazette*, June 25, 1887, July 16, 1892, Mar. 20, 1897; Indianapolis *Freeman*, Aug. 3, 1912, Aug. 1, 1914, Sept. 4, 1915; Wright, "Negroes of Xenia," 1026–27; Census Office, *Eleventh Census*, I, pt. 2, pp. 596–597; City directories: Columbus, 1871, 1879, 1891; Cleveland, 1900; Steubenville, 1895, 1896.

[62] Columbus *Free American*, Mar. 19, 1887; Cleveland *Gazette*, Aug. 22, 1883, Feb. 25, 1888; New York *Freeman*, Jan. 15, 1887; Irvine Garland Penn, *The Afro-American Press and Its Editors* (Springfield, Mass., 1891), pp. 114, 280–286.

[63] Cleveland *Gazette*, June 16, 1888.

tunity. Blacks were generally barred from the respectable positions of clerk, cashier, and sales manager in retail stores; instead, their opportunities were limited to sweeping up and carrying boxes. So rare was the employment of a black clerk in Ohio, even in those stores which courted black customers, that the hiring of black individuals to clerk was reported joyfully in the race press.[64] On those occasions when blacks were given clerkships, white customers and employees were known to object. The hiring of a black clerk at a Columbus dry goods store in 1887, for example, led to a walkout by white clerks, who successfully demanded that the black be fired. "This should show the race," said the *Gazette*'s Columbus correspondent, "that we must have our own businesses." [65]

That blacks did not have their own businesses in large enough numbers or in a wide enough variety of fields to please these commentators may be explained by several factors. There is some truth in the observation of the sociologist E. Franklin Frazier [66] that blacks before emancipation had no practical business experience, and thus after 1865 had no entrepreneurial heritage to motivate them. At the same time, the very severe limitations on black employment in the late nineteenth century reinforced slavery's limitations on commercial skills. As the failure of white businesses to hire black sales and managerial personnel suggests, few blacks were in a position to obtain business training. Moreover, as other observers have frequently noted, the chronic poverty of most blacks militated against the gathering of capital with which to open stores. The American banking establishment also had traditionally shown itself unwilling to grant blacks loans with which they might start businesses.

Yet each of these arguments only explains part of the situation in Ohio and, doubtless, elsewhere as well. Black Ohioans and black Americans generally were not so isolated from American society that they were unaffected by the boosterism, hucksterism, and materialism and the strong emphasis on entrepreneurial activity which pervaded American life. The Protestant ethic and the "better mousetrap" philosophy of individual success and enterprise were part of the cultural baggage of many blacks as well as whites, and they contended against the social and psychological results of the race's ongoing lack of opportunity to acquire commercial skills and enter business.

[64] Ibid., Apr. 26, 1884, Oct. 16, 1886, May 23, 1891, Nov. 19, 1892.
[65] Ibid., June 4, 1887.
[66] E. Franklin Frazier, *The Negro in the United States* (New York, 1949), p. 411, and Frazier, *Black Bourgeoisie: The Rise of a New Middle Class* (New York, 1957), p. 165.

Then, too, the argument that blacks lacked the capital to enter business and were hindered in acquiring capital by the bias of credit institutions overlooks several important factors. The type of commercial activity frequently engaged in by socially marginal groups is the tiny "Mom and Pop" corner grocery store and other very small businesses. Not only do such enterprises require little prior commercial skill or experience, but they are also characterized by limited inventories and hired labor, and thus they require relatively little capital. Small stores are rarely financed by bank loans; usually they depend on individual savings, loans from family and friends, and informal credit arrangements among members of a common social group.[67]

While it cannot be denied that most black Ohioans were poor, enough capital was present in black communities that such small commercial enterprises, and even some larger ones, were possible. Through lives of ceaseless toil and thrift, some people acquired savings. In addition, a number of blacks had settled in Ohio communities in earlier decades; by wisely investing in land, they were reaping harvests of profit by the late nineteenth century. An example was Nelson Gant of Zanesville, who had come to Muskingum County as a recently self-purchased freedman in the 1840s. He began to use his savings to buy land, eventually accumulating 450 acres in Zanesville and its immediate vicinity. As the town expanded, and particularly after the discovery of coal in the area, Gant was able to live off his investments, and to build his daughter a large home as a wedding present.[68] The net worth of Gant's holdings is not known, but that of James Madison French is known. At his death in 1922 the Sandusky real estate dealer and speculator left Oberlin College $100,000.[69] Few of the men whom the Negro press occasionally reported [70] as having made large sums in real estate were probably as wealthy as either Gant or French, but that is hardly the point. The careers of such men suggest that some blacks outside of service businesses were skillful at making and manipulating money, and that capital did exist for commercial activity.

Yet those with capital from savings and real estate investment tended not to establish businesses with their funds. Only occasionally

[67] Ivan H. Light, Ethnic Enterprise in America: Business and Welfare among Chinese, Japanese, and Blacks (Berkeley, 1972), p. 20.

[68] J. Hope Sutor, Past and Present of the City of Zanesville (Chicago, 1905), pp. 374–377; Zanesville Courier, Oct. 14, 1903.

[69] [James M. French], Crisis, XXIV (Sept., 1922), 222, and XXV (Nov., 1922), 24 (obituary).

[70] Xenia Torchlight, Nov. 23, Dec. 7, 1887; Cleveland Gazette, Jan. 30, Nov. 27, 1886, Feb. 10, 1894, Jan. 7, July 15, 1899; Cleveland Leader, Jan. 29, 1900; Indianapolis Freeman, Aug. 7, 1915.

were such monies used to begin service enterprises; for example, one young Cincinnatian in 1885 used his inheritance to open a well-equipped downtown barbershop. But most used their funds to invest or reinvest in real estate, or to buy homes for themselves and further improve them over the years.[71] Among other things, such a use of capital reflected a sense of where profit lay. Few blacks felt that it would be profitable to attempt to compete with established white enterprises for an overwhelmingly white commercial market. Blacks with capital not only failed to enter commerce, but they also failed to investigate the vast possibilities which would have been available by pooling their resources through incorporation. Needed was some realistic expectation that a market might be tapped by black enterprise outside of service operations. Yet, in the late nineteenth century, Ohio's blacks did not act as if they believed such an impetus to enterprise existed.

V

During the post-bellum decades, great opportunities to obtain advanced education and training and to enter the professions were opening up for Ohio's blacks. Before the war a few blacks had graduated from Ohio colleges, particularly Oberlin, but their opportunities to obtain dignified professional employment had been proscribed by exclusion from law and medical schools as well as more general racial prejudice; at most they had been able to attend lectures without being allowed to matriculate and obtain a degree. The late nineteenth century saw increasing eradication of the color line in professional education and a growing black presence in the professions. "We are knocking on the doors of all the professions asking for admission," said the *Gazette's* Columbus correspondent in 1884. This remark was made on the occasion of the graduation from Columbus Medical College of Dr. Isaiah Tuppins, said to be "the first colored graduate from a medical college in Ohio." [72] Tuppins was then thirty and had worked for years as a barber while patiently saving money to enter medical school; he was one of a small but growing number of men, often of similar age and background, who were entering and graduating from professional schools in law, medicine, and various business fields such as

[71] Cleveland *Gazette,* Jan. 20, 1885, Nov. 27, 1886, Feb. 10, 1894; New York *Freeman,* Feb. 6, 1886; Carrie Clifford, "Cleveland and Its Colored People," *Colored American Magazine,* IX (July, 1905), 365–380; Cleveland *Leader,* Jan. 29, 1900; Cleveland *Plain Dealer,* Oct. 14, 1900; Indianapolis *Freeman,* Aug. 7, 1915.

[72] Cleveland *Gazette,* Apr. 5, 1884.

accounting after 1870. In 1874 William Parham, who had been elevated from a principalship to the superintendency of the city's black schools, added to his accomplishments when he became the first black graduate from Cincinnati Law School. Blacks also began to appear in small numbers on the rosters of graduates of Toledo's Ohio Business College, Toledo Medical College, Cleveland's Union Law School, Western Reserve University Law School, Western Reserve University Medical School, and Cincinnati's Eclectic Medical School.[73]

In addition, more blacks began to receive important aid in the launching of their careers from influential whites. This was particularly the case among those who aspired to be lawyers; some were invited by respected attorneys to read law in their offices. John Green, who financed his education largely by waiting on tables and doing odd jobs, supplemented a legal education at Cleveland's Union Law School in the late 1860s and early 1870s with practical training in the office of Judge Jesse Bishop. William R. Steward, the son of bricklaying contractor Lemuel Steward, prepared for a legal education at Cincinnati Law School in the mid-1880s by reading law in the office of Youngstown's congressman, a prominent attorney. Similarly, Charles Chesnutt studied in the office of a Cleveland judge, while George Washington Williams supplemented his studies at Cincinnati Law School with practical experience in the office of Cincinnati's influential Judge Alonzo Taft. These men commonly opened offices in downtown buildings near the courts in order to stay at the center of local legal affairs and retain contact with whites. Some, like John Green, might form partnerships with whites; others, such as John Hargo, a graduate in 1884 of Cincinnati Law School, begin their careers as associates of well-known white law firms.[74] These contacts with whites were enormously helpful for men like Williams, Green, and Steward who had political ambitions. Each of them, in fact, served one or more terms in the legislature during the 1880s and 1890s at a time when the relatively small size of the Ohio black electorate made the active support of white politicians a necessity for nomination and election.

Black professionals were also winning increasing acceptance from the white public and from white colleagues. Because of the small black

[73] Ibid., Dec. 7, 1885, June 16, 1888, Dec. 10, 1892, Dec. 7, 1895; "Dr. Frank Johnson," *Colored American Magazine,* III (Aug., 1901), 317.

[74] Youngstown *Vindicator,* May 5, 1958; New York *Globe,* Feb. 24, 1883; Cleveland *Gazette,* June 7, 1884; William J. Simmons, *Men of Mark: Eminent, Progressive, and Rising* (Cleveland, 1887), pp. 371–383; John Green, *Fact Stranger Than Fiction: 75 Years of a Busy Life* (Cleveland, 1920), pp. 117, 171–181; Helen M. Chesnutt, *Charles W. Chesnutt: Pioneer of the Color Line* (Chapel Hill, 1952), p. 40.

populations in most localities, many black professional men depended as much, if not considerably more, on white patronage than on black to make a living. Steward and attorney John Oatneal of Washington Court House both worked for many years settling the pension claims of white Civil War veterans. Green, who acquired a reputation as one of Cleveland's leading defense counsels in criminal cases, had a large number of whites seeking his services. Black physicians also enjoyed white patronage. Dr. Thomas Burton of Springfield, a slave-born surgeon who became a specialist in the removal of tumors, based his practice largely upon whites. Gradually, too, professional recognition came in the form of invitations to join professional societies. Some black doctors were asked to join local medical societies; respected ministers were invited to affiliate with ministerial associations composed almost totally of whites; and an occasional attorney joined the more socially exclusive bar associations.[75]

Nevertheless, progress in numbers was painfully slow. In 1890 there were but fourteen black attorneys and thirty-two black doctors in Ohio, and professionals made up only 2.4 percent of the black work force. Moreover, the vast majority of black professionals remained in two areas: clergymen trained almost exclusively (to the extent they received advanced training) at black seminaries and preaching at black churches; and black public school teachers who remained at their posts in some southern Ohio towns where the dual school system lingered after 1887. The teachers themselves illustrate the limits of acceptance of the black professional, for very few school systems were willing to employ black teachers to instruct white pupils, because of doubts about their ability and the belief that they could never be fitting models for the moral and intellectual development of white children.[76] Nor did discrimination end in professional education. Occasional cases of refusal of admission because of race continued to arise in professional schools, and it was a well-known fact that some professional schools and seminaries in Ohio had never, and by their own admission would never, admit blacks.[77] No matter how many whites might seek his help at his office, the black doctor was not likely to be

[75] Thomas Burton, *What Experience Has Taught Me* (Springfield, 1910), pp. 68, 86–87; Green, *Fact Stranger That Fiction*, pp. 171–181; Cleveland *Gazette*, Nov. 11, 1899, Apr. 18, 1903; Youngstown *Vindicator*, May 5, 1958; interviews with Dr. Richard Winn and Dr. S. S. Jordan, n.d., W.P.A. Project, Springfield, Ohio, typescripts at OHS.

[76] Census Office, *Eleventh Census*, I, pt. 2, pp. 596–597; see also ch. 8, below, on black teachers.

[77] W. E. B. Du Bois, *The Negro Church* (Atlanta, 1903), pp. 196–197, and Du Bois, *Negro Health and Physique* (Atlanta, 1906), pp. 100–101, and Du Bois, *The College Bred Negro* (Atlanta, 1910), pp. 67–75.

admitted as a resident at either a public or a private hospital, even though blacks were usually admitted as patients.[78] Black nurses were not admitted to white nursing schools or hired to work at white hospitals. They received private training and worked for individual doctors, and they were barred from the nurses' professional organization, which served as an important source of employment information.[79]

Yet the growing recognition of black professionals suggests the willingness of at least some whites to acknowledge black aspirations and talents, and it was not without important implications. By the mid-1890s, when the first post-Reconstruction generation of blacks began to go out in search of advanced training, students found most of the state's better professional schools ready and willing to receive them. Moreover, by calling attention to the desire of the black professional for a conventionally respectable lifestyle and to his respect for solid middle-class values, the acceptance, even if partial, of blacks within the professions reinforced the claims of all blacks with similar values and aspirations to equality and consideration outside economic life as well as within it. Such acceptance might serve as an impetus to socioeconomic uplift among ambitious but poor individuals seeking to break the cycle of economic degradation. Again, the new era had revealed its limitations and its possibilities.

[78] Generally blacks were either barred from practice at both public and private hospitals, or admitted to one of them only in the larger cities. Davis, *Black Americans in Cleveland,* pp. 175, 179; Associated Charities of Columbus, *Third Annual Report, 1901–1902* (Columbus, 1902), pp. 15–18; *Crisis,* V (Mar., 1913), 233–234 (statement on discrimination in Cincinnati's hospitals). There is no evidence, however, of widespread rejection of black patients at Ohio hospitals.

[79] James H. and Mary Jane Rodabaugh, *Nursing in Ohio* (Columbus, 1951), pp. 156–157; Jane Edna Hunter, *A Nickel and a Prayer* (Cleveland, 1940), pp. 71–74.

5

Class, Lifestyle, and
the Conditions of Black Life

As the black population slowly grew before the Civil War, a class structure began to appear among black Ohioans. In every community in which blacks were found, some were more skilled, learned, affluent, propertied, and respected than others; out of combinations of such differences the black population became stratified. A small, self-conscious group of refined, cultivated, and economically secure artisans, servants, shopkeepers, service entrepreneurs, some assorted general laborers and menials, and a very few professionals (mostly teachers and preachers) emerged as a higher status, upper-class group. Below them on the social scale were the poor, unskilled, uneducated, and unpropertied. This group was by no means monolithic in that there were different degrees of poverty and that steady work, ambition for the conventional symbols of success, and respectable lifestyles might separate some from others. The extent of such stratification varied considerably from place to place. It found its greatest development in the cities and towns; there economic and educational opportunities for blacks were greater and more varied than in the rural areas, where most blacks were landless agricultural laborers and where black public education was slow to develop. Moreover, among the urban centers themselves, in long-established and relatively large black communities such as at Cincinnati, Xenia, Cleveland, Columbus, Zanesville, and Chillicothe, class lines had tended to harden more than where populations were smaller or newer. In particular, at Cincinnati, where some commercial businessmen had prospered from the economic boom of the pre-war years, black service enterprise had developed greatly before 1860, black educational opportunities were large, and the schools provided respectable employment for a corps of black teachers; there was an especially large, affluent upper class with a lifestyle mirroring that of the white upper class.

The tendency toward class stratification was greatly accelerated in the new era of race relations, which offered blacks the legal and political bases upon which to protect and enlarge their citizenship, and at the same time provided greater opportunities for social acceptance, educational opportunity, and economic security. The demographic trends of the immediate post-war decades also provided a basis for increased stratification, because increasing black urbanization brought growing numbers into the stratifying economic, social, and cultural environment of the city. Particularly for an ambitious minority of higher status and upwardly mobile blacks, the new era offered a chance to consolidate its social position. As substitutes for the isolation and hopelessness of its position in the years before the Civil War, this minority was now afforded unprecedented opportunity to mingle more freely with whites of equivalent social status and to gain political power, and with it the potential to more effectively lead the fight for equality.

I

Approximately two-thirds of the black population constituted a lower class. For the large majority of these people, daily life remained a struggle for survival, little affected by the benign changes brought by the new era. As is the case with so much of the social history of the nineteenth-century northern black masses, origins tend to be obscure.[1] Many persons had been slaves and had migrated— more recently than not—from the southern states; some were the sons and daughters of ex-slaves, while others were the descendants of the poorest rural Ohio blacks of the ante-bellum period.[2] Yet, regardless of origin, all shared a common fate. Mired in menial and unskilled employment, the lower class was made up almost exclusively of the hardworking, ordinary poor who lived perpetually in an unsuccessful race with poverty. Like whites of the lower class who lived alongside them (especially in the large cities), their lives were circumscribed by want and lack of opportunity, both of which affected the scope of their ex-

[1] The outstanding exception to the lack of scholarship on the social history of the northern black masses is found for the city of Philadelphia; see W. E. B. Du Bois, *The Philadelphia Negro: A Social Study* (Philadelphia, 1899), and Theodore Hershberg, "Free Blacks in Ante-Bellum Philadelphia: A Study of Ex-Slaves, Freeborn, and Socio-Economic Decline," *Journal of Social History,* V (Winter, 1971–72), 183–209. Important as well is the work done on Detroit; see David Katzman, *Before the Ghetto: Black Detroit in the Nineteenth Century* (Urbana, Ill., 1973).

[2] Works Progress Administration, Federal Writers Project, interviews with Springfield blacks, transcripts (undated), OHS.

pectations and aspirations. Because of the obstacles which racial discrimination placed in the path of their mobility and advancement, poverty and lack of opportunity perpetuated themselves from one generation to the next in a vicious, almost inexorable cycle. Struggling to emerge from slavery, poor blacks were reminded of their lowly status at every turn; since their economic position changed little during the period, there was a bleak uniformity of basic social and material conditions over time and throughout the state.

Mobility out of the lower class was difficult. For one thing, few had more than a slight exposure to formal education. Indeed, when many of those reared in slavery were still alive in the late nineteenth century, at least one out of four Ohio blacks was illiterate, and the incidence of illiteracy no doubt was considerably higher within the lower class.[3] Few had skills which allowed them to compete for better jobs. Yet, in truth, what incentive was there for them to seek such skills, especially given the difficulties which blacks experienced in becoming apprentices, when the terms of competition were so weighted against the black artisan? Thus their employment was inevitably low-paying; in addition, because of the long periods of joblessness and underemployment to which common laborers were subject, for many it was not very dependable.

While the wages earned as a porter or hod carrier might provide a decent life for an individual, for a family they did little more than offer subsistence and little, if any, security. Many experienced a desperate struggle to maintain family life. While there is little evidence of widespread family disintegration among the black masses during the period,[4] there is ample evidence that all members were pressed into

[3] U.S. Census Office, *Population of the United States in 1860 . . . Eighth Census* (Washington, 1864), I, 507; *Ninth Census of the United States . . . 1870* (Washington, 1872), I, 394–396; *Statistics of the United States at the Tenth Census* (Washington, 1883), I, 918–921; and *Negro Population in the United States, 1790–1915* (Washington, 1918), p. 415.

[4] Investigating a number of Ohio Valley communities in the years between 1850 and 1880 through the use of manuscript census returns, Paul J. Lammermeier in "The Urban Black Family of the Nineteenth Century: A Study of Black Family Structure in the Ohio Valley, 1850–1880," *Journal of Marriage and the Family* (Aug., 1973), 440–456, found that the overwhelming majority of black families were two-parent, male-headed households. For example, for the Ohio communities he investigated, in 1880 at Cincinnati approximately 80% of black families were two-parent, male-headed households, while for several small cities taken in the aggregate (Steubenville, Portsmouth, Marietta, with some data for Wheeling, West Virginia) the percentage in 1880 was approximately 82. He found only a slight rise in the number of female-headed households during those three decades. It is interesting to note how little the issue of family breakup among blacks preoccupied both black and white commentators in late nineteenth and early twentieth century Ohio. While there is some evidence of family disorganiza-

work in the struggle to sustain family life. Women were often required to work—while only 10 percent of Ohio's white women were at work in 1890, 18 percent of all black women were employed. The gap between the races in the extent of female employment was often greater in the cities, where there were greater opportunities for black women to find work, particularly in domestic service. In 1890 at Cincinnati, Cleveland, Columbus, and Dayton, 36 percent, 24.5 percent, 23 percent, and 26 percent respectively of the total black female population was at work, compared to percentages of 18 for white women at Cincinnati and 15 for white women at Cleveland, Columbus, and Dayton.[5] A few years later the black sociologist R. R. Wright, Jr., found that women were earning fully 20 percent of the incomes of black families at Xenia. Because of the irregular work and small incomes of the many day laborers at Xenia, Wright stated, "It often happens that the only income which a family may have for several weeks is that earned for the labor of the wife or some other female member of the family." [6]

Poverty tended to force children to concern themselves with bringing money into the home. Children received an early initiation into the frustrations of seeking work in a proscriptive job market; the experience no doubt marked an important, if cruel, step in their understanding of their own destiny in a hostile world. Like their parents, black youngsters were limited to certain low-paying, back-breaking work. Though young blacks were found working as newsboys, and a few delivered special mail for the post office at Cincinnati, for example, at the turn of the century only white youngsters obtained employment as messengers for the city's telegraph companies and as delivery boys for its larger department stores, florist shops, and other retail businesses, the kinds of jobs likely to produce the greatest income because of tips.[7] It was not unusual for black children to be

tion among the very poor of Cincinnati's waterfront wards during the 1870s, these areas contained substantial numbers of transient riverboatmen and prostitutes who were involved in informal liaisons; see O. W. Frost, ed., *Children of the Levee* (Lexington, 1957), pp. 5, 17–18, 35, 41; Cincinnati *Commercial,* June 27, Aug. 22, 1876. On the other hand, the available printed records of white public and semi-public charitable organizations and institutions for Columbus, Cincinnati, and Cleveland, and of state custodial and reform institutions catering to the young, do not mention family disorganization among blacks. Consulted were the printed records of Associated Charities of Cleveland, Columbus, and Cincinnati, and of the Cincinnati House of Refuge, and of the state girls' and boys' homes.

[5] U.S. Census Office, *Report on the Population of the United States, Eleventh Census . . . 1890* (Washington, 1897), I, pt. 2, pp. 596–597, 652–659.

[6] R. R. Wright, Jr., "The Negroes of Xenia, Ohio: A Social Study," U.S. Department of Labor *Bulletin* no. 48 (Sept., 1903), 1029.

[7] E. N. Clopper, "Children of the Streets of Cincinnati," *Child Labor and Social Progress,* Proceedings of the Fourth Annual Meeting of the National Child Labor Committee, *Annals,* XXIX (July, 1908), Supplement, 116–121.

doing several menial tasks at once, searching constantly for a number of petty jobs in order to earn some change. Reverdy Ransom, a bishop of the A.M.E. Church in the early twentieth century, recalled that the lack of work for young blacks at Cambridge in Guernsey County, where he grew up in the 1870s, forced him to carry laundry to and from customers for his mother, who supplemented family income with domestic work; at the same time, he had to do general labor in a brickyard and work as a clean-up man in a barbershop and a saloon, while also struggling to attend the primary grades.[8]

Work often required poor black students to attend school irregularly. Teachers and principals were sometimes forced to make special arrangements to teach large numbers of students at the latter's convenience rather than see them leave school permanently.[9] Many, however, left school of necessity, and throughout most of the period before World War I there was a gap between the percentage of the school-age populations of both races actually attending school. This discrepancy was especially great before the strengthening of compulsory education legislation in the 1880s and the coming of school desegregation in 1887, and in the villages and rural areas where black schools were poorly located to begin with.[10] Of course, in the late nineteenth century most white children also left school before completing the upper grades, but for them lack of education was not a permanent bar to finding respectable employment; the skilled trades and clerkships in retail stores, for example, were open to them. For young blacks, however, lack of education was but one more disability in the struggle for stable, fulfilling employment. The contemporary black press periodically bemoaned the small, if slowly increasing, number of black children educated beyond basic literacy training, and it warned parents of the adverse effect upon racial and individual advancement which resulted from allowing children to drop out of school after the early grades. Said a Cleveland *Gazette* correspondent in 1885, such individuals became nothing more than "common hirelings." [11]

They left school to help their families fight poverty, but behind that

[8] Reverdy Ransom, *The Pilgrimage of Harriet Ransom's Son* (Nashville, n.d.), p. 25.

[9] Dayton *Journal*, July 25, 1885; Hillsboro *Gazette*, Mar. 5, 1887, for comments by teachers, principals, and parents on such special arrangements.

[10] During the late nineteenth century the percentage of school-age populations of both races actually attending school was 82 for whites and 40 for blacks in 1860, 77 and 52 in 1870, 70 and 43 in 1880, and 75 and 68 in 1890; see Census Office, *Eighth Census*, I, 507; *Ninth Census*, I, 394–396; *Tenth Census*, I, 918–921; *Negro Population . . . 1790–1915*, pp. 389–402, and *Eleventh Census*, I, 733; II, 137.

[11] Cleveland *Gazette*, Mar. 21, 1885.

tendency lay a set of realistic expectations based on what they saw around them. Many realized early in life that education alone gave blacks no guarantee of a better job or a better life. Many probably left school with few reservations, believing that education would be of little use to them in the menial work which they, like their fathers and mothers, seemed destined to do. Around 1900 one black teenager told an investigator of Springfield's social problems that he would not enter high school because "in Springfield I can get no better work even if I have an education." [12] Instead of advanced learning, one might more reasonably hope for steady employment at work neither too servile nor too low-paying, but even this was not easily obtained.

Poverty also placed the Negro masses in the poorest housing in locations often both unsafe and unhealthy. The poor in the countryside lived in crude huts in the crossroad settlements; in the small villages, they often resided in shanties on the edge of town. In the large cities, to which a growing number of rural blacks were migrating, many lived in shanties and crowded tenements in deteriorating neighborhoods of the downtown fringe, where filth gathered in the streets, mortality rates were high, and conditions of social disorder were endemic. In the late nineteenth century, however, the black ghetto had not yet appeared. For the most part, Ohio's black population was too small for blacks to occupy exclusively the central neighborhoods of the cities and towns.

The closest they came to doing so was not in the major cities, but in the medium-sized urban centers of southern Ohio, such as Xenia, Gallipolis, Portsmouth, and Chillicothe. Here throughout the years before 1916 a large percentage of local blacks occupied one ward or a section of a ward, often known to white contemporaries as "Africa," and they made up a large, though rarely dominant, percentage of the total ward population.[13] Xenia's East End was typical of the black neighborhoods of such towns. The center of local black settlement before 1860 and during the large influx of freedmen just after the war, the East End by 1870 had become, as one resident said many years later, a type of "Negro town." Here, in a large section of the Fourth Ward and a small contiguous area of the Third Ward, altogether not much more than a mile square, there lived some 75 percent of local blacks, about 1,400 persons. By 1900 the black population had become even more concentrated there. R. R. Wright, Jr., estimated that 90 per-

[12] E. S. Todd, *A Sociological Study of Springfield and Clark County, Ohio* (New York, 1904), p. 103.

[13] Census Office, *Ninth Census*, I, 226–241. Aggregate decennial census data, census district enumeration maps, and local city directories have been used in tracing all urban residential patterns.

cent of Xenia's blacks (some 1,791 of 1,900) lived in the East End around 1900. Xenia, however, was exceptional to the extent that blacks achieved numerical dominance in a ward: in 1870 blacks made up slightly more than 53 percent of the Fourth Ward's population, and they would continue to linger around the 50 percent mark thereafter.[14]

Lacking high population density, tenements, and congestion, the East End, like the Irish West End across town, was not a classic urban slum. Within it were small sections of decent housing, particularly along major streets, where affluent blacks resided. Yet for the most part its inhabitants were the black poor, and large areas of the East End, such as "Frog Hollow," had the appearance of a shanty town. Relatively few of the shacks and cottages in the East End were rented; at the turn of the century, slightly over 63 percent of the black families in the district owned their own homes. But the distinction of being a homeowner in this case was lessened by the sorry condition of the average dwelling, which was a small, dilapidated, poorly insulated, and poorly floored frame structure, lacking any but the crudest sanitary facilities and often too small even for a family of four. Over half of the structures were assessed by their owners and local tax collectors as having a value of $200 or less—often much less.[15] Rain, storms, and winters brought great suffering to the poor of this section. "The great need is for fuel," said the Xenia *Torchlight* in 1887, when subzero temperatures brought the danger of disease and exposure to the poor people of the Fourth Ward. "Many of the houses occupied by these poverty stricken people are almost as bad as no house at all. The cracks in them are many and broad, and the amount of coal and wood required to keep them inhabitable is consequently increased." Yet each family had a bit of land, where vegetables were often grown and a cow or some chickens might be raised to help supplement the family diet. Residents recalled that flowers bloomed everywhere in the spring, turning the East End into a sweet-smelling garden, and good weather brought the residents out to make repairs on their humble homes.[16]

The benefits of elbow room, a garden, and privacy were less attainable for the lower-class poor of the cities who lived amidst squalor in the crowded neighborhoods at the fringes of bustling business districts. More than in the towns, the black poor were relatively few in the areas where they clustered, when compared to the white lower class living

[14] Helen Hooven Santemyer, *Ohio Town* (Columbus, 1962), pp. 83–84; Wright, "Negroes of Xenia," 1012; Census Office, *Ninth Census*, I, 231.

[15] Santemyer, *Ohio Town*, pp. 84–85, 90–94; Wright, "Negroes of Xenia," 1038–39.

[16] Xenia *Torchlight*, Dec. 3, 1887; Santemyer, *Ohio Town*, pp. 92–99; Wright, "Negroes of Xenia," 1036.

alongside them. Furthermore, in cities they tended to be scattered throughout various neighborhoods, rather than concentrated in one area.

At Cincinnati in 1870 approximately 60 percent of the city's blacks (some 3,457 of 5,900 persons) lived spread throughout seven wards of the city's basin, near the waterfront and on the southern, eastern, and western fringes of downtown. This area had been the primary place of settlement for black migrants in the immediate post-war years. Especially large concentrations of blacks were found in three non-contiguous neighborhoods in these wards. The one farthest to the east, comprising parts of the First and Thirteenth wards, contained approximately one-fourth of the city's blacks, generally the ordinary, hard-working poor but with a small admixture of the more affluent and a larger one of paupers, criminals, and prostitutes. Located in an area centered along Sixth from Broadway to Culvert, and derisively called "Bucktown" by white contemporaries because of its long-time association with blacks, the area was hardly a racial ghetto. Though the Thirteenth Ward contained the largest percentage (18.5) of Cincinnati's total black population in 1870 and a larger number (1,092) of blacks than any other ward, the blacks formed only 15 percent of the ward's population and were clearly eclipsed by the surrounding whites. A second area of black concentration was several blocks to the southwest, comprising a small section of the First Ward and a substantial corner of the riverfront Fourth Ward. Here blacks were found particularly along Front Street between Ludlow and Walnut near the docks, in sections called the "Levee," "Sausage Row," and "Rat Row." Some 400 blacks, about 7 percent of the black population, lived here, constituting at most a quarter of the total population of these small sections. Many of the residents of both races were dockworkers and transient riverboatmen who lived here with their families and (like sailors everywhere with girls in every port) their mistresses. Little Bucktown, a third area of black concentration much farther to the west in the Fifteenth and Sixteenth wards along Sixth between Freeman and Baymiller, contained about 15 percent (some 900 persons) of the city's black population. As the neighborhoods farther east of Little Bucktown became more devoted to wholesale business, mills, and factories with the decline of the river trade in the late nineteenth century, Little Bucktown became the major focus of black settlement in Cincinnati.[17]

[17] Census Office, *Ninth Census* I, 231; Paul Lammermeier, "Cincinnati's Black Community: The Origins of a Ghetto, 1870–1880," in John Bracey, August Meier, and Elliot Rudwick, eds., *The Rise of the Ghetto* (Belmont, Calif., 1971), pp. 24–27; Works Progress Administration, Writers' Project, *Cincinnati: A Guide to the Queen City* (Cincinnati, 1943), pp. 78–79, 195–196.

These three neighborhoods, especially the eastern ones, were the site of Cincinnati's earliest settlement in the 1790s and early 1800s. By 1870 the eastern neighborhoods had become decayed, dirty, and congested, taking their place among the notorious slums of the era. Located in the river bottoms, much of Rat Row and Sausage Row and part of Bucktown were subject to flooding when the river rose; their poorly drained streets, paved and unpaved, were often filthy breeding places for disease. "The black hollows are foul, noisome, and miasmatic," wrote Cincinnati newspaperman Lafcadio Hearn, later a well-known writer of fiction. In 1876 he described the riverfront areas as "full of damp corruption and often under water, or better expressed, liquid filth." [18]

Because the hollows were periodically filled with dirt to check erosion and disease, many of the buildings were practically buried. Since the streets were sometimes several feet above the front door, stepladders were required at entrances. In this bizarre setting, in crude shacks and tenements, some of which had once been warehouses, dilapidated, their wood rotting "from a thousand petty inundations," lived the poor. On the fringes of Bucktown they also lived in the decayed and subdivided mansions of wealthy whites who had long ago left for better neighborhoods. The population here was denser than elsewhere in the city. Five or six families "are smothered into seven rooms to swelter and bake," wrote Hearn of Bucktown one July. "Ten to twenty in one two-story, underground den is common enough," he said of the Levee. By the late 1870s the municipal Board of Improvements was forcing a clean-up in the basin neighborhoods, condemning property and paving the streets. Yet the mortality rate remained high for both races, and the damp and crowded tenements were prime breeding grounds for tuberculosis. [19]

Crime and vice abounded. Bucktown and the Levee were the "red light zones" and "tenderloins" of the day, where illegal trafficking in liquor, gambling, drugs, and especially prostitution ran rampant. In some tenements families with young children lived next door to brothels. Many of the prostitutes were "morphine eaters"; some died from the effects of withdrawal when they were too poor to buy the drug, and even short stays in the workhouse meant agony for those with an advanced habit. Abandoned children of prostitutes and of the broken poor roamed the streets, to die of hunger or exposure or to be taken in

[18] Frost, ed., *Children of the Levee*, p. 3; Cincinnati *Commercial*, Aug. 22, 1876, Jan. 18, 1877.
[19] Cincinnati *Gazette*, July 26, 1876; Census Office, *Eleventh Census*, Part II, *Vital Statistics* (Washington, 1896), pp. 182–183, 185–191.

by some saintly soul like "Aunty" Porter, an aged, turbaned, pipe-smoking black woman who claimed in 1876 to have raised some nine-teen abandoned children. Because brothel-keepers of both races often had political influence, and the police desired to keep what they be-lieved to be necessary evils contained in one district of the city, officers rarely interfered. Periodic crackdowns were usually prompted only by some instance of murder, mayhem, or scandal which particularly quick-ened the public conscience. In truth, the job may have been too much for even the most conscientious police force. No sooner were the prosti-tutes out of the workhouse than they were back at their trade in the wretched tenements and houses of assignation. In addition, the police had all they could do to deal with violent crime. Rarely did a day pass in Bucktown of the 1870s without the usual "carvings" and shootouts, frequently arising from quarrels over gambling or the favors of a pros-titute. The prostitutes themselves were said to be adept with razors. Professional thieves, con men, and muggers gathered here. The repu-table poor of both races, depending on the prosperity and vulnerability suggested by dress and demeanor, might be attacked by gangs of mug-gers and rowdies who roamed the streets. With the decline of the river trade in the late nineteenth century, these neighborhoods grew some-what more orderly because of the diminishing number of transients, and toward the end of the century the police began to clear the streets of thieves.[20] By the 1890s violent crime had decreased to the point, said Dabney ironically, that "murder had become a lost art, and some-times several nights would pass without anyone being murdered." [21]

Yet "dissolute women and gambling men" of both races remained. As the eastern neighborhoods were given over to industry and com-merce, they began to appear more frequently on George Street, on the eastern fringe of the Little Bucktown section. Every manner of brothel came to exist on that notorious street, which catered to affluent visitors for whom slumming brought special pleasures. (Traveling southern gentlemen were known to request young black women of the "servant type" such as they knew at home.) In bold defiance of the color line, there were white-staffed brothels catering to blacks. This was the environment in which many poor black children came of age. The very conditions of poverty which placed them in such neighborhoods tempted them to take advantage of the fast money to be made in the

[20] Cincinnati *Commercial,* Aug. 21, 1872, Mar. 17, June 27, July 14, Aug. 22, 1876, Aug. 20, 1879; Cincinnati *Enquirer,* Sept. 22, 25, 1877; Wendell Phillips Dabney, *Cincinnati's Colored Citizens: Historical, Sociological, and Biographical* (Cincinnati, 1926), pp. 153–157.

[21] Dabney, *Cincinnati's Colored Citizens,* pp. 156–157.

streets. In the environment of Bucktown or the Levee it was not difficult to understand how men became thieves, pimps, and murderers,
and why women sold their bodies on the streets. Most, of course,
simply remained poor and honest, faceless to the society around
them.[22]

The poverty and squalor of the slums established a possible basis for
solidarity between black and white residents. Moreover, throughout
the period before World War I, large concentrations of recently arrived immigrants and their American-born children (pariahs despite
their white skins, in the eyes of many old stock Americans) resided
here. Indeed, these slums were the crucible of poverty and pain in
which their Americanism was forged. The Irish poor, with whom
blacks had worked on the docks for years, lived in large numbers in
Bucktown. In Little Bucktown blacks mingled with large numbers of
Germans, who by the 1870s were becoming prosperous enough to begin to leave for better neighborhoods. Later in the century, when only
the poorest of the immigrant Irish and Germans remained, newer immigrants from southern and eastern Europe and poor native whites
from the border states lived in these same neighborhoods. Blacks remained throughout, locked here like no other single group for decades
and decades by poverty.[23]

Yet the immigrants tended not to view the blacks as comrades in
misery. While Hearn remarked in 1876 about how strikingly the blood
of County Cork and Killarney "seems to predominate in the veins of
half the mulattoes of Bucktown," the immigrants' desire more often
than not was to widen their distance from the blacks, whom they regarded as beneath them. Blacks and whites rarely lived together in
the same tenements, though they might live next to one another in
separate buildings. Had blacks sought residence in a white building,
doubtless as dilapidated and cramped as their own, they would have
been rebuffed.[24]

The matter was probably not of great importance to the black poor
who found enough fulfillment in the company of their own people. But
hostilities were sometimes more overt. As Cincinnati's interracial battles of the ante-bellum and Civil War years suggest, the races lived
together in an uneasy peace. Serious conflict continued intermittently
after the war—particularly after enfranchisement, when clashes be-

[22] Ibid., pp. 164–167.
[23] Cincinnati *Commercial*, Oct. 7, 1877; Lammermeier, "Cincinnati's Black
Community," 25–26; G. A. Dobbert, "The 'Zinzinnati' in Cincinnati," *Cincinnati
Historical Society Bulletin*, XXII (Oct., 1964), 217–218.
[24] Cincinnati *Commercial*, June 27, 1876; Lammermeier, "Cincinnati's Black
Community," 26.

tween the Democratic Irish and Republican blacks sometimes accompanied close elections.[25] Gangs of white, generally Irish, rowdies were known to attack innocent blacks in the streets. The trustees of Allen Temple, A.M.E. Church, located in the heart of Bucktown, complained in 1869 that black worshippers were constantly harassed:

> On every Sabbath, we are insulted on the very threshold of our house of worship for no reason whatever. . . . On Easter Sunday, we had eggs thrown upon us as if we were heretics. Our chapel is regularly stoned, and if we dare to speak we are threatened with having our [church] mobbed and the whole body of us killed. Our wives are insulted; our children beaten with boulders as they go to Sabbath School. If anyone will look at the front of the chapel today they may readily see the evidence of abuse; windows are broken and some filled with mud.[26]

In the 1870s similar circumstances had not emerged at either Columbus or Cleveland or at the smaller Miami valley cities of Dayton and Springfield. The fewer than 2,000 blacks at each of the four cities in 1870 were overwhelmed by the surrounding whites, and they tended to live in greater peace and amidst more pleasant surroundings than was the case at Cincinnati. At Dayton and Springfield, most blacks lived in small clusters scattered throughout neighborhoods bordering the central business districts, or near industry, the railroads, and the canals; in such locations small rented bungalows and apartments were found more often than tenements.[27]

Blacks also clustered throughout the capital city. In 1870 almost 85 percent of the city's Negroes lived in five of Columbus's eight wards, in percentages of no less than 11 and no greater than 35 in relation to the total black population of the city. Several separate neighborhoods had served as foci of black settlement and would continue to be among the most prominent black neighborhoods throughout the late nineteenth and into the twentieth centuries, as the city's black population grew. In none of them, however, did blacks constitute more than about 30 percent of the population before 1916.[28]

The largest concentration of blacks appeared in an area several

[25] Cincinnati *Gazette,* Oct. 7, 1872, Oct. 13, 14, 1880; W. A. Knapp to E. F. Noyes, Oct. 14, 1872, Box II, folder 2, Governor Edward Noyes Papers, OHS.

[26] "An Appeal to the Mayor of the City" (dated May 3, 1869), quoted in Centennial Commission, Allen Temple, A.M.E., *Centennial Guide, Allen Temple, A.M.E.* (Cincinnati, 1924), p. 36.

[27] Census Office, *Ninth Census,* I, 229, 236, and *Eleventh Census,* I, 474–475; Todd, *Springfield and Clark County,* pp. 72–99.

[28] Census Office, *Ninth Census,* I, 230.

blocks north and east of the corner of Broad and High Streets, the center of downtown Columbus. Along East Long, East Lafayette, and East Spring to North Fourth Street on the east, some 650 blacks, about 35 percent of the total black population, resided in 1870 in a neighborhood mixed by class as well as race. Here a good many affluent blacks and whites lived in homes not far from the back alley and side-street shacks and bungalows of the poor. Another, smaller concentration of blacks was found several blocks northwest of Broad and High, along West Long and West Spring streets from North Front on the east to the walls of the state penitentiary on the west, an area generally lower- and working-class in character, but where many people lived in small, neat cottages. Blacks also lived in a shantytown along the bottoms of the Scioto River immediately southwest of downtown, and in a neighborhood of small homes and apartments around Seventh and Main, about fifteen blocks southeast of the center of town.[29]

At Cleveland, however, the black majority was more concentrated; in 1870 some 84 percent of the 1,292 blacks resided in three contiguous wards immediately southeast of the Public Square, the center of the city's downtown, and directly east of the bustling canal, railroad, and factory complex along the Cuyahoga River. Yet the black area was a large one, and it encompassed as wide a variety of neighborhoods as was found at Columbus. There were essentially two main clusters of blacks. A little over a quarter of the black population lived in an area surrounding the Haymarket, the central market place, not far from the river. Most of them resided on and near Ohio Street (later a part of the main thoroughfare, Central Avenue), from Erie Street (later East 9th) east toward Brownell (later East 14th). (The names of Cleveland's major north-south streets changed in 1906.) This was a thickly settled, multinational, commercial and industrial area; though poor and congested, it lacked the decay and disorder of Bucktown. From here black population shaded off to the east until it reached a section some fifteen blocks away, not far to the south of some of the most aristocratic homes in Cleveland; there another one-fourth of the local blacks resided along Garden (also later part of Central) and Perry (later East 30th), and several smaller streets to the east and immediately to the west of Perry. Like the East Long Street area, this neighborhood was mixed by class as well as race; it was characterized by homes as well as bungalows and apartments of varying degrees of quality. Both sections had been the main foci of black settlement before 1860 and

[29] Mary Louise Mark, *Negroes in Columbus* (Columbus, 1928), pp. 17, 19; Cleveland *Gazette*, Jan. 7, 1899; Ben Hayes, "Negro—No. 10," undated clipping, Columbus *Citizen-Journal*, on file at OHS; Census Office, *Ninth Census*, I, 230.

would continue to be so until 1916, as a slowly growing black population filled in the gaps between the two. Yet in the late nineteenth century the Cleveland black population was small, still under 5,000; its growth barely kept pace with the explosion of white population, which within several decades led prosperous, rapidly industrializing Cleveland to replace Cincinnati as Ohio's largest city. Though blacks might cluster together in small enclaves, they were easily outnumbered by whites in the neighborhoods where they resided. In no ward did blacks constitute as much as 10 percent of the total population.[30]

As at Cincinnati, these Cleveland, Dayton, Springfield, and Columbus neighborhoods were convenient to the places where many blacks worked—the railroad yards, the canal, lake, and river docks, warehouses, stores, hotels, laundries, and the homes of affluent whites. The availability of cheap, often relatively decent housing made them suitable locations for many low-income blacks. In 1870 the black areas of all four cities had yet to undergo the serious decay that the older, generally more densely populated areas of Cincinnati had experienced. In addition, the small number of blacks at each city tended to live in peace with their white neighbors; absent were the riotous scenes of contemporary Bucktown.

Yet each city's potential for economic development and population growth, and the proximity of black neighborhoods to central commercial and industrial districts, destined them to become more congested, more filled with tenements, crime, and vice, and more singularly poor and slumlike in character as the century waned. The process was apparent at Cleveland, which was undergoing intensive industrial development and accommodating growing numbers of European immigrants. The area of congestion and poor housing spread eastward from the Haymarket, and though streets of homes and better apartments remained, tenements began to make their appearance. So did vice and crime; by the turn of the century, brothels and saloons were plentiful along Central Avenue.[31] Similarly, at Springfield and Dayton, brothels and saloons began finding their way into the neighborhoods where the black poor resided. Springfield had its own "Levee," the name perhaps

[30] Census Office, *Ninth Census*, I, 227; Wellington G. Fordyce, "Immigrant Colonies in Cleveland," *Ohio State Archeological and Historical Quarterly*, XL, 4 (1936), 333–336; Kenneth Kusmer, "Black Cleveland: The Origins and Development of a Ghetto, 1890–1930" (Master's thesis, Kent State University, 1970), pp. 13, 18; see also Kusmer, *A Ghetto Takes Shape: Black Cleveland, 1870–1930* (Urbana, Ill., 1976). Russell H. Davis, *Black Americans in Cleveland from George Peake to Carl B. Stokes* (Washington, 1972), p. 128.

[31] Cleveland *Gazette*, Dec. 30, 1887, Sept. 22, 1888, Oct. 1, 1898; Jane Edna Hunter, *A Nickel and a Prayer* (Cleveland, 1940), pp. 66–68; Judith Trolander, "Twenty Years at Hiram House," *Ohio History*, LXXVIII (Winter, 1968–69), 28.

borrowed from Cincinnati, and Dayton its Joe Street. Both were high crime areas, known for vice of all sorts which was sanctioned for many years by public officials.[32]

Columbus's black areas were particularly ripe for such a transition, lying as they did in the immediate path of downtown expansion, and it came rapidly. The section of East Long Street nearest to downtown Columbus changed dramatically during the last decades of the century. Cheap tenements, boarding houses and hotels of dubious character, wholesale houses and warehouses, and saloons proliferated. Single-family dwellings were razed or divided into small, cheap apartments. The demimonde made its appearance as well. By 1881 the Visiting Committee of the Negro schools of Columbus complained of the "unhealthy moral atmosphere [of] saloons and streetcorners" which surrounded the city's largest black public school. In the 1890s the neighborhood became known as the "Bad Lands" for its pervasive crime, gambling, and prostitution, and it was here that "Smoky" Hobbs kept his opium den. The other neighborhoods of Columbus blacks experienced similar physical and moral deterioration. The area around Seventh and Main became such a center for prostitution that a Seventh Street address was in itself a stigma. Residents of a more respectable section of the street eventually petitioned to have its name changed.[33]

As the number of urban blacks increased, the condition in which the lower class lived grew more uniform throughout Ohio's major urban centers. Regarding the situation across distances of physical space and culture, upper- and middle-class whites and conventionally respectable people generally were prone to see the conditions of poverty and disorder in these neighborhoods as they related particularly to blacks, less as the result of social and economic forces which proscribed the lives of the struggling poor than of black racial character. Poverty and crime were not simply deprivation and violence, but "Negro crime" and "Negro poverty"—conditions to which race, rather than social circumstances, predestined them.

Tendencies toward racial determinism were clear in the late nineteenth century press. All but the most circumspect Ohio daily papers gave ample coverage to petty crimes committed by blacks (always identified by race), and to more general evidence of social and moral

[32] Todd, *Springfield and Clark County*, pp. 106–107, 112–113; Dayton *Daily News*, Jan. 11, 12, 13, 15, 1906.

[33] Cleveland *Gazette*, Oct. 1, 1892; Mark, *Negroes in Columbus*, pp. 20–21; Richard Clyde Minor, "Negroes in Columbus" (Ph.D. dissertation, Ohio State University, 1936), pp. 116–118; Columbus Board of Education, *Annual Report, 1881–1882* (Columbus, 1882), p. 193.

chaos in the neighborhoods and lives of the black poor—fighting spouses, abandoned children, dispossessed persons sleeping in alleys and on sidewalks.[34] Such reportage, often humorous in tone (except when the victims of crime were whites), revealed a deep-seated belief that fighting, drinking, gambling, and prostitution were the peculiar characteristics of an undisciplined, irresponsible people. Such antics, while too familiar to contemporary readers to be shocking, reaffirmed the decision to ignore their aspirations to a better life and their very humanity. When some of the crimes reported were against whites, however, as in the minority of cases, the emphasis changed: viciousness and depravity were then suggested. The occasional violent clashes between police and urban blacks who were angered by police mistreatment, and the periodic protests to civil authorities against such mistreatment,[35] revealed that this attitude was commonly held by law enforcement agents, society's emissaries to the black masses. Whatever the particular components of the racial stereotype at any given time, the message was clear, and the constant repetition served only to reinforce it: these people are not worthy of better regard.

The social and cultural distance was great on both sides of the color line. Then emerging from slavery, the masses of blacks lived in a world of distinctive frames of reference, forged over centuries of oppression. Their own cultural modes—their shared symbols, meanings, and values —provided a foundation for their struggle for self-respect, dignity, fulfillment, and a measure of self-determination. Assimilated, however marginally, into the economic system, they were at best, by the standards of the larger society, imperfectly acculturated. Belief in the values which daily governed that society must have been especially difficult. Why work to succeed in conventional terms, when so few blacks could achieve success along lines approved by the white majority? Better to lower one's expectations in order to avoid continual and tragic disappointment. How could one make long-range plans based on saving and thrift and the grasping of every possible opportunity when unmanage-

[34] Examples of such reportage abound; see Columbus *Ohio State Journal*, Feb. 8, 1866, July 27, 1868, July 11, 1872, Aug. 6, 1879; Cleveland *Leader*, Apr. 6, 1870; Cincinnati *Enquirer*, Sept. 22, 25, 1877; Cincinnati *Commercial*, Aug. 21, 1872, Aug. 17, 1877.

[35] One serious and particularly violent example of black-police tensions in the Cincinnati slums was prompted by the killing of a black by a U.S. marshal during an election; it led to a shoot-out on the streets. See Cincinnati *Commercial Gazette*, Oct. 15, 1884. Five years before at Columbus, an off-duty white policeman shot and killed a black laborer who tipped his hat to two white women on the street one evening. The incident intensified long-standing black demands for black policemen. See Columbus *Democrat*, Aug. 17, 1879; Columbus *Ohio State Journal*, Sept. 14, 15, 16, 17, 1879.

able circumstances played havoc with life? Better to live for the day
and the hour than for a highly unlikely future gratification. How could
one seek fulfillment in the acquisition of the conventional success symbols when these were beyond reach? Easier were the joys of enthusiastic religion and the fellowship of the front stoop and the tavern. One
sought in possessions not the symbols of arrival at a certain social rank,
but expressions of a self which yearned to be free of the psychic prison
of degradation and poverty.[36]

For those then emerging from slavery but mired in poverty and social isolation, the new era in race relations posed a difficult dilemma:
how to find meaning in the American Dream and the symbols and
values which sustained it from the vantage point of their own lives.
Some struggled to believe in that dream, while for others it seemed a
cruel deception, or at best irrelevant to the struggle for survival. Each
pointed to changes and continuities to justify the chosen position.
There was freedom from the lash, freedom from forced removal of
loved ones, freedom to roam; there were wages, basic guarantees of
civil rights, and the central symbol of citizenship—the vote. But there
was at the same time a basic continuity between the past and the
emerging present: they were black in a world in which black and white
were potent symbols, a world which rejected them, yet sought to control their lives and limit their horizons. Though the constraints were
now more subtle, they were no less tangible to blacks pondering the
matter from the standpoint of oppressive poverty and lack of opportunity.

As long as this duality and isolation existed, they would reflect contradictory impulses regarding their citizenship. Years after Republicans
ceased to be concerned with their welfare, they might still be swayed
by powerful black oratory and by white promises to show enthusiastic
gratitude to the party of Lincoln. The masses were not without pride
in the accomplishments of those very few, slave-born like themselves,
who had struggled from southern plantations to the national capital
and attained positions of power and respect, and who spoke to them
of racial interest and advancement. Yet at the same time they remained
wary of those, black and white, however sincere, who approached
them from outside their own immediate experience. When leaders
spoke of social mobility and equality as if these were practical reali-

[36] Little has been written about the emergence of lower-class black culture in
the late nineteenth century northern city. Lafcadio Hearn's sketches of recreational life and lifestyles among Cincinnati's black riverboatmen in the waterfront
neighborhoods are suggestive, however, even if these relatively rootless transients
are singular social types. See Cincinnati *Commercial*, Mar. 17, Apr. 9, June 27,
Aug. 22, 1876.

ties, or easily within their grasp with the vote, their suspicion must have run deep.

They needed at the same time to respect those whose experience paralleled theirs, and to find sources for self-regard in their own struggles. The central act of their newly obtained citizenship—casting a ballot—often meant making a few extra dollars on election day or earning the gratitude of an admired black political boss who could be of practical assistance in the emergencies which often beset the poor: no coal in winter, no job, no money in time of illness, a son in trouble with the law. In this respect they were no different from the immigrants. Yet they watched the immigrants suffer, but later often prosper and obtain acceptance as they themselves could not, and they also watched these same immigrants assume the racial attitudes of the white majority. They alone seemed to remain at the bottom.

The black men who occasionally emerged from among them to aid them in relating to a hostile world suggest their needs. There was Henry "Old Man" Pickett, reputedly a former brothel-keeper, but in the 1870s the proprietor of a combination dance hall, restaurant, and saloon on Sausage Row. An occasional Democratic operative at a time when such an affiliation was considered apostasy by most blacks, he had his political base among the dockworkers and riverboatmen to whom he extended credit during the period of winter unemployment.[37] There was "Smoky" Hobbs, whose immunity from police harassment was largely due to control over lower-class votes in the East Long Street area. Hobbs used these votes to make deals with various factions of Columbus's Republican party, which in turn protected his interests.[38] Crude and corrupt, Hobbs was also a man who understood the needs of his people and who gained a reputation for helping the down-and-out during his many years in Columbus. His outspoken, aggressive public manner, which made him an object of contempt in the Columbus press and among respectable people generally,[39] identified him to his constituents as a man of spirit who refused to accept the role which society had laid out for him. Those who lived in poverty and degradation longed for examples which proved their power and worth. Yet allegiance to men like Hobbes promised few permanent changes that would once and for all lift their sons and daughters out of the circumstances in which they themselves were confined. Thus, in their relation to society, they were left where they had begun.

[37] Ibid., Oct. 11, 1871; Cincinnati *Enquirer*, Feb. 21, 1875.
[38] Ben Hayes, "Negro—No. 5," undated clipping, Columbus *Citizen-Journal*, on file at OHS; Minor, "Negroes in Columbus," pp. 116–118.
[39] Columbus *Dispatch*, Sept. 9, 1907, Sept. 11, 23, 1908.

II

Shading off from the upper reaches of the more reputable lower-class poor there was an upwardly mobile group of perhaps 25 to 30 percent of the black population, the contemporary black version of a middle class. The ambitions and values of this little-understood, middling group particularly tended to distinguish it from the lower-class poor. Life for it was a constant struggle for order, security, and respectability; these values placed it more firmly within the framework of white American values. Very few objective indicators, however, showed the middle group of blacks as bearing much resemblance to the white middle class. They were generally without advanced training, let alone advanced education, and had very little in the way of capital. Indeed, most lived not far above the thin line separating poverty and want from security and comfort, and doubtless some lived below it.

In fact, they bore many similarities to the black lower class. Many had roots in the South and in slavery; those who had come North before the war were more recently manumitted slaves than representatives of the older, well-established southern free people of color. Some had come with skills in the building trades or in shoemaking, blacksmithing, and other crafts, but most were unskilled and had come in poverty. Few had education beyond basic literacy. Many worked as porters, menials, and common laborers, just as did members of the lower class. Indeed, in towns and villages with smaller black populations and limited opportunities for a black artisan and shopkeeper group, there was often little difference between the work of this middle group and the lower classes.[40]

At the same time, there were differences of objective circumstance. In its desire to lift itself above poverty and degradation, the middle class magnified these differences and used them to reinforce a distinctive social position and the values which sustained it. Those who were employed as unskilled laborers and menials often had more secure positions, less subject to periodic layoffs and to long seasonal unemployment. Among them were messengers for commercial businesses and porters in the better stores and office buildings; as the century waned, Ohio blacks also found their way into factories as unskilled but steadily employed laborers in Xenia's cordage works, Columbus's rail-

[40] Wright, "Negroes of Xenia," 1042; Francis Charles Hubbard, "A Short History of the Colored People of Barnesville, Ohio" (1942), typescript, OHS; Florence Brown, "Things I Remember and Things That Have Been Told to Me about the Colored People of Albany" (1955), typescript, Ohio University Library; Santemyer, *Ohio Town*, pp. 109–113.

road shops, or Springfield's iron mills. The men in domestic and personal service were those who worked, often for many years, for the
same few substantial (if not wealthy) white families as handymen,
servants, and gardeners. Women of the middle group often worked as
cooks, nurses, or maids for the same types of families, or as laundresses,
scrubwomen, and chambermaids in hotels, offices, or public institutions. Also working in domestic and personal service were the barbers
and hairdressers without their own shops, waiters in better hotels and
restaurants, or janitors in charge of smaller office buildings, warehouses, commercial business buildings, or the better apartment houses.[41]

The upper reaches of the middle class encompassed those who had
gone into business for themselves as well as some on the fringes of the
professions, or farmers who owned moderate-sized parcels of land.
Their business activities were most often small operations requiring
little capital, frequently offshoots of previous employment in domestic
and personal service. Some barbers and hairdressers opened small
shops in the neighborhoods, and an occasional cook opened a small
diner. A few others were the proprietors of more respectable saloons.
Independent teamsters or cabbies sometimes had contracts with small
businesses to do delivering and carrying, or arrangements with hotels
and restaurants to carry baggage and patrons. A very few had their
own small retail businesses of the corner store or newsstand variety.[42]

In relation to the lower class, the economic base of the middle class
was to some extent distinctive in its security, greater self-employment,
and greater prosperity. However, it was as much in the subjective indicators of social position that the middle class became distinctive.
Middle-class lifestyle was defined by a commitment to bourgeois values
and an aspiration for order and security. The middle class believed in
the value of hard work, thrift, saving, and adequate planning for the
future; it respected all the evident and accepted signs of breeding and
respectability. Its often close relations with higher-status whites, in
whose homes middle-class domestics worked, no doubt helped to
create, reinforce, and amplify these values, but relations with the small
black upper class were no less important. In the late nineteenth century the middle class played a prominent and increasingly active role
in the black voluntary associations which upper-class persons usually
led. From the churches and lodges they expected an atmosphere of re-

[41] Cleveland *Gazette,* Dec. 6, 1884, June 1, Dec. 12, 1901, June 1, 1902,
June 15, 1907; Indianapolis *Freeman,* Aug. 3, 1912, Aug. 29, Sept. 12, 1914;
Cleveland *Journal,* Sept. 19, 1908. (Citations refer to biographical sketches.)

[42] Cleveland *Gazette,* Apr. 26, 1884, Oct. 16, 1886, May 23, 1891, June 9,
1904; Columbus *Free American,* Mar. 19, 1887; Cincinnati *Colored Citizen,*
May 19, 1866.

spectability and guiding principles which stressed the values of right living and the dignity of the straight and narrow path. The lodges also enhanced security through their sickness, death, and burial insurance.[43]

Their commitment to these values grew out of their own experience as blacks facing a hostile white world; as such, it was tailored to suit their needs and horizons as they themselves saw them. These values were cherished not so much in themselves, or because the middle class believed that deference to them would open the doors of the nation's colleges, businesses, industries, social circles, or government to their sons and daughters, even though they might have wished it to be so. Instead, in daily life these values served as the instruments which provided the economic and social cushion protecting them against unforeseeable but easily imagined threats to security, gratuitous insults from the white world, and the alienation of so much of lower-class life. The order and predictability they wished to impose upon life was thus defensive, dictated largely by a knowledge of their own vulnerability.

Private strivings tended to focus on the struggle for a secure domesticity. Above all, those in the middle class desired homes of their own as a basis for respectable family life and as shelters against the outside world. Ideally such homes were owned outright, but the large majority were of necessity rented. Also, middle-class providers protected their families through the purchase of life insurance. Middle-class parents felt a particularly profound anxiety for their children because of the temptations of the street, and in light of the hopelessness that young blacks might so easily feel as they surveyed their limited opportunities. Home life, supplemented by church, was to inculcate values which would lead youngsters to pursue the safety, security, and comfort available to them. They desired to make it possible for their children to stay in school long enough to acquire basic education, and some even aspired to have them go to high school, but they tended to be distrustful of book learning alone. They wanted their children to have definite skills in the trades or in domestic service, the proven paths of black opportunity. The resistance of young people unwilling to become barbers, waiters, butlers, etc., because they found these jobs demeaning must have caused many a middle-class parent anxiety.[44]

Preparing a path toward middle-class goals required careful planning, hard work, sacrifice, and patience, especially for economically marginal people. In the career of Columbus's Mrs. M. E. Williams one sees middle-class goals and the decisions they required at work. Born

[43] See ch. 6, below.
[44] Cleveland *Gazette,* Dec. 30, 1887, Sept. 22, 1888, Jan. 31, 1891, June 2, 1894.

in 1839 of poor parents who had settled at Chillicothe after their emancipation some years before, Mrs. Williams found herself at Columbus
in the late 1860s, a young widow with two small children, few friends,
and little security. Aware of her vulnerability, she wanted a trade by
which she might acquire security for her family. Particularly troubling
was the money she spent on rent, which ate up a large share of her
earnings but brought her no closer to having a home of her own. She
decided to take up hairdressing and turn the front room of her rented
flat into a beauty salon. Through hard work and single-minded dedication, with time she had a home and a successful business. Even then
she did not stop planning for the long-range future, or for her children's security. Although her son and daughter aspired to more challenging employment, she insisted that they learn the hairdressing trade.
Carrie, her particularly spirited daughter, consented—but she also
went to normal school for teacher training, and she married a young
man who became a prominent politician. Her mother, however, always
had the reassuring knowledge that her daughter would have a trade to
fall back on in hard times.[45]

Most were not as successful as Mrs. Williams and did not have their
own businesses. Indeed, her success probably catapulted her (and certainly her children) beyond her class in a way that the always hard-
working, unpretentious woman was perhaps unconcerned about. Most
people experienced smaller triumphs over circumstance. They found it
particularly important to free themselves from the physical decay and
moral chaos of the slums. For those who were not able to do so, or who
lived in close quarters in small-town neighborhoods like Xenia's East
End, life must have been a continuing battle against influences they
considered debilitating.

During the late nineteenth century these middling blacks began to
leave the older areas of the cities and cluster in better neighborhoods.
Cincinnati's Walnut Hills section served as the focal point for settlement of middle-class blacks who wished to leave the lower river basin
wards. The movement to Walnut Hills had begun in the 1860s, when
large numbers of southern blacks began moving into the already congested slums of the river basin. In 1860 the black population of Walnut
Hills, then an independent village, was very small; but when the area
was annexed by the city in 1870, some five hundred blacks resided
there. The number rose steadily, reaching about two thousand at the
turn of the century, with the greatest concentration in an area around

[45] Carrie Clifford, "The Business Career of Mrs. M. E. Williams," *Colored
American Magazine*, IX (Sept., 1905), 477–481; Cleveland *Journal*, Mar. 28, 1903
(obituary of Mrs. Williams).

Alms and Chapel Streets. This neighborhood was convenient for black domestics because it was near the homes of affluent whites residing in Cincinnati's exclusive hilltop sections and suburbs. But proximity to wealthy whites does not suggest that the Walnut Hills blacks were themselves affluent. Many were common laborers; in 1870 most lived in single-family dwellings, often owned by their occupants, but the number living in homes subsequently declined. Most blacks came to the hills to reside in apartments, a considerable improvement over the tenements and hovels of Bucktown and Rat Row.[46]

The pattern at Columbus and Cleveland was similar, though the exodus began about two decades later. While on a smaller scale than at Cincinnati, in the late nineteenth century some Cleveland blacks began to move much farther east to the rapidly developing area just north of Hough Avenue between East 84th and East 95th streets. There they were not far from the homes of affluent whites in the growing neighborhoods of the far east side. Most, however, did not go that far, instead settling in more convenient neighborhoods. Those who stayed closer to downtown, around Central Avenue and East 30th Street and east, found that housing was cheaper but still in good repair, and that there were less congestion and better moral conditions than in the older sections to the west.[47]

By 1880 there was considerable incentive to leave Columbus's downtown districts; the East Long Street section had become particularly decayed and congested. In the 1880s a few blacks began to rent inexpensive homes in developing sections of the city far to the north and west. Much the largest new concentration of blacks was found farther to the east, down Long Street itself. This area was accessible both to the shops of the Pennsylvania Railroad a mile or so to the north, and to the homes of whites in the exclusive and growing East Broad Street section a few blocks to the south. In the late 1880s black laborers and domestics began to rent (and sometimes buy) small, inexpensive homes. White real estate dealers found an unexpectedly large market of black working people who wanted to move to orderly, convenient neighborhoods. Unlike the black influx at Walnut Hills and in eastern Cleveland, however, the movements of blacks here was rapid, involving almost a thousand persons within a single decade. Feeling threatened by the tide of blacks, white residents resorted to informal agreements in an attempt to exlude them. But because real estate dealers and black clients utilized block-busting techniques, keeping the race

[46] WPA, Writers' Project, *Cincinnati,* pp. 291–292; Lammermeier, "Cincinnati's Black Community," p. 26.
[47] Kusmer, "Black Cleveland," p. 18; Cleveland *Gazette,* June 25, 1904.

of prospective lessees secret until arrangements for rental were final, the whites failed and ultimately began to leave certain streets. Yet the larger area remained generally white; blacks constituted only about a quarter of the population by 1900. For the most part, they were concentrated on or near a few streets such as East Long, Ohio, and Champion, and sections of Mount Vernon Avenue.[48]

Largely defensive, the movements to better neighborhoods were attempts to safeguard the family circle, the children, and the values which sustained individual lives. As such, they were symptomatic of the marginal and precarious position of an emerging class. Yet at the same time, a change of residence marked a grasping for opportunity, new expectations, and greater self-consciousness. The tendencies of marginality and insecurity combined with those of aspiration and striving were particular realities of middle-class life. To balance the drives and attitudes created by such antagonistic tendencies, and to consolidate its position and create a more secure base, a group acquiring confidence in its abilities needed leadership. Such leadership was to come from a small but articulate and relatively secure upper class; it produced the interracial interpreters who pleaded the race's cause before the bar of white opinion and provided guidance for those struggling to emerge from poverty and social isolation.

III

It was not unusual for talented, ambitious individuals of middle-class origin to move upward on the social scale. Though Mrs. Williams never traveled in upper-class social circles, her daughter Carrie used the financial security, education, and higher expectations provided by her mother's success to ascend into the upper class. While working as a teacher in West Virginia, she met and married young William Clifford, who had been born in Cleveland in 1860 and educated in the city's public schools. The couple settled at Cleveland, and both gained prominence: William was active in local politics and eventually held state and local offices, and Carrie participated in local women's club affairs, eventually becoming a leader in the national black women's club movement.[49]

Some, like Cincinnati's William Porter, went from slavery to the upper class in one generation. Born in bondage in Tennessee in 1850, Porter came to Cincinnati with the influx of freedmen in 1865. Lacking education and a trade, he worked for ten years as an independent

48 Mark, *Negroes in Columbus,* pp. 16–19.
49 Cleveland *Gazette,* Dec. 30, 1893; Cleveland *Plain Dealer,* May 18, 1902.

hackman. In 1875 two changes profoundly affected his social status: he began the first black undertaking business in the city (and for many years the only one in the state) catering only to blacks, and he married Ethlinda Davis, a respected young public school teacher. The business grew extraordinarily profitable—so much so that Porter became one of the wealthiest blacks in the city. By the turn of the century he had begun to expand his operation into a few other towns in Ohio and Kentucky.[50]

Cases like Carrie Clifford's were not unusual. Those like William Porter's, however, were rarer. The lines of socioeconomic demarkation and lifestyle which separated the upper class of not more than 5 percent of the black population from the rest of the race were less ambiguous than those which separated the lower and middle classes. Hence, while mobility into the upper class was not unusual, it was difficult. None of the objective indicators of class (such as income, education, or occupation) or the subjective ones (such as refinement or taste) by which the upper class tended to differentiate itself were in themselves enough to insure entrance into the upper class. In toto, however, they tended to create backgrounds for individuals of unusual opportunity, and in some cases extraordinary preparation, which, in turn, produced expectations quite different from those of people outside the upper class.

Their origins tended to be removed from slavery by the time of general emancipation.[51] Relatively few were those like Porter who traveled in upper-class circles in the late nineteenth century after spending many years in slavery. Those who were slave-born often experienced a very unique form of bondage. Robert Harlan, for example, was for many years a dominant figure in Cincinnati's black community and served as an influential Republican operative until his death in 1897. Born in Mecklenburg County, Virginia, of a white father and a quadroon mother who was a slave, his status, according to southern law, followed his mother's. Under circumstances which remain a mystery, at an early age Harlan was taken to Kentucky to be raised by James Harlan, the father of Supreme Court Justice John Marshall Harlan. He lived at the family's Boyle County estate, and he was allowed to take the prestigious family name. Young Robert was given an unusual degree of freedom. Taught to read and write by the Harlan family,

[50] Dabney, *Cincinnati's Colored Citizens*, pp. 182–183; Booker T. Washington, *The Negro in Business* (Chicago, 1907), pp. 96–97.

[51] Of a sample of 95 prominent black community leaders and others traveling in black upper-class circles whose biographies were investigated, only 9 (9.4%) were found to have been slaves.

he was later permitted to hire out his time and became an apprentice barber. He opened a barbershop at nearby Harrodsburg, and then his own grocery store at Lexington, some fifty miles away. Then, while still a slave, he went to Cincinnati. Harlan lived there from 1835 until 1848, when the Gold Rush lured him to California; there he made a quick fortune of $50,000, reputedly profits from gambling. Returning to Cincinnati, he made substantial investments in real estate and commercial enterprise before proceeding to the London World's Fair in 1851. He eventually returned to Kentucky to purchase his freedom from the Harlans.[52]

To be sure, Harlan's was an extraordinary case. Few upper-class individuals who had been slaves had had his opportunity for close relations with important whites, or for far-ranging geographic mobility and business enterprise—not to mention, of course, the accumulation of wealth. Yet even those who lacked such outstanding opportunities were usually free before 1860, or, as was the case with Wilberforce professor William Sanders Scarborough, their bondage might be nominal. Scarborough's father, Jesse, a literate, skilled railroad worker emancipated in 1845, was married to Frances, a slave whose owner made no claims upon her time. The couple had their own home in Macon, Georgia, and were independent in every sense; yet, because his status followed that of his mother, William was a slave during his early years. More distinctive were the experiences of those like Porter and his good friend George W. Hayes. For many years the court crier of the federal district court at Cincinnati and a church and fraternal organization activist, the young Hayes was a slave in Kentucky under not very unusual circumstances. At fifteen he ran to Ohio and freedom, rather than serve in the Confederate Army.[53]

Many were deeply rooted in freedom. Some had been in their Ohio communities for decades prior to general emancipation—often long enough to qualify as pioneers. The Reverend James Poindexter, long a prominent figure in Columbus before his death in 1907, had come to the city in 1829; he was twelve years old, and the future metropolis was a village of less than 2,500 persons.[54] Others younger than Poindexter, such as A.M.E. minister J. W. Gazaway, were rooted in families (like the Gazaway clan of Muskingum County) which had been present in the state since the 1820s and 1830s.[55] Some had come either be-

[52] William J. Simmons, *Men of Mark: Eminent, Progressive, and Rising* (Cleveland, 1887), pp. 421–422.

[53] Sarah C. B. Scarborough and Bernice Sanders, eds., "Autobiography of the Life of William Sanders Scarborough" (undated typescript in the possession of T. K. Gibson); [George W. Hayes], *Crisis,* X (Sept., 1915), 221–222.

[54] Simmons, *Men of Mark,* pp. 259–260.

[55] Cleveland *Journal,* June 15, 1907.

fore or after the Civil War from elsewhere in the North; in a few cases, their parents had lived for years in Canada. Jere Brown, for example, was born at Pittsburgh of parents who had come North in the 1820s and 1830s. The father purchased freedom for himself and five members of his family; the mother was manumitted by her master. Eventually the Browns accumulated a large amount of property in Pittsburgh. Jere spent years steamboating with his father, who was the chief steward aboard a large passenger boat on the rivers; in 1869 he settled in Cleveland, having decided that the city offered as free an environment as a black man was likely to find. He believed especially that he would be able to practice his carpenter's trade unhindered there. At about the same time, his parents settled at Wilberforce so that their younger children might be educated in the university's high school department.[56]

Free birth did not imply a lack of familiarity with the South. Many had left the ante-bellum South with their parents, who were often long free either by birth or manumission, or by themselves as young adults. There were those like Parham, whose parents had left the South so that their son might be educated in Northern public schools;[57] others, like the Chesnutts, and Hortense Green and her children, had left to escape repression.[58] Though some came North during the Civil War, relatively few came with the large influx of freedmen immediately after the war. In the late 1860s and throughout the 1870s, however, some young men of older free families, like George Myers, did come to Ohio in search of work.[59]

Origins were important in defining the upper class. Even if not backed by the rights of citizenship before the 1860s, traditions of freedom over several generations, or for many years in one individual's life, created powerful feelings of pride, ambition, and higher expectations than were practically possible for the average bondsmen. In turn, these feelings tended to heighten self-confidence. Though free in a color-conscious society anxious to check their advancement, such blacks did have a head start in economic life. They were often acquiring commercial and mechanical skills while most of their brethren were in bondage and deprived of advanced training.

Early in their lives, a few upper-class individuals had actually enjoyed some economic security because of their parents' prosperity. Yet security, not to mention affluence, was unusual. Most parents could

[56] Simmons, *Men of Mark*, pp. 55–59; Cleveland *Gazette*, May 22, 1886.

[57] Cleveland *Gazette*, Dec. 7, 1895.

[58] Helen M. Chesnutt, *Charles W. Chesnutt: Pioneer of the Color Line* (Chapel Hill, 1952), pp. 1–34; John P. Green, *Fact Stranger Than Fiction: 75 Years of a Busy Life* (Cleveland, 1920), pp. 44–62.

[59] Cleveland *Gazette*, June 1, 1895.

provide little more than strong affection and encouragement; occasionally they settled purposely at places like Oberlin or Wilberforce or Cincinnati, where their children could obtain advanced education and be exposed to helpful influences like dedicated black teachers. Careers were built and material success attained through single-minded, patient labor; these children were sustained less by parental material assistance than by great effort, dedication, and the same values which influenced the middle class. They began working early in life, often after only rudimentary education. Indeed, those born before the Civil War rarely had advanced education. Most went no further than normal school, as had Parham and A.M.E. Bishop Benjamin Arnett of Wilberforce, both of whom began their careers as teachers. Those who went to professional schools often did so only after years of work in other fields, particularly domestic and personal service, financing their education with earnings made while working as barbers or waiters or menials. In the late nineteenth century more men and women went to professional schools; as the need for black teachers rose because of the larger black student population following the immediate post-war migrations, some even attended normal schools. But most—whatever their aspirations—could not afford advanced training, and the teachers, lawyers, doctors, and seminary-educated ministers among them were a small, though highly influential, minority.[60]

Generally, therefore, the upper class carved out a secure economic base for itself not in fields which required education or much advanced training, but in those traditionally associated with the upper levels of black opportunity. Many worked in domestic and personal service, but their work was often characterized by greater dignity, responsibility, income, or prestige than that of the average service worker. Some were menials, porters, or messengers; but those who were so employed worked for many years at local banks, for example, and often became highly trusted and well-regarded employees. Others had risen from service work to quasi-managerial positions as headwaiters, chefs, superintendents of service, chiefs of bellhops and footmen, and head janitors in the larger hotels, restaurants, stores, and office buildings. Servants or butlers in private homes might be employed (as were, for example, Cincinnati butlers Ben Hunter and Alex Norris) by the wealthiest and most prominent white families, sometimes working for the same family for years and occasionally receiving pensions at retirement.[61]

[60] Ibid., Apr. 5, 1884, Jan. 9, 1892, Dec. 7, 1895, Nov. 11, 1899; Cleveland *Journal*, June 27, 1903; Indianapolis *Freeman*, Aug. 29, 1914; Baltimore *Afro-American Ledger*, Oct. 13, 1906 (all biographical sketches).

[61] Dabney, *Cincinnati's Colored Citizens*, pp. 185–187; Cincinnati *Enquirer*, Aug. 8, 1897; Minor, "Negroes in Columbus," p. 40; Green, *Fact Stranger Than*

As was the case for the few middle-class individuals who entered business, the upper class found that domestic and personal service was the primary route to enterprise. Yet upper-class service business, like upper-class service work, brought distinctive prosperity and prestige, and it generally served the most affluent and influential whites. The barbershop owners (once, like George Myers, barbers themselves) were likely to own the prosperous shops in hotels and office buildings. Caterers had often (like Cleveland's William N. Alexander) served previously as chefs and headwaiters, providing food and service for the weddings and other celebrations of affluent whites. A few owned restaurants, and a number of others owned fleets of carriages and taxis. These enterprises, like the Lewis family barbershop or the Fossett family catering firm, were occasionally built up over several generations.[62]

Outside the professions and services, a few upper-class individuals were found following a wide variety of pursuits. Prominent among them were skilled artisans, especially the more prosperous artisan-contractors like the Berrys and Stewards of Youngstown and the Roneys and Mitchells of Columbus.[63] Cleveland's Jacob Reed was a poor boy who joined with a white partner to become a proprietor in one of the city's most prosperous fish markets; others like him and Columbus's C. I. Hood were food retailers and wholesalers, catering for the most part to whites.[64] Like M. E. Berryman of Jamestown in Greene County, some owned stables and hauling and delivering businesses, often uniting them in one enterprise or combining both with the delivery of coal and ice.[65] A handful like Harry Smith of Cleveland, Dan Rudd of Springfield, and Walter S. Thomas of Columbus attempted to earn their livings by publishing black weekly newspapers and doing job printing on the side.[66] Among upper-class enterpreneurs were those like undertaker William Porter, in business fields in which they were the race's only representatives at the time. Such business-

Fiction, p. 86; Indianapolis *Freeman,* June 26, 1897, Sept. 4, 1915; Cleveland *Gazette,* Feb. 22, 1913; Cleveland *Plain Dealer,* May 18, 1902.

[62] Dabney, *Cincinnati's Colored Citizens,* pp. 180–185; Ben Hayes, "Negro—No. 1," undated clipping, Columbus *Citizen-Journal,* on file at OHS; Cleveland *Gazette,* Feb. 20, 1904.

[63] Cleveland *Gazette,* May 12, 19, Aug. 11, 1888; Cleveland *Journal,* July 18, 1908; Indianapolis *Freeman,* Sept. 9, 1911, Sept. 11, 1915.

[64] Cleveland *Gazette,* June 25, 1887, Mar. 20, 1897; Cleveland *Gazette,* Sept. 23, 1905; Indianapolis *Freeman,* Aug. 1, 1914.

[65] Cleveland *Gazette,* June 25, 1887, June 17, 1889, Oct. 15, 1910; Indianapolis *Freeman,* Sept. 11, 1911.

[66] Irvine Garland Penn, *The Afro-American Press and Its Editors* (Springfield, Mass., 1891), pp. 114, 280–286; Columbus *Free American,* Mar. 19, 1887; Cleveland *Gazette,* Aug. 22, 1883, Feb. 25, 1888; New York *Freeman,* Jan. 15, 1887.

men included Athens hotel owner E. C. Berry, Ripley flour mill proprietor J. P. Parker, Dayton carpet-cleaner John Finley, Columbus house-mover Charles W. Bryant, and the owners of two small factories, C. R. Patterson of Greenfield, who produced carriages, and A. R. Cooper of Findlay, who manufactured an orthopedic shoe for which he held a patent.[67]

A few worked in particularly prestigious clerical positions. Alfred Merchand was for many years assistant librarian at Cincinnati Hospital; Walter Wright of Cleveland served for decades as the personal secretary of railroad executive G. W. Caldwell. A very few, like Cleveland's C. L. Lacy, were clerks in white-owned retail stores at a time when blacks rarely rose above the rank of porter in such businesses. Prestigious as such work might have been, however, there were definite limits placed upon black aspirations. Caldwell was known to have said that Wright knew the business well enough to be purchasing agent for any large railroad, but he feared to promote him because whites might refuse to accept Wright as their boss. In an attempt to compensate, Caldwell gave Wright frequent pay raises and bequeathed him a large sum.[68]

Investments in real estate reinforced the economic position of the upper class. So large were Robert Harlan's returns from real estate investments that he seems to have done little work for much of the 1860s, until a combination of unwise speculation and temporarily adverse local conditions made his situation more difficult. Normally he was able to breed horses, travel, and live in the grand style that befitted a man who thought of himself as the descendant of Kentucky aristocrats. Real estate investments, on the other hand, allowed Harry Smith to keep working. Income from property enabled him to publish the *Gazette* every week between late 1883 and his death in 1941, a remarkable record in the black journalism of that time.[69]

The upper class also consolidated its economic base, as well as its racial leadership, and expanded its job opportunities through political patronage. Much of the political activity in the black community was not so much a matter of partisanship or ideology as of ambitious in-

[67] Washington, *Negro in Business*, pp. 62–67, 289; New York *Freeman*, Jan. 23, 1886; Cleveland *Journal*, Oct. 27, 1906; Cleveland *Gazette*, July 22, 1912; Indianapolis *Freeman*, Aug. 3, 1912, Aug. 29, 1914.

[68] Dabney, *Cincinnati's Colored Citizens*, p. 99; Cleveland *Gazette*, Mar. 18, 1899, Jan. 25, 1900; Cleveland *Plain Dealer*, May 18, 1902; Ransom, *Pilgrimage*, p. 71.

[69] Cincinnati *Commercial*, Apr. 4, 1870, Aug. 29, Sept. 6, 1872; Cleveland *Gazette*, Nov. 27, 1886, Feb. 10, 1894; Cyrus Field Adams, "Harry C. Smith," *Colored American Magazine*, VI (Mar., 1903), 385–386.

dividuals, frustrated by racial discrimination, aspiring to dignified work. For those who eschewed service work as demeaning but lacked the capital for business or training for a profession, patronage was an avenue to opportunity—if one had the right connections. As the established political leaders of the race (i.e., those blacks who had frequent contact with and trust of the most politically powerful whites), the upper class monopolized the well-paying and prestigious local, state, and federal clerkships which normally were the highest black appointments. Upper-class politicians sometimes helped lower- and middle-class blacks to obtain political jobs as laborers and porters, but generally they concentrated on feathering their own nests. This was an incessant activity, for, dependent as it was on the vagaries of politics, patronage was not a stable source of employment.

A series of federal posts sustained Robert Harlan when he could no longer live solely from investments.[70] Some, like Cleveland's William Clifford, Toledo's Charles Cottrill, and Springfield's Charles Fillmore, all of whom embarked on political careers in the 1880s, served for several decades in local, state, and federal patronage posts and spent much of their time pursuing jobs with yet more security, pay, and prestige.[71] For fathers worried about their sons' futures, patronage offered one means of helping to insure their security. Bishop Arnett, for example, devoted considerable energy to using his influence to help his sons.[72]

The more prosperous situation of the upper class and its vision of "the good life" established its lifestyle. Though a few upper-class women were practicing professionals (mostly unmarried public school teachers),[73] upper-class women usually did not work, devoting themselves instead to home and children and to the religious and literary concerns of their independent or church-affiliated women's clubs. While it was not unheard of for upper-class children to work, they did so much less because of economic necessity, and they had consider-

---

[70] Cleveland *Gazette*, May 1, 1886, Oct. 2, 1897 (obituary of Harlan); Cincinnati *Enquirer*, Sept. 22, 1897 (obituary of Harlan).

[71] Cleveland *Gazette*, June 16, Dec. 1, 1888; [Charles Fillmore], *Colored American Magazine*, XII (Apr., 1907), 306, 311–312; William H. Crogman, *Progress of a Race* (Chicago, 1925), pp. 352–353.

[72] Ralph Tyler to George Myers, Oct. 7, 1896, Box II, folder 4, George A. Myers Papers, OHS; Benjamin Arnett to William McKinley, Mar. 11, 1901 (letter with enclosed memorandum), Reel 76 (microfilm ed.), William McKinley Presidential Papers, LC.

[73] Ruth Young White, ed., *We, Too, Built Columbus* (Columbus, 1936), pp. 371–379; Carrie Clifford, "Cleveland and Its Colored People," *Colored American Magazine*, IX (July, 1905), 372–373, 375; Cincinnati Board of Education, *Minutes*, XXIII, 60 (Aug. 30, 1897).

ably greater opportunities not only to finish high school but also to go on to college. It was not at all unusual for parents to dedicate themselves to that goal. Cleveland's John Bolden, born to free parents in Tennessee before the Civil War, was a prosperous carpenter; it was said that "his chief aim was to have his children well-educated and his family placed in comfortable circumstances." Both Bolden children received high school educations. Upon graduation the son, John, Jr., did well enough on a competitive civil service examination to become a letter carrier, a prestigious job for blacks at the time, and he eventually went on to medical school at Western Reserve University. The daughter, Helen, went directly to Western Reserve after high school and later became a local school teacher.[74] To be sure, not all families produced college graduates or professionals, nor indeed did all upper-class children find dignified work; some entered the services, spent their lives waiting on whites, and were neither bosses nor entrepreneurs. But usually more choices and opportunities for developing individual talents were open to them than to the large majority of the race.

Upper-class marriages tended to occur within class boundaries, as people of similar tastes, hopes, and backgrounds sought out one another. The lines were not strictly drawn, and those from the upper reaches of the middle class might enter into marriage with members of the upper class; nevertheless, a class rule in marriage was especially pronounced the further one traveled up the social scale. Because the upper class was itself quite small, the result was often a complex pattern of family interrelationships transcending geographical lines. An example is the Payne-Clark-Steward connection. After the death of his first wife, the eminent A.M.E. Bishop Daniel Payne, whose episcopal seat was at Wilberforce for many years, married the widow Clark of Cincinnati. One of her sons by her first husband was the black high school principal, Peter Clark. Peter's daughter Consuelo, the Bishop's step-granddaughter, was a physician; she married Youngstown attorney William R. Steward of the Steward artisan clan and continued to practice medicine at Youngstown.[75]

Marriage sometimes helped to establish the financial security of upper-class individuals, aiding them in the pursuit of careers which might not otherwise have been possible. Cincinnati attorney and political leader George Jackson was born of free parents who were descen-

---

[74] Cleveland *Gazette*, Sept. 3, 1892; Cleveland *Journal*, July 11 (obituary of Bolden), 25, 1908; Clifford, "Cleveland and Its Colored People," 376.

[75] Hallie Q. Brown, ed., *Pen Pictures of Pioneers of Wilberforce* (Xenia, 1937), pp. 49–52; Youngstown *Vindicator*, Apr. 5, 1958.

dants of slaves of the prominent Custis family of Arlington, Virginia; they had fled to Canada from Lafayette, Indiana, in order to escape racial persecution. Jackson went to Cincinnati in 1849 to enter the black public schools, and he was eventually trained by Peter Clark to become a teacher. In the late 1870s, when he was past thirty and had been teaching for a number of years in various cities in the Ohio Valley, he met Virginia Gordon; her father, the Cincinnati coal dealer Robert Gordon, had made a fortune during an ante-bellum coal famine. After his marriage in 1879 the now financially secure Jackson quickly gave up teaching and entered law school.[76]

Complementing the material security and the more conventionally bourgeois family roles and patterns of the upper class was a strong home-centeredness shared with the middle class. Unlike the latter group, however, upper-class families could afford to buy their own homes; they comprised a large portion of the slightly over 4,000 blacks (5 percent of the black population) who owned homes in Ohio in 1890.[77] If greater prosperity made homeowning easier, it also allowed for greater opportunity to live in better neighborhoods. While the middle class was at the mercy of opportunistic real estate agents and white prejudice in its attempts to move into better areas, the upper class might surmount prejudice by purchasing rather than renting. A local correspondent of the Cleveland *Gazette* in 1893 commented on the growth in home-buying in the better residential neighborhoods by Cleveland blacks: "The owners of rentable property are doing us no harm by refusing to rent us property. The answer, 'It is rented.' or 'I don't rent to colored people.' is a constant reminder of our dependency. These words have driven many to purchase who otherwise would not have done so." [78] While they might still encounter those unwilling to sell them homes and others hostile to their presence as neighbors, it was testimony to the possibility of at least partial acceptance by white social counterparts that a few affluent, refined blacks were able to live peacefully in neighborhoods almost exclusively white in all of the state's major cities and towns.

This relatively wide-ranging choice of residential neighborhood caused the upper class to be scattered throughout the cities and towns, and for it often to be separated residentially from the large majority of the black population. Some, like Robert Harlan and George Jackson,

[76] Cleveland *Gazette*, Aug. 22, 1891.
[77] Bureau of the Census, *Negro Population, 1790–1915*, p. 470.
[78] Cleveland *Gazette*, Nov. 25, 1893. For similar statements on home-buying as a response to discrimination encountered as renters, see, for Cincinnati, New York *Freeman*, Feb. 6, 1886; for Steubenville, Cleveland *Journal*, Dec. 5, 1903.

owned or rented homes on the fashionable streets left in the fringes of Cincinnati's Bucktown and Little Bucktown after the Civil War; others lived in respectable, overwhelmingly white sections north of the lower river basin and the downtown fringe. Some were servants in the homes of wealthy whites, living in servants' quarters on their employers' property. Others, however, were owners and renters working outside domestic service. A good portion of the upper class residing outside the central city lived on the better streets of Walnut Hills (as did Parham), but a small though growing number found their way (as did Peter Clark) to fine neighborhoods like Cumminsville, Avondale, and other hilltop sections, overlooking the congested city and far to the north and west of downtown.[79] At Cleveland and Columbus, the immediate post-war decades found most upper-class blacks living along the fringes of the main areas of black settlement on the more affluent streets, but they began to leave these areas as they became decayed. Some at Columbus would continue to live on the remaining fashionable streets (Spring, Hickory, North Fourth) in the downtown East Long Street area, but growing numbers settled along the northern fringe of the newly developing black area further to the east down Long, or moved to widely scattered locations on the north and west sides. By 1899 one Columbus black noted the liquidation of the once extensive holdings of the first families of black Columbus, the Bookers, Jenkinses, Lankins, Hills, Respesses, Johnsons, Butchers, Roneys, and others, all of whom had once lived and owned property in the area of downtown East Long High to North Fourth. Whites now owned the property, and the black families were scattered throughout the city.[80] At Cleveland, many continued to live in the eastern Central Avenue section, moving increasingly to the East 40s and East 50s. But a sizable number of others, including George Myers, Charles Chesnutt, and John Green, moved far to the east in the area of Carnegie Avenue and East 105th Street; a few, such as Walter Wright, moved west of the Cuyahoga River, or to newly developing areas on the fringes of the city.[81]

Along with family and home, the upper class enjoyed an active social and cultural life. Though many had begun life poor and few became wealthy, they were distinguished for their cultivation of ele-

[79] WPA, Writers' Project, *Cincinnati*, pp. 78–79, 291–292; Cincinnati city directories, 1879, 1880, 1900, 1901.

[80] Cleveland *Gazette*, Jan. 7, 1899; Columbus city directories, 1870, 1880, 1896, 1901.

[81] Cleveland *Gazette*, Nov. 25, 1893; Cleveland *Plain Dealer*, Oct. 14, 1900; Clifford, "Cleveland and Its Colored People," 365–380; Davis, *Black Americans in Cleveland*, pp. 129–132.

vated (if conventional) tastes in the arts, entertainment, dining, and dress which they shared with affluent whites. Many could afford to dine out and attend the theater; however, even though the new era offered unprecedented opportunity for participating in the cultural and recreational life of white society, the continuing possibility of insult in public places made them cautious about doing so. Their literary societies, lyceums, debating groups, drama clubs, fraternal and sororal orders, churches, and women's clubs provided the fellowship, recreation, and stimulation that were difficult for them to find outside the race. At the same time, such organizations served as schools for those who were deeply desirous of learning but unable to obtain anything more than a basic formal education. While some were temperance oriented, most of the women's clubs were devoted to literary subjects. Some of them, and some of the literary societies, aided their members in their quests for self-improvement by maintaining libraries and reading rooms; a few individuals like George Myers and Walter Wright had large libraries, accessible to friends, in their homes. Entertaining also played a prominent role in the lives of upper-class blacks, and the celebration of weddings, birthdays, anniversaries, and holidays as well as excursions, dances, supper parties, and theater parties were more than occasional occurrences.[82]

Though few could afford the several trips to Europe taken by John Green, rented summer homes and short vacations were within the grasp of most. In the 1880s there were blacks who spent the summer in the beautiful rural area around Wilberforce; the *Gazette* received weekly letters on the comings and goings of the various families who vacationed there in order to take advantage of the cultural life of the university and the healthful natural springs of the area. Others sought the watering places along the Atlantic, where a few small black summer resorts were located, or rented cottages on Lake Erie. Tourists rarely lacked for extensions of hospitality from local people of their class wherever they visited. Through close contacts maintained by correspondence between relatives and friends and the medium of the chatty, weekly local letters and social notes sent to black newspapers throughout the nation, members of this small class were often well known to one another throughout the country. It was not uncommon for out-of-town travelers to attend the literary and social club meetings

[82] Memphis *Colored Tennessean* (Cincinnati letter), Mar. 24, 31, May 19, 1866; Cleveland *Gazette*, Nov. 3, 1883, Jan. 24, Feb. 14, Nov. 28, Dec. 12, 1885, Mar. 26, 1887, July 30, 1892, Dec. 19, 1896; Columbus *Standard*, July 27, 1901; Cleveland *Plain Dealer*, May 18, 1902.

of the communities which they visited and to be guests at one another's homes—especially at a time when hotel accommodations for blacks were problematic in many areas of the nation.[83]

IV

While members of the upper class shared a core of common origins, economic bases, values, tastes, and lifestyles, skin color divided them against each other during the late nineteenth century. There was a pronounced tendency for the lighter-skinned to set themselves apart socially from the darker members of their class and to some extent from the race itself.

The upper class, en bloc, was probably lighter than the balance of the race, for to an important extent its origins lay in the frequent blood relations between slave ancestors and their masters. As the natural offspring of the union of black slave and white master, individuals sometimes were accorded greater access to manumission by masters who wished either to aid loved ones across the color line or to remove symbols of sexual transgression from their midst. But the advantages enjoyed by the light-skinned often stopped abruptly at the point of manumission. The lighter-skinned freedmen were not allowed to emerge as a large, privileged middle caste between black and white, possessed of citizens' rights and relatively open access to social and economic mobility. Even in ante-bellum Ohio, where the courts tended to enlarge the scope of the rights of the light-skinned, custom severely limited the application of court rulings. White blood mattered only when it facilitated "passing" as one of the white race. Yet while upper-class blacks were entering a color-conscious society in which their status was sharply proscribed, the freedom allowed many of their ancestors helped set in motion the cultural and socioeconomic process by which their class gradually came to be separated from the masses.

Light-complexioned individuals might continue to hope for more. As "passing" illustrated, the power of whiteness was enormous. The minor differences in skin tone and the nuances of physiognomy by which hair became straight enough and lips and noses Caucasian enough to transform "black" to "white" had the power to elevate one from a member of a reviled minority to a privileged, powerful majority. It was not surprising that the lightest-skinned tended to absorb the physio-aesthetic standards of the dominant culture, for everywhere around them whiteness was overwhelmingly dominant. They might

[83] Cleveland *Gazette*, Aug. 28, 1886; Green, *Fact Stranger Than Fiction*, pp. 224–259, 279–333; Chesnutt, *Chesnutt*, pp. 63–68.

continue to hope that lightness of color would eventually earn them special consideration, and that a middle position might be eked out if the proper standards of taste, conduct, and belief, as well as color, were carefully cultivated. Perhaps they might also hope that generations of intragroup marriage and eventually marriage with whites would one day establish a basis for a merger with the dominant race.

Before general emancipation there had begun to appear within the upper class, North and South, especially in the larger cities, a socially exclusive light-skinned "high society" [84] which was conscious of its physical distinctiveness and eager to cultivate the refinements which might make it even more distinct from the balance of the race. Not every light-skinned person fit easily into these elevated circles. Those lacking the values, styles, and manners of the upper class would certainly not have been accepted on the basis of light color alone, but light skin was definitely necessary for recognition. As the ranks of the light-skinned "high society" were filled from within the upper class, darker individuals were not admitted to their social sets, no matter how refined or intellectual they were. Such exclusiveness caused jealousy among some rejected Negroes and pity among others.

Whatever one's perspective, there was a tendency to call members of the elite "blue veins," [85] in the popular (no doubt false) belief that in order to gain admission to their elevated circles one had to be so light that the veins on the underside of the arm were visibly blue in color, as is the case among whites.

Blue vein social life was really very much like the social life of the black upper class. Blue veins organized themselves into small formal and informal social circles in which there were no whites; typical was the Cleveland Social Circle, which found its complement in Columbus's Douglass Literary Society. Membership in the Social Circle was

[84] E. Franklin Frazier, *The Negro in the United States* (New York, 1949), pp. 275–276; Du Bois, *Philadelphia Negro*, pp. 22, 198–199, 203; Dabney, *Cincinnati's Colored Citizens*, pp. 150–151, 175–176. For work by two contemporary scholars on the emergence of a light-skinned social elite, see Laurence Glasco, "Black and Mulatto: Historical Basis for Afro-American Culture," *Black Lines* (Fall, 1971), 20–30; Theodore Hershberg, "Status at Birth, Color, and Social Structure in Nineteenth Century Philadelphia: A Comparison of Ex-Slaves and Free-Born" (paper presented at University of Rochester, Mar., 1972), pp. 23–34.

[85] The history of this term is unclear; apparently it was too commonly understood in the late nineteenth century black community for any to have sought a lengthy explanation. In his short story, "The Wife of His Youth," Charles Chesnutt briefly discusses the term "blue vein"; he attributes it to "some envious outsider" who invented the notion of a physical test for recognition within light-skinned social circles. See Charles Chesnutt, *The Wife of His Youth and Other Stories of the Color Line* (Boston, 1899), pp. 1–3.

said to be the *"sine qua non* of social standing" among Cleveland blacks in the 1870s and 1880s; the organization was founded in 1869 for the purpose of "social intercourse and cultural activities among the better-educated people of color in Cleveland"—not all of whom, of course, were allowed to join. Members were light-skinned, prosperous, often self-employed artisans and caterers or occasionally teachers or servants, and their wives and unmarried children; altogether they probably numbered between thirty and fifty. As the number of black professionals in Cleveland grew, the circle picked up several prominent attorneys: John Green, who served as the organization's president in the 1880s; Leon Wilson, son of an ante-bellum Philadelphia doctor and brother-in-law of the Mississippi black politician Blanche K. Bruce; and Charles Chesnutt, who had largely forsaken an unprofitable law practice for the lucrative profession of court reporting. The circle held formal meetings twice a month in the homes of members for evenings of debate, music, dramatic reading, discussion, and light refreshment. In addition, it published a small monthly paper of poems, essays, and chatter.[86]

Out-of-town guests were usually present, for the circle members were connected by family and friendship with similar societies in other cities. Out-of-town visitation also gave the eligible bachelors and young ladies a wider field in which to search for a spouse than their own small, inbred local circles. Under any circumstance, they were expected to marry within the ranks of the blue veins, for marriage was the central act by which they consolidated their group's position—and, quite possibly, insured that the next generation might be just a shade lighter (if partners were matched accordingly) than themselves.[87]

The Social Circle's simple, unpretentious meetings demonstrated the membership's lack of great wealth, as well as its moderate and intellectual tastes. At Cincinnati, however, the blue veins of the 1870s and 1880s were more extravagant in their entertaining. A few had made considerable sums as stewards, headwaiters, and servants in private clubs, aboard steamboats, and in private homes, and as owners of prosperous service and commercial businesses. A number of families

[86] Chesnutt, *Chesnutt,* p. 61; Julian Krawcheck, "The Negro in Cleveland," #2, Cleveland *Press,* May 30, 1963; Cleveland *Leader,* Aug. 25, 1874; *Social Circle Journal,* XVIII (Nov., 1886); Patrick Reason to John Green, Nov. 5, 1879, Box I, folder 1, John P. Green Papers, WRHS; Cleveland *Gazette,* Jan. 15, 1887; Columbus *Ohio State Journal,* Mar. 22, 1879; City directories: Cleveland, 1874; Columbus, 1879.

[87] Cleveland *Leader,* Aug. 25, 1874; Columbus *Ohio State Journal,* Mar. 22, 1879. Charles Chesnutt's story "A Matter of Principle" indicates blue vein anxieties in regard to the color of a marriage partner. See Chesnutt, *Wife of His Youth,* pp. 94–131.

(the Harlans, Troys, Tinsleys, Dunlaps, Sheltons, Fossetts, and Rox-boroughs) appear to have lived and entertained lavishly. Robert Har-lan could afford to invite two hundred people into his home to cele-brate the marriage of Ernestine Clark, daughter of Harlan's friend and sometime political rival Peter Clark. When the daughter of Alex Thomas, a wealthy photographer, was married in 1874, over three hundred persons were invited and entertained. The chief social rivals of the Thomases were the Tinsleys; the latter family owned a large, three-story home, filled with expensive furniture and paid for with the large tips which John Tinsley had received as chief steward at a pri-vate gambling club.[88]

While those responsible for such opulent displays risked eventual impoverishment, the less ostentatious blue vein circles were by no means stable either. Cleveland's Social Circle was barely able to limp into the 1890s. With its members increasingly scattered around the city, it grew more difficult to gather for the round of meetings and lesser social events and visiting which had sustained the close circle. A number of older members had died, leaving in their places newer ones who slowly began to allow their darker-skinned upper-class friends to become members. Cynics assumed that money alone was sought from the newer, darker members, because the circle's declining membership made it more difficult to support the style of entertainment to which members were accustomed. Whatever the weight of these various fac-tors, by the turn of the century the Social Circle was clearly dying, with few members and without its former ability to excite either envy or loathing in non-members.[89]

Yet only a part of blue vein life revolved around formally organized groups; social exclusivity also assumed informal guises. Not only were there close friendships and familial relations among them, but their aloofness was occasionally enhanced by social relations with whites—particularly in the Western Reserve, where the color line was weakest to begin with. John Green enjoyed a long, cordial friendship with Cleveland's John D. Rockefeller; Green and his family occasionally visited the Rockefeller home on Cleveland's east side, not far from their own.[90] A few individuals had business and professional contacts almost exclusively with whites; they maintained personal friendships with members of both races and found their way into professional, civic, and social organizations to which no other Negroes were allowed

[88] Cincinnati *Enquirer,* July 30, 1879; Dabney, *Cincinnati's Colored Citizens,* pp. 95, 150–153.
[89] Cleveland *Gazette,* Jan. 22, 1887, Aug. 6, 12, 1898.
[90] Green, *Fact Stranger Than Fiction,* pp. 210–211.

admittance. At Cleveland in the twenty years after the war two Social Circle members, Leon Wilson and shoemaker John Hope, belonged to white Masonic lodges. Leon Wilson was for many years the
only Negro member of the Cleveland Bar Association. After the turn
of the century, with his reputation as a writer now firmly established,
Chesnutt became a member of several white booster and civic organizations and social clubs.[91]

A much more common tendency throughout the state was for mixing
with whites to be limited to church. While the upper class generally
belonged to either the black Baptist or Methodist churches, many of
the light-skinned elite belonged to predominantly white, higher-status
denominations and church congregations. Most were Episcopalians,
with minorities of Congregationalists, Presbyterians, and Unitarians.
In all of these denominations it was rare for blacks anywhere in post-
bellum Ohio to be organized in separate, all-black congregations. Only
at Cleveland did an all-black Congregationalist church exist, organized
in 1864. Usually blacks worshiped with whites, or (among the Episcopalians in the state's three largest cities and the Presbyterians at Cincinnati) they were organized in small black missions, which were ad-
juncts of large white congregations. These missions shared close relations with the larger churches—even to the point of worshiping in
small chapels in their church buildings. Even where such missions existed, however, some Negroes continued to worship with whites.
Charles Chesnutt and his family worshiped at a white Episcopal
church, though membership in St. Andrew's Mission, organized in 1890
by black Episcopalians, was open to them.[92]

Yet even at the height of their organized existence, and in spite of
such contacts with whites, the blue veins did not completely separate
themselves from the race and its darker-skinned members. It is true
that some of them appear rarely, if ever, to have participated in racial
affairs; their names are conspicuously absent from the lists of those
helping to plan the annual celebrations of emancipation or participat-

[91] Charles Wesley, *The History of the Prince Hall Grand Lodge of Free and
Accepted Masons of the State of Ohio, 1849–1960: An Epoch in American Fraternalism* (Wilberforce, 1961), p. 63; Cleveland *Gazette*, Nov. 11, 1899; Chesnutt, *Chesnutt*, pp. 240–247.

[92] Cleveland *Leader*, Sept. 12, 1864; Cleveland *Gazette*, Feb. 2, 1889, Oct. 11,
1890, Dec. 7, 1901, June 27, 1903, Feb. 22, 1913; Cincinnati *Commercial
Tribune*, July 1, 1901; Indianapolis *Freeman*, June 12, 1909, June 5, Aug. 11,
Sept. 14, 1915; Dabney, *Cincinnati's Colored Citizens*, pp. 150–151; Simmons,
Men of Mark, p. 245; George Bragg, *History of the Afro-American Group of the
Episcopal Church* (Baltimore, 1922), pp. 136–137; Green, *Fact Stranger Than
Fiction*, pp. 277–278; Chesnutt, *Chesnutt*, pp. 46, 49; Minor, "Negroes in Colum-
bus," p. 84.

ing in the widely held demonstrations of gratitude and hope held when the Fifteenth Amendment was ratified in the spring of 1870. It is also true that some lived only at the edge of the race. Though his fiction was deeply embedded in black themes and rich in references to black folk tradition, Charles Chesnutt had as many ties with white society as with black, and he rarely took an active part in black affairs or associational life in late nineteenth century Cleveland.[93] Leon Wilson, whose wife was white,[94] had virtually passed permanently into white society. Finally, there were those like the Tinsleys and Thomases whose lives, except for occasional and always generous gifts of charity to the black poor and black churches, seem to have been a whirl of partying, entertaining, matchmaking, and cultivating reputations for display and high living within their own limited circle.

Counterbalancing these tendencies toward aloofness was the fact that, like it or not, their larger destinies were inextricably bound up with those who were obviously Negro. This high society was vulnerable to the same gratuitous insults and inhumane treatment that the darker-skinned daily suffered. For those who did not or would not see this themselves, there were always incidents to make it clear to them. For example, their desire for integrated worship on occasion brought crisis to individual white churches. At Columbus in 1889 some whites threatened to resign from a Congregational church unless the application for membership of an aristocratic, blue-vein music professor was refused. Some Cincinnati Congregationalists voiced a similar threat in 1898, demanding that a Negro family found passing for white must themselves resign from the church.[95] Such insults to blue veins were rare in late nineteenth century Ohio, for these people were too skilled in the etiquette of race relations to place themselves among whites who

[93] It was not unusual for Chesnutt to slip into the third person plural when writing of the race in his private correspondence. In the context of his aloofness from the black community, this would seem more than just stylistic artifice. In a letter to Albion W. Tourgee in 1885, for example, he responded to Tourgee's inquiries as to why his magazine *The Basis* was failing to attract attention among blacks whose rights it was dedicated to protecting: "I think it is accounted for not by indifference to their own fate or lack of appreciation for those who are trying to serve their best interests but by the fact that their own efforts in behalf of their race are distributed over so wide an area." Charles W. Chesnutt to Albion W. Tourgee, Sept. 3, 1895, letter #8826, Albion W. Tourgee Papers, CCHS.

[94] Charles W. Chesnutt to C. W. Burrows, Mar. 20, 1927, Charles W. Chesnutt Papers, FU, contains a short history of the Wilson family.

[95] Cleveland *Gazette*, Feb. 2, 1889; Dabney, *Cincinnati's Colored Citizens*, pp. 98–99. At Columbus the incident ended with the Negro congregant going to another white church. However, at Cincinnati the family was backed by the Reverend Herbert Seeley Bigelow, a well-known local exponent of social justice; they stayed, despite determined efforts by some church members to force them out.

would resent their presence. Yet when incidents such as these did occur, their message was sadly clear.

If there were reasons for them to doubt the possibility of full, unquestioned acceptance by their white social counterparts, there were at the same time compelling bases for identification with the struggles of the masses. The cruel logic of racial stereotyping meant that whites tended to judge all Negroes, however high their attainments and aspirations by contemporary standards, on the basis of the actions of those few blacks who committed crimes or failed to support their families, or of the many whose adherence to the survival-oriented culture of the masses set them off from white society. The situation provided blue veins with ample reason to become involved in the cause of racial advancement. To the extent that both might work to undermine racial stereotypes, the socioeconomic uplift and acculturation to conventional norms of the masses were, therefore, in a vital sense sources of their own advancement as well. Their motives need not have been solely calculated self-interest, however, for their high expectations, personal and group pride, and substantial intellectual attainment based on generations of freedom, greater opportunity, and constant struggle for recognition produced solid emotional and intellectual bases for an idealistic commitment to fighting all forms of oppression.

With their own opportunities for fulfilling, dignified employment within the economic mainstream often limited, and their sense of responsibility heightened by self-interest, ideals, and feelings of noblesse oblige, many found their life's work in the black public schools, the institution which was particularly charged with speeding the acquisition of respectable aspirations and conventional standards by the masses. Before the desegregation of Ohio's schools in 1887, members of the light-skinned set were particularly prominent as teachers and principals of the black schools. Peter Clark of Cincinnati, W. O. Bowles of Dayton, and E. J. Waring of Columbus, the principals of black schools, all traveled in blue vein circles. Others, like Robert Harlan and John Green, were active in Republican politics as representatives of their race.

Blue veins did not, however, monopolize all positions of power within the institutions of the black community, for the very reason that they often chose to remain outside them. The most continuously powerful institution of the black community, the church, would not be controlled by them as long as so many found their religious home outside the denominations and churches attended by darker-skinned Negroes. And since they often participated in their own social and literary societies rather than in racial fraternal and sororal associations, or sometimes belonged to the latter alongside much larger numbers of darker-skinned members, they could not monopolize power within this important segment of racial community life.

Nor did they exclusively control the few positions of power, authority, and prestige available to blacks in politics. While business and personal ties afforded them a disproportionate influence with powerful whites, practically speaking they could not have viable alliances with each powerful, competing white faction. To the extent they were aloof from the race, they could not have the firm black political ties which were enjoyed by darker upper-class politicians, who maintained especially solid ties with the black middle class. Indeed, their aloofness and sense of superiority might well alienate the rest of the race.

These forces working to check the political influence of the blue veins were apparent in the Cleveland *Gazette's* successful 1885 campaign to block the nomination of Republican State Representative John Green, then president of the Social Circle, for a second term. Though himself light-skinned (probably not light enough, however, to earn admission to the circle had he desired), Harry Smith led a movement among darker politicians to deny Green renomination because of his blue vein ties. The *Gazette* hammered away at Green, whose power was based primarily on ties with white ethnic political interests in both major parties; at the same time the increasingly powerful Mark Hanna faction of Cleveland's Republicans worked against Green because of his negative votes on certain street railroad bills, which had been intended to give Hanna control over Cleveland's streetcar lines. Due to a defection from the Green candidacy by a successful alliance of black and white politicians, Green was defeated at the county Republican convention by Jere Brown, the *Gazette's* candidate. Green would have to make his peace with darker politicians like Brown and Smith before he would again, four years later, be able to stand successfully for a nomination. He would also eventually establish ties with Hanna. As far as Smith was concerned, however, his was a temporary rapprochement with Green. Largely because of Green's blue vein ties during Smith's formative political years, he would never really trust Green and would work to check his political ambition for years to come.[96]

White politicians were not usually sensitive to the nuances of the black community, and they tended to lump all black politicians together, regardless of color. Politics, in fact, often made very strange

---

[96] Cleveland *Gazette*, Sept. 12, 1885, Apr. 5, 1913; New York *Freeman*, Sept. 19, 1885; Cleveland *Plain Dealer*, Sept. 5, 8, 11, 14, 1885; George A. Myers to John Green, Nov. 18, 1902, Box VII, folder 1, Green Papers.

bedfellows. The *Gazette* found considerable irony in the nomination for municipal office in 1885 of Powhattan Henderson, a member of the Social Circle. White Republicans had charged two very dark Negro politicians with the responsibility of nominating and seconding Henderson, thinking perhaps that this triad of color would make a nice symmetry and hoping to mollify those Negroes who claimed that the race was not allowed enough participation in local conventions. Smith said with bittersweet glee that Henderson would no more have associated with his new racial allies voluntarily "than with *the most prejudiced poor whites,* because they are so black." [97]

Some might find humor here, yet the incident was sadly illustrative of the larger social contradiction in the life of blue veins. Despite intellect and refinement, their aspirations rendered them socially marginal. In attempting to straddle the fence between both racial camps, they fit comfortably into neither one.[98]

V

As in all social structures in societies where a broad range of both opportunity and inequality is possible, the black social structure in late nineteenth century Ohio contained mutually repelling and attracting forces that held the parts together, while at the same time keeping them at a distance from one another. Although the extent and intensity with which discrimination proscribed black life varied from class to class, a shared social disability worked to unify all classes of blacks— as did the tendency of many whites to view all blacks, whatever their accomplishments and aspirations, in the same harshly negative light. Yet, at the same time, reflecting the varying experiences in historical development of the segments of black society, individual blacks were separated by cultural and material gaps. They held different expectations for their own lives as citizens and social beings, and they lived in patterns and with values which might have seemed mysterious or incor-

---

[97] Cleveland *Gazette,* Apr. 4, 1885.

[98] No one understood the dilemma of the blue veins better than the more perceptive people within their own ranks. Charles Chesnutt, whose early stories particularly dealt with the question of intraracial color division, had one of his characters express the following cogent views on the plight of the lighter complected: "We people of mixed blood are ground between the upper and nether millstone. Our fate lies between absorption by the white race and extinction in the black. The one doesn't want us, but may take us in time. The other would welcome us, but it would be for us a step backward. 'With malice toward none, with charity for all,' we must do the best we can for ourselves and those who are to follow us. Self-preservation is the first law of nature." See Chesnutt, "The Wife of His Youth," in *Wife of His Youth,* p. 7.

rect to blacks outside their group. Among the upper and middle classes, however, there was a relatively broad consensus on values regarding the relationship of the individual to opportunity and advancement: one struggled to improve his or her material and social circumstances, and to live a respectable life according to patterns dominant within the larger society. The masses had little reason to develop these same aspirations and expectations. For whatever might be said in praise of the few individuals who grasped every opportunity to lift themselves from abject poverty, improve their social circumstances, and provide a path to yet greater attainment for their posterity, the way was extremely difficult, and the opportunities which might have motivated the majority to absorb bourgeois lifestyles and values were sadly lacking for the overwhelming majority. Under the circumstances, the culture which sustained the masses yet separated them from higher-status blacks and whites provided them with a coherent patterning of perspectives and values from which came the strength to survive in a relentlessly hostile world. At the same time, however, the cultural gap among blacks had serious consequences for the struggle for racial advancement. It threatened to divorce the attitudes of the black upper class, which was most likely to speak for the race before the powerful white majority, from the self-perceived needs of the masses. While the black masses might accept those from the upper class as leaders in racial struggles, they could not be assured that such leadership would serve their interests, no matter how dedicated or how lofty its aims.

To be sure, such differences in values and perspectives were present among whites, but for blacks they were exacerbated by the nature of material development. It was not simply that the path out of poverty was more difficult for individual blacks, limited as they were by the mutually interacting factors of discrimination and lack of vocational skills. Unlike its white counterpart, the black economic elite was unable to generate the material preconditions for socioeconomic mobility and acculturation of the masses. The black upper class lacked an economic base from which to establish itself as a powerful material force within American society and, indeed, within the race itself. Lacking capital and economic autonomy, it derived its prosperity from a relatively few opportunities made available by whites, and its dependence upon whites hindered the development of economic ties with the masses. Blacks did not own the banks, stores, mills, and factories that could provide employment and advanced training to millions of blacks, supplying opportunities which whites did not provide and creating capital to further black economic development. Instead, the upper class was largely involved in small, service-oriented businesses—when it was en-

gaged in enterprise at all. While providing a basis for individual prosperity and respectability for a few, service enterprises employed only
a handful of persons, and the profits from them were not used for
creating other enterprises. The lack of economic relations between segments of black society reinforced their different perspectives and values,
which resulted from different degrees of acculturation to American
bourgeois norms. Upper-class blacks were not able, just as white society was not willing, to create opportunities for the development of
bourgeois norms among the black masses.[99]

No one was more aware of the chasm which separated blacks than
those who struggled to place the race in the social mainstream, for the
masses were often an embarrassment to their efforts. "Whereas, there
are a few persons of color in our midst of low class that may use language to cause disturbance to others, therefore, Resolved, That we,
as colored citizens of Xenia, will do all in our power to put from our
midst such persons whenever properly reported to [our] Committee"—
so stated a self-designated committee of four prominent Xenia blacks
in 1862.[100] Such social divisions did not cease because of threats, and
they continued to rear their heads in similar forms. At Xenia at the turn
of the century, higher-status blacks were again scandalized by the
actions of those outside their ranks. This time, on three separate occasions, the majority of voters in the largely black Fourth Ward approved an attempt, spearheaded by Xenia's churches and respectable
moral reformers of both races, to bar the local sale of alcohol. On the
third occasion, reported in the daily press throughout Ohio and the
nation, Xenia was solidly "dry" until the Fourth Ward was polled; it
distinguished itself by becoming the only ward in which the majority
voted "wet." The black Cleveland *Journal* commented bitterly, "The
Negro can always be counted on to make a fool of himself at the wrong
time. He is oft times a mule when he should be influenced by reason
and common sense, especially when a moral issue supported by the
best people of all classes is at stake." Liquor interests had spent liberally to influence the votes of the black poor. Commenting on the
tallies from the Fourth Ward, the *Journal* concluded sadly, "It is safe
to say that 90 percent of the 359 [voting "wet"] are irresponsible and
shiftless; at least 75 percent of them sold their birth-right for a mess
of pottage. . . . The 166 intelligent, wise, moral-loving Afro-Americans
[voting "dry"] must suffer, more or less, for the misdeeds of 359 lager-

[99] E. Franklin Frazier, *Black Bourgeoisie: The Rise of a New Middle Class*
(New York, 1957), pp. 43–59, 153–173.
[100] Xenia *Torchlight*, Sept. 3, 1862.

heads." [101] Thus the masses came to be seen as a barrier to the advancement of an aspiring minority.

Yet for the one-third who allied themselves with the "best people," the results of the election were also a challenge. The outcome served as a powerful reminder that they might well be judged on the basis of attitudes and actions of those who did not live according to conventional standards of respectability. As such, it was a reminder of the necessity of assuming responsibility for uplifting the masses. How the obligations of the one-third to the rest of the race were interpreted and then acted upon depended on how the former interpreted the new era in which it lived and struggled.

[101] Cleveland *Journal*, Aug. 6, 1904; Wright, "Negroes of Xenia," 1042.

6

Black Institutions

The black social structure tended to impede racial unity, but the race's venerable religious and fraternal institutions to some extent counterbalanced the divisive forces of class. These institutions were a product of black initiative, and they were sustained by profound emotional needs, shared to one extent or another across class lines by all blacks, for greater dignity, security, self-determination, and spiritual sustenance than white society offered. The churches were channels for the expression of unique black cultural practices, embodied in ways of worship and attitudes toward the divine. The lodges offered a generally poor, or often at best economically marginal, people material security in the form of insurance. Both institutions provided settings for friendly, empathetic fellowship which few blacks found among whites, and both offered opportunities for leadership to a people proscribed in its chance to learn new social skills and exercise its talents.

Yet while serving needs found throughout the race, these institutions were limited in their ability to serve a cohesive role in racial life. On the one hand, they took root within the black social structure of the time and mirrored its cleavages. They were dominated not by the Negro masses, whose socioeconomic circumstances and cultural values failed to lend themselves to a broad range of social interaction and to participation in formal institutions. Instead, a relatively narrow, higher-status segment of black society used these institutions to reinforce its values and consolidate its social position, hence further isolating the poor and lowly. On the other hand, black institutions were themselves subject to the limitations of their voluntary associational format, which, in its flexible allowance for diversity within a larger common setting, tended at the same time to a fragment efforts and resources as new congregations and lodges continually emerged.

I

At the dawning of the new era, the most stable, prestigious, and widespread racial institution was the church. Blacks were concentrated in Baptist and Methodist denominations which had, during the eighteenth century, sought converts among the downtrodden of colonial America, regardless of race and slave status. In colonial times it was not uncommon for black and white Baptists and Methodists to worship together in the same churches, but after the American Revolution, as the racial liberalism of the period waned, there was an increasing reaction among whites of both denominations to black participation as worshipers in white churches. In response to incidents of discrimination and insult, free urban blacks in the northeastern and the eastern border states began to organize their own churches, the foundation of the separate black denominations. Out of one of the earliest independent churches, organized at Philadelphia by the prominent local black leaders Richard Allen and Absalom Jones, sprang the African Methodist Episcopal Church; by 1845 it had some 10,000 members, primarily in the East and frontier regions of the Old Northwest, but also in the slave South. Comparable developments among Baptists during the same era produced independent black Baptist churches. The Baptists, however, were slower to break away from their white regional connections.[1]

The A.M.E. and Baptist faiths were so well entrenched in early nineteenth century Ohio that the state became an episcopal seat of the A.M.E. Church in 1832, and in 1836 the site of the organization of the nation's first independent black regional Baptist conference, the Providence Baptist Association; another Ohio Baptist conference was established in 1845. Congregations arose wherever there were blacks; by 1860 one church of each denomination was present in most centers of black population, from humble villages to large cities. At Columbus, Cleveland, and Springfield, congregations of each denomination were located in black neighborhoods. Xenia claimed one A.M.E. and two Baptist congregations, all located in the East End. At Cincinnati there were five black congregations in 1860; two were Baptist, and the rest were affiliated with the A.M.E. connection, the Disciples of Christ, and the Methodist Episcopal Church, North. These were located primarily

---

[1] Carter Woodson, *History of the Negro Church* (Washington, 1921), pp. 34–165; Daniel Payne, *History of the A.M.E. Church*, ed. C. S. Smith (Nashville, 1891), pp. 44, 61–62, 97, 118, 180, 205; Carol V. R. George, *Segregated Sabbaths: Richard Allen and the Rise of Independent Black Churches, 1760–1840* (New York, 1973).

in the area between Little Bucktown in the West End and the higher-status residential areas of the northwestern fringe of the river basin wards, where many more affluent blacks lived. Black urban churches were usually small but comfortable and well-constructed buildings; however, in towns and villages they often started as little more than crude shacks, hand-built by members of an impoverished community. Unadorned by religious art and handsome oaken pews, such churches were lit as much by the zeal of the congregants as by the few lamps which lined their small chapels. Elsewhere blacks were sometimes too poor to have any church structure at all, and they worshiped in small black school buildings, or in one another's homes.[2]

Wartime migrations pressed the congregations to meet the needs of even more parishioners. Some churches were already overcrowded because of an inability to keep up with the ante-bellum migrations. While there are no data on the increase in church membership among the Baptist majority during the war era, information on the growth of A.M.E. congregations is suggestive. According to A.M.E. episcopal district records, between 1865 and 1871 the church's membership in Ohio increased by 55 percent from 3,050 to 4,743. In several rural areas new A.M.E. parishes were created, while those cities and towns which experienced an influx of migrants saw a substantial increase in A.M.E. membership. Xenia experienced an increase of 88 percent (113 to 212) among A.M.E. affiliates during 1865–71; the figure for Columbus was 62 percent (211 to 342), Cincinnati 43 percent (227 to 325), Cleveland 152 percent (70 to 177), Chillicothe 62 percent (80 to 130), and Steubenville 94 percent (36 to 70). Such growth caused a wave of church-building and renovation following the war.[3] Usually, the affiliating migrants simply fit into existing congregations, but where de-

2 Woodson, *History of the Negro Church*, p. 107; Russell H. Davis, *Black Americans in Cleveland from George Peake to Carl B. Stokes, 1796–1969* (Washington, 1972), pp. 104–108; Benjamin Arnett, ed., *Proceedings of the Semi-Centenary Celebration of the African Methodist Episcopal Church of Cincinnati* (Cincinnati, 1874), pp. 55–62, 117; Columbus *Ohio State Journal*, Nov. 7, 1868; Richard Clyde Minor, "Negroes in Columbus" (Ph.D. dissertation, Ohio State University, 1936), pp. 80–84; Ivan Tribe, "The Development of a Rural Community: Albany, Ohio, 1840–1880" (Master's thesis, Ohio University, 1967), pp. 95–102; Francis Charles Hubbard, "A Short History of the Colored People of Barnesville, Ohio" (1942), typescript, OHS; Jennie Braddock, "The Colored People and Greene County, Ohio, 1800–1865" (Senior thesis, Antioch College, 1953, rev. 1962), pp. 60–66; B. F. Prince, ed., *The Centennial Celebration of Springfield, Ohio . . . 1901* (Springfield, 1901), pp. 45–47.

3 Hillsboro *Highland Gazette*, Apr. 6, 1865; Xenia *Torchlight*, Oct. 13, 1869; Cleveland *Leader*, May 16, 1865, July 30, 1872, June 16, 1873; Columbus *Ohio State Journal*, Sept. 13, 1870, July 22, 1872; A.M.E. Church, Ohio Conference, *Minutes of the 35th Session* (Pittsburgh, 1865), pp. 19–20, and *Minutes of the 41st Session* (Cincinnati, 1871), pp. 25–26.

nominations appeared for the first time, the newcomers probably took a large role in establishing churches. Washington Court House's Rogers A.M.E. Church, founded in 1867, was composed solely of southern ex-slaves who had recently migrated to the town and its immediate vicinity.[4] In at least one case the church was brought to the migrants. At Cincinnati, members of an existing Baptist church founded a mission, which later became Plum Street Baptist Church, in an area of the levee called "Hell's Half Acre." [5]

In the late nineteenth century the churches continued to proliferate. Most people continued to worship in all-black Baptist and A.M.E. churches. Indeed, the Baptists created two new regional conferences to facilitate communication among their growing number of churches, and the African Methodists divided the state into two episcopal districts to provide more efficient governance for their expansion.[6] In 1900, the first time data are available by race for all the denominations with which Ohio blacks were affiliated, Ohio's 27,723 black congregants were found in 300 black churches. Of these, 16,213 (58%) were Baptists in approximately 175 congregations, and 6,308 (23%) were African Methodists in 100 congregations. The remaining 19 percent were spread through several denominations. Three integrated denominations with separate black congregational affiliates, the Disciples of Christ, the Wesleyan Methodists, and the Methodist Episcopal Church, North, claimed 1,000 (4%), 557 (2%), and 1,645 (6%) respectively. Most of the remaining 7 percent of black affiliates were found among the Episcopalians, with a small number scattered among Presbyterians, Congregationalists, Roman Catholics, and Unitarians. The approximately 2,000 blacks in these five denominations generally worshiped with whites or were members of small black missions affiliated with white congregations, as was often the case among urban Episcopalians. Throughout the late 1800s the only black Catholic church, St. Anne's, was located at Cincinnati, while Cleveland claimed the only black Congregational church, Mt. Zion. The first black Episcopal church, St. Andrew's, was established at Cleveland in 1892.[7]

---

[4] Naomi Terry, "An Historical Sketch of Rogers A.M.E. Church" (undated typescript at Carnegie Public Library, Washington Court House, Ohio).

[5] Arnett, ed., *Proceedings of the Semi-Centenary*, p. 61.

[6] G. Lincoln Caddell, *Brief History of the North Ohio Annual Conference, Third Episcopal District of the A.M.E. Church* (n.p., 1948), p. 1; Western Ohio Anti-Slavery Baptist Association, *Minutes of the First Anniversary* (Cincinnati, 1873); Eastern Union Anti-Slavery Baptist Association, *Minutes of the Twelfth Anniversary* (Ripley, 1884).

[7] R. R. Wright, Jr., "The Middle West, Ohio," in W. E. B. Du Bois, ed., *The Negro Church* (Atlanta, 1903), p. 94; Davis, *Black Americans in Cleveland*, pp. 107–108, 184; John H. Lamott, *History of the Archdiocese of Cincinnati,*

While the earlier development of Ohio's black churches had been spread throughout rural and urban areas, the later decades of the century marked the beginning of a new pattern of development which paralleled the general demography of Ohio's black population. With the growth of black populations in the larger cities, based largely on migrations from Ohio's small villages and rural areas, there was a pronounced increase in the number of black urban church members, coupled with little or no growth or an actual decline in the numbers of rural members. According to available Baptist church records, between the early 1870s and 1900 the number of small rural Baptist parishes dwindled, and in small towns like Sidney, Piqua, and Oxford there was little growth or a decline in the numbers of black Baptist congregants. Simultaneously, in the four large cities for which there are data, increases were two- or three-fold or even more. The number of Columbus Baptists grew from 497 to 1,278, Cincinnati's from 1,027 to 2,011, Springfield's from 173 to 525, and Dayton's from 32 to 314. The same tendency was present in the A.M.E. church. Between the early 1870s and 1896 in towns like Portsmouth, Gallipolis, and Chillicothe the number of A.M.E. affiliates grew very little after the migrations of the war era, while a number of small rural churches and missions closed. But growth in the cities was substantial—Columbus's A.M.E. congregants increased from 342 to 770, Cincinnati's from 325 to 512, Cleveland's from 177 to 320, and Springfield's from 123 to 484.[8]

A growth in the number of urban churches accompanied this increase in the number of congregants. The proliferation of churches did not necessarily result from increasing numbers of affiliates alone; though migrants to the cities might establish their own congregations, other factors also helped to account for the increased number of congregations. First, large black urban populations and more complex black social structures were products of the greater social, economic, and cultural opportunities existing even for blacks in cities. Such complexity facilitated the emergence of subgroups based on common interests, ideas, friendships, etc., which might desire congregational autonomy. Larger social divisions were mirrored in the sort of bitter

1821–1921 (New York and Cincinnati, 1921), p. 144; Cleveland *Leader,* Sept. 12, 1864; Cleveland *Gazette,* Feb. 2, 1889; Oct. 11, 1890, Dec. 7, 1901; Cincinnati *Commercial-Tribune,* July 1, 1901; Indianapolis *Freeman,* June 12, 1909, June 5, Aug. 11, Sept. 14, 1915.

8 A.M.E. Church, Ohio Conference, *Minutes of the 41st Session,* pp. 25–26, and *Minutes of the 66th Session* (Cincinnati, 1896), pp. 107–108; A.M.E. Church, North Ohio Conference, *Minutes of the 14th Session* (Springfield, 1896), pp. 108–110; Western Ohio Anti-Slavery Baptist Association, *Minutes of the First Anniversary,* p. 16; Western Union Baptist Association, *Proceedings of the Thirty-first Annual Session* (Cincinnati, 1903), p. 41.

intracongregational feuding which caused the breakup of large, prosperous congregations like Columbus's Second Baptist Church in 1869 and Cleveland's Shiloh Baptist Church in 1893. Feuds sometimes resulted from the emergence within a congregation of self-conscious groups desiring greater recognition, perhaps in the belief that positions of prominence and power in church affairs were being monopolized by other groups. At the same time, feuds were also the product of specifically congregational issues, such as the activities of a controversial minister or the allocation of scarce resources. In either case, the possibility of fragmentation was present.[9]

While feuding and the desire for congregational autonomy were traditionally aspects of both black and white congregational life, in the late nineteenth century distance and location became factors in the proliferation of urban black churches. This was the result of the tendency of upper- and middle-class blacks to leave the central neighborhoods for newly emerging urban and suburban ones. In the Cincinnati metropolitan area, residential mobility began on a large scale in the 1860s. Both Baptist and A.M.E. denominations had established themselves in Walnut Hills between 1862 and 1868, and movements of both into other hilltop residential areas continued throughout the later nineteenth century. At Cleveland a small mission of the long-established St. John's A.M.E. Church, located in the Central Avenue area, was begun in 1894 on Hudson Street near East 105th to accommodate the small but growing affluent black population on the far east side; this mission eventually became the city's second A.M.E. church, St. James'. At Columbus in the 1890s Baptist congregations were established on the north side and in the newly developing black area down Long Street when established downtown churches became too distant.[10]

As a consequence of these various factors, all of Ohio's major cities saw a growth in the number of churches. This was less the case among the African Methodists, because their centralized system of governance made the establishment of churches subject to the scrutiny of economy-minded bishops, who opposed the creation of small congregations which might not prove financially viable, and who demanded that feuding congregants settle their differences and remain together. Thus

---

[9] Reverdy Ransom, *The Pilgrimage of Harriet Ransom's Son* (Nashville, n.d.), p. 70; Cleveland *Gazette*, Aug. 3, 1901; Minor, "Negroes in Columbus," pp. 80–84; Western Ohio Anti-Slavery Baptist Association, *Minutes of the First Anniversary*, pp. 4–5, and *Minutes of the Tenth Annual Meeting*, p. 9.

[10] Arnett, *Proceedings of the Semi-Centenary*, pp. 55, 62; Wendell Phillips Dabney, *Cincinnati's Colored Citizens: Historical, Sociological, and Biographical* (Cincinnati, 1926), pp. 372–375; Cleveland *Plain Dealer*, May 18, 1902; Ransom, *Pilgrimage*, p. 68; Minor, "Negroes in Columbus," pp. 80–84.

urban A.M.E. congregations tended to have larger memberships. Dayton, Springfield, Cleveland, Columbus, and Cincinnati each had two A.M.E. churches in 1900; all but two had well over a hundred members. (The exceptions, two newly established congregations at Dayton and Springfield, both grew rapidly in the next years.) Larger urban A.M.E. congregations like Cincinnati's Allen Temple, Columbus's St. Paul's, Cleveland's St. John's, and Springfield's North Street A.M.E. all had memberships between 325 and 700.[11]

But the Baptists were not subject to any centralized authority, and the picture there was quite different. While the Cincinnati area had six Baptist churches in 1874, by 1900 there were thirteen in the city and eight in suburban areas. Membership levels varied greatly among them. Three of the churches, all founded before 1870, had three to six hundred congregants, but four of the newer ones in the city had only 54 to 71 members. Distance was a factor here; three of the four were located in hilltop neighborhoods far from one another and from the inner city. At the same time, there were tendencies toward a duplication of effort within the same residential areas. Two churches were located in Walnut Hills; four were found in and near the West End–Little Bucktown section; and two were located in and near the East End–Little Bucktown section. In 1870 Columbus had two Baptist churches, the result of a recent split in the Second Baptist Church. By the turn of the century there were seven; some were in new residential areas, and three had memberships of less than a hundred. At Dayton, Springfield, and Cleveland the ante-bellum Baptist congregations were all complemented in the next decades with two additional churches, none with more than 150 members and at least one with fewer than 50. At Cleveland feuding had caused a split in Shiloh Baptist Church and led to the founding of Antioch Baptist several blocks away.[12]

Though the late nineteenth century saw increasing numbers of urban congregants and churches, there probably was no substantial growth in the percentage of persons within black communities who were formally affiliated with churches. Throughout the late nineteenth century, membership levels suggest that many were not regular members. Some persons might have attended church occasionally or even

[11] Prince, ed., *Centennial Celebration of Springfield*, pp. 45–47; A.M.E. Church, Ohio Conference, *Minutes of the 66th Session*, p. 41, and *Minutes of the 72nd Session* (Hamilton, 1902), Table A; Cleveland *Plain Dealer*, May 18, 1902.

[12] Ohio Baptist State Convention, *Proceedings of the Fifth Annual Session* (Urbana, 1900), p. 12; Western Union Baptist Sunday School Convention, *Minutes of the 27th Annual Session* (Columbus, 1900), Statistical Table; Western Union Baptist Association, *Proceedings of the Thirty-first Annual Session*, p. 42; Eastern Union Baptist Association, *Minutes of the Twenty-ninth Annual Meeting* (Urbana, 1903), p. 32.

regularly on a less than formal basis; however, they probably had little role in church governance and lacked the regular contact which members enjoyed with the social and cultural functions of the church outside of worship.

Membership levels ranged between 30 and 40 percent of Ohio's adult and near-adult black population. According to the federal census of 1890, 19,723 blacks, or one-third of the total black population fifteen and over, were formally affiliated with churches. R. R. Wright, Jr., conducted a thorough investigation, based on records and interviews with church leaders, of affiliational levels among Ohio blacks at the turn of the century; he found that approximately 28,000, or 40 percent of the black population fifteen and over, were formally affiliated. While this level of affiliation is near that found among white Ohioans during the same years, it was much lower than the nationwide figure for blacks. In 1890 63 percent of the nation's blacks fifteen and over were formally affiliated. This high level of affiliation was considerably greater than that of American whites; it was due to the fact that rural southern blacks, who constituted about three-quarters of the total Afro-American population in the late nineteenth century, were likely to be church members.[13]

Unfortunately, data correlating age and membership levels are not available for late nineteenth century Ohio communities. Approximations can be made, however, on the basis of *total* black populations, utilizing extant denominational records. At Cincinnati approximately 1,990 blacks (29%) of the black population) were affiliated in 1874, while some 3,925 (24%) were affiliated in 1902–3. At Columbus approximately 956 (39%) were affiliated in 1875, compared with 2,344 (24%) in 1902–3. In the smaller cities and larger towns the extent of formal affiliation was greater. Membership levels of 37 and 35 percent of Springfield's black population were present in 1874 and at the turn of the century, while Chillicothe recorded 57 and 36 percent in 1873 and 1903, Portsmouth 32 and 29 percent in 1875 and 1903, and Xenia 50 and 54 percent in 1873 and 1902. For the sake of comparison, it should be noted that while Ohio's 28,000 church members in 1900 make up 40 percent of the black population fifteen and over, they were 29 percent of the *total* black population in that same year.[14]

---

[13] U.S. Census Office, *Report on Statistics of Churches in the United States at the Eleventh Census, 1890* (Washington, 1894), p. 49, and *Negro Population, 1790–1915* (Washington, 1918), pp. 92, 170–171; Wright, "The Middle West," p. 94. In 1890 the extent of affiliation for whites in Ohio was 51%, and for whites in the nation at large 53%.

[14] Extant yearly church state convention and connectional records were the basic source employed to find levels of black affiliation in cities and towns. These data are good, though the Baptists collected statistics less frequently, and more

Who were the unaffiliated Ohio blacks, and why did they fail to become church members? First, it must be said emphatically that church membership among black Ohioans was not defined strictly by high social status, although, given the bottom-heavy nature of the black social structure, low membership levels suggest that many lower-class persons were not formally affiliated. Some churches, like Cincinnati's Plum Street Baptist, were located in the slums and drew their members from the ranks of the lower class; there were also missions, opened by established congregations, which catered to the poor. Furthermore, lower-class persons might be members of churches with a generally upper- and middle-class membership. This was probably particularly true of lower-class women for, like their higher-status sisters, their greater isolation relative to men made church an especially important center for their social interaction. In fact, women constituted approximately two-thirds of black church members in Ohio and throughout the nation at the turn of century.[15] At Xenia, for example, R. R. Wright, Jr., found evidence of substantial activity of lower-class individuals in congregational life. On the one hand, he stated that "invariably those in the most lucrative . . . employment are church members," and he found 84 percent (80 of 95 persons) of black high school graduates and 91 percent (288 of 318 persons) of black home-owners were church members. But he also found that fully 84 percent of the total number of black families (421 of 501) at Xenia had at

A.M.E. records survive. A problem, however, arises in that while the large majority of blacks were affiliated with these two churches, a minority were affiliated with churches for which there are no extant membership data. To approximate this minority membership, I utilized the percentage of 20—according to R. R. Wright, Jr., approximately this percentage of black churchgoers were affiliated with churches outside the Baptist and A.M.E. connections. For the nation at large around the same time, the figure is similar: 18% of all U.S. blacks belonging to churches were affiliated outside the A.M.E. and Baptist churches. Furthermore, it was necessary to presume even rates of black population growth between censuses in order to compute population totals for individual years. On the few occasions when I had the opportunity to check such estimates against complete local membership total for all denominations, my estimates were between 2 and 5% higher. No data were available for Cleveland until after the turn of the century. Wright, "The Middle West," pp. 92, 99; Arnett, *Proceedings of the Semi-Centenary*, pp. iv, 117; E. S. Todd, *A Sociological Study of Springfield and Clark County, Ohio* (New York, 1904), p. 86; Western Ohio Anti-Slavery Baptist Association, *Minutes of the First Anniversary*, p. 16; Western Union Baptist Association, *Proceedings of the Thirty-first Annual Session*, p. 41; Eastern Union Baptist Association, *Minutes of the Twenty-ninth Annual Meeting*, pp. 31–32; A.M.E. Church, Ohio Conference, *Minutes of the 41st Annual Session*, pp. 25–26; *Minutes of the 44th Annual Session* (n.p., 1874), pp. 40–43, *Minutes of the 72nd Session*, Table A, and *Minutes of the 73rd Session*, (n.p., 1903), Table A.

[15] Bureau of the Census, *Religious Bodies, 1906, Summary and General Tables* (Washington, 1910), I, 554–558.

least one person who was a formal church member. It seems evident that many of these families, and hence their (probably female) representatives in church, were on the lower rungs of the black social ladder.[16]

Yet while lower-class persons were found on church membership rolls, it was also likely that they would be prominent among the unaffiliated, especially in the large cities. The complex interrelationships between affiliation, black urbanization, and social stratification suggest reasons for this. Membership data for Ohio and the nation at large reveal a negative relationship between black urbanization and church membership. In Ohio, the towns and smaller cities and the state at large (reflecting the rural experience) show a greater degree of black church membership than the cities of Columbus and Cincinnati. National data, heavily reflecting the experience of the southern rural black majority, which made up 75 percent of the national black population and 85 percent of the southern black population, reveal that non-Ohio blacks were more likely to be formally affiliated than their Ohio brethren, the majority of whom were living in urban areas after the 1880s. These relationships suggest that, in the smaller urban centers and rural areas, where the church was usually the center of black social life, the pressure to affiliate was greater. In the cities, however, church competed with other amusements and centers for socializing, such as street corners, front stoops of tenements and apartments, cafes, and taverns, for the loyalty of those seeking community. For those who did not particularly care about the final disposition of their souls, and for those, particularly lower-status persons, whose cultural perspectives did not necessarily equate social respectability with church attendance, the latter path might prove considerably more attractive.

Then, too, in both rural and urban areas the lower class often had to relate to churches controlled by upper- and middle-class persons, and some must have found it difficult to do so. It was not so much that lower-class persons could not afford to join, for membership costs were minimal, and the churches themselves, through periodic revivals, actively sought members. Nor did the reviewing procedures for membership function restrictively. The A.M.E. churches were asked to require a six-month probation period for prospective members, during which the candidate was to receive instruction on the obligations of practicing Christians; however, as R. R. Wright, Jr., observed at Xenia, application of this policy was uneven. The Baptists took their

[16] Wright, "The Middle West," p. 100, and Wright, "The Negroes of Xenia, Ohio: A Social Study," U.S. Department of Labor *Bulletin* no. 48 (Sept., 1903), 1041. Wright gave no data on the sex of church members.

members directly after their declaration for Christ. If an applicant left one local Baptist church for another, he needed only a letter attesting to his or her good character.[17]

Instead, subtler differences in cultural and socioeconomic standing separated the classes. Dress, manners, and lifestyles differentiated lower-class poor people and might serve as a reason for others to look down on them. Because they did not measure up to bourgeois standards, they themselves no doubt often felt ill at ease in the company of higher-status individuals. Overt demands for respectable conduct might also be intimidating. Among Ohio Baptists, for example, the late nineteenth century saw increasing efforts to press members to take vows of temperance and to publicly censure those who were seen frequenting saloons, the social clubs of the poor.[18]

Different styles of worship also separated blacks, tending to make worship in churches controlled by those outside their ranks less satisfying for the lower-class majority. Not unlike the Christianity of the white lower classes, the folk religion which the masses brought from slavery was characterized by improvisation, religious ecstasies, and active congregant participation. In contrast, the religion of higher-status blacks, though containing unique black elements, resembled that of their white social counterparts in its more formalized and decorous practice. These differences became especially important in the late nineteenth century as the leadership of Baptist and A.M.E. churches began to encourage the development of an educated ministry. Growing numbers of educated, sometimes seminary-trained, ministers now entered local churches. They brought with them more restrained styles of preaching and a more intellectual approach than that of past generations of preachers who had been schooled only in the ways of "old-time religion." They also possessed a missionary desire to speed racial uplift by inculcating conventionally respectable religious mores.[19]

In 1874 Ohio A.M.E. Bishop Daniel Payne, a leader in the struggle for an educated ministry and the person responsible for the initiation of a theology curriculum at Wilberforce University in 1866, spoke of the differences in religious practices among blacks. He suggested the need

[17] Wright, "The Middle West," p. 97; Eastern Union Anti-Slavery Baptist Association, Minutes of the Twelfth Anniversary, p. 12.

[18] Western Union Anti-Slavery Baptist Association, Minutes of the Tenth Annual Meeting (Springfield, 1883), p. 11; Eastern Anti-Slavery Baptist Association, Minutes of the Twentieth Annual Meeting (n.p., 1894), p. 17.

[19] Woodson, History of the Negro Church, pp. 224–241; Western Union Anti-Slavery Baptist Association, Minutes of the Tenth Annual Meeting, p. 11; Eastern Anti-Slavery Baptist Association, Minutes of the Twentieth Annual Meeting, p. 17; Frederick A. McGinnis, A History and Interpretation of Wilberforce University (Blanchester, Ohio, 1941), pp. 60–62.

for patience and understanding in the important work of changing them—along lines favorable to higher-status black practices. Payne stated, "The religious errors and wild enthusiasms of the freedmen are the result of slavery which had been operating on their forefathers for nearly 250 years, and cannot be removed in a day, nor by one man, nor one kind of human agency." He went on to urge a broad attack by both teachers and ministers upon religious ignorance and unorthodox practice.[20]

Although there were a number of reasons why blacks were separated from one another in religious affairs, both the formally affiliated and the occasional congregants of all classes sought primarily the same benefits from their churches: the comfort of prayer and the spiritual sustenance of an organized religious community. Like Christian churches across the nation, black churches responded by dedicating themselves to the saving of souls and the inculcation of morality with the added advantage for blacks: the practice and upholding of Christian virtue showed the worthiness of a scorned people and gave them a source of pride.

The churches devoted considerable energy to serving individual and group spiritual needs. Denominations and individual congregations sponsored organized missionary activities for propagating the gospel at home and abroad, and they made intensive efforts to win converts. Local churches were scenes of constant religious activity, tied to the rhythms of the week and the seasons. There were two or three services on Sunday in the larger churches, with additional midweek prayer meetings and occasional weekly religious instruction for adults.[21] Sunday schools provided the early exposure of the young to Christian teaching; they were popular even in the smallest hamlets, and in the cities it was not uncommon for large congregations to boast enrollments of several hundred, with teaching staffs and libraries of proportionate size. The Sunday schools were an object of considerable pride and effort everywhere. As early as 1872 Baptists went so far as to organize annual conventions for the purpose of exchanging ideas about instruction among teachers and gathering elaborate data on the progress of the individual schools.[22]

Revivals were often held early in the year. Lasting from a week to

[20] From the Reverend Daniel Payne, "Semi-Centennial Sermon," in Arnett, ed., *Proceedings of the Semi-Centenary,* p. 84; Josephus R. Coan, *Daniel Payne— Christian Educator* (Philadelphia, 1935), pp. 61–62; McGinnis, *History of Wilberforce,* pp. 47, 60–62.

[21] Wright, "The Middle West," pp. 100–101.

[22] A.M.E. Church, Ohio Conference, *Minutes of the 35th Session,* pp. 23–24; Western Ohio Anti-Slavery Baptist Association, *Minutes of the First Anniversary,* pp. 14–15; Western Union Baptist Sunday School Convention, *Minutes of the Twenty-seventh Annual Session* (Oxford, 1899), Statistical Tables.

as long as two months, they were the setting for formidable efforts at obtaining commitments to Christ and to formal church affiliation, especially among young adults and teenagers. At the same time, the revivals served to strengthen the faith of congregants. Here especially, in these intensive weeks of religious activity, the effective preacher could shine brightly as the guiding light of his congregation's spiritual life. R. R. Wright, Jr., visited Greene County's black churches during the revival season and spoke of the preachers' frenetic efforts. Their impassioned sermons, he said, "are chiefly on hell and its terrors; the love of Christ and God are shown in the suffering and death of Christ. . . . They abound in pathetic stories, which are related with great feeling, and which seldom fail the desired result . . . a large number of conversions and accessions to the church." Several weeks during the summer might again be reserved for revivals, which were often held in open-air camp meetings and presided over by traveling evangelists.[23]

But however much the effective preacher was the spiritual leader of a religious community, he also had to be the financial administrator of a business which utilized the hard-earned savings of pious people of generally humble means. Along with the spiritual concerns of the church were the additional imperatives of congregational survival, growth, and development; the individual clergyman had to be part businessman and part public relations expert, as well as the shepherd of his flock.

Stimulating membership growth was but one factor in a minister's practical calculations. In fact, when reading the Negro press of the day one cannot help but be impressed by the great energy and effort expended by ministers and congregations alike in building, enlarging, and refurbishing church structures. This was particularly the case in the large cities, where post-bellum populations grew rapidly and forced the churches to accommodate growing numbers of affiliates. Then, too, blacks saw their churches as certain signs of racial progress and autonomy. They lent prestige to a scorned people, and they provided opportunities for independent action and self-help. Each was, in fact, a type of self-financing Negro government, and the espiscopal denominations resembled small polities. Black congregations did not hold back when it came to making churches objects of dignified beauty and, occasionally, grandeur. While most churches were valued at considerably under $20,000, values were significantly greater in the larger cities, where congregations might be larger and their members more affluent.

[23] Wright, "The Middle West," pp. 96–97, 100; Columbus *Ohio State Journal,* Aug. 11, 1879; Columbus *Free American,* Mar. 19,' 1887; Cleveland *Gazette,* Oct. 25, 1890.

Cincinnati's imposing Allen Temple, A.M.E., located at Sixth and Broadway in the heart of Bucktown, had been purchased in 1870 from a congregation of Sephardic Jews which was moving elsewhere. Valuable as the large structure was, with its seating capacity of 12,000, after two decades of improvements by the black Methodists the property's worth had jumped from $40,000 to $80,000. Among the improvements were rows of chandeliers worth about $1,000 apiece. Most congregations could not afford such expensive fixtures, yet many aimed to purchase carpets, stained glass windows, pipe organs, frescoed and varnished interiors, parsonages and pastor's studies, small libraries, and kitchens. At the same time, they had to pay their pastors.[24]

In addition to the individual congregation's goals for itself, there were its financial obligations to its own regional denominational connections and episcopal districts, and to the national offices, agencies, and missions of the denomination. Such contributions were never large, but they were certainly expected (indeed, among the African Methodists, with their tight episcopal organization, they were required), and the individual congregations certainly conceived of them as an important part of their larger obligations. After the 1868 enactment of its "dollar law," the A.M.E. Church required one dollar per year per congregant collected at the local level for the support of retired, itinerant, and supernumerary preachers and the widows of preachers, and for the maintenance of denominational publishing efforts. A.M.E. members were also expected to make regular contributions for the support of sub-regional presiding elders. Among Baptists and Methodists there were periodic collections for the support of denominational educational institutions, largely in the South, though Ohio African Methodists naturally felt special obligations to Wilberforce University. Domestic and foreign missions and a variety of occasional special projects also received support. Collections from poorer congregants and congregations were erratic, but apparently no one was chastised or humiliated for failure to pay as much as was asked. An important part of the obligations of membership, however, was to strive to make such payments whatever the difficulties. Connectional records are filled with evidence of such struggles in the form of references to fifty cents, or

<hr>

24 Centennial Commission, Allen Temple, A.M.E., *Centennial Guide, Allen Temple, A.M.E.* (Cincinnati, 1924), p. 25; Wright, "Negroes of Xenia," 1040; "History of Zion Baptist Church" and Marietta Gales, "History of Third Baptist Church," both undated typescripts appended to Braddock, "Colored People and Greene County"; Hillsboro *Highland Gazette*, Apr. 6, 1865; Cleveland *Leader*, Sept. 22, 1863, May 16, 1865; Columbus *Ohio State Journal*, Sept. 13, 1870, July 22, 1872; Cincinnati *Commercial*, Feb. 22, 1874; Columbus *Free American*, Mar. 19, 1887; Cleveland *Gazette*, Oct. 25, 1890.

thirty cents, or even as little as a dime *per congregation* per annum contributed for the support of missions or denominational schools.[25]

Church decoration and construction inevitably imposed even greater burdens for both individuals and congregations; along with new, enlarged, or refurbished churches came large debts. The burden of these was likely to be greater for the smaller congregations, such as the growing number of urban Baptist churches, than for the A.M.E. churches, which, especially in the cities, tended to be larger in membership. For both Baptists and African Methodists the burden of debt was doubtless increased psychologically by the fact that mortgages and notes were almost invariably held by whites, compromising the quest for self-determination. The Cincinnati correspondent of the Cleveland *Gazette*, himself a member of Allen Temple, suggested the importance of this issue in 1890 when he reported with a sigh of relief that Ohio's "Citadel of African Methodism" was finally out of debt and "entirely free of the claims of *any white man.*" [26]

Efforts at attaining such financial autonomy were led, in spirit or in deed, by the ministers. Many a minister's reputation appears to have been based on his ability to lead his congregation out from under a burden of debt. Congregational histories are laden with references to ministers remembered for their "financial ability," or their success as "financiers," or their accomplishment in placing the church on a "splendid financial basis" or "in first class condition with mortgages paid." [27] Such reputations helped to set the course of a minister's career. Whether his parish was chosen for him (as in episcopal churches, by bishops who kept close watch on his activities) or sought by him individually, a reputation for financial ability might well make a significant difference. A minister could find employment in a wealthy, urban church offering a parsonage, a handsome salary ($1,300 at Allen Temple at the turn of the century), and have a chance to live in a cosmopolitan setting; on the other hand, he might end up with a small, impoverished

---

[25] On the origin of "dollar money" see Bureau of the Census, *Religious Bodies: 1916*, II, 494. On collections for denominational responsibilities: Western Union Anti-Slavery Baptist Association, *Minutes of the Tenth Annual Meeting*, pp. 34, 39–40; and *Proceedings of Thirty-first Annual Session*, p. 41; A.M.E. Church, Ohio Conference, *Minutes of the 41st Session*, p. 28, and *Minutes of the 72nd Session*, Tables B, C, D. To illustrate the struggle to collect denominational monies: in 1885 the recently established North Ohio Conference, A.M.E., with 3,255 members in 55 churches, collected 16¢ per congregant in dollar money and 21¢ per congregant for presiding elder's support. In 1892 the conference collected almost 13¢ per congregant in support of Wilberforce University. See Caddell, *Third Episcopal District*, pp. 10–11.

[26] Cleveland *Gazette*, Oct. 25, 1890.

[27] Urbana *Informer*, Aug., 1902; Allen Temple, A.M.E., *Centennial Guide;* Terry, "Rogers A.M.E. Church"; Marietta Gales, "Third Baptist Church."

church where he would earn as little as $300 a year and suffer a standard of living akin to that of the proverbial church mouse.[28] Thus a minister must take seriously not only his charge as a spiritual leader, but also his obligation to inspire congregants to raise money. When it was consistent with dignity, he might take an active role in fundraising, urging his congregants on and often seeking aid from wealthy whites, such as Cleveland's John D. Rockefeller, who gave liberally for the support of local black Baptist congregations. If he was lucky, he would preside over the ritualistic "mortgage burning" ceremonies which were the capstone of successful efforts to relieve the burden of debt.[29]

While they demanded a large share of the minister's and congregation's time and energy, fiscal imperatives were not the only secular concerns of the churches. Even the poorer congregations commonly engaged in informal, unsystematized distribution of food, clothing, and small sums of money to needy congregants and, when possible, to the general community. The economic marginality of the churches and their members, however, must have limited the scope of this activity. The men's and women's church organizations visited sick, aged, and bereaved congregants and arranged to help them with shopping, housework, and child care. Some of the larger urban churches sent packages of food and clothing to impoverished southern co-religionists. Cleveland's large St. John's A.M.E. women's missionary society helped to support several African students at Wilberforce in the late 1890s, while Cincinnati's Union Baptist Church maintained a black cemetery for many years. Church buildings served as community meeting halls, and the congregations themselves were the basis for church literary, Bible study, and temperance societies. As for the ministers, they were called upon to arbitrate personal disputes, to consult on family and individual problems, to act as the interracial interpreters of their local communities, and to help occasionally to find work for individuals. They, too, visited the sick and comforted the bereaved.[30]

[28] Among both Baptists and African Methodists salary ranges in 1900 varied according to congregational size and location. Most salaries were between $500 and $750, with the higher ones found among the large urban churches and the lower ones in the rural areas. Only about half of the churches in both denominations had parsonages. A.M.E. Church, Ohio Conference, *Minutes of the 72nd Session*, Tables A, C; Western Union Baptist Association, *Proceedings of the Thirty-first Annual Session*, p. 43.

[29] Hillsboro *Highland Gazette*, Apr. 6, 1865; Cleveland *Leader*, May 16, 1865, Feb. 1, 1867, July 30, 1872, June 14, 20, July 16, Aug. 8, 20, 1873; Xenia *Torchlight*, Apr. 12, 1869; Columbus *Free American*, Mar. 19, 1887; Cleveland *Gazette*, June 3, 1899; Urbana *Informer*, Aug., 1902; Ransom, *Pilgrimage*, p. 70; Marietta Gales, "Third Baptist Church," p. 3.

[30] Cincinnati *Gazette*, Sept. 18, 1865; *Columbus Ohio State Journal*, July 13, 1870; Warren *Western Reserve Chronicle*, Apr. 28, 1875; Columbus *Free Amer-*

Yet efforts to bring the churches into more comprehensive relations
with their communities and to guide them toward broader roles in
racial affairs developed slowly. For contemporaries wishing a more
activist church, this was not a matter of having ministers, denominations, and congregations more involved in partisan politics. Both congregants and churchmen had too much respect for the traditional moral
and religious functions of the church, and for the doctrine of separation
of church and state, to lead black religion or religious institutions in
that direction; this reticence was reflected in the political activity of
denominations and of individual ministers and congregations. The extent of ministerial involvement in politics varied greatly among individuals. There were those like Arnett and Poindexter, whose personal
ambitions and sense of racial need led them to become deeply involved
in politics. But other laymen and ministers agreed with "Deacon," an
anonymous black who wrote in the Cincinnati *Commercial* in 1874 that
constant political activity by ministers depressed the "moral standard"
of the church. "Politics has taken hold of the pulpit," he observed,
claiming with sarcasm that since Hiram Revels, a black Mississippi
minister, had entered the U.S. Senate in 1870, "each of our elders thinks
he must too." "Deacon" particularly singled out for abuse those ministers who attempted to use the church, primarily through publishing
and disseminating their sermons, in order to gain reputations which
would serve them in politics.[31] A viewpoint like his kept many ministers
from entering political life actively and attempting to bring their congregations with them, except when unusually pressing racial, moral, or
religious issues like the suppression of vice, the preservation of the
Sabbath, and the use of the Bible in the public schools were under
intense debate.[32]

Nor was it thought desirable for the denominations to take active
political stands on public questions. While the Baptists did not begin
the practice of issuing yearly statements on national and international
questions until after 1900, the A.M.E. Church's annual district convention reports all contained pious, polite, and reasoned reports on
secular issues, with occasional comments on controversial ones. These
were not, however, for the purpose of stimulating further debate and
eventually forging a connectional stand. Though the reports never
shrank from a broad defense of racial interests, they were more for the

ican, Mar. 19, 1887; Minor, "Negroes in Columbus," p. 84; Benjamin Arnett, ed.,
*Centennial Thanksgiving Sermon Delivered . . . at St. Paul's A.M.E. Church,
Urbana, Ohio . . . 1876* (Urbana, 1876), pp. 55–56.

   [31] Cincinnati *Commercial,* Feb. 22, 1874.

   [32] Ibid., Mar. 31, 1870; Cincinnati *Times-Star,* Feb. 12, 13, 14, 1889; Cleveland
Gazette, Feb. 13, 1904.

purpose of reference for posterity and served a largely symbolic fulfillment of the moral obligation to see Christian values realized in the
world. There was a ritualistic quality in the way the reports were read
into the record, approved quickly, and succeeded by the next order of
business.[33]

Contemporary critics of the churches wanted them to do more to
reach out to those beyond the sphere of their normal activities. While
most saw the inculcation of morality through suasion from the pulpit
as the church's chief social obligation, these spokesmen wished to see
the church develop programs to deal with practical needs, especially
those of young people. Like Bishop Payne, some lamented the fact that
the churches did nothing to help worthy young men and women pursue their educations, particularly toward racially beneficial teaching
and ministerial careers.[34] Others, especially in the large cities, wished
to see the churches fill the leisure needs of young people. A Columbus
resident spoke in 1887 of the failure of local churches to compete with
"the saloons and houses of ill-repute" for the attention of young people in the city's decaying older neighborhoods: "Our churches are
closed six nights a week as far as the young are concerned for in no
church here have we meetings to which the young may go and men-
tally benefit." [35]

Though he was not able to offer practical advice as to how the
church might better relate to the needs of the young, a number of
others in the next decade would try, with modest results. The members
of Allen Temple established a small congregational YMCA, more on the
order of the traditional lyceum than a multi-faceted social center. Similar YMCAs were established outside the church, but under the leadership of ministers, at Springfield and Dayton.[36] A few congregations, like
Cleveland's Antioch Baptist, began to interest themselves in the problems of the indigent, the homeless, and juvenile offenders.[37] The Baptists began on the local and eventually on the connectional level to
establish Baptist Young People's Unions for the purpose of involving

[33] A.M.E. Church, Ohio Conference, Minutes of annual conference, 1865, 1871,
1874, 1879, 1881–89, 1896. A representative example of a statement on national
affairs is found in the 1889 published proceeding. Said that year's Committee on
the Church and the State of the Nation, "The South is in such a condition that we
are unable to give an idea of what is to be developed. But one thing we are safe
in saying and that is that the Sons of Africa are feeling the iron hands of oppression. We pray God that soon things may change for the better." A.M.E. Church,
Ohio Conference, *Minutes of the 52nd Session* (n.p., 1889), p. 50.

[34] Payne, "Semi-Centennial Sermon," p. 83.

[35] Cleveland *Gazette*, Dec. 10, 1887.

[36] Ibid., Oct. 25, 1890, Apr. 28, 1893, July 20, 1895, Jan. 18, 1896.

[37] Cleveland Plain *Dealer*, May 18, 1902.

young people in religious affairs and reinforcing the straight and narrow path to morality.[38] Yet at the close of the century a *Gazette* correspondent at Columbus could still describe as "splendid progress" the innovative work of a young Columbus minister, the pastor of the three-hundred-member Mt. Vernon A.M.E. Church, who had organized a "missionary and saving society" to provide clothes for poor children "that they might attend Sunday School and church." [39]

While the churches were slow to find a role in secular community affairs, they failed completely to appreciate their potential role as advanced agents of racial unity by cooperating with one another in community endeavors. It was not that the major black denominations were bitterly set against one another; seldom were interdenominational rivalries matters of serious or prolonged community conflict. Usually they involved little more than the failure to agree on plans for participation in some event, resulting in separate participation. Instead, it was simply that with the notable exceptions of occasional cooperation in organizing revivals and participating in general celebrations of religious holidays, or, in a few instances within local ministers' associations, the churches and their pastors felt little stimulus to initiate interfaith cooperation.[40] Each denomination had worked reasonably well at saving souls and building congregations with its own forms of ritual and governance, and most asked only for the chance to continue to profit from the status quo. Thus the churches continued to pattern most of their activities in predictable and traditional molds.

II

National black fraternal orders made their appearance in the same era when the black churches emerged. The Masons were for many years the most prestigious of black lodges. The order had been founded by Prince Hall, a Boston artisan who was a leader in early mutual aid efforts among Boston Negroes, after he had obtained instruction in Masonry from British soldiers during the American Revolution. The order spread through the North and, where possible, the South; before 1860 it had developed all of the national and much of the regional and female-affiliate apparatus for wives, daughters, and

[38] Western Union Baptist Association, *Twenty-first Annual Meeting* (Urbana, 1893), pp. 10, 14–15, 35; Ohio Baptist State Convention, *Proceedings of the Fifth Annual Session* (Urbana, 1900), p. 5.
[39] Cleveland *Gazette*, Oct. 29, 1898.
[40] Hillsboro *Highland Gazette*, Aug. 3, 1865; Columbus *Ohio State Journal*, Nov. 17, 1868, Aug. 11, 1879; Cincinnati *Enquirer*, July 16, 1877; Cleveland *Gazette*, Apr. 18, 1903, May 14, 1904.

relatives of male members which was necessary for the success and further spread of Masonry. Then, in 1843 and 1864, came the next large orders, the Odd Fellows and the Knights of Pythias. During the same years a number of smaller ones, like the United Brothers of Friendship and the Good Samaritans, were also established.[41]

By 1870 several of the orders had found their way into Ohio. Their impressive combination of ritual, social, and insurance features and their national reputations enabled them to replace the older local mutual aid societies; few of these latter organizations survived into the 1890s outside small towns.[42] Though neither the Knights of Pythias nor (except at Cleveland) the Odd Fellows would begin to organize in Ohio until the late 1870s, the Masons had been present at Cincinnati as early as 1848. In that year, following several unsuccessful attempts to obtain instruction in Masonry and the warranting of separate black lodges from local white Masons, a small group of Cincinnati blacks established contact with black Masons at Pittsburgh. These men provided the Ohioans with instruction and warranted the state's first black lodges. In 1849 the three recently established Cincinnati lodges founded an Ohio Grand Lodge, which then warranted lodges throughout Ohio and surrounding states. By 1870 there were approximately thirty Masonic lodges, with some 720 members, scattered throughout Ohio. In the large cities few additional lodges were providing additional work toward advanced Masonic degrees.[43] In addition, a number of lesser national orders were also found in Ohio, especially in the cities. At Cincinnati, for example, there were lodges of the United Brothers and Good Samaritans and their sororal affiliates, the Daughters of Hope and the Daughters of Samaria. In addition there was a host of independent local or regional, often ephemeral, orders, such as the Daughters of the West and Zeribabel's Commandery. Most of these established themselves after 1865 and had only small memberships.[44]

In the immediate post-bellum decades the Masons were the most successful and well established of the orders in Ohio. Their numbers grew considerably, from 720 members in 30 lodges in 1870, to 2,615

[41] Harry E. Davis, *A History of Free Masonry Among Negroes in America* (n.p., 1946); Charles H. Brooks, *A History and Manual of the Grand United Order of Odd Fellows in America* (Philadelphia, 1902); W. E. B. Du Bois, *Economic Cooperation among Negro Americans* (Atlanta, 1907), pp. 110–126.

[42] Cleveland *Gazette*, Dec. 13, 1884, Feb. 11, Mar. 18, 1893.

[43] Charles Wesley, *The History of the Prince Hall Grand Lodge of Free and Accepted Masons of the State of Ohio, 1849–1960; An Epoch in American Fraternalism* (Wilberforce, 1961), pp. 28–49; Cincinnati *Colored Citizen*, May 19, 1866.

[44] Arnett, ed., *Proceedings of the Semi-Centenary*, pp. 117–127; Cincinnati *Colored Citizen*, Jan. 18, 1868.

members in 60 lodges by 1887. The order derived its status as much from its social basis within the black community as from its early start and its roots in an ancient tradition. Ohio's early Masonic lodges (those founded before 1880) drew most of their membership from the established upper class of artisans, teachers, shopkeepers, service entrepreneurs, and higher-level service workers, many of whom had been in the state for many years. "The early rosters of our lodges here," said the historian of black Masonry at Cleveland, "show that they comprised most of the founders of our old families." [45] Similarly, at Columbus, Cincinnati, Xenia, Toledo, and other places which had early lodges of large size, prominent individuals played active roles in the creation and development of lodge life. Particularly visible were a large number of school teachers such as Peter Clark, William Parham, Samuel Clark, and Lewis Easton, all of Cincinnati, William Lucan of Cadiz, and James and Augustus Guy, members of a prominent southern Ohio family originating near Zanesville. All of these men were high officers in Grand Lodges during the post-bellum period.[46]

Middle-class blacks also belonged to the Masons and other orders. Though the upper class continued to provide leadership in high lodge offices on the state and local levels, the representation of the middle class in the fraternal orders expanded considerably. This was especially evident in Ohio between 1880 and 1900 in the impressive growth of the newer national orders, the Knights of Pythias and the Odd Fellows. As the result of aggressive, innovative methods of recruiting among a broader segment of the black population, each order had over 2,000 members in 1897–98. Information on the Odd Fellows indicates that they were organized into 71 lodges. They had not only checked the Masons' growth, but had even cut sharply into their ranks: during the 1890s the number of Masons actually declined by more than half to slightly over 1,000. While the Masons had traditionally depended on their reputation, word of mouth, and contacts among friends to bring members into their ranks, the newer orders employed public re-

---

[45] *History, Constitution, and By-Laws of the Excelsior Lodge #11 Free and Accepted Masons* (Cleveland, 1926), quoted in William Muraskin, "Black Masons: The Role of Fraternal Orders in the Creation of a Middle Class Black Community" (Ph.D. dissertation, University of California, Berkeley, 1970), p. 36. Muraskin's study has appeared as *Middle Class Blacks in a White World: Prince Hall Masonry in America* (Berkeley, 1975).

[46] Wesley, *Prince Hall Grand Lodge*, pp. 38–42; Arnett, ed., *Proceedings of the Semi-Centenary*, pp. 127–128; Columbus *Ohio State Journal*, June 29, 1870; Xenia *Torchlight*, June 28, 1871; Cleveland *Leader*, Aug. 24, 1872; Cincinnati *Commercial*, Sept. 11, 1873; Columbus *Dispatch*, Aug. 17, 1876. City directories: Columbus, 1870, 1875, 1876; Xenia, 1870, 1871, 1872; Cleveland, 1872; Cincinnati, 1873, 1874, 1875, 1876.

lations techniques, such as seeking out publicity in the black press and boasting in print of their accomplishments in providing benefits and an active recreational life. The Masons had always avoided such practices, perhaps as much because they believed them beneath their dignity as because there had been no need for them. Moreover, the newer orders had discovered unique ways of incorporating more middling social types. For example, during the late 1890s the Columbus Knights of Pythias affiliated a lodge which had been organized within an all-black local of the Hod Carriers' Union.[47]

Though the lodges provided both middle- and upper-class persons with the same social, economic, and recreational benefits, they were particularly important to the middle class. Fraternal life was but one segment of the active associational life of the upper class, and the small insurance benefits were of less importance to the more affluent. In contrast, the lodges were vital, along with the churches, in providing the respectability and wholesome association which the middle class hungered for; the insurance features were highly regarded by this economically marginal, security-conscious group. Thus, in a period in which the middle class was attaining greater self-consciousness, fraternal life helped it to consolidate its distinctive position.

The male lodges and their sororal affiliates had traditionally been deeply concerned with upholding bourgeois values and lifestyles— "Our organization is a moral normal school," said Benjamin Arnett of the Odd Fellows. They therefore offered both models and incentives for the patterning of life which, though isolating the poor, aided the middle class in its gradual social differentiation. All orders insisted that candidates for membership be recommended by a member in good standing, and those who could not meet standards of sobriety, sexual fidelity, honesty, industriousness, and dedication to family were rejected. The orders were especially sensitive to any scandal or irregular behavior which might tarnish their good names and the reputations of their members. When a member of Cleveland's first and most prestigious Eureka Masonic Lodge witnessed the near takeover of a lodge fund-raising excursion and public picnic by persons whom he described as "followers of Bacchus" and "lewd and unchaste women," he wrote Masonic brother George Myers to express outrage. "The very

[47] Wesley, *Prince Hall Grand Lodge* pp. 80, 101; Dabney, *Cincinnati's Colored Citizens,* pp. 415–418; Davis, *Black Americans in Cleveland,* pp. 74, 212–213; Benjamin Arnett, *Biennial Oration before the Second B[iennial] M[ovable] C[ommittee] of the Grand United Order of Odd Fellows* (Dayton, 1884), p. 19; Cleveland *Gazette,* Nov. 15, 1884, Jan. 26, 1889, Aug. 22, 1891, June 30, 1894, May 8, 1897, Aug. 13, Nov. 12, 1898, July 1, 1899, May 12, 1900; Columbus *Standard,* July 27, 1901.

words 'the Masons,' " he wrote, "are and always should be synonymous with decency, order, and regularity. We cannot [go] too far in prohibiting the use of our name from a repetition of such scenes as were enacted under the auspices of this lodge." He emphasized in closing the need to keep the matter from reaching the press and falling among gossips, suggesting further that it go immediately to the lodge's committee on jurisprudence for full review.[48]

Not all benefits of membership were tied to what the lodges did not allow members to do, for the lodges made numerous tangible contributions to racial and individual life. While state and local offices tended to be held by the upper class, local lodge autonomy allowed for much self-government. This increased the opportunity, denied many in daily life, for average middle-class members to learn leadership skills and to share local power with upper-class brethren. In 1887 fully 1,095 of a total of 2,615 Masons had been officers in local lodges.[49] Furthermore, the good fellowship of the lodge hall and its calendar of inexpensive social events created a world of respectable recreation, the occasional intrusion of Bacchus notwithstanding. Such events were important to the middle class, which did not enjoy (and could not afford) the full round of social activities which characterized upper-class life. Also, the quasi-religious rituals of the orders, the regalia and pomp of their ceremonies, and their humanistic cosmologies allowed for a feeling of dignity and spiritual unity which the objective circumstances of those struggling to stay one step ahead of poverty and degradation might rarely provide.

But for the ambitious of all classes and for the politically powerful and socially prominent, fraternalism was more than a series of compensatory strivings. The lodges served as a setting in which the ambitious might make contact with the powerful. The latter, in turn, saw in the lodges an opportunity to consolidate their leadership; they could make alliances with other powerful individuals and build a constituency of loyal followers from among the rank and file. Thus, fraternal connections helped to maintain networks of influence within the black community, and they provided a basis for sympathetic understanding, cooperation, and trust among black politicians. Many of Ohio's leading black politicians of the era—men like Parham, Myers, Clark, and Brown—were Masons and often affiliated with other orders as well. It

[48] Arnett, *Biennial Oration*, pp. 14–15; Muraskin, "Black Masons," pp. 26–30; Cleveland *Gazette*, Nov. 15, 1884; Alex ? to George Myers, enclosed in Jere Brown to George Myers, July 22, 1893, Box I, folder 3, George A. Myers Papers, OHS.

[49] Benjamin Arnett, ed., *The Centennial Jubilee of Freedom at Columbus, Ohio* (Xenia, 1888), p. 78.

is to be expected, therefore, that ambitious young men like Cottrill (Masons and Odd Fellows) and Fillmore (Masons, Odd Fellows, and Knights of Pythias) belonged to several orders so that they could get to know many of these powerful men, who might help them to obtain patronage posts or admit them to their political circles. Then, too, the lodges provided these young men with one basis for forming their own constituency.[50]

The insurance program was the most compelling practical benefit of fraternal affiliation for those who were neither affluent nor ambitious for social or political prominence. It was illustrative of a heightened concern for both planning for the future and family stability. All major orders provided money for funerals and regular, systematized relief for widows and orphans. The benefits were not large. The Masons, for example, provided $45 per funeral in 1887, a not insubstantial sum, but in that year they were paying only $19.68 to each widow and $13.15 to each sick member per year.[51]

Low benefits were as much the result of the manner of funding as they were of the members' poverty. With the exception of the Pythians, the orders operating in Ohio failed to implement centralized insurance schemes supervised at the Grand Lodge level. Nor were any of the lodges in Ohio connected with the few national lodge insurance schemes which then existed. Though in the 1870s the Masons had talked of implementing a state insurance scheme perfected at the national level, neither program appears to have gotten off the ground. The result was that the Masons, like most other orders, left the matter solely up to the local lodges. Even there, however, the procedure involved something less than the calculating, businesslike methods of the insurance industry. Usually each member made a regular yearly contribution, either fixed or based on what he could pay, for the relief of widows and orphans; he also gave a set sum for the funerals of lodge members.[52]

The strain upon the local lodges was exacerbated by their small memberships. At the turn of the century the Odd Fellows averaged twenty-one members per lodge, while the Masons averaged about sixteen. As was the case among the churches, lodge size was often a function of distance and location. Many of the Masonic lodges war-

[50] Cleveland *Gazette*, May 22, 1886, June 16, 1888, Jan. 16, 1892, Dec. 10, 1892, Dec. 16, 1893, Feb. 1, 1896; Baltimore *Afro-American Ledger*, Oct. 13, 1906.

[51] Arnett, ed., *Centennial Jubilee*, p. 78.

[52] Jere Brown to George Myers, July 20, 1893, Box I, folder 3, Myers Papers; Muraskin, "Black Masons," pp. 133–134; Cleveland *Gazette*, June 30, 1894, Aug. 13, Nov. 12, 1898.

ranted after 1870 were located in isolated towns and villages where black populations were small, and there were no other lodges for miles around. Yet proliferation of lodges within individual communities, especially the cities, was also apparent—partly due to distance, but also the result in the more socially complex, large urban communities of the desire of small subgroups, sharing common employment, interests, and friendships, for a measure of self-determination. At Columbus at the turn of the century there were twenty-two lodges—four of Masons, eleven of Pythians, two of Odd Fellows, and five scattered among the smaller orders. At Cleveland there were then thirteen lodges—seven of Masons, two apiece of Odd Fellows and Pythians, and one each of Good Samaritans and True Reformers. Springfield's lodges, for which we have data on the size of membership, averaged forty-nine members per lodge among nine Masonic and five Pythian lodges; eight were smaller than average, while six were considerably larger.[53] The situation was complicated by tendencies toward multiple membership. "If you can find a colored man who does not belong to from one to ten secret societies, we should like to look him in the face," said the Cleveland *Journal*[54] of a situation which became increasingly common as the orders established themselves in the state. As they sought to get the best from each national order, widen their circle of friends and contacts, and increase their opportunities for recreation and entertainment, some people belonged to several local lodges. One result was that money was spread in small sums around many lodges when it could have been more effectively concentrated in larger sums in one.

A variety of responses checked attempts to begin serious efforts in the direction of more rationalized and effective benefit programs. Some members simply could not or did not wish to pay more for the sake of larger benefits. Others argued that while centralized procedures administered from a distant office would bring together money in a large common pool and insure larger benefits, such procedures would at the same time remove the ethos of mutual aid among comrades so important to lodge life, at the same time encouraging apathy in local lodges while subverting local lodge autonomy. Finally, though some argued that larger benefits would help in the competition for members, there were those (particularly among the proud Masons) who rejected tailoring their activities in the name of drawing members, feeling that such competition was degrading.[55]

[53] Wesley, *Prince Hall Grand Lodge*, p. 115; Cleveland *Gazette*, Aug. 13, 1898; Columbus *Standard*, July 27, 1901; Cleveland *Plain Dealer*, May 18, 1902; Prince, ed., *Centennial Celebration of Springfield*, pp. 213, 215.

[54] Cleveland *Journal*, Jan. 23, 1909.

[55] Wesley, *Prince Hall Grand Lodge*, pp. 124, 129; Muraskin, "Black Masons," pp. 127–134; William H. Rogers, ed., *Senator John P. Green and Sketches of*

While the pattern of lodge development retarded the growth of effective benefit programs, it also drained the lodges of their entertainment and operating funds. Each small lodge spent money for the purchase or rental of meeting halls, entertainments, and all of the relevant accouterments of affiliation. There was no public discussion of the possibility that the consolidation of local lodges within the individual orders, or the building of a common lodge-temple to be shared among lodges and perhaps among the orders themselves, would be practical; the desire to maintain the intimate community of the individual lodge, with all its substantial emotional benefits, was too great. Nor did Ohio's lodges or orders move toward entrepreneurial schemes to finance their activities and accumulate capital. A very few large, prosperous urban lodges bought property, and in the 1890s a Columbus Odd Fellows Lodge, said to be composed of the "best educated colored businessmen of the city," decided to erect a meeting hall for themselves which would also contain office space, stores, and an auditorium available for rent to the community.[56] But such self-promoting business activities were expensive, and few local lodges could afford to make such investments, let alone to gather the $15,000 in capital which had been raised by the Columbus lodge in order to launch themselves into business. Under the circumstances, the lodges and orders could not afford to consider extending the scope of their activities to encompass the welfare needs of their members, or the race generally; thus no lodge or order attempted, for example, to establish homes for the aged or for orphans.[57] Like the churches, the lodges had developed in patterns which offered benefits to their members but made service to the racial community difficult.

III

While the nationally affiliated lodges and churches proliferated, few indigenous racial institutions arose through local initiative in response to specific local needs. There were few rescue missions catering to the black impoverished, homeless, and despairing. Those that did exist (such as the one at Lockland, an industrial suburb of

Other Prominent Men of Ohio (Cleveland, 1893), p. 106; Cleveland *Gazette,* Aug. 13, 1898.

[56] Cleveland *Gazette,* Feb. 20, 1892; Minor, "Negroes in Columbus," p. 207; Dabney, *Cincinnati's Colored Citizens,* pp. 415–416.

[57] Only the Odd Fellows appear to have gotten as far as discussing the matter of building such a facility—this one for their indigent brethren—but the idea was dropped because of an inability to gather the funds. Cleveland *Gazette,* Aug. 13, 1898.

Cincinnati where some five hundred blacks lived at the turn of the century) were directed by white churches and philanthropic groups which were aided by interested individual blacks.[58] Despite the observation at Columbus that the temptations of the street might prove too great for a number of young people, with the exception of the organization of the black YMCAs at Springfield and Dayton and a black YWCA at Dayton, no settlement houses or neighborhood centers arose among urban blacks during the late nineteenth century. Even the Y's at Springfield and Dayton were more like reading and debating societies than recreational centers, and they were most likely to attract upper-class youth.[59]

Some interest was taken in developing institutions for the care of black dependents. There was a movement toward the creation of old people's homes in the three major cities. The needs of the aged were particularly compelling, for the private Protestant homes controlled by whites were sometimes closed to blacks or were too expensive or too crowded to take them in, leaving the ill-suited county infirmaries to house homeless and incapacitated old people. Columbus blacks had begun to take an interest in opening such a home in the late 1880s; their fund drive went on for years, but by 1900 they had still failed to collect enough money.[60] Clevelanders were more successful. After an impressive fund-raising campaign was initiated by several upper-class women in the early 1890s, a small home was opened in 1897.[61] At Cincinnati two homes appeared. One opened in 1888 as the direct result of the gift from a white benefactor of a suburban College Hill estate for use as a home for aged men; the other, a small home for aged women, opened in 1897 after a six-year fund drive by a number of local black women.[62] In addition to its old people's homes, the Cincinnati black community continued to maintain the Colored Orphan Asylum, another gift of white philanthropy, under the direction of a black Board of Trustees composed of prominent upper-class leaders like Peter Clark and George Hayes. During its first half-century the home had been too small to accommodate more than a few children, but it was given the opportunity to expand its services considerably during 1896 as a result of the gift of a large new building donated by the Emerys, a charitable white family.[63]

[58] Ibid., Sept. 3, 1898.
[59] Ibid., Apr. 28, 1893, July 20, 1895, Jan. 18, 1896; Gerda Lerner, ed., *Black Women in White America: A Documentary History* (New York, 1973), p. 478.
[60] Columbus *Press*, Sept. 23, 1903.
[61] Cleveland *Gazette*, Mar. 27, May 22, Aug. 14, Sept. 11, 1897.
[62] Dabney, *Cincinnati's Colored Citizens*, pp. 95–96, 396.
[63] Ibid., pp. 238–239, 357; Cleveland *Gazette*, Nov. 30, 1895, Jan. 18, 1896.

Among upper-class leaders such efforts to create and maintain a network of racial institutions outside the traditional church-lodge sphere were exceptional. They were more likely to be found at Cincinnati, where the racial climate fostered separateness, and where there was a unique history of black institutional development dating back to the ante-bellum period. Just as upper-class leadership showed little interest in broadening the concerns of the churches and lodges or of its women's clubs and social circles, which were dedicated largely to genteel home entertainments and literary discussion, it showed little interest in developing new racial institutions and in initiating and maintaining innovative, group-oriented self-help programs for racial advancement. It was not that black leaders were uninterested in the uplift of their people. Rather, group-oriented self-help tended to imply a delay in pursuing the new era's most important possibility: a chance to obtain the means by which they might win permanent and imminent integration within a color-blind American society.

7

Pathways to Racial and Individual Advancement: Racial Leadership and Priorities

Between 1830 and 1860 northern black leaders had shifted their views on strategies for racial advancement. Buoyed with hope by the rise of militant antislavery and racial liberalism among whites, they had at first emphasized essentially integrationist goals for northern black advancement, stressing cooperation with whites in racially mixed forums, the destruction of segregation, and the pursuit of civil and political equality. But by the end of the ante-bellum period black leaders had begun to turn inward, increasingly emphasizing goals which furthered racial solidarity, self-help, and pride. This gradual transition was seen most dramatically in the growing support for emigration and colonization during the 1850s. It was the product of deepening feelings of hopelessness about the race's future. Blacks lacked tangible gains in the struggle for emancipation in the South and equality in the North; in fact, in the Fugitive Slave Law and the Dred Scott decision, they actually saw slavery grow more secure and their own position as free men grow more vulnerable. In addition, they despaired at the extent to which the power of the slaveholders, their northern allies, and all foes of racial justice remained entrenched in government and society. In 1860 there was little reason to believe that blacks would ever find their way into the American mainstream, and many had come to believe that the race must seek its own salvation through its own resources.[1]

Within a few years, however, there were new bases for optimism. Thus the pendulum of racial thought now shifted back in the direction of integration, a goal appropriate to a time of expanding black citizen-

[1] Howard H. Bell, "A Survey of the Negro Convention Movement, 1830–1861" (Ph.D. dissertation, Northwestern University, 1953).

ship. Concern for racial solidarity, pride, and self-help did not disappear entirely during the new era, for as long as racial prejudice and discrimination remained daily facts of life, there would be racial spokesmen who felt to one degree or another the need for a protective racial community based on varying combinations of black pride and intraracial cooperation. Yet such ambivalence, even among those in whom it was most pronounced, could not mask a growing desire to grasp at new opportunities for integration and social acceptance. The trend of race relations was progressive; consequently, the dominant ideological thrust among black leaders was a belief in the possibility of a relatively imminent, final entrance into the American mainstream. The dominant practical quest among them was the fashioning of racial priorities fitted to the achievement of that end.

I

On the evening of April 1, 1870, William Parham rose to address a meeting of Cincinnati blacks. The group had assembled for two related purposes: discussing plans for the celebration of the final ratification of the Fifteenth Amendment, and debating the issues before Cincinnati voters in the upcoming municipal election, the first held since the enfranchising amendment became the law of the land. The Cincinnati *Commercial* reported the next day that the hall "was filled with colored people, including the most intelligent of that class in the city . . . and . . . a crowd of the more ignorant of the new fledged citizens of color." Rising to the podium, Parham began his address, which was intended to offer suggestions for the new voters as they sorted out issues and candidates. "My fellow citizens," Parham began —and then he suddenly paused. Regaining his composure, he explained, "You know I have not gotten used to calling you fellow citizens yet; it ["citizen"] is a new kind of word to us. I guess I will try the new word, fellow citizens, just to see how it stands." It stood well. The business of the meeting continued, to the delight and interest of an enthusiastic audience.

Perhaps for that second Parham had been distracted by a sudden recognition of the rapid, dramatic, and comprehensive changes in the race's status. Black leaders like Parham felt joy, wonderment, and a deep sense of renewed hope; these feelings were matched only by their sense of the great challenges and dangers which the new era presented blacks as they attempted to define their citizenship and struggle for equality. They realized that many whites doubted the race's capacity for citizenship and moral commitment. Despite the black man's proven loyalty to the Union and his sacrifices on the nation's battlefields in all its major wars, said the Reverend S. D. Fox at an 1865 Emancipation Day celebration at Clermont County, "We are now looked down upon . . . and excite only the pity of whites."[2] Racial leaders also knew that many Americans were bitter over the racial consequences of the Civil War and Reconstruction. Warning of the dangers posed by unreconstructed Southerners and their northern allies in the Democratic party, the Reverend James Poindexter told a Columbus black audience in 1869, "However apparent and auspicious the result of the Emancipation Proclamation and the abolition of slavery, we cannot shut our eyes to the fact that there are those who feel uncomfortable about it. They and their friends lost heavily by it, and they curse the name of Mr. Lincoln, and would blot his acts and the days on which they occurred from the calendar."[3] For some, their own respect for the memory of Lincoln and their faith in his party were tempered by the knowledge that emancipation and enfranchisement were not, in the words of Peter Clark in 1873, ". . . done from any original impulse to benefit us. They were merely steps needed to carry out the central purpose of the Republican party: the preservation of the Union." "I am sorry," Clark stated, "that the motive which prompted the gift of freedom had not more kindly feeling toward the negro in it. . . ."[4]

In coming to terms with these challenges and dangers, blacks were armed with what many of them regarded as the ultimate civil equalizer. The ballot, said Poindexter in 1870, "lifts the colored man and sets him on his feet and gives him for the first time a fair start in the race of life."[5] The vote was seen as the means by which they might consolidate and build upon the gains of the 1860s. "We must see to it," said the call of a black state convention in 1871, "that every vote we cast repeats the story: that no man by any vote of ours can be elected to make and administer the laws who will not hold the scale of justice with an even hand and dispense equal rights to all, without reference to color." Black voters must be organized "so that their votes shall be available for securing and maintaining for ourselves and our children the legitimate benefits resulting from our newly acquired rights under the Constitution. . . ."[6] On the question of how blacks shall vote, most members doubtless found it inconceivable that the day would ever come when they could in good faith vote regularly, if at all, for

[2] Cincinnati *Gazette*, Aug. 9, 1865.
[3] Columbus *Ohio State Journal*, Sept. 23, 1869.
[4] Cincinnati *Commercial*, Aug. 23, 1873.
[5] Columbus *Ohio State Journal*, Jan. 13, 1870.
[6] Ibid., Jan. 7, 1871.

the Democracy. Nevertheless, the convention resolved to guard an independent spirit, maintaining that blacks must "inform themselves and then canvass men and measures, supporting in every case the great principles on which their own and their country's interest and liberty depend." [7]

While the vote was seen as the most potent weapon for pursuit of racial interest, supplementing it in the minds of the delegates was a knowledge of and willingness to employ the law so that blacks might win in the courtroom that which was withheld in daily political and social affairs. Delegates to the 1871 convention regarded the use of law as important enough that they resolved to encourage legal studies among young men; in the event that interested and qualified blacks found law schools closed to them, they planned to discuss the possibility of founding a black law school in Ohio. [8] Based on the same deeply felt need for lawyers and legal knowledge was the creation of a small law department at Wilberforce University in the early 1870s. [9]

Thus, though the times brought solid achievements and rapid gains, racial spokesmen continued to be disturbed by the presence of racial oppression; they refused to relax their vigilance and to cease agitation for equality and a fuller citizenship. This refusal made even the race's firmest white allies uncomfortable, for whatever their feelings about racial and governmental action that might be needed to reconstruct the South and rid it of the influence of rebellion, they tended to view enfranchisement as ending the need for public debate and action of the racial question in Ohio. The staunchly Radical Republican Cleveland *Leader,* for example, expressed the opinion of many of the more tolerant white opinion leaders when it stated in 1873 that the soundest racial strategy for blacks in the post-enfranchisement era was "to await the gradual work of time in allaying prejudice against their race and raising them to an equal condition of education and intelligence." The blacks "have full rights now and their future is in their own hands." [10] Yet, though they fully realized the gap between white expectations and their own desires, the blacks knew that the struggle must not end. "In my youth," said Peter Clark in 1873, considering the appropriateness of continued agitation, "I was proud to sit at the feet of Frederick Douglass from whom I learned that it is never premature to demand justice." [11]

[7] Ibid., Jan. 19, 1871.
[8] Ibid., Jan. 19, 1871.
[9] Frederick A. McGinnis, *A History and Interpretation of Wilberforce University* (Blanchester, Ohio, 1941), pp. 47–49.
[10] Cleveland *Leader,* Aug. 28, 1873.
[11] Cincinnati *Commercial,* Sept. 23, 1873.

Yet while eager to pursue justice, black leaders did not ignore the need to come to terms with the legacy of poverty, ignorance, and lack of skills which limited the race's full participation in social and political affairs and made winning acceptance more difficult. What was needed, in the words of the Reverend S. D. Fox, was a racial "career of improvement." [12] Proceeding from the bourgeois values dominant within their class and American society, the upper-class black leadership of the late 1860s and early 1870s continually emphasized their brethren's obligation to assimilate and practice habits of economy, industry, and morality, and to seek education, all of which would arm them to compete successfully and ultimately, through their proven worthiness, to surmount the walls of prejudice. A typical statement emphasizing such obligations was that of a convention of Franklin County black leaders held at Columbus in 1869. Mixing God and Mammon with that peculiar lack of self-consciousness common to their white counterparts, the convention resolved that it was

> . . . alive to the truth that others may help lift us up and set us on our feet, but none can walk for us, and knowing that a large liberty brings corresponding duties and obligations, and yet more, that there are certain duties which no people can ignore and yet hope for success: such as love and fear of God, good business habits, industry, punctuality, sobriety, economy, and education, we urge our people to labor without ceasing for the acquisition of these virtues.[13]

Elsewhere, too, blacks were enjoined of the need to "purchase homes for our families, schools for our children, and churches for our people, and under God, possess ourselves of all the advantages of Christian civilization." [14] They were told to be "industrious; enter any pursuit; remain humble; be frugal; be honest; perform faithfully your duties to God and man, and no government will be able to resist your claims to all the rights and privileges of men." [15] The well-respected Poindexter urged them "to inculcate upon your children and let us cultivate ourselves habits of industry, economy, and sobriety. . . ." [16] And they were made aware of the "imperative necessity of acquiring property and educating our children." [17]

Such statements inspired the race to greater self-reliance, self-sacri-

---

[12] Cincinnati *Gazette,* Aug. 9, 1865.

[13] Columbus *Ohio State Journal,* Nov. 17, 1869.

[14] A.M.E. Church, Ohio Conference, *Minutes of the 35th Session* (Pittsburgh, 1865), p. 25.

[15] Cincinnati *Gazette,* Aug. 9, 1865.

[16] Columbus *Ohio State Journal,* Apr. 14, 1870.

[17] Cincinnati *Commercial,* Apr. 15, 1870.

fice, and practical struggle for material and moral improvement, while emphasizing that its efforts on its own behalf were as important as its insistence on changes in white attitudes and actions. However, noticeably missing from the statements of contemporary racial leaders and the resolutions of racial conventions were discussions of the ways in which mutual self-help among members of the race, inspired by racial pride and feelings of group solidarity, might be mobilized for this "career of improvement." During the 1860s and early 1870s, the formative years of racial strategy in the new era, the state and regional conventions of Ohio's black leadership concerned themselves at first with the struggle for the vote. Then, after January, 1870, and enfranchisement, they were concerned largely with the organization of the black vote and the question of the extent to which the race should attempt to stake out a politically independent position in state and local affairs; this issue remained largely symbolic as long as large segments of the Ohio Democracy remained unreconstructed. The coming of the vote also brought discussions of long-term racial goals. From these discussions emerged a concern for safeguarding the civil and legal advances of the last years, gaining open access to public accommodations and publicly supported institutions and asylums, impressing upon Republican leaders blacks' desire for a fair share of political patronage, and changing the Ohio school laws in order to obtain equal educational facilities.[18] These were to remain the chief objects of racial strategy for most of the late nineteenth century.

Absent were discussions of interracial cooperation in the economic realm, where it might be employed to provide some alternative to absolute dependence upon the few opportunities available in a white-controlled, white-dominated economy. Urging the race on to material improvement as a basis for sustained moral improvement and social advancement, and promising that moral improvement and education would be rewarded with increased opportunity, security, comfort, and social acceptance, black leadership in the early years of the post-bellum era implicitly established a racial strategy in which advancement was ultimately dependent on the good will and tolerance of whites—and thus as fragile as a house of cards. In truth, of course, as long as blacks had few material resources to fall back on, and as long as racism remained a potent force in American life and whites controlled capital, institutions, and sources of opportunity and advancement, there was

[18] Xenia *Sentinel,* Jan. 20, 1865; Cincinnati *Commercial,* Jan. 9, Feb. 23, 1867, Apr. 2, 1870, Aug. 23, 25, 26, 1873. Columbus *Ohio State Journal,* Feb. 13, 27, July 4, 1867, Oct. 20, Nov. 17, 1869, Jan. 19, 1871, Aug. 28, 1873; Xenia *Torchlight,* July 20, 1871, Sept. 10, 1873; Cleveland *Leader,* Mar. 14, 1872.

174 Black Ohio and the Color Line

little room in which racial strategy might maneuver. In establishing a program for racial advancement, a leap of faith was required.

That leap implied a triumph of the optimism born of the changes of the 1860s over a pessimism that might have resulted from the awareness of persistent white racism and of complex white motives in assenting to the ameliorative trend. But it was by no means a blind one for those who made it. At bottom, it reflected the strong commitment of Ohio's black leaders, reinforced by their personal experiences and achievements, to fundamental American ideals tailored to the race's needs in the context of its position in the American social system. Black leaders did not emphasize group solidarity and collective action in pursuit of uplift and advancement, because they believed that racial progress would come through the struggles of individual blacks. Persons of intelligence, refinement, and high morality who had proven themselves in the struggle for success and status would be accepted by a society valuing individual excellence.

Thus, while there were few, if any, public discussions of the deliberate organization of interracial unity and self-help, there was a decided emphasis on clearing the way for individual achievement. This approach was evident from the earliest years of the new era in the effort to define broad racial goals and to achieve civil and political equality. Black spokesmen insisted that their goal was not to obtain "social equality" for the black race *en masse;* for contemporaries, such equality implied the completely unfettered intermingling of the races in all contexts. Rather, as Poindexter maintained, the intent was to lift the black man up and set him on his feet as a citizen, hence giving him "for the first time a fair start in the race of life." The manner in which the race was then run, rather than the disabilities suffered by blacks at the starting gate, would now determine the fate of the individual. Denying that there ever was "such a state of society as social equality farther than persons chose to allow," M.P.H.J., writing in the Cincinnati *Colored Citizen* in 1863, gave voice to the spirit behind the black suffrage campaign of the late 1860s and the struggle for equality throughout the remainder of the century. He asked only that each be given the opportunity to realize an individual potential. "All we ask is give us our common and natural rights as men," he said, "and every other condition of the human family will find its own level." [19] It remained for Bishop Benjamin Arnett some years later to find the metaphor appropriate to an age that saw a fundamental relationship between material and moral improvement, which best characterized the society for which he and others were striving. It was one in which a

[19] Cincinnati *Colored Citizen*, Nov. 7, 1863.

man might be allowed to pass in his community for whatever value he represented in human currency. "If he is a dollar, he will pass for a dollar—he may be silver, paper, or gold, but still be a dollar," said Arnett before a mixed audience at Columbus in 1888. "What we want is that everyone stand on his merits or demerits. In the name of our sons and daughters, we say judge each individual of our race as is done in all other cases and to all other races." [20]

At the same time, black leaders believed deeply in the ultimate justness of the American socioeconomic order. While they were certainly aware of racial discrimination, they retained a faith in the ability of the American system to generate individual opportunity and success for anyone who worked hard and well. With the exception of Peter Clark, who was familiar with and sympathetic to Marxism and was briefly associated with the Socialist Labor party in the late 1870s, they were deeply and conventionally conservative in their views on political economy and greatly distrustful of radicalism. It was not an unthinking or opportunistic acceptance of American capitalism, but a positive ideological commitment. While campaigning for the state Republican ticket at Xenia in 1877, just months after violent struggles between railroad workers and their employers had paralyzed the nation's transportation system from Baltimore to St. Louis, George Washington Williams warned voters that the program of the Socialist Labor party, then fielding candidates for state office in Ohio, was "impractical, absurd, and dangerous in the extreme," interfering with "the natural laws of economy" and likely to produce "centralized despotism." Williams urged the cooperation of labor and capital, between whom he believed there to be no natural antagonism; however, his own commitment to classical economic theory and capitalism led him to the position that control over workers' wages must remain firmly in the hands of the employer, who, said Williams, "knows best what wages to grant . . . because he knows what the demand [for labor] is." [21]

This ideological conservatism was strengthened rather than weakened by perceptions of racial needs. Though himself a conservative in political and social affairs, Harry Smith was less concerned that radicalism would interfere with natural economic laws than that it would result in a wholesale assault upon the structure of law and order which helped to keep the forces of lawless racism in check. Smith's editorials

[20] Benjamin Arnett, ed., *The Centennial Jubilee of Freedom at Columbus, Ohio* (Xenia, 1888), pp. 12–13, 80.

[21] Cincinnati *Commercial*, Sept. 6, 1877; Herbert Gutman, "Peter Clark: Pioneer Negro Socialist, 1877," *Journal of Negro Education*, XXXIV (1965), 413–418.

on radicalism continually emphasized the need to preserve law and order. Commenting upon the hanging of the four anarchists charged with murdering policemen during Chicago's Haymarket riot, Smith asserted in 1887 that ". . . It seems to us like playing with a dangerous animal to allow even the demonstrations which took place on the day of the funeral. To do so was to give seeming countenance to the open display of all outer signs of rebellion against society. . . . It is time to put down the foot of American law, promptly and fearlessly, upon every effort, no matter how small, to rouse the people to revolution against it [the law]." [22] Smith's concern for law and order was made more acute by the rise in anti-black mob violence and lynching at the century's close. He ultimately emerged as a leading advocate for legislation to repress mob demonstrations of all types.[23]

Opposition to labor unions was fed as much by racial need as by ideology. Unions were not only an assault on conservative values but also, because of the frequency with which they adopted racially exclusionist policies, a threat to black opportunity. For many years George Myers kept a strictly, self-consciously nonunion shop; he had a deep distrust and dislike for labor unions, particularly the Journeymen Barbers International Union. While that union did its only organizing among Ohio blacks in a few small towns and among the minority of black barbers working in integrated shops, it was not overtly hostile to blacks. Yet Myers feared that the union's strong support for legislation establishing minimum licensing and sanitary standards for the trade in Ohio was nothing less than an effort to drive the black barber from the trade, and for years he led black efforts against union-supported bills.[24] Harry Smith's anti-unionism was more opportunistic than Myers's, but it grew as intense during the late nineteenth century. During the 1880s the Knights of Labor made gestures of friendship and solidarity to black workers; Smith then printed articles favorable to the Knights and urged black cooperation with them. After the Knights declined, however, he grew more and more hostile to unions, largely because of their exclusionist policies. While he had neither discouraged nor encouraged black strike-breaking before the 1890s, by 1892 his opinions were beginning to change. In that year, at the time of the strike against

[22] Cleveland *Gazette*, Nov. 26, 1887.
[23] See ch. 9, below.
[24] John A. Garraty, ed., *The Barber and the Historian: The Correspondence of George A. Myers and James Ford Rhodes, 1910–1923* (Columbus, 1956), p. xviii. On Myers's years of conflict with the barbers' union, see the series of letters: folder 1, Box XI (1902), folder 6, Box XII (1904), folder 1, Box XV (1910), folder 2, Box XIV (1913), folder 6, Box XVI (1915), George A. Myers Papers, OHS.

the Carnegie steelworks at Homestead, Pennsylvania, Smith attempted to discourage the use of black strike-breakers, but only on the grounds that nationwide sympathy for the strikers would do the race harm. Less than a year later, however, Smith noted with pleasure that black strike-breakers were being used increasingly at Homestead and other locations in place of "an ignorant and rough foreign element." The contemporary labor movement provided little incentive for Smith to change his views, and he continued in future years to be sympathetic to strike-breaking.[25]

On the other hand, Myers's friend and Smith's rival John Green was known as a friend of the labor movement, largely because he introduced a bill to establish an Ohio Labor Day in 1890. The nature of that friendship testified to the usual limits of the Ohio black leadership's sympathy with the workers' movement. Green's affection for labor sprang not from feelings of class solidarity or a vision of a new world, but from a belief in the worthiness of the sturdy, independent, upwardly mobile worker, armed (as Green himself had been as an aspiring but poor boy in the 1860s) with strong desires for wealth and respectability—the classic "man on the make." Green did not doubt that American society would recognize the merit of such men. In 1895, on his way home from an extended vacation in Europe, Green recalled an unlikely shipboard debate with the pioneer British socialist Keir Hardie. Green stated at that time that, while socialism might be necessary in aristocratic Europe, in the democratic United States "every man is in theory and law, at least, the equal of every other man; and may, if he will, aspire to any gift of the people." Doubtless his own political career seemed proof. He also drew similar conclusions about the openness of American society from his friendships with John D. Rockefeller and other prominent white men. Reflecting on these relationships, Green stated, "A colored person in the United States can make a place for himself in the hearts and homes of the foremost white citizens by modest, respectful, and honorable conduct in his daily walk of life." [26]

Though champions of individualism and individual mobility and achievement, Ohio's black leaders were not without ideas on how the separate striving of individual blacks might serve the race. Those like Bishop Payne felt the need to combine individual excellence with service in behalf of larger racial needs, generally for education and the assimilation of bourgeois values. They wished to systematize the work of fostering individual achievement by creating patterns of obligation

[25] Cleveland *Gazette*, Feb. 20, July 17, 1886, July 23, 1893, Apr. 28, 1894.
[26] John P. Green, *Fact Stranger Than Fiction: 75 Years of a Busy Life* (Cleveland, 1920), pp. 333–335, 337.

and cooperation within the black community. Speaking before congregants of Allen Temple in 1874, Payne chastised his fellow African Methodists for failing to actively support the education of highly motivated, intelligent young men and women. He felt this deeply, not only because individuals with talent and the desire to advance themselves were being deprived of opportunity, but also because their services were ultimately being lost to a race which badly needed them. The bishop was particularly concerned about wasting the talents of young women, whom he believed to be in need of community support if they were to embark upon suitable teaching careers. Payne stated, ". . . Whenever a young woman of talents and piety is found who has an aptness for teaching, and who is desirous to qualify herself thoroughly for such work, but has not the means to meet the expenses, this church ought to undertake to educate her." He was also concerned with the plight of aspiring young men; in line with his own religious commitments, Payne felt that they and the race would be best served if they obtained community support for entering the ministry.[27]

Yet opinions such as Payne's, which sought to emphasize racial service and solidarity while attempting to create the institutional supports to foster them, were decidedly in the minority. The fact that the bishop felt the need to criticize his co-religionists, and that they failed to take up his challenge, is only one indication of this. Based on the available evidence, the emphasis of most racial leaders was on individual struggle, achievement, and initiative and the ways in which the individual, largely by setting an example before both races, might influence the work of advancement. Bishop Arnett offered a commonly held view of individual racial obligation and service when he spoke of the daily efforts by which he felt individual blacks might help eradicate discrimination in public places. Noting that there were places in Ohio "where we cannot be accommodated as travelers," Arnett stated, "We will not stand and complain, but we will work to meet the demand of the day and time, and by our individual efforts use the weapons that most effectively destroy . . . [racial] distinction. As individuals, we will have to have daily conflicts, and if we gain 365 victories and good impressions by work and deed, that is the thing that will help us most in this battle." [28]

While daily individual efforts at the color line were important in influencing whites, the biographies of conventionally successful individual blacks were seen as very important sources of inspiration and

[27] Benjamin Arnett, ed., *Proceedings of the Semi-Centenary Celebration of the African Methodist Episcopal Church of Cincinnati* (Cincinnati, 1874), pp. 83–84.
[28] Arnett, ed., *Centennial Jubilee*, p. 80.

models for inculcating morality and values for blacks. Blacks had their equivalent of the contemporary Horatio Alger success stories, in which the worthy hero rises from poverty and obscurity to affluence and social prominence through a combination of virtue, talent, and luck; sketches of the lives of black politicians, professionals, and community leaders who exemplified this pattern appeared frequently in the contemporary black press and in pamphlets and books. These were, in the language of contemporaries, "representative men"—representative not in the sense of being numerically typical, but instead in typifying the very best in moral excellence, refinement, and practical worldly achievement.

Invariably these sketches emphasized the subject's commitment to the values of personal sacrifice, deferred gratification, self-reliance, hard work, education, religiosity, general self-improvement, and even personal hygiene, all of which were thought to aid individuals in their struggle for positions of respect and prominence, acknowledged occasionally by whites as well as blacks. Typical was a sketch of the life of Cleveland's Reverend Daniel Shaw,[29] born free but poor in Louisiana in 1857. Before his tenth birthday, the author notes of Shaw, ". . . his passion for books and learning was so strong that he tramped his way many a day through mud and rain and densest forests to the schoolhouse." Encouraged by his family, he came North when just fifteen in search of an education and, on the advice of a devoted teacher, went to Baldwin University at Berea near Cleveland. Shaw was admitted as a student, but the poor lad suffered many hardships in pursuit of learning: "Many a time his table was spread with *crackers* and *milk* only, while at other times a more simple fare satisfied his board." None of these hardships turned him from his pursuit of knowledge. He agreed to go without the luxuries and pleasures which the less provident around him sought: "He was never foppish, cared not for the fineries of dress . . . and was courageous enough to forego pleasures which might achieve the desires of the heart." Financing an education also required time-consuming, back-breaking labor for the impoverished boy: "Some days he rose at 4:00 AM and went out under the first grey dawn . . . and began his work, going many days without breakfast, because he so prized the opportunity to make money to help himself through school." He took every job, no matter how menial: "He sawed wood, put up trellis work for vines and flowers, painted, and oiled floors, sodded yards, kept up lawns, and in short was ready for any work." Of Shaw's struggle for an education, the author drew the

[29] Found in William H. Rogers, *Senator John P. Green and Sketches of Other Prominent Men of Ohio* (Cleveland, 1893), pp. 37–62.

following lessons: "Let no young man feel that he has only play before him when he goes out to make his way through the schools. For as we gather up the record of this young man, we catch sight of a tremendous struggle and a vast outlay of energy. . . . Let no young man say that he cannot get an education, for he may if he will." Of Shaw's progress from humble rural southern origins to a successful, widely admired and racially beneficial pulpit in a large, cosmopolitan city, it was said, "His culture finds equal recognition among his brethren in white." Here was proof, the author concluded, that for "the young colored man there is open a way to honor and usefulness if he has energy, ambition, and health, to which shall be added the Christ[ian] life."

At first glance, such tales appeared only to be the usual didactic celebrations of individual success. However, racial hagiography was also a potent source of racial pride and group solidarity in common struggle, perhaps the source of these group-oriented emotions which had the greatest resonance for Ohio's black leaders as they strove for personal accomplishment and racial equality. Suggesting an ambivalence among black leadership, which sought protective and compensatory benefits from the racial community while at the same time seeking to enter the wider, often still hostile American mainstream, the inspirational message of these sketches came not only from individual example, but also from the comment on the ability of blacks, when properly reinforced by appropriate values and adequate preparation by family, church, and school, to enter and succeed in the competitive struggle. Thus the sketches marshaled feelings of race pride and solidarity to serve the dominant goals of the time. Here pride and solidarity were oriented toward inspiring confidence, particularly in black youth, countering the negative images of the race which were transmitted daily to young blacks in a thousand different ways, and arming youngsters to fight the battle for acceptance and achievement.

Both this racial ambivalence and the instrumental use of feelings of pride and solidarity in struggle were particularly evident in the story of the black hero's struggle against white prejudice and indifference. While inspiration was to be derived from the success of blacks like Shaw, who obtained their goals while subscribing to the best moral and motivational standards, it was just as inspiring that they achieved their objectives even on the harsh terms set down for black advancement by the hostile white world. All along his path the hero encountered the gross devices, double standards, and petty insults typically employed by whites to gain advantage at the starting block in the "race" of life. Shortly after his father's death, young Shaw and his family were cheated out of the farm and homestead where they had lived and worked for years "by oppulent whites of the neighborhood." They were then forced to pay rent "as a stranger and alien would be required to do." No sooner had he arrived at Berea in search of an education than he discovered that it "was known as a town in which the Negro found no welcome." The town was, in fact, an aberration in the Western Reserve: since the Civil War, when Copperhead Democrats had chased out the few black families living there, blacks coming to live or to attend school in Berea had been told to go to nearby Oberlin. Shaw refused to do so: "He had come to attend school and there he would remain." Persecution began, but Shaw, as far as was consistent with dignity, replied in kind: "When fifty boys pelted him with snow balls and shouted vile epithets, he pelted fifty boys with rocks until they flew from the field of battle." Throughout his years in college he was "never known to sit calmly by under insult. . . . Although he was the only colored student at the University, he demanded fair and courteous treatment, and was ready to contend for it if it could not be won easily." Not all whites were tormentors ("As elsewhere, the objecting element was the riff-raff of society"), but most were either indifferent or desired to be shown the boy's qualities before befriending him. Shaw impressed more open-minded whites and intimidated the overtly hostile by excelling at sports and self-defense. "He made impossible catches. . . . He was the strongest and longest thrower, the fleetest runner and almost a perfect base-runner. . . . He was also so skilled in the art of self-defense that not many boys would put on gloves with him unless they made great restrictions as to where and how hard one should strike." He excelled in his studies, in the quasi-social literary societies, and finally, symbolic of his acceptance and ultimate victory over bigotry, in his role as a commencement speaker at his own graduation in 1883. By the time he was ready to leave Berea for graduate study at Boston University Theological Seminary, he had "won for himself a host of friends who may be named among the foremost citizens of the town." Thus had Shaw, beginning from a position of weakness and oppression shared with fellow blacks, conquered white society on its own exacting terms. In so doing, he contributed to its transformation.

For contemporaries, the principal importance of biographical sketches like Shaw's lay in the fact that they directly related the strivings of successful, highly motivated blacks to the most important goal of Ohio's black leaders—individual achievement and recognition within the American mainstream. But while they were for this reason considered key sources of confidence, inspiration, and pride, they were by no means the only source. Others, taken more from group than individual life and experience, were also accepted.

The most important of these was the study of racial history. Few would have disagreed with Peter Clark's contention that the race had deep roots in Western culture and American history. Said Clark in 1874, "The colored people of the United States are not exotic. Centuries of residence, centuries of toil, centuries of suffering have made us Americans. In language, in civilization, in fears, and in hopes we are Americans." [30] From such a recognition came a close identification with the American past and the democratic institutions of the nation; quickened by emancipation and the coming of civil and political equality, blacks felt a deep patriotism founded upon a belief in the continuing evolution of American society. Yet at the same time, there were those who recognize the race's unique origins in non-Western culture and its unique history in the New World; they felt that these, too, were worthy of study and were vital sources of pride and inspiration. Ohio's first black legislator, George Washington Williams, believed in the usefulness of the study of racial history. While practicing law, preaching, and doing newspaper and political work in the late 1870s, he began his monumental *History of the Negro Race in America*. He found reason for optimism about the race's future in its past; the historical record, he said, revealed that blacks possessed the qualities of "courage and endurance" which "fit a people for long existence and qualify them for highest civilization." Believing that blacks needed greater self-discipline and greater assimilation of conventional moral and motivational standards, he emphasized that the study of their history would "incite . . . greater effort in the struggle for citizenship and manhood." [31] Benjamin Arnett also found a source of pride and inspiration in the race's past. From the large personal collection of books, pamphlets, and memorials written by and about blacks which was housed at his library at Wilberforce, he compiled a ten-volume historical collection of Negro literature. [32]

While Harry Smith was also interested in racial history, he was concerned with finding proper self-descriptive terms for the race and with countering negative images of dark skin in order to bolster pride and confidence. In his *Gazette* he refused generally to use the popularly accepted terms "Negro" and "colored," and the much less accepted term "black." All, he felt, were "mongrel" terms foisted upon a defenseless people during slavery; at the very least, they were simply inaccurate as descriptions of physical characteristics and unrevealing of

30 Cincinnati *Commercial*, Jan. 9, 1867.

31 John Hope Franklin, "George Washington Williams, Historian," *Journal of Negro History*, XXXI (Jan., 1949), 64–65; George WashingtonWilliams, *Oration Delivered 4 July 1876 at Avondale, Ohio* (Cincinnati, 1876), pp. 28–29, 36.

32 William J. Simmons, *Men of Mark: Eminent, Progressive, and Rising* (Cleveland, 1887), pp. 627–628.

origin. He would employ "Negro" after the turn of the century as its usage became more popular, but throughout the period Smith preferred "Afro-American," taking great pride in his contention that he was one of its pioneer popularizers. He felt that "Afro-American" was superior in its prideful refusal to shrink from an association with Africa at a time when whites held it in low regard, and that it was more in line with the self-describing terms used by other American ethnic groups. He went further than simply to acknowledge origins in Africa, for the *Gazette* from time to time reported African political affairs.[33]

In addition, in an era when skin bleaches and hair straighteners challenged racial pride, Smith tried to resist the temptation to allow advertisements for such products to appear in the *Gazette*. The precarious financial condition of black journalism in the late nineteenth century made such a refusal difficult to sustain, however, and Smith (one suspects especially in hard times) was forced occasionally to include such advertising in his columns.[34] He showed greater constancy in his long struggle against blue-veinism and the exclusive Cleveland Social Circle; while he was still an upstart young editor in his early twenties, this battle pitted him against some of the city's most powerful, well-established black community leaders. Though at first the campaign was waged in the name of destroying all vestiges of color prejudice, black and white, and it was maintained that Negroes who drew the color line could hardly expect more considerate treatment from whites, the rhetoric of race pride also entered the conflict. Smith and his anti–blue vein correspondents in Cleveland, Cincinnati, Columbus, and elsewhere chided blue veins with suggestions that they used "anti-Curl," a hair straightener, and accused them of lacking both racial and personal pride.[35] Finally, in a particularly zealous moment, Smith stated that the race was beginning to realize that greater beauty and ability lay with the darker majority—a position which contradicted the thrust of previous statements, but helped to compensate for the widespread negative images of dark complexion and to bolster the confidence of darker Negroes. When informed in 1887 that the Social Circle was dying, Smith commented, "Yes, it will die, we're afraid, for 'yalla' [yellow] folks 'ain't' above par like they used to be *when* we were *more ignorant*. It's more fashionable and intelligent in this day and time to be highly tinted with the rich brown characteristic of sunny Africa's children. Blue-veins are below par." [36]

[33] E.g., Cleveland *Gazette*, Dec., 1884–Mar., 1885, passim (comments of Berlin African conference), Feb. 19, 1887, Nov. 12, 1889, Aug. 4, 11, 1900.

[34] E.g., ibid., Mar. 19, 1898.

[35] Ibid., June 27, Sept. 29, 1885, Mar. 13, Apr. 24, 1886.

[36] Ibid., Jan. 22, 1887.

While feelings of race pride and solidarity derived from such sources as racial history and a positive identification with Africa tended to run deep, black spokesmen were ambivalent as to their value and meaning. True, they were sources of inspiration and confidence. But at the same time, unlike biographical sketches, they related indirectly to their larger individualistic, integrationist goals. At the same time, an emphasis on group-oriented feelings might be self-defeating, giving the appearance of racial chauvinism, and thus widening the gap between blacks and American society.

The limitations of feelings of racial pride and group solidarity were revealed by an ambiguous attitude toward racial institutions, which in themselves were practical embodiments of these feelings. Few, if any, racial leaders would have agreed with such a sweeping statement as that of W. H. Davidson, a Columbus artisan who wrote the New York *Freeman* that the first step in preparing the race "to receive the blessing and exercise of American citizenship" required destruction of the specifically racial character of such institutions. "I would abolish colored schools, colored fairs, colored literary societies . . . and above all colored churches. I would erase 'A' from the A.M.E. Church [and] eliminate 'Colored' from Colored Baptist Church, thus removing their racial feature, and erect a broad catholic altar, around which all could worship, irrespective of race . . . and upon which would be laid the prejudices of past generations." [37] But those who disagreed with Davidson would have done so for a variety of reasons. Of course, there was an emotional attachment to institutions which in themselves embodied the struggles of a hard-pressed but resilient people for dignity and self-respect, offering them opportunities for employment, leadership, and a measure of self-determination. Many recognized that the church played a vital role in stimulating individual uplift through its moral teaching. To some extent, there was also a feeling that such institutions, particularly the church, embodied unique racial values and traits. Yet (and here lay the ambiguity) there was at the same time a feeling that the time was not right to consider such a radical step—not because of a great loyalty to racial institutions, but simply because white prejudice was too great. But what would be the fate of such institutions if white prejudice were to end? Would there be no bases on which to sustain loyalty to them? Or would the existing bases prove too weak to sustain loyalty?

This dilemma was particularly evident in the early 1870s, a time when there were discussions among some whites and blacks on the possibility of bringing the races together in what the Zanesville *Courier,* a participant in the discussions, called "the higher walks of religion."

[37] New York *Freeman,* Nov. 13, 1886.

In the midst of this dialogue, Peter Clark addressed the celebration of the fiftieth anniversary of the presence of African Methodism in Cincinnati on the subject of "The Developing Power of African Methodism." Clark spoke compellingly of the social and cultural importance of the church to the race. Born of a refusal to accept insult, it embodied "a manly self-respect, a confidence in the manhood of the race, [and] an opportunity to demonstrate more by deeds than words the ability of the colored man to plan, to lead, to execute." In addition, he found that African Methodism was better suited to the "ardent temperament which we inherit from our African ancestors" than white Methodism. Though they sprang from the same roots in eighteenth-century America, the whites had replaced "the warmth" of the original Methodist worship "with a decorous and formal mode of worship," while the black church had retained the original emotional quality of the faith. Blacks were "ill at ease in a church where the audience sits quietly in the pews, while a trained choir, aided by an organ, gives voice to its religious emotions. No man can tell the Father for us our hopes, our wants, our fears, no man or choir of men can replace for us the privilege of announcing by the loud shout, the resounding hallelujah, and the triumphant hymn, the stream of joy which fills us, when the blessing is felt pouring like a flood into the soul." Methodism, therefore, said Clark, "is adopted to our wants, and we have, therefore, taken it into our hearts and made it our own." [38]

Yet when discussing the desire of the white Methodists to begin a dialogue on the possibility of efforts "to draw the colored man into the bosom of the mother church," Clark did not dwell upon these cultural differences, which he had described with so much feeling. Rather, he stressed the racial disabilities which had driven the blacks from integrated Methodist worship and which would continue to keep them away: "The existence of the African Methodist Church is a protest against prejudice and an assertion of the equal humanity of the African race, and there is a necessity for it to continue until the prejudice is dead and that equality is acknowledged." [39] Though he failed to mention cultural differences which might have separated the races in worship and in values, a like-minded man was Zanesville's Dr. J. C. McSimpson, a well-respected practitioner of herbal medicine. He answered some local whites' talk of integrating worship with a bitter statement about the prejudice which he and other blacks had encountered at local white churches. "When we go to a white church or Sabbath school we are afraid to seat ourselves for fear we will be invited to take a back seat, or a side seat, or a front seat as your humble servant has been

[38] Arnett, ed., *Proceedings of the Semi-Centenary*, pp. 98–99.
[39] Ibid., p. 102.

many times." Yet the same whites would on occasion go to black churches, he charged, sit next to blacks (so close that the blacks "squeeze them hard enough to make them look like oil cakes"), and conduct themselves disrespectfully. This kind of Protestantism, Mc-Simpson concluded, would eventually lead thousands of blacks to Catholicism: "We are constantly invited into Catholic churches and schools where proscription is not known." [40]

As he and Clark rightly suggested, it was not likely that most blacks would find decent, respectful treatment in white churches. Yet both strongly implied a willingness under more tolerant conditions to consider leaving the racial church, demonstrating a feeling that black institutions were in a sense transitory. Clark, who would become a Unitarian within the next decade in his own quest for spiritual fulfillment, voiced the belief that "there may be some young people here who will live to see the day when the dissolution of the [A.M.E.] church will be a proper and wise thing." [41] While agreeing with the basic integrationist thrust of Clark's remarks, others would have found such a prediction inordinately optimistic. They may in fact have felt, along with Bishop Payne, that the churches should play larger roles in their communities, thus strengthening themselves by assuming greater responsibilities in the work of racial advancement. It is difficult to say to what extent black leadership had nagging doubts about the ultimate future of racial institutions—doubts growing out of their own identification with the dominant society and their desires for equality and acceptance. Since the actual opportunity for wholesale institutional integration was far from presenting itself, there was little reason for general discussion of the issue. Yet to the extent that others felt like Clark, questions might be raised as to whether or not their feelings of racial pride and solidarity, for all their powerful compensatory and inspirational value, were not (like their attitudes toward racial institutions, the living embodiments of those feelings) contingent on the extent to which they were rejected and abused by a hostile world. When considered along with their commitment to individual mobility and acceptance, such doubts checked the development of commitment to a broad, unifying racial nationalism as a basic element in racial strategy.

II

Given the bourgeois, individualistic premises of black leadership, it was not unexpected that its most intense post-bellum struggles

[40] Zanesville *Courier*, Sept. 13, 1873.
[41] Arnett, ed., *Proceedings of the Semi-Centenary*, p. 102.

—the efforts for a civil rights act safeguarding access to public facilities, and for quality public school education for black youngsters—were ones which approached the question of racial advancement from the standpoint of the individual's preparation for competition in society, and which worked to speed social acceptance in everyday affairs.

The struggle for equality in public accommodations intensified first. It was spurred by Senator Charles Sumner's introduction in 1870 of a bill to prohibit discrimination in a broad range of facilities and institutions licensed or incorporated by public authority; these included schools, juries, common carriers, hotels, restaurants, and places of amusement. Ohio black leaders who desired passage of the bill became increasingly impatient with the inaction of successive Republican-controlled Congresses between 1870 and the summer of 1872. Their discontent declined later in 1872, when Republicans adopted a platform which included a plank promising a civil rights law. But when the Sumner bill languished throughout 1873, despite large new Republican majorities, black leaders again became restless, and local and state race conventions began once more to discuss the matter at length. Few spokesmen emphasized school integration; perhaps they doubted that wholesale integration of the nation's schools could be accomplished in light of white sentiment against integrated education, and they may have been wary that too much talk about the sensitive subject would jeopardize local race relations. Instead, they dwelled on the compromise of egalitarianism which discrimination in public accommodations constituted. According to Poindexter, as long as blacks daily encountered discrimination "in dining rooms, parlors and staterooms of steamboats on our rivers . . . in first class cars on railroads . . . in hotels and admission to public amusements . . . our citizenship is a cheat." [42] Though he went further than most by including the schools in his discussions, Peter Clark highlighted what was for many the most important larger issue: the mobility of aspiring individuals. Dismissing social equality as a racial goal, Clark said, "We do not care about social mingling, but we demand the opportunity to make ourselves the social equal of any man in this land and derive whatever benefits we can from concerts, art galleries, theaters, and schools." [43] Others spoke simply and with emotion of the insults and inconveniences they had suffered and demanded passage of Sumner's bill.[44]

Yet while blacks desired civil rights legislation, they were at the same time sensitive to the backlash which might result from a sudden,

[42] Columbus *Ohio State Journal*, Aug. 5, 1873.
[43] Cincinnati *Commercial*, Sept. 23, 1873.
[44] Ibid., Aug. 23, 1873.

widespread assault on the color line. They were cautious when approaching the issue of discrimination in local communities, where jobs, alliances with influential whites, and even lives might be threatened by hasty and premature attempts to eradicate color lines. Such caution was particularly well illustrated at Columbus in November, 1873, when discrimination in public accommodations became a hotly debated issue. Precipitating the debate was an incident of discrimination and its bloody aftermath. A theater doorkeeper had refused to allow a young black man, Richard Porter, access to seats in the parquette section, for which he held tickets bought for him by a white friend. Porter assaulted and badly injured the hapless doorkeeper when he chanced upon him several days later; he narrowly escaped going to jail for this action.[45]

The well-publicized incident sent shock waves through the Columbus black community. Encouraged by the city's leading Republican newspaper, the *Ohio State Journal,* some blacks felt that the issue of discrimination in public accommodations should now be pressed further, and that an attack should be made on the restrictive seating policies of those Columbus theaters which continued to practice such discrimination. Yet the older, established leaders of the black community were hesitant. Poindexter, who was himself deeply involved in the struggle for passage of the Sumner bill, and his friends barber John Booker and shopkeeper J. S. Tyler, worried along with the Columbus *Dispatch* that pressing the issue too vigorously in the face of white opposition would only generate serious racial conflict. At a black meeting called to discuss the affair, which Poindexter and his allies attended only reluctantly, there were bitter debates. Porter and his friends, most of them young men, wanted to draft resolutions strongly denouncing segregation and the particular theater involved. Poindexter and his allies, however, wanted to select an investigation committee to talk with the theater owner in order to determine whether color was the cause of the refusal. After hours of heated debate their suggestion was adopted, and they were given control of the committee.[46]

Shortly after the meeting, just as the committee was beginning its investigation, the city council registered its approval of discrimination in theater seating policies. Prodded by the *Ohio State Journal,* a Republican councilman had introduced an amendment to an ordinance regulating the sale of theater tickets; the amendment would have opened all sections of theaters to anyone who could afford to sit in them. Several Republicans and all of the Democrats united to defeat

---

[45] Columbus *Dispatch,* Nov. 26, 1873.
[46] Ibid., Dec. 1, 2, 1873

the measure, but only by one vote. Expressing the conventional wisdom of the day, members of the majority stated that the proposal was an encroachment upon the personal leisure of white patrons and an interference with the right of businessmen to run their businesses as they chose. When interviewed by the committee of blacks, the theater owner pleaded his case along similar lines. While it was unimportant to him personally where his patrons sat, he said, his white patrons felt differently. He feared that they would stop patronizing his theater if he were forced to integrate all sections of the house.[47]

Having discovered the limits of white tolerance, the black committee's report urged a moderate approach to ending discrimination in public accommodations and institutions which reflected the tendency of men like Poindexter to support agitation only on particularly pressing matters in which immediate results were needed. While urging "a manly resistance at whatever cost to every encroachment upon their rights as citizens," the Columbus *Dispatch* reported, the committee sought to distinguish between two kinds of discrimination: that which inflicted "real injury" (such as inconveniences to the black traveler in public carriers, and denials of admittance to asylums for the aged, the infirm, and the destitute), and that which was less crucial to racial welfare. "It is unwise," said the committee's report, "to worry at an exclusion from amusements." Such matters, it was implied, would be best resolved on an individual basis as Arnett's "dollars" slowly differentiated themselves from "dimes." [48]

In 1875 a weakened version of Sumner's bill, most notably excluding a provision for school integration, finally passed successfully through Congress. The statements of black leaders on the likely uses of the new law reflected a similar line of thinking. Poindexter warned Columbus blacks "to be wise," not seeking "privileges which are of no practical value," but instead waging "a manly struggle for those rights and privileges which involve . . . real comfort, prosperity, and happiness." To Columbus whites, on the other hand, he promised that blacks would not use the law to force social equality; equal status would only come to those with "brains and culture" who had earned it.[49] At Cleveland, the *Leader* reported similar comments by John Green at a race meeting called to celebrate the passage of the law. Green maintained that blacks must make themselves worthy of their newly expanded rights by becoming equals in fact, rather than depending on the possibility that the law would gain access for them where they were not

[47] Ibid., Dec. 6, 16, 17, 1873.
[48] Ibid., Dec. 18, 19, 1873.
[49] Columbus *Ohio State Journal,* Feb. 25, Mar. 10, 1875.

wanted.[50] At Cincinnati, the *Commercial's* reporters talked with local racial spokesmen about the uses to which the law would be put. "Thinking men among the colored people state that they don't want to see any fuss in this city over the civil rights bill. Things are fair enough now they claim and only trouble all around will result." One of the blacks interviewed stated that there had already been sufficient progress outside the law for his sake: "I have never been refused at the Opera House. I go there and take my seat in the parquette and my daughter, who is as dark as I am, frequently attends matinee performances, sitting in the best seats." [51]

Desirous of legal protection of their rights to equal access to public accommodations, black leaders were willing, at the same time, to leave the progress of blacks to social acceptance to the slow and deliberate course of individual achievement and excellence. Their failure to press for the filing of lawsuits under the federal law during its eight-year existence showed this willingness. For them, much depended on the quality of individual preparation and the individual character. Thus they were led to an intense struggle for better education for their children, their most important struggle of the late nineteenth century.

III

After the Civil War, the black public schools, to which parents and racial leaders looked to prepare a new generation for racial service and individual excellence, were far from adequate and farther still from the equal of white schools. The greatest problem involved locations for schools. Relative to that of southern states, Ohio's black population was small; blacks remained largely rural until the 1880s, scattered in small numbers, compared to the whites who lived around them, in crossroads settlements, villages, and farm districts. This situation had been reinforced by the wartime migrations which brought large numbers of blacks to rural areas. Under such demographic circumstances, it was difficult to provide schools convenient to all black children, and the problem was occasionally exacerbated by the refusal of local white school officials even to consider the educational needs of blacks.

The matter posed serious difficulties both for local school boards and for the legislature, which, when conscientiously seeking to provide for black education, were caught between two equally unpopular alternatives: the creation of a large number of conveniently located but costly

50 Cleveland *Leader*, Mar. 24, 1875.
51 Cincinnati *Commercial*, Mar. 9, 1875.

schools for a small number of children, or school integration. The legislature attempted to work through and around the former. Legislation in 1864 sought to maximize the number of children brought into the black school system by lowering the requisite number of students needed to create a black school from thirty to twenty-one. In the event there were fewer than twenty, school officials could combine adjoining districts, thus bringing together enough blacks to establish a school.[52] The new law did not explicitly bar integration by local initiative (no Ohio school law had ever done so), but at the time of its passage there was no reason to believe this would be a widely considered alternative.

While the 1864 legislation did provide more schools, in the late 1860s over half of Ohio's school districts where blacks resided still lacked provisions for Negro education. Even where black schools were established, children often had to walk great distances to reach inconveniently located schools. In rural areas, under conditions created by joining together districts to form one large black school district, it was common for children to walk ten miles a day to and from school. In the cities the situation was not much different, though distances were not as great. Unlike large towns like Xenia, where blacks were concentrated in one neighborhood, city blacks were often scattered throughout many wards—a tendency which actually increased with the intracity migrations of higher status blacks. Centrally located urban schools were usually difficult to establish. As a result, in the cities and in many rural districts, where schools had been provided by existing legislation, many children were in effect denied educations because the distance to school was too great, or they were attending very irregularly, especially during inclement weather. Of those school-age blacks who lived outside black school districts, only a few were found in mixed schools; they were generally in districts where blacks lived in very small numbers, or, as in the Western Reserve, in districts where integration was esteemed for its own sake.[53] Locational factors, when combined with the chronic poverty and lack of motivation which kept many black children out of school, help to account for the fact that in 1870, when 77 percent of white school-age children were attending schools, only 52 percent of black children were likewise enrolled.[54]

Where black schools did exist, they were usually of low quality.

[52] Ohio, *Laws, 1864*, pp. 32–33.

[53] Leonard Erickson, "The Color Line in Ohio Public Schools, 1829–1890" (Ph.D. dissertation, Ohio State University, 1959), pp. 214–219, 224, 228, 239–240.

[54] Census Office, *Ninth Census of the United States . . . 1870* (Washington, 1872), I, 394–396.

While there was a post-war trend toward replacing the decrepit shacks and church back-rooms which had often served as schools, blacks sometimes received abandoned white schools and equipment, usually old and in poor condition.[55] Exacerbating the inadequate physical plant was a weak curriculum, a lack of attention to the educational needs of various age groups, a briefer school year, and a shortage of faculty. Black schools were generally ungraded facilities in which one or two teachers taught a relatively large number of pupils of all ages and degrees of academic progress; students received, on the average, one month per year less instruction than their white peers. High school instruction was absent everywhere except at Cincinnati before 1870, and those black students seeking advanced education were forced, if they could afford the cost, to make private arrangements for instruction.[56] Those who could not no doubt shared Reverdy Ransom's experience at Cambridge. As a young man he wanted to go beyond elementary school, but he lacked the money to make special arrangements for his education, and he was refused admission to the regular high school. So he remained in elementary school, "covering the same ground year after year," occasionally glimpsing the high school texts of white friends and receiving lessons in various subjects from interested individuals.[57] Even at Cincinnati, where skilled black administrators, black school directors, and a generally cooperative board of education made serious efforts to provide conveniently located, quality school buildings and a curriculum equal to that of white schools, the black schools were not wholly adequate. Though by the early 1870s there were three black elementary schools and a high school, with values per building up to $35,000, the schools were overcrowded and understaffed. Twenty teachers taught over 1,000 students. In addition, with only one black high school, black students often went miles to attend classes, passing white high schools on their way.[58]

The weaknesses of Ohio's black schools and the dearth of educational opportunity for blacks were placed in sharp relief after 1865, when immense changes of black civil and political status created new expectations for quality education. Reflecting the population geography of Ohio's blacks, concern for educational inequality among both whites and blacks focused first on the rural areas. The black, suffrage-

[55] Erickson, "Color Line in Ohio Public Schools," pp. 238–239.

[56] Ibid., pp. 235, 246–247.

[57] Reverdy Ransom, *The Pilgrimage of Harriet Ransom's Son* (Nashville, n.d.), pp. 22–23.

[58] Arnett, ed., *Proceedings of the Semi-Centenary*, pp. 65–68; Cincinnati *Commercial*, Sept. 23, 1873; Columbus *Ohio State Journal*, Feb. 11, 1878; Cincinnati *Colored Citizen*, May 19, 1866.

oriented Ohio Equal Rights League attempted in the 1860s to gain legislation providing for the establishment of black schools in any district where there were black children. Though these efforts failed,[59] in some localities changes were occurring. Prompted by a rapid growth of black population after the war, officials at Brown and Highland counties (in the southwest) began to establish schools.[60] At the same time there were a few localities (such as Berlin in Jackson County in the south-central region) where blacks took an interest in establishing their own private schools when officials refused to act.[61] Yet even where there were schools, the problem of distance often remained unresolved. Because they proved inaccessible to some children, the new schools which had been created to meet the educational needs occasioned by black population increase actually exacerbated tension between blacks and school officials. Problems of location led to agitation for the integration of black children in more conveniently located white schools by several black parents in two rural Franklin County townships in the early 1870s; one case eventually resulted in an unsuccessful lawsuit to compel integration.[62] Though conditions varied around the state, the problem of distance was not resolved in most rural areas until the passage of the school desegregation law in 1887, and it continued to cause periodic complaints and lawsuits by parents.[63]

Increasingly, however, black protests centered in the cities and the large towns, where greater concentrations of blacks made protest easier to organize. Moreover, in the large cities, population trends were plac-

[59] Ohio Equal Rights League, *Proceedings of a Convention of the Colored Men of Ohio* (Cincinnati, 1865), p. 151; Cincinnati *Commercial,* Jan. 11, 1867.

[60] Frederick A. McGinnis, *The Education of Negroes in Ohio* (Blanchester, Ohio, 1962), pp. 46–48.

[61] Columbus *Ohio State Journal,* Sept. 25, 1869.

[62] Erickson, "Color Line in Ohio Public Schools," p. 241; Xenia *Torchlight,* Nov. 29, 1871. The suit attracted attention because the plaintiff alleged that his children, kept from the local black school by the long distance they would have to walk to attend, were being denied rights guaranteed under the Fourteenth Amendment. But courts, all the way up to the state supreme court, contended that school officials had the right to classify students by race and thus to exclude blacks from white schools. State of Ohio ex rel William Garnes v. John McCann et al., 21 Ohio State Reports 198 (1871), 198–212.

[63] Erickson, "Color Line in Ohio Public Schools," pp. 239–245; Cincinnati *Enquirer,* Apr. 29, 1881; Cleveland *Gazette,* June 7, 1884. In 1881 a black parent at Washington Township, Clermont County, sued school trustees and a teacher for refusing to admit his son to the regular public school which was more convenient to him. He was awarded damages of $50 in federal district court at Cincinnati on the basis of the judge's contention that the boy was refused admission solely on the basis of race. This is the only case involving the question of distance and location which appears to have been won in a court. United States v. Buntin, 10 Federal Reporter 730 (1883). It did not, however, lead to a wholesale assault on segregated education by black parents in rural areas.

ing growing burdens on black school systems. Black urban populations were continually rising, pressuring antiquated, understaffed public schools to accommodate still more students, and the increasing movement of blacks into newly developing residential areas created needs for black schools in locations far from the older centers of black residence.

The urbanization trend also had important social implications. It accelerated the pace of socioeconomic stratification among blacks and reinforced the assimilation of white middle-class norms among the aspiring and ambitious. In the context of urban culture and the urban job market, the relationship between education and socioeconomic mobility was more evident than in rural areas. In an era of racial optimism, when increasing numbers of blacks became interested in individual and racial mobility, the urban school became an important focus for black aspirations and strategies for advancement.

Symptomatic of the mobility-conscious mood were the frequent protests of a small by vocal number of black parents, at Columbus, Zanesville, and Xenia in 1873 and thereafter at Springfield, Marietta, Lancaster, Urbana, Bellefontaine, Gallipolis, Circleville, and Portsmouth, who wanted high school instruction for their children. The most practical arrangement, and the one favored by black parents at Columbus, Xenia, and Zanesville, would have been to admit the few black scholars (less than five at each of the three locations) to the regular high schools. As some locations, such as Columbus and Springfield, thrifty school boards did open the doors of the regular high schools to blacks, rather than go to the expense of providing separate facilities. Elsewhere, as at Xenia and Zanesville, vigorous white resistance to high school integration forced officials to establish separate facilities for blacks. Given the sorts of arrangements which were made, however, this was never very costly. At Xenia, a room at the black elementary school was utilized for advanced instruction; the principal of the black schools served as the teacher. Students were given access, at special times and in isolation, to scientific, art, athletic, and musical equipment and to language instruction at the white high schools. Eventually Xenia blacks were given an abandoned white school building for use as a high school.[64]

64 Erickson, "Color Line in Ohio Public Schools," pp. 247–252; Zanesville *Courier,* Sept. 2, 9, 10, 14, Oct. 8, 1873; Cincinnati *Commercial,* Sept. 10, 17, 1873; Xenia *Gazette,* Sept. 16, 1873; Columbus *Dispatch,* Jan. 20, 1874; Norris F. Schneider, *Y-Bridge City: The Story of Zanesville and Muskingum County* (Cleveland, 1950), p. 255; "History of East High," undated typescript appended to Jennie Braddock, "The Colored People and Greene County, Ohio, 1880–1865" (Senior thesis, Antioch College, 1953, rev. 1962).

Because it involved relatively few blacks, the high school question did not precipitate serious, prolonged conflict in those communities where it arose. Integration of three students hardly threatened the existing pattern of race relations, and the separate facilities which were arranged did not drain local funds for education. The elementary schools posed a more complex problem: the number of black children involved was much greater, their educational needs were subsequently more expensive, and the prospect of their integration in large numbers into the regular public schools was more threatening for many whites. In the 1870s and 1880s there were some communities, such as Steubenville, Marietta, Troy, and Piqua, where school officials chose to integrate the schools independent of black demands. Motivations were not explained, but the expense of maintaining separate schools seems to have played a role; at Steubenville, for example, integration came just after an attempt to create more precisely graded black schools left as few as six pupils per teacher. At the same time, integration here was doubtless facilitated by the tolerant ethos of local race relations. In none of these communities was there white resistance to integration.[65]

More often, however, the elementary schools were the source of protracted and occasionally quite bitter conflict. The progress of the issue in those communities where it became the source of serious conflict followed a pattern of events similar to that which occurred in 1869–71 at Toledo, the first city to experience sustained debate on the elementary schools. Dismissing integration as unlikely in the light of the strength of white opposition, or simply not desiring it, blacks and their white allies (most notably Toledo *Commercial* editor Clark Waggoner) petitioned for improvement of existing separate schools, or for the creation of additional black schools in more convenient locations. They were soon frustrated by white officials' indifference or inability to ameliorate poor conditions. Faced with mounting protests and the threat of black lawsuits, and confronted with the prospects of rising costs if the black school system was to be made equal to the white, officials at Toledo chose integration. It was accomplished in only two years, and with little white resistance.[66] But elsewhere school boards were more reluctant to integrate a large number of black children, and the process took longer. Yet even in these cases a sustained white backlash was rare; Springfield and Lancaster stand alone as communities where blacks were re-segregated after a short period of integration.

[65] Erickson, "Color Line in Ohio Public Schools," pp. 241–295; Joseph E. Doyle, *Twentieth Century History of Steubenville and Jefferson County, Ohio* (Chicago, 1910), p. 395.

[66] Leonard Erickson, "Toledo Desegregates," *Northwest Ohio Quarterly*, XXI (Winter, 1968–69), 5–12.

The Columbus and Springfield experiences illustrate this pattern and are particularly important. After years of unsuccessfully struggling for equal facilities, blacks in both cities became leaders in the struggle for repeal of the Ohio separate school law, and in the articulation of the belief that racial and individual advancement depended not only on quality education, but also on the integration of all children in the public schools.

In the late 1860s, Columbus's black school system consisted of two small, dilapidated buildings. One was southeast of downtown; the other, known as the "Alley School," was located at the juncture of two alleys in the downtown East Long Street area, where most blacks resided. In the late 1860s the two buildings housed six black teachers, including the principal E. J. Waring, catering to the needs of over 400 pupils.[67] Black protests during the 1860s focused on the school board's failure to distribute funds equitably; blacks demanded the creation of a black board of directors, similar to Cincinnati's, to oversee their schools. Failure to secure necessary legislation in 1869, and enfranchisement in 1870, led to a partial change in tactics. While blacks continued to hope for some independent body to monitor their schools, they now threatened to use lawsuits and votes to compel a fair apportionment of school funds. In 1871 the board responded to these threats by giving the blacks an abandoned white school in the heart of the East Long Street area to replace the Alley School. The new black school was named for Dr. Sterling Loving, their most constant ally on the board.[68]

Population changes quickly made this settlement obsolete. Between 1870 and 1880 Columbus's Negro population rose by 1,100. Attendance at the Loving School tripled during 1872–79, straining both the physical plant and the small teaching staff. More important, the growing black population did not settle exclusively in the East Long Street area. Though the largest concentration of blacks was in that vicinity, from 6 to 10 percent of the total black population settled in various individual wards of north, south, and east Columbus. Complaints about the distances which children had to walk from these wards to the Loving School led some parents not to send their children to school at all; these complaints now combined with criticism of the inadequacy of the decaying school. In addition, the school board had to contend with a 56 percent rise in the white population during the same decade, which caused overcrowding at many of the white schools. New schools were

[67] Richard Clyde Minor, "Negroes in Columbus" (Ph.D. dissertation, Ohio State University, 1936), pp. 145–146.

[68] Columbus *Ohio State Journal*, June 25, 29, 1867, Apr. 8, 14, Sept. 27, 30, 1870; *Ohio Senate Journal*, 1869, pp. 94, 107, 183, 207, 254.

needed for whites, and, if the dual school system was to be preserved, they were also needed in the scattered, growing black enclaves throughout the city and for the nearly half of the black population living near East Long Street. Yet money for such comprehensive improvements was lacking.[69]

Integration seemed inescapable, and the board eased haltingly into this course. In September, 1881, faced with overcrowding, Negro demands for new schools, and serious decay of the Loving School, it voted to close the latter at the end of the year and build another black school. The two actions were in a sense contradictory, for it was doubtful that any adequate school building could be built in time for the start of the 1882–83 school year, Then, in June, 1882, when blacks in southeastern Columbus demanded a separate and more convenient school, the board refused and invited them to send their children to nearby white schools wherever it was convenient to do so. Though they were not specifically asked to do the same in their neighborhoods, blacks elsewhere in Columbus took this as an invitation to resolve similar problems, and when the new school year began, they sent their children to nearby schools. Integration brought little conflict. Blacks were only 6 percent of the population, and with half of the city's total of 3,000 blacks scattered throughout Columbus and the other half in the downtown East Long area, few whites probably felt directly threatened by mixed schools.[70]

Poor location and overcrowding also posed serious problems at Springfield, but black school conditions there were made worse by a hostile school board. A jump in black population from 276 to 2,360 during 1860–80 strained the only black school, the Pleasant Street School, to its limits. Moreover, as elsewhere, the school was inconvenient for many students; only 35 percent of the black population lived in the ward where the school was located, while the remainder lived in the city's other four wards. Some children were walking as far as five miles a day to and from school.[71] For years the school board offered no relief and occasional insult; when blacks petitioned for more

[69] Minor, "Negroes in Columbus," pp. 147–149; Columbus *Ohio State Journal,* Feb. 9, 1878; *Columbus Dispatch,* Sept. 22, 1880; Columbus Board of Education, *Annual Report . . . 1872–1873* (Columbus, 1873), p. 71, and *Annual Report . . . 1876–1877* (Columbus, 1877), p. 166.

[70] Columbus *Dispatch,* Feb. 9, May 4, June 1, Aug. 24, Sept. 7, 28, 1881, Sept. 5, 6, 20, 1882; Columbus Board of Education, *Annual Report . . . 1881–1882* (Columbus, 1882), p. 193, and *Annual Report.. . . 1882–1883* (Columbus, 1883), p. 95; Erickson, "Color Line in Ohio Public Schools," pp. 272–284.

[71] Census Office, *Ninth Census* I, 228, and *Report on the Population of the United States, Eleventh Census . . . 1890* (Washington 1894), I, pt. 1, p. 475; *The History of Clark County, Ohio* (Chicago, 1881), pp. 526–529; Springfield *Republic,* Oct. 27, 1862; Cleveland *Gazette,* Jan. 17, 1885.

conveniently located schools in 1872, they were treated, they said, "with disrespect and effrontery." [72]

At the start of the 1881–82 school year, a dozen black children were denied admission to the conveniently located white Shaffer School in the northern part of the city, to which an increasing number of blacks employed in the nearby iron mills were moving. Springfield blacks then pressed for a final confrontation with the board. All wanted quality education, but they were divided on the question of wholesale integration. At a meeting attended by 125 blacks, among them the most influential and wealthy, two factions emerged. One was represented by the chairman of the meeting, blacksmith Frederick Dent, and by George Reynolds, a machinist whose children were among those refused at Shaffer School. This group wanted improvements in the existing system, asking for larger and more conveniently located black schools. The second faction, composed of parents for whom distance and location were less of a problem, argued against the principle of segregation in education. While the board was willing to cooperate with the former, it remained adamantly against integration; it was supported in this opinion by the overwhelming majority of local whites, who voted against school integration at referenda in the spring and fall of 1882. White opposition was doubtless strengthened by a rapid rise in Springfield's black population; blacks made up over 11 percent of the city's population by the 1880s, a figure equaled in few northern cities of comparable size at the time.[73]

Black integrationists and white allies, among them the editor of the influential Springfield Republic, pressed for a legal confrontation with the board, which agreed to participate in a test case in the federal courts, contesting the constitutionality of school segregation under the Fourteenth Amendment. Eva Gazaway, daughter of A.M.E. minister John Gazaway, was chosen as the plaintiff and was summarily refused admission at a white school. For a year blacks, aided by the Republic, raised money to finance the expensive suit—but the case as framed was a tactical blunder. By failing to base their claims on the essential inequality of their school system, which was inconvenient and overcrowded and unlikely to improve in the context of the city's dual school system, they allowed the court to stay within the legal confines of an accepted judicial canon: separation per se was not evidence of inequality. The case did not get beyond the district court at Cincinnati, where it was lost in November, 1882.[74]

72 Xenia Torchlight, Mar. 20, 1872.

73 Springfield Republic, Sept. 5, 13, 17, 1881; Cincinnati Enquirer, Nov. 3, 1882.

74 Springfield Republic, Sept. 15, 27, 29, Oct. 3, Nov. 17, Dec. 20, 1881, Jan. 26, Feb. 2, Nov. 4, 9, 1882; Cincinnati Enquirer, Nov. 3, 1882.

The failure of the suit left blacks more vulnerable than ever to the vagaries of the school board. Though a teacher was soon hired for black children in the northern area of the city, no school was built. Though plans were drawn to build another school for whites, in 1884 the budget of the black school was actually cut. That same year, while providing school districts for newly annexed parts of the city, the board extended segregation to blacks who had previously been attending mixed schools, forcing them into inconvenient black facilities in the city or just beyond the annexed sections. Partial integration came briefly in 1885–86, when a Republican school board allowed blacks to attend the schools nearest their homes. But those opposed to mixed schools seized an opportunity presented by the use of black strikebreakers in the farm machinery industry early in 1886 to begin a campaign for resegregation. Democrats won control of the board in that spring's local elections; at the end of the school year the board passed a resolution returning all blacks to Pleasant Street School.[75]

IV

The emergence of militant school integrationism at Springfield was part of a trend among vital segments of Ohio's black leadership toward the belief that school integration was essential to the securing of racial equality. At the same time, the appearance of an articulate, public integrationist position and the possibility of school integration mobilized blacks who favored separate schools. The first public confrontation between these forces took place in 1878 and resulted from the appearance in Ohio's House of Representatives of a politically motivated, Republican-sponsored bill to repeal the state's separate school law. The bill appeared to have no chance of passing a Democratic-controlled legislature, but the Democrats were not about to be embarrassed in their occasional quest for Negro votes. The result was the 1878 school law, which facilitated the creation of black schools by ending the requirement that a certain number of school-age blacks were necessary for the establishment of a separate school. However, the law would have little effect because school officials refused to sanction the proliferation of schools for a very few students.[76]

The debate between blacks was prompted by the news that several black teachers were lobbying for defeat of the desegregation bill and

[75] Cleveland *Gazette*, Jan. 12, Apr. 12, Aug. 30, 1884, July 21, 24, 1886.

[76] Ohio, *House Journal, 1878*, pp. 48, 647, 669–670; Ohio *Senate Journal, 1878*, pp. 801; Ohio, *Laws, 1878*, p. 513; Erickson, "Color Line in Ohio Public Schools," p. 202.

attempting to impress the legislature with the claim that blacks desired separate schools. The teacher's efforts were first revealed in a public letter, addressed to a legislator, written by Dayton teacher Solomon Day. Day explained that while he was not against school integration in principle, "regarding the immediate and future interests of the colored race" integration would be harmful. Whites, he said, would never allow blacks to teach their children, and the black teachers would lose their jobs and be forced to search for work in the South, where separate schools were legion but where prejudice would destroy them. Of integration Day concluded: "I know of no better scheme to reduce the most intelligent classes of colored people to penury and want, or to drive them from the state to become the victims of southern barbarism. . . . Where else is the colored teacher to go but the South? . . . For the colored teacher to go South and carry his opinions with him is to die." [77]

While Day and other teachers were not motivated solely by the desire to keep their positions, this was an important consideration. Some, like Peter Clark, openly stated that they were not opposed to integration if it applied to faculties as well as to student bodies. The teachers did indeed have much to lose if integration were accomplished. The creation of Ohio's separate school system, with its 7,000 to 10,000 pupils during 1865–87, had in turn created a self-conscious corps of black educators. Black teachers and principals numbered between 144 and 262, and after 1878 consistently over 225. The great demand for black teachers in Ohio and throughout the nation in the late nineteenth century created high salaries, making teaching one of the best paying, most prestigious, and most readily available positions for educated blacks in a time of limited opportunity.[78] Too, salaries earned by black teachers, representing the largest sustained income drawn by blacks at the public till, were necessary for the support of black families, lodges, and churches, and there was little prospect for their replacement. These facts were in themselves powerful arguments in favor of separate schools for some outside the teachers' ranks. Thus, at a meeting at Columbus in 1878 which had been called to discuss school legislation, both porter Robert Hodge and barber James Hill emphasized that

[77] Columbus *Ohio State Journal*, Feb. 9, 1878. For the other letters in the exchange between Day and others arguing for integration, ibid., Feb. 7, 11, 14, 20, 21, 1878.

[78] Erickson, "Color Line in Ohio Public Schools," pp. 210, 216–219, 236. The professional self-consciousness of the Ohio black teachers was reflected in the organization in 1861 of an Ohio Colored Teachers Association, which held meetings periodically during the next years. "Ohio Colored Teachers Association," *Ohio Educational Monthly*, IV, 3 (1863), 159.

Ohio blacks could ill afford to sacrifice the "$320,000 annually" which Hodge estimated as the teachers' earnings.[79]

Because the debate began on this footing, however, it tended to obscure larger issues and made it too easy to identify every teacher defending separate schools with a selfish espousal of inferior facilities. While self-interest played a role in their thought, a small but vocal minority of teachers also believed deeply, though in varying combinations, in the benefits of separate schools, black teachers for black students, and the utility of separate institutions in the struggle for racial advancement. Thus, they saw their own employment as but one part of a larger educational structure essential to racial needs. They did not argue that Ohio's dual school system provided educational settings equal in quality and convenience; such an argument was impossible for men who wished to preserve their integrity. Instead, they maintained that, given the special problems of the black community and its children, separate schools brought benefits outweighing their known defects. Nor did they seek to supplant black leadership's desire for equality and social acceptance within American society by arguing that separate institutions were a long-term alternative to integration. Instead, even those who argued most articulately for separate institutions and schools saw them not as ends in themselves, but as means for preparing the race for the American mainstream. Thus, though reflecting a pronounced ambivalence on integration, the teachers argued within the larger confines of contemporary black goals.

Those who defended separate schools were decidedly a minority among those racial spokesmen who were active in the school debate. To the extent that a defense of separate schools threatened to compromise or postpone the attainment of equality and social acceptance, even if undertaken in the name of larger racial goals, it constituted a basic challenge to the racial articles of faith of most Ohio black leaders. But it was a coherent position, forged by a highly respected, articulate, and intellectual, if small, group. As a result, the issues raised by some of the teachers attracted considerable attention and precipitated the sharpest post-war ideological conflict within black leadership.

In the years between the initial airing of views in 1878 and the repeal of Ohio's separate school law in 1887, those teachers who defended separate schools as essential to the cause of racial advancement emphasized the corrective influence of the separate school and the sympathetic black teacher upon the ambition and self-esteem of a child growing up black in a hostile white world. Integrated schools would not only neglect what were perceived to be the special emotional and

[79] Columbus *Ohio State Journal,* Feb. 12, 1878.

educational needs of black children, but would daily exacerbate their difficulties by placing them in a demanding, unfriendly environment. Inevitably, predicted Hamilton principal Ira Collins, "Many will absent themselves completely" from such segregated schools.[80]

Hillsboro principal John Q. Price pointed out that poverty would affect black students' regular attendance and possible success in integrated schools. "Their parents are too poor to buy them the proper kind of clothes to wear," he said, "and they will not stand being the objects of ridicule, preferring to live in ignorance." In addition, Price explained that many of his students had to work and could only attend school part-time, coming when they could for brief periods of instruction. "Some only stay an hour," he stated, "but I let them, spending as much time as I can with them while they are in school, letting them leave when they have to." Indeed, over ninety of his pupils were attending school on this basis. Some who were between sixteen and twenty years old were still in the primary grades as the result of part-time attendance. "Their pride will not allow them to be in class with the young white children," Price said of these older students. Implicit in such statements was a feeling that black children would not receive such sympathetic understanding and attention from white teachers.[81]

Teachers like Price also saw themselves as important role models for black children, whose circumstances continually worked to sap them of ambition. Collins warned that with labor unions drawing the color line, with prejudice keeping blacks from clerkships in stores, and with teaching now in jeopardy, "What has the average colored child to inspire him to educate himself?" Dayton principal W. O. Bowles cautioned against eliminating this "opportunity for the development and employment of race talent," pointing out the irony of sacrificing the unparalleled opportunity of teaching in the name of racial advancement.[82]

Such arguments were not incompatible with an underlying desire for school integration, for the same racial needs might be served if black teachers were retained in integrated schools. Yet a few teachers developed the defense of separate schools into part of a more generalized defense of separate institutions. W. O. Bowles saw such institutions as a product of "a Chinese wall of prejudice and exclusiveness [which has] barricaded the way against the ambition and aspirations of the Negro"; but, rather than tearing them down, he felt that they must be kept alive "until the causes which produced them shall cease to exist

[80] Cleveland *Gazette*, Feb. 6, 1885.
[81] Hillsboro *Gazette*, Mar. 5, 1887.
[82] Cleveland *Gazette*, Feb. 6, 1885; Dayton *Journal*, Feb. 20, 1885.

and to operate to our detriment." While most black leaders shied away from espousing the strengthening of such institutions in order that they might become centers of self-help and solidarity, Bowles moved toward such a position. For the present, he argued, blacks needed to play a major role in their own uplift and through the inculcation of middle-class habits and standards make themselves more acceptable to whites. Moral and social uplift through self-help would "do more toward destroying existing racial antipathy than any act of legislation compelling race associations." The chief requirement for the immediate future, he said, was "a manly independence to be secured by an accumulation of wealth, the improvement of morals, the development of intellect, and the courageous support and exhaltation of our race institutions." [83]

Agreeing with Bowles was Columbus principal E. J. Waring, who compared the black situation with that of other proscribed racial and ethnic groups. Waring believed that separate development in educative and value-inculcating contexts was more conducive to group and individual advancement during the transitional phase of a group's progress into the social mainstream; integrated development offered, Waring said, only the benefit of contact, and that on another's terms. Integrated settings in these particular contexts, therefore, were not necessarily "conducive to the greatest growth" and the "highest culture of the individual or the masses of a proscribed class." Said Waring, "All growth is from within outward, and is the result of exercise, not merely of contact. Hence organizations, schools, and churches based on language or color may, during the period of transition of any class . . . produce grander results than mixed organizations." [84]

School integrationists were considerably less patient than Waring. "Ours is a work of assimilation," said Columbus's J. S. Tyler in 1878 during a heated exchange with Solomon Day, "and the more vigorous and earnest the efforts the more speedy the results." [85] Tyler and others believed that compromises with inequality would postpone full citizenship, social acceptance, and individual mobility. While Waring and his allies stressed the debilitating effect of interracial contact in a white-dominated setting and saw separate schools as countering the harm done by racism, integrationists like Tyler stressed the dangers inherent in the inequity of separate schools, which they saw as more a burden than an opportunity.

Led particularly by Columbus and Springfield blacks, most of whom

[83] Dayton *Journal*, Feb. 18, 1885.
[84] Columbus *Ohio State Journal*, Feb. 18, 1878.
[85] Ibid., Feb. 11, 1878.

were prominent in the frustrating struggles for equal facilities in their cities, the school integrationists argued from bitter experience that separate schools could never be equal in the context of American race relations. They emphasized the biases of funding, inconvenient locations, and the lack of adequately trained, effective black teachers—a point dwelled on with greater candor than tact. In 1878, after systematically outlining the failings of the dual school system, Tyler warned that inferior schools would produce adults inadequate in those qualities, "a well-balanced brain and proper culture," which might speed social acceptance. Speaking as a parent, he said, "I want my child to be brought into contact with everything that conduces to the development of those qualities among the whites." [86]

In addition to providing inadequate education, integrationists argued that segregated schools were vital to the process by which children of both races learned about their places in the social order. Black children, forcibly set off in unmistakably inferior schools, were obviously not equal to their white peers. They vividly described the lasting effects of such childhood experiences. Poindexter, for example, stated that in separate schools "the white child imbibes the false idea that the color of his skin makes him the colored child's superior, while the colored child grows sour under the weight of invidious distinctions made between him and the white child, and in many cases in the very beginning . . . loses that ambition which would be the greatest spur to his success in life." [87] Thus, by destroying an inequitable school system and initiating contacts between the children of both races in the neutral setting of the schools, integration would help to eliminate the images which sustained racial prejudice.

Usually school integrationists were also concerned with more general efforts to end discrimination and change white attitudes, so that upon leaving school daily or upon graduation the children would step into a more tolerant world. Yet, during the early 1880s, as the school issue intensified, they were coming to place a primary emphasis in their evolving conception of racial strategy on school integration, for it seemed to offer the best immediate hope for changing white attitudes and preparing blacks for equality and social acceptance. Teachers who argued for separate schools sometimes saw the schools as but one link in a chain of racial activities and institutions working for advancement and against prejudice; in contrast, their opponents saw school integration as the most important remaining step to assuring black advancement, now that political and civil equality had been attained. Im-

[86] Ibid., Feb. 11, 1878.
[87] Columbus *Ohio State Journal*, Feb. 7, 1878.

pressed with the new possibilities for race relations, and less sensitive than the teachers to the need for group identity and solidarity, the school integrationists tended to believe that there was a single, integrated path to equality, and that it was shorter and less perilous than the teachers argued.

Illustrative of their view of race relations was the ease with which the school integrationists became allied with activist Cleveland blacks, particularly Harry Smith, whose perspective on school integration and broader racial strategy was influenced by the uniquely tolerant atmosphere of the Reserve. At Cleveland, mixed schools had been the rule for decades. Black teachers taught white students, and interracial contacts were generally freer and more frequent than in southern and central Ohio. Though he showed more concern for the fate of the black teachers than most southern and central Ohio spokesmen, Smith seemed to believe that conditions elsewhere were as malleable as those around him. If blacks simply exerted enough pressure, he believed that their teachers might be retained in integrated schools. He also suggested a quota system for hiring black teachers, which would make their employment dependent on the size of the black student population. But he was frank enough to state that the teachers' fate was a "secondary consideration." [88]

It is difficult to weigh the strengths of the opposing positions in black communities around Ohio; there is simply not enough evidence. Yet the lack of sustained protest against the dual school system in some communities must be explained. Given the inequities of the dual school system, support for integration might well be expected, especially among the aspiring upper-class leadership. Indeed, the weight of the evidence certainly suggests that articulate and vocal professionals, businessmen, artisans, higher-level service employees, and others of the upper class (except for some teachers) favored integration.

Yet there were communities where sustained protest, either on the scale of that present at Columbus and Springfield or on the less intense order of that appearing over the high school question at Xenia and Zanesville, failed to materialize. Coercion and fear of reprisal are factors which must not be overlooked in any explanation, and these probably figured prominently in small southern Ohio communities, where caste relations were firm and repression easiest to marshal. At the same time, however, there were larger communities which seemed content, at least for the present, to make the most of their separate opportunities, even if such opportunities were the product of racial preju-

[88] Cleveland *Gazette,* Sept. 22, 1883, Mar. 29, Apr. 12, 1884, Feb. 21, 1885, Mar. 17, 1886.

dice and were hardly equal to those of whites. At Cincinnati, for example, there is little evidence of continual protest against educational inequality, and until the school issue appeared in the state legislature in the 1880s, culminating in the passage of the 1887 desegregation law, no evidence of a widespread desire for integration. A number of factors stemmed discontent with the dual school system and desire for school integration. As blacks were only too well aware, local white opinion was hardly favorable to racial mixing. At the same time, though Peter Clark had himself acknowledged the defects of the black schools, blacks had pride in their long-established schools and confidence in their teachers, many of whom were trained under Clark. Even after the legislature's 1873 passage of uniform local school laws led to the abolition of the black board of directors, the school board continued to cooperate in efforts to improve the black schools, increasing the number of schools as populations grew and shifted. During 1874–87 four new black schools were opened, bringing the total to seven black elementary schools.[89]

Dayton blacks more actively and directly expressed their belief in the utility of separate schools. In 1884 and 1885, when their school board took steps to integrate the schools because of the expense entailed in providing convenient facilities for blacks, local blacks split on the question. Many were concerned particularly with the impact of integration upon their children and the loss of teaching opportunities; they joined forces with W. O. Bowles in a successful fight to retain separate schools.[90]

Yet the idea of equality was a powerful force on the side of school integrationists, and the lack of equality in Ohio's dual school system was fast winning them converts as the issue was raised around the state in the early 1880s. To the extent that blacks came to consider equality in education as contingent upon integration, their battle for black opinion would be won. Nor did blacks lack examples of the issue's resolution elsewhere in the North to spur them on in pursuit of full equality. In parts of New England there had never been dual school systems, and elsewhere integration had been achieved long ago; closer to home,

[89] Cincinnati Board of Education, *Minutes*, v. 1870–73 (June 16, 1873), p. 596, and v. 1873–76 (May 4, 1874), p. 203 (May 3, 1875), p. 413 (Aug. 23, 1875), p. 475 (Oct. 18, 1875), p. 519 (Nov. 29, 1875), pp. 539–540; Cincinnati *Commercial*, Sept. 30, 1873; Cleveland *Gazette*, Sept. 6, 1886. For Peter Clark's remarks about the inadequacies of black schools, see Cincinnati *Colored Citizen*, May 19, 1866; Cincinnati *Commercial*, Sept. 23, 1873; Columbus *Ohio State Journal*, Feb. 11, 1878.
[90] Cleveland *Gazette*, Aug. 9, 16, 1884, Aug. 29, 1885; Dayton *Journal*, Feb. 14, 16, 18, 20, July 25, 1885, May 15, 1887.

Iowa, Michigan, Illinois, and (in 1881) New Jersey and Pennsylvania had opted for comprehensive integration or local option during the past twenty years.[91]

While the school issue intensified, a series of unexpected shocks suggested to Ohio blacks that the battle for equality was in need of especially vigorous champions. In October, 1883, the Supreme Court declared the 1875 Civil Rights Law unconstitutional. Though the law had not effectively checked discrimination, blacks still desired the protection which it might provide to those who wished to use it aggressively. At race meetings in Ohio and in other states speakers expresesd dismay at the backward-looking decision, especially because it had come from a court dominated by Republicans. Yet the court left open a possibility for continued protection when it ruled that such legislation was the proper domain of the states, rather than the federal government.[92] Then, early in 1884, Ohio blacks learned that the state's dormant anti-intermarriage law, passed in 1861, had been employed at Toledo; a black bridegroom was sent to the workhouse for two months at hard labor for marrying a white woman. Few black leaders advocated intermarriage, and the subject was never discussed in the public forums on racial strategy; the strength of white opinion against intermarriage was enough to convince blacks of the issue's dangers. Yet the existence of the law smacked too much of coercion and insult, and in its curbing of individual freedom and mobility it posed a sharp, if largely symbolic, challenge to black aspirations and goals. In addition, while in the past it had simply been a troublesome reminder, along with the separate school law, of the continued existence of discrimination in Ohio's statutes, and hence it had stood as an annoying compromise of full equality before the law, its sudden use signaled a possible wave of repression against Ohio's few interracial couples.[93]

The school issue, the civil rights decision, and the use of the anti-intermarriage law all touched upon the most basic goals of black leadership. Though it was an accident that they arose at the same time, the fact that they had done so lent a particular urgency to coming to terms with them. It was as if, in the early 1880s, black leaders faced the possibility of winning or losing the future to which they aspired. Confronting the three issues called for strong, creative leadership which could maximize what tools blacks had for ameliorating their situation.

[91] Gilbert Stephenson, *Race Distinctions in American Law* (New York, 1910), pp. 177–189.

[92] New York *Globe*, Nov. 20, 1883; Cleveland *Gazette*, Nov. 20, 27, Dec. 4, 11, 18, 1883.

[93] Cleveland *Gazette*, Mar. 22, 1884; Harrisburg *State Journal*, Feb. 23, Mar. 1, 1884.

Their most important tool was politics, and the three issues would give black leaders the most compelling impetus since enfranchisement to flex the race's political muscle for the sake of winning major legislative victories.

8

Amelioration through Politics: Black Politics and Black Welfare

Ohio black leaders hoped to pursue two related ends by exercising political power and organizing blacks into an effective voting bloc. In an effort to consolidate and make more effective their leadership and to expand, for the most part, their own employment opportunities, they sought political patronage and elective office. At the same time, they desired to protect the racial gains of Civil War and Reconstruction eras and to fulfill the larger ends of racial strategy. Because the political situation across the state and in individual localities was often uncertain enough for the black vote to emerge as a strategic element in contests between the major parties, political activity aided black leaders considerably in both efforts. But before the black vote could realize its full potential, and thus effectively pursue racial and individual aspirations, blacks had to develop a tendency toward political independence in which their own needs were balanced against partisan loyalty. Given impetus in the 1870s by disappointments in the quest for patronage and elective office, and by the retreat of Republicans from the policies of congressional Reconstruction, that tendency gradually evolved. In the 1880s black politics in Ohio came of age. By the end of the decade, blacks had used political power to achieve repeal of the separate school and anti-intermarriage laws; they had also obtained passage of civil rights legislation and won an expansion of their political opportunity. These triumphs heightened their faith in the benign course of the new era, and in the efficacy of politics as the key weapon in the struggle for racial advancement.

I

During the months after Ohio's ratification of the Fifteenth Amendment, white politicians responded to the prospect of black political participation with deep interest and feverish calculation. Republicans gloated and matched their old majorities up against those which they assumed would result from black loyalty to the party of Lincoln.[1] Democrats, on the other hand, showed reactions at once bitter, yet strangely hopeful. They were bitter that a new political factor had been introduced without their consent—and more bitter, perhaps, that they seemed so unlikely to profit from it. Yet there were strains of hope. At least one Democrat was reported to have left the very session of the House at which, in spite of Democratic opposition, the Fifteenth Amendment had been ratified, saying, "We'll have 'em; we'll have the bulk of the darkey vote after all." [2] Searching desperately into Ohio's past, Democrats discovered that in 1849 and 1850 they had helped to repeal some of the more repressive black laws and to establish black public education when Free Soilers, who held the balance of power, forced them to do so or lose control of the legislature. De-emphasizing the expedient nature of their role, Democrats now began to speak of themselves as "the party that repealed the black laws." Then too, as Columbus's Democratic *Ohio Statesman* pointed out in March, 1870, the Democracy was Ohio's "poor man's party," defending his interest in low prices by its advocacy of low tariff rates.[3] Democrats thus began to marshal arguments to impress blacks that class interests should outweigh racial ones in their political calculations. Said a leading Democratic state senator, "Sambo will learn as he progresses in historical knowledge that this high tariff system originates in the same spirit of avarice which long ago caused New Englanders to drag his ancestors from Africa and sell them into cruel and hopeless slavery." [4] To be sure, these were rear-guard actions. While in 1871 the Ohio Democracy would take its New Departure, accepting the wartime amendments though rejecting the use of federal power that produced and sustained them, its record was too laden with racial intransigence and hostility for it to extend its hand very far in the direction of the black voter. Then, too, as the senator's use of the term "Sambo" suggests, Democrats would have to come to terms with their low regard for blacks before attempting to court their vote. Yet the Democracy realized that the black vote was worth contending for, and eventually refined its approach and became considerably more effective in its appeals.

A survey calculating the number of black males over twenty, who

[1] Cleveland *Leader*, March 2, Apr. 5, 1870; Xenia *Torchlight*, Apr. 6, 1870.
[2] Cincinnati *Commercial*, Jan. 21, 1870.
[3] Columbus *Ohio Statesman*, Mar. 30, 1870.
[4] McConnelsville *Democrat*, Aug. 4, 1871.

were the eligible voters of color, had first tempted the Ohio Democracy to begin seeking out bases of common interest. Early estimates of the size of the black electorate tended to be conservative. Republican newspapers suggested that it was approximately 10,000; of these, it was said, perhaps as many as 40 percent had voted, regularly or irregularly depending on the region, under earlier court decisions enfranchising the light-skinned.[5] Such estimates failed to take into account the magnitude of the post-war migrations. While in 1860 the size of the potential black vote was 8,711, by the next federal census it was 15,614, an increase of almost 80 percent. When Republicans stopped to consider that they had won the governorship in 1867 by a mere 2,900 votes and in 1869 by 7,500 in an electorate of about 500,000, they were unavoidably impressed with the fact that the black vote, though only 3 percent of the total electorate, would provide important padding for their gubernatorial majorities.[6]

Black voting potential was particularly impressive in the Miami and Scioto valleys of southern and west-central Ohio, where two-thirds of the prospective black voters resided in 1870. In Brown, Clark, Franklin, Gallia, Greene, Montgomery, Pickaway, and Ross counties, the new voters numbered usually between 400 and 1,000. The figure reached as high as 1,700 in the case of Hamilton County (Cincinnati and vicinity), and blacks often constituted between 5 and 10 percent of the electorate.[7] The implications of this configuration were evident in the 1870 congressional elections. Although Republican voting was down throughout the state, new black voters turned out in very large numbers to vote in their first national election. Their participation helped to insure continued Republican hegemony in two uncertain congressional districts of the seven Miami and Scioto valleys. In a third district they provided the margin of victory by which one seat was taken from the Democracy. The state's First District encompassed eastern Hamilton County, including Cincinnati's eastern wards, where 800 of the city's almost 1,200 new black voters lived. Republicans had lost in 1868 by 211 votes, but they were able to obtain a respectable 695-vote majority in 1870.[8] To the northeast in the Seventh District, which Republican

[5] Columbus *Ohio State Journal*, Sept. 11, 1867; Cleveland *Leader*, Mar. 2, 1870.

[6] U.S. Census Office, *Population of the United States in 1860 . . . Eighth Census* (Washington, 1864), I, 370–371, and *The Statistics of the United States Embracing Tables of Race, Nationality, Sex, Selected Ages, and Occupations . . . from the Original Returns of the Ninth Census* (Washington, 1872), p. 619.

[7] U.S. Census Office, *Ninth Census of the United States . . . 1870* (Washington, 1872), I, 226–241; Cincinnati *Commercial*, Apr. 5, 1870.

[8] Cincinnati *Commercial*, Oct. 13, 1870.

observers saw as "doubtful" on election eve, they had won in 1868 by a narrow 114-vote margin in an electorate of almost 28,000; in the upcoming election they faced an apathetic white Republican electorate and a vigorous Democracy at Columbus. Encompassing large black populations at Columbus, Springfield, and Xenia, the district contained almost 1,800 black voters; the Republicans were able to establish a respectable 1,334-vote majority.[9] Just to the southwest, in the Sixth Congressional District, Republicans had been prepared for defeat. Their 1868 majority had been only 343 in an electorate of over 26,000, and they now faced the challenges of a renegade Republican who was running as an independent in his home county, combined with an apathetic corps of white Republicans. The black vote of approximately 1,500 saved the day, however, and the Republicans were able to eke out a narrow majority of 236. After settling upon blacks as the main factor leading to Republican success in the district, the Wilmington *Clinton Republican* said, "Their actions show how thoroughly they can organize and what a power they will be in future elections if they work as they have done in this one. . . ."[10]

The black vote could be even more influential in local contests, for, depending on the size of the local black electorate, political power would increase as the size of the district decreased. In some larger towns (Xenia, Gallipolis, Chillicothe, and Portsmouth) and a few of the small ones (such as Oberlin) blacks comprised 10 to 25 percent of the total electorate; they had to be recognized in both party and government affairs. Oberlin moved immediately to accept and reward its black voters, electing a black town councilman in April, 1870. Xenia blacks made up a majority of the Fourth Ward's voting population; they eagerly awaited the 1871 municipal elections, at which they elected black grocer E. C. Jackson to represent them on the town council. Both Oberlin and Xenia continued to have a black councilman for many years. While blacks did not control Chillicothe's Second Ward, constituting only slightly more than 30 percent of its population in 1870, they did find themselves with a balance of power. They demonstrated unusually vigorous independence of judgment in their early use of the vote, helping to keep in office a Democratic councilman who had brought sidewalks and gas lamps to an area of the town that had been long neglected. At Gallipolis and in Gallia County, Republicans were at war with one another in the early 1870s over the liquor issue. There blacks not only held a balance of power between Republican factions, but they also came to provide the votes to keep the party in

9 Ibid., Oct. 11, 13, 1870.
10 Ibid.; Wilmington *Clinton Republican*, Oct. 20, 1870.

power once factionalism began to change to political independence for some whites.[11]

Black populations were generally much larger in Cleveland, Columbus, Cincinnati, and other cities than in all the towns but Xenia, and they would grow still larger during the 1870s. However, black political influence in the cities tended to be lessened for two reasons: blacks were vastly outnumbered by whites, and they were much more scattered residentially than in the towns. At Cleveland, where blacks were only about 1 percent of the population, their vote was overwhelmed in citywide contests. Though not holding the balance of power in the Sixth Ward, where their vote was most concentrated, they were nevertheless an important element in Republican success because the party balance was fairly close.[12] While 6 percent of the population at Columbus, blacks were scattered throughout the largely Democratic city. In the Eighth Ward, where they had their greatest voting strength, blacks helped to pad the Republican majority in council elections. The party's majority rose from 2 in 1868 to 164 in 1870; the ward's black vote was estimated at 180.[13] At Cincinnati, where blacks were 3 percent of the population in 1870, their vote was also scattered. It tended to be eclipsed in the lower river basin wards by Democratic Irish influence. Yet in the very first municipal contest in which they voted, blacks demonstrated their potential power. In the April, 1870, elections there was considerable nonpartisan contention in local school board elections over the use of the Bible in the schools. The question tended to separate Protestants, white and black, from Catholics, who were against religious instruction in the Protestant-controlled public schools. While the Cincinnati *Commercial* found nothing remarkable in regard to the first appearance of blacks at the polls that spring, it was impressed with the political muscle they had shown in the school board elections. "The Bible candidates carried several of the closely contested wards," said the newspaper, "and will have a small majority on the Board. They are indebted to the colored voter for their success." [14]

White Republicans moved to recognize the power shown by blacks in these early contests by integrating them into the party structure and rewarding them for loyalty at the polls; blacks, in turn, actively sought opportunities to enter their party's affairs. Beginning in the very first year of black voting, racial leadership began to play a role in party

[11] Cleveland *Leader,* Apr. 11, 1870; Xenia *Torchlight,* Apr. 5, 1871; Cincinnati *Commercial,* Aug. 23, 25, 1873; Ironton *Register,* Oct. 23, 1973; Gallipolis *Journal,* Apr. 1, 8, 1875.

[12] Cleveland *Leader,* Mar. 23, Apr. 5, 1870.

[13] Columbus *Ohio State Journal,* Feb. 16, Apr. 5, Oct. 13, 1870.

[14] Cincinnati *Commercial,* Apr. 2, 4, 5, 1870.

activities. A small number of blacks—rarely in proportion to their population of any district—took part in ward, city, and county nominating conventions. In 1870 hairdresser William Ambush, a leader of Cleveland's Sixth Ward blacks, and the Reverend James Poindexter of Columbus were delegates to the state convention; in 1872 Toledo's Madison Bell attended the Republican National Convention as a delegate-at-large, as would Poindexter in 1876. After serving in the bodies which nominated candidates, black leaders began to appear on ward, county, and state Republican central committees which directed election campaigns. The Reverend Benjamin Arnett represented Toledo and Lucas County on the state central committee in 1871, while the next year Robert Harlan was chosen to fill one of Cincinnati's two seats on the committee. Ohio's leading black orators—Poindexter, Clark, Arnett, and others—began to address Republican rallies; while they were usually assigned to speak before blacks, they also occasionally appeared before whites.[15]

Further serving to integrate blacks into party affairs was the formation of black political clubs, such as Cleveland's Sixth Ward Union Republican Club and Cincinnati's West End Grant Club and East End Colored Republican Club. These clubs were the earliest black political organizations, founded by various racial leaders soon after enfranchisement. Unlike the informal structures of political influence which were developing around men like Henry Pickett in the slums, the clubs were formal organizations with a regular membership, an elected body of officers, an organized round of campaign activities, and a casual recreational role in the lives of their members. Their structure and functions at this early date resembled those of the clubs of later decades. They were supported more by small subsidies from the party than by dues. They had perhaps one or two dozen members, a mixture of all social types, but with middle-class laborers and service workers predominant; at election time, however, regular members were joined by supporters seeking to participate in the various aspects of club-sponsored campaigning. The clubs usually had a handful of elected officers, but their posts, however prestigious, were often only ceremonial and secretarial. Officers did not necessarily have final say over club political strategy— that authority, not of necessity formalized in elected officership, went to the most influential black political leaders and their circle of advisors. At the summit of the clubs were articulate, upper-class men of forceful personality such as Harlan or Poindexter, who enjoyed mutu-

[15] Columbus *Ohio State Journal*, Apr. 5, July 4, 6, Oct. 1, 12, 1870, Sept. 1, 4, 1871; Cleveland *Leader*, Aug. 1, 1870; Cincinnati *Commercial*, Sept. 20, 1870; Toledo *Commercial*, Jan. 20, 1871, Mar. 29, 1872; Xenia *Torchlight*, Apr. 3, 1872; Ironton *Register*, Aug. 21, 1873; Steubenville *Herald*, Mar. 19, 1875.

ally reinforcing reputations for influence in both white and black communities based on varying combinations of personal friendship, informal connections, and business, professional, church and fraternal ties. Yet individual contacts, reputations, and charisma were politically valuable only insofar as they brought organization and regularity to black relations with the party, facilitated an efficient, thorough black canvass, and got out the black vote, for these levels of black politics were most on the minds of vote-conscious white party leaders. In fact, the creation of such clubs demonstrated the awareness of blacks that as a minority, however great their potential power, they would succeed in politics only to the extent that they presented an active, organized front before white Republicans when pressing their claims for patronage, nominations, and other considerations. Only then could the leader's extensive contacts and political skills be used to maximize racial and individual interests. Under these circumstances, political rivalries among blacks centered as much on winning the brethren into contending clubs with promises of various benefits as on the pursuit of reward from the party, for white party leaders expected their black counterparts to have a significant number of followers (hence, potential party workers and voters) among the black electorate.[16]

Despite their increasing organization and their eagerness to participate in politics, the ascension of blacks to appointive and elective office came much more slowly than integration into the party's structure and campaign activities. A very few, like Cleveland's J. H. Washington and Allan Medlin, were elected ward constable or ward assessor, and Jere Brown was appointed a bailiff and subsequently deputy sheriff of Cuyahoga County. Fewer still were the blacks nominated for significant state and local offices. The only important electoral victory in the early 1870s was that of John Green, whose wide contacts among white Republicans and Irish Democrats helped him to win a 3,000-vote majority in a race for justice of the peace in 1873, a year when the Cleveland Republican mayoral candidate lost by over 2,000 votes. The only significant federal appointment was Harlan's—a sinecure as special postal agent at Cincinnati—given in return for the power he wielded among Cincinnati blacks, and for his extensive influence among whites.[17]

[16] Cleveland *Leader*, Mar. 23, 29, 1870, Aug. 26, Sept. 22, 1871, June 13, Aug. 15, 1872, Oct. 7, 1874; Cleveland *Plain Dealer*, Sept. 11, 12, 20, 1874; Cincinnati *Commercial*, Sept. 1, 13, 1870, Sept. 4, 6, 1872. In the early days of black politics, when black participation was still a novelty, newspapers frequently carried articles on the activity of these clubs, which facilitated the gathering of names of members and officers. Their names were then traced in city directories for Cleveland, 1869, 1870, 1871, and 1874, and Cincinnati, 1870, 1871, 1872.

[17] Xenia *Torchlight*, Dec. 29, 1869; Cleveland *Leader*, Mar. 30, 1872; Cincinnati *Commercial*, Aug. 23, 1873; Cincinnati *Enquirer*, Mar. 22, 1875; Jackson

On the other hand, ample evidence was already accumulating to suggest that many white Republicans were more anxious to use blacks than to share power with them. At Cincinnati in 1871, blacks were publicly encouraged to compete for nomination to the legislative slate, only to be double-crossed by alleged friends in the balloting. One white Republican was said to have been heard muttering that "he would not vote his delegation for any damned nigger" when he was asked to place his forces behind Harlan's legislative candidacy. The nominating convention had been set up, said one black bitterly, "to tickle the nigger admirably and then slaughter him as a butcher slaughters cattle." At Columbus two years later, Poindexter was nominated to run for the legislature—a largely symbolic honor, since the city regularly sent Democrats to the General Assembly. Yet few local blacks expected the respected minister to make as poor a showing as he did, running over a thousand votes behind the lowest Republican tallies. At Greene County, a white Republican candidate for the sheriff's nomination was defeated in a local party convention when it was discovered that he had promised a deputyship to a young, qualified black. (In the sheriff's office at Hamilton County, a young black man who did work as a deputy sheriff was paid a janitor's wages.) Many were most angered, however, by the Republican legislature's refusal in 1871 to consider the application for sergeant-at-arms of David Jenkins. Legislators were surely aware that he was well qualified for the post, after nearly three decades of observing their sessions in his role as a lobbyist in behalf of black welfare.[18]

These examples of greed, prejudice, and treachery among white Republicans were profound disappointments for blacks. Not only did they compromise the party's principles and signal a merely superficial commitment to equality, but they also posed a serious immediate threat to the ambitions of black politicians. Black leaders looked to the coming of political equality for more than the ballot. They hoped that along with enfranchisement would come the opportunity to participate alongside whites in every level of government, helping to prove the capacity of blacks for directing public affairs and for democratic self-government. Any denial of that opportunity to wield power not only blocked racial advancement, but was in itself a negative comment on black ability, and as such nothing less than an insult. Moreover, blacks hoped that enfranchisement would bring the opportunity

Standard, Apr. 15, 1875; John P. Green, *Fact Stranger Than Fiction: 75 Years of a Busy Life* (Cleveland, 1920), pp. 150–168.

[18] Cincinnati *Commercial,* Sept. 12, 21, 1871, Aug. 23, 1873; Columbus *Dispatch,* Sept. 8, 1873; Columbus *Ohio State Journal,* Sept. 1, Oct. 17, 1873.

for qualified persons to obtain steady, well-paying, dignified employment of the type they were denied by private employers. Few had
great hopes that Ohio blacks would be amply rewarded with federal
patronage, for the northern black vote was simply too small to bring
black leaders the patronage opportunities that their southern counterparts enjoyed. However, on the state and local levels their votes might
be important for Republican majorities, and where they were proving
themselves diligent workers in party affairs, blacks did expect patronage. Yet in the early 1870s a small number of black men competed for
an even smaller number of jobs; the better the job, the smaller the
chance that it would be within the grasp of even the most qualified
blacks.

This situation posed a cruel dilemma and raised difficult questions,
initiating a serious debate about the proper direction and basic goals
of black politics. Most blacks felt a deep attachment to the party of
Lincoln and emancipation. In the early 1870s the party was the chief
source of the protection of the race's newly won civil status and of the
basic welfare of the southern freedmen, and it had also proven itself
equal to the task of maintaining basic rights in the South. Most blacks
then would have agreed with Frederick Douglass's dictum: "The Republican party is the deck; everything else, the sea."

The extent of this commitment to the Republican party and the
identification of the party with racial welfare was evident during the
1872 presidential campaign. Many felt that the forces of Liberal Republicanism represented racial reaction in the South, and they were
deeply distrustful of any alliance with Democrats. J. S. Tyler accused
Charles Sumner and other white Republicans backing Horace Greeley
of "apostasy." When Sumner issued a public letter in July stating that
Greeley represented the best hope for the race because he would bring
peace to the South, Tyler said emphatically, "We are opposed to all
Republicans who seek to form alliances, offensive or defensive, with
the party that has been an uncompromising enemy of our race." Tyler's
friend, John Booker, accused Sumner, who was then struggling for passage of his civil rights bill, of attempting to trade on his record in order
to get blacks to betray their best interests. Sumner's statement urging
blacks to vote for Greeley was "a political trick to cheat the colored
voters of this country—to take advantage of the colored man's sincere
devotion to Mr. Sumner to transfer the colored vote, body and soul, to
the enemies of liberty." [19] Forceful as such statements were, they paled
in comparison to the treatment accorded a black Liberal Republican,
Tabbs Gross of Arkansas, who attempted to present Greeley's positions

[19] For Tyler and Booker quotes, Columbus *Ohio State Journal*, Aug. 3, 1872.

to black audiences at Springfield and Cincinnati during the fall campaign. His efforts were greeted with threats upon his life that forced him to flee from Ohio. ". . . No colored man," said the Cincinnati *Commercial's* Dayton correspondent, "can speak for Greeley in this community without great personal peril." [20]

But there were blacks who recognized the great danger in unquestioning, unyielding partisanship. They were wary that slavery would be replaced by political bondage to the Republican party, and they believed that black politics could not be based solely on the vagaries of white men, no matter how lofty the principles they proclaimed, but must retain an independent, critical spirit. Their wariness was reinforced by a realistic appraisal of the forces which had led Republicans to champion emancipation and black citizenship; they displayed varying degrees of appreciation for the complexity of Republican motives, if not occasional distrust of the party. Objecting to the fawning, uncritical tone of a resolution thanking Republicans legislators for voting to place an enfranchising proposition before the voters, Dr. J. C. McSimpson of Zanesville said at an 1867 race convention that Republicans had been "as loathe to give us our rights as any, and we are not indebted to them for any privileges we enjoy." Blacks owed more to the avenging arm of "old John Brown"; regardless of which whites had been or were allies, blacks had won their rights through sacrifices on southern battlefields.[21]

To the extent that such attitudes implied that blacks should deal with the party which made them the best offer, they seemed superfluous in the early 1870s when the Republicans were the only champions of equality and citizenship. But even though they were practically tied to the Republican party, some black leaders sought to preserve freedom of action within partisan constraints. They were willing to remain loyal but refused to subordinate racial welfare to political expediency—a position challenged by those black politicians calling for partisan loyalty. At the first state racial convention after enfranchisement there was a discussion of the propriety of voicing grievances against the party outside Republican forums; Columbus A.M.E. minister J. P. Underwood then warned against "submerging the colored vote." Such a course would only be practical, he said, to the extent that Republicans remained completely true to the best principles of their party—a quite unlikely contingency. David Jenkins agreed; he argued against "silent movement," i.e., working gradually and unobtrusively through the party, because it left too much up to white Republicans.

[20] Cincinnati *Commercial*, Aug. 19, 20, 21, 26, Sept. 3, 6, 7, 1872.
[21] Columbus *Ohio State Journal*, July 4, 1867; Cincinnati *Gazette*, July 4, 1867.

He urged blacks to be prepared to take issues vital to their welfare directly to the state legislature and other governmental agencies when racial welfare so dictated, rather than waiting for the party to initiate action in their behalf. Opposition to such views came from Booker of Columbus and Dr. R. J. Robinson of Wellington in Lorain County. Both men argued that, given their numerical weakness in Ohio and the debt of gratitude they owed Republicans, blacks must accept party discipline, using their loyalty and party labor to convince their allies of the need to work for black advancement. The convention debates ended inconclusively, with no formula for balancing racial advancement and partisan loyalty.[22]

The problem surfaced again two years later. A number of the black political leaders who had grown highly critical of the Republicans for inaction on racial matters began searching for ways of dealing with the dearth of black patronage and electoral opportunity in Ohio. They also wished to protest the failure of congressional Republicans to act upon Sumner's civil rights bill, despite overwhelming majorities in both houses. In the process, they gave rise to one of the decade's sharpest clashes between the two outstanding tendencies in black politics: the desire for greater independence, and the belief in the necessity of partisan loyalty. This clash was precipitated by the convening, largely under the direction of Peter Clark, of a state racial convention at Chillicothe in late August, 1873, for the purpose of holding extensive discussions on the political condition of Ohio blacks.[23]

Two influences led Clark to call the convention and to quickly emerge as the leading critic of the party. He was deeply disturbed by the party's failure to live up to its principles of racial justice, particularly in the matter of patronage and electoral opportunity for blacks; he was also disgusted by the fact that black men were set against one another in a struggle for a very small number of well-paying posts, while the few who did obtain public employment were more often than not merely menials. He had received reports of broken promises, greed, and treachery in Republican ranks. "I was constantly in receipt of letters from all over the state," said Clark, explaining the reason for the convention, "and was constantly met by men who complained that the Republican party was not doing justice to its colored members." Prominent among those complaining to Clark were talented, aspiring "young men of this generation" who had been frustrated in their search for respectable public employment and were now searching for an established racial leader to help them press their cause.[24]

22 Columbus *Ohio State Journal,* Jan. 7, 19, 1871.
23 Ibid., July 31, 1873.
24 Cincinnati *Commercial,* Aug. 30, 31, Sept. 4, 1872, Aug. 23, Sept. 23, 1873.

Yet while they were anxious to pursue justice from the party, Clark and other convention organizers were at the same time bent on finding a new direction for black politics in Ohio. They hoped to forge out of the existing frustration and bitterness a viable tendency toward political independence. Clark was especially impressed by signs that political solidarities which had developed out of sectional conflict over slavery were now eroding. He himself had remained a loyal Republican in 1872, believing that the fate of the southern freedmen was at stake. But he had now begun to realize that many of the race's allies, including those who "would lay down their lives on the altar of the colored man's freedom," had become Democrats or Liberal Republicans in response to various issues (such as the tariff and the corruption of the Grant administration) which were of great concern to the white majority, but had no direct bearing upon the civil and political goals of contemporary black leadership. Like others who were to involve themselves in the Chillicothe movement, Clark still considered himself a loyal Republican in 1873. But the changing nature of national political groupings and of the issues which moved the white majority were breaking down the earlier political polarization over race and slavery, suggesting the opportunity for increased black political independence. By showing a willingness to vote for Democrats concerned with, or at least not hostile to, black welfare, black voters might encourage Democrats to court their votes and to take an interest in black advancement. Finally, Clark and his followers felt that the time was right for a movement toward greater political independence. The Republican campaign of 1872 had left the party in control of two-thirds of the states, both houses of Congress, and the presidency, securing several more years of safety for the freedmen, and insuring that blacks discussing the need for a new political strategy could not be accused of immediately jeopardizing racial or party interest.[25]

From its first session, the well-attended convention of nearly a hundred delegates from around Ohio showed an openness toward controversial opinion and a militant spirit of independence. The sessions were invigorated by the presence of many of the embittered young men with whom Clark had been in contact, and strengthened by the judgments of older leaders such as Clark, Xenia councilman E. C. Jackson, and long-time activist Alfred Anderson of Hamilton. The convention was definitely a meeting of the "outs," however; those with power and influence in the higher reaches of the Republican party, such as Poindexter, Arnett, Parham, and Harlan, were not present.[26]

25 Ibid., Aug. 23, 26, Sept. 23, 1873.
26 Ibid., Aug. 23, 1873.

John Booker, who had become increasingly critical of Republicans because of the party's failure to act on its promise of civil rights legislation, was elected president of the convention. He set its tone in his acceptance speech. The delegates' purpose must be to warn Republicans that blacks were "no longer footmats to be trodden on, for them to wipe their feet on and then be thrown away when done with." Speech after speech made the same point. The resolutions, adopted without dissent, called upon the party to "sustain its claim to being the special friend of the colored man . . . to do something for the colored man to which it is not driven by necessity." A long statement of complaints singled out grievances: the failure of congressional Republicans to pass a civil rights law, the refusal of the party's conventions to nominate qualified black men for state and local office, and the unwillingness of party officials and officeholders to appoint loyal, worthy Ohio blacks to patronage posts. With the fall state elections in view, blacks were urged toward political independence. They were told "to refrain from unconditionally pledging themselves to the nominees of local conventions and to use their best discrimination in determining for themselves in each locality whom to vote for." In order to provide for a perpetuation of the movement, a committee of three was appointed to call another convention when the time was thought right.[27]

The reaction to the Chillicothe movement began before the convention ended. After being denied permission to address the convention, Colonel Harlan, the Grant administration's leading black officeholder in Ohio, proceeded anyway. Amidst hooting and booing he offered his own resolutions, expressing confidence in the administration and in the likelihood of the passage of a civil rights law. In the following weeks the opposition gathered force; local meetings, often the scene of bitter contention, either denounced the Chillicothe resolutions or failed to espouse them firmly. A week after the convention, Cincinnatians met at Allen Temple to hear Harlan, Arnett, and Parham denounce the movement as destructive and disloyal to both race and party. Clark and his followers attempted to speak but were menaced by toughs from Harlan's East End Colored Republican Club. The chair was controlled by Republican partisans, and though the voice vote on the partisan resolutions offered by Harlan was, according to a Cincinnati *Commercial* reporter, extremely close, there was a quick ruling in favor of the colonel. Meetings at Chillicothe, where the willingness of Second Ward blacks to vote for an effective Democratic councilman was a living example of the political independence which the convention had advocated, and at Dayton denounced the Chillicothe resolutions. A meet-

[27] Ibid.

ing at Columbus settled upon a compromise offered by Poindexter
which accepted the resolutions—with the contradictory proviso that
they were not to be seen as critical of the Republican party.[28]

That fall's state election campaign proved a poor occasion for attempting to implement the convention's goals. The Democratic gubernatorial candidate was seventy-year-old William Allen, an "Old
Time Democrat" who had been allied with Copperheads during the
war. He had helped to raise the spectre of mass black migration in
order to turn Ohioans against the war and emancipation, and he was
thus a symbol of reaction for whom few blacks could vote in good conscience. Federal officeholders John Mercer Langston and Frederick
Douglass, armed with lists of 500 blacks (mostly Southerners) holding
positions under the Grant administration, entered the state in September in behalf of the Republican ticket. They specifically criticized
Clark and the Chillicothe movement, extolled the virtues of the Grant
administration, and warned of the dangers of a Democratic revival.
Then in late September the bottom began to fall out of the economy,
and it became evident that Ohio Republicans would need every vote
they could muster in fending off Democratic charges that the administration was to blame. The panic meshed well with Allen's continued
emphasis on the tariff, inequitable taxation, and the corrupting influence of corporate interests in scandal-ridden Republican Washington.
Democrats took control of the legislature, and Allen secured a narrow 817-vote majority. For first time in well over a decade the Democrats held the governorship and the legislature at the same time.[29]

In the next few years the same story was repeated elsewhere. Because of the economic situation, Democrats made gains in northern
states. In the South, the transition from Republican rule to Democratic
control was accelerated by campaigns of terror and intimidation of
black voters. By the 1876 presidential election only South Carolina,
Florida, and Louisiana were still in Republican hands, dependent on
the possible intervention of federal troops to check the growing force
of the Democracy. In the 1874 congressional campaign the Republicans
lost control of the house for the first time since the war. The political
situation, therefore, again appeared uncertain and threatening for
blacks, and it gave Ohio Republicans a new opportunity to secure
their loyalty without making significant changes in the patronage situa-

[28] Ibid., Aug. 23, 25, 26, Sept. 6, 17, 1873; Columbus *Ohio State Journal,*
Aug. 26, 28, 1873; Xenia *Torchlight,* Sept. 10, 1873.
[29] Cincinnati *Commercial,* Sept. 17, 23, 24, 1873; Cleveland *Leader,* Sept. 25,
1873; Philip D. Jordan, *Ohio Comes of Age, 1873–1900* (Columbus, 1943),
pp. 28–30.

tion; indeed, they added only a few clerkships connected with the legislature (such as engrossing clerk) and a few minor local posts. In
Congress, the passage of a weakened civil rights bill was delayed until
1875. Under the circumstances, no sequel to the Chillicothe convention
was held, and the independent thrust initiated by Clark collapsed.[30]

But the debate over political strategy was revived in 1877 with the
appearance of Rutherford B. Hayes's southern policy. The recently in-
augurated Ohioan planned a pull-out of remaining federal troops, with
the implicit promise of an end to federal action in southern racial affairs and a pledge of close political and economic ties between the
administration and southern conservatives. Reactions among black
Ohioans ranged from full support to outrage. Poindexter, Arnett,
Green, Anderson, and George Washington Williams all were ardent
defenders of the new policy. Poindexter, who had close ties with Hayes
and had encouraged him to take a new direction in southern affairs,
was the most vocal defender. Arguing that the old policy was a failure because white opinion and the courts refused to sustain the federal power needed to protect freedmen in the South, Poindexter envisioned an alliance between southern blacks and responsible, wealthy,
and conservative southern whites, who wished an end to violence and
disorder in their section. By stimulating southern economic development
and giving political encouragement to southern conservatives, Poindexter contended, the new policy benignly tied black labor to southern
capital, offered blacks greater opportunity for socioeconomic mobility,
and at the same time provided a means for their political protection
without requiring that they take the active role in politics which so in-
furiated southern whites. "I have found great comfort in the reflection,"
said Poindexter in June, "that the South would soon turn to the colored man for labor . . . and I have thought that if the colored man
would be wise, would cultivate habits of industry, sobriety, and honesty . . . and let politics alone, except for voting for the best man and
accepting an office when sought after . . . prejudice against him
would soon die in the South; his color would cease to be a detriment to
him, and he would be respected the country-over as any other man." [31]
But Poindexter, and Anderson as well, had additional reason for supporting Hayes: dangling before each of them in the first months of the
administration was the possibility of appointment as U.S. consul to

[30] Cincinnati *Enquirer,* Sept. 25, 1873; Xenia *Gazette,* Oct. 7, 1873; Cleveland
Leader, Mar. 8, Apr. 3, 7, 1875; Columbus *Ohio State Journal,* Jan. 1, 1876.

[31] Columbus *Ohio State Journal,* June 7, July 2, Aug. 13, Sept. 17, 1877;
Richard Williams, ed., *Diary and Letters of Rutherford B. Hayes* (Columbus,
1925), III, 417.

Haiti, one of the richest patronage plums then available to blacks. Both actively sought the position, but in August it was given to Langston. He had left Ohio to reside in Virginia in the early 1860s, and his influence among the southern black majority made him more important to the party than a Northerner would be.[32]

For others, however, the new policy was seen as a betrayal. Columbus's Fred Roney believed that advancement of the freedmen would be "woefully retarded" by the Hayes policy, and he helped found a movement to influence Ohio Republicans of all colors to register their protest by staying away from the polls in that fall's state elections. Partisan though he was, Harlan admitted in a letter to Ohio Senator John Sherman that he and other blacks were angry. "Nineteen out of twenty colored men I know believe that the Republican party wishes to unload them. This belief is so strong that thousands of them will not go to the polls this fall." "As for myself," he concluded, "I am done with politics." Harlan's retirement was short lived, however. He continued to be active in Republican politics, but he seldom played as unquestioningly partisan a role as he had in the early 1870s.[33]

Talk of bolting the party was everywhere. Angered by the southern policy and the lack of patronage at all levels, a small but vocal group of black politicians turned toward political independence. Feeling that the party could no longer ask them to compromise their interests in the name of the freedman's welfare, they demanded a correction of the patronage situation and threatened to desert the Republican ticket. An Independent Union of Colored Voters was organized at Cincinnati in August. Angered that they had been helping white Republicans for years in exchange for "promises of political recognition and proportionate representation" which were "totally ignored," the Cincinnati independents demanded fair representation at party nominating conventions and proper shares of nominations and patronage.[34]

More surprising was the emergence of a small black Democracy at Columbus and Cincinnati. Previously there had been a handful of blacks who had worked with Democrats in return for cash and promises of minor office—generally nothing more than ward assessorships,

[32] Columbus *Ohio State Journal*, July 2, Sept. 17, Oct. 3, 1877; Cincinnati *Commercial*, Sept. 3, 1877; Alfred J. Anderson to W. J. West, Aug. 5, 1877, Rutherford B. Hayes Papers, HL; Alfred J. Anderson to W. J. West, Aug. 10, 1877, v. 145 (1877), W. J. West to John Sherman, Aug. 22, 1877, v. 146 (1877), John Sherman Papers, LC.

[33] Cincinnati *Enquirer*, Aug. 10, 1877; Columbus *Ohio State Journal*, Aug. 10, 1877; Columbus *Dispatch*, Sept. 6, 1877; Cincinnati *Commercial*, Sept. 30, 1877; Robert Harlan to John Sherman, Aug. 20, 1877, v. 146 (1877), Sherman Papers.

[34] Cincinnati *Enquirer*, Aug. 7, 31, Sept. 7, 1877; Cincinnati *Commercial*, Aug. 18, 19, 21, 1877.

but then the Republicans promised little more. Henry Pickett of Rat Row had worked for the Democracy in return for boodle for himself and friends; several opportunistic Clevelanders, such as excavating contractor Madison Tilley, realizing that the city's black patronage was monopolized by a few upper-class influentials and their followers, made an alliance with local Democrats. It was hardly a respected position, and the obscure names of those in the "Colored Democracy" suggest that the individuals involved were, like Pickett, hardly frequenters of upper-class social circles. No effort was made to bring these blacks into the party. The Democrats used them for propaganda, and they in turn used the Democrats. While there was for a brief time a black Democratic club at Cleveland, these did not exist elsewhere, nor did blacks appear on the hustings in behalf of the Democracy.[35]

In 1877 the situation began to change. Democrats initiated concerted efforts to make inroads into the black vote. A few party-financed black Democratic clubs emerged, and for the first time blacks began to address Democratic audiences, black and white. The most prominent of these orators was Athens attorney Andrew Jackson Davidson, born a slave but raised at Ashtabula, where he had read law with a white attorney. Calling for a coalition of the poor of both races within the Democracy, Davidson and a few others attacked Republicans as the party of corporate greed and accused them of hypocrisy on the race issue. In 1879 Davidson served as the first black delegate at a Democratic state convention.[36]

Fearing a massive black defection to the Democracy or a stay-at-home protest, Cincinnati Republicans also faced, in a year of economic depression and labor militance, the appearance of Peter Clark as a leader of the Ohio Socialist Labor party; he was running for state school commissioner. In response to the economic crisis and the misery it created among Cincinnati's poor of both races, Clark emerged in 1877 as a socialist—a commitment which waned considerably in a few years. These challenges to black loyalty forced Republicans to take extraordinary measures. They nominated George Washington Williams for the legislature—the first time since enfranchisement that a Cincinnati black had been put forward for anything but a minor post. At Cleveland, though no black socialist appeared, the situation was simi-

[35] Cincinnati *Commercial*, Oct. 13, 1870, Oct. 11, 1871; Cleveland *Leader*, Mar. 30, 31, 1871; Cleveland *Herald*, Mar. 29, 1871; Columbus *Ohio State Journal*, Oct. 10, 1870.
[36] Cincinnati *Commercial*, Aug. 11, 1877; Cincinnati *Enquirer*, Aug. 15, Sept. 15, 18, 22, 28, 1877; Cleveland *Leader*, Sept. 19, 1877; London *Madison County Democrat*, Sept. 19, 1877; Columbus *Ohio State Journal*, June 5, 1879; Charles H. Harris, *The Harris Story* (Athens, 1957), pp. 27–29.

lar. Fearing that close local contests might require the loyalty of every Republican, the party nominated John Green as the first black Clevelander on the legislative ticket. Both nominations seem to have had the desired effect. At Cincinnati, a number of independents rallied to Williams's cause; though the black Democracy did not affiliate with his campaign, its talk of political bondage faded during the weeks before the election. The Green candidacy served to revive partisan loyalty among Cleveland's Sixth Ward blacks who were bitter over patronage, and the Republican cause was helped immeasurably by the abusive racial rhetoric used against Green by Cleveland's Democratic press. In addition to providing two legislative nominations, Republicans flooded the state with the most prominent black orators, who justified the southern policy, soothed tempers over patronage, and attempted to counter the impact of the Clark candidacy by raising the spectre of anarchism.[37]

The election resulted in the most sweeping Democratic victory in Ohio since the organization of the Republican party two decades before. Republicans lost both the governorship and the legislature which they had won by narrow margins in 1875. Democrat Richard Bishop obtained the largest Democratic majority (22,250) in a gubernatorial election since the war. The fate of the two black legislative candidates certainly offered grist for the black Democracy's propaganda mill. Both Green and Williams lost, running substantially behind the other Republicans on local legislative tickets. Williams was more than 1,500 votes below the tallies of three-quarters of the Republican legislative candidates, but the whole ticket went down to defeat along with him. Green also ran behind the Republican ticket, but (much to the disgrace of local Republicans) that ticket won, while Green fell far enough behind to lose to the Democratic front-runner.[38]

Carefully analyzing election returns, the Columbus *Dispatch* cited a large stay-at-home protest against the southern policy, particularly in the Western Reserve, as the primary cause of the Republican debacle. It is very difficult to gauge the extent to which blacks stayed at home or defected to other parties as a protest against Republican policy. There is a lack of data for many smaller constituencies, and, given the stay-at-home tendency among white Republicans, it is impossible to isolate the electoral protest of the party's black minority—especially because, except in several medium-size urban centers, blacks almost

[37] Cincinnati *Commercial*, Mar. 27, July 23, 26, Aug. 12, 19, 23, 28, 31, 1877; Cleveland *Leader*, Sept. 10, 1877; Cleveland *Plain Dealer*, Sept. 18, 28, Oct. 8, 1877.

[38] Cincinnati *Enquirer*, Oct. 12, 23, 24, 1877; Cleveland *Plain Dealer*, Oct. 10, 11, 12, 1877.

always voted in racially mixed districts. Growing radicalism resulted in more Socialist Labor voting in cities and towns, but it is not easy to discover the extent to which Clark drew blacks to that ticket. However, in no large constituency did the press note a significant black electoral protest against the southern policy, as opposed to specific local racial problems.[39]

While black discontent may have been muted by the nominations of Green and Williams, 1877 marked a turning point in the development of a tendency toward politics based on racial needs, rather than on gratitude for favors gone stale. Hayes's southern policy made political independence a more responsible and respected position. An influential minority of black politicians, whose proclivities tended to be Republican, finally became convinced that blacks must make the best terms with each party without coming to depend too heavily on either, and that they must be willing to vote Democratic in order to penalize Republicans for indifference to black welfare. Moreover, encouraged by new chances for creating dissension among black Republicans, those who were Democrats continued to support the semblance of a black Democracy, small but monied (thanks to the party), vocal, and grasping at every opportunity to expose Republican perfidy. Their practical success was no doubt minuscule, especially in the face of continuing Democratic repression of southern blacks. But the impact upon Republicans was predictable—they were forced to combine appeals for black gratitude with more substantive bases upon which to call for black loyalty. In 1877 blacks had new expectations for representation in the legislature. Renominated in 1879, Williams was elected; although Green failed to obtain renomination in that year, he was subsequently nominated and elected to the legislature in 1881. Precedents were set, and blacks continued to be sent to the legislature from both Cleveland and Cincinnati at regular intervals for most of the period before 1916. Republicans also began to give blacks more prestigious appointive offices. In 1880, newly elected Republican Governor Charles Foster

[39] Columbus *Dispatch*, Oct. 10, 11, 1877. The situation at Xenia was complex. Campbell Maxwell, a young black lawyer who had been one of the Chillicothe rebels, ran for state representative on the Socialist ticket. Maxwell's candidacy resulted more from a desire to protest local Republican failures to appoint, nominate, and elect blacks than from either ideological affinity with socialism or a desire to penalize the Republican party for the policies of President Hayes. Maxwell won 84 votes (26%) in the largely black Fourth Ward, doing slightly better than Peter Clark, who won 73 votes (22%) in his race for state school commissioner. In both contests, the rest of the vote went almost wholly to Republican candidates. While local Republican voting was down throughout Xenia and Greene County, this was less the case in the Fourth than elsewhere. Cincinnati *Enquirer*, Sept. 5, 1877; Xenia *News*, Aug. 25, Sept. 22, Oct. 6, 13, 20, 1877; Xenia *Torchlight*, Oct. 10, 17, 1877.

appointed Poindexter to the board of trustees of the Ohio Institution for the Education of the Blind in reward for his years of loyalty; this choice established a precedent which admitted blacks in growing numbers to the governing boards of state institutions.[40]

The most evident benefits were found at the local level, for there it was easiest for the black voter and politician to demonstrate an interest in Democratic candidates. If Democrats were to subsidize temporary black campaign newspapers and, on occasion, the regular black press, Republicans had to do likewise. Both parties of necessity courted independents, Republicans in the hope of deepening their usual affinity for Lincoln's party, and Democrats in the hope of wooing them from independent Republicanism. If Democrats subsidized clubhouses and provided cash, uniforms, and other accouterments of partisan loyalty, Republicans had to make sure that their already subsidized black clubs were maintained in similar, if not better, style.

There were occasionally more substantive benefits from the new competition between the parties and the new spirit of black independence. Columbus provides an example. In 1879, after recently elected local Republican police commissioners failed to keep a promise to appoint a black policeman, black Democrats began an embarrassing campaign to expose the betrayal and to ask what was to be done about it. Black Republicans, urged on by their more independent element's threat to bolt the entire Republican ticket in that fall's county elections, vowed to fight the election of one commissioner who had been nominated for sheriff. Some weeks before the election two black policemen were appointed by frightened Republicans, but the ticket-splitting campaign continued, supported by even the partisan Poindexter. The election returns indicated that very few blacks had defected,[41] but militant rhetoric and constant criticism from black Democrats had done their work effectively. Backed by growing numbers of black voters in the city, the formula would be used again to good effect in coming years.

In 1880 Columbus blacks contended successfully for the creation of a black-staffed firehouse. More important was Poindexter's election in

[40] Cleveland *Plain Dealer*, Aug. 30, Sept. 1, 1879; Cleveland *Herald*, Oct. 11, 12, 13, 1881; Cincinnati *Commercial*, Aug. 8, 11, 22, 24, 25, Oct. 9, 12, 13, 16, 1879; Richard Clyde Minor, "James Preston Poindexter: Elder Statesman of Columbus," *Ohio State Archeological and Historical Quarterly*, LVI, 3 (1947), 276.

[41] Columbus *Democrat*, Aug. 17, 19, Sept. 4, 14, 1879; Columbus *Ohio State Journal*, June 28, July 2, 3, 5, 7, 1879. There was little difference in the tallies of the Republican gubernatorial candidate and the candidate for sheriff in precincts with large numbers of blacks; Columbus *Ohio State Journal*, Oct. 15, 1879.

1880 as Ninth Ward city councilman, which opened the door for other black councilmen, such as Pennsylvania Railroad clerk I. D. Ross and caterer Ed Tripplett, to be elected from shifting political districts along East Long Street. Blacks would also begin in 1884, several years after school integration in Columbus, to represent the Ninth Ward on the board of education. In the 1880s the Ninth was largely Republican; while blacks were a power within the ward, with approximately 30 percent of the population, they did not hold the balance of power. Recognition at the time was largely due to their growing willingness to make demands and threats which led to nominations at ward conventions. Ward Democrats acceded to the power of the blacks; as gestures of good will, they occasionally refused to nominate candidates to oppose popular black Republicans. During the early 1880s, when black Republicans began to be elected to minor ward positions, such as constable and assessor, not to be outdone, the Democracy nominated blacks for the same positions. In the spring of 1884 Columbus blacks appeared on the tickets of both parties for the first time.[42]

The same dynamic influenced the patronage situation in other areas. While black patronage opportunities rarely corresponded to the proportion of the race among local voters, there was nevertheless a noticeable tendency toward improvement beginning in the 1880s, as blacks grew more willing to threaten and demand. While Cincinnati and Cleveland blacks lacked the electoral opportunity of those in Columbus, their patronage situation was by no means bleak. From a mere handful of black appointees in 1880, by 1891 there were 164 black employees earning over $120,000 for their work in municipal and county positions at Cincinnati; at Cleveland, where there were many fewer blacks, there were 18 black employees. The range of black jobs was expanding to include small numbers of more respectable jobs as clerks, engineers, and policemen, as well as the more common (and menial) messengers and porters.[43]

The new political situation had a vital impact on major racial issues of the 1880s, particularly on the status of civil rights, school, and intermarriage legislation. In the wake of the 1883 decision invalidating the civil rights law, black meetings in Ohio sought a strategy for regaining legal protection.[44] They heeded the court's suggestion that they look

[42] Richard Clyde Minor, "Negroes in Columbus" (Ph.D. dissertation, Ohio State University, 1936), pp. 172–179; Cleveland *Gazette*, Mar. 29, Apr. 26, Dec. 30, 1884, Apr. 18, 1885; Columbus *Ohio State Journal*, Mar. 17, 1893.

[43] Cleveland *Gazette*, Aug. 23, 1890, Apr. 25, May 2, July 4, 18, Aug. 1, 1891, July 6, 1893.

[44] Ibid., Nov. 3, 1883; Cincinnati *Enquirer*, Oct. 23, 1883; Cincinnati *Gazette*, Oct. 23, 1883.

to the states, but the likelihood of obtaining Ohio legislation was dubious. The 1883 state elections had resulted in a substantial Democratic victory; Democrats gained 36,000 votes over their 1881 total to win the governorship back from the Republicans by a majority of 12,529, and they took control of the legislature, doubling their number in the Senate and almost doing likewise in the House.[45] While Democrats courted the black vote in various ways, beneficial legislation was not normally expected of them.

Yet Ohio politics were in flux, and blacks were in a position to profit from the situation. During 1873–83, as its electoral triumphs in 1873, 1877, and 1883 suggest, the Ohio Democracy had begun to threaten the hold which Republicans had enjoyed since the late 1850s as the result of the sectional crisis. Between 1855 and 1873 Democrats had failed to win the governorship even once and had taken control of the legislature only twice; in contrast, the 1873–83 decade was characterized by fluctuating control of both the governorship and the legislature. In an electorate of between 450,000 and 720,000 during 1873–83, on only one occasion (1881) were Republicans able to obtain a majority of over 20,000 in a gubernatorial election. At the same time, their presidential majorities in Ohio fell from 57,000 and 47,000 respectively in 1868 and 1872 to only 7,600 in 1876—and this for favorite son Rutherford B. Hayes, who had twice recently been elected governor. In the next three presidential contests, margins were between 21,000 and 35,000. Moreover, third and fourth parties, led by socialists, Greenbackers, and temperance advocates, reflecting the conflicts of the emerging post-Reconstruction era, threatened to cut into the support of both parties on all levels, and they added even more uncertainty to politics.[46]

Political instability and narrow margins of victory in presidential and gubernatorial elections highlighted the importance of Ohio's estimated (in 1880) 22,000 black voters,[47] for their numbers were roughly equal to or greater than Republican majorities. In many counties and districts where the two parties ran neck and neck, the black vote was obviously important to Republican success.[48] As observers in the early

[45] Ohio, *Statistics, 1883*, pp. 254–256, 312–315.

[46] Jordan, *Ohio Comes of Age*, pp. 144–188; Thomas E. Powell, *The Democratic Party of Ohio* (n.p., 1913), I, 250–289; W. Dean Burnham, *Presidential Ballots, 1836–1892* (Baltimore, 1955), pp. 248–249; Ohio, *Statistics, 1873–83*.

[47] U.S. Census Office, *Statistics of the United States at the Tenth Census* (Washington, 1883), pp. 618–619.

[48] Many legislative seats were at this time being won by narrow majorities, particularly in the counties with voting populations under 5,000 and in the two leading urban counties, Hamilton and Cuyahoga, where voting populations were approximately 60,000 and 40,000 respectively. In 1881, 67 of 105 seats in the

1880s sorted out the various factors defining Ohio politics, they came to realize that blacks might well hold the balance of power. In 1883 Harry Smith maintained that there had not been a single election in Ohio since 1879 which would have been won by Republicans if blacks had voted Democratic. Joseph Benson Foraker, the central figure in Republican state politics during the 1880s, agreed. Reflecting years later on the gubernatorial politics of the period, he said, "The Negro vote was so large that it was not only an important but an essential factor in our considerations. It would not be possible for the Republican party to carry the state if that vote should be arrayed against us." [49] The argument was often extended to include presidential elections in Ohio; it was frequently claimed that, given a solidly Democratic South, it was the Republican black vote in New York, Indiana, and Ohio which kept Democrats from regularly electing their presidential candidates. George Washington Williams claimed in 1884 that Garfield owed his election in 1880 "to the clannishness of the Negro vote in the North"; he went on to prove, on the basis of inflated estimates of black voting potential, that blacks in these three states held the key to that contest. Harry Smith felt less bound to offer proof, although he frequently made the same point in the *Gazette*. Such observations on Ohio and the North usually overestimated the size of the black vote, and they always proceeded upon the dubious premise that all blacks voted. They also failed to admit that blacks were not likely to align en masse against Republicans, and that general fluctuations from election to election were determined by the votes of white independents and special interest groups like temperance advocates.[50] But as long as white Republicans such as Foraker and vocal blacks such as Smith and Williams were impressed with the importance of black voters, the argument had a life of its own.

Ohio Democrats were realistic enough to know that blacks were not likely to consider voting Democratic in any but local elections, and then not regularly. Yet the 1883 state elections led them to unprece-

lower house were won by less than 1,000 votes; in 1883, 75 of 105 seats were won likewise. Ohio, *Statistics, 1881*, pp. 352–355, and *1883*, pp. 254–256, 312–315.

[49] Cleveland *Gazette*, Sept. 1, 1883; Joseph Benson Foraker, *Notes of a Busy Life* (Cincinnati, 1916), I, 177.

[50] George Washington Williams, *The Negro as a Political Problem: Oration . . . at the Asbury Church, Washington, D.C. April 16, 1884* (Boston, 1884), pp. 29–30; Cleveland *Gazette*, Nov. 8, 1884. Presidential majorities in the two other states which made up this triumvirate of black political power during 1876–84 were, for Indiana: 1876, 6,600 (Democratic); 1880, 7,400 (Republican); 1884, 6,500 (Republican); and for New York, 1876, 33,000 (Democratic); 1880, 16,000 (Republican); and 1884, 1,000 (Democratic). Burnham, *Presidential Ballots*, pp. 390–391, 632–633.

dented optimism. For the first time since enfranchisement, blacks were thought to have deserted the Republican ticket in large numbers. Indeed, the day after the election the Democratic Cleveland *Plain Dealer* estimated that fully a third of Ohio's black voters had cast their ballots for the Democratic gubernatorial candidate, George B. Hoadley of Cincinnati, providing more than half of the 12,529 votes by which he defeated Foraker. Hoadley himself agreed, estimating that as many as 8,000 blacks had voted for him.[51]

The dramatic shift in black voting was thought to result from several factors. Foremost was a widespread unhappiness with the Foraker candidacy. Years later, while serving in the Senate, Foraker would be known as an outstanding crusader for black rights because of his lonely defense of the black soldiers who were summarily dismissed from the army for unproven charges of rioting at Brownsville, Texas. However, in 1883 rumors sweeping Ohio accused Foraker of racial prejudice and insensitivity to black welfare. The most damaging charge was that he had been chief counsel for the Springfield superintendent of schools, G. W. White, in the Gazaway school integration case. Though the Reverend Mr. Gazaway and his black attorneys, Graham Dewell and W. S. Newberry, all stated during the campaign that they were certain that Foraker had acted out of a sense of personal and professional obligation to White, an old friend from college days, and that he had shown no evidence of prejudice in his dealings with them during the case, many blacks remained unenthusiastic about the candidacy. Six weeks before the election, only 27 of 200 black voters at a Foraker rally in Cleveland pledged to vote a straight Republican ticket. Smith's *Gazette* gave Foraker less than wholehearted support, stating only that as the Republican he was the lesser of two evils. John Green also lacked enthusiasm, but he felt obligated to support the ticket on which he himself appeared as a legislative candidate. Black Republican politicians were noticeably inactive during the campaign.[52]

Foraker's record was set in bold relief by the career of his opponent, for Hoadley was surely the most compelling Democratic candidate ever placed before Ohio's black voters. He had not been involved in abolitionist organizations, but his sympathy for fugitive slaves had led to an arrest for refusing to help a sheriff apprehend a runaway. He had been a staunch foe of slavery's extension into the western terri-

[51] Cleveland *Plain Dealer*, Oct. 18, 1883; Cleveland *Gazette*, June 28, 1884; George B. Hoadley to Daniel Lamont, Mar. 28, 1885, Grover Cleveland Papers, LC.

[52] Foraker, *Notes of a Busy Life*, pp. 175–188; Springfield *Republic*, June 14, 1883; Cleveland *Gazette*, Sept. 1, 1883, Mar. 14, 1885.

tories, a commitment which followed him into politics. His first affiliation was with the Free Soil party, and in the late 1850s he joined the
newly organized Republicans. In 1872 he broke with the party on the
tariff issue, joining first the Liberal Republican movement and then
the Democracy. But in Cincinnati he retained a reputation as an ardent
defender of Negro rights, and his record gave black Democrats, more
active in 1883 than in any previous campaign, ample propaganda.[53]

With the Black Democracy was Peter Clark, who joined the party in
1882. His conversion followed years of wandering across the political
landscape; in 1879 he left the Socialist Labor party, still an exponent
of socialism but disillusioned by the doctrinaire tendencies within the
party, which he said tried "to hold members down to a rigid pattern
of ideas." [54] Moreover, at that time he was grateful to Cincinnati blacks
for standing by him when powerful local politicians unsuccessfully
attempted to remove him from the principalship of the black high
school because of socialist affiliation. His gratitude, he said, led him
back to the Republicans as the best vehicle for combating Democratic
repression in the South—but not for long. The motives for his subsequent Democratic affiliation were complex. Clark was not without personal ambition, and he was bitter that prominent white Republicans
had refused to support his bid for the Haytian ministry during the
first months of the Garfield administration. At the same time, he
quickly grew disgusted with Republican hypocrisy on the race issue,
coming to feel again, as he had almost a decade before while leading
the Chillicothe movement, that blacks must make the best possible
terms with both parties. He felt special urgency at the prospect of a
Democratic presidential victory in 1884. Under the first Democratic
administration since 1856, and possibly a Democratic Congress, it
would be folly for blacks to be antagonistic to the Democracy and the
South, which would no doubt play a larger role than in any administration since the 1850s. Black voices were needed to help influence the
Democracy's policies. According to T. Thomas Fortune, who admired
his independent spirit, Clark felt "that for the Democracy to triumph
entirely without the aid of the colored man would be a great calamity
and with this view he joined . . . that party and urged other colored
men to do so." With funds supplied by Democrats, Clark and his son
Herbert established and edited the Cincinnati *Afro-American* as the
organ of Ohio black Democrats. Herbert Clark took charge of the black

---

[53] Powell, *Democratic Party of Ohio*, I, 288–289; Wendell Phillips Dabney,
Cincinnati's Colored Citizens: Historical, Sociological, and Biographical (Cincinnati, 1926), pp. 87–88.
[54] Cincinnati *Commercial*, July 22, 1879.

Democratic campaign in 1883, climaxing his efforts with a state convention shortly before the election.[55]

The black vote was probably not as influential in 1883 as politicians and racial spokesmen assumed. Much more significant was a split among Republicans on the liquor issue, then before the voters in the form of two proposed state constitutional amendments. This matter kept thousands of prohibition-minded Republicans away from the polls and led others to make deals with Democrats on liquor control in local communities in exchange for votes for Hoadley. Few blacks appear to have stayed away from the polls or split their tickets, even at Springfield, where Foraker's role in the Gazaway case should have hurt him the most.[56] But, regardless of its lack of factual basis, politicians' widely held belief of a black defection had its own uses. The situation was ripe for exploitation by black Democrats, who certainly deserved recognition from the governor and legislature they were supposed to have been instrumental in electing, and they soon began to stake their claims. Meeting early in December, they and a number of independents who had worked for Hoadley resolved to petition the new legislature for a civil rights law.[57] Hoping to check the influence of the black Democrats and to take advantage of the Democratic quest for black votes, Republicans plotted their own course. When they met at Columbus on Christmas, they resolved to create a network of local "equal rights leagues" which were to be loosely governed by a state central committee. The immediate purpose of organizing was to launch local campaigns for civil rights legislation; larger purposes were also considered, for the long-range goal of the leagues was the repeal of

[55] Ibid., Oct. 2, 1879; Columbus *Ohio State Journal*, Sept. 21, 1883; Cincinnati *Enquirer*, Oct. 3, 1882; New York *Freeman*, Jan. 3, 1885; Cleveland *Gazette*, Mar. 8, 1886; Peter Clark to John Sherman, Apr. 10, 1881, v. 250 (1881); Edwin Baltzby to Peter Clark, Apr. 13, 1881, v. 6 (letterpress copybook, 1880–81), John Sherman to Peter Clark, Apr. 27, 1881, v. 250 (1881), Peter Clark to John Sherman, Apr. 24, 1881, v. 252 (1881), Sherman Papers.

[56] Jordan, *Ohio Comes of Age*, pp. 179–182; Cleveland *Herald*, Oct. 10, 11, 1883; Cincinnati *Commercial*, Oct. 12, 13, 1883. The lie in Democratic claims of a large black defection was revealed in local election results. In Xenia's largely black Fourth Ward, the Republican vote was actually higher than in 1882. Foraker ran but eight votes behind his running mate, while Hoadley bettered the Democratic mark in 1882 by only five votes; Xenia *Torchlight*, Oct. 13, 1883. At Springfield, not only were voting levels higher than in 1882 throughout the city, but no more than six votes separated Foraker from his more popular running mate in any ward; Springfield *Republic*, Oct. 11, 1883; E. L. Buchwalter to Joseph Foraker, Oct. 13, 1883, Box IV, folder 1, Foraker Papers. In Columbus's Ninth Ward precincts A and B, where there was a large black vote, Foraker received two votes fewer than his running mate; Columbus *Ohio State Journal*, Oct. 10, 1883.

[57] Cleveland *Gazette*, Dec. 8, 1883.

both the separate school law and the anti-intermarriage law, the last remaining statutes making distinctions between citizens on the basis of color. Unlike the campaign for repeal of the school law, that for the repeal of the marriage law was a pursuit of largely symbolic consequence, intended to complete the work of banishing legal color distinctions; it became a matter of practical necessity in the minds of many, however, when a few weeks later the marriage law was employed against a black Toledo man. Under convention-appointed organizers, such as attorney Graham Dewell and Professor William Sanders Scarborough, leagues were in time set up in many of the two hundred urban centers where the organization hoped to spread its influence.[58] In an era when black leaders had failed to consider the possibility of such well-coordinated efforts, the leagues demonstrated the urgency with which the civil rights situation was viewed, and the hope of many that the new political situation might be used for the sake of progressive change.

Democrats lost no time in staking their claim to Negro gratitude. Hoadley's inaugural address in January, 1884, was a dramatic gesture of friendship. Using rhetoric which, in the words of Fortune's New York *Globe,* "would have fitted well in the mouth of the immortal Sumner," he called for the removal of the two remaining racially offensive laws. Placing particular emphasis on the inequity of the dual school system, he also called for comprehensive school integration. Hoadley quickly appointed a few blacks, perhaps ten in all, to offices bearing varying degrees of honor and profit; yet numbers were deceptive, for more blacks were given posts by Hoadley than by any other Democratic administration (and several Republican ones) since enfranchisement. Ripley's J. S. Attwood, a businessman and outspoken Republican, was chosen to fill Poindexter's seat on the board of trustees of the school for the blind, and precedent was set by the appointment of Peter Clark and principals Ira Collins of Hamilton and J. R. Blackburn of Xenia to the boards of the state universities. Herbert Clark, Andrew Jackson Davidson, and several others were given clerkships on state agencies and with the legislature.[59]

Democratic legislators were also active. A civil rights bill was drafted by Senate Democrat Crowell of Coshocton County and then submitted amidst considerable fanfare to Peter Clark for his approval. The bill, which guaranteed protection in all facilities but eating places

[58] Ibid., Dec. 29, 1883, Jan. 12, 1884.
[59] Ibid., Jan. 19, 1884; Cleveland *Herald,* Sept. 16, 1884; W. A. Taylor, *Ohio Statesman and Hundred Year Book* (Columbus, 1892), pp. 596–618; New York *Globe.* Feb. 2, 1884.

and barbershops and failed to include juries, was quickly shepherded through committee and passed by a vote of 30 to 1. It then went to the House, where the benefits of the new competition between the parties were already apparent. The representatives were in the midst of debating a similar but more comprehensive bill introduced by a Gallia County Republican. Democrats claimed that the bill's universality was not desired by blacks, who did not wish to push themselves where they were not wanted. But, as if to disprove the contention that they wished a limited law, large numbers of Columbus blacks came to the chamber to lend moral support when the Republican bill appeared for its first reading. It passed at the time but was soon buried in committee. House Democrats were not opposed to the Crowell bill, however; they were even willing to accept the extension of protection to juries, though they refused to include eating places and barbershops. Ultimately, after much debate, they joined with Republicans in unanimously approving the Crowell bill.[60]

The new law was not popular among Ohio blacks, and it came under criticism from lawyers on the central committee of the Ohio Equal Rights League almost immediately after passage. In its failure to include some facilities, the law was actually proscriptive; since no minimum fine was stated in the law, judgments against violators could be so small as to be meaningless. Also, the maximum penalty, except in relation to discrimination in jury service, was $100. Jurisdiction for such suits was in the hands of justices of the peace, in whose courts plaintiffs losing damage judgments but winning cases were themselves liable for all court costs. In response to criticisms, and no doubt believing that the law would not be enforced anyway where white opinion was against it, Democrats consented to amendments extending protection to barbershops and eating places, but they still refused to change the weak machinery of the law. Thus, while the law was a groundbreaking effort by white Democrats to recognize black welfare, it was at best an ambiguous contribution.[61]

Democratic legislators showed themselves considerably less progressive than Hoadley in their reluctance to initiate action on either the school or intermarriage questions. In truth, as the experience of the first two black legislators attested, Republicans had been no more

[60] Cleveland *Gazette*, Jan. 12, Feb. 9, 1884; Ohio, *Senate Journal, 1844*, pp. 95–96, 100 (the one "no" vote was cast by a central Ohio Democrat); Ohio, *House Journal, 1884*, pp. 155–158.

[61] Cleveland *Gazette*, Mar. 8, 15, 22, 29, 1884; Ohio, *Senate Journal, 1884*, pp. 300, 305, 320, 331–334 (the vote was 28 to 2, both dissenters Democrats); Ohio, *House Journal, 1884*, pp. 587–631 (the vote was 70 to 2, both dissenters Democrats); Ohio, *Laws, 1884*, pp. 15–16.

eager to confront those issues. During his tenure in the House in 1880 and 1881, Williams tried unsuccessfully to garner Republican support for repeal of the anti-intermarriage law.[62] Though Williams had not broached the school issue, Green had tried, but he failed because of a combination of white prejudice and black apathy or circumspection. In 1882 and 1883, when he attempted to interest the Republican majority in the House in repeal of the separate school law, southern Ohio Republicans had argued that blacks did not desire school integration. Green felt, therefore, that his best course was to call for petitions from blacks demanding repeal. But none came, so he felt that it was impossible for him to proceed.[63]

A combination of forces on both sides of the color line were at work to push the issues in 1884. Not only did the escalating competition for the black vote suggest that controversial racial questions might be taken up by white politicians, but among blacks themselves a growing concern for both questions was evident in the intensification of the school controversy and in the reaction to the prosecution of the black Toledoan under the anti-intermarriage law.

Caught in a confluence of these forces was Springfield Republican John Littler, who introduced a bill to repeal the separate school law during the first week of the 1884 session. The blacks in his community were usually important to Republican success in county elections, because they combined with the Republican rural vote to counter the weight of Democratic Springfield. Those blacks were becoming increasingly militant on the school question. No evidence illuminates Littler's motivations, but while he may have been one of the minority of Springfield whites who desired integration on principle, he also had ample reason to be concerned with the way in which the changing views of black constituents might effect their political allegiances.[64]

Though the equal rights leagues were not yet organized enough to make sustained efforts for the Littler bill, by February black teachers and school administrators were ready to protect their interests and those of the race as they saw them. Because of his influence with the Democrats, Clark emerged as the leading figure in the teachers' lobby, though he himself refused to defend separate schools and argued only that, in fairness, school integration must encompass faculties. Aiding

[62] George Washington Williams to John P. Green, Dec. 24, 1879, Box I, folder 1, John P. Green Papers, WRHS.

[63] Green, *Fact Stranger Than Fiction*, pp. 178–179; Cleveland *Gazette*, Mar. 13, 1886.

[64] Springfield *Republic*, Oct. 19, 1882; Cleveland *Gazette*, Jan. 19, 1884; E. S. Todd, *A Sociological Study of Springfield and Clark County, Ohio* (New York, 1904), pp. 66, 78–79.

him were the Cincinnati teachers, who had the informal support of their board of education, and two respected black principals, Zanesville's James Guy and Springfield's S. T. Mitchell. Clark's appearance as the leading spokesman for the teachers presented Democratic legislators with the problem of balancing off their obligation to their leading black supporter and their quest for black voters, many of whom appeared to desire integration. A compromise was struck in late March in the House Judiciary Committee: the Democratic majority, in consultation with Clark, amended the Littler bill to provide for the establishment of separate schools upon petition of the majority of blacks in any school district.[65]

The amended Littler bill reached a vote in the House on April 9. Most Democrats were hostile to repeal even with the local option cause, and some Republicans did not wish to face the issue at all. Though the bill received the favorable votes of forty Republicans and ten Democrats, compared to the thirty-one Democratic opposing votes, it lacked three votes of obtaining a constitutional majority. The cause of repeal was hurt by the absence of almost a quarter of the legislators, including eleven Democrats and Republicans from northern districts which had long ago done away with separate schools. From Springfield and Cleveland came bitter criticisms of the teachers' lobby; it had unexpectedly come out against even the amended Littler bill just before the vote in the House, and the *Gazette* credited it with changing the vote of at least twelve members of both parties. No further action was taken in 1884.[66]

At the start of the 1885 session, Hoadley again called upon the legislature to repeal the two laws. While Littler reintroduced his bill, containing a local option clause allowing blacks to choose separate schools, Republican Senator George Ely of Cleveland introduced legislation in the Senate embodying Hoadley's more universal proposal. The Ely bill would repeal the separate school law without making provision for local option, and it would also abolish the anti-intermarriage law.[67]

The 1885 session saw important changes in tactics by black integrationists and the teachers' lobby. Learning from their failure to organize quickly in 1884, integrationists took their cause to the legislature at the very beginning of the session. Leading them and constituting the largest local delegation in behalf of repeal were Springfield blacks, who

65 Cleveland *Gazette*, Feb. 16, Apr. 19, 26, 1884; Ohio *House Journal, 1884*, p.678.

66 Cleveland *Herald*, Apr. 8, 1884; Cleveland *Gazette*, Apr. 12, 19, 1884; Ohio *House Journal, 1884*, pp. 770–771.

67 Columbus *Ohio State Journal*, Jan. 7, 1885.

spent several months at the capital. The teachers also changed their tactics. Desiring to lessen the impact of the integrationist press's bitter criticism of Peter Clark and to have less attention called to their efforts, they hired a lobbyist.

Yet there were serious problems within the teachers' ranks, and they were encountering their first open, organized opposition in their own stronghold, Cincinnati. During the 1884 session some Cincinnati blacks had grumbled about the teachers' lobby; such talk grew out of complaints about the inadequacy of local black schools and of individual animosities against Peter Clark, who, in his long, controversial career, had (not surprisingly) alienated some local blacks. But the earlier discontent had been unorganized. Now for the first time blacks began to hold mass meetings on the school issue and to circulate pro-repeal petitions.[68]

The changing mood among Cincinnatians resulted as much from conflicts in local politics as from a disgust with unequal school facilities. Many were coming to find the close relationship of the teachers' lobby to the Ohio Democracy particularly distasteful. Most blacks in the city were Republicans, of course, and as such had occasionally been faced with Democratic attempts to suppress their votes in local elections. Such efforts generally grew out of not completely unfounded charges that blacks from across the river in Kentucky were brought into the city on election day to vote Republican. Prior to the 1884 fall campaign these attempts at political repression had not been serious, but on election day in October all previous efforts were eclipsed by the illegal mass arrests of black voters by Democratic police. The incident left Cincinnati blacks understandably distrustful of their erstwhile Democratic allies and angry at those blacks who supported and dealt with them. In this acrimonious climate, criticism of the teachers and of Clark, who was especially vulnerable as a Democrat, intensified, and the first significant breach in the teachers' ranks occurred. At a race meeting early in February, 1885, Charles D. Bell, a respected teacher and local political activist, addressed the crowd by personal request and pledged that he would no longer support the teachers' lobby. The meeting then passed resolutions calling for repeal of the separate school law, but agreeing to work for both the Ely and Littler bills, thus obscuring whether its preference was for local option or wholesale integration.[69]

The Democratic legislative majority was well aware of these shifts

[68] Cleveland *Gazette*, Mar. 29, May 17, 1884, Jan. 17, Feb. 28, 1885; Cincinnati *Commercial Gazette*, Feb. 5, 6, 1885; Cincinnati *Enquirer*, Feb. 11, 1885.
[69] Cincinnati *Commercial Gazette*, Oct. 15, 16, 18, 1884, Feb. 11, 1885.

in black opinion. By the time the Littler bill came up for a vote in the House in mid-March, Democrats had been holding closed caucuses for weeks in order to determine the political risks of opposing or backing repeal. The debates revealed the opportunistic calculus behind the growing number of decisions to vote for repeal. Doubtless attuned to the opinions of the Cincinnati mass meeting a month earlier, Representative Thompson of Cincinnati outlined the political components of the situation for his fellow Democrats in a long, frank speech. Proceeding from the premise that blacks desired repeal and would hold Democrats responsible if it were not forthcoming, he warned that close contests in that fall's state elections might well hinge on black votes. Moreover, if repeal were not achieved and the Republicans won the fall elections, a Republican legislature would certainly accomplish it in 1886 and win the undying loyalty of the now wavering black vote.[70]

Abandoning Peter Clark, Thompson then introduced an amendment to the Littler bill nullifying the local option clause. Though several southern and central Ohio Democrats had spoken bitterly against repeal prior to the Thompson speech, the 59-13 vote in favor of the Thompson proposal suggested that many Democrats respected his compelling political logic. All of the no votes were cast by Democrats, largely from southern and central counties, but 26 Democrats from northern and central Ohio and from Cincinnati—16 more than had voted for the Littler bill with the local option clause in 1884—combined with 33 Republicans to assure passage. The bill then went to the state senate, where the school and intermarriage issues had created intense political tension during the session. Senate Democrats, themselves divided on repeal, had been very reluctant to take up both the school and intermarriage issues together as the Republican-backed Ely bill required. They attempted to put forward a bill which dealt only with repeal of the school law, but they could not unite on it, and it was defeated. Though five Democrats joined eight Republicans to vote for repeal, ten Democrats from throughout the state voted against it; a number of senators, including a few southern and central county Republicans, did not vote at all. The bill fell four votes short of a constitutional majority. The House bill did little better when it came to the Senate. Action was thus postponed until the seating of a new legislature in January.[71]

That fall's campaign, a rematch between Foraker and Hoadley, found Republicans making intense efforts to keep blacks loyal. It be-

70 Ibid., Mar. 14, 1885; Columbus *Ohio State Journal*, Mar. 14, 1885.

71 Columbus *Times*, Apr. 24, 30, 1885; Ohio, *House Journal, 1885*, pp. 453–454; Ohio, *Senate Journal, 1885*, pp. 735–736.

came apparent in the months before the state convention that Foraker would be renominated, and a number of black politicians simply climbed on the bandwagon; black Foraker clubs soon appeared at Springfield and Cincinnati. Others, like Poindexter, accepted the likelihood of a Foraker nomination, just as they had accepted his 1883 candidacy, with resignation. But some, like Smith and Green, continued to distrust Foraker and to predict black defections in the event of his nomination. Conscious of the doubts about him and believing that the black vote might make the difference between defeat and victory, Foraker devoted much time to courting blacks. His nomination was seconded by a young black politician, and his very first campaign address, given before a black audience at Wilberforce University, resounded with praise for black accomplishments and pledged to further the work of achieving equality in Ohio. The Republican Central Committee quickly printed the address in pamphlet form and circulated it among blacks throughout the state. Foraker's cause was strengthened considerably by Hoadley's association with the Cincinnati Democracy and his political ties with some of those responsible for the 1884 mass arrests; throughout the campaign Foraker's speeches neatly wove together Democratic repression of black votes in the South and in Ohio. Also serving to tie blacks to the party were three legislative nominations, the largest yet in one campaign. Harlan and Brown were chosen at Cincinnati and Cleveland; Arnett, who was now living at Wilberforce, was nominated at Greene County, largely in the hope among local Republican leaders of both races that he might secure state aid for near-bankrupt Wilberforce University. The lively black campaign was amply funded by the party, and it was not long before Smith and his *Gazette* were enthusiastically defending the Foraker record. Sensing perhaps the futility of defending their party's recent performance in the legislature and at Cincinnati, black Democrats lay low throughout the campaign.[72]

Foraker's 18,000-vote majority highlighted the importance of the black vote for those who saw it as the balance of power, and the governor soon demonstrated his understanding of the obligation he had incurred. The Foraker administration widened the scope and in-

[72] At *Wilberforce: Speech of Judge J. B. Foraker before the Alumni Association . . . June 18, 1885* (n.p., 1885); Foraker, *Notes of a Busy Life*, I, 175–200; Cleveland *Gazette*, June 13, 20, Aug. 8, 1885; Cincinnati *Commercial Gazette*, Aug. 12, 29, 1885; Joseph B. Foraker to S. E. Huffman, Feb. 2 and Feb. 13, 1885, Box XXVII, folder 3, Joseph B. Foraker to the Reverend R. G. Mortimer, May 22, 1885, Box XXVIII, folder 2, Joseph B. Foraker to W. H. West, July 15, Box XXVIII, folder 2, Foraker Papers, CHS; Joseph B. Foraker to Mark Hanna, June 20, 1885, Foraker Papers, LC; Asa Bushnell to Charles Kurtz, July 21, 1885, Box IV, Charles Kurtz Papers, OHS.

creased the number of black appointments, soon besting Hoadley's creditable record. It continued to appoint blacks to trusteeships of state institutions, increased the number of black clerks in state agencies, and added work as pages, messengers, laborers, and prison guards to the range of black jobs. Smith was rewarded with the lucrative job of deputy state oil inspector, the first black to hold that post. By the start of Foraker's second year in office well over thirty blacks, earning thousands a year, had received state patronage posts.[73]

Not unexpectedly, Foraker's inaugural address called upon the legislature to repeal the separate school and anti-intermarriage laws. However, at the start of the 1886 session the legislature's ability to act upon that request was in doubt. While Republicans held firm control of the House, among the new members of which were Harlan, Arnett, and Brown, the situation in the Senate was confused. When the legislature convened, there were 17 Republicans and 20 Democrats, but four of the Democratic seats were contested. They were ultimately rewarded to Republican challengers, but it took almost the entire session to resolve the question, leaving little time for other matters. Arnett had promised white constituents at Xenia that he would take no initiative on the school issue; however, much to their dismay, he introduced a bill to repeal both laws. The vote on his bill suggested a declining Democratic interest in wooing the black vote at the expense of the color line. The bill passed the House 59 to 25, with 54 Republicans and 5 northern county Democrats voting for it. All negative votes, except for that of one renegade northern Republican, were cast by Democrats representing districts throughout the state. Approval of Arnett's bill by the Senate had to wait one more year.[74]

Though frustrated by the delay, black school integrationists continued to lobby throughout the session. They could take heart at their increasing success in winning converts, not only among white legislators, but also among blacks. Of special importance for them was a petition, signed by 3,000 Cincinnati blacks, which placed them firmly behind wholesale school desegregation. The petition signaled the final collapse of the Cincinnati teachers' lobby—a victim not only of a sense of impending defeat, but also of a serious erosion of Peter Clark's influence. In December, 1885, Clark admitted attempting to bribe a key witness in a conspiracy to cover up the activities of those involved in

[73] Cleveland *Gazette*, Jan. 9, May 22, June 19, July 17, 1886, Jan. 29, 1884.

[74] Cincinnati *Commercial Gazette*, Jan. 2, 13, 1886; Cleveland *Gazette*, Jan. 9, 23, 1886; Columbus *Ohio State Journal*, Jan. 13, Mar. 11, Apr. 2, 30, 1886; Xenia *Torchlight*, Jan. 16, 20, 27, Apr. 3, 1886; Ohio, *House Journal, 1886*, pp. 95, 342; Ohio, *Senate Journal, 1886*, pp. 44, 52, 592.

the 1884 mass arrests. The disclosures brought a sad end to the thirty-year career of the once-revered Clark, whose pursuit of political independence had led him into the arms of some of the most disreputable elements of the Cincinnati Democracy. When a Republican school board replaced a Democratic one in 1886, it was expected that, after years of dedicated service, Clark would be removed from his position as principal of the black high school. Local blacks were forgiving and petitioned for Clark's retention, but in vain. Shamed and bitter, the aging Clark, whose singularly unconventional activities and opinions had done so much to pave the way for racial progress in Ohio, wandered from job to job for several years before taking a position in the black schools of St. Louis.[75] Under less trying circumstances, a number of Cincinnati teachers were giving up the fight, and some were reported applying for jobs in southern and border-city separate schools.[76]

Though teachers from Zanesville and Xenia continued to appear before the Senate's committee on schools in behalf of the dual school system, and a few black petitions against integration continued to reach the legislature, there was never any doubt that the Senate would favor repeal if and when the four Republicans were seated. It was no surprise, then, that the Arnett bill was approved on February 16, 1887. The 24 to 7 vote, which found only four Democrats voting for repeal and no Republicans voting against it, was witnessed by several hundred enthusiastic black spectators in the galleries.[77]

It had taken three years for the legislature to repeal Ohio's last discriminatory laws, and even then the course of events had been determined by competing forces: political expediency and prejudice versus idealism and egalitarianism. While there had been no moral revolution accompanying the ameliorative trend of the 1880s, a high point in the history of racial advancement in Ohio had nonetheless been reached—a high point which, though dependent upon enfranchisement, in an important sense exceeded it as a racial landmark. While obtaining the vote had been vital to the achievement of citizenship and hence of the gains of the 1880s, enfranchisement was an act done for blacks by whites with little reference to black feelings and aspirations. However much moral support blacks had lent the process, they had lacked the power to be among its prime movers; instead, they had been

[75] Cincinnati *Commercial Gazette*, Nov. 29, Dec. 1, 6, 19, 1885; *Xenia Torchlight*, Apr. 3, 1886; Cleveland *Gazette*, June 12, 19, 24, 1886; New York *Freeman*, June 19, 26, July 3, Aug. 7, 1886.

[76] Cleveland *Gazette*, Mar. 27, 1886.

[77] Ibid., Jan. 15, 22, Feb. 19, 1887; Columbus *Ohio State Journal*, Feb. 17, 1887; Ohio, *Senate Journal, 1887*, pp. 212, 255–256; Ohio, *Laws, 1887*, p. 34.

placed in the degrading position of watching and waiting while others determined their fate. In contrast, the achievements of the 1880s had been deeply influenced by black political power and black activities in pursuit of racial welfare. As voters, lobbyists, legislators, and politicians, blacks had proven to be skilled manipulators of the party system and of government, and they had significantly furthered their own advancement.

The ameliorative legislation of the decade and the vital role of black political activity and power in helping to bring about its passage further impressed black leaders with the larger progressive trend of race relations and strengthened their faith in the race's future. In politics they had found their most effective weapon for protecting and expanding black rights and opportunities, and they had achieved racial goals, particularly in the school desegregation law, which they believed capable of generating an irresistible trend toward equality, opportunity, and fuller citizenship. In 1887 Harry Smith spoke dramatically of a "revolution" in Ohio's race relations, one with unstoppable momentum because of school desegregation. "Revolutions never go backward," said Smith confidently, adding, "Education has always been the handmaiden of freedom, progress, and reform." [78] For Smith and others who shared his view, all that this revolution needed to fulfill its promise was time and a continuance of the relatively open, flexible conditions they found in the Ohio of that day.

[78] Cleveland *Gazette*, Mar. 26, 1887.

Part II

Black Ohio in the Age of Jim Crow

9

Reaction

It has long been recognized that there was a precipitous decline in black-white relations during the last years of the nineteenth century and the first years of the twentieth. While this trend was present throughout the nation, it was most dramatic and evident in the South, where over 90 percent of black Americans resided in 1900. At the very time when Ohio blacks were celebrating the victories of the 1880s and looking with hope to the future, they were beginning to witness the early stages of a full-scale reaction against black rights in the South. Dramatically apparent in the alarming increase in lynchings in the late 1880s and early 1890s, the forces of reaction soon gathered momentum. By 1910 the social and political gains made by the southern freedmen since emancipation had been wiped out by political disfranchisement, mob violence, and an increase in both the scope and severity of customary and legal segregation. The federal government, which was the only possible source of protection for the freedmen once southern whites were won over to reaction, did little to arrest the course of decline. The Supreme Court acquiesced in state legislation which accomplished disfranchisement and segregation. Reflecting the changing concerns of the dominant Republican party, now interested in economic issues and foreign affairs rather than race, Congress and the Executive refused to protect the constitutional rights of southern blacks. Indeed, Republican presidents McKinley, Roosevelt, and Taft exacerbated the southern situation. First, they generally failed to speak out against disfranchisement, segregation, and anti-black violence. Second, in the name of sectional reconciliation, and in order to lay foundations for a viable white Republican party in the South, all three in varying degrees courted southern whites with praise of their sectional traditions and, at the expense of southern black Republican politicians, with patronage and political influence.[1]

[1] C. Vann Woodward, *The Origins of the New South, 1877–1913* (Baton

These events had an impact on northern blacks, but that impact was to a considerable extent indirect and subtle. The forces which caused the collapse of the fragile structure of black citizenship which Reconstruction had brought to the South were intimately tied to the singular historical development of the region, and they could not be replicated in the North. Yet the *example* of the South had importance. That the overwhelming majority of black Americans could be subject to lynching and segregation and be deprived of their constitutional rights certainly did not foster positive images of black citizenship. The southern example not only bolstered the confidence of those northern whites who wished to turn back the clock on black advancement in their section, but also helped to convince Northerners generally that second-class citizenship was the natural and proper state of affairs for blacks.[2]

Other forces also helped convince them. As the reactionary trend in the South gathered force, it was complemented and intensified by intellectual influences from natural and social science, humane letters, popular literature, and practical social and political polemics. These helped to reshape the racial consciousness of Americans, independent of section, and gave racial prejudice a new respectability. Founded upon ideas of a natural racial hierarchy, the new intellectual trend served the changing racial status quo by singling out black inferiority, criminality, and lechery as its causes. It offered deterministic scientific and historical explanations for the increasing subordination of southern blacks, as well as for the concurrent triumph of Western imperialism.[3] Popularized by such propagandists for the subordination of blacks as South Carolina Senator Ben Tillman (who frequently spoke in the North, and whose oratory reveled in defamations of Negro character)

Rouge, 1951), pp. 321–395, and Woodward, *The Strange Career of Jim Crow* (New York, 1974), pp. 3–125; Thomas Cripps, "The Lily White Republicans: The Negro, the Party, and the South in the Progressive Era" (Ph.D. dissertation, University of Maryland, 1967); J. Morgan Kousser, *The Shaping of Southern Politics: Suffrage Restriction and the Establishment of the One-Party South, 1880–1910* (New Haven, 1974).

2 The southern example was not, however, carried to Ohio by white Southerners, for after the turn of the century Southerners continued to make up between 5 and 6% of the total Ohio population and around 10% at most major cities; U. S. Bureau of the Census, Census Reports, *Twelfth Census of the United States . . . 1900* (Washington, 1901), I, pt. 1, 634–635, 698–701, 704–706, and *Thirteenth Census of the United States . . . 1910* (Washington, 1913), I, 730, 775–777. In 1910, 207,750 persons born in the South lived in Ohio; their numbers in the major cities ranged from 40,563 at Cincinnati to 6,881 at Dayton.

3 George Frederickson, *The Black Image in the White Mind: The Debate on Afro-American Character and Destiny, 1817–1914* (New York, 1971), pp. 228–319.

and divorced from whatever sophistication they might attain in the works of scholars and scientists, such ideas left a vicious legacy of crude racist notions. Their impact upon popular racism was evident in a personal conception of the hierarchy of the races which was expounded in 1908 by a Dayton informant to an investigator of that city's race relations. "This is the way I class the nigger among the races: (1) the white man, (2) the Mongolian, (3) the Japanese, (4) the Chinese, (5) the dog, and last, the nigger." Such opinions, heard increasingly from quarters in the North and South alike, caused John Green to conclude in 1906 that whites were speedily growing less tolerant. In a *Gazette* article in which he described the direction of the times, he said simply, "The general trend of popular feeling toward our class of American citizens is rapidly downward."[4]

I

Green had to look no further than his own Ohio for evidence of the practical implications of changing racial attitudes. Slowly in the 1890s, and more rapidly thereafter, Ohio's race relations deteriorated. Blacks did not lose their vote, nor were laws passed to segregate them, but there was a marked increase in racial conflict and de facto segregation. The negative trend took hold not only in southern and central Ohio, where it might have been expected, but also in the once uniquely tolerant Western Reserve. The old pattern of intrastate variation in racial tolerance did not completely disappear, but the gap began to close. Throughout Ohio the deterioration of race relations was complemented, as we shall later see, by other disturbing trends: declines in black employment opportunity and political influence, both of which added significantly to black anxiety.

One early sign of worsening race relations was no doubt directly influenced by southern events; it surfaced in the early 1890s, when what Harry Smith called "the lynching disease" entered Ohio and other northern states. While the Old Northwest had not experienced serious racial violence since the riots of the Civil War, the years after 1890 saw an increase, by no means approaching that found in the South but alarming in itself, of lynchings, attempted lynchings, and race riots. In Ohio, the 1892 lynching of an Oxford black, who was accused of murdering a white woman and assaulting her daughter, was the first of a series of six, and almost as many serious but unsuccessful attempts at lynching, to occur in central and southern counties

[4] Frank U. Quillin, *The Color Line in Ohio* (Ann Arbor, 1913), p. 140; Cleveland *Gazette*, Oct. 6, 1906.

in the next decade and a half. As was the case in most such incidents, North and South, Oxford authorities made no serious attempt to bring either the leaders or members of the lynch mob to justice, even though the crime of murder was compounded with breaking into the town's jail to seize a prisoner, and despite the fact that members of the mob were well-known local citizens. The lynching received sensational treatment in one of the state's most widely circulated newspapers, the Cincinnati *Enquirer*: "RED SPOTS STAIN THE WHITE SNOW," the story-line proclaimed. The *Enquirer* assumed the guilt of the black suspect immediately upon learning of the charges against him, and it spoke of him as "the colored fiend" and "the colored murderer." That news-paper was by no means alone among Ohio's papers in giving sensa-tional treatment to mob violence, whether in Ohio or elsewhere; nor was it unique in giving tacit approval to mob vengeance in cases where blacks were accused of serious crimes.[5]

Ohio blacks responded to this incident and others like it taking place in the South by organizing rallies; at these gatherings partici-pants passed resolutions calling upon state and federal officials to take action to stop lynchings and to bring members of lynch mobs to justice.[6] However, it was not until after the shocking lynching of a black teenager who had been accused of murdering an aged white couple at southern Adams County in January, 1894, that black leaders began to search for a legislative remedy. Cooperating were Harry Smith, then serving his first term as a state representative, and his white friend Albion W. Tourgee of Westfield, New York, a longtime crusader for black rights who had been a Republican official in North Carolina during Reconstruction, and had later continued the fight for that cause through a series of organizations, personally edited news-letters, and syndicated columns in black and white newspapers, in-cluding Smith's *Gazette*.[7] For several years Tourgee had been seeking a federal anti-lynching law based on the principle of community responsibility and financial liability for mob violence. Proceeding from the premise that lynchings, North and South, "never take place except in a community whose citizens favor and approve such outrage," Tourgee posited that the most efficient means to check them was to make the entire community responsible before the law. This could be

[5] National Association for the Advancement of Colored People, *Thirty Years of Lynching, 1889–1919* (New York, 1919), pp. 7–10, 85; Cincinnati *Enquirer*, Jan. 14, 15, 16, 1892.

[6] Cleveland *Gazette*, May 7, 14, 28, June 4, 11, July 9, 1892.

[7] Ibid., Jan. 20, 27, Feb. 3, 17, 1894; Otto Olsen, *Carpetbagger's Crusade: The Life of Albion W. Tourgee* (Baltimore, 1965).

accomplished, he said, by "touching the pocket nerve"—that is, making communities financially responsible for lynching, just as railroads were required to compensate victims of accidents in which the operators were found negligent.[8] Frustrated in attempts to impress the Harrison administration with the need for such legislation and unlikely to obtain a sympathetic hearing from Democratic President Cleveland, Tourgee was persuaded to turn his efforts to Ohio by the Adams County lynching, the presence of Smith in the Ohio legislature, and the militantly anti-lynching statement made by recently elected Governor William McKinley when he learned of the Adams County affair.[9]

Hoping to take advantage of the legislature's willingness to act on questions involving black welfare, Smith introduced a bill embodying Tourgee's ideas during the 1894 session. Yet divisions existed among the House's black legislators; Cleveland's other black representative, William Clifford, introduced his own, much weaker anti-lynching proposal. Moreover, the opposition of southern county legislators of both parties, who were frightened that the bill might have ramifications for their own communities, and the change after 1894 of the legislature from annual to biennial sessions, caused the Smith bill to lie dormant until 1896.[10]

During the balance of 1894 and throughout 1895, public opinion in Ohio was influenced in favor of legislative action, not only by the continued lynchings in the South, but also by two lynchings (at Bellefontaine and New Richmond) and several serious attempts at lynching in Ohio. Particularly tragic were events at Washington Court House in October, 1894; several attempts to lynch a black man found guilty of rape, at a trial held amidst threats of violence from a mob stationed near the courthouse, led to clashes between mob members and state militia called to the scene by Governor McKinley. The unsuccessful effort to take the prisoner from the town's jail left five young mob members dead and some twenty others wounded. In the wake of the incident, several leading Ohio newspapers and many legislators fell behind the recently reelected Smith's effort to gain passage of his bill during 1896.[11]

The bill which finally passed late in that session despite continued

[8] Cleveland *Gazette*, Mar. 3, 1894.
[9] Olsen, *Carpetbagger's Crusade*, pp. 310–313, 333.
[10] Cleveland *Gazette*, May 12, 19, 1894; Columbus *Ohio State Journal*, Apr. 18, 19, May 1, 2, 9, 1894.
[11] Bellefontaine *Examiner*, Apr. 19, May 17, June 7, 1897; Washington Court House *Cyclone and Fayette Republican*, Oct. 11, 18, 1894; Cleveland *Gazette*, Oct. 20, 27, Dec. 1, 22, 1894, Aug. 31, Nov. 23, 1895; Batavia *Clermont Sun*, Aug. 28, 1895.

opposition from southern county legislators [12] was the most comprehensive measure against mob violence anywhere up to that time; [13] it
served as a well-respected model for future legislation in both northern
and southern states, and in the NAACP's campaign for federal anti-
lynching legislation.[14] The Smith Law provided that a county where
lynching and other mob violence against individuals occurred might be
sued for $500 to $1,000, depending on the seriousness of the injury
sustained by surviving victims, or for $5,000 by the next of kin of those
murdered by mobs. The money was to be raised through county taxes;
the county might in turn recover the amount of judgments rendered
against it by suing mob members. The law did not relieve mob members from criminal prosecution for homocide or assault.[15]

Comprehensive though it was, the new law was based on certain
questionable assumptions about motivation, violence, and interclass
relations. Smith and Tourgee assumed that the principle of community
financial responsibility would move the wealthy individuals who were
the leading taxpayers to actively oppose lynch law. They would be
discouraged from joining mobs (which in small towns were often said
to be composed of leading citizens) and forced instead to use their
prestige and power to restrain those very mobs and to bolster the
efforts of law enforcement agents. Among the more affluent prospective mob members, the law might cause circumspection, though its
penalties were small enough that the financial loss would be minimal.
The social composition of lynch mobs was by no means constant, however, and to the extent that leading citizens were neither mob members nor leaders, the law perhaps depended too heavily on an

[12] Columbus *Ohio State Journal*, Jan. 21, Feb. 6, 27, Apr. 9, 1896; Cleveland
Gazette, Jan. 25, Feb. 29, Mar. 7, 14, 21, 28, Apr. 4, 11, 1896; Ohio, *House
Journal, 1896*, pp. 313–314, 320, 699–700, and Senate *Journal, 1896*, pp. 602–603.
The votes of 21–2 in the Senate and 61–22 in the House found legislators of both
parties from southern Ohio opposed to the bill.

[13] Up to that time only two states had passed laws specifically aimed at stop-
ping lynching. A Georgia law of 1893 penalized sheriffs who were found negligent
in the protection of prisoners and allowed law enforcement agents to deputize
local citizens to aid in such protection; no penalty was greater than a misdemeanor. A North Carolina law made counties in which lynchings occurred liable
for costs of investigations and prosecution of members of mobs. *Code of the State
of Georgia . . . 1910* (Atlanta, 1911), II, 74–75; Thomas Womack et al., *Re-
visal of 1905 [Statutes] of North Carolina* (Raleigh, 1905), p. 363.

[14] James Harmon Chadbourn, *Lynching and the Law* (Chapel Hill, 1933),
pp. 149–213; J. E. Cutler, "Proposed Remedies for Lynching," *Yale Review*, 2
(1904), 194–212; Edward Leight Pell, "The Prevention of Lynching Epidemics,"
Review of Reviews, XVII (Mar., 1898), 321–323; Charles Flint Kellogg, *NAACP:
A History of the National Association for the Advancement of Colored People*
(Baltimore, 1967), I, 214.

[15] Ohio, *Laws, 1896*, pp. 136–138.

exaggerated appreciation of the leading citizens' influence. Perhaps the most fundamental problem was the law's dependence on a rational calculation of self-interest to dissuade an enraged mob, especially when that rage was fueled by racial prejudice. As a tool for preventing mob violence, such a law was no substitute for the most determined, unyielding law enforcement by local officials, supplemented when necessary by state militia.

The lynching of a young black man at Urbana in June, 1897, a year after the passage of the Smith Law, revealed both the law's limitations and the encouragement which mobs received from signs of weakness among authorities. The young man was taken from the local jail and lynched after being charged with the rape of a wealthy widow, who was said to be mortally wounded. Yet evidence gathered in the weeks after the lynching suggested that no rape or assault of any kind had taken place. Indeed, the alleged victim watched the lynching from her porch at the very time when the local press was proclaiming her to be at death's door. It was also apparent that glaring cowardice and very poor judgment had been displayed by officials at every level. Governor Asa Bushnell, who had distinguished himself many years before by integrating his factories at Springfield, had refused, in spite of pleas from the local sheriff, to send in the National Guard to supplement inadequate local militia forces. Only after attacks upon the county jail left several persons dead did Bushnell finally act. But Urbana's mayor and a committee of local citizens met these reinforcements at the train station and sent them back, and they then walked to the jail and persuaded the sheriff to surrender his black prisoner to the waiting mob. The lynching took place almost immediately.[16] As usual, local inquiries, grand jury hearings, and even state investigations initiated in deference to black protests brought no punishment to the mob.[17] The failure to pursue justice in this case appears certainly to have been an accurate reflection of the sentiment not only of Urbana residents, but of a large number of other Ohioans as well. Many newspapers rushed to the mob's defense; while others denounced lynching in principle, they were enraged enough by the alleged rape of a white woman by a black man to express sympathy with the passion of Urbana whites.[18]

[16] Urbana-Champaign *Democrat*, June 3, 10, 1897; Urbana *Citizen and Gazette*, June 7, 1897; Cincinnati *Enquirer*, June 3, 4, 5, 6, 1897; Cleveland *Gazette*, June 19, 1897.

[17] Cleveland *Gazette*, June 26, July 10, Aug. 7, 14, 21, Oct. 9, 30, 1897, Apr. 16, 23, 1898; Columbus *Dispatch*, Aug. 6, 9, 10, 1897.

[18] For summaries of editorial opinion around the state: Cleveland *Plain Dealer*, June 5, 7, 1897; Urbana *Citizen and Gazette*, June 7, 1897.

Lynching in Ohio and elsewhere declined after the late 1890s, but in the few incidents of racially inspired violence which did take place in Ohio thereafter—riots at Akron in 1900 and at Springfield in 1904 and 1906—the scale of violence surpassed anything seen in the past. The Akron riot [19] resulted from a mob's attempts to wrest from jail a black prisoner charged with the rape of a white child. Although this incident did not involve a wholesale assault on local blacks, the Springfield riots did. In both 1904 and 1906 white mobs became enraged by the prevalence of vice and violent crime, which were mistakenly blamed on local blacks; their wrath led them to conduct pogrom-like riots in lower-class black neighborhoods. Destructive, brutal, and not unlike mob demonstrations in the contemporary South, the Springfield riots attracted national attention as symptoms of deteriorating race relations in the North.[20]

Springfield blacks became associated with vice and crime in the minds of whites because of the "Levee," a 300-foot row of black- and white-owned saloons, brothels, and gambling dens located along the railroad tracks in a small, slum-like black neighborhood not far from the central business district.[21] Yet behind the existence of the Levee was a pervasive, systemic corruption which had existed for years, and which guaranteed Springfield's reputation throughout the Miami Valley as a "wide-open town" where gambling and prostitution thrived and saloons stayed open till dawn seven days a week in flagrant defiance of closing laws. Venal public officials, their political machines oiled by monies from saloon and brothel proprietors, were naturally reluctant to interfere in the Levee's affairs. The courts were also lax and inconsistent in enforcing the laws. Gamblers, saloonkeepers, and pimps with influence were rarely convicted, no matter how great the evidence against them. Even murderers with influence were allowed to go free—a source of particular anguish to many in a city with a growing number of homocides, particularly after the turn of the century. For all this, the city lacked a strong municipal reform tradition. Indeed, in the year before the 1904 riot the reform candidates suffered their usual devastating defeat. Yet here, too, the association of blacks with the Levee and corruption was strengthened, for it was

[19] Akron *Democrat*, Aug. 21, 22, 23, 1900; Akron *Beacon Journal*, Aug. 22, 23, 24, 1900; Cleveland *Gazette*, Sept. 1, 3, 29, 1900; C. R. Quine, *The Akron Riot of 1900* (Akron, 1951), pp. 1–23.

[20] Ray Stannard Baker, *Following the Color Line* (New York, 1908), pp. 201–210; New York *Times*, Mar. 8, 9, 1904, Feb. 28, Mar. 1, 1906.

[21] E. S. Todd, *A Sociological Study of Springfield and Clark County, Ohio* (New York, 1904), p. 106; Baker, *Following Color Line*, p. 202.

well known in Springfield that the impoverished blacks of the Levee regularly sold their votes.[22]

The Levee was not the only factor embittering race relations. On the surface of daily life a series of lingering problems further increased tensions between the races. While the schools had been peacefully integrated in 1887, a vocal minority of white parents continued to demand the separate seating of black and white children within integrated classrooms.[23] In addition, the bitter memory of the role black strike-breakers had played in breaking the power of unions in the city's large factories lived on from the 1880s into the new century. The head of Springfield's Labor Union Council told one investigator several years after the riots that the outstanding reason why blacks were barred from local craft unions was because of their past willingness to be used as strike-breakers; other commentators likewise spoke of the bitterness which white workers held for local black labor.[24] Yet blacks continued to come to Springfield for steady work in the major factories, and the 1890s saw a large influx of single young black men in search of work.[25]

The events of 1904 unfolded amidst the sudden conjunction of several of these points of tension. A drunken black man, recently arrived from Kentucky but already twice arrested for being drunk and disorderly, killed a policeman who was attempting to arrest him for shooting a black woman companion in a Levee apartment they shared. The next day he was taken from jail and lynched; the determined mob was unfettered by local militia, which, though called to the scene by the mayor, did not arrive until after the lynching. Reporters heard mob members discussing the recent rash of murders, the impotence of the courts, and the continued failure of local authorities to prosecute criminals to the fullest extent of the law. Few whites felt remorse about the incident. "Everywhere the verdict is the same," said the Springfield *Press-Republic* after sampling local opinion, ". . . the lynching was a good thing." [26]

After the lynching, rumors circulated that the destruction of the Levee by a mob was imminent, but officials chose to disregard such

[22] Todd, *Springfield and Clark County,* pp. 69–70; Baker, *Following Color Line,* pp. 201–204.

[23] Todd, *Springfield and Clark County,* p. 66.

[24] Ibid., p. 67; Quillin, *Color Line in Ohio,* pp. 155–156; *Voice of the Negro,* III (Apr., 1906), 245.

[25] Todd, *Springfield and Clark County,* pp. 43–47.

[26] Ibid., p. 111; Baker, *Following Color Line,* pp. 205–206; Cleveland *Gazette,* Mar. 12, 1904; Springfield *Press-Republic,* Mar. 8, 1904.

statements. Thus, the next evening, when white mobs attacked the Levee and set its buildings ablaze, authorities were unprepared. Their lack of preparation was supplemented by a lack of will: police, firemen, and local militia took several hours to mobilize, in spite of the fact that they had been trained to do so in an hour; even after their arrival they did nothing but attempt to stop the fire from spreading into a neighboring white residential area. Eventually the presence of several companies of National Guard, sent to the city by Governor Myron T. Herrick, discouraged the mob from continuing its work.[27] Though the destruction of the Levee obliterated the homes of many of the black poor, there was rejoicing over the excision of what many Springfielders saw as a moral cancer.[28]

Given the attitudes prevalent at the time of the riot, it was not surprising that those responsible for either the lynching or the riot escaped prosecution. Nor did local officials correct the conditions which had fostered the rioting. Grand pronouncements of a war against the "criminal element" resulted only in the closing of a few saloons, all owned by blacks. The chief effect of the 1904 riot was, in fact, the removal of vice and crime and some of the black poor from the Levee to a white working-class area, soon to be known as the "Jungles," several blocks away.[29]

Conditions were ripe for more violence. On an evening in February, 1906, two separate incidents in which several whites were attacked by blacks set the stage. The blacks were quickly apprehended and sent to Dayton to prevent lynching, but an angry mob attacked and set fire to the saloons and tenements of the Jungles. During the 1904 riot, attacks upon individual blacks were subordinated to the destruction of property; this time, though, innocent blacks were beaten. The rioting went on for two days without much interference from authorities, and only after the rioters began to leave the streets did police finally act. The official response was mixed. Largely because many of those brought to trial were young men without criminal records, few of the mob were jailed, but those local authorities who had failed to check the riot were reprimanded and in some cases dismissed from office. In addition, an effort was made to regulate saloons more care-

[27] Ohio Adjutant General, *Annual Report . . . 1904* (Springfield, 1905), pp. 416–444; Springfield *Press-Republic*, Mar. 9, 10, 1904.

[28] Springfield *Press-Republic*, Mar. 11, 1904.

[29] Ibid., Mar. 8, May 1, 1904, Mar. 20, Apr. 4, 1905; Cleveland *Gazette*, Apr. 2, 9, May 7, 1904, Oct. 7, 1905; Dayton *Daily News*, Jan. 2, 1906; Baker, *Following Color Line*, p. 209.

fully, and a Civic League composed of white businessmen and professionals was organized to fight municipal corruption.[30]

II

While some, like Harry Smith, expected there to be more violence at Springfield,[31] no third act would be played there, and in the subsequent decade neither lynchings nor riots again occurred in Ohio. Yet there were less dramatic, though no less troublesome, signs of deteriorating race relations. The color line was growing more rigid in daily life, as whites from all ranks of society began increasingly to accept and demand the separation of the races. The access of blacks to public accommodations grew more limited, and even the openness of public institutions was threatened. Most evident everywhere was the erosion of the old bias in favor of giving fair treatment in public places to more affluent and conventionally respectable blacks.

While it had never been good in the past, the situation at Cincinnati grew worse in the very last years of the nineteenth century and continued to decline in the first years of the twentieth. Better public accommodations, which had once grudgingly opened their doors to occasional upper-class blacks, were now said by one investigator to be "universally closed" to the race. A black notable or a respectable traveler might once have hoped to find a room in a better hotel, if he was willing perhaps to forego the dining room, but Wendell Phillips Dabney's Cincinnati *Union* lamented in 1915 that "colored people not only cannot get a room in a hotel, but are even forbidden the elevators and told to ride in the freight elevators." Such was the case during the 1908 presidential campaign, when blacks visiting the Taft headquarters at the Taft-owned Sinton Hotel were not even allowed to enter the lobby. Instead, they were asked to take a freight elevator, approachable only by a back door, to the floor occupied by the Republican campaign. Theaters, which had once allowed blacks access to all seats or restricted them to certain sections of the house, now either excluded them completely or charged them higher prices for the same segregated seating arrangements. At the same time, Cincinnati blacks were being given a first-hand example of the north-

[30] Springfield *Daily News,* Feb. 26, 28, Mar. 1, 2, 3, 1906; Cleveland *Gazette,* Mar. 3, 10, 17, 31, Apr. 7, 14, 1906; Baker, *Following Color Line,* p. 210; Ohio Adjutant General, *Annual Report . . . 1906* (Columbus, 1907), pp. 305–315; *Voice of the Negro,* III (Apr., 1906), 245.

[31] Washington *Bee,* Mar. 10, 1906; Cleveland *Gazette,* Mar. 24, 1906.

ward migration of the southern example: as southern states increasingly segregated their railroad cars, more and more trains came across into Ohio with "White Only" signs illegally but prominently displayed.[32]

While Republicans usually controlled Cincinnati's municipal government, neither Republican administrations nor Republican boss George B. Cox's powerful political machine did anything to combat discrimination. Despite the party loyalty of many blacks in every election, increasingly there was not even the appearance of concern. In a pamphlet written in 1901, Dabney charged that by both omission and commission local Republicans were actually encouraging discrimination. Earlier in the year President Roosevelt had invited Booker T. Washington to dine at the White House; but, Dabney exclaimed, "The Republicans of Cincinnati won't even sell a colored man a dinner! Think of all the race prejudice here in a Republican city. Restaurants, saloons, theaters . . . controlled and owned by Republicans . . . refusing citizens in public places on account of color." When civil rights cases were brought before them, Republican judges engaged in legal hair-splitting in order to invalidate the 1884 Civil Rights Law. The Republican-controlled municipal licensing board refused to consider using its power to enforce equality of access to public accommodations. In fact, one board member was the owner of a tavern well known for refusing to serve blacks.[33]

While at Columbus conditions in the past had been somewhat flexible, favoring the upper class and black notables, they changed rapidly in the late 1890s. In 1900 the International General Conference of the A.M.E. Church was held in the city, with bishops from throughout the United States, Africa, and the Caribbean in attendance. The conference had to some extent been brought to Columbus because of the planners' expectation that the bishops would receive fair treatment in the city; the event was publicized in all of the city's daily newspapers, and doubtless the bishops were men who by dress (with clerical collars) and manner were not difficult to identify. Yet while they found rooms in the city's better hotels, a number of them were refused service in eating places. About a decade later they would have faced even more difficult conditions. By then Columbus hotels barred blacks, though the managers of two of them said that for an extra charge they accommodated the servants of southern

[32] Quillin, *Color Line in Ohio*, pp. 126–128; Cleveland *Gazette*, Mar. 26, 1898, Aug. 1, 1908; Cincinnati *Union* quoted in Cleveland *Gazette*, Apr. 10, 1915.
[33] Wendell Phillips Dabney, *Why the Negro of Hamilton County Should Stay Away from the Polls at This Election* (Cincinnati, 1901), pp. 1–3.

guests in a back room where they were obliged to take their meals. Bars, restaurants, and soda fountains were almost all discouraging black patronage, placing blacks at isolated back tables and charging them inflated prices when they did not simply refuse to serve them altogether. Theaters showed a mixed record and were characterized, to some extent, by inconsistent practice. A few had flirted with separate seating arrangements around the turn of the century, only to return to egalitarian policies in the last years before World War I. But the balance was definitely struck in favor of segregation, for the tendency of most Columbus theaters, particularly the now proliferating motion picture houses, was to exclude blacks completely or to limit them to the galleries or the last five rows of the first floor. A number of these theaters also borrowed one of the most insulting fixtures of southern segregation: in the last years of the period, they began to place signs boldly announcing their racial policies at entrances and ticket booths.[34]

Nowhere was the trend toward a more rigid color line more dramatic than in the Western Reserve. There a number of cities and towns which had acquired reputations for tolerance began to weaken their commitment to equality. Beginning in the late 1890s, Cleveland *Gazette* correspondents in such Reserve communities as Elyria, Lorain, Akron, Warren, and Ravenna began for the first time to report instances of discrimination in public accommodations. At Lorain in 1902 the extent of discrimination was such that the famed black Jubilee Singers, in town to perform at a white church, were refused accommodation at two hotels and a restaurant; they were ultimately forced to sleep in the homes of a few kind church members. Several years later a white clergyman attempting to find a hotel room for Booker T. Washington, who was to address a church congregation, was given an emphatic refusal by one Akron hotel. Most of the city's hotels, it was said, had begun to change their policies in deference to the complaints of traveling salesmen. In these communities, where discrimination represented a sharp and unprecedented turn in race relations, blacks responded immediately with lawsuits, but these brought mixed results. Some at Ravenna, Warren, and Elyria, were won, but even in the Western Reserve there were courts which showed little sympathy for blacks. A suit against an Akron skating rink in 1908, for example, was lost in circuit court; the judge ruled that there was no cause for

[34] Columbus *Press Post*, May 8, 1900; Cleveland *Gazette*, June 1, 1901, Aug. 27, 1910, Feb. 10, 1912, Feb. 15, 1913, Mar. 21, 1914, Apr. 10, 1915; Richard Clyde Minor, "Negroes in Columbus" (Ph.D. dissertation, Ohio State University, 1936), pp. 239–241; Quillin, *Color Line in Ohio*, pp. 146–149.

action, despite the fact the rink owner had stated frankly that race was his sole reason for refusing the black plaintiff admission.[35]

Though Oberlin continued to graduate more blacks than any other integrated college in the nation, the racial climate changed greatly as new generations of faculty and students entered who lacked the intense egalitarian commitments of the school's founders. Student literary societies had been integrated, but the Oberlin *Alumni Magazine* was unhappy to announce in March, 1910, that black male students had formed their own literary society after one of them was refused admission to two white-controlled societies. In that same year the track team, which in the past had accepted inferior accommodations on road trips in order that blacks and whites might stay at the same hotel, decided that the blacks would now have to shift for themselves; white teammates would no longer sacrifice comfort for the sake of solidarity. The color line also entered student religious life. There was talk of forming separate Bible study classes, and churches attended by students were now excluding blacks from their choirs. These incidents brought storms of outrage from alumni and from Oberlin president H. C. King, who remained true to the school's proud past. Yet the separation of black and white students continued, and it was increasingly evident that students of both races were coming to share expectations about interracial mingling on and off campus which were quite different from those of past generations of Oberlin students.[36]

Conditions were also changing at Cleveland. Segregation and general mistreatment of blacks in restaurants rose alarmingly in the late 1890s; by May, 1900, an unprecedented number—twelve—of Civil rights suits against restaurant owners were being fought in Cleveland courts. Some restaurants were openly and publicly changing their policies. Such was the case in 1904, when a downtown proprietor informed blacks that they would in the future be seated only in the basement or in the second-floor dining area, in order to separate them from white patrons. But most restaurants, as well as the dining rooms of chain and department stores, appear simply to have discouraged black patronage without explanation or compensating arrangements, either by turning blacks away at the door or by resorting to such

[35] Cleveland *Gazette*, Aug. 5, 1899, Mar. 10, 1900, Mar. 15, 1902, Apr. 28, 1906, Sept. 25, Nov. 20, 1909; Akron *Beacon Journal*, Sept. 17, 18, 1909.

[36] From *Oberlin Alumni Magazine* (1910): "Literary Societies for Colored Students," Mar., 224; "Literary Society for Colored Students," Apr., 254–255; "Social Distinctions in Oberlin Societies," May, 316–317; H. C. King, "The College and Democracy," Dec., 94–102. Cleveland *Gazette*, Apr. 23, 1910; Cincinnati *Enquirer*, Apr. 20, 1910.

devices as pouring salt in their coffee in order to discourage future visits. Individual protest to the management of the Bailey and May companies' department stores, the Union Station restaurant, and the Standard Drug Company won promises of equal treatment,[37] but many better eating places were now closed to blacks. In 1908 the Cleveland *Journal*, a black paper established in 1903, was forced to agree with the Cleveland *Plain Dealer*, which in the past decades had gone from negrophobia to sincere concern for the welfare of local blacks. "With two or three exceptions" the better downtown eating places and the dining rooms of the better hotels, not to mention the hotels themselves, were closed to the race, and lawsuits and individual appeals to owners had done little to change conditions. It had now become, said the *Plain Dealer*, "extremely difficult" for even the most well-groomed, well-mannered blacks to obtain a meal downtown without insult. In 1916 George Myers agreed, stating in a letter to a city official, "There is scarcely a restaurant or cafe downtown that we are permitted to enter and be served, no matter how respectable, with or without families." [38]

When Cleveland hosted the 1908 National Education Association convention, the dearth of hotel and dining facilities for black delegates threatened to create chaos. Local blacks pleaded with the Chamber of Commerce to ask proprietors to make exceptions during the convention week so that black visitors might be accommodated. In this way hotel rooms were secured for many of the blacks, and several downtown restaurants pledged that there would be no discrimination. Yet after the convention Harry Smith noted that there had been "more than a half dozen cases of hotel and restaurant refusals on account of race." [39]

Conditions were also declining in recreational and cultural facilities. Segregation in theater seating became widespread, and some theaters attempted to exclude blacks completely. Of the six major theaters in 1905, the only two which drew no color line at all were the prestigious Cleveland Opera House and the Star, which had ended a policy of separate seating in 1898 after a black woman and a white companion launched a private crusade against the theater's discriminatory policy.[40]

[37] Cleveland *Gazette*, Nov. 21, 1896, Aug. 14, 1897, May 28, Oct. 1, 1898, July 29, 1899, Jan. 20, May 26, 1900.

[38] Ibid., Feb. 15, May 24, 1902, May 27, 1905, Aug. 11, 18, Sept. 15, 1906, May 8, 1909, Aug. 6, 1910, June 10, 1911, Aug. 24, 1912, Aug. 14, 1915; Cleveland *Journal*, May 9, 1908, quoting Cleveland *Plain Dealer*, May 3, 1908; George Myers to F. H. Goff, Jan. 17, 1916, Box XVII, folder 1, George A. Myers Papers, OHS.

[39] Cleveland *Journal*, May 9 ,16, 30, 1908; Cleveland *Gazette*, July 11, 1908.

[40] Cleveland *Gazette*, Apr. 9, 1898, May 27, 1905.

But efforts to end discriminatory seating at the Empire led the management to attempt to exclude blacks completely—unless they consented to stand in the back of the theater. The Cleveland, Hippodrome, and Prospect theaters restricted blacks to the balconies. So adamant was the Hippodrome that in 1908 the sons of John Green and Charles Chesnutt, both respectable young men light enough to be taken for white, were almost carried out of the theater when they attempted to take main floor seats for which they had been mistakenly sold tickets.[41] A few successful lawsuits, individual appeals, and letters to management led to some changes, and by late 1908 the *Journal* was able to report that blacks were now receiving "a fair degree of respect and good judgment in selling tickets" by theater managers, who were beginning once more to seat respectable-looking blacks on the main floor.[42] But at most theaters the rule remained: blacks were to sit in the balcony.[43]

Roller skating rinks and bowling alleys were excluding blacks or limiting them to special days of the week. Luna Park, a popular amusement park, also began to mistreat blacks. Even on the day when one of the city's leading black organizations held its annual outing there, swimming, roller skating, and dancing were either denied blacks or allowed them only for a few hours, and signs were posted everywhere noting the restrictions.[44] A popular desire to segregate municipal beaches, bath houses, and dancing pavilions also became apparent. By 1908 a de facto color line had actually begun to emerge at Lake Erie beaches; in that year a young black bather was stoned and chased for blocks for swimming at a municipal beach considered "white." Talk of establishing municipal segregation as public policy was squelched, however, during 1911–15 by Mayor Newton D. Baker.[45]

Because it compromised the ideal of Christian fellowship which had informed the founding of the YMCA and YWCA movements, the change in membership policies of both at Cleveland was particularly disturbing to many blacks. Cleveland had been almost alone in Ohio

[41] Ibid., Feb. 14, Mar. 21, 1903, Sept. 10, Oct. 15, 22, 1904, Apr. 29, 1905, Oct. 6, 1906, Feb. 1, Apr. 18, 1908; Cleveland *Journal*, Jan. 20, 1906.

[42] Cleveland *Journal*, Nov. 21, 1908.

[43] George Myers to F. H. Goff, Jan. 17, 1916, Box XVII, folder 1, Myers Papers; Cleveland *Gazette*, Apr. 2, 1910, Mar. 11, 1911, Jan. 31, Mar. 21, May 9, 1914.

[44] Cleveland *Gazette*, Feb. 1, 1902, Feb. 4, 1905, Sept. 15, 1906, Jan. 23, 30, 1909, Aug. 3, 1912, July 26, Oct. 4, 1913, June 27, 1914, July 17, 1915; Cleveland *Journal*, May 14, 1905, July 17, 24, Aug. 7, 1909; Cleveland *Plain Dealer*, Aug. 2, 1911.

[45] Cleveland *Gazette*, June 27, 1908; George Myers to F. H. Goff, Jan. 17, 1916, Box XVII, folder 1, Myers Papers.

in opening its Y's to blacks, if only in small numbers. Yet, as the purpose of both movements began to shift in the late nineteenth century from the original evangelical mission to general recreational service, whites no doubt felt greater justification for excluding blacks. The appointment in the early 1890s of a new YMCA secretary, G. K. Shurtleff, signaled a change in policy. Under his direction blacks seeking membership were refused; after 1900 black members were gradually dropped. In 1907 Shurtleff finally admitted that he desired segregation, justifying his course by stating that blacks should not push themselves where they were not wanted. The refusal to admit a black girl to a training program in 1903 was the start of a shift in YWCA policy. Black girls were not excluded completely, but after 1903 their numbers were kept very small on the grounds that more black participation would cause a white exodus.[46]

III

The trend toward greater racial conflict and segregation in public accommodations had its complement in the public schools. The matter was very complex, for not only were there particularly strong continuities with the past, but elements of racial progress also mingled with ones of prejudice and discrimination in defining the new black school situation. This situation was a product of local responses to the 1887 school desegregation law in southern and central Ohio, the two regions where many schools still remained segregated at the time. Because the response coincided with the emerging era of reaction in race relations, the late 1880s and the 1890s found many communities trying to adjust to the demands of school desegregation at a time when the larger context of race relations was increasingly hostile to integration. On the basis of post-Reconstruction race relations in these southern and central communities, where racial contacts had always been relatively proscribed, the response to the law was by no means unexpected. Years of warning from both within and outside the race had prepared many black Ohioans to face the fact that integration would be accomplished at the expense of black teachers' positions. Moreover, in certain southern Ohio towns strong, and ultimately successful, resistance to desegregation could be expected.

The bitter choice between integration and black teachers was faced in many communities. Whatever their past feelings about the efficacy

[46] Cleveland *Gazette*, Nov. 16, 1895, Oct. 30, 1897, Aug. 4, 1900, Jan. 31, 1903, Mar. 9, 1907; Jane Edna Hunter, *A Nickel and a Prayer* (Cleveland, 1940), pp. 90–94.

of separate schools, in the years following the passage of the Arnett Law most blacks apparently concluded that integrated schools meant better lives for their children, and they thus abandoned the separate schools. Some parents with lingering doubts found their decision assisted by school officials, who seized upon the occasion to close costly separate schools which had long placed financial burdens on their communities. The result was that while many black children now enjoyed unprecedented opportunities for quality, integrated education, black teachers lost their jobs in the desegregated districts. Sometimes integration was accomplished quickly and peacefully (as at Dayton, Springfield, and the majority of school districts),[47] or over a period of years (as at Cincinnati),[48] or only through the filing of lawsuits (as at College Hill, Yellow Springs, and Oxford),[49] or was accompanied by a brief period of violence and intimidation of blacks (as at Ripley, Felicity, and New Richmond, all southern communities with relatively large black populations).[50] But in any case, black teachers were always its victims, fired almost as soon as black schools closed. No amount of black protest or complaint could alter this situation. In response to requests that black teachers be retained, school officials were often quite frank in stating that this might happen only if blacks consented to the preservation of separate schools, or to the initiation of separate classrooms within otherwise integrated

[47] Cleveland *Gazette,* June 4, 18, Sept. 17, Oct. 1, 29, 1887; Steubenville *Herald,* Sept. 9, 1887; Belmont *Chronicle,* Sept. 15, 1887; Jackson *Herald,* Sept. 8, 15, 22, 1887; Columbus *Ohio State Journal,* Sept. 12, 1887; Circleville *Democrat,* Sept. 23, 1887; Lebanon *Gazette,* Sept. 15, 1887; Cleveland *Plain Dealer,* Sept. 14, 1887; Ironton *Register,* Sept. 15, 1887; Cincinnati *Enquirer,* Sept. 22, 1887; Zanesville *Signal,* Sept. 12, 14, 27, 1887; Springfield *Champion City Times,* Sept. 6, 27, 1887.

[48] Cleveland *Gazette,* June 25, Sept. 17, 1887, June 15, 1889, Sept. 13, 1890; Cincinnati *Commercial Gazette,* Sept. 16, Oct. 18, 1887; Cincinnati Board of Education, *Minutes,* v. 19, "Special Report" (May 20, 1887), pp. 410–411 (June 20, 1887), pp. 494–495 (Aug. 29, 1887).

[49] Cleveland *Gazette,* Oct. 1, 8, 22, Nov. 26, 1887, Mar. 10, 1889. In all three towns the cases were won by the blacks at various levels of the courts; the College Hill case went to the Ohio Supreme Court, while the others were fought at lower levels. State of Ohio ex rel. Wilson Hunter v. Board of Education of College Hill, 45 Ohio State Reports 556 (1889); State of Ohio ex rel. Perry Gibson of Oxford, 2 Ohio Circuits 557 (1887).

[50] At Ripley, where blacks were about 20% of the population, an economic boycott was employed against black farm labor and farm tenants, in the hope that they would move from the area and that the schools would thus escape integration. This boycott appears to have failed, however; Cincinnati *Enquirer,* Sept. 22, 1887, Feb. 15, 1889. At New Richmond, all but the lower grades were integrated after a year of conflict, while at Felicity blacks entered the public schools after two years of periodic violence and intimidation. In both towns blacks were about a quarter of the population. Ibid., Dec. 5, 8, 1888, Jan. 24, Feb. 9, 1889; Batavia *Clermont Sun,* Feb. 23, Aug. 17, Sept. 12, Nov. 21, Dec. 12, 1888.

schools.[51] At Dayton, the latter arrangement was reluctantly agreed to at one school after a few years of threats and demands failed to obtain a black teacher.[52] But most blacks appear to have found that price too high, and they took the same path as black Cincinnatians. When protests and attempts to take the issue into politics failed to gain employment for black teachers, except in the one Walnut Hills school which blacks controlled because of their large numbers in the surrounding neighborhood, Cincinnati blacks simply gave up the fight.[53] Given the strength of local attitudes, no major black political figure seems to have even considered bringing the issue into the legislature. Between 1887 and 1916 only three of Ohio's integrated school systems (Cleveland, Youngstown, and Columbus) regularly employed black teachers for integrated classrooms—and then, except at Cleveland, only in very small numbers, and often much to the dismay of white parents.[54]

Black teachers did remain securely at their posts, however, in the few southern Ohio school districts which retained the dual school system. Black political power in these communities was often well developed because of the large and concentrated black vote; but whites were too unanimous and too adamant in their desire to retain school segregation for blacks to use their power to bring about change. Xenia blacks found themselves unable to force integration where their school board, backed by all segments of white opinion in their overwhelmingly Republican community, responded to the desegregation law with a gerrymandering of school districts. The entire, largely black, East End of Xenia was placed in one district. The gerrymander was approved by local and county courts.[55] After Republican and Democratic school board members at Chillicothe united to gerrymander districts in order to avoid wholesale integration, black attempts to take the matter into local politics and courts likewise failed to produce relief.[56] At both towns blacks learned to accommodate

51 Cleveland *Gazette*, June 4, 1887; Zanesville *Signal*, Sept. 12, 1887; Cleveland *Plain Dealer*. Sept. 14, 1887; Jackson *Herald*, Sept. 8, 15, 22, 1887.

52 Richmond *Planet*, Mar. 7, 1896.

53 Cincinnati *Enquirer*, Mar. 30, 1897, June 1, 1900; Cleveland *Gazette*, Aug. 7, Oct. 19, 1897.

54 Cleveland *Gazette*, Aug. 10, 1889, Oct. 12, 1895, Oct. 8, 22, 1898. There were approximately a dozen black teachers in Cleveland in 1905, and about 20 ten years later; Carrie Clifford, "Cleveland and Its Colored People," *Colored American Magazine*, IX (July, 1905), 372–373; Cleveland *Gazette*, Feb. 28, 1914.

55 Xenia *Torchlight*, Sept. 14, 21, Nov. 23, Dec. 10, 14, 1887; Cleveland *Gazette*, Sept. 18, 1888.

56 Portsmouth *Tribune*, Aug. 24, 1887, Jackson *Herald*, Oct. 27, 1887; Cleveland *Gazette*, Jan. 20, Sept. 15, 22, 1894; Chillicothe *Advertiser*, Nov. 24, 1893, Jan. 12, Feb. 16, Apr. 13, Aug. 31, Sept. 14, 21, 28, Oct. 12, Nov. 2, 9, 1894.

themselves to the situation, and the overwhelming number of their children remained in separate schools until well into the twentieth century.[57] In some communities, such as Hillsboro and Gallipolis, coercion does not appear to have been present in the retention of the dual school system; black parents there apparently made a tacit agreement to allow segregation to remain, even though it was illegal.[58] At Gallipolis and eventually at Xenia, the consent of black parents was obtained through promises of excellent facilities, highly qualified black teachers, and a continuing commitment to equality with local white schools. But this was surely not the case everywhere; at Hillsboro and Baltimore, not far from Columbus, for example, the black school buildings were decrepit and inadequate.[59] Moreover, at a time when school integration was desired by most Ohio blacks and gaining acceptance, however reluctant, among many whites, the retention of separate schools in these communities bespoke a rigidity of race relations in some communities that blacks were powerless to change— a rigidity that could only become more oppressive, in light of the larger trend of race relations.

Once schools were integrated successfully, whites almost never launched a serious and sustained movement for their resegregation. Indeed, only at Columbus was this to happen, and there the final result was a partial compromise of the city's commitment to mixed schools. Though the city's schools had been integrated without incident by local initiative in 1882, and several years later the school board had begun the relatively progressive practice of hiring black teachers (usually only to teach in schools with substantial black enrollment), opposition to integration began to gather force after the turn of the century, just when segregation in public accommodations began to increase. At monthly meetings beginning in 1901, school board members, often at the urging of white constituents whose

[57] G. Gwendolyn Brown, "The Influences Surrounding the Establishment of the Present Segregated Schools in Selected Cities of Ohio" (Master's thesis, Howard University, 1947), pp. 1–5, 37; George David, The Effect of School Segregation in Xenia, Ohio (Wilberforce, 1939), pp. 14–15, 23–24.

[58] Columbus Ohio State Journal, Sept. 12, 1887; Gallipolis Journal, Sept. 7, 1887; Portsmouth Times, Sept. 7, 1887; Cleveland Gazette, Oct. 8, 29, 1887, Sept. 29, Oct. 25, 1888, July 27, 1895; Hillsboro Gazette, Sept. 10, Nov. 5, 1887.

[59] Columbus Ohio State Journal, Sept. 12, 1887; Gallipolis Journal, Sept. 7, 1887; Xenia Torchlight, Dec. 17, 1887; Cleveland Gazette, Sept. 18, 1888; R. R. Wright, Jr., "The Negroes of Xenia, Ohio: A Social Study," U.S. Department of Labor Bulletin no. 48 (Sept., 1903), 1020–23, 1041–42; Mame Charlotte Mason, "The Policy of the Segregation of the Negro in the Public Schools of Ohio, Indiana, and Illinois" (Master's thesis, University of Chicago, 1917), pp. 49–52; William Giffin, "The Negro in Ohio, 1914–1939" (Ph.D. dissertation, Ohio State University, 1969), pp. 40–45.

children attended school with blacks, began to introduce proposals calling for the creation of separate schools, separate classrooms within integrated schools, or the reassignment of black pupils in pre- dominantly white schools to buildings with larger black enrollments. These periodic proposals were by no means the work of racist cranks. In 1907, for example, two were initiated by well-respected and dis- tinguished members, one a Democratic politician who would the next year become the board's president, and the other Ohio State University President Walter Oxley Thompson.[60]

Fearing perhaps that it might run afoul of the state's school laws, the board always defeated these resolutions, though seldom by large majorities. Yet the search for remedies continued, and the board was finally led to experiment with gerrymandered school districts. During 1907 and 1908 land was acquired and plans were drawn for the construction of a large junior high school in the rapidly growing black section of East Long Street. This area was at the time adequately served by a conveniently located integrated school, but boundaries were redrawn in 1909 so that as many students as possible would be brought into the new school. In addition, when the new Champion Avenue School, one of the city's best equipped and most modern, opened to 300 black students in 1911, all four black teachers in Colum- bus's schools were reassigned to a new building, supplemented by six more black teachers and a black principal. Of course, many black students lived outside the gerrymandered district and continued to attend mixed schools. Moreover, even within the area served by the new school, high school and primary-grade blacks went to integrated schools. Yet the establishment of a segregated school marked a signifi- cant departure from the policy of integration which been pursued, albeit grudgingly at times, in the past, and it contributed to the deterioration of race relations in the city.[61]

IV

Segregation in individual communities usually remained in- formal, lacking legal standing and government approval. However, white social workers and state institution heads tried to make it the

[60] Cleveland *Gazette*, Oct. 22, 1898, Sept. 16, 23, 1899, Aug. 22, Sept. 26, 1903; Columbus *Dispatch*, Mar. 7, 1901, Sept. 3, 17, Oct. 15, 1907; Columbus *Press*, Aug. 12, Sept. 23, 1903.
[61] Columbus *Dispatch*, Oct. 15, 1907, Jan. 7, 1908, Feb. 2, 16, Aug. 31, Nov. 28, 1909, Sept. 2, 1910, Mar. 15, 1911; Columbus, Board of Education, *Minutes*, July 20, Aug. 3, 31, 1908; Columbus *Ohio State Journal*, June 6, Sept. 6, 1910; Brown, "Influences Surrounding Segregated Schools," pp. 65–66.

official policy of state custodial institutions caring for young dependents and delinquents. The complex motivations behind these efforts
were revealed in the campaign for a black orphanage waged by the
Reverend Rufus Longman, a visiting agent for the semi-public Cincinnati Children's Home and president in 1911 of the influential Ohio
Board of Charities and Corrections. In an address before the annual
Ohio Conference on Charities and Corrections in 1910, Longman stated
that years of research into the care of black dependents in Ohio revealed that many were woefully neglected, either committed to re-
formatories though innocent of wrong or allowed to shift for themselves. While this was bad enough, Longman found the situation in
existing integrated homes not much better. In seeking "to approximate
the family home," these facilities fostered an unwholesome familiarity
between black and white children. They grew so close to one another
that they were utterly without racial awareness; Longman contended,
though offering no proof, that this closeness easily lent itself to subsequent interracial sexual and marital relations. Relatedly, he charged,
the circumstances in such homes failed to prepare black children to
enter a segregated society, in which they would have to mingle almost
exclusively with their own people and live with limited opportunities.
Longman therefore proposed the creation of a well-financed state
home for black dependents, staffed by black social workers.[62]

Without recent precedent as it was in Ohio and involving a large
expenditure in an area in which the legislature felt little urgency, the
Longman proposal never received serious attention. Yet even before
Longman's address, segregation was quietly and informally being
instituted at existing state facilities. In 1909 the twenty black girls at
the state orphanage for veterans' children, located at Xenia, were
placed in a separate cottage, with a black matron to care for them;
the girls continued to share all recreational and educational activities
with whites. The black girls themselves were said to have asked for the
change, but events the next year made this claim somewhat dubious.
In 1910 black boys were placed in a separate cottage under a black
matron, and they were to engage only in segregated sports, dining,
and trips to town; no mention was made of their having asked for
separation.[63] Similar arrangements were made at the home for
delinquent girls at Delaware. In 1909 the home's hundred black girls
were placed in a separate building under a black matron. Here separa-

[62] Rufus Longman, "Dependent Colored Children in Ohio," *Ohio Bulletin of
Charities and Corrections,* XVII (July, 1911), 30–33; Cleveland *Gazette,*
Oct. 20, 1909, Jan. 28, Feb. 4, 1911; Cincinnati *Enquirer,* Oct. 16, 1910.
[63] Cleveland *Gazette,* Aug. 28, Sept. 4, 11, 18, Oct. 30, 1910.

tion heralded inferior treatment, for the ratio of white girls to matrons was nineteen to one. In addition, the black girls' building was in such poor condition that a state inspector soon suggested that it should be vacated immediately.[64]

Longman's concern with miscegenation was a facet of yet another aspect of deteriorating race relations—an increasing repression of interracial sexual relations. This preoccupation assumed its most dramatic form in a number of lynchings and attempted lynchings prompted by rumors of the rape of white women by black men, but it could be seen as well in the harassment of interracial couples. Probate court judges now blocked the issuance of marriage licenses to interracial couples in settings as different as Ashtabula (in the Reserve) and Columbus.[65] Nowhere was this repression more intense than at Cincinnati. When police there began a long-awaited crackdown on vice at the turn of the century, they set out with particular vehemence to bring all interracial aspects of prostitution under control. Brothels were for the first time segregated—to the extent that black men could no longer frequent white prostitutes. Many blacks would have agreed that the crackdown was necessary, even if capricious, but few appreciated the accompanying bullying of interracial couples of all classes. White women seen with black men were arrested and fined, though little concern was shown for white men with black women. In 1901, after the police arrested a light-skinned Negro woman of social prominence and beat up the darker companion with whom she was dining, black leaders secured mayoral promises that such harassment would end. But several months later an off-duty policeman shot an unarmed and respected black man when a registered white prostitute complained of his alleged advances.[66]

The efforts to repress interracial sexual relations reached a peak in 1913. The legislature considered an anti-intermarriage bill which not only made such marriages illegal in the future, but reached back with dubious legality to comprehend every interracial marriage which had ever taken place in Ohio. Similar bills were introduced that same year in fourteen other northern and western states, and Congress debated such a measure for the District of Columbia. The Ohio bill,

[64] Ibid., Dec. 16, 1905, Nov. 18, Dec. 25, 1909, Jan. 7, 1911, Dec. 18, 1915; Cleveland *Journal*, Dec. 4, 25, 1909; Special Legislative Committee, "Girls Industrial Home . . . Report," *Ohio Bulletin of Charities and Corrections*, XVII (Feb., 1911), 30.

[65] Cleveland *Gazette*, Apr. 17, 1909; Portsmouth *Blade*, Jan. 26, 1910.

[66] Cleveland *Gazette*, Dec. 9, 1899; Dabney, *Why the Negro*, p. 3, and Dabney, *Cincinnati's Colored Citizens: Historical, Sociological, and Biographical* (Cincinnati, 1926), pp. 165–167.

which carried penalties of up to five years in prison, was particularly vicious. All of these proposals were largely the response of an angered and threatened society, increasingly insistent on a rigid color line, to the well-publicized marital and extramarital affairs of one man, Jack Johnson, the first black heavyweight champion of the world, whose boxing ability and relations with white women emphatically challenged the canons of white supremacy. In Ohio and elsewhere, vigorous lobbying by blacks and their white allies combined with strong doubts among legislators about the rightness, enforceability, and consequences of anti-miscegenation legislation to bring about the bill's defeat.[67]

This victory represented but one triumph against racial intolerance at a time when new challenges to equality and black citizenship were multiplying ominously. A few months earlier, Ohio voters had refused by a majority of over 25,000 to erase the word "white" from the suffrage and militia provisions of the state constitution as part of a general charter revision then underway. A similar change had been blocked in 1874, when voters struck down in its entirety a new charter, leaving an ante-bellum constitution. Few blacks had felt threatened at that time, for both the Reconstruction amendments and the progressive trend of the times made this remnant of pre–Civil War years a quaint, if bitter, reminder of a less enlightened past. Now Harry Smith saw the matter quite differently. He actually envisioned the results of the referendum as a portent of disfranchisement in state elections if the tide of political repression swept northward. "Ohio joins the ranks of all the other Negro-hating states—all 48," said Smith.[68]

Thus on the eve of World War I Ohio's racial environment bore little resemblance to the open, malleable, and hopeful one of the immediate post-bellum decades. It signaled the end of the promising new era of the late nineteenth century, and it mocked the optimism of the 1880s.

[67] David Fowler, "Northern Attitudes toward Interracial Marriage: A Study of Legislation and Public Opinion in the Middle Atlantic States and the States of the Old Northwest" (Ph.D. dissertation, Yale University, 1963), pp. 298–301; Cleveland *Gazette,* Jan. 18, Feb. 8, 15, Mar. 1, 15, 22, 29, Apr. 19, 1913.

[68] Cleveland *Gazette,* Sept. 14, 1912.

10

Migration, Urbanization, and the City

The alarming deterioration of race relations caused Ohio's black leaders to review the basic premises of a racial strategy framed in more hopeful times. Yet they could not sort out and react to the new trend in isolation from important, though less dramatic and often less visible, developments internal to Ohio's growing black urban communities. At the same time they faced growing racial intolerance, they had also to come to terms with the serious implications of increasing black urban populations and resurgent migrations from the South. In both objective and subjective ways the two trends mingled to pose what many considered to be the sharpest challenge to racial strategy in the years between enfranchisement and the World War.

I

The 1880s marked a significant watershed in the urbanization of Ohio's black minority, which numbered 87,113 by 1890. Not only did the decade see the transition of the black population from rural to predominantly urban (in centers with populations over 2,500), but black urban growth also shifted away from the towns and villages to the major metropolitan centers—Cincinnati, Cleveland, Columbus, Dayton, Springfield, Toledo, and Youngstown. After 1890 the tendency of Ohio blacks to settle in the major cities increased; by 1910, 74 percent (82,282) of Ohio's 111,452 blacks were found in urban areas, and close to half (54,454) resided in the seven major metropolitan centers. Table I illustrates these trends in black population development.[1]

Though the population trend is impressive, it was probably even

[1] Unless otherwise noted, in this chapter all statistical references in regard to population, urbanization, and migration are taken from the following decennial

TABLE I. BLACK URBANIZATION, 1870–1910

	Ohio Urban Blacks		Blacks in Seven Major Metropolitan Centers	
	No.	%	No.	%
1870	24,200	38	11,554	18
1880	38,200	48	17,954	22
1890	51,124	59	27,601	32
1900	64,986	67	38,936	40
1910	82,282	74	54,454	49

deeper than the data reveal. When the black populations in the industrial and residential suburbs of Cincinnati, Columbus, and Cleveland are included, by 1910 almost three-quarters of the black urban population and two-thirds of the state's total black population were found in the major cities. Moreover, because the data are derived from the federal census, which has consistently encountered difficulties in obtaining a full count of lower-status persons (particularly rural southern blacks in the late nineteenth century and northern metropolitan blacks in the twentieth), the figures probably substantially underestimate the extent of black urbanization.[2] Yet the demographic trend is clear: within five decades Ohio blacks had been transformed from a rural to an urban people.

More dramatic proof of the urban trend is available in the individual metropolitan centers. While blacks remained a small percentage of the total population within each one, all of the major cities experienced substantial increases in their black populations. While urban population growth was continual during 1870–1910, the most substantial absolute gains occurred after 1890 (except in Springfield). The largest absolute gains took place at Toledo and Cleveland during the 1890s, and at Columbus, Cincinnati, Dayton, and Youngstown during 1900–1910. Table II summarizes the data on black population for the major cities.

census volumes or compilations of census data: U.S. Census Office, *Ninth Census of the United States.. . . 1870* (Washington, 1872), I, 226–241, 536–539, 540–541, *Statistics of the United States at the Tenth Census* (Washington, 1883), I, 422–423, *Report on the Population of the United States, Eleventh Census . . . 1890* (Washington, 1895), I, pt. 1, pp. 546–549; and U. S. Bureau of the Census, *Census Reports, Twelfth Census of the United States . . . 1900* (Washington, 1901), I, 358–365, 522–539, *Thirteenth Census of the United States . . . 1910* (Washington, 1913), III, 502–505, 547–552, and *Negro Population, 1790–1915* (Washington, 1918), pp. 43–45, 51–52, 150.

[2] For a discussion of undercounting, see Bureau of the Census, *Negro Population, 1790–1915*, pp. 26–28.

The black metropolitan population grew mainly through the entrance of outsiders, rather than from the natural increase of earlier black residents. As contemporary observers often pointed out, northern black populations in large cities were usually characterized by rates of little or no natural increase. As the result of the tragic toll in the lives of the urban black poor taken by disease, particularly tuberculosis which festered in the decaying, ill-ventilated tenements of the slums, black death rates often tended to equal or exceed black birth rates.[3] According to the decennial census and to special yearly censuses of mortality taken in 1900 and thereafter by the Bureau of the Census, deaths among blacks exceeded births at Columbus, Cleveland, Cincinnati, and Dayton in 1890, 1900, and 1910; in smaller cities births occasionally appear to have exceeded deaths, although the gap even then was quite small.[4] At Springfield, for example, birth and death records indicate that because of the low rate of black natural increase during 1880–1900, at least two-thirds of black population increase was due to the entrance of outsiders. The pattern was almost exactly the opposite for Springfield whites; births accounted for at least 59 percent of their population increase during 1880–1900.[5] In the larger cities, the entrance of newcomers as a factor in urban black

[3] R. R. Wright, Jr., "The Migration of Negroes to the North," *Annals*, XXVII (May, 1906), 559–560, 563, and Wright, "The Growth of the Northern Negro Population," *Southern Workman*, XXXXI (June, 1912), 333–334. Negro mortality as the result of tuberculosis was great, both in Ohio and in the nation at large. In 1910, for example, the national Negro mortality rate for tuberculosis was more than three times greater than that for whites. In Ohio between 1910 and 1915 tuberculosis accounted for 20% of all black deaths and 22.5% of all black deaths in the cities, compared to 8% and 9% respectively for whites; Bureau of the Census, *Special Reports, Mortality Statistics* (Washington, 1910–15), (1910), p. 252, 268, (1911), pp. 26, 274, (1912), pp. 52, 66, (1913), pp. 246, 260, (1914), pp. 306, 322, (1915), pp. 300, 318, and *Negro Population, 1790–1915*, pp. 313–315.

[4] The gap between births and deaths could be relatively great in the major cities. Deaths per 1,000 blacks at Cincinnati exceeded births by 4.4 in 1890, 12.9 in 1900, and 15.9 in 1910, while Cleveland's figures were 10.2, 3.7, and 5.7 during the same years. At Columbus, the gap was 9.0, 6.3, and 5.8, and, according to one local observer, 3.2 between 1909 and 1915. Births exceeded deaths at Toledo in 1890, Youngstown in 1900, and Springfield in 1910, but the gap was small: 2.2 per 1,000 at both Toledo and Youngstown and 1.3 at Springfield. See Census Office, *Report on the Vital and Social Statistics of the United States . . . 1890*, Part 1, *Analysis and Rate Tables* (Washington, 1896), pp. 628–632, and *Twelfth Census*, I, pt. 2, pp. 126–127, 145–146, *Thirteenth Census*, III, 399, *Special Reports: Mortality Statistics, 1900–1904* (Washington, 1906), pp. 4–12, *Special Reports: Mortality Statistics, 1910* (Washington, 1913), p. 71, and *Negro Population, 1790–1915*, p. 320; Richard Clyde Minor, "Negroes in Columbus" (Ph.D. dissertation, Ohio State University, 1936), pp. 14–15.

[5] E. S. Todd, *A Sociological Study of Springfield and Clark County, Ohio* (New York, 1904), pp. 42–47, 57–59.

TABLE II. BLACKS IN OHIO'S MAJOR CITIES, 1870–1910

	1870		1880			1890		
	(1)	(2)	(1)	(2)	(3)	(1)	(2)	(3)
Cincinnati	5,896	2.7%	8,179	3.2%	2,283	11,655	3.9%	3,476
Cleveland	1,292	1.3%	2,038	1.2%	746	2,989	1.1%	951
Columbus	1,847	5.9%	3,018	5.8%	1,171	5,525	6.2%	2,507
Dayton	548	1.7%	991	2.5%	443	2,158	3.5%	1,167
Springfield	1,227	9.6%	2,360	11.3%	1,133	3,549	11.1%	1,189
Toledo	612	1.9%	928	1.8%	316	1,077	1.3%	149
Youngstown	132	1.6%	320	2.0%	288	648	1.9%	328

	1900			1910		
	(1)	(2)	(3)	(1)	(2)	(3)
Cincinnati	14,482	4.4%	2,827	19,639	5.4%	5,157
Cleveland	5,988	1.6%	2,999	8,488	1.5%	2,500
Columbus	8,201	6.5%	2,676	12,739	7.0%	4,538
Dayton	3,387	4.0%	1,229	4,842	4.2%	1,455
Springfield	4,253	11.1%	704	4,933	10.5%	680
Toledo	1,710	1.3%	633	1,877	1.1%	167
Youngstown	1,015	2.0%	367	1,936	2.4%	921

(1) total number of local blacks
(2) % of blacks in local population
(3) net increase in black population during intercensal decade

population increase was actually greater than the absolute gains recorded by the census. Newcomers not only comprised the absolute gains over a previous decade, but also made up for the net loss of population attributable to high death rates and out-migration. Thus, for example, Cleveland's black population growth due to in-migration was greater than the 2,500 during 1900–1910 and 2,730 during 1910–14 as recorded by federal and local police censuses.[6] More accurately, the increase equaled 2,500 and 2,730 *plus* the number of deaths over births *and* the number of out-migrants during the two periods.

Between 1870 and 1910 these were several sources for this entrance of black outsiders into the cities. Throughout these decades, as the result of aggressive municipal annexation policies, blacks living on the fringes of large cities were increasingly brought into urban populations. This pattern of development was present almost exclusively in southern and central Ohio, for the overwhelming majority of rural blacks lived there to begin with, and it helps to account for the rela-

[6] For data from the Cleveland police census, Cleveland *Gazette*, May 9, 1914.

tively large increase in black population at Dayton, Columbus, Cincinnati, and Springfield during the 1870s and 1880s.[7]

Migration was an even more important source of urban black population growth. In the late nineteenth century the major source of this urban migration seems to have been from within Ohio rather than from the South; there are strong indications that after the Civil War, which brought large numbers of southern blacks to Ohio, the extent of southern migration fell considerably. Though imperfect because they fail to take into acount both mortality and out-migration, census data on the percentages and absolute numbers of southern-born blacks residing in Ohio suggest such a trend. While half of black Ohioans had been born in the South in 1870, the figure had fallen to 37 percent in 1890; while the number of southern born was 31,378 in 1870, it was only 902 more (32,280) in 1890.[8]

The intrastate migrants of the late nineteenth century came from the rural areas and small towns of southern and central Ohio. As for many whites, opportunities for blacks were in decline in the countryside at the time. The mechanization of Ohio agriculture was rapidly undercutting the position of farm labor; the growing costs of land, equipment, and maintenance, and the increasing marginality of the family farm within the larger economy also checked the growth of the black farm owner and tenant populations. At the same time, the cities offered greater economic opportunities, even for blacks, and their varied social attractions and excitements exerted a powerful pulling force upon rural folk.[9] The result was a long period of black population decline or stagnation beginning in the 1870s and 1880s in rural southern counties such as Clermont, Brown, Gallia, Meigs, Pickaway, and Ross, and in the central counties of Miami, Darke, Logan, Shelby, Mercer, and Champaign. All of these had been major foci of black migration from the South before the 1870s. The same phenomenon was occurring in a number of other counties with smaller black populations, such as Delaware, Madison, and Union, which were immediately adjacent to metropolitan counties. As the quite skewed sex

[7] Zane Miller, *Boss Cox's Cincinnati: Urban Politics in the Progressive Era* (New York, 1968), p. 108; Charlotte Reeve Conover, *The Story of Dayton* (Dayton, 1917), p. 26 and passim; Todd, *Springfield and Clark County*, pp. 24–28; Cleveland *Gazette*, Jan. 12, 1844; Indianapolis *Freeman*, Aug. 3, 1912.

[8] Bureau of the Census, *Negro Population, 1790–1915*, p. 68.

[9] Philip D. Jordan, *Ohio Comes of Age, 1873–1900* (Columbus, 1943), pp. 105–106; Ivan Tribe, "The Development of a Rural Community: Albany, Ohio, 1840–1880" (Master's thesis, Ohio University, 1967), p. 19; Alma May, "The Negro and Mercer County" (Master's thesis, University of Dayton, 1968), pp. 49, 55; W. E. B. Du Bois, "Long in Darke," *Colored American Magazine*, XVII (Nov., 1909), 353–355.

ratios at Columbus, Dayton, and Cleveland in 1890 suggest, the migrants were often single men.[10]

A shift in the source of the urban migration began to occur during the 1890s and proceeded rapidly thereafter. While the intrastate migrants continued to come to the large urban centers, now vying with them for predominance in the urban migrant population were numerous southern blacks, part of a larger stream now leaving for northern cities.[11] The southern migrants accelerated black population growth in all of the large cities except Springfield by helping to produce the greatest population gains experienced between 1870 and the World War. Springfield experienced its largest gains in the 1880s as the result of annexation and the entrance of rural blacks attracted by the availability of work in factories recently opened to the race. After 1890 Springfield also attracted southern migrants, but its rate of black population growth began to fall at the same time—particularly after 1900, when its reputation for offering economic opportunity to blacks was offset by a reputation for race violence.

The extent of southern migration into Ohio is suggested by the census. After declining by only 1 percent between 1890 and 1900, the percentage of black Ohioans born in the South rose by 4 percent (from 36 percent to 40 percent) in the following decade. The total number of Ohio blacks of southern nativity rose from 32,280 in 1890 to 34,848 in 1900 and 44,439 in 1910; the gain of 12,159 in that period should be compared to that of 902 in the previous twenty years.[12] Mortality and out-migration can be taken into account through use of a method developed by demographers; when this technique is used in analyzing the 1870 and later censuses, the extent of the southern migration becomes even more impressive. During 1870–90 approximately 9,000 blacks arrived from outside the state, the overwhelming majority of them Southerners; between 1890 and 1910 there were 24,200 migrants.[13]

The large majority were bound for the cities, and the changing

[10] Sex ratios based on the 1890 census: Columbus (120.1), Cleveland (116.5), and Dayton (110.1). Cincinnati was Ohio's only large city with a predominance of females in 1890; its sex ratio was 97.1. This may have reflected the fact that a significant number of black men who were employed as steamboat deckhands would not have been in the city at census time.

[11] C. Warren Thornwaite, *Internal Migration in the United States* (Philadelphia, 1934), p. 12; George E. Haynes, *The Negro at Work in New York City* (New York, 1912), p. 17.

[12] Bureau of the Census, *Negro Population, 1790–1915*, p. 68.

[13] Simon Kuznets and Dorothy Thomas Swaine, directors, *Population Redistribution and Economic Growth, 1870–1950*, v. I, *Methodological Considerations and Reference Tables* (Philadelphia, 1957), p. 332. The method employed is based on "forward census survival ratios" computed from national mortality data. For a discussion see ibid., pp. 15–16, 57–65, 81, 95.

nature of the migrant population was apparent to contemporary observers. In his study of turn-of-the-century Springfield, Todd noted
that prior to 1890 the black migrants had been rural Ohioans from the
surrounding Miami Valley counties; in contrast, the 1890s found about
80 percent of the black in-migration composed of Southerners.[14] A
student of Columbus race relations stated in 1904, "It cannot be
denied that since 1900 there has been a great in-rush of southern
negroes into Columbus. Different estimates place these migrants at
from 750 to 1000 yearly." Noting persistent intrastate migration, he
added, "Almost rivaling the inflow of southern negroes is the coming
of negroes from the southern portions of the state. . . ." Yet, with its
extensive rural hinterland and central location, Columbus appears to
have been relatively unique in its continuing significant intrastate
migration.[15] The different patterns of migration were apparent in the
nativity of local black population. While the 1910 census found that
47 percent of Columbus's blacks were born outside the state, nearly
60 percent of the blacks at Cleveland (which had few rural counties
with significant black populations around it) and 70 percent of the
blacks at Cincinnati (which had a strategic position on the river-
border) were natives of other states. The census does not provide data
on the more specific regional origins of urban blacks, but it seems
likely that, in a year when 90 percent of those born outside the state
were native Southerners, the large majority of urban blacks not born
in Ohio would also be Southerners.[16]

Like the migrants of the Civil War era, the new southern migrants
came largely from Kentucky, Virginia, North Carolina, and Tennessee,
in that order; only a few natives of the Deep South reached Ohio.[17]
Little is known about whether southern migrants came from the
countryside or cities. Contemporaries, though, assumed that after 1900
northern cities were siphoning off from southern ones a growing
number of rural southern blacks who were leaving the soil to seek
urban employment. While some of the migrants had probably been
city dwellers in the South, these commentators contended, most of
them were a rural farming and village folk with little past experience
of urban life who were seeking relief from the poverty and isolation of
southern sharecropper and farmworker communities, and from south-

---

[14] Todd, *Springfield and Clark County*, pp. 37–44, 110–111.
[15] J. B. Malone in J. E. Hagarty, *The Columbus Negro: A Social Study* (1904),
quoted in Mary Louise Mark, *Negroes in Columbus* (Columbus, 1928), p. 10. An
exhaustive search has failed to locate the Hagarty volume.
[16] Bureau of the Census, *Negro Population, 1790–1915*, p. 74.
[17] Ibid., p. 83.

ern racial repression.[18] They were spurred on by rumors and oral tradition which spoke of the great opportunties and racial openness of the North. Speaking just weeks after the 1904 Springfield riot, which lent a tone of irony to his claim, Todd observed that "all negroes in Virginia, the Carolinas, and Kentucky know of Xenia and Springfield." Underscoring the high expectations of the migrants, he added, "They regard these places as a Mecca. . . ."[19]

The individual characteristics of the migrants are only slightly better known. Unlike the southern migrations of the 1860s which brought people of all ages, the new migrations brought young men and women [20]—members of a new free-born generation who could not feel, as their slave-born elders might, a sense of growing opportunity in the South. Those who were alone at the time of migration might have family ties which they hoped eventually to reestablish in Ohio. For example, at Xenia, alone among the larger towns in attracting southern migrants (perhaps a few hundred), an in-migration of young men from Caswell County, North Carolina, began in the late 1890s because of reports from a black woman who had left Caswell for Xenia many years before. When she returned home for the first time, she informed local blacks of her prosperity and of the opportunities for blacks; the young men left for Xenia soon afterward. They served as a vanguard, first establishing themselves at Xenia and then, after several months or a year, sending for their families. Their example undoubtedly influenced unrelated townspeople to consider going North.[21]

Men and women participated about equally in the 1890–1910 migration from the South.[22] But in order to be fully appreciated, the influx

[18] Wright, "Migration of Negroes," 564–573; Lillian Brandt, "The Make-up of Negro City Groups," Charities, XV (Oct. 7, 1905), 7–11; George Haynes, "The Movement of Negroes from Country to City," Southern Workman, XXXXVII (Apr., 1913), 230–236; Carl Kelsey, "Some Causes of Negro Emigration," Charities, XV (Oct. 7, 1905), 15–17.

[19] Springfield Press-Republic, Apr. 30, 1904.

[20] Bureau of the Census, Thirteenth Census, III, 619–620, 643–644, 648, and Negro Population, 1790–1915, pp. 180–181.

[21] R. R. Wright, Jr., "The Negroes of Xenia, Ohio: A Social Study," U.S. Department of Labor Bulletin no. 48 (Sept., 1903), 1016.

[22] Because census data make it impossible to trace out-migration from the cities, it is difficult to approximate the sexual component of migration at particular times and places. If we can assume no particularly significant out-migration of one sex as opposed to the other, some estimate might be made. The declining male-dominated sex ratios at Cleveland and Toledo between 1890 and 1910 suggest strong female components in those cities. At Cleveland the rate of female increase was over 15% greater than that for males during 1890–1910. On the other hand, men appear to have dominated the migration at Cincinnati, Springfield, and Youngstown, though the rate of female increase in the latter two rose

of young women must be taken on its own terms. Because many migrant women had to work, they entered the labor force in large numbers; between 1890 and 1910 the number of black working women in Ohio rose by 128 percent from 7,796 to 17,843. While the percentage of white working women rose only from 15 in 1890 to 18 in 1910, the percentage of black women at work rose from 22 to 33. The increase among urban black working women was greater, ranging from 12 percent at Cincinnati and Dayton to 15 percent at Cleveland. By 1910, 38 percent of all black working-age women at Cleveland, Columbus, and Dayton, and a very high 49 percent at Cincinnati, were in the labor force. These figures are 15 to 20 percent greater than those for white women in these four cities.[23]

II

Both rural Ohio and southern migrants faced a variety of problems in relating to urban life. These were likely to be worse for those from the South, who were less familiar with the fast-paced, crowded, impersonal world of the northern industrial city. Indeed, some of the Ohio migrants, especially those from rural areas immediately adjacent to large cities, had probably visited those cities on occasion; experience or hearsay gave them some familiarity with the cities' geographies and economic opportunities for blacks. At the same time the Southerners probably suffered considerably from the lack, relative to that offered the Civil War era migrant, of guidance, general aid, and concern for the newcomers present during most of the period of the urban migration. Unlike the migration of the 1860s, the new influx was neither sudden nor dramatic. It took place over decades, and it was not accompanied by events of overwhelming historical importance which had focused the nation's attention on the plight of blacks and inspired an ethos of public service and self-sacrifice among many. The migrations of the war era came at the beginning of the most significant ameliorative trend in the history of American race relations; in contrast, the new migration came during a period of precipitous decline in race relations, a period of reaction and of

considerably between 1900 and 1910. At Dayton and Columbus, the female population rose about 10% over male increase, only to have the discrepancy erased in the next decade.

[23] Census Office, *Eleventh Census*, I, pt. 2, pp. 596–597, 652–659; *Special Reports: Occupations at the Twelfth Census* (Washington, 1904), pp. 358–365, 522–539, and *Population, 1910, Occupation Statistics* (Washington, 1914), IV, 502–505, 547–552.

deflated expectations and pessimism. Blacks and whites in Ohio, as elsewhere, were in the midst of a painful search for new, seemingly more appropriate ways of relating to one another. With racial prejudice becoming increasingly respectable, fewer Ohio whites felt the moral pressure and inspiration to offer a helping hand. Indeed, reserves of racial tolerance which might check overt hostility were running dangerously low. And, as we shall see, established Ohio blacks often regarded the new migrants as a disturbing presence which shook the foundations of their attitudes toward racial progress and their belief in the uniqueness of northern race relations, and which often forced difficult adjustments in perspective.

Work was the migrant's first difficulty, essential to survival and the key to raising money to send for family members left behind in the South. Yet in the large cities the search for regular employment could be frustrating; the complex, impersonal, and biased labor market was far different from that of the rural South, where farm work was readily available and blacks had long-time contacts with white employers and labor recruiters.[24] Opportunities for migrants were at a premium, said the Cleveland *Journal* in 1906, and the paper confessed sadness and dismay at the "inflated ideas" about local opportunities which brought many blacks to a city with a national reputation for tolerance. Because of discrimination in Cleveland's factories and commercial businesses and the barring of all but a handful of blacks from the skilled trades, even those few migrants with skills and education beyond basic literacy were having difficulty finding work, and the *Journal* warned only those with work prearranged to consider making the long trip in search of a new home. Most would eventually enter the menial, unskilled, and service employment at which blacks had traditionally labored in Ohio. But some migrants found it impossible to build a solid economic base for themselves and were forced to seek charity. Attempting to quicken public sympathy for the plight of Columbus migrants, Otto Davis, the superintendent of the city's semi-public Associated Charities, which specialized in aiding impoverished families, stated in a newspaper interview in 1908 that few citizens appreciated the grave problems created "by the great influx of colored families into Columbus." "Many of these families are illiterates and few have trades," he said; the inability to support themselves had created a situation in which fully a third of all those seeking assistance were black,

[24] For perceptive comments on the problems of shifting from rural to urban job settings for southern blacks gone North, see Booker T. Washington, "The Negro and the Labor Unions," *Atlantic Monthly*, CXI (June, 1913), 756–757.

largely migrant, families—and the number was said to be growing rapidly.[25]

Finding adequate housing also posed a considerable problem; the choices were often as narrow as those faced in the labor market. This was partly a result of the migrants' own predilections. Most desired to find lodging in sections with already established black populations, and such neighborhoods, often decayed and overcrowded, were usually close to the main railroad terminals and served as convenient targets for those seeking lodging on their first day in the city. But, at the same time, poverty condemned newcomers to the very worst housing in these neighborhoods. "They are generally found living in miserable hovels and big 'rat and fire trap' tenements," said a black businessman regarding local migrants in Columbus.[26] Associated Charities of Columbus found most needy migrant families paying relatively high rents for crowded, unsanitary tenement housing.[27] At Cleveland in 1913, migrant families resided in what the chief of Cleveland's Bureau of Sanitation described as some of the worst tenement housing in the United States, located in the area of Central Avenue and East 34th Street in the Twelfth Ward. Here the poor of both races found residence in tenements which were overcrowded and often characterized by dilapidated exteriors, leaking roofs, defective and insufficient plumbing, poor lighting and ventilation, and wooden frames which easily caught fire and wooden backstairs which occasionally collapsed.[28]

For those who were without families, the housing situation could be particularly depressing. At Cleveland, for example, it was not uncommon for young black newcomers to pay the better part of a week's already slim wages for a small, unventilated bedroom in a rooming house, and to pay extra for light and hot water. Though the rooming houses were bad in themselves, for single young girls they posed a special danger: there was often a thin line between those rooming houses catering to young women and the brothels, which were widespread in inner city neighborhoods. When prostitution had not actually established itself within them, the rooming houses might

[25] Cleveland *Journal*, Feb. 2, 1906; Columbus *Dispatch*, May 27, 1908; Associated Charities of Columbus, *Considerate Charities: Ninth Annual Report of Associated Charities, 1908–1909* (Columbus, 1909), pp. 20–21.
[26] Quoted in Frank U. Quillin, *The Color Line in Ohio* (Ann Arbor, 1913), p. 150.
[27] Associated Charities of Columbus, *Considerate Charities*, pp. 25–27.
[28] Mildred Chasey, "Report on Housing Conditions in Cleveland in 1913," *Cleveland Medical Journal*, XXIII (Apr., 1913), 223–252.

serve as the places where parasitic pimps and their fast-talking agents of both sexes recruited unwitting and lonely, or simply impoverished, girls. Reflecting on her experiences in a similar setting, Jane Edna Hunter, a nurse who came to Cleveland from South Carolina in 1905 at age twenty-three and eventually dedicated her life to helping migrant and poor black girls, stated that "a girl alone in a large city must needs know the dangers and pitfalls awaiting her." [29]

The brothels were but one of a multitude of negative influences in the lives of the young migrants. Yet the migrations found blacks and sympathetic whites ill prepared to aid them in their time of adjustment. Throughout the late nineteenth century Ohio's black communities had had difficulties relating their charitable and social activities to the urban lower class, non-church members, and young people. For those affiliated with churches, congregational life offered the supportive and guiding influence of an organized community. But many of the migrants would not formally affiliate, and thus were unlikely to derive full benefit from church—if they took any interest in organized religion at all. Yet, other than churches, black urban communities were able to offer little in the way of institutionalized guidance. If the migrants had been prone to seek them out, they would have found few black community centers, with the exception of the small lyceum-like black YMCAs at Dayton and Springfield and the YWCA at Dayton, for most of the period before 1916. Nor did the white-administered settlement houses offer havens or guidance. Though settlement houses like Columbus's Godman House and Cleveland's Hiram, Alta, and Goodrich houses did not draw the color line and in fact encouraged black participation, often they were either too far from the main centers of black population or dedicating their work almost exclusively to the larger numbers of European immigrants settling in the cities.[30]

At the same time, unknowing of the value and unskilled in the formation of voluntary associations, which served higher-status persons in protecting their interests and fulfilling their lives, the young migrants did not seek to organize themselves (for example, by place of origin in the South) into mutual benefit associations that might have

[29] Jane Edna Hunter, *A Nickel and a Prayer* (Cleveland, 1940), p. 77.

[30] Jon A. Peterson, "The Origins and Development of a Social Settlement: A History of the Godman Guide Association, 1898–1958" (Master's thesis, Ohio State University, 1959), pp. 1–8; Mark, *Negroes in Columbus,* pp. 19–20; Judith Trolander, "Twenty Years at Hiram House," *Ohio History,* LXXVIII (Winter, 1969), 28, 31–32; Cleveland *Journal,* June 17, Dec. 2, 1905; Columbus *Citizen,* Mar. 1, 1912; Cleveland *Gazette,* Feb. 21, 1914.

aided them in their transition to urban life.[31] Nor had the storefront evangelical church, the transplanted religious community of southern lower-class migrants of a later day, yet made its apperance in the city.

"The downfall of a large percentage of the 'strangers' who come to Cleveland," the *Journal* said in 1904, "is due to the unfortunate absence of a convenient place where they might get wholesome information about board, lodging, and work, and good wholesome association." In lieu of any other alternatives, the paper said, "People not accustomed to city life follow the path of least resistance."[32] Whether or not the "strangers" might be persuaded to make use of facilities offering "wholesome information" and "wholesome association" is, of course, debatable. But there can be little doubt of the availability of a broad, sometimes perilous, path of least resistance. That path, which was particularly accessible in the slums and most likely to appeal to the young, lonely, and impressionable, frequently led to the ever-growing numbers of pool halls, saloons, gambling dens, and brothels which sprang up to accommodate the black and white poor. According to two contemporary social workers in a report on recreation in the Central Avenue area, pool halls "are practically the only recreational places open for boys and young men. . . ."[33] They had neglected to mention saloons. Thomas Fleming, who came to Cleveland from Meadville, Pennsylvania, in the 1890s at age eighteen and later became an important figure in municipal politics, recalled spending most of his early evenings in the city in saloons like Dean's Place in a tough neighborhood near the Haymarket. It was "patronized by the low element . . . and no place for a small town boy," he said, remembering an evening spent "inhaling rotten cigar smoke [and] seeing men and women of the underworld drinking. . . ."[34]

Trouble was never far from the pool halls, brothels, street corners, and saloons, and when it came to those like Fleming it usually presented itself as conflict with the law and its agents—not always seri-

[31] Cf. Gilbert Osofsky, *Harlem: The Making of a Ghetto* (New York, 1966), p. 32. To the best of my knowledge, Osofsky was the only student of pre–World War I northern black communities who has found evidence of such mutual benefit societies, organized by place of origin in the South, among black urban migrants in the North. Unfortunately, he does not note either the extent or class basis of their membership.

[32] Cleveland *Journal*, Jan. 23, 1904.

[33] Russell and Rowena Jelliffe, "Report to the Men's Club [of the Second Presbyterian Church], 1915," quoted in John Selby, *Beyond Civil Rights* (Cleveland and New York, 1966), p. 19.

[34] Thomas Fleming, "My Life and Persecution" (c. 1932), typescript, WRHS; Cleveland *Journal*, July 18, 1908; Cleveland *Leader*, Feb. 19, 1912.

ous, but occasionally so. To a large extent, this conflict was the
product of the difficulty which both black and white rural folk might
experience in learning urban ways. One had to learn not only *where*
one might get in trouble, but also *how*. In particular, it was necessary
to learn that certain forms of relatively innocent exuberance were
not always acceptable in the city as they were in the countryside.
Attempting to explain the social geography of lawbreaking, the 1910
federal census of crime pointed out that the category "violating city
ordinances," the general category of misdemeanor frequently en-
trapping the rural-bred newcomer to the city,

> . . . covers actions which for the most part in a distinctly rural com-
> munity either could not occur at all or would be inoffensive if they
> did occur. There are, in fact, many lines of conduct which in the cities
> are offensive . . . and inevitably lead to arrest but in rural areas are
> innocuous, at least as far as the general public, and may escape notice.
> This is to a large extent true of those acts which are punished as "dis-
> orderly conduct" and "disturbing the peace." It is also true to some
> extent of drunkenness, which in sparsely settled regions may occur
> without causing much annoyance to the community-at-large.[35]

Thus, the villagers' custom of standing along the local Main Street
to talk and pass time now brought arrests. At Cleveland in July, 1907,
on two successive nights police arrested "loitering" groups of blacks
who were engaged in conversation and horseplay along Central
Avenue in an effort to escape the heat and humidity of the tenements
and to entertain themselves as best they could afford to.[36] Public
conversation and horseplay had become "disorderly conduct" and
"disturbing the peace" in the city. At Columbus, loitering was accompanied by an attempt to transfer other southern rural customs to
the northern city. The same Columbus black businessman who had
described the migrants' housing characterized many migrant tenement
dwellers as "one day-livers"—"their ambition is to make enough money
to get intoxicated Saturday night and to feast and carouse all day
Sunday." He complained that they appeared in the streets below the
"rat and fire trap" tenements to enjoy their lone day a week free from
back-breaking, ill-paid toil. Their Sunday activities consisted of
nothing more scandalous or illegal than the continuation of Saturday
night's drinking and the tendency to "hold dog, cat, and chicken fights,
play the banjo, [and] dance the cake-walk. . . ." Occasionally, too,
the men were known to appear in public with the unbuttoned top of

[35] Bureau of the Census, *Prisoners and Juvenile Delinquents in the United
States, 1910* (Washington, 1918), p. 22.
[36] Cleveland *Gazette,* July 27, 1907.

their undergarment exposed, rather than in conventionally proper style. No mention was made of violence, theft, or abuse of passersby or property. Yet so different in their values and so unabashed in their style, the "one day-livers" were said emphatically by the same Columbus commentator "to make the day hideous for their neighbors." [37] Doubtless they offended a broad range of local respectables and antagonized the police; the latter, sworn to uphold the letter of the law and sharing the cultural premises and increasingly intolerant attitudes of their society, went about their duty in a vigorous way.

As the steadily increasing representation of blacks in the jails of urban counties suggests, conflicts with the law appeared in more serious form as well. Commitments to county jails, which were the middle rung of the contemporary penal ladder, are an excellent gauge of the more serious run-ins with law enforcement agents. Unlike the city jails and workhouses, where vagrants and drunks were sent for a night or several days, or state and federal penitentiaries which confined serious offenders sentenced to a year or more, the county jails held those incarcerated for the less serious forms of assault and petit larceny, sentenced to no more than a year and most often to two months or less. Thus while they did not house prisoners who had been found guilty of committing those crimes *most* common to lower-status groups (misdemeanors such as loitering, vagrancy, and drunkenness), they were used for those charged with the less serious felonies, particularly stealing and fighting, for which members of those groups were also likely to be arrested. In addition, they were used for the incarceration of those poorer persons unable to pay fines and therefore sentenced to terms in jail which the more affluent offender might escape.[38]

In light of racial discrimination in the administration of justice and the poverty and social and cultural isolation of blacks, it is not surprising that the period began and ended with blacks constituting a disproportionate percentage of county jail populations.[39] This tendency was strongest in the urban counties, and it would become more

[37] Quoted in Quillin, *Color Line in Ohio,* pp. 150–151.

[38] Bureau of the Census, *Prisoners and Juvenile Delinquents in Institutions, 1904* (Washington, 1907), p. 29, and *Prisoners and Juvenile Delinquents . . . 1910,* pp. 43–44.

[39] The following data are gathered from the annual reports of the Ohio secretary of state, Ohio *Statistics,* between 1872 and 1916. Sheriffs in each of Ohio's 88 counties annually reported on the number of prisoners of each race committed to their county jails between July 1 and June 30. Because county jail populations were generally shifting (prisoners within them were rarely sentenced to terms of more than one year), the problem of counting prisoners who were serving longer sentences twice or more for consecutive years is alleviated.

pronounced as the black population became more urbanized. While constituting less than 3 percent of Ohio's total population and an even smaller percentage of the total population of the seven major urban counties during the 1870s, blacks comprised 10 percent (1,811 prisoners) of the county jail population of the seven urban counties and 8 percent (2,757 prisoners) of the county jail population of the remaining, largely rural eighty-one counties of Ohio. While the percentage of blacks in the total state or urban populations did not grow greatly in the next decades, blacks came to make up a larger percentage of urban county jail populations, and the gap between the number of black prisoners in rural and urban counties widened. By 1900–1915, blacks comprised 17 percent (11,757 prisoners) of the county jail population in the seven urban counties and 10 percent (24,071) elsewhere.

The trend toward greater representation of blacks in the urban jails was first seen during the 1880s in Franklin and Clark counties, where Columbus and Springfield are located; these areas at once received the largest number of intrastate migrants and experienced the greatest growth rates of black population. Blacks rose sharply as a factor in jail populations, from 13 percent during the 1870s to 25 percent during the 1880s in the case of Franklin County, and from 18 to 29 percent in the case of Clark. During the 1890s, as the source of in-migration shifted to the South, the trend continued; blacks comprised 32 percent of Franklin and 38 percent of Clark county jail populations. After 1900, as migration to Springfield declined, blacks in the Clark County jail population dwindled. But since Columbus continued to attract large numbers of migrants, the Franklin County percentage dropped somewhat during 1900–1909, only to rise again during the next six years.

Other urban counties experienced their most rapid black population growth after the 1880s; from 3, 6, and 14 percent of the county jail populations at Cuyahoga, Montgomery, and Hamilton counties respectively during the 1880s, blacks during 1900–1909 came to comprise 13 percent of the prisoners at both Cuyahoga and Montgomery county jails and 26 percent at the Hamilton County jail. While the black population of Cuyahoga County (site of Cleveland) increased by 302 percent during 1880–1910, the number of black prisoners rose 2012 percent, from 149 during the 1880s to 3,148 in 1900–1909. At Montgomery County (Dayton), black population increased by 319 percent during 1880–1910, but black prisoners increased by 625 percent (from 83 to 602). At Hamilton County (Cincinnati), the two rates of growth were more in line; black population rose by 131 percent, while the number of black prisoners increased from 1,758 to 5,082, or 189 percent. The next six years witnessed an acceleration of this trend in most urban counties. By the end of 1915, the number of black prisoners at four of the seven counties was already greater than it had been for the entire 1900–1909 period, and in five of the seven counties the number of black prisoners during 1910–15 was growing much more rapidly than the number of white prisoners.

These statistics might be thought to suggest that the urban migrations brought a black "crime wave," but there is little evidence to sustain such an interpretation. Because of discrimination on the part of the overwhelmingly white police and the courts and in the sentencing of those too poor to pay fines, the increasing presence of blacks in urban county jails does not necessarily represent either a growing number or an increasing seriousness of crimes. Doubtless some of the new black city-dwellers turned to serious crime, and in their alienation from a society which despised them they no doubt did so in greater numbers than migrant whites. Yet at the same time, growing black jail populations may well have been a product of a conscious or unconscious desire of the police and the courts to show offensive blacks their "place." Longer sentences and fines too high to be paid were reminders that while one was indeed freer in the urban North than in the rural South, certain types of behavior and petty criminal activity were still considered more serious when indulged in or committed by blacks.

In the highly charged racial situation of the time, the trend toward increased conflict between blacks and police was capable of generating its own destructive dynamic. It might precipitate racial violence, as it did at Springfield in 1904, and Harry Smith continually warned after each incident of black crime and conflict between blacks and the police which reached the daily press at Cleveland in the prewar years that Cleveland and other cities had the potential to become interracial battlefields.[40] Perhaps even more destructive, however, were the long-range but less sensational implications for race relations. In response to Cleveland blacks' complaints that the seriousness and extent of black crime were blown out of proportion by the white press, Smith pointed out in 1906, "That the whites do even more . . . that is coarse, bad, loud, and criminal than Negroes is no excuse and does not help our cause in the slightest. We are in the minority in the North and cannot control public sentiment, which has everything to do with our success in every community." [41] As Smith and others knew

[40] Cleveland *Gazette*, July 20, 27, 1907, Mar. 6, 1909, Feb. 17, 1912.
[41] Ibid., Oct. 19, 1906.

only too well, by helping to revitalize already existing and time-honored stereotypes of the criminality and barbarism of the Negro masses in an era when other forces were already legitimizing such views, the growing numbers of blacks in conflict with the law would be used to justify growing repression and discrimination.

III

The urban migrations helped establish and accelerate two important trends in black urban residential patterns. The first, and most influential, was a tendency toward increasing concentration of blacks, particularly the poor, in certain inner city neighborhoods. While these were not new areas of black settlement, under the weight of migrations the black presence, relative to that of whites, was rapidly growing; at the same time, growing percentages of total local black populations now existed in these sections. Second, as the older inner-city areas grew more dilapidated and crowded, more upper- and middle-class blacks sought housing in neighborhoods away from the disease, crime, vice, and decay of congested tenement districts. These centripetal and centrifugal trends were found almost exclusively in Ohio's four largest cities: Cincinnati, Dayton, Cleveland, and Columbus. While black populations grew considerably at Toledo and Youngstown after 1890, they still remained under 2,000 in each case. The black population of Springfield was larger, but the lower rates of black growth there after 1890 worked against the emergence of the patterns of the larger cities. Even among the four major cities there were variations: Columbus blacks were more scattered, while at Dayton the largest area of black settlement contained a significant number of the affluent as well as the poor.

While signs indicated that a basis for the black ghetto was being established, black ghettoes like those which would exist in later decades had not yet emerged in Ohio's largest cities. True, some streets and blocks in certain sections were becoming more black, and the number of these was growing. Yet such areas were small, and blacks were still no more than about 30 percent of the population of any urban ward during 1900–1910. Nor could more than 30 to 40 percent of a city's black population be found in a given ward. Furthermore, in 1910 blacks comprised less than 8 percent of the population in each of the four largest cities; native white rural migrants and European immigrants were much more important factors in population growth than black migration. While blacks might be clustering together more in the cities, all around them (if not necessarily in the same buildings or on the same blocks) were poor, often ethnic whites. The settlement of these Europeans—now Slavs, Italians, and Eastern European Jews as well as Irish and Germans—was an especially important check on the creation of the black ghetto, for the numbers of these immigrants were large, and their poverty and foreign tongues and habits kept them huddled together in sections of their own, surrounding and interspersed among those of blacks.

Then too, an escape route from the inner city continued to exist for more affluent blacks, who might move to small black districts in better neighborhoods; discrimination had not yet rigidly locked them into neighborhoods where they had no desire to live. Though disturbing signs indicated that whites were perfecting techniques for keeping blacks out of better neighborhoods, the number of blacks seeking escape was still too small to necessitate a full-scale reaction which would close the escape route. The fact that the number of blacks in the cities was still small helped check the rise of a defensive, frightened "enclave mentality" among whites in better neighborhoods.

Of course, it would not be many years before this situation would begin to change radically: migration from abroad would abruptly end during World War I and revive briefly thereafter, only to be limited by legislation; the ethnic groups would be rapidly assimilated into American socioeconomic life with results that took many out of the slums; industrial booms occasioned by two World Wars within a quarter-century would combine with the steady deterioration of the economic position of the southern black peasantry to bring hundreds of thousands of southern blacks North. However, none of this was apparent in 1900 or 1910. The black ghetto was the work of the future, of more massive migrations from the South and of a more socially and culturally homogeneous white population.

The situation that existed during the first decade of the century is best illustrated by examples from the individual cities. At Cleveland there was a continual line of black settlement in the Central Avenue section, an area bounded by East Ninth and East 55th between Woodlawn and Cedar, with Central Avenue bisecting the section. In 1890 this large area contained about 1,500 blacks, approximately half of the local black population; but by 1910 5,000 blacks lived here, about 58 percent of the black population. Black settlement in the section began to taper off after the East 30s, and the East 40s and 50s were better neighborhoods than areas to the west. The demographic and approximate geographic center of black population here was the Twelfth Ward, located between East 24th and East 37th, a vice-ridden and congested tenement area where a third of the black population (2,792 persons) lived in 1910. Along the East 30s black settlement became particularly thick during the pre-war black migrations. While the concentration of blacks in the Twelfth Ward in 1910 comprised a larger percentage of the total black population than had existed in any one ward since 1860, when Cleveland's black population was a tenth the size, blacks were still only 16 percent of the ward's population. By contrast, the foreign-born (largely Russian Jews, Slavs, Germans, and Irish) and their American-born children were 69 percent of the ward's population in that same year.[42]

At Cincinnati, the focus of migrant settlement was the western fringe of the central business district; it had become the center of black residence as Bucktown and other areas to the east were taken over by industry and commerce, forcing out the poor. Considerably larger than the western Little Bucktown of 1870, the West End of 1900 was an area of tenements and apartments of different, though generally lesser, degrees of quality with some better dwellings on its fringes. George Street, the city's major red-light zone, was located within it.[43] Near the central terminus of railroads converging upon Cincinnati, the West End was a relatively short walk for the newly arrived migrant.[44] In 1890 some 3,500 blacks lived here; the number rose steadily, reaching 8,600 in 1910. Comprising slightly less than 31 percent of the city's black population in 1890, the area claimed 44 percent by 1910. The heart of the black area was the dilapidated Eighteenth Ward, just up from the banks of the Ohio; around West Fifth and Central, in the heart of the ward, blacks were thickly concentrated. With the largest black population of any ward in a large Ohio city at the time, the Eighteenth was home to about 4,000 blacks in 1910—a bit over 20 percent of the city's black population. Yet blacks were still in a minority here; they constituted only 27 percent of the ward's population in 1910. By contrast, first- and second-generation foreign stock, mostly Russian Jews and Italians, made up 38 percent.

At Dayton, the immediate post-Reconstruction decades found the small black population around the fringes of the central business district. But as the city's boundaries pushed rapidly west across the Great Miami River, the center of the growing black population followed them; most migrants also came to the West Side. By 1910, 54

---

[42] Cleveland *Journal*, June 9, 1906; Cleveland *Gazette*, Nov. 7, 1914; William F. Moore, "Status of the Negro in Cleveland" (Ph.D. dissertation, Ohio State University, 1953), pp. 37–38; Cleveland, *Ordinances of the City of Cleveland* (Cleveland, 1907), p. 14; *Cleveland City Directory: 1913*, pp. 2253–54 (contains ward boundary information).

[43] Miller, *Boss Cox's Cincinnati*, pp. 28, 251 (n. 8).

[44] *William's Cincinnati City Directory*, June, 1910, pp. 31–35 (ward data).

percent of Dayton blacks (some 2,600 persons) lived in an area bounded on the east and south by the broad meanders of the Great Miami, on the west by Broadway, and on the north by West Third Avenue. The heart of the West Side black section was the Sixth Ward, where about 40 percent of the city's blacks (1,960 persons) resided in 1910; this was the largest percentage of a local black population to be found in a single ward of a large Ohio city at the time. Around the major thoroughfares of Broadway and West Fifth and on the streets nearest the river there were cheap apartments and bungalows, but away from the river and major streets there were more expensive single-family dwellings where more affluent blacks resided. Though central Ohio cities attracted fewer immigrants than Cincinnati and Cleveland, blacks in the Sixth Ward were outnumbered by Irish, Germans, Italians, and their American-born children, who were 19 percent of the ward's population in 1910, compared to the 14 percent which was black. Dayton blacks also continued to live east of the river, along the fringes of the downtown wards; there they were never more than 5 percent of the population. In one such area, along Joe Street, the city's turn-of-the-century red-light zone was concentrated; as a result, at least at that time, the West End was unique among Ohio's major black neighborhoods for being relatively free of vice.[45]

Much more than the other three cities, Columbus blacks had always resided in various neighborhoods; the immediate pre-war years found them still, according to one observer, "scattered to the four parts of the compass." [46] Rather than settling in any one district, Columbus migrants were likely to be attracted to several neighborhoods near the downtown area. The three major sections each had 10 to 20 percent of the city's 13,000 black residents in 1910. The first of these was the downtown area of East Long Street, which was a short walk from the railroad station and known for its cheap housing as well as its notorious vice-ridden "Bad Lands." This was the old center of black population, but the percentage of city's blacks here had fallen from 35 percent in 1870 to just below 20 percent in 1910. The other low-rent districts where the migrant poor settled were around Seventh and Main, to the southwest of downtown, and an area west of High Street, the main north-south thoroughfare several blocks west of the downtown East Long Street section. The latter district, one of the city's poorest, was located amidst the confluence of several railroad routes and near the walls of the state prison. While

45 *William's Dayton City Directory*, 1909–1910, pp. 86–88 (ward data); Dayton *Daily News*, Jan. 12, 1906.
46 Indianapolis *Freeman*, Aug. 29, 1914.

traditionally blacks had not been allowed to proceed beyond West Goodale into a more northerly section called "Flytown," the pattern of settlement began to change after 1900. The equally unpopular Italians moved in, sending established residents in flight. On the heels of the Italians came some blacks, mostly Southerners, all encouraged by real estate agents who were taking advantage of the increased demand for housing by buying up residential property north of West Goodale and renting it to blacks at high prices. While there were pockets of black concentration in these sections, such as on West Spring and West Chestnut near the state prison or on East Long Street between Third Avenue and High or on Sixth and Seventh streets south of Mound, in none of these neighborhoods do blacks appear to have constituted more than 10 percent of the total. While Columbus attracted relatively few immigrants, blacks were outnumbered even here by Slavs, Germans, Irish, Italians, and Russian Jews.[47]

As the poor concentrated in certain neighborhoods, more affluent blacks, in turn, tended to move to better sections. Though some migrants would settle there, fewer lived in the section of East Long Street on the East Side, where a quarter of Columbus blacks resided throughout the years 1890 to 1910. The black population here had grown rapidly, from 1,250 in 1890 to 3,332 in 1910; it was concentrated along Ohio, Champion, and Mt. Vernon avenues, and began filling up sections of Clifton and Granville avenues, all in the Ninth Ward, where 16 percent of the population was black in 1910. But the high property values in the Ninth, and the neighborhood's reputation among local whites as "the aristocratic colored section,"[48] suggests that black population growth here continued to result from an exodus of upper- and middle-class blacks from the inner city. The emergence of this section as a haven for higher-status blacks was underscored in 1904 by a decision of the officers of St. Paul's A.M.E. Church, the oldest and one of the more prestigious black congregations. For many years the church had been located in the downtown East Long Street area, but now it was to move to a site at East Long and Jefferson, midway between downtown and the eastern black area. Columbus's Odd Fellows had made the same decision a few years before, moving still further east.[49]

The same tendency was at work at Cincinnati, where by 1910 al-

[47] Mark, *Negroes in Columbus*, pp. 15–29; Columbus *Dispatch*, May 31, 1900.

[48] Mark, *Negroes in Columbus*, p. 18; Roderick Duncan McKensie, "The Neighborhood: A Study of Local Life in the City of Columbus, Ohio," *American Journal of Sociology*, XXVII (Sept., 1921), 153.

[49] Cleveland *Gazette*, Jan. 7, 1899; Nimrod B. Allen, "East Long Street," *Crisis*, XXV (Nov., 1922), 12–16.

most a third of the blacks lived in higher-status neighborhoods far from the inner city. The most populous such area was the well-established black neighborhood along the southern fringe and up toward the central section of Walnut Hills. There were an ample number of affluent black homeowners, and, especially as the migrations from the South gathered force after 1900, some poorer newcomers. But generally the norm was the ordinary middle-class apartment dweller. Walnut Hills's black population had grown slowly between 1860 and 1890, reaching 1,900 persons in the latter year; it almost doubled in the next two decades, reaching 3,600 in 1910—18 percent of the city's black population and about a fifth of Walnut Hills. By then other pockets of black population, representing altogether some 2,500 persons, could also be found in the central hilltop communities of Clifton and Avondale, not far from Walnut Hills, and in several western residential areas far across the tracks from the West End.[50]

Cleveland's eastern neighborhoods, and to a lesser extent the eastern suburbs, continued to serve as a safety valve for upper- and middle-class blacks. But more than at Columbus or Cincinnati, the movement of blacks out of the inner city at the turn of the century was novel and therefore seemed precipitous. The tendency of many Cleveland blacks who had wished to move to better areas was to move further east down Central Avenue to contiguous areas, rather than to escape to outlying residential neighborhoods on the fringe of the city. Thus in 1890, when blacks were pushing down Central into the East 40s and East 50s, there were fewer than 600 blacks residing east of East 90th. As the migration from the inner city gathered force, that figure tripled. Symbolic of the increased number of blacks on the far East Side was the evolution of the St. James A.M.E. Mission, which had been opened in 1894 to cater to the small black community in the area of East 100th and Cedar and Hudson streets, into a regular congregation in its own right after the turn of the century.[51]

Because of this relatively rapid movement, white residents felt more threatened by the mobility of the black population than they did at Cincinnati, where there was a long history of such mobility, and at Columbus, where blacks had always been scattered throughout the city. From the 1890s to the close of the pre-war period, incidents of

[50] Miller, *Boss Cox's Cincinnati*, pp. 30–31; Wendell Phillips Dabney, *Cincinnati's Colored Citizens: Historical, Sociological, and Biographical* (Cincinnati, 1926), pp. 242, 252, 278, 284, 296, 301, 316–320, 349, 360; *William's Cincinnati City Directory*, June, 1910, pp. 31–35.

[51] Russell H. Davis, *Black Americans in Cleveland from George Peake to Carl B. Stokes* (Washington, 1972), pp. 186–187.

intimidation and violence aimed at black homeowners and renters multiplied in eastern Cleveland. The most serious of these occurred in 1901: a house on the far southeast side had been purchased by blacks as a new site for the black Old Folks' Home; it was set afire by arsonists, to be followed, one local black resident said, by "quiet general rejoicing" among neighborhood whites.[52] Cleveland blacks, however, were not the sole targets for such abuse. A good deal of animosity was also directed against Jews and other white groups then searching for better housing. During the years just before the World War, one important sign of these racial and ethnic tensions was the use of the restrictive covenant as a device for limiting the mobility of groups offensive to urban property holders. Claiming that blacks and others lowered property values, whites in the East 105th Street and Greenlawn Avenue area began to insert clauses in their deeds which restricted the transfer of property.[53] This device was new to Ohio,[54] for in the past whites had been content to rely on informal pressures to keep blacks from their neighborhoods. Now, however, threatened with a growing black movement out of the slums, Cleveland whites felt the need for formalized methods of residential discrimination. This was an ominous note; on the eve of the massive black migrations of the World War years, it pointed to a growing commitment among whites to blocking the mobility of blacks. Though Cleveland had shown itself to be not much different from the rest of Ohio in its capitulation to segregation in public accommodations, it revealed in at least one instance that it was equal to accelerating the forces of reaction in Ohio's race relations.

As was the case with rising rates of black incarceration, conflict over black residential mobility implied that the major trends of the time—black migration and urbanization and the concomitant rise in racial tension, prejudice, and discrimination—would be joined, locked menacingly as the first exacerbated the second. Blacks were only too

[52] Cleveland *Gazette*, May 16, 1897, Dec. 7, 1901, Jan. 4, 1906.

[53] Ibid., July 3, 1915.

[54] Though other cities had begun to employ the restrictive covenant as a device for limiting black residential mobility before Cleveland, its use was still relatively new in the United States. The years after 1900 saw the first widespread efforts, particularly in southern and border cities, to develop formalized methods to insure residential segregation. In addition to the racially restrictive covenant used by individual property owners, there were municipal race segregation ordinances (actually first employed in California against the Chinese in 1890) and racially restrictive agreements. In the latter a number of property owners, usually organized in neighborhood "improvement associations," agreed to bind each other not to sell to blacks. See Clement E. Vose, *Caucasians Only: The Supreme Court, the NAACP, and the Restrictive Covenant Cases* (Berkeley and Los Angeles, 1959), pp. 5–9, 50–52.

well aware of the situation, and they began to see the habits and maladjustments of the migrants as an important factor in determining the downward course of northern race relations. Reflecting on the fact that the 1904 Springfield riot had been precipitated by the murder of a white policeman by a drunken black Kentuckian, the Washington *Bee* said, "Trouble and race friction frequently are brought to northern cities by the influx of the idle and loafing Negro of the South." [55] A Columbus minister found the untidy appearance and improper attire of the migrants partly responsible for the increasingly negative views of blacks found among Columbus whites. The migrants were going about the streets "dirty and half-clothed"; they were "used to doing this in the South, and they never thought of being tidy, and did not realize that they were making themselves and their race offensive to the white people." [56] A Clevelander found that the actions of migrants in public places were largely to blame for the rapid descent of the color curtain in northern public accommodations. Commenting on the undignified behavior in a local cafe of an elderly bootblack just up from the South, he said bitterly, "This kind of Negro is doing the race here in the North untold harm and causing almost as much prejudice as Tillman. . . . It will not be long before the old man and his kind close the doors of this restaurant and others to our people just as they have already done in numerous places in Cleveland and elsewhere in the North." [57] The relationship between the migrations and the deterioration of race relations cannot be clearly delineated, especially in light of the fact that the latter was a national trend. Yet the existence of such a relationship is undeniable, and it is not surprising that black efforts to check that deterioration often proceeded on the premise that the migrants' behavior had to be changed for the sake of racial harmony.

Yet at the same time black migration and urbanization were not without more positive possibilities for racial development. At the turn of the century the outlines of a positive relation between the northern city and racial welfare were faint, and contrary tendencies were working to blur them. But a critical mass of black population was beginning to gather force in inner-city neighborhoods, and imaginative minds came increasingly to be excited by its potential. The political, socioeconomic, and cultural bases provided by the growing numbers of urban blacks offered footing for the first deliberate steps in the struggle to forge a unifying spirit of racial community, rooted

[55] Washington *Bee*, Mar. 26, 1904.
[56] Quoted in Quillin, *The Color Line in Ohio*, p. 145.
[57] Cleveland *Gazette*, Jan. 26, 1907.

in the urban neighborhood. Here, in this center of racial institutions, residence, and enterprise, a black metropolis, a city within a city, might be molded. Much depended on the readiness of black leaders to take up the challenge, and therefore much depended on how black leadership saw itself and its opportunities in changing times.

11

Employment and Economic Opportunity

The last years of the pre–World War period found black
Ohioans locked into essentially the same economic situation that they
had endured throughout the late nineteenth century. Most black workers continued to be employed in menial service work or unskilled,
common labor. The 1910 census found that of Ohio's 38,018 black
working men, at least three-quarters were common laborers or service
workers, while of 17,843 black working women, 15,615 (87%) were
employed as service workers, generally scrubwomen, laundresses, and
domestics.[1] Yet the situation was not static, and several trends were
then in the process of partially redefining black economic opportunity.
Blacks continued to enter factories in small but growing numbers. At
the same time, however, their own traditionally weak competitive position, technological displacement, the changing nature of several key
service fields, and changing black attitudes toward service work combined to cause decline or stagnation in other fields, with implications
not only for black employment, but also for black enterprise in traditionally important fields like barbering, livery, hauling, and carrying.

In the midst of this complex situation, it was becoming increasingly
clear that the rapid growth of black population in the cities was offering unprecedented opportunities for black enterprise. For the first
time, Ohio black urban populations were becoming large enough and
concentrated enough to allow aspiring black enterpreneurs to dream of
tapping a Negro market for goods and services. The result was a rapid
expansion of black retail and service businesses, which began in the

[1] All statistical data on occupations and employment in this chapter are taken
from the following: U.S. Census Office, *Report on the Population of the United
States, Eleventh Census . . . 1890* (Washington, 1897), I, pt. 2, pp. 596–597,
652–659; Bureau of the Census, *Special Reports: Occupations at the Twelfth
Census* (Washington, 1904), pp. 358–365, 522–539, and *Population, 1910, Occupation Statistics* (Washington, 1914), pp. 502–505, 547–552.

1890s and accelerated after the turn of the century. Also, at a time when more blacks were obtaining professional training, expanding black urban populations offered new opportunities for black professionals, who in the past had had to compete with whites for white clients. Now they could base their practices as much, if not more, on the needs of their own people. Thus, while from a social viewpoint the migrations had a negative impact because they contributed to the deterioration of race relations, from a black commercial and professional perspective they held out the possibility of new opportunity.

I

The progress of black factory employment followed lines established in the late nineteenth century. As before, the race's outstanding chance lay in the metal industries, where increases in black employment were quite impressive. The 1890 census listed 286 blacks employed in Ohio foundries and steel mills, but as these industries expanded rapidly, so did black employment. By 1900 there were 700 blacks working in foundries and mills; by 1910 the number reached 1,560. The overwhelming majority (87%) of these workers were unskilled and semi-skilled. Blacks continued to be underrepresented in iron and steel, constituting 3 percent of Ohio's work force but only 2 percent of its metal workers in 1910. Yet their numbers were growing more rapidly (representing a 455% increase during 1890–1910) than the black male labor force as a whole, which had increased by 34 percent (from 28,331 to 38,018) during 1890–1910.

In light of labor union weakness in the iron and steel industries, and the preoccupation of existing unions with organization of skilled workers, blacks had occasionally enjoyed access to unskilled and semi-skilled, and at Springfield even skilled, metalwork unfettered by hostile unions. Yet blacks did not have a clear field even then. Black opportunities at local foundry centers varied considerably, depending on whether their numbers allowed them to emerge as an important local labor source. At Cleveland and Cincinnati, where there were large pools of cheap immigrant and second-generation ethnic laborers who had little choice but to do heavy, dirty work in the stiflingly hot mills and foundries, blacks had less opportunity to enter metal industries than in other Ohio cities like Columbus and Springfield, where foreign and ethnic populations were smaller. At Cleveland and Cincinnati, where first- and second-generation labor of foreign stock made up from three-quarters to 90 percent of workers in iron and steel during 1900–1910, black employment was insignificant. The number of black metalworkers in Cleveland had risen from 3 in 1890 to 49 in 1910, and at Cincinnati from 13 to 22; in both cases blacks were less than 1 percent of local metalworkers. The situation was quite different at Columbus, where the first- and second-generation component of the population fell from 44 to 32 percent during 1890–1910, and where the immigrants and their children were approximately 35 percent of the local metal-work force in 1910. Columbus's expanding iron industry came to depend on black labor after 1890. Companies aggressively recruited blacks, offering them not only the chance for steady, indoor employment, but also, in the case of Ohio Malleable Iron Company, low-cost company housing not far from the mill. While there were only 16 blacks in Columbus foundries in 1890, there were 343 in 1910. At a time when blacks were 7 or 8 percent of the local labor force, they had gone from 2 to 21 percent of Columbus's metalworkers. Data are lacking on the number of black metalworkers at Springfield, where blacks had established a foothold in the iron industry in the 1880s and where immigrant and second-generation ethnic workers were no more than a quarter of the work force. According to local black commentators, blacks continued after the turn of the century to work in large numbers (probably a few hundred) in iron foundries. Most were unskilled, but a few black iron molders also found work in Springfield's foundries. The balance of black metalworkers in Ohio before the World War were employed largely at the foundry centers of northeastern Ohio, particularly Youngstown, Salem, Lisbon, and Steubenville, all of which had ethnic work forces that made up less than half of local laboring populations.[2]

Outside the metal industries, early twentieth-century black factory employment was greatest where the black presence in factory work was already well established and where blacks were a significant part of the local labor force. Opportunities at Columbus were especially good: when combined with black employees in the iron industry, blacks working in other industrial plants brought the number of black factory workers up to about a quarter of the approximately 5,000

[2] Bureau of the Census, *Thirteenth Census of the United States . . . 1910* (Washington, 1913), III, 423–430; David Brody, *Steelworkers in America: The Nonunion Era* (Cambridge, 1960), pp. 50–79, 126; Charles D. Swayne, *Facts and Figures about the Negro in Springfield and Clark County, Ohio, as They Stood December 31st, 1907* (Urbana, 1908), p. 16; Richard Clyde Minor, "Negroes in Columbus" (Ph.D. dissertation, Ohio State University, 1936), p. 172; Mary Louise Mark, *Negroes in Columbus* (Columbus, 1928), p. 22; C. S. Bonsall (Salem, Ohio) to Booker T. Washington, June 6, 1910, Box 402, Booker T. Washington Papers, LC; Cleveland *Gazette*, Mar. 16, 1902, May 23, 1908, Sept. 15, 1915; Cleveland *Journal*, June 13, 1903; Indianapolis *Freeman*, Sept. 9, 1911.

black working men in the city just before the World War. Around 1900 blacks began taking jobs at a local fertilizer plant, where an estimated 550 Negroes worked by 1908; numerous blacks also worked for the Jeffries Manufactory Company, which produced mining, conveying, and elevating machinery, and for the Killbourne Jacobs Company, which produced wheelbarrows. Unions blocked the entrance of blacks at some plants, but local labor organizations were not strong before the war.[3] At Xenia, where many blacks were already employed in the four cordage factories and the distillery at the turn of the century, the opening of two cigar factories subsequently gave work to at least 225 black men and women. Some of the men worked as cigarmakers and shop foremen, but the large majority of blacks were engaged in the tedious work of stemming and shredding tobacco leaves. Owners of the companies had actively sought black workers, not only because Xenia's large black population was a convenient source of labor, but also because the management of at least one firm believed that blacks had a "natural adaptation for handling tobacco."[4] At Springfield just after 1900 blacks also enjoyed more wide-ranging factory employment. They began to enter a rapidly developing new industry when the owner of the Champion Chemical Company turned over the management of his plant to Charles Lester Johnson, a young black man, and gave him permission to employ large numbers of blacks. In this case, however, the decision appears to have been motivated less by economic than by personal considerations, for Johnson was said to be the owner's natural son. Johnson used his authority to hire blacks, so that by 1911 the plant had 85 black employees, working in all positions from laborer to chemist.[5]

Elsewhere black factory opportunities were generally much narrower in scope. Cincinnati blacks worked at the Jarecki Chemical Company and the Williamson Furnace Company, among other industrial establishments, but the percentage of local blacks employed in factories seems to have been much smaller than at Columbus.[6] Although Dayton blacks did not gain a foothold in industrial work, they had obtained

---

[3] Indianapolis *Freeman,* Aug. 29, 1914; Walter Thomas to Joseph B. Foraker, Sept. 24, 1907, Box 73, Joseph B. Foraker Papers, CHS; J. S. Himes, "Forty Years of Negro Life in Columbus, Ohio," *Journal of Negro History,* XXVII (Apr., 1942), 142.

[4] R. R. Wright, Jr., "The Negroes of Xenia, Ohio: A Social Study," U.S. Department of Labor *Bulletin* no. 48 (Sept., 1903), 1028–29; Cleveland *Journal,* Mar. 10, 1906; Cleveland *Gazette,* July 2, 16, 1910; Indianapolis *Freeman,* Aug. 1, 1914.

[5] Indianapolis *Freeman,* Sept. 9, 1911. August Meier kindly provided me with information on Johnson's background; letter to author, May 31, 1974.

[6] "Report of the Ninth Street Branch YMCA . . . January 31, 1915," Julius

factory employment. One of the city's largest employers, the prosperous National Cash Register Company, employed them in relatively large numbers as plant clean-up personnel. In 1906, however, the company fired all 83 of its black workers, some of whom had been with the firm for many years, and replaced them with whites. The reason given was that since black employees were barred from promotion to industrial and managerial positions as a matter of company policy, it was better "to engage the services of young white men with a view to their gradual advancement in the services of the company."[7] As a result of such policies, black industrial opportunities at Dayton came more and more to be the product of special circumstances in which white philanthropists and capitalists put up money to create small factories where blacks might work. In 1906 a tobacco plant employing about fifty blacks was established in this way; several years later C. H. Baldwin, a wealthy local businessman, opened a small factory which was engaged in light industry and handicrafts and which used blacks as the sole source of labor.[8]

While technological innovation helped industry to create new opportunities for blacks, it was also responsible for the decline of black opportunity in other areas. The development of the internal combustion engine jeopardized various employment opportunities utilizing horses. Between 1890 and 1910 the number of Negro blacksmiths, hostlers, and livery stable owners (unfortunately, the census does not separate the latter two occupations) declined as the automobile replaced the horse. The situation was exacerbated by the weak competitive position of those blacks who were attempting to obtain white patronage in shrinking fields. While the total number of Ohio blacksmiths declined by 5 percent (from 16,693 to 15,858) during 1890–1910, the number of blacks at work in the trade declined by 60 percent (from 257 to 158). The total number of Ohioans engaged in the care and breeding of horses increased slightly from 4,701 to 4,832 in those decades, but the number of blacks so employed decreased from 458 to 438. Nor did the coming of the truck and automobile bode well for the independent black teamster and cabbie, who could afford little more than his team and wagon or cab, and who was less than likely to have the money for a motorized vehicle. While blacks were making up a growing share of Ohio's teamsters and cabbies, rising from 6 percent

Rosenwald Papers, University of Chicago; Zane Miller, *Boss Cox's Cincinnati: Urban Politics in the Progressive Era* (New York, 1968), p. 16.

[7] Dayton *Journal*, Jan. 1, 1906; Dayton *Daily News*, Jan. 3, 1906; Cleveland *Gazette*, Jan. 13, 20, 1906.

[8] Cleveland *Gazette*, Oct. 27, 1906, Jan. 21, 1911.

(1,125) to 7 percent (1,600) of Ohio haulers during 1890–1910, with larger increases at Cleveland (2 to 7%), Cincinnati (4 to 8%), and Columbus (18 to 24%), they were acquiring a larger share of occupations which did not have much of a future. It was illustrative of the competitive strength of motorized vehicles that the smallest increases in the number of black haulers came in urban centers outside the three major cities; the smaller cities, towns, and villages accounted for less than 10 percent of the increase. In smaller urban centers a truck could easily corner the local hauling market which had once been shared by several horse-drawn drays.

In the railroad and building and decorating trades, blacks were threatened less by technology than by their own traditionally weak competitive position and by union hostility. The decimation of the skilled black railway force, which had begun in the 1880s with the rise of the powerful, exclusionist railroad workers' brotherhoods, continued after the turn of the century. From a total of 355 blacks in skilled and semi-managerial (for example, conductor and freight agent) positions in 1890, the number fell to 202 in 1900 and 147 in 1910, as long-time black employees retired and were replaced by whites. Black railroad employment was soon limited to common labor and service jobs, such as sleeping car and train porter.

The greatest losses were among black conductors, engineers, and trainmen (switchmen, flagmen, and brakemen); in these fields the unions were most active in limiting black competition. Yet in one sense the exclusion of blacks in skilled train work was more apparent than real. In Ohio and other states, unorganized black porters continued to be required to do brakemen's work in addition to their own duties, though they received no extra compensation for it. However, this situation began to change in 1902, when the Brotherhood of Railway Trainmen lobbied through the Ohio legislature, just as affiliates in other states would do during the next decade, a "full crew law" aimed at carefully defining the tasks and regulating the size of train crews. From the union's point of view, the law was intended not so much to insure safety, as it publicly contended, as to create additional job security and better working conditions. Thus, while the law was not primarily aimed against blacks, it was hardly accidental that it threatened the jobs of black train porters who, though doing brakemen's work, had never been officially classified as "brakemen" because of management's acquiescence in the exclusionist policies of the trainmen's union. Though the law was not strictly enforced for almost a full decade, its full implementation in 1911 by the state railroad commissioner resulted in the immediate firing of approximately thirty black porters (some long-time employees) working for the Big Four Railroad.[9]

Union hostility also prevented blacks from working at newer building trades, particularly plumbing and the electrician's trade, which were developing rapidly in response to technological innovation and consumer demand. The national plumbers' union not only openly discouraged black membership and apprenticeship, but sought (especially in the South, where black competition was most threatening) to exclude blacks from the trade by lobbying for proscriptive state licensing laws. While no such legislation was considered by the Ohio legislature during the period, union-sponsored local ordinances accomplished the same thing. These were not aimed at blacks; nor need they be, for there was little prospect that enough blacks would enter the trade to challenge white predominance. Rather, the ordinances had both an explicit and an implicit purpose; the latter had an impact on men of both races who wished to become plumbers. The ordinances were passed in the name of imposing much-needed sanitary standards to the practice of plumbing by tightening union supervision of the trade. But it was not accidental that these laws gave the unions control over the licensing of men who wished to enter plumbing, thus allowing plumbers' locals to regulate competition between plumbers and hence keep wages higher. At Cleveland, for example, one who wanted to receive a plumbing license now had to have the approval of two master plumbers willing to attest to his knowledge of the trade. Since there were no black master plumbers in Cleveland until *one* appeared in 1910, and white master plumbers could not be counted on to aid black aspirants, black plumbers had only two options: to work outside the law and risk getting caught (as did one who was arrested in 1904 for working without a license), or to work outside the city limits. This situation no doubt contributed to the fact that there were only five black plumbers at Cleveland in 1910—of the fifty-nine in the entire state.[10] Fewer still, however, were the black electricians. The electricians' locals were strongly exclusionist. This, when combined with the weak contracting position of the lone non-union black electrician, made the chances of finding work small indeed. One black electrician,

[9] Sterling D. Spero and Abram L. Harris, *The Black Worker: The Negro and the American Labor Movement* (New York, 1931), pp. 306–307; Cleveland *Gazette*, Apr. 30, May 14, 1904, Oct. 14, 1911, Apr. 13, 1913, Mar. 27, 1915; Chicago *Broad Ax*, Nov. 2, 1907; *Crisis*, II (Oct., 1911), 254.

[10] Cleveland *Gazette*, Apr. 16, 1904, Oct. 9, 1909; Spero and Harris, *The Black Worker*, pp. 59–60; Frank U. Quillin, *The Color Line in Ohio* (Ann Arbor, 1913), p. 130.

who eventually left Ohio to find work elsewhere, described his frustrating attempts to earn a living at Columbus during 1912–13:

> First I tried to secure work at my trade, but found it impossible because of the unions and my color. The best I was able to do was find employment as an elevator operator in a department store with no chances of advancement and small wages. . . . I stayed for awhile and then began to practice my trade independently, but I find it impossible to compete with the large contracting firms and therefore it is very hard to make expenses.[11]

In the older building and decorating trades (carpentry, plastering, bricklaying, painting, varnishing, and glazing) where blacks had earlier gained a foothold despite varying degrees of union hostility and fierce competition, the picture was not as bleak—but neither was it consistently promising. The years from 1890 to 1910 produced absolute gains in the number of black carpenters (277 to 361), bricklayers (280 to 345), painters, varnishers, and glaziers (207 to 256), and plasterers (285 to 413) in the state. But only in plastering, a trade unattractive because of its working conditions, did the pace of growth surpass the 34 percent increase in the black male labor force in Ohio during those decades, and in other trades it fell short of that mark. In addition, while blacks had increased from 8 to 12 percent of Ohio's plasterers, they remained underrepresented among carpenters, painters, varnishers, and glaziers, and their numbers among its bricklayers barely equaled their representation in the male work force. In the last years of the period, blacks in the smaller towns were notably pessimistic about the future of skilled craftsmen, and they complained that younger men were not entering the trades in nearly the numbers that they had in the past. Portsmouth, Oberlin, and Ironton informants for the 1912 Atlanta University survey of the status of black artisans all noted that while a few individual black craftsmen were prospering in their towns, the black artisan force was growing older, and men were being lost to sickness, retirement, and death.[12] To some extent, perhaps, prospective local artisans were joining the urban migration. If such young men planned to enter skilled trades in the large cities, they probably faced considerable difficulty. It was no doubt symptomatic of the competitive situation faced by the urban black artisan that black gains in individual building and decorating trades in Ohio's three largest cities during 1890–1910 ranged from as few as three or four to no more than thirty in each city.

[11] R. M. Tyler to Emmett Scott, June 25, 1913, Box 466, Booker T. Washington Papers; Spero and Harris, *Black Worker*, p. 58.
[12] W. E. B. Du Bois, *The Negro American Artisan* (Atlanta, 1912), pp. 71–72.

While black artisans had always faced harsh competition in skilled industrial fields, the same could not be said of blacks engaged in barbering, waiting table, and other more prestigious service fields like butlering; here blacks had enjoyed relatively great opportunity. Yet in Ohio and elsewhere throughout the North and South,[13] serious setbacks in these fields jeopardized not only individual employment, but also one of the race's most successful service enterprises—the barbershop. While the total number of Ohio barbers increased from 5,716 to 10,371 during 1890–1910, the number of black barbers dropped from 1,372 to 1,172. The trend was present both within and outside the largest cities. Although the total number of barbers increased at each of Ohio's three largest cities, the number of black barbers dropped slightly at Columbus (from 87 to 85) and Cincinnati (150 to 124), while growing a bit at Cleveland (80 to 109). In all three cities the percentage of blacks among local barbers fell, at Columbus by as much as 15 percent. Elsewhere the trend toward decline was greater. The number of black barbers fell by 199, and the percentage of blacks among barbers fell sharply from 32 to 13 percent. In barbering, therefore, blacks were not simply failing to obtain an increased percentage of a growing trade, but actually losing past gains.

While the number of black women employed as waitresses and servants was growing rapidly everywhere in Ohio, and black women were coming to comprise a greater percentage of the female work force in these fields,[14] opportunities for black men were at a standstill. The number of black men employed as servants and waiters grew at Cleveland (392 to 514) and Columbus (327 to 522), though declining at Cincinnati (949 to 790); however, in all three cities the percentage of blacks in the total servant-waiter group declined, by as much as 10 percent at Columbus and 12 percent at Cincinnati. Elsewhere the trend was similar: a slight growth in numbers (1,514 to 1,584), accompanied by a decline in percentages (36 to 31 percent).

According to contemporary commentators like John Green,[15] the

[13] For comments on the situation nationally, see Booker T. Washington, "Negro Disfranchisement and the Negro in Business," *Outlook*, LXXXXIII (Oct. 9, 1909), 313.

[14] During 1890–1910, while the percentage of working black women employed as service workers stayed around 88, black women actually took control of the Ohio's female service work. In 1890 they were 46% of Ohio's women service workers, but by 1910 they were 62%. No doubt the migration of young working women with few other job opportunities accounts for this. By way of proof, it should be noted that the largest increases in Ohio, both in absolute numbers and as percentages of the female work force in the categories "waitresses and servants" and "laundresses," were found among black women in the large cities, the target of the migrations.

[15] Cleveland *Leader*, May 11, 1910.

root of the problem in black male service employment was the competitive challenge of growing numbers of white men then entering the services. Because of very high rates of southern and eastern European immigration during both decades, there were more whites desperate enough to take low-status service positions. Coming at a time when growing color prejudice placed blacks at an initial disadvantage, the result was a profound challenge to black opportunity.[16] Data for Ohio indicate that, particularly in the large cities, where that challenge was likely to be the greatest, whites of foreign stock were acquiring a larger and larger share of service fields. While the number of black barbers in the three largest cities rose by only 1 percent in 1890–1910, the number of first- and second-generation ethnic barbers rose by 58 percent. The number of black male servants and waiters there rose by 9 percent, compared to the increase of 40 percent for foreign stock.

At the same time, less obvious factors were affecting the situation. Given the strong advantage held by white competition at the time, these factors were not necessarily definitive in themselves, but they did make it more difficult for blacks to compete for service work with the singleness of purpose which the new situation required. According to contemporary observers, attitudes toward service work among black men were changing. While they were certainly aware that service work reinforced caste relations, earlier generations of black men either had been resigned to service work for the security it provided, or had willingly embarked upon service careers because these might provide a path to business or to positions of authority and responsibility of the type usually forbidden blacks. But at the turn of the century young men were growing more reluctant to enter the services. They found jobs which required serving whites at table or cutting their hair particularly undignified and demeaning, because they highlighted the race's subjugation to the vagaries of the white world. Such young men sought service work as a last resort, rather than as a positive alternative.[17] The Cleveland *Journal*, for example, complained in 1906

[16] There is no evidence that labor union hostility in the two service areas—the food services and barbering—in which unionization was taking place had any impact upon this situation. Labor unions were very weak in the food services in Ohio at the time, and at any rate they were not hostile to black membership. The barbers' union, while it did not organize significant numbers of black barbers, showed no desire to strike out against the black presence in the trade. See above, p. 72, and W. Scott Hall, *The Journeyman Barber's International Union of America* (Baltimore, 1936), pp. 20, 43–44.

[17] W. E. B. Du Bois spoke of this same orientation toward service work, particularly the barbers' trade, in his careful, empirical study of Philadelphia's black community published in 1899. Young black men, he said, tended generally to see service "as a relic of slavery and longed to get other work as their fathers had

that many local young men saw the barber's trade as "a social stigma"; because they refused to be trained for it, the better local black-owned shops were having difficulty finding men to staff their chairs.[18] The same contempt existed for other forms of service which had once been seen as likely avenues of security and prestige. William Hunley, the black superintendent of service at Cleveland's Hollenden House, complained in 1904 that previously sought-after positions in hotel service were now being scorned. Young blacks were looking for work they considered more dignified, and they resisted being trained as waiters, bellboys, footmen, and stewards. Hunley maintained that these young men saw hotel service as menial when in fact occupations like that of hotel dining room waiter actually required greater skill and were far more challenging and exacting than ever before.[19]

To the extent that the practice of such servile work as waiting table is considered unchanging, Hunley's argument might seem unconvincing. Yet at the turn of the century there was mounting evidence of the changing requirements in this trade, with important implications for all those, whatever their race, who clung to old ways. Hotel dining rooms and restaurants were converting from American to European-style service, a reflection of changing standards of sophistication among American diners. American-style service demanded only that the waiter bring diners their selections from a limited menu; he need not prepare checks, because the price of meals was fixed. The European style of dining, however, introduced a more varied menu with prices which differed from item to item. Waiters now had to take complex orders and make out bills; illiterates and those not adept at thinking on their feet, whether black or white, were hurt as a result. In addition, because of attempts to replicate the luxury of European dining, waiters were now asked to prepare food at table. Their range had to be greater than standard American dishes; the growing number of European chefs working in the United States, as well as American

---

longed to be free." As for the barbers' trade, "One would have to look a long time among young and aspiring Negroes to find one who would willingly become a barber—it smacks perhaps a little too much of domestic service, and is a thing to fall back on rather than to aspire to." At the same time, however, Du Bois was also aware of the force of color prejudice and ethnic competition upon the position of black skilled workers generally and black barbers particularly at Philadelphia. In his post-1900 writings, he came to dwell more upon these factors than upon black attitudes and actions in explaining overall trends in black employment. W. E. B. Du Bois, *The Philadelphia Negro: A Social Study* (Philadelphia, 1899), pp. 116–137; August Meier, *Negro Thought in America, 1880–1915* (Ann Arbor, 1963), pp. 193, 196.

18 Cleveland *Journal*, May 26, 1906.
19 Ibid., Dec. 24, 1906.

travels abroad, were influencing the tastes of diners, and thus creating a demand for those skilled in preparing continental cuisine. The emergence of these new conditions obviously gave a competitive advantage to waiters trained in Europe, if they knew English.[20]

The ethnic challenge and other factors had uneven effects upon black opportunity. Among barbers and barbershops, those catering to the affluent white trade in the central business districts were particularly hurt. Dabney's Cincinnati *Union* noted in March, 1910, that several such shops had closed within a few weeks' time because of the "rapid march of white competition." [21] But others, like George Myers's shop or that of Cincinnati's Lewis family, proved equal to the challenge. Myers responded particularly effectively. Constantly interested in improving his business, he installed all of the most modern sanitary equipment and most comfortable chairs; he even hired a stenographer to take dictation for busy professionals and businessmen as they waited their turns or sat in the barber's chair. Faced with a shortage of black barbers in Cleveland, Myers brought willing young men up from the South to work for him.[22]

In food service, blacks also kept some old opportunities while losing others. The situation at Columbus was similar to that of other cities and towns. As late as 1910, the waiters at Columbus's three finest hotels (the Neil House, the Southern, and the Chittenden) were all black, and black headwaiters managed their dining rooms. But other hotels and a number of restaurants were then replacing blacks with white help.[23] However, after the turn of the century blacks at Cleveland, Columbus, and Youngstown began to respond to new conditions. In varying combinations representing labor, management, and enter-

[20] Matthew Josephson, *Union House, Union Bar: The History of the Hotel and Restaurant Employees and Bartenders International Union, AFL-CIO* (New York, 1956), p. 5 and passim. I thank David Katzman for sharing with me his very valuable insights on factors affecting the situation of black waiters at the turn of the century.

[21] Cincinnati *Union*, n.d., quoted in Cleveland *Journal*, Mar. 5, 1910. For general comments on the downward trend in barbering, see Wendell Phillips Dabney, *Cincinnati's Colored Citizens: Historical, Sociological, Biographical* (Cincinnati, 1926), pp. 183–185, and Russell H. Davis, *Black Americans in Cleveland from George Peake to Carl B. Stokes* (Washington, 1972), pp. 160–162, which discuss the decline of the black barber catering to the white trade in those two cities.

[22] Washington, "Negro Disfranchisement," 313; John A. Garraty, ed., *The Barber and the Historian: The Correspondence of George A. Myers and James Ford Rhodes, 1910–1923* (Columbus, 1956), pp. xvi–xvii; George Myers to Mark Hanna, draft dated Feb. 4, 1902, Box XI, folder 1, George A. Myers Papers, OHS; George Myers to John Green, Feb. 10, 1902, Box VI, folder 3, John P. Green Papers, WRHS.

[23] Columbus *Dispatch*, Mar. 6, 1910; Indianapolis *Freeman*, Aug. 29, 1914; Quillin, *Color Line in Ohio*, pp. 148–149.

prise, black cooks, waiters, headwaiters, and caterers formed service associations. While the associations in all three cities had savings, insurance, and recreational features, they also acted as clearing houses for information about employment opportunity and orchestrated cooperation between workers, employers, and employers' representatives. Cleveland's "Caterers Association" was founded in 1905 and had a membership of about a hundred caterers, headwaiters, and waiters by 1909; its boosters contended that the organization was responsible for "allowing colored men in this profession to keep up their monopoly." [24] The claim was something of an exaggeration, for blacks certainly did not have such a monopoly. But there was little doubt that the association had aided a number of men in getting and keeping work, an important contribution in the context of the contemporary competitive situation.

II

Prior to the urban migration, black businessmen made few specific attempts to tap the Negro market for goods and services, and blacks had given little thought to the possibility that new opportunities for enterprise might lie in the race itself. Until the 1880s the black population was largely rural and scattered, and thus not a temptation for the prospective black entrepreneur. In the cities and a few of the larger towns, particularly Xenia, there had occasionally been black-owned eating spots, saloons, and a grocery or two catering to blacks; there were also black barbershops and beauty salons reversing the traditional pattern by tapping the black rather than the white market for tonsorial services. A struggling race press was bent on forming a race market. But even urban black populations were too small and unstable to excite the potential entrepreneur. Thus, although the Bucktown of the 1870s possessed Ohio's largest concentration of urban blacks, the neighborhood's Irish majority owned the stores—such as they were.[25] The most successful black retailers and service entrepreneurs of the late nineteenth century depended almost exclusively upon white trade. No doubt the knowledge that they, too, would have to compete with established white businesses for white patronage in a highly race-conscious society kept many blacks from entering business. The last years of the period witnessed new developments in the

[24] Indianapolis *Freeman*, Sept. 27, 1913, Jan. 17, 1914; "The Spirit of Progressive Cleveland, Ohio," *Colored American Magazine*, XV (Mar., 1909), 138–140.

[25] Cincinnati *Gazette*, July 26, 1879.

scope, scale, and target of Negro enterprise, largely in response to the growing number and increased concentration of blacks in the major cities and urban wards. The expansion of Negro business was clearly demonstrated by federal censuses of enterprise. While there were only 73 blacks engaged in wholesale and retail business in 1890, the number had reached 246 by 1900 and 477 by 1910. The number of black-owned eating places and saloons rose, too, from 28 in 1890 and 50 in 1900 to 254 in 1910. During twenty years in which Ohio's black population increased by one-fourth, the number of black businesses increased sixfold.

The shifting of Negro enterprise from dependence on white patronage to attempts to tap the growing Negro market was evident in the major cities. New black business centers arose after the turn of the century. Usually composed of several blocks of new black enterprises, interspersed among established white ones, and located in the midst of the major black concentrations of population and black churches and lodge halls, these commercial districts furthered the association of urban blacks with specific areas of the city. They were an important part of the process by which distinct black neighborhoods were emerging out of amorphous blocks of houses, tenements, shops, and institutions.

The heart of Dayton's black business district was Dunbar Avenue, named for the black poet Paul Laurence Dunbar, born and bred at Dayton, after his untimely death in 1906. Located in the heart of the Sixth Ward black residential area, the street was convenient not only for black shoppers on the West Side but also for blacks who lived just across the Great Miami River on the fringes of the central business district.[26] At Columbus, both the downtown and East Side sections of East Long Street developed black business areas; but as the latter neighborhood grew rapidly after 1900, the downtown business section was eclipsed. Black businesses soon lined both sides of East Long Street and Mt. Vernon Avenue; it was estimated in 1914 that well over a hundred black enterprises were located in the neighborhood.[27] According to one local black, Cincinnati's "Brownsville," a section of the Eighteenth Ward on Fifth Street between Central and Smith, had "become a Mecca for Negro enterprise" by 1910. At any time of the day or night, it was said, blacks from throughout the Miami Valley and from nearby Kentucky and Indiana could be found shopping in the area.[28] The expansion of Cleveland's black enterprise was quite rapid just

[26] Indianapolis *Freeman*, June 19, July 24, 1909, Aug. 3, 1912.
[27] Cleveland *Gazette*, Jan. 7, 1899; Indianapolis *Freeman*, Aug. 29, 1914.
[28] Indianapolis *Freeman*, Aug. 13, 1910.

after the turn of the century; Central Avenue between East 25th and East 35th streets served as the black commercial center. The boom was evident to Harry Smith. Speaking of the developments along Central Avenue, he stated happily in 1904, "During the last two years business activity among our people has been growing steadily until now we have a great number of places doing fairly better than ever before." [29] Even at Youngstown, where the small black population was growing rapidly, a section of Federal Street convenient to nearby centers of black population emerged as a black business section.[30]

The expansion of Negro enterprise often followed predictable lines. To some extent, it involved the opening of small service-oriented businesses, such as tailor shops, shoeshine parlors, and barbershops, fields in which blacks had had ample experience catering to whites. At the same time, however, some were striking out in new directions. Grocery, drug, and candy stores opened in most major cities after the turn of the century, and some clothing, furniture, and notions shops also appeared.[31] Even in service enterprises, new paths were taken. Though undertaking was a field with a constant market, and one in which blacks had occasionally encountered discrimination at the hands of white businessmen, William Porter's successful operation at Cincinnati stood virtually alone in the nineteenth century. After 1900, however, black funeral parlors staffed by black morticians appeared in all of the state's major cities.

Discrimination by white hotels had long inconvenienced the Negro traveler, who often found it necessary to stay with friends and relatives or in cheap rooming houses. From the late 1890s on, the increasing establishment of black-owned hotels in the major cities brought some relief. Columbus's Litchford Hotel, opened in 1906 by a local native, William Litchford, was typical of the better new hotels. It was small (containing twenty-six rooms), clean, and pleasantly furnished, and it offered guests a lobby, sitting room, and dining facilities. Restaurants, larger and with better service and a wider selection of food than the black-owned eateries of the past, and ice cream parlors and candy shops were also appearing in cities.[32]

[29] Cleveland *Gazette*, June 9, 1904; Carrie Clifford, "Cleveland and Its Colored People," *Colored American Magazine*, IX (July, 1905), 378–380.

[30] Indianapolis *Freeman*, Sept. 11, 1915.

[31] Cleveland *Gazette*, Sept. 7, 1901, June 14, 1902; Urbana *Informer*, Feb., 1903; Cleveland *Journal*, Dec. 2, 23, 1905, Jan. 6, Apr. 28, Dec. 15, 1906.

[32] Cleveland *Gazette*, Jan. 7, 1899, May 11, 1901, Apr. 11, 18, 1903, Jan. 2, Mar. 19, May 11, 28, Aug. 24, 1904, Apr. 14, 1906, Aug. 7, 1909, Feb. 5, 1910; Cincinnati *Enquirer*, Jan. 8, 1902; Indianapolis *Freeman*, Aug. 3, 13, 1910, Sept. 9, 23, 1911, Aug. 3, 1912, Aug. 1, 29, 1914, Aug. 7, 14, Sept. 11, 1915;

The new enterprises also attempted to tap the growing market for leisure services. There were two levels of such activity. One, involving saloons, pool halls, brothels, and gambling dens, encompassed the illegal or simply not wholly reputable. The times produced their own "shadies"; their manner of operation was not unlike that of older counterparts like Smoky Hobbs, but their clientele was now more black than white. An example is Cleveland's A. D. "Starlight" Boyd, nicknamed for his flashy diamond ring. Boyd was a Mississippian of unknown age and obscure origin who turned up at Cleveland after the turn of the century. At various times he owned legitimate enterprises, including a restaurant and a saloon, but behind these fronts there is evidence that he was deeply involved in gambling and prostitution. A classic "shady" politician, Boyd used his position as a Republican precinct captain to build a power base among the black and white poor in the Central Avenue slums. His control over a large number of local votes helped to insure his freedom from police harassment.[33]

On another level were conventionally respectable and legitimate enterprises. Especially welcome to those seeking amusment in an era of increasing theater segregation was the appearance of a black vaudeville and the opening of a number of race theaters to accommodate it, both illustrative of a developing urban black popular culture. The increasing professionalization and expansion of the black theater was attested to in 1910 at Cincinnati, which had become a center of black vaudeville because two popular theaters were located there. The Afro-American Booking Company, the only operation of its kind at the time, created a circuit of race-operated theaters for the leading black entertainers and musical revues to travel.[34]

Black amusement parks were also opened. Columbus native Billy Smith, who owned the Dunbar Theater and had for years been a performer himself, opened a "Crown Garden Theater and Airdome" in 1914. Featuring motion pictures, dancing, and refreshments, this outdoor recreation park was conveniently located near Columbus's several centers of black population. It accommodated up to 2,000 persons and was frequently crowded to capacity during its first summer.[35]

Dabney, *Cincinnati's Colored Citizens*, pp. 183–184, 194, 385; "Litchford Hotel," *Colored American Magazine*, XIV (Nov., 1908), 584–588.

[33] Davis, *Black Americans in Cleveland*, pp. 144–145; Jane Edna Hunter, *A Nickel and a Prayer* (Cleveland, 1940), pp. 120–129; Cleveland *Plain Dealer*, Apr. 7, 1903; Indianapolis *Freeman*, Sept. 9, 1911, Sept. 11, 1915.

[34] Cleveland *Journal*, Feb. 22, 1908, Mar. 27, 1909; Cleveland *Gazette*, Jan. 22, 1910, Dec. 30, 1911; Indianapolis *Freeman*, Jan. 22, June 25, 1910, Jan. 27, July 20, 1912, Jan. 17, Apr. 4, 25, June 27, Aug. 29, 1914, Feb. 20, 1915.

[35] Indianapolis *Freeman*, Sept. 12, 1914.

Even more ambitious was much-heralded Dahomey Park, opened at Dayton in 1910. This largest black-operated, black-patronized amusement park in the nation was the brain child of Moses Moore, a long-time black resident who had made a fortune in real estate speculation and had for some years been concerned with the lack of recreational facilities available to Dayton's growing black population. As its name (after the old West African kingdom) suggests, Dahomey Park was at least partly conceived of as a living symbol of racial pride and solidarity. Whites were admitted and "civilly treated and served," but their patronage was not sought. Representing an initial investment of $40,000 by Moore himself, the park featured a wide range of services and amusements, including a zoo, movie theater, roller skating rink, ice cream parlor, and several eating spots; it attracted not only black Daytonians, but also excursionists from throughout Ohio and other states. An added attraction was the Marco Baseball Club, owned by a corporation composed of Moore and several other blacks, which made its home at a stadium on the grounds.[36] The Marco Club was one of many professional and semi-professional black Ohio baseball teams participating in the new all-black leagues established throughout the North after the turn of the century.[37]

As much a departure from the old pattern of black business in Ohio was the development of black real estate firms in the cities—a direct result of more affluent blacks' desire to leave congested inner-city neighborhoods. In the 1890s the black real estate firms were generally one-man operations concerned with finding property for blacks to rent or purchase, but after 1900 there appeared a small number of firms organized as joint stock companies and involved in construction and development.[38] One such firm, Cleveland's Mohawk Realty Company, was the product of a partnership between two young men, Welcome T. Blue, a realtor, and S. C. Green, a Virginia-born Clevelander who manufactured a sofa-bed, on which he held the patent, and was at the same time involved in various amusement enterprises. The company not only built several apartments in better residential districts along

[36] Ibid., June 12, 1909; Cleveland *Gazette,* Apr. 2, 1910; "Dayton's Exclusive Colored Park," *Colored American Magazine,* XVII (Oct., 1909), 290–294.

[37] Cleveland *Gazette,* Apr. 4, 1906; Columbus *Ohio State Journal,* May 18, 1908; Cleveland *Journal,* Apr. 10, 1909. Illustrative of the growing popularity and increasing organization of Negro sports in northern cities after the turn of the century was the creation of a "sports section," with player profiles, game coverage, and box scores, in the Indianapolis *Freeman,* one of the most popular northern black papers.

[38] Cleveland *Gazette,* Apr. 8, 1893, Feb. 11, Mar. 4, 1899, Sept. 13, 1902, Dec. 10, 1904, Dec. 16, 1905; Cleveland *Journal,* Dec. 3, 1904, Jan. 19, 1907; Indianapolis *Freeman,* June 19, 1909, Aug. 3, 1912, Oct. 4, 1913, Aug. 19, 1914.

Central Avenue and on the east side, but also developed a suburban tract southeast of Cleveland for blacks wishing to leave "the crowded, smoky city" (as their ads described it) and have a garden and some chickens in their backyard. The idea appealed to some. In 1907 the company claimed that approximately one hundred property owners and their families were now living on small plots of land, available at easy terms, at a site forty-five minutes from downtown at the end of a street-car line.[39] A similar development was planned at Youngstown in 1912 by H. J. Jeffe, a Negro realtor who headed a small corporation. Explaining the origin of his efforts, Jeffe said that many Youngstown blacks wanted to leave congested areas but could not because of residential discrimination. He bought a large plot of land near an integrated (but largely white) area and subdivided it into 250 lots. Nearly half of them were sold almost immediately.[40]

As the use of the corporate format in real estate suggests, blacks were becoming increasingly aware of the benefits of incorporation and shareholding as means for pooling small individual resources in order to sustain large projects. The corporate format had not been utilized during the late nineteenth century, and it appeared now for two reasons. First, of course, entrepreneurs and investors wanted to cash in on the growing race market in the cities. In addition to real estate corporations, grocery stores at Cleveland, Columbus, and Cincinnati and a drugstore at Cleveland were financed through shareholding after 1900. Typically, the number of stockholders was small (in the range of ten to thirty) and stockholding was limited to the proprietor, his friends and relatives, and their acquaintances.[41]

Incorporation and shareholding were not utilized only in the large cities. A number of small towns were experiencing no expansion of the Negro market (if anything, black populations were declining), but in these towns the same types of enterprises were being financed through the same methods. After 1900 groceries were established through shareholding at Urbana, Zanesville, Gallipolis, and Washington Court House. The reason given for resorting to the corporate format was typified by the complaints of Gallipolis blacks: when they opened their grocery in 1910, they announced that they were tired of seeing local blacks spend "from $200 to $300 monthly" on groceries, most of which "made wealthy a few white merchants." Shareholding here was divided among many of the town's higher-status blacks; they

---

[39] Cleveland *Journal*, Aug. 17, 1907.

[40] Indianapolis *Freeman*, Feb. 10, 1912.

[41] Urbana *Informer*, Feb., 1903; Cleveland *Journal*, Dec. 2, 23, 1905, Jan. 6, 1906; Indianapolis *Freeman*, Sept. 12, 1914.

subscribed not only with an expectation of individual profit, but also in the hope of making work for a few black clerks and circulating the race's money within its own ranks. Thus, in an era of repression and reaction in race relations, in which a consciousness of racial separateness and a feeling of the need for protective and collective action might easily develop, black corporations were practical embodiments of natural desires for intraracial unity and self-help—and on practical investment terms which higher-status blacks could easily appreciate.[42]

Doubtless both racial and profit motives were present in a number of particularly ambitious urban corporate endeavors. Corporate organization was utilized to establish building and loan associations at Cleveland, Dayton, Youngstown, and Toledo after 1900.[43] These associations were the immediate product of growing desires for movement and homeownership among the more affluent, but at the same time they reflected a desire to systematize economic self-help. More grandiose corporations were founded at Springfield and Cincinnati. In 1897 blacks established a Springfield Weekly Savings Corporation, capitalized at $5,000, which then organized a dime savings bank. At $25 a share, stockholding was no doubt limited to the more affluent; however, accounts at the bank, in the interest of racial inclusiveness, could be maintained through deposits of as little as ten cents a week. The next year, a number of Springfield blacks involved in the former endeavor founded a National Agitator Printing and Publishing Company for the dual purpose of publishing a daily black newspaper and doing job printing. At Cincinnati around the turn of the century, some of the more affluent race leaders founded an Ohio Cooperative Company, chartered for many kinds of mercantile business and for real estate sales.[44]

This impressive expansion of enterprise should not be allowed to obscure the substantial difficulties which blacks faced in succeeding at their businesses. The reach of the new endeavors often exceeded their grasp. Cincinnati's Ohio Cooperative Association died aborning, its officers and stockholders unable to agree on where to put their money and generally unable to get along with one another. Springfield's black savings bank, on the other hand, based its hopes on the

[42] Urbana *Informer*, Aug., 1902, Feb., Apr., 1903; Cleveland *Gazette*, Sept. 7, 1901, June 14, 1902; Gallipolis *Weekly Tribune*, Aug. 23, 1901; Cleveland *Journal*, Jan. 6, Apr. 28, 1906.

[43] Cleveland *Gazette*, Aug. 10, 1901, Mar. 7, 1903, Mar. 31, 1906; Indianapolis *Freeman*, Apr. 25, 1914.

[44] Cleveland *Gazette*, Sept. 17, Oct. 29, 1898; Dabney, *Cincinnati's Colored Citizens*, p. 437; "Springfield's Negro Bank," W.P.A. Project Interviews, Springfield, Ohio, OHS.

ability and willingness of a poor people to put away as little as a dime a week. Good idea though it was, the bank did not receive the broad base of support its founders had hoped for, and it closed in 1899. The National Agitator Printing and Publishing Company found that it faced the traditional problem of black journalism: large costs exceeded the return from subscriptions, even in the large potential race market of Springfield and the surrounding Miami Valley. In addition, the firm's attempts at job printing faced sharp competition from well-established white job printers. Thus, it limped along for years, sporadically publishing papers.[45]

The new entrepreneurs faced especially formidable difficulties, and the rate of attrition among businesses attempting to tap the Negro market appears to have been quite high. This was largely the result of overexpansion in certain fields, particularly the services, in which so many ambitious men had training. Some saw the prosperity of others as auguring their own success, without considering that only so many similar businesses could tap a limited, if expanding, market within the usual ten-block area. Toward the end of a decade of expansion of black business along Central Avenue, Harry Smith began to chastise local entrepreneurs for their insensitivity to the laws of the market. In 1909, when another black eating spot opened on Central, he remarked sarcastically, "All that is needed in the vicinity now is another barbershop."[46]

Then, too, the new enterprises were established on the questionable assumption that they would have the unqualified loyalty of blacks. In fact, many of them offered little incentive to black consumers. Fledgling black businesses frequently opened with limited inventories and little experience in the display and care of merchandise; in addition, their prices were not always competitive. On the other hand, there were a few established white stores and shops in the same neighborhoods that had always actively encouraged black patronage and were able to offer good, attractively displayed items at reasonable prices. So, however deep their feelings of race loyalty may have been, many blacks continued to patronize whites. One black commentator at Columbus singled out the care and display of goods as especially important in determining consumer preferences. He wrote thus in 1914 concerning one prosperous black Columbus grocery:

> One gets the impression that it is not a colored store as its appearance is so unusual. Everything—the counters, cases, floors, figures, and stock

[45] E. S. Todd, *A Sociological Study of Springfield and Clark County, Ohio* (New York, 1904), p. 67; "Springfield's Negro Bank," W.P.A. Project Interviews; Dabney, *Cincinnati's Colored Citizens*, p. 437.
[46] Cleveland *Gazette*, Aug. 7, 1909, July 30, 1910, Aug. 12, 1911.

are neat and clean, and seem to have just been polished. . . . When our business people learn to show respect for their customers that is due them by keeping their stores or places of business clean, orderly, and respectable, then they will find that the colored customers will prefer to trade with our own businesses.[47]

In this competition with white business, location could work either for or against the black entrepreneur. While the black commercial districts were located in or near Negro population centers, those centers were themselves no more than a short walk or streetcar ride from the central business district. At Columbus, for example, local boosters of black business pointed out that one factor working against East Side entrepreneurs was the convenient streetcar connection between the East Side and downtown; a short, inexpensive ride could bring black shoppers to the city's best stores, such as Lazarus', the biggest downtown department store, and one which had always encouraged their patronage.[48] Only at Cleveland did poor streetcar connections isolate many black shoppers—not only from the central business district, but also from shopping and commercial districts near Central Avenue. To some extent, this was the result of racial animosity; white residents of East 25th Street north of Central had balked at the thought of riding on streetcars with blacks, and they had been instrumental in blocking the construction of a streetcar line between Central and Cedar avenues in 1906. The isolation of Central Avenue was also the result of inaccessible streetcars and poorly planned routes; streetcar stops along Central were sometimes as much as half a mile apart, and as late as 1912 the streetcar line linking the populous Central district with downtown only brought riders within a quarter-mile of the central business district.[49] As a result, the neighborhood shopping area had a distinct advantage over similar areas in other cities.

The weak position of the new black businesses had ironic implications. While many of the new businessmen hoped that racial loyalties would help them to tap the Negro market, the Cleveland *Journal* observed that the most successful moneymakers based their appeal less on race than on the excellence of their product and their competitive prices. Their businesses were so well run that they could count on the patronage of discriminating consumers of both races. The *Journal* noted that even the most lucrative neighborhood barbershops and res-

[47] Quoted in Indianapolis *Freeman*, Aug. 29, 1914. See also Cleveland *Journal*, Dec. 24, 1904, Sept. 25, 1909; Cleveland *Gazette*, Dec. 19, 1914; Booker T. Washington, *The Story of the Negro* (New York, 1909), II, 199–200.

[48] Indianapolis *Freeman*, Aug. 28, 1914.

[49] Cleveland *Journal*, May 25, 1907; Cleveland *Gazette*, Aug. 29, Dec. 5, 1908, Oct. 19, 1912.

taurants (businesses which, because of the personal nature of their services, came closest to having a largely Negro clientele) were able to attract some whites. Less well-run black enterprises, on the other hand, could count on neither blacks nor whites.[50]

But though the competitive position of the new black enterprise was often difficult, this did not deter blacks from entering business. The Indianapolis *Freeman* surveyed black commercial activity in major Ohio cities between 1909 and 1915 and found intense effort everywhere.[51] As neighborhoods filled up with blacks, the impetus to try for a business success was greater than ever. At a time when many black economic trends, not to mention the more general course of race relations, were headed downward, the new opportunity for enterprise was one of the few bright spots in the black situation. For this reason, as we shall see, it was an important element in shaping the thought of many of those who looked for ways of coming to terms with racial needs in a perilous time.

III

This sudden burst of individual and corporate entrepreneurial energy in the cities had its parallel in the professions. As the racial market for the services of black attorneys, doctors, and dentists grew in the cities, Ohio appeared hospitable to the growing number of aspiring young men and women then graduating from the nation's black and white professional schools. However, in absolute numbers the increases remained small. Though their numbers more than doubled between 1890 and 1910, there were still only 39 black lawyers (all men) and 99 black doctors and dentists (24% women) in all of Ohio in 1910. Similarly, in 1910 Cincinnati, Cleveland, Columbus, Dayton, and Toledo possessed only 4, 11, 7, 2, and 1 black attorneys and 14, 8, 13, 10, and 5 black doctors and dentists. Moreover, most of Ohio's black professionals remained concentrated in the more traditional black professional pursuits: preaching and teaching in separate public schools.[52]

Yet, from a black viewpoint, other factors compensated for the small numbers in the prestigious upper reaches of the professions. When they had embarked upon their careers in the 1870s, 1880s, and early 1890s, the older generation of urban black attorneys and physicians

---

[50] Cleveland *Journal,* Sept. 25, 1909.

[51] Indianapolis *Freeman,* June 19, 1909, Sept. 9, 1911, Aug. 3, 1912, Sept. 12, 1914, Aug. 14, Sept. 4, 11, 1915.

[52] As in the late nineteenth century, professionals continued to account for slightly under 3% of Ohio's working blacks.

often had to depend on the patronage of whites because of the relatively small urban black populations. But now a new career pattern was emerging. Younger professionals like Columbus dentist R. M. Tribbitt and Dayton attorney William O. Stokes were attempting to draw their clients largely from the race itself; they often set up their offices in the black commercial districts (rather than downtown, as in the past) in order to facilitate contacts with the growing Negro community.[53] They were not only an important addition to racial welfare, but also part of the larger process by which demographic and economic trends were interacting to create a stronger black presence in urban neighborhoods. Once again, the migration and urbanization trends had shown their potential for exerting a dynamic influence on racial life.

[53] Cleveland *Journal,* Mar. 19, 1910; Indianapolis *Freeman,* Sept. 9, 1911, Aug. 3, 1912, Sept. 12, 1914, Aug. 14, Sept. 11, 1915.

12

The Social and Political Crises
of the Old Order

Immediately after the Civil War, the progressive trend of the times, the self-confidence and optimism of the black upper class, and the considerable degree of black political influence in Ohio had all combined to provide black Ohio with aggressive, successful leadership. The elements in this complex of factors had asserted important positive influences on each other, heightening the motivation of black leaders to pursue the goals they set for racial advancement. Yet this situation had weak bases: the tenuousness of race relations, the instability of Ohio politics, and the precarious social and economic arrangements which sustained the upper class. By 1900 this structure of interdependent, positive influences had begun to collapse. Not only did race relations deteriorate, but the balance of political forces shifted to the detriment of black influences. Furthermore, under the pressure of menacing times and in response to new developments, the larger, debilitating contradictions in upper-class life began to assert themselves. The former combination of positive influences ultimately became a web of negative ones which weakened late nineteenth century black leadership's ability to confront the challenges of a new time.

I

When he sought a title for his autobiography, John Green settled upon *Fact Stranger Than Fiction*. Though he never explained his choice, it quickly becomes clear to the reader that the odyssey of Green's life, his rise from poverty and degradation in the ante-bellum South to prominence in his adopted Cleveland, was always a marvel to him. Born in 1845 of light-skinned, free parents in the small eastern North Carolina town of New Bern, he grew up desperately poor. His father, an artisan, died when John was five, leaving his wife with a small home and little else. John's mother, Hortense, fought poverty by working as a seamstress and laundress. In the hope that they might someday advance themselves, she sent her children to the little school for free children of color that New Bern whites then tolerated.

Yet times were very hard. The family often depended on small gifts of food from friends and relatives. Moreover, the 1850s were a time of growing repression of North Carolina's free blacks; many, including Mrs. Green and her children, were forced to flee northward. After selling her home and meager belongings, Hortense Green bought tickets in June, 1857, aboard a coastal ship bound for New York City. Her destination was Cleveland, which she would reach by the Erie Canal. There she hoped to find safety and prosperity, as had other North Carolina refugees who had settled in the Oberlin-Cleveland area. John remembered the years following their migration as "bittersweet." He was apprenticed to a black artisan at Oberlin in 1857, but, lonely and desirous of education, he ran away after only six weeks. That fall he entered school with his mother's encouragement, but lack of money forced him to quit after only two years. He worked hard and long, waiting tables, doing errands and odd jobs, and working aboard the trains between Cleveland and Pittsburgh, in order that he might re-enter school and pursue a legal career. He pushed himself through Cleveland's Central High School and Union Law College; in 1870, he was admitted to the bar.

Throughout his life Green enjoyed help from people of both races: black ministers who inspired him and provided fatherly advice; a black man who gave him a crucial loan; a white judge in whose office he read law and clerked; and an Irish Democrat who was his law partner and helped him make vital political contacts among the Cleveland Democracy. With their support and through his own efforts, Green enjoyed great success. By the time of his fifty-fifth birthday in 1900 he had attained a reputation as an able defense counsel; he had served with distinction as an elected justice of the peace and state legislator; and finally, under McKinley, he held federal office. His friends included John D. Rockefeller, and his travels took him to Europe.[1] By 1900 many blacks throughout the nation viewed him as a sage—"one of the smartest colored men in Ohio," said a black newspaper [2]—and he was recognized as one of the most prominent members of that first generation of blacks to participate actively in American party politics.

---

[1] Remarks on Green's life are based on *Fact Stranger Than Fiction: 75 Years of a \Busy Life* (Cleveland, 1920).

[2] Undated clipping from either Cleveland *Journal* or Indianapolis *Freeman*, Box XVIII, folder 8, George A. Myers Papers, OHS.

For years, the outlines of racial history had appeared to follow the same progressive course as Green's personal history. This mixture of racial and personal triumphs had inspired Green and others to envision the day when American society might allow each person, regardless of color, to realize his or her potential. Yet, as they grew into middle and old age, Green and his peers witnessed a steady erosion of black citizenship, and their world became confused and menacing. In 1906 Green himself sensed a deep crisis in race relations, one which presented a fundamental contradiction of the racial articles of faith upon which Ohio's late nineteenth-century racial leaders had based their hopes. Illustrative of his commitment to the goals framed by black leadership in that hopeful time, for Green the ultimate import of the crisis was that it compromised his hope for the creation of a color-blind society in which each individual would be judged (as Green himself claimed to have been judged) on the basis of individual talents and worth. After describing the more obvious components of the new situation, he wrote in a letter to the Cleveland *Gazette:* ". . . The white citizen has departed from the fundamental idea and theory of a republican form of government and society. . . . Whereas they live and thrive on an *individual basis* . . . the colored citizen, no matter what his ambition and merits, must wear the same mark and suffer death if he dares venture beyond the dead line from his whole class." His concern for the race's future became especially clear when he reflected upon the impact of this compromise of egalitarian theory upon young people. It would be "fatal to the aspirations of the ambitious, energetic colored youth, for he knows that every discrimination which confronts any unworthy member of the race must be shared and endured by the most worthy." He concluded with the sad prediction that the reinvigorated spirit of caste would take a terrible toll in the hopes and lives of black youngsters: "While smallpox, cholera, yellow fever, bubonic plague or even leprosy may be healed, there is no . . . Jordan whose waters are potent enough to cleanse them of the fatal effects of color caste and proscription." [3]

By challenging the fundamental tenets of a racial strategy which was not simply the result of a rational calculation of alternatives but, in a sense, a living commitment acted upon daily by racial leaders like Green, who had succeeded as individuals on their own merits and against the odds, the sharp downward trend of race relations shook the very foundations and premises upon which they had lived so much of their lives. What was challenged was not simply an intellectual com-

---

[3] Cleveland *Gazette*, Oct. 6, 1906.

mitment to a policy, but the validity of a human experience and of the perspectives and values which that experience had created and sustained. The times seemed to demand that Green and others who had risen to prominence during the more hopeful late nineteenth century repudiate not only a notion of racial alternatives, but also the relevance of their own experiences—a much more difficult process. The crisis of race relations was thus transfigured: it became the crisis of a social class and its leadership as both confronted times which mocked them.

Although the crisis in race relations had created intellectual and psychological challenges, destructive forces were also working within the black upper class and leadership group which had been instrumental in bringing about the ameliorative trend of previous decades. These forces sapped vital energies and diminished the resiliency and emotional and intellectual toughness necessary to confront the times.

In part, of course, the decline was inevitable: by the first decade of the twentieth century many leaders of the post–Civil War era were dead or aging. Bishop Payne and Colonel Harlan had died during the 1890s; Bishop Arnett died at sixty-eight in 1906, and Poindexter at eighty-eight a year later.[4] William Parham, George Jackson, Jere Brown, and John Green reached their sixties and seventies after 1900.[5] Others had left the state and died elsewhere. While on assignment for the Freedmen's Bureau at Canton, Mississippi, David Jenkins had fallen victim to a fever.[6] Peter Clark spent his old age in exile at St. Louis, dying almost a centenarian, many years after leaving Ohio.[7] Shortly after his House term ended in 1881, Ohio's first black legislator, George Washington Williams, left Ohio for the East, and spent the next years concentrating on his historical writing. He died prematurely in 1891 at age forty-two in England.[8]

But the weakness of the older leadership group also reflected the insecure economic position of the black upper class. By 1900 its members had begun to suffer the effects of several economic shocks which forced unusual adjustments on the part of families and individuals, and made the passage of leadership from one generation to the next difficult. These economic trends had roots in the late nineteenth century, a time

[4] Josephus R. Coan, *Daniel Payne—Christian Educator* (Philadelphia, 1935), p. 117; Cincinnati *Enquirer*, Sept. 22, 1897; Baltimore *Afro-American*, Oct. 13, 1906; Columbus *Dispatch*, Feb. 11, 1907.

[5] Cleveland *Gazette*, Aug. 22, 1891, Dec. 7, 1895, Apr. 5, 1913.

[6] Ben Haynes, "Negro—No. 3," undated clipping, Columbus *Citizen-Journal*, OHS.

[7] Cleveland *Gazette*, June 20, 1896; Wendell Phillips Dabney, *Cincinnati's Colored Citizens: Historical, Sociological, and Biographical* (Cincinnati, 1926), p. 114.

[8] Cleveland *Leader and Herald*, Aug. 7, 1891.

when the upper class had been most successful and secure. That very success had set in motion one of the economic shocks weakening its position. As the black public school teachers had themselves predicted during the intraracial debate on school integration, their positions had been sacrificed in the name of the panacea of mixed schools. Black teachers and school administrators had been forced out into a market which did not welcome the talents of educated, intellectual blacks; some went immediately to nearby border states in order to continue their teaching careers, thus depriving Ohio of their leadership, while others had stayed in Ohio to seek other dignified and well-paying work. Some succeeded. Ira Collins lost his position as principal of Hamilton's black schools when they finally closed in the 1890s; he then entered the church, the only other racial institution which could offer a career and livelihood, and resurfaced a decade later as an A.M.E. minister at Cleveland.[9] Most, however, found the transition more difficult. Having lost his position as principal of Dayton's black school, W. O. Bowles also surfaced at Cleveland in the 1890s—but as a barber who owned a small shop catering to whites. He unsuccessfully attempted to play a role in local politics; at the same time, bad investments, first in an ephemeral race newspaper and then in a printing firm, worsened his financial situation.[10] Others came to depend on the uncertainties of patronage, or on the civil service. After losing his job at Cincinnati's Gaines High School, Samuel Clark used his influence with black politicians and fellow Masons Jere Brown and George Myers to win a clerkship with the state legislature in the early 1890s; he continued to feed at the political trough until his death in 1903, though not without having to change jobs periodically.[11] After Daniel Guy finished his thirteen years as principal of the black school at Newark, Ohio, he labored at various trades before finally entering the postal service.[12]

Teaching was not the only employment opportunity lost to many upper-class blacks, for, as was noted earlier, the service trades and enterprises had begun to slip away from the race. Barbershops closed and waiters and cooks found it difficult to get employment, bringing crises to a number of once-secure families. The decline of the livery business after the development of the internal combustion engine

[9] Cleveland *Gazette*, Aug. 13, 1908; Cleveland *Plain Dealer*, Nov. 3, 1908.
[10] Cleveland *Gazette*, Apr. 15, 1893, June 23, Dec. 22, 1894, Jan. 5, 1895.
[11] Ibid., Feb. 28, 1903; Jere Brown to George Myers, July 5, Aug. 12, 1893, Box I, folder 3, Samuel Clark to George A. Myers, Feb. 22, 1894, Box I, folder 4, and Oct. 7, 1895, Box I, folder 6, and undated clipping, source unknown, "Masonic Authority, Samuel Clark" [obituary], Box XVIII, folder 3, Myers Papers.
[12] [Daniel M. Guy], *Colored American Magazine*, XI (Dec., 1906), 418–420.

caused grave problems for the Harlan family, for example; the Colonel's grandson found that he was unable to earn a living at this formerly money-making enterprise, a difficult situation for a young man just starting out in the world. Robert Harlan, Jr., whose own father had made sure before his death that his son was provided with a patronage post in a federal agency, wrote in the same vein in 1910 to a friend with political influence: "Automobiles have put the livery business to the bad; hence, my son finds it a desperate struggle to meet obligations, and very slight prospects of saving make him anxious to retire from that business if he can get employment. Can you help him?" [13]

Most upper-class families with such service businesses probably lacked the political influence of the powerful Harlans. At the same time, few if any showed the desire to make a transition from the old white-oriented service enterprises, with their genteel traditions forged over decades of catering to affluent whites, to the new race-oriented ones appearing in the inner city neighborhoods. The result was that children who did not desire to go to college and then obtain professional training, or who could not afford to do so, might very well have to start out at the bottom, walking the uncertain avenues of black opportunity in Ohio. George Myers's son Herbert was in some ways atypical, for his father's barbershop was very prosperous and the elder Myers had influential political ties. But George Myers's ruggedly individualistic, conservative attitudes toward the value of hard work and the character-building function of individual struggle led him to refuse to intervene too actively in his son's behalf. ("I paddled my own canoe," he wrote to a friend, reflecting on his son's problems in making a career.) Herbert Myers's situation at the very end of the period suggests the plight of those without influence and without the benefit of the old service opportunities. In 1915 young Myers was at work as a laborer in an automobile factory, hoping, in spite of discrimination in the hiring of skilled employees, that he might eventually be promoted to the drafting department.[14]

Under such circumstances a number of young men undoubtedly left the state to try their luck elsewhere. They joined others of the upper class who were also in search of better positions. A number of these transplanted black Ohioans were chronic officeholders and minor political time-servers who had come to depend on patronage for a livelihood and who went where the political breezes took them. By the early twentieth century there was at Washington, D.C., what George

---

[13] Robert Harlan, Jr., to Whitefield McKinlay, Sept. 13, 1910, Box II, folder 28, Carter Woodson Collection, LC.

[14] George Myers to Daniel Murray, Sept. 20, 1915, Daniel Murray Papers, HU.

Myers referred to as an "Ohio Colony"[15] of black civil servants and patronage employees which had been built up during the decades since the race had obtained the vote and a measure of political power. It was composed of some temporary appointees whose jobs would end with a change of administrations or at the whim of their political patrons, and of others who were firmly entrenched in the civil service. Milton Holland of Athens was a Civil War hero who had left Ohio in 1880 to take a government clerical post and returned now and then only to vote and campaign for Republican candidates;[16] William Clifford and Charles Fillmore left Ohio in the late 1890s for clerkships at the War Department, where Robert Harlan, Jr., already worked.[17]

Complementing the economic difficulties were destructive forces of a more social and cultural nature—old sources of weakness and disunity. One of these involved "passing," which ultimately weakened the race and the upper class, even though it tended to work to the benefit of the individual. There is, of course, no way to estimate the number of persons whose ancestors were Negro, by their own reckoning and the conventional categorization of the day, but who themselves had been bleached "white" by 1910. Harry Smith was willing to venture in 1914 that fully 3,000 of what he estimated to be 20,000 Cleveland Negroes (much above the official police and census figures) were light enough to elude racial identification by the average white citizen, such as the census-taker; by implication these people were able to pass between the races at will.[18] Yet the very nature of "passing," totally dependent on the ignorance and credulity of the white world and the ability of those in racial transit to keep their origins secret, precludes an accurate accounting. However, given the lightness of much of the late nineteenth-century Negro upper class and the prevalence of the "blue vein" ethos, with its insistence upon marrying lighter and lighter until the goal of whiteness was achieved, it is more than likely that at least a few were attempting a change of identity by 1910. The increasing rigidity of the color line provided more than ample reason for a light-skinned individual to opt for, at the very least, the *convenience* of being white—even if at the same time not believing in the superiority attributed to whiteness. Furthermore, "passing" may well have become easier by the turn of the century, for the presence of millions of

[15] The term is frequently mentioned in Myers's correspondence.

[16] Milton Holland to Charles Kurtz, Nov. 26, 1880, Box X, folder 4, Charles Kurtz Papers, OHS.

[17] Cleveland *Gazette*, Feb. 1, 1902; Baltimore *Afro-American Ledger*, Sept. 5, 1908; [Charles Fillmore], *Colored American Magazine*, XII (Apr., 1907), 306, 311–312.

[18] Cleveland *Gazette*, May 9, 1914.

swarthy southeastern European immigrants, particularly Italians, then streaming into the nation helped to further confuse the physiognomy of racial and ethnic identity. Dabney, that perceptive chronicler of Cincinnati's black community, noted the case of a turn-of-the-century family composed of a light-complexioned mother and three probably still lighter children, the product of her liaison with a southern white man. The four turned white en route from their native Alabama to their new home at Cincinnati. In an effort to further this transition, the mother attempted to learn Italian with native fluency. She died before her own experiment with identity could be completed, but one of her daughters, whether posing as an Italian or not is unclear, did succeed in marrying the son of a white businessman.[19]

This is but one of several local examples which Dabney records of affluent upper-class Negro families in transit between races.[20] Elsewhere there is little direct evidence, but the historian must look skeptically at the mysterious disappearance of certain once-prominent Negro families from mention in the extant records of black community affairs after the turn of the century. Columbus's Roneys were said to be the color of "spring butter" in the 1870s—light enough, at that time, to have been the cutting edge of a Columbus theater owner's unsuccessful attempt to begin seating mulattoes in the white-only parquette section of the main floor.[21] The Roney family is conspicuously absent from community activities in the later years of the period, following very intense involvement in all facets of Columbus's black affairs in the immediate post-bellum decades. They are but one example. To be sure, impoverishment, death, aging, barrenness, emigration, social and political quietism, and simply the incompleteness of the historical record must also be considered in appraising such cases. But so must "passing," the act by which descendants of families like the Roneys could move to another city or state and cast off old ties, freeing themselves forever of the burden of being black.

If the extent of passage between the races is unclear, it *is* clear that the light-skinned tendency toward social exclusivity remained a source of tension and division within the upper class. The formalized blue vein structures were dead by 1900, but an informal pattern of personal relations among the near white continued to separate them from the dark complected. This was particularly evident at Cleveland. Though the city's Social Circle had collapsed, a victim of the changing interests and residential dispersal of its members, its spirit lived on. A young

19 Dabney, *Cincinnati's Colored Citizens*, pp. 175–176.
20 Ibid.
21 Columbus *Dispatch*, Dec. 2, 6, 1873.

Cleveland black anxious to dispel a long-standing local reputation wrote in 1903 that blue veinism "only existed years ago when meritorious people were more light than dark," averring that "People are now judged on merit alone." [22] But a less partial observer from Columbus noted three years later that Cleveland possessed "a class of fair-skinned Negroes who . . . scorn the darker-skinned Negroes" and remained isolated in their own exclusive circles, hindering the development of racial unity.[23]

While they might try to remain aloof from the race, the old light-skinned elite was not everywhere as prominent as it was at Cleveland. Cincinnati's much more ostentatious aristocracy was clearly in eclipse by 1900; the old big-spending, high-living, party-throwing elite of affluent stewards, butlers, and shopkeepers had burned itself out. Said Dabney of this decline: "Sadly, certain families began to realize that the imitation of millionaires has pain as well as pleasures." Such was the tragic history of the Tinsleys, whose lavish parties, opulent lifestyle, and large charitable contributions had caught up with them. John Tinsley had been a steward at a gambling club and received large tips out of winnings; he had lived beyond his means for years, and finally brought misery upon his family. His wife died an aged pauper, leaving behind only her blind daughter, once a favorite of Negro society, now alone, impoverished, and dependent.[24]

Perhaps, as Dabney suggests, Mrs. Tinsley's tragedy was "not that she outlived her contemporaries, but that she had outlived her money"; she was forced by a "reckless imitation of millionaires" to live out her days with only daydreams of a vanished glory to sustain her. Yet in the light of contemporary racial history, her tragedy becomes more a part of the larger crisis of her class, and hence, ultimately, of the people it was supposed to lead. The Tinsleys' fall did not mark the passing of a family deeply involved in racial life—with the exception of their charities, they, like many other members of Cincinnati's post-bellum black high society, had been aloof from the struggles of the masses. Yet the social and economic ills of the upper class had great ramifications. Faced with deteriorating race relations, the upper class was at the same time the victim of its own weaknesses. Marginal within the economy, and sharing the bourgeois culture of a respectable white America which increasingly refused to accept it, black high society

[22] Nahum Brascher, "Cleveland: A Representative American City," *Voice of the Negro*, II (Aug., 1905), 532–533.

[23] Pearl Chavers, *Conditions That Confront the Colored People* (Columbus, 1908), p. 8.

[24] Dabney, *Cincinnati's Colored Citizens,* pp. 152–153.

lived untenably between two worlds: one white, powerful, and confident; the other black, poor, and despised. From this increasingly insecure racial netherworld, it was forced to respond to time, which signaled the bankruptcy of its hopes.

Early hints of a recognition that the crisis in race relations threatened past goals and of a questioning, still tentative, assessment of past
racial strategy took two related forms. First, there was a growing tendency to seek intraclass unity in order to relate more effectively to the
trends of the times; second, a quiet, voluntary, and partial retreat from
the integrationist ethic of the past, which had insisted on maintaining
contacts with higher-status whites, was evident. The movement toward
intraracial unity, as well as growing concern for the crisis in race relations, was evident in the changing orientation of Ohio's black women's
clubs. At the turn of the century they began to seek greater contact
with one another and to express less interest in their traditional activities—art, teas, and luncheons—and more in racial service. The immediate catalyst of this development was the founding in 1896 of the
National Association of Colored Women, dedicated to a national unification of club women and to relating club work to racial advancement.[25] The N.A.C.W.'s Ohio branch was formed in 1901 by a small
coalition of older upper-class women, such as Carrie Clifford, Jere
Brown's sister Hallie Quinn Brown of Wilberforce, and the wives of
Cleveland artisan John Bolden, Wilberforce Professor Horace Tolbert,
and Columbus ex-city councilman I. D. Ross. Its first convention set
the tone for the branch's interests in coming years and demonstrated
the extent to which the ethos of the N.A.C.W. took root in Ohio. Resolutions denounced lynching, segregation, and disfranchisement, and
discussions examined how black constitutional rights might be conserved. A paper given by a Cleveland school teacher denounced blue-
veinism as "a social cancer," while other papers dealt with the need to
inculcate bourgeois standards of conduct and values in the masses. A
similar unification of clubs was concurrently taking place at the local
level throughout Ohio.[26]

While the club women had never had contacts with their white
counterparts, black doctors had often had professional contacts with
white colleagues. For this reason their movement toward professional
solidarity along racial lines was a significant departure from past prac-

[25] Robert Factor, *The Black Response to America: Men, Ideals, and Organizations from Frederick Douglas to the NAACP* (Reading, 1970), pp. 111–115.

[26] Cleveland *Gazette*, Dec. 28, 1901, Jan. 4, 1902, Aug. 1, 1903, July 22, 1905;
Cleveland *Leader*, Dec. 28, 1901; Cleveland *Plain Dealer*, Dec. 28, 29, 1901;
Xenia *Gazette*, July 21, 1903.

tice. The impetus for this movement was provided in 1897 by a well-established physician, Springfield's Thomas Burton, who organized a black "Ohio Mutual Medical Society." Burton explained that while black doctors "in good standing" were admitted to Ohio's medical societies, the time had arrived for them to seek greater professional contact with one another. At first even he seemed unsure of the wisdom of such separation—he insisted that, if they cared to join, qualified whites would be accepted. The movement suffered for several years from this lack of ideological certainty and a division among upper-class physicians on the need for such professional separation. After a lapse into inactivity, it was revived in 1905; increasingly legitimized by an era of racial hostility, its annual meetings were attended by growing numbers of black doctors.[27]

An even more certain sign of changing times was the growing tendency of upper-class black members of prestigious white denominations to organize their own congregations. After 1890 at each of Ohio's three largest cities, black Episcopalians who had been members of missions which shared close relations with white parent congregations departed to establish independent congregations. After some years of mission status, black Presbyterians at Cincinnati did the same; in 1901 they founded Ohio's first black church of the faith. Where black Episcopalians for many years had worshiped right alongside whites, black missions were now being founded—one at Youngstown in 1908, at the initiative of Lenora Berry of the Berry artisan clan, and one each at Dayton and Toledo in 1909. While tied to white churches, these missions were steps in the direction of congregational autonomy. There is no evidence that the new black missions and churches were a product of forced separation.[28] Instead, they appear simply to mirror the mood of the times: a mood which caused even higher-status whites, who had supported that religious connection and had desired it as a recognition of their humanity, to perceive race as a potent, perhaps immutable barrier. The fact that moves toward congregational autonomy were initiated by blacks themselves confirms the changing mood of race relations. To be sure, there was still no sign that the black upper class had renounced its commitment to entering the American mainstream, or to its post-Reconstruction racial strategy. Yet, marking a compromise of the single most prevalent form of contact it had enjoyed with whites

[27] Thomas Burton, *What Experience Has Taught Me* (Springfield, 1910), pp. 67–75; Cleveland *Gazette*, May 27, 1905, June 17, 1911.
[28] Cleveland *Leader*, June 17, 1901; Cincinnati *Commercial Tribune*, July 1, 1901; Cleveland *Gazette*, Apr. 12, Dec. 7, 1901, June 27, 1903; Indianapolis *Freeman*, June 12, 1909, June 19, Aug. 14, Sept. 11, 1905.

of equivalent social status, the retreat from religious bonds signaled the depth of its crisis of confidence.

All that remained for that crisis to be complete was for politics, the primary means by which equality had been pursued, to be rendered a less potent weapon.

II

In the first years after their legislative triumph of 1887 there was little sign that politics had lost its ability to interest blacks and to work for their benefit. Those years found the black position in Ohio politics very much the same as before, aided by the unstable political situation in which third- and fourth-party movements remained active, control over state politics fluctuated, and Republican majorities stood at less than 20,000 and dipped as low as Harrison's 1,072 in the 1892 presidential election.[29] Blacks could continue to claim control of a balance of power, not only in a number of smaller constituencies, but in the state at large; hence they could threaten political independence if their power was not recognized by the Republicans.

Legislators and governors, whether Republican or Democratic, remained sensitive to the will of black voters. Black legislators and a respect for black opinion and political power among their white colleagues checked segregationists' efforts to reintroduce separate school legislation during the 1888 and 1889 sessions of a Republican-controlled legislature. Democrats accepted the new racial status quo created by the legislation of the 1880s and remained concerned with the race's desires. When that party regained control of the legislature in 1890, black petitions and the efforts of Representative John Green conveyed strong enough opposition to a local option bill on school integration that Democrats did not even allow the bill to leave committee.[30]

Backed up by lobbying and petitions, black legislators made more positive gains. In order to take financial pressure off struggling Wilberforce University, Representative Arnett won the creation of a small, state-supported teacher training and vocational program, open to both races, at the Wilberforce campus in 1887. The amount of state support was pitifully small at first, just over $2,000 a year. Black legislators gradually won larger appropriations for the program, reaching $16,000

[29] W. Dean Burnham, *Presidential Ballots, 1836–1892* (Baltimore, 1955), p. 249; Ohio, *Statistics, 1913*, pp. 261–264.

[30] Cleveland *Gazette*, Jan. 7, Mar. 10, 1888, Feb. 2, 9, Mar. 23, 1889, Mar. 9, 15, 29, Apr. 5, 1890; Ohio, *House Journal, 1888*, p. 52, *1889*, p. 538, and *1890*, p. 408.

a year in 1893. In 1889 Jere Brown gained a significant measure for racial welfare when he pushed through a bill to outlaw the common practice of charging blacks higher rates for life insurance. Not long after, changes were won in the weak 1884 Civil Rights Law, which fared poorly in its few court tests. In 1893 State Senator John Green and Representative George Jackson introduced competing bills to amend the law, but the Republican legislature was so impressed with the need to pass such a bill that it refused to act until the two men resolved their differences. In the following year a bill introduced by newly elected Representative Harry Smith passed by wide margins in both houses of the Republican-controlled assembly. Rounding out this run of positive legislation was the 1896 anti-lynching law. Also initiated by black legislators, its history was similar to that of the amendments to the Civil Rights Law. Here also the white majority sought to discover whether Ohio black opinion favored William Clifford's or Harry Smith's anti-lynching measure; this division among the blacks helped to cause a delay in final action on anti-lynching legislation, from 1894 until 1896.[31]

Blacks continued to receive state patronage no matter which party was in power. Democrats like Herbert Clark and Hamilton's Joseph Alexander and Republicans like Jere Brown and Chillicothe's Charles R. Doll continued to hold clerkships in various departments of state government when their respective parties were in power. After 1890 blacks won the right to contend actively, and often successfully, for positions as chief legislation clerks and sergeants-at-arms of both houses, whether controlled by Republicans or Democrats. Andrew Jackson Davidson was sergeant-at-arms of the Democratic House in 1890 and 1891. Following the Republican takeover, John Cisco of Cleveland and B. F. Allen of Findlay were appointed as Senate enrolling clerk and House engrossing clerk for the 1892 and 1893 sessions; they were replaced by other blacks in Republican legislatures between 1894 and 1897. Black men did not yet serve as members of a governor's cabinet, leading large bureaucracies and determining major policies. But some of the most articulate and able black men, like George Hayes and

31 On the aid to Wilberforce: Frederick A. McGinnis, *A History and Interpretation of Wilberforce University* (Blanchester, Ohio, 1941), pp. 56–57, 110–128; Ohio, *Laws, 1887*, p. 127; Ohio, *Laws, 1892*, p. 340; Cleveland *Gazette*, Dec. 1, 1888. But though open to students of both races, the state-supported program attracted only blacks until well into the twentieth century, largely because it existed on a black campus. On the insurance law: Ohio, *Laws, 1889*, pp. 163–164; Cleveland *Gazette*, Jan. 28, Feb. 11, 1888, Feb. 2, Mar. 30, Apr. 3, 1889. On the amendments to the Civil Rights Law: Cleveland *Gazette*, Jan. 14, 28, Apr. 1, 8, 15, May 6, 1893, Jan. 27, Feb. 3, 10, 1894; Ohio, *Laws, 1894*, pp. 17–18. On the anti-lynching law: see above, pp. 250–253.

Ira Collins, continued to serve as trustees of important state welfare and educational institutions and helped to set policies and standards which governed their activities.[32]

In recognition of their power, blacks continued to sit in the highest councils of the Republican party. In 1892 three blacks served on the state central committee which managed Ohio's Republican presidential campaign; they continued to serve regularly on that committee throughout the next twenty-odd years. Blacks regularly acted as full delegates at state Republican conventions. While Republican leaders did not consider their numbers large enough to merit choice as delegates to national conventions, they regularly served as alternates. By their own admission, black Republicans would have served in larger numbers had they united behind the candidacies of several prospective delegates, rather than standing divided along factional and geographic lines.[33]

As before, blacks frequently had to make threats and demands, and they often failed to get their way. In constituencies where the balance-of-power argument did not apply, they were unable to force recognition in the distribution of patronage. The dearth and the narrow range of patronage, relative to what they thought they deserved, were primary sources of local grievances. In 1890 Cleveland blacks were angered over the failure of local Republicans to appoint a black fireman; this issue would go unresolved for many years, largely because white firemen resisted the integrated living conditions which their work would require if blacks were appointed. Ironton blacks were angered in that same year because they had been promised a letter carrier's job, only to find after election day that an Irish policeman, already making a respectable $50 a week, was given the spot. The next year found Cincinnati blacks angered over their failure to obtain Republican patronage in proportion to their numbers, and displeased that what jobs they did get were usually low-paying and menial.[34] At Dayton, Chillicothe, and Springfield, white Republicans seemed more willing to corrupt blacks with beer and boodle on election day than to find them public employment.[35]

[32] W. A. Taylor, *Ohio Statesman and Hundred Year Book* (Columbus, 1892), pp. 415–416, 577, 606; Cleveland *Gazette*, June 23, 1890, June 21, 1891, Aug. 13, Dec. 3, 10, 17, 1892, Jan. 14, 1893, Jan. 6, 1894, Nov. 16, 23, 1895, Jan. 11, 18, 1896.
[33] Cleveland *Gazette*, Apr. 30, June 25, July 2, 1892.
[34] For these incidents and aspects of the patronage situation at Cleveland, Ironton, and Cincinnati: Cleveland *Gazette*, July 19, Oct. 10, 1890, July 4, 1891; Cleveland *Plain Dealer*, Apr. 1, 1902.
[35] Cleveland *Gazette*, Apr. 18, July 18, 1891, Feb. 29, 1896; Chillicothe *Advertiser*, Feb. 23, Aug. 31, 1894.

But tough talk and a willingness to consider an independent or even Democratic course continued to exert some influence. As long as Cleveland's Democracy consented to nominate a black politician for the legislature (as it did in 1891), and as long as Harry Smith's *Gazette* continued to threaten to lead a boycott of Republican candidates, Cleveland Republicans had to be cautious in the handling of their black allies. Thus, while Cleveland blacks did not get their fireman, they did get a policeman, and the number of blacks on the municipal payroll rose steadily during the 1890s.[36] As long as Cincinnati blacks were willing to consider what William Parham characterized as "a political revolution among the colored voters," white Republicans could not disregard their demands for more and better jobs. By 1896, in fact, black public employment at Cincinnati had been upgraded; though the numbers were still small, black deputy sheriffs and clerks were by no means as rare as they once had been.[37] Moreover, at both Cleveland and Cincinnati, black Republicans continued to be nominated and elected to the legislature.[38]

Though they were unsuccessful in obtaining nominations for the legislature, tough talk was no longer necessary for Columbus blacks wishing power in local affairs. Blacks, such as teacher J. J. Lee and lawyer Wilbur King, continued to be elected to both the city council and the school board; the growing black population in East Long Street wards only reinforced this unparalleled situation. While at Columbus the growing black vote played a significant, though not conclusive, role in establishing black political influence, this could not be said of Youngstown, where the black vote in the 1890s was too small to be crucial. Yet so respected was black attorney William R. Steward that he received an overwhelming vote in the 1895 local Republican nominating convention; he ran in front of several white Republicans on the ticket that fall.[39]

In the smaller municipalities, where blacks constituted much larger percentages of local populations, their power continued to be great. Xenia's blacks controlled the politics of their Fourth Ward, regularly electing black councilmen and ward assessors.[40] Oberlin

[36] Cleveland *Gazette*, Aug. 23, 1890, Apr. 25, 1891, July 6, 1893; Cleveland *Plain Dealer*, Sept. 19, 24, 27, 1891.

[37] Cleveland *Gazette*, May 2, 1891, Apr. 30, May 2, 30, Sept. 3, 1892, May 30, 1896.

[38] Cleveland *Plain Dealer*, Nov. 4, 1891, Nov. 9, 1893, Nov. 11, 1895; Cincinnati *Times-Star*, Nov. 4, 1891, Nov. 9, 1893, Nov. 11, 1895.

[39] Cleveland *Gazette*, Apr. 8, 1893, May 25, 1895; Youngstown *Telegraph*, May 20, 27, Nov. 6, 1895.

[40] Cleveland *Gazette*, Apr. 16, 1892, Apr. 8, 1893.

blacks boasted in 1891 of their "five important positions in municipal government," which included a councilman; they regularly enjoyed representation on important municipal boards through election at the hands of the entire community.[41] And at Rendville, in southern Perry County, a situation existed which was without equal in contemporary Ohio. This 1,000-member mining community was populated by almost equal numbers of blacks and whites. The races cooperated to such an extent that during the 1880s and 1890s the town had several black mayors, and blacks had ample, sometimes controlling, representation on all municipal boards.[42]

During the early 1890s, therefore, Ohio blacks were gaining power and influence while also obtaining the passage of ameliorative legislation. Their victories were helping them to consolidate the racial program of the immediate post-bellum decades which had sought strong civil rights legislation, public employment, and public power as integral parts of a larger strategy aimed at bringing about equality and social acceptance. Yet these very successes contained within them the germ of a new black political situation. After the passage of Harry Smith's innovative anti-lynching law in 1896, Ohio blacks believed that their major legislative requirements had been completed. There would not be another major proposal for comprehensive legislation to correct racial injustice before 1916. Those few black-sponsored bills were aimed not at positing bold remedies for racial ills, but at strengthening the civil rights and anti-lynching laws in response to newly revealed constitutional and practical defects.[43] The fulfillment of the black legislative program demanded thought and intraracial debate about the purposes of black politics. Blacks could devote themselves solely to the continued pursuit of patronage and public power, assuming a purely defensive stance on legislation, as they did in opposing the 1913 anti-intermarriage bill and bills introduced in 1902, 1904, 1910, 1913, and 1915 to regulate and license barbers, elevator operators, masseurs, manicurists, and chiropodists.[44] But if

---

[41] Ibid., Apr. 4, 1891, Apr. 15, May 6, 1893.

[42] Ibid., Mar. 24, 1888, Apr. 11, 1891, May 6, 1893.

[43] Ibid., Apr. 23, Sept. 17, 1898, Mar. 10, 31, Apr. 21, 1900, Feb. 5, Apr. 16, 1910.

[44] Much to the dismay of barbers' union officials and public health and safety officers, their efforts were always successful—except in 1915, when the issue was compromised. Under any circumstances, their concerns were probably exaggerated, for the legislation they opposed was invariably aimed only at enforcing in these trades and professions minimum safety, sanitary, and technical standards which had been sorely lacking in the past. Yet the barbers' union, which campaigned for legislation to regulate its trade, was the object of intense suspicion among blacks; though it contained a few black members in Ohio, it did not

they chose not to adopt such a defensive position, new concepts of racial goals would have to evolved to suit a new situation and regain an initiative. Blacks might reflect, for example, on how their political power could be used to counter the growth of reaction and repression in the South. Or, closer to home, they might ask what new relationships could be established between government, the growing reform movement of white social justice advocates, and racial welfare. How might blacks relate their needs and influence to movements for social insurance or workingmen's compensation, or for better public recreational and health facilities?

But such questions were not debated among Ohio's established black leaders. In the first place, forums in which such questions might be discussed had all but disappeared by the 1890s. With the accomplishment of major black goals in the 1880s, the times had seemed to call for a relaxation of organized efforts. The first and almost immediate victims of this attitude were the equal rights leagues, which had been organized in the mid-1880s to lobby for a civil rights bill and had also lobbied for repeal of the separate school and anti-miscegenation laws. The leagues were disbanded or fell into disuse once their goals had been enacted by the legislature.[45] State and regional racial conventions, which had been the most important forums for discussing racial issues, declined sharply in number after the 1880s. Harry Smith, for one, believed that they were no longer needed because Ohio blacks could bring up problems and issues for discussion in integrated forums. As early as 1885 he had stated, "Instead of holding black men's conventions, let us meet each other, both white and black, in our representative gatherings and there fight it out on the line."[46]

Given this relaxed, optimistic mood, a perfect forum for the evolu-

actively organize the black barbers working in black-owned shops who constituted the large majority of blacks in the trade. In addition, similar laws in Ohio and other states which regulated plumbers (above, p. 303) and electricians did ultimately work against blacks. However, the bills introduced to govern barbering did not give unions anywhere near the power which these laws did. Doubtless suspicion of the barbers' union and of unions generally spilled over into suspicion of proposals to regulate the practice of barbering. For black lobbying efforts: Columbus *Dispatch*, Feb. 5, 1902, Mar. 9, 1904; Cleveland *Journal*, Feb. 27, 1904; Cleveland *Gazette*, Jan. 9, Mar. 27, Apr. 24, 1915; George Myers to Henry Eubanks, Feb. 8, 1910, Box XV, folder 3, and B. F. Stewart to George Myers, Mar. 6, 12, 13, Apr. 28, 1913, Box XVI, folder 2, Myers Papers; W. Scott Hall, *The Journeyman Barber's International Union of America* (Baltimore, 1936), pp. 61–86.

45 Only at Cincinnati does it seem possible that one of the leagues was retained for a few years, for a "Civil Rights League" existed in the city in the late 1880s and early 1890s. It is not known, however, if this organization was an outgrowth of the earlier one; Cleveland *Gazette*, May 6, 1886, Mar. 12, 1887, Feb. 7, 1891.

46 Ibid., May 2, 1885.

tion of new goals, T. Thomas Fortune's Afro-American League, had little chance of surviving in Ohio. By the late 1880s Fortune, the influential editor of a New York City race newspaper, had begun to believe that a nonpartisan, national black organization was needed to influence public opinion on racial questions and to press black legal and constitutional claims in the courts. A national steering committee was selected in 1890, and local organizations began to appear in Ohio and other states. But while there was interest in Ohio, there was little of the urgency which Fortune felt. From the beginning local leagues and the state organization were divided by political and other rivalries, all of which took precedence over the larger aims suggested by Fortune. Within a few years the movement was dead in Ohio.[47]

Yet if forums were lacking, so were the ideas to debate within them. The development of new legislative and reform concerns was checked by the commitment of black leaders to the conservative ideology of the dominant white elite. Like the white upper class, the black one was dedicated to the values of hard work and thrift, to individual pursuit of wealth and status, and to a neutral role of government in the economy. Race leaders had been willing to see the role of government grow in order that black rights might be established and conserved— but this was very different from an espousal of the welfare state as then advocated by a vanguard of white social reformers. The intention was to clear the field of caste restraints so that blacks might compete for wealth, status, and power on the same terms with whites. Beyond that, black leaders were loath to envision the expansion of government protection of anyone's welfare—black or white. Black Ohioans who considered the legislative requirements of black citizenship in their state demanded only protection of basic civil rights, quality integrated education, and freedom from mob violence. After these were guaranteed by law, they trusted the courts to see to the matter of enforcement. Yet such a conceptualization of the relationship of law and the state to race relations was quite advanced for the time. Black rights were daily violated or simply nullified in the South; in the North, few states with black populations as large as Ohio's had come as far in integrating education, protecting civil rights, and opposing lynching by the turn of the century.[48]

[47] Emma Lou Thornborough, "The National Afro-American League," *Journal of Southern History*, XXVII (Nov., 1961), 494–512; Cleveland *Gazette*, Nov. 9, 16, 30, 1889, Jan. 18, Feb. 1, 22, May 24, 31, Aug. 23, Oct. 18, 1890; New York *Age*, Dec. 7, 14, 1889; Columbus *Dispatch*, May 20, 21, 22, 1890.

[48] By the first years of this century most northern states had relatively comprehensive civil rights laws. In the matter of school segregation, however, New

If ideology checked the possible emergence of new goals, a changing balance of political forces in Ohio and the nation also fostered the belief that blacks would not continue to have their former influence. The unstable political situation between 1876 and 1896 had allowed northern blacks to claim that their united vote determined Republican victory or defeat in presidential elections; however, the firm establishment of Republican hegemony in the 1894 midterm elections and McKinley's decisive victory over Bryan in 1896 destroyed that argument. Until the 1910 Democratic congressional victories and Wilson's 1912 triumph, the Republicans were more secure than at any time since Reconstruction. This situation had its complement in Ohio. After Harrison's mere 1,072-vote majority in 1892, Republican majorities in the elections of 1896, 1900, 1904, and 1908 ranged between 48,500 and 255,421 (the latter for Roosevelt's victory in 1904). In 1912 and 1916, Wilson received majorities of 90,000 and 100,000, and became the first Democrat since Franklin Pierce in 1850 to win Ohio's electoral votes.[49]

A similar trend was present in Ohio's internal affairs. With McKinley's 81,000-vote majority in the gubernatorial election of 1893, the largest of any candidate for governor since 1863, Ohio Republicans had begun to establish the foundations for more than a decade of firm control of state politics. Their gubernatorial majorities averaged 72,000, ranging as high as 93,000 in 1895 and 114,000 in 1903, and with lows of 49,000 in 1899 and an uncharacteristic 28,000 in 1897. Substantial legislative majorities often accompanied these victories.[50] While blacks might still claim to hold strategic positions in some counties and muncipalities, the size of their vote was not as impressive as it had once been: according to the census, black males over twenty years of age numbered 25,976 in 1890 and 38,290 in 1910.[51] Even taking into account the possibility that urban black males were undercounted,

York did not integrate until 1900; Indiana chose local option on the question in 1877, and this remained the state's policy until well into the twentieth century. Indiana continued to have an anti-miscegenation, anti-intermarriage statute as well. Ohio's anti-discrimination insurance law of 1889 was a pioneering effort, copied by New York, Massachusetts, Michigan, and Connecticut before 1910. With regard to remedies for lynching, many states eventually copied the Ohio anti–mob violence law, but often not until after 1916. Gilbert Stephenson, *Race Distinctions in American Law* (New York, 1910), pp. 55–56, 120–121, 163–164, 177–189; James Harmon Chadbourn, *Lynching and the Law* (Chapel Hill, 1933), pp. 149–213.

[49] Ohio, *Statistics, 1913*, pp. 261–264; Hoyt Landon Warner, *Progressivism in Ohio, 1897–1917* (Columbus, 1964), pp. 375, 481.

[50] Ohio, *Statistics, 1905*, pp. 163–165, and *1913*, pp. 261–264.

[51] Census Office, *Eleventh Census*, I, pt. 2, pp. 72–73; *Thirteenth Census*, I, 394.

and assuming that *every* eligible black voted regularly, the old balance-of-power argument had been dealt a severe blow. Harry Smith saw the new trend and dropped the argument from his established repertoire of editorials threatening white Republicans with a black electoral boycott. At the turn of the century he began to notice an ill omen: white Republicans seemed much less concerned with pleasing black voters.[52]

Republicans were not to exercise uninterrupted control over the state from 1900 to 1916. Beginning in 1905 Democrats, elected by large majorities, held the governorship continuously for a decade; in addition, they shared control of the legislature during the long session of 1906–8, and took control of it with large majorities in 1911–12 and 1913–14. (A constitutional amendment approved in 1905 shifted state elections to even years; thus terms which would have expired in 1907 were extended through 1908.) Democratic victories accounted for the fact that the long session was the first in over a quarter-century which lacked even a single black legislator. As usual, black candidates for the House had run at Cleveland and Cincinnati, but both had been defeated, along with the rest of the local Republican legislative tickets. The same situation would occur in the 1911–12 and 1913–14 sessions as the result of Democratic triumphs in legislative contests throughout Ohio. While Republicans retrieved control of the legislature in 1915, the black nominees for representative at both Cleveland and Columbus again went down to defeat with their tickets. The pre-war period ended as the post-enfranchisement period had begun: without a black in legislature.[53]

Difficult as it was for most black voters and politicians to confront a strong Democratic trend, it was even harder for them to come to terms with the underlying social and political ferment which the trend signaled. Unlikely as it might have seemed to those who remembered the opportunistic Democracy of the 1880s, Ohio Democrats would emerge as the political wing of the state's reformist progressive movement. This was especially true in the cities, where Democrats, under the lead of reformers such as Tom L. Johnson and Newton D. Baker of Cleveland and the Reverend Herbert Seeley Bigelow of Cincinnati, mobilized voters against the bossism, graft, and corruption which infested urban politics. Their success was by no means even; they were not in control everywhere or at all times in the last years of the period. But their movement was the dominant challenge to the political status

---

[52] Cleveland *Gazette*, Oct. 29, 1898, May 21, 1902, Nov. 12, 1910.
[53] Ibid., Nov. 7, 1914; Ohio, *Statistics, 1913*, pp. 261–264.

quo, and as such it commanded the attention of all those, black and white, who were active in political life.[54]

The transformation of the Democracy into a vehicle for reform brought thousands of once-partisan Republicans into a period of unprecedentedly independent voting.[55] Few of these new independents, however, were black. This is not because the reform movement was associated with the Democracy, or because reformers were anti-black. In fact, reformers often enjoyed reputations for tolerance and egalitarianism. Cleveland Mayor Tom Johnson had given George Myers a small loan to help him into business at the Hollenden, and he remained Myers's friend for many years. In an era when blacks never worked on urban streetcar lines as anything but unskilled laborers, after 1900 Johnson began to hire them as skilled workers on the streetcar line he owned.[56] His protege, Mayor Newton D. Baker, blocked efforts to segregate Cleveland's pubic recreational facilities.[57] Cincinnati's Bigelow, a Congregationalist minister who was chairman of the highly progressive 1912 Ohio constitutional convention, took pride that his church had been a stop on the Underground Railroad; at one point Bigelow had almost lost his job while successfully defending the right to membership of a Negro family.[58] Toledo Mayor Sam "Golden Rule" Jones, a Republican turned independent, invited leading black men and their wives into his home to visit *after* his 1897 electoral victory—a simple but dramatic and rare gesture, and one which could not be attributed to a desire for black votes.[59]

Black political leaders admired these men for their personal qualities and for such acts of racial liberalism, but they feared the likely consequences of much of their reform program for the precarious structure of black political influence. As a result, they found it difficult to contemplate alliances like the ones they had once made with the old Democracy in order to penalize Republicans for indifference to individual or racial welfare; this refusal narrowed the range of their political tactics. But black opposition to reform bore little resemblance

[54] Warner, *Progressivism in Ohio.*

[55] Ibid., pp. 23, 46.

[56] George Myers to James Ford Rhodes, Mar. 15, 1921, in John Garraty, ed., *The Barber and the Historian: The Correspondence of George A. Myers and James Ford Rhodes, 1910–1923* (Columbus, 1956), p. 127; Tom L. Johnson to George Myers, May 28, 1894, Box I, folder 5, Myers Papers; Cleveland *Gazette*, Oct. 8, 1892, July 13, 1897, May 4, Oct. 12, 19, 1901, Mar. 22, 1902, May 15, Oct. 23, 1909.

[57] George Myers to F. H. Goff, Jan. 17, 1916, Box XVII, folder 1, Myers Papers.

[58] Warner, *Progressivism in Ohio*, pp. 122–123; Dabney, *Cincinnati's Colored Citizens*, pp. 98–99; above, ch. 5, n. 95.

[59] Toledo *Bee*, March 14, 1899.

to that of deeply entrenched, machine-affiliated elements among white Republicans. Blacks did not seek the power to ride roughshod over an ignorant, apathetic electorate and fill their pockets with tens of thousands in graft; rather, they desired opportunities for a measure of power and decent employment for themselves and their people. Their opposition to reform was bred not of contempt for democracy, but of need and victimization, and it pitted black politicians against reformers not only in Ohio, but also in other places where reform challenged the political status quo.[60]

The gap between the reformers' program and the race's self-interest as its political leaders saw it was particularly evident in the struggle against bossism. Black leaders had been known to oppose Republican municipal bosses. At Cincinnati in 1891, a coalition of fifty-two highly respected racial spokesmen led by William Parham protested a system for dispensing black patronage which had developed under the aegis of the recently emerged, powerful machine of boss George B. Cox. They claimed in a declaration of principles not only that jobs awarded to blacks were menial, but that positions were assigned only "to some tool, sycophant, or favorite of some boss of high or low degree, and not from respect to the will or wish of colored men." They resolved that the rule of "acceptability to their people," which they thought would lead to recognition of more widely respected and respectable black men, rather than acceptability to white bosses, must govern dispensing of black patronage.[61] Harry Smith inveighed for almost two decades against Cleveland's "Little Black Tammany," averring that it attempted, on the basis of its ties to white bosses, "to boss, direct, control, and pose as leaders." He took special note of the tendency of white bosses to choose black men with vice and saloon connections (but with ties among the black poor in the neighborhoods) for appointments.[62]

Yet, rhetoric aside, these criticisms were not aimed as bossism per se, but at its function within and its effects upon the black community. As such, they boiled down to a matter of which black politicians were suffering most from the current workings of bossism. After the 1891 protests the Cox machine attempted to upgrade the quality of black appointments and the character of the men appointed; it secured legislative nominations not, as in the 1880s, for machine characters

---

[60] See, for example W. E. B. Du Bois, *The Philadelphia Negro: A Social Study* (Phildelphia, 1899), pp. 383–384, and David Katzman, *Before the Ghetto: Black Detroit in the Nineteenth Century* (Urbana, Ill., 1973), p. 165.

[61] Cleveland *Gazette*, Jan. 24, July 4, 1891.

[62] Ibid., Dec. 22, 1894, Feb. 1, Apr. 4, 1896, May 22, 1897.

like Colonel Harlan and William Copeland, a Cox regular who based his livelihood on patronage, but for respectable lawyers and teachers like George Jackson, Samuel Hill, and Parham himself. Blacks were also appointed to clerkships and inspectorships as well as menial and janitorial jobs. Criticisms of Cox and his allies then, diminished considerably.[63]

Smith's transparent criticisms of bossism always ultimately revealed his animosities toward black rivals in Cleveland. When members of the "Little Black Tammany" enjoyed unprecedented influence in the late 1890s with the elevation of George Myers's patrons (McKinley to the presidency and Hanna to the Senate), Smith watched his words, praised Myers for his work in their behalf, and waited patiently for his reward. When his hopes were dashed, he not only revived his criticisms of the "Little Black Tammany" and the dictates of black and white bosses; he even joined forces with the chief rival of the Hanna interests, the machine of Cleveland Mayor Robert McKisson.[64]

Thus, as long as the bosses triumphed and served black interests and needs, an opportunistic black leadership quite wisely chose to do business with them. Then came the reformers with their principled criticisms of machine politics. Reformers quickly placed black politicians in the same camp with the white bosses and their lieutenants, making them targets of the same criticisms leveled at white spoilsmen. Cleveland's progressive Municipal Association, founded in 1894 to promote clean government, refused to endorse Smith's legislative candidacy in 1899; allegedly he was subject to "machine domination" because of his affiliation with McKisson. When Smith's enemy, Henry Eubanks, proprietor of the Kennard House barbershop and a sometime Myers' ally, ran for the city council in 1901, he, too, failed to obtain the association's endorsement. Like other machine candidates, he was judged short on ability. The association instead endorsed a young white attorney, Frederic C. Howe, who had close ties with Tom Johnson and would emerge as one of the nation's leading reform intellectuals with the publication of his *The City: The Hope of Democracy* in 1905.[65]

Blacks greeted other parts of the reform program with the same ambiguity, opposing the reformers who they felt jeopardized race interests, but using the rhetoric and results of reform when such were

[63] Ibid., Sept. 3, 1892, Dec. 16, 1893, Dec. 7, 1895, May 30, 1896.
[64] Ibid., Feb. 18, Mar. 11, 1899, June 29, 1901; Cleveland *Plain Dealer*, Sept. 7, 1899.
[65] Cleveland *Leader*, Nov. 4, 1899, Feb. 18, 1901; Cleveland *Gazette*, Nov. 4, 1899.

beneficial. Placing civil service on the merit system, rather than on the basis of partisan reward, was of obvious concern to reformers. Even though it would potentially jeopardize the opportunities for poorly educated blacks to take government jobs, black politicians were little concerned with the problem for three reasons: the merit system did not yet govern every job; it could be circumscribed through influence; and literate blacks often passed civil service examinations. At Cleveland the merit system had made substantial inroads by 1910; Harry Smith reported that blacks were scoring well on exams, and he lamented that too few blacks were taking civil service tests.[66] Unsuccessful applicants could still get jobs through the right connections, particularly in the federal service. When Arnett's son Alonzo failed the examination necessary to placement as a census clerk, the bishop wrote to Ohio Congressman Charles Dick: ". . . I trust you will see your way clear to have him put on the roll as they do hundreds of others." In the case of his own son, Robert Harlan, Jr., wrote to his Washington contact: ". . . Don't let civil service stand in your way; if that is the only reason, it can be overcome," and he went on to imply that Ohio congressmen and senators were willing to exert their influence.[67] Thus reform did not need to be opposed at all; it became irrelevant.

Ohio blacks eventually became as blasé about the direct primary, a leading reform proposal for returning power to the public. When a system combining the direct primary and the nominating convention was introduced at Cuyahoga County in the late 1880s, Harry Smith feared that elimination of convention deals in exchange for places on the ticket would prevent blacks from receiving future nominations. The new system, he said, "allows race prejudice to go full sway. As part of this community we have a right to vote *and* nominate *and* be nominated *and* hold office. But this plan denies us the latter two privileges and we will not tolerate it." [68] But machine endorsement helped blacks to do well in the newly mandated primaries, and Smith himself obtained several nominations for the legislature. The system was dropped at the turn of the century because of opposition by the

[66] Cleveland *Gazette,* Jan. 30, Feb. 6, 1897, Feb. 14, 1914; Russell H. Davis, *Black Americans in Cleveland from George Peake to Carl B. Stokes* (Washington, 1972), pp. 96–97, 148–150.

[67] Benjamin Arnett to Charles Dick, July 8, 1900, Box VIII, folder 5, Myers Papers; Robert Harlan, Jr., to Whitefield McKinlay, Sept. 13, 1910, Box II, folder 28, Woodson Collection. Though he tried for some weeks, for some reason Dick was unable to fulfill the bishop's request; Benjamin Arnett to Charles Dick, Aug. 14, 1900, Box VIII, folder 5, Myers Papers.

[68] Cleveland *Gazette,* Mar. 30, 1889; Cleveland *Leader and Herald,* Sept. 28, 1889.

Hanna interests; Smith and other political "outs," black and white, naturally protested being thrown back into hostile nominating conventions.[69] A 1907 law making the direct primary mandatory in all state and local contests evoked little, if any, criticism from blacks, who henceforth continued to be nominated for office.[70]

Many did believe strongly that other proposals to establish greater popular control of government would harm the race. When confronted in 1912 by the campaign to ratify a highly progressive state charter, black politicians were concerned about provisions for municipal home rule and initiative and referendum. They feared that direct democracy and greater self-government for the cities would allow the worst racial passions of the white majority to find their way into law without checks from more judicious assemblies, particularly the state legislature. George Myers and other Clevelanders wrote a pamphlet calling for blacks to oppose both provisions: "If these amendments carry, a small minority of the voters can petition and may have laws passed that will affect us as a race. If you do not want segregation, separate schools, Jim Crow streetcars, and other discriminatory laws passed, urge every man to vote 'NO.'" [71] Both amendments passed decisively, and all blacks who shared these fears must have felt great anxiety as Toledo, Dayton, Columbus, and Cleveland took the challenge of the home rule amendment and drafted new charters providing for initiative and referendum.[72]

Columbus blacks had special fears. The new municipal charter contained provision for at-large elections for all local offices and municipal boards; reformers hoped these would check the political power of the easily corruptible inner-city poor and the ward heelers who controlled their votes, instead guaranteeing the hegemony of the respectable middle class. After the new charter was passed in 1914, blacks had little opportunity for representation on either the city council or the board of education for the first time in three decades.[73] In no other Ohio city did reform result in such a comprehensive political centralization, yet blacks outside the capital might logically see events there as illustrating a dominant trend: blacks were slowly losing the

[69] Cleveland *Gazette,* Apr. 4, June 6, 1903.

[70] Warner, *Progressivism in Ohio,* pp. 196–197.

[71] Cleveland Association of Colored Men, *Letter to the Public,* dated Aug. 21, 1912, Box XVI, folder 1, Myers Papers.

[72] Warner, *Progressivism in Ohio,* pp. 440–460.

[73] Ibid., pp. 444–445; J. S. Himes, "Forty Years of Negro Life in Columbus, Ohio," *Journal of Negro History,* XXVII (Apr., 1942), 136–137; William Giffin, "The Negro in Ohio, 1914–1939" (Ph.D. dissertation, Ohio State University, 1969), p. 101.

significant degree of political influence and power they had enjoyed in previous decades.

III

Ironically, while Democratic and reformist trends were gathering force around the turn of the century, there was a brief interlude in which Ohio black political influence, in state and nation, reached its zenith. This was the result of the close ties which George Myers and his political intimates (Jere Brown and John Green of Cleveland, William Parham of Cincinnati, Charles Cottrill of Toledo, Charles Fillmore of Springfield, and Ralph Tyler of Columbus) and their adversary Benjamin Arnett enjoyed with William McKinley and his alter ego, Cleveland millionaire businessman Mark Hanna. Between McKinley's presidential nomination in 1896, his assassination in 1901, and Hanna's death in 1904, a group of Ohio black politicians were to sit closer to the throne than ever before. While they obtained expanded patronage opportunities and new heights of influence within the Republican party, the long-run benefits were less than satisfactory. The lack of northern and Ohio black voting power relative to that in the South continued to work against the Ohioans. Moreover, while they proposed no concrete program for racial welfare, they did wish to see black constitutional rights preserved. But they soon discovered that the white leaders in whom they so profoundly wished to believe were following the path of least resistance in race relations, acquiescing in (and indeed hoping to profit from) the course of racial reaction in the South.

Myers's influence arose from a long history of quasi-personal and political relations with the Hanna family and with McKinley. As a young man working as a barber and shop foreman in Cleveland's Weddell House from 1879 through 1888, Myers had met Hanna and his brother Leonard, who were regular customers, and McKinley, who came in occasionally when sojourning from his native Canton. Myers had no doubt exchanged with them the good-natured, shallow pleasantries which prosperous men of affairs reserve for their servants. There were greater advantages than such banter, however, for when Myers moved to the Hollenden, Leonard Hanna was one of his white benefactors, and the Hanna brothers, as well as many other prominent whites, brought their business to Myers's new shop.[74]

Not until the 1892 Republican convention did Mark Hanna take

---

[74] Garraty, ed., *Barber and Historian*, pp. xvi–xix.

serious note of the Negro barber and begin to see the potential for a mutually beneficial political relationship. Like other young men of both races, Myers was, and always remained, thrilled by the intrigues of politics. In order to become more actively involved, he had joined the black Young Men's Foraker Club in the late 1880s; the name connoted a respect for Foraker's power more than loyalty to his faction of the Ohio Republican party, for the club was actually not closely allied with any white faction. Myers's club, to which Jere Brown and John Green also belonged, was one of the most powerful in black Cleveland, equaled in influence only by Smith's Onward Foraker Club, which was more truly identified with Foraker.[75] His club's influence afforded Myers the chance to attend the 1892 Republican national convention at Minneapolis as an alternate, the role ordinarily played by Ohio blacks at national conventions. Usually the alternate did little more than view the political drama—but, at least in Myers's case, the 1892 convention was quite different. The regular delegate from Ohio's 21st congressional district became ill, leaving Myers with a vote. He cast an enthusiastic ballot for northern Ohio's favorite son, Governor William McKinley, whose presidential possibilities Hanna had been booming for several years—to the dismay of Cincinnati's equally ambitious and conservative Foraker. But 1892 was not McKinley's year. Incumbent Benjamin Harrison got the nomination and went on to lose to Grover Cleveland. McKinley, on the other hand, won another term as governor in 1893; he and Hanna eagerly awaited the 1896 convention and the opportunity to again seek the presidential nomination.

Myers's role in the presidential balloting was actually less important than his crucial vote on the selection of the state's Republican national committeeman. This contest was seen by the Hanna-McKinley forces as the first step in their effort to take control of Ohio politics in preparation for 1896; it placed McKinleyite William Hahn against Foraker's man. At the outset the result was not predictable. The delegates voted according to the numbers of their Ohio congressional districts. When the vote came to Myers, of the 21st and final district, it was tied. Myers cast his lot with Hahn, an act which he said vaulted him into "the national political arena." That vote, he later recalled, "brought me to the attention of Governor McKinley and Mr. Hanna in a more personal way than my previous thirteen years of acquaint-

[75] Cleveland *Gazette*, Jan. 28, 1893; circular announcing a "literary and musical entertainment" of the Young Men's Foraker Club with roster of members, Box I, folder 2, Myers Papers.

ance. From then until the death of both, I enjoyed perhaps a closer relation with Mr. Hanna than was accorded to but a few." [76]

As the 1896 convention approached, Myers became more of a political confidante of Hanna, a brusque, matter-of-fact, but withal likeable man with no apparent racial prejudices or obsessions about social equality. (Myers affectionately referred to him as "Uncle.") If Hanna proved a compelling figure for Myers, Governor McKinley was showing himself to be a good friend of both the race and its political leaders. His statements denouncing lynching and his outspoken approval of Smith's anti-lynching bill were admirable; the fact that he furnished Brown, Cottrill, and a few others with jobs in state government was important to Myers, who understood the difficulties his friends experienced in finding dignified employment.[77] Finally, the conservative Myers had much ideological sympathy with the stand-pat Republicanism of Hanna and McKinley. Impressed by both men and excited by Hanna's increasing confidence in him, Myers entered the political battle. Backed by the Hanna interests at Cleveland, Myers was chosen as a delegate-at-large to the 1895 Republican state convention which nominated Springfield's Asa Bushnell for the governorship. In addition, he began a political correspondence with a Louisiana black Republican, J. Madison Vance, whom he courted for the McKinley forces.[78]

It was in relation to southern black politicians like Vance that Myers was to perform his most valued service for Hanna in the drive to win McKinley's nomination. They represented a declining constituency, decimated by an apathy born of poverty and social isolation, by violent repression, and increasingly by disfranchisement; nevertheless, Hanna took seriously the potential power these southern black politicos might wield in the presidential balloting at the convention, and he set out to woo them. In 1895 he retired from business and bought a home at Thomasville, Georgia. From this convenient spot he made contacts among black (and the few white) important southern Republicans. Hanna eventually paid the travel and lodging expenses of many of these men when they became delegates to the St. Louis convention in 1896. In addition, he and McKinley courted them with

[76] Cleveland *Gazette*, June 1, 1895; George Myers to James Ford Rhodes, Mar. 8, 1920, and Feb. 16, 1923, in Garraty, ed., *Barber and Historian*, pp. 123, 146.

[77] Cleveland *Gazette*, Mar. 26, June 16, Aug. 13, Dec. 3, 10, 1892, June 10, 1893, May 30, Sept. 19, 1896.

[78] Ibid., June 1, 1895; J. Madison Vance to George Myers, Box I, folder 6, Myers Papers.

the platform's anti-lynching plank, supplemented by the usual token statement affirming blacks' right to vote.[79]

Myers felt that the black delegates might be even more firmly secured if the McKinley forces were to provide them with entertainment and aid them in finding hotel and dining accommodations in a city in which segregation was firmly entrenched. Perhaps also sensing an opportunity to glean useful bits of political intelligence, Hanna agreed. He provided money for the establishment of a Negro Entertainment Bureau, headed by Myers and staffed by Brown, Parham, Cottrill, and William R. Steward.[80]

The success of the bureau, the southern delegates' overwhelming support for McKinley, and that candidate's nomination and eventual election all placed Myers in an excellent position to obtain a fine political plum. But though Hanna and McKinley both approached him with offers, Myers refused them. He had the good fortune to own "a business that was far more remunerative than any position that either would have given." [81] Instead he sought federal jobs for some of his close friends, particularly Brown and Fillmore, who then worked in state agencies, and Cottrill, who was employed as deputy recorder of Lucas County. He received some general assurances on patronage from McKinley,[82] but Hanna, who disliked having to commit himself in advance to any particular course, made no promises, and he simply gave Myers assurance that he would try to help his friends. He frequently made it known that he would prefer to end his obligation with Myers.[83] Hanna realized that the southern black politicians wielded power on both convention and popular ballots; their influence might be useful if McKinley were to seek reelection and if the Hanna-McKinley forces were to consolidate their position within the party, and thus he would have preferred to give the better jobs to southern blacks and those who enjoyed firm contacts among them. Perhaps sensing this, and understanding the psychology of obligation, Myers knew that as long as he himself refused to accept reward,

[79] Thomas Cripps, "The Lily White Republicans: The Negro, the Party, and the South in the Progressive Era" (Ph.D. dissertation, University of Maryland, 1967), pp. 22–24, 31; Stanley Jones, *The Presidential Election of 1896* (Madison, 1964), pp. 112–113, 128–129.

[80] Jere Brown to George Myers, Mar. 14, Apr. 18, 22, 1896, Charles Cottrill to George Myers, Apr. 19, 1896, William Hahn to George Myers, Apr. 30, 1896, Box II, folder 1, Myers Papers; Cleveland *Gazette*, June 27, 1896.

[81] George Myers to James Ford Rhodes, Feb. 16, 1923, in Garraty, ed., *Barber and Historian*, p. 146.

[82] George Myers to James Ford Rhodes, Feb. 16, 1923, ibid., p. 149.

[83] George Myers to James Ford Rhodes, June 11, 1917, ibid., p. 70.

Hanna incurred a continuing debt to him, and hence to his friends.

This predominance of southern black politicians in the calculations of powerful whites like Hanna was a source of aggravation for Myers and his friends; it contributed greatly to the emergence of another goal, less formally articulated than their claims to patronage: the hope that the influence of *northern* blacks in national politics might be increased through his own closeness to Hanna and McKinley. The Northerners had long been subordinated in patronage, party affairs, and the advising of white statesmen on racial affairs. Since enfranchisement, northern black politicians had limped along on minor patronage, far from the real corridors of power; hence, among them, there was a feeling of blocked mobility and frustration—a feeling that no matter how strenuous their partisan efforts and how great their abilities, they would never be allowed to have real influence or access to the better "Negro jobs" in the federal service. During the early 1890s most Ohio blacks were too far from the inner circles of political power to clash directly with southern black influence. Therefore the tension between their aspirations and the entrenched power of the Southerners manifested itself as a somewhat diffuse anger over the party's tendency to bring the political relics of black Reconstruction—in the form of Blanche K. Bruce and others of the aging breed of southern office-holders of the 1870s—into Ohio at election time in order to allay and mask discontent.[84]

But in the mid-1890s, as Myers and his allies came in closer contact with southern politicians and moved nearer the throne, their criticisms became more pointed and their efforts to upset the old pattern of influence grew more aggressive and direct. Much of this was the work of one of Myers's trusted political advisors, Ralph Tyler, the son of J. S. Tyler, who had been a leader of the Columbus black community in the 1870s and 1880s. Though but twenty-seven at the time of the 1896 convention, Tyler had already been active in Columbus's racial affairs for a decade. He had matured into a tough-minded, ruthless practitioner of *realpolitik,* best at gut-fighting behind the scenes while effusing the milk of human kindness in public. He was then employed as the personal secretary of Robert Wolfe, the publisher of the Columbus *Dispatch,* a Republican daily with independent leanings, and he occasionally did reporting for the paper. His well-paying, prestigious job afforded him a large bank account and a fine home in a wealthy white neighborhood. For this reason Tyler, like

[84] Cleveland *Gazette,* Aug. 1, 29, Oct. 7, 1891.

Myers, at this time at least was playing the political game for the sake of power and influence, rather than for a sinecure in Washington.[85]

While he had sympathy for the plight of allies like Brown who made a living from politics, Tyler placed little faith in them as racial political leaders because their dependence made it impossible for them to put racial interest above self-interest. Since Northerners had less opportunity to use patronage and graft as a means of livelihood, he came quite naturally to believe that they offered a superior source of national black political leadership. His contacts with southern politicians (at St. Louis while helping Myers) crystallized these views and made him all the more desirous of bringing about a change in the sectional center of black politics. Shortly after the convention, he wrote Myers of his "disgust with the average southern colored man in politics . . . with whom to work candidates for money is the great desideratum. . . ." "I hope the day is not too far distant when the colored man in the North will be recognized as the proper one for leadership, and my observation of this convention impresses me with the fact that colored leadership is gravitating from South to North very rapidly." [86]

It was wishful thinking. The North could not yet provide the demographic basis for such a transition, and disfranchisement had not yet completely erased black influence in the South. Yet Tyler might still hope that the new administration would begin the transition. To his mind, one certain sign of the willingness to do so would be the appointment of John Green, the one black Ohioan with a national reputation among both races, to one of the top "Negro jobs" in the federal government. Such an appointment would place Green in an excellent position to expand the influence of Myers and Tyler and to work for jobs for their circle.[87]

Unfortunately for Myers and his allies, they were not without rivals in Ohio itself, let alone in the nation at large. They faced one stiff challenge from Bishop Arnett, a wily strategist whose arsenal of political tricks was at least equal to Myers's. Groomed in the labyrinthian complexities of church politics, the thick-set, dark bishop was reputedly a particularly effective and ambitious operator. His rise to prominence in church affairs had been rapid and was accompanied by growing political influence. Born in Pennsylvania in 1838,[88] Arnett

[85] For the most complete biographical sketches of Tyler's early life and career see Cincinnati *Times-Star*, Feb. 1, 1907; Cleveland *Leader*, Apr. 10, 1907.

[86] Ralph Tyler to George Myers, June 20, 1896, Box II, folder 2, Myers Papers.

[87] Ralph Tyler to George Myers, Dec. 5, 1896, Box II, folder 6, ibid.

[88] For biographical information on Arnett, see William J. Simmons, *Men of Mark: Eminent, Progressive, and Rising* (Cleveland, 1887), pp. 883–891; Balti-

had not entered the ministry until 1867, when he became a preacher in Bishop Daniel Payne's Ohio Conference. He must have greatly impressed the benignly autocratic Payne, for he was soon assigned to some of the wealthiest, most prestigious churches in the conference—hardly those given to the average novice preacher. Starting out at Walnut Hills in 1867, he then went to Toledo, to Cincinnati's Allen Temple, and, after two years at Urbana, to Columbus's St. Paul's, leaving a trail of published commemorative pamphlets and booklets bearing his name and advertising him as a dynamic, intellectual minister. In 1870 Arnett was ordained an elder of the conference, and in 1876 he was appointed assistant secretary of the national A.M.E. General Conference. All the while he was recognized as a skilled political orator, and he regularly traveled the campaign circuit on behalf of Republican candidates.

The 1880s brought continued recognition in both politics and the church; indeed, success in one seemed to reinforce success in the other. In 1880 and again in 1884 he was elected financial secretary of the A.M.E. Church, a position which gave him significant control over the denomination's money. The office allowed him to settle permanently at Wilberforce, the intellectual center of the church in Ohio, and he quickly became involved in local politics. In 1885 he was chosen by the Wilberforce faculty during one of the school's periodic financial crises to run for the Greene County Republican legislative nomination, in order that he might eventually lobby for state aid. Arnett not only obtained the nomination (tantamount to election in partisan Greene) and obtained aid in the form of a state facility on the Wilberforce campus; by introducing one of the final bills, he was also able to take credit for the passage of school desegregation legislation, which was well advanced when he took office. But his work on behalf of mixed schools contradicted the wishes of an overwhelmingly white constituency—a constituency which he had promised, as part of the bargain for nomination, that he would not pursue desegregation.[89] As a result, his career in Greene County electoral politics ended in 1887, at the close of his term. But nonetheless Arnett found himself at the height of his power among blacks, who greatly admired his legislative achievements. A year later his eighteen-year episcopal reign commenced with his election as a bishop.

more *Afro-American Ledger,* Oct. 13, 1906. There is a biography of Arnett up to 1890; it is worshipful and somewhat in the Horatio Alger vein—Lucretia Coleman, *Poor Ben: A Story of Real Life* (Nashville, 1890).

[89] Xenia *Gazette,* Mar. 10, 1885, Mar. 11, Apr. 1, 1887; Xenia *Torchlight,* Jan. 16, 20, 30, Apr. 3, 1886; Cleveland *Gazette* Jan. 30, 1886.

Arnett was not without his problems. An excellent church administrator, he was strangely improvident in personal affairs. He
allowed his fire insurance to lapse shortly before his home burned
around the turn of the century, and he lacked the savings to rebuild;
Mark Hanna ultimately provided him with the money.[90] The rebuilt
house had to be sold at a sheriff's auction a few years after his death to
help pay debts owed by his estate, leaving his widow without a roof
over her head.[91] Moreover, Arnett faced the problem of what to do
with his three sons, Ben Junior, Henry, and Alonzo; the three were
reaching or well into manhood by 1896, but without well-paying,
stable employment and family wealth. Between 1894 and 1896 the
bishop tried to have Ben Junior appointed a professor of literature at
Wilberforce; this effort failed when the faculty nearly staged an
open revolt at the prospect of turning the untrained young man loose
on undergraduates.[92] About this time, the bishop began to view
patronage as a means for securing the future of his sons. In addition,
he wanted to help several church intimates in their attempts to
become army chaplains. Thus Arnett entered politics in 1896 with
tremendous determination. But he did not cast his lot with Myers's
circle, even refusing Jere Brown's request for a consultation before the
convention. Instead he allied himself with southern black politicians
whom he knew through the church and personal relations.[93]

Arnett did not work for McKinley's nomination with the same
fervor which Myers brought to his labors at St. Louis, and he did not
have a comparable clique of hard-working Ohio black allies. Even so,
the McKinley organization put great value on his support. White politicians astutely sensed the great opportunity to mold and mobilize
black opinion which was open to leading A.M.E. clergymen relative to
ministers from the nonepiscopal denominations. This, coupled with
the bishop's wide circle of southern contacts, made him a welcome
member of the McKinley camp. Soon after the convention his power
was recognized: his second son, twenty-eight-year-old Henry, who
had been a teacher in South Carolina and had enough contacts there
to manage McKinley's interests with the South Carolina convention delegation, now became head of the well-funded black Mc-
Kinley drive in Ohio. Throughout 1896 rumors spoke of the bishop's

[90] Reveredy Ransom, *The Pilgrimage of Harriet Ransom's Son* (Nashville, n.d.),
p. 70.

[91] Indianapolis *Freeman*, Oct. 9, 1909.

[92] W. E. B. Du Bois, *Autobiography* (New York, 1968), pp. 189–190.

[93] Jere Brown to George Myers, May 3, 1896, Box II, folder 1, Myers Papers,

presumed power over the best Ohio appointments, and Myers's circle wondered, worried, and waited for the first year of the new administration to indicate just how true those rumors might be.[94]

Between these two camps was Harry Smith, an ambitious loner whose influence as the editor of a black weekly made up for the fact that he had no contacts in the South and no firm power base in Ohio. The McKinley forces recognized Smith's influence, appointing him to assist Henry Arnett in the management of the Ohio black campaign, and providing him with a full round of speaking engagements throughout the state and the North. Smith undertook his assignment with vigor, for he deeply respected McKinley for his opposition to lynching and his views on the need for sound money and a high tariff.[95] It was quite another thing, however, for Smith to cooperate with the other Ohio blacks involved in the McKinley campaign. Smith had an acid pen and a compulsion for fault-finding, and events of 1896 severely tested his rarely exercised power of self-control. But he was by no means immune to the lure of a good spot in Washington from which he might have some national influence in racial affairs, and he did his best to win the friendship of both Ohio power blocs after the convention. Earlier in the year Smith had criticized Bishop Arnett for taking meals in his suite at a Boston hotel which refused to allow him in the dining room and then failing to file a lawsuit; however, the post-convention period found Smith full of praise for his boss Henry Arnett, whose lack of experience did not stop Smith from boosting him as a race leader, and without a harsh word for the temporizing bishop.[96] Smith even ceased his criticism of Myers and other members of the "Little Black Tammany." He praised Myers for his excellent convention work and observed a journalistic moratorium on the discussion of local political rivalries.[97]

But either this effort simply proved too much for him or, as Myers's circle suspected,[98] he decided to cast his lot with the Arnetts. Even before the fall canvass had ended, Smith was involved in intrigues against Myers. He reportedly made sarcastic remarks about "Mark Hanna's barber" posing as a political kingpin, and he conspired in October to have these thoughts anonymously printed in a Buffalo,

[94] Jere Brown to George Myers, July 15, 1896, Box II, folder 2, and Ralph Tyler to George Myers, Oct. 7, 1896, Box 2, folder 4; ibid.; Henry Y. Arnett to John Green, Mar. 29, 1896, Box I, folder 1, John Green Papers, WRHS; Cleveland *Gazette*, Nov. 14, 1896.
[95] Cleveland *Gazette*, Aug. 22, 29, Sept. 5, 19, 1896.
[96] Ibid., Feb. 1, Sept. 5, Nov. 14, 1896.
[97] Ibid., June 27, 1896.
[98] Ralph Tyler to George Myers, Oct. 7, 1896, Box II, folder 4, Myers Papers.

New York, black Democratic weekly.[99] The covert anti-Myers campaign was the worst blunder of Smith's political career, for it gave his enemies a chance to strike a lethal blow. Myers took Tyler up on the latter's offer to write a series of articles damaging to Smith; these were to be printed in early December in the Washington *Colored American*, a paper which was edited by Myers's ally E. E. Cooper and carefully circulated throughout the nation.[100]

The title of Tyler's article was innocuous enough—"Prominent Colored Men in Ohio Politics"—but its treatment of Smith was vicious. In discussing the Cleveland editor, Tyler concentrated on a controversial speech which Smith had delivered in January, 1896, before the annual fete given by Columbus blacks for Ohio's black legislators. Reminiscent of Frederick Douglass's classic "What Is the Fourth of July to the Slave?" Smith's speech had graphically portrayed the wrongs daily done to the race in the South—wrongs which, he said, made it impossible for him to sing "My Country Tis of Thee, Sweet Land of Liberty" or to salute the flag without feeling hypocritical. The words were honest, spoken from a tortured heart. While subsequent speakers had criticized the remarks as excessively emotional, Smith's speech had elicited rounds of applause from a largely black audience.[101]

Tyler's poisoned pen, however, carried Smith from the realm of heartfelt criticism to that of traitorous disloyalty, causing a storm of righteous indignation from a black leadership both patriotic and at the same time eager to prove itself worthy of white regard.[102] The article had an immediate, withering impact on Smith's chances, isolating him from those, black and white, with influence, and making it impossible for him to be considered seriously for an office in the new administration.[103] Embittered, Smith spent the next months lashing out

[99] Ralph Tyler to George Myers, Aug. 19, 1898, Charles Fillmore to George Myers, Sept. 16, 1896, Box II, folder 3, Jere Brown to George Myers, Nov. 8, 1896, Box II, folder 5, ibid.

[100] Ralph Tyler to George Myers, Oct. 13, 23, 26, 27, 28, 29, 1896, E. E. Cooper to George Myers, Oct. 30, 1896, Box II, folder 4, and James A. Ross to George Myers, Nov. 11, 1896, Charles Anderson to George Myers, Nov. 17, 1896, J. Madison Vance to George Myers, Nov. 17, 1896, E. E. Cooper to George Myers, Nov. 25, 1896, Box II, folder 5, ibid.; E. E. Cooper to John Green, Nov. 25, 1896, Box III, folder 3, Green Papers.

[101] Columbus *Ohio State Journal*, Jan. 21, 1896; Cleveland *Gazette*, Jan. 25, 1896.

[102] Unfortunately, there are no extant copies of the relevant issues of the *Colored American*, but the articles are described in the Cleveland *Gazette*, Dec. 19, 1896, Jan. 2, 9, 1897.

[103] E. E. Cooper to George Myers, Dec. 17, 31, 1896, Box II, folder 6, Myers Papers; George Myers to John Green, Aug. 5, 1897, Charles Chesnutt to John Green, Aug. 14, 1897, Box IV, folder 2, Green Papers.

at Myers and Green, and eventually (though less stridently) at the Arnetts, who turned on him when it became clear that he could no longer be of use. Though he served another term in the legislature during 1900–1901, largely as the result of ties with the anti-Hanna McKissonites, Smith could never again make the political alliances which would help him extend his influence beyond Cleveland; the Tyler charges came back to haunt him on occasion when he tried.[104] His thwarted ambition welling up in him like venom, Smith would now gradually begin to slip from cranky, yet often constructive, nay-saying to cold negativism. It was a sad setback for an able man who was but thirty-seven at the turn of the century.

With Smith out of the picture, the Ohio factions enter the critical year of 1897, when the McKinley administration would firmly establish its black connections. From the beginning, the results were hardly satisfactory for Myers. The drive to assign Green to one of the higher federal "black" posts, Washington recorder of deeds, failed in the face of an onslaught of southern influence; Henry P. Cheatham of North Carolina got the position. Instead, in late July amidst considerable fanfare, Green was appointed superintendent of postage stamps. He was the first Negro to hold the position, but it hardly signaled an improvement in the race's fortunes. As the title suggests, it was little more than an elevated clerkship, totally without influence, prestige, and larger possibilities; when Green's long tenure ended in 1906, the position was abolished. With an already inflated staff of eight white clerks ("to help him with the arduous task of putting in time to draw a salary," the Cleveland *Plain Dealer* snidely remarked), there was not even an opportunity to hire a black clerk. Green happily settled back to enjoy his expanded free time—"Well, old boy, this is a sinecure sure enough," he wrote to Myers shortly after taking office. However, his Ohio friends began to sense the collapse of their hopes. Tyler was especially depressed, seeing the Green appointment as "insignificant and not at all . . . commensurate with the race's voting strength or fealty [in Ohio] or Green's prominence." [105]

Arnett's star, on the other hand, was clearly rising. His southern friends and allies swept into office, and Southerners profited from the

104 Cleveland *Gazette*, Jan., Feb., Mar., 1897, July 17, 1897, Oct. 28, Nov. 4, 11, 18, 1899; Cleveland *Journal*, Oct. 19, 1907.
105 Edward A. Brown to John Green, Feb. 13, 1897, George L. Knox to John Green, Mar. 31, 1897, Box III, folder 4, Mark Hanna to John Green, May 10, 1897, Box IV, folder 1, Mark Hanna to John Green, July 10, 1897, Box IV, folder 2, Green Papers; Ralph Tyler to George Myers, July 22, 1897, Box III, folder 5, and John Green to George Myers, Aug. 4, 1897, Box III, folder 6, Myers Papers.

fact that McKinley distributed patronage to blacks more liberally than any previous president. Henry Arnett got a federal clerkship (nothing more was expected), and the bishop himself often consulted with the president on patronage.[106] Later in the year Myers's forces, through Green, attempted to undermine Arnett's influence among the Southerners and to establish themselves as southern allies. But it was too late, and the effort failed almost from the beginning.[107] By the winter of 1897 it was clear that Myers's faction would have to take whatever it was given.

The disappointment of Myers and his friends was at first checked by their new and unprecedented power to manage the black campaign in the 1897 state elections. Normally, the odd-year election would decide the governorship and the legislature—important, of course, but by no means as important as the particular U.S. Senate seat to be filled when the new legislature convened in January, 1898. In order to bring Hanna to power at Washington and to fulfill his life-long ambition to sit in the Senate—and at the same time to balance the power of Foraker, who had been elected senator in 1896—McKinley appointed aging Ohio Senator John Sherman as secretary of state, leaving vacant the Senate seat which Sherman had held since 1881. Hanna was quickly, though doubtless reluctantly, appointed by Governor Asa Bushnell, a Foraker loyalist, to finish Sherman's term. It was naturally assumed that Hanna would fight to retain the seat when his term expired.[108]

But Hanna was far from popular in Ohio. While McKinley enjoyed a reputation as a pious, dignified, and unquestionably honest statesman, Hanna had an unenviable image as a plutocrat and spoilsman who had corrupted municipal officials and state legislators in order to obtain a competitive edge over his leading opponent, Tom Johnson, in a struggle for control of Cleveland's streetcar lines. Hanna also had many enemies within the party. Foraker partisans throughout the state could not be counted on to bring out the vote for Hanna's sake, and in Cleveland itself, where Hanna was never able to assume complete control, the followers of Robert McKisson were his bitter enemies.[109]

Under these circumstances, the black vote again took on the impor-

---

[106] Indianapolis *Freeman*, June 5, 1897; Cleveland *Gazette*, June 26, 1897; H. Y. Arnett to Albion W. Tourgee, Feb. 12, 1897, item #9225, Albion W. Tourgee Papers, CCHS.

[107] George Myers to John Green, Nov. 11, Dec. 6, 19, 25, 1897, Box IV, folder 4, Green Papers.

[108] Herbert Croly, *Marcus Alonzo Hanna: His Life and Work* (New York, 1923), pp. 228–241.

[109] Warner, *Progressivism in Ohio*, pp. 4–6, 16–17, 112–113.

tance which had been attributed to it in previous years. But both the Hanna forces and those convinced partisans who simply desired to keep Ohio firmly Republican were worried about a discernible restiveness among black voters during the summer of 1897. The discontent was almost exclusively the result of blacks' belief that Governor Bushnell, by failing to act quickly and decisively to send the Ohio National Guard to Urbana in order to reinforce local militia units, had contributed to the June 5 lynching of a young black man accused of rape.[110] Though Bushnell was easily nominated for a second term at the Republican state convention later in the month, feeling among blacks was running strongly against him. In an unprecedented politicization of the pulpit, the Reverend Joshua H. Jones, the influential presiding elder of the A.M.E. Church in the Columbus area, was delivering weekly sermons at the Second A.M.E. Church, denouncing the governor, demanding a public investigation, and calling for a revolt at the polls if the matter was not cleared up. The resolutions of a mass meeting at Columbus in late June said no less.[111] The anger of blacks was only heightened by Bushnell's efforts in August to begin proceedings to dismiss Urbana's mayor and the county sheriff on the grounds that they failed to do all they could to prevent the lynching. It was widely believed among blacks that the governor's culpability was just as great, if not greater. Furthermore, many agreed with Harry Smith that the suits against the local officials were "a gigantic bluff intended to hang fire in the courts until election day when all legal proceedings will disappear." (Smith was genuinely angry, and he also hoped to use the issue to compromise his political enemies should they work for Bushnell.) This view gained credibility when the taking of depositions was indefinitely postponed only one week after the preliminary state investigation had begun.[112]

Myers and Tyler sensed the possibility of a black defection as early as the state convention. Their warnings to Republican officials were taken seriously. In late July, Myers was unanimously elected to the state executive committee; he was given carte blanche and a great deal of money to organize a black counterattack. With the aid of such allies as Parham and Fillmore and Bishop Arnett, cooperating for Hanna's and hence for his own sake, Myers established an office at

[110] Cincinnati *Enquirer*, June 5, 6, 1897; Cleveland *Gazette*, June 12, 19, July 17, 1897.
[111] Columbus *Dispatch*, June 11, 21, 28, 30, 1897; Cleveland *Gazette*, June 12, 19, July 17, 1897.
[112] Cleveland *Gazette*, Aug. 7, 1897; Columbus *Dispatch*, Aug. 6, 9, 10, 11, 1897. The cases were eventually brought to the state supreme court by the attorney general; they were quickly lost.

Columbus to coordinate the efforts of loyal black Republican clubs in every important county. The office was managed by Jere Brown, who worked closely with Myers throughout the campaign. Never before had such organization been brought to a black canvass in Ohio. Equally out of the ordinary was the creation of a *state* black political organ, the amply endowed *Republican Vindicator*. The publication was edited by Tyler and circulated at no cost to the reader in order to counter the influence of Smith's *Gazette*, which by late August was urging an electoral revolt against Bushnell. Supplementing the *Republican Vindicator* were thousands of copies of two popular out-of-state race papers, the Indianapolis *Freeman* and the Washington *Bee*, with appropriate pro-Hanna copy; these were also circulated without cost. Finally, several anemic Ohio black papers were subsidized, and speakers were brought in from all over the nation to generate enthusiasm among black voters.[113]

In late September, just as Myers's machine was reaching peak efficiency, it was confronted by a unique challenge. At Columbus, a closed meeting of black Democrats and a few independents established a "Negro Protective Party," with a full slate of candidates for all state executive offices and a platform protesting mob violence and all forms of racial discrimination. The N.P.P. was financed (secretly at first, until Republican papers revealed the connection) by the white Democracy, with particularly strong backing from the Cincinnati *Enquirer's* publisher John R. McLean, who hoped not only to upset Hanna's plans, but also to get himself elected to the Senate if Democrats took control of the legislature. The N.P.P. was the last hurrah of the old black Democracy before reform Democrats bade it goodbye; its founders intended simply to create a little confusion in the ranks of the opposition and to make a little money. Though its state and some local candidates spoke the heady language of political revolt, the speed with which local slates disappeared after being paid off suggests that more than a few were boodlers. (One of Myers's agents, Charles R. Doll, convinced the entire N.P.P. ticket in Highland County to resign.[114]) When the

---

[113] Ralph Tyler to George Myers, June 5, 14, 26, 29, 1897, Box III, folder 4, George Knox to George Myers, July 6, 1897, E. C. Cooper to George Myers, July 7, 1897, Box III, folder 5, and W. C. Anderson to George Myers, Aug. 16, 1897, John R. Rudd to George Myers, Aug. 18, 1897, Box III, folder 6, Myers Papers; George Myers, "The Ohio Campaign of 1897," typescript dated Mar. 19, 1898, Box VI, folder 2, ibid.; Cleveland *Gazette*, Aug. 21, Sept. 4, Oct. 30, 1897; Cleveland *Leader*, Oct. 14, 1897.

[114] Ohio, *Annual Report of the Secretary of State . . . 1897* (Norwalk, 1898), pp. 276–277; Columbus *Dispatch*, Sept. 18, 20, 22, 23, Nov. 1, 1897; Cincinnati *Enquirer*, Sept. 26, 27, 28, 29, 1897; Cincinnati *Commercial-Tribune*, Oct. 2, 4, 7, 9, 10, 12, 1897; Columbus *Press-Post*, Oct. 8, 11, 1897; Hillsboro *News Herald*,

returns came in, the N.P.P. had only 477 of the 3,000 votes which gubernatorial candidate Sam Lewis, an old Cincinnati Democrat, had predicted he would receive. But Bushnell's majority dropped from 93,000 in 1895 to 28,000, with Republican voting down in all areas and among both races.[115]

The Republican legislative majority was reduced to only five votes on a joint ballot of both houses such as would decide the fate of the Senate seat, and in the weeks before the balloting some feared that Hanna would be defeated. When the new legislature convened in January, Democrats and anti-Hanna Republicans had chosen McKisson as an alternate candidate. Bribes were being offered on both sides, and the adversaries had hired detectives to catch each other in the act.[116] At this point, Myers said years later, he put his "head in the door of the Ohio penitentiary." The unpredictable William Clifford, just elected for a second House term, began to flirt with the McKissonites; they made him a handsome cash offer, but Myers successfully countered with a better one. Clifford's vote provided the decisive margin in the contest. Had the investigation of the ensuing election been more thorough, Myers might well have been martyred to the career of his "Uncle." [117]

Myers did not undertake these efforts for Hanna as the quid pro quo for future favors, but it would have been natural for him to hope for closer relations with the administration as a reward for his labors. This was not to be. Indeed, the struggle to elect Hanna to the Senate marked a turning point in the relationship between Hanna and McKinley and the black politicians centered around Myers. In the few years before McKinley's assassination in September, 1901, the influence of the blacks did not markedly increase, and for various reasons they became disillusioned with both white men. As a result, some of them chose to lessen their political activity.

The first source of tension was patronage. Some members of Myers's circle received minor posts in 1898 and 1899: Brown worked at inter-

Oct. 21, 28, 1897; Charles Doll to George Myers, Oct. 20, 21, 1897, Box V, folder 3, Myers Papers.

[115] Ohio, *Statistics, 1897*, pp. 287–480, for N.P.P. vote data. Lewis polled best in his hometown, where he received pitifully few (60) votes; in no other city or town in the state did he receive more than 20 votes. Where they were left on election day, N.P.P. local tickets did even worse.

[116] Croly, *Hanna*, pp. 242–271.

[117] George Myers to James Ford Rhodes, Apr. 30, Sept. 20, Oct. 27, 1920, in Garraty, ed., *Barber and Historian*, pp. 118, 121, 141; George Myers to John Green, Dec. 19, 1897, Jan. 18, 1898, Jere Brown to John Green, July 18, 1898, Box IV, folder 4, Green Papers; Eugene Roseboom and Francis Phelps Weisenburger, *A History of Ohio* (New York, 1934), p. 376.

nal revenue, Fillmore received a commission in the army during the
Spanish-American War and then a clerkship under the auditor of the
navy, and Cleveland minister W. T. Anderson became an army chaplain.[118] But at around the same time the group suffered two major
disappointments. The most important was Green's failure to obtain appointment as register of the treasury when McKinley's original ap-
pointee, Blanche K. Bruce, died in office early in 1898. Bruce's body
had hardly been laid to rest before intense competition for the job
began. While Green actively sought the post, he was hardly given a
second thought, and Judson Lyons of Augusta, Georgia, was appointed.[119] Also deeply felt was the failure to obtain the post of first
assistant surgeon at Washington's Freedmen's Hospital for Tyler's
brother James, an experienced physician. Green actually had difficulty
getting an appointment with Hanna in order to discuss the matter.[120]

On the other hand, Arnett remained powerful. A Xenia attorney
named Campbell Maxwell, who was a friend of Arnett's, had been active in Wilberforce University affairs in various capacities and in local
Republican politics; late in March he was appointed ambassador to
Santo Domingo—far from Washington, to be sure, but the best-paying
and most prestigious job yet given to an Ohioan of color. Three months
later Ben Junior, now a preacher, became an army chaplain.[121] Tyler
was beside himself. The Maxwell appointment was "not a recognition
of those who did the work" in 1896 and 1897; the Arnett appointment,
coming on the heels of his brother's failure, led him to swear that he
would not work in the fall congressional canvass as long as the bishop

---

[118] Ralph Tyler to George Myers, Dec. 28, 1897, Box V, folder 5, and Mark
Hanna to George Myers, June 9, 11, 1898, Box VI, folder 1, Myers Papers; Jere
Brown to John Green, Mar. 13, Apr. 7, 1898, Box V, folder 1, Green Papers.

[119] Green at least was not surprised. "I did not expect to get the appointment,"
he wrote Myers; "Southern statesman of color get the big, juicy, fat offices." John
Green to George Myers, Mar. 23, 1898, Box VI, folder 2, Myers Papers. But
Myers was very disappointed: George Myers to John Green, Apr. 1, 1898, Box V,
folder 1, Green Papers; John Addison Porter to John Green, Mar. 21, 1898, William McKinley Papers, LC.

[120] Dr. J. A. Tyler to John Green, Nov. 6, 1897, Box IV, folder 3, Ralph
Tyler to John Green, George Myers to John Green, both dated Feb. 18, 1898,
Box V, folder 1, Green Papers; Ralph Tyler to George Myers, Feb. 13, 24, May 14,
1898, John Green to George Myers, Feb. 19, 1898, Box VI, folder 1, Myers Papers.

[121] John Addison Porter to Benjamin Arnett, Nov. 9, Dec. 30, 1897, Mar. 14,
23, May 5, 1898, McKinley Papers; Ralph Tyler to George Myers, Mar. 29,
May 14, June 22, 1898, Box VI, folder 2, Myers Papers. Maxwell had been appointed to the same position in 1892, and served very briefly during the last
months of the Harrison administration; Cleveland *Gazette*, Jan. 9, 15, 1892. On
some of Maxwell's earlier political activities, see above, p. 237n39.

was running "the whole damn business." [122] By 1898 Myers, too, had profound doubts about Hanna. In early June he wrote to Green, lamenting that Hanna "has fallen short of my expectations. I have never forgiven him for not doing better by you, though he has done better for white men who have done less than you and I. I hate to think that Uncle is suffering from negrophobia, but sometimes I am almost constrained to believe so." [123] Though Myers went on to pledge continuing loyalty to Hanna despite these nagging doubts, he and Tyler, Parham, and others were conspicuously absent from the 1898 congressional campaign. [124]

More disturbing was the administration's apparent lack of concern for black rights. McKinley and his war department were slow to commission and promote black officers for the war with Spain, and still slower to get eager black troops into battle. [125] Worse yet was the seeming insensitivity to increasing racial repression in the South throughout 1898. McKinley did not publicly protest the lynching of a black postmaster and members of his family at Lake City, South Carolina, early in the year, though Myers and Tyler begged Hanna to get him to do so. Nor did the president denounce Louisiana's strict disfranchisement law, the first passed during his term, or speak out after the bloody pogrom which followed the fall elections at Wilmington, North Carolina, or support a bill introduced by Representative George White of North Carolina, the last southern black to serve in Congress for many decades, to make lynching a federal crime. [126] Rubbing salt in these

[122] Ralph Tyler to George Myers, May 14, 1898, Box VI, folder 2, Myers Papers.
[123] George Myers to John Green, June 10, 1898, Box V, folder 2, Green Papers.
[124] William Parham to Ralph Tyler, undated, enclosed in Tyler to George Myers, June 2, 1898, Box VI, folder 2, Myers Papers.
[125] Ralph Tyler to George Myers, Aug. 27, 1899, Box VII, folder 3, ibid.; Edward A. Johnson, *History of the Negro Soldiers in the Spanish-American War* (Raleigh, 1899), pp. 127–135. Myers and his friends had to look no further than their own Ohio to see the workings of prejudice in the war effort. Some of black Ohio was eager to go to war, but was frustrated in attempts to get to the battlefield. The black Ninth Battalion of state militia, organized years before by Governor Foraker, was mustered into the regular army in 1898 with other militia units. But the Ninth was an "immune" regiment, and like almost all the other black militia companies brought into the army, it spent the war in a camp waiting for orders—a source of frustration attributable to prejudice in the war department. Cleveland *Gazette*, Mar. 5, 19, 26, May 21, July 9, 26, Oct. 8, 1898. See also Willard B. Gatewood, Jr., *Black Americans and the White Man's Burden, 1898–1903* (Urbana, Ill., 1975).
[126] Mark Hanna to George Myers, Dec. 15, 1898, Box VI, folder 7, Myers Papers; Rayford Logan, *The Betrayal of the Negro from Rutherford B. Hayes to Woodrow Wilson* (New York, 1965), pp. 97–100.

wounds, McKinley began to court the white South in 1899 as the spirit of sectional reconciliation fostered by the Spanish-American War gathered force across the nation. Climaxing these overtures, in December he journeyed to Atlanta to praise southern traditions, and, while wearing a badge of Confederate gray, he saluted the rebel war dead and offered federal care for their gravesites.[127]

Ohio blacks watched these developments with growing anger. When weeks passed after the Wilmington riot without a word from the White House, Cleveland blacks met to pass angry resolutions denouncing the administration for "criminal neglect" in its disregard for violations of the Fifteenth Amendment and its failure to protect black federal employees from mob violence.[128] At another meeting at Cleveland and one at Columbus similar resolutions were passed before the end of 1898; within a year a meeting of Oberlin blacks felt desperate enough to call upon foreign governments to protect the race from lynching.[129] In the midst of McKinley's 1900 reelection campaign, censure of the once-popular president came from sources which were rarely outspoken on public issues. In August the convention of Ohio black Odd Fellows denounced the administration, signaling the first known instance of a fraternal order taking a political stand during the period. October brought another surprise: the annual meeting of the North Ohio Conference of the A.M.E. Church passed a resolution criticizing McKinley's inaction on disfranchisement and defeated another one urging support for his reelection.[130]

There was an official explanation for McKinley's actions, conveyed to black politicians in 1899 and used publicly during the 1900 campaign. He had supposedly been warned by black advisors, particularly Arnett, Lyons, and Cheatham, that presidential statements would worsen the situation, embittering southern whites and driving them to new heights of lawlessness. It was a lame explanation. Parham, for one, was disgusted by it. "It is no excuse," he wrote Myers in June, 1899, "that certain Negroes in high places advised that silence. Those Negroes are certainly not the keepers of the President's conscience and sense of right and duty. . . ." He then concluded bitterly, "But you cannot expect much of a President who marches through the streets of a southern city decorated with a Confederate badge and feels that the nation

[127] Margaret Leech, *In the Days of McKinley* (New York, 1959), pp. 348–349; Paul Buck, *The Road to Reunion,* 1865–1900 (Boston, 1937), p. 309.
[128] Cleveland *Gazette,* Dec. 10, 1898.
[129] Ibid., Dec. 10, 1898, June 3, 1899; Columbus *Ohio State Journal,* Dec. 21, 1898; Ralph Tyler to George Myers, Dec. 17, 21, 1898, Box VI, folder 7, Myers Papers.
[130] Cleveland *Gazette,* Aug. 18, Oct. 27, 1900.

should care for and keep green the graves and memories of men who gave their all for the overthrow of the government." [131]

As the administration's course in race relations became clear, members of Myers's circle drifted apart politically. Brown and Green, officeholders under McKinley, were obliged to defend the administration. Brown did so quietly through letters to friends, but Green took a more active public role. Much to the dismay of Myers and Tyler, when interviewed in August, 1899, by the Columbus Ohio State *Journal*, Green contended that the cause of black discontent was due to nothing more than the machinations of the black Democracy and a few frustrated officeseekers. To those angered by the lack of commissions and promotions of black soldiers, Green's interview offered a questionable solace: the exploits of black heroes would be enshrined in the archives of the war department. Moreover, he argued that the president lacked the constitutional authority to send troops into the South to stem the tide of racial violence, neglecting the vast number of other options open to the administration. [132] In the face of strong criticism of the administration at the 1898, 1899, and 1900 annual meetings of the Afro-American Council, a revival of the Afro-American League undertaken in 1898 by Fortune and A.M.E. Zion Bishop Alexander Walters, Green and other federal officeholders defended the administration. In spite of Green's especially vigorous efforts to politicize the nonpartisan deliberations of the Council in 1900, it refused to pass his resolutions endorsing McKinley's reelection and the Republican party. [133]

Other members of the group took different directions. Parham and Tyler did not defend the administration publicly; both men fluctuated between disillusionment and a hope that, by working in the 1900 campaign, they might be able to gain enough esteem to influence a change in the southern policy. Yet they had no concrete proposals for such a new policy. More than anything else they wanted some display of concern from the president, but they knew that his efforts to befriend the white South made this extremely unlikely. With no specific proposals to impress upon their party, and with little faith in McKinley, their despair easily triumphed over their hope, and both put comparatively

131 Ibid., Sept. 22, 29, Oct. 27, 1900; William Parham to George Myers, June 30, 1899, Box VII, folder 2, Myers Papers.

132 Columbus *Ohio State Journal*, Aug. 23, 1899; Ralph Tyler to George Myers, Aug. 26, 1899, John Green to George Myers, Aug. 29, 1899, Box VII, folder 3, and Ralph Tyler to George Myers, Sept. 11, 1899, Box VII, folder 4, Myers Papers.

133 Cleveland *Gazette*, Sept. 8, 29, 1900; George Myers to John Green, Dec. 9, 20, 28, 1899, Box V, folder 3, Jere Brown to John Green, Jan. 21, 1899, Box V, folder 7, F. L. Barnett to John Green, Aug. 9, 1900, Box VI, folder 1, Green Papers; John Green to William McKinley, June 29, 1899, McKinley Papers.

little effort into that campaign. Parham, in fact, gave up politics after decades of activity, instead devoting himself entirely to his law practice.[134]

The disenchanted Myers also believed that campaign activity was a necessary prelude to any attempt to influence the president. His role, however, was different from that in the last presidential campaign. McKinley's renomination was never in doubt, and Southerners were in firm control of the black aspect of the convention. With the support of Hanna and McKinley, Myers did again serve on the state executive committee, and with Brown's aid he directed the black canvass in Ohio. It was a difficult job. Myers found McKinley unpopular, and he had a difficult time inspiring blacks with a platform that contained a bland statement on voting rights and no anti-lynching plank.[135]

Just days after McKinley's enormous triumph, Myers wrote to the president. His letter, stylistically embellished by Tyler, politely observed that the votes which McKinley had received from Ohio blacks were the result of their faith that, during his second term, the president would speak out against disfranchisement and racial violence and would award patronage to northern blacks. The desired results were never obtained. McKinley's second inaugural spoke of sectional reconciliation but said nothing of black rights, and the last months of his life saw no change in racial policy. Indeed, in the hope of building the bases for a white Republican party in South Carolina, McKinley courted conservative white Democrats with patronage.[136]

The assassination ended Ohioans' slim hopes for influence at Washington. McKinley's successor, Theodore Roosevelt, developed his black political ties through Booker T. Washington. Though Roosevelt attempted to check the influence of southern black placemen and grafters, just as Tyler might have wished, he continued to depend on southern blacks for talent and advisement, now looking for individuals of high personal integrity and respectability. While Washington respected Myers's political acumen, and they would enjoy cordial relations, there

[134] William Parham to George Myers, June 30, 1899, Box VII, folder 2, July 23, 1899, Box VII, folder 3, Ralph Tyler to George Myers, Sept. 11, 1899, Box VII, folder 4, Mar. 8, 1900, Box VIII, folder 1, Myers Papers.

[135] Jere Brown to George Myers, June 30, 1900, Box VIII, folder 1, ibid.; Cleveland *Gazette*, June 23, 30, Oct. 20, 27, 1900; Ralph Tyler to George Myers, July 10, 1900, Box VIII, folder 4, Jere Brown to George Myers, Sept. 21, 1900, Box IX, folder 3, Myers Papers.

[136] George Myers to William McKinley, draft dated Nov. 15, 1900, Box IX, folder 5, Myers Papers (carbon of final copy is in Box VI, folder 1, Green Papers); Cripps, "Lily White Republicans," p. 91; Cleveland *Gazette*, May 4, 25, 1901.

was little reason for him to consult Myers often.[137] At the same time, in the years before his death in 1904, Hanna had little to offer Ohio blacks. His rivalry with Roosevelt left him with little say in the dispensing of major black appointments. With the exception of a war department clerkship which he obtained for Clifford in 1902, to repay him for his key vote in 1898, he gave little evidence of caring about the minor offices.[138]

Under these circumstances, it is not surprising that the decline of political activity among Myers and his allies continued after McKinley's death. Their own opportunities had lessened considerably with the death of the patrons on whom they had so depended. Moreover, the national Republican party was rapidly changing, taking a form that blacks could not accept but were powerless to oppose. The party displayed a growing willingness to assent to southern repression. Proposals to lessen southern representation at national conventions in recognition of the impact of disfranchisement first appeared in 1899; although McKinley had refused to consent to them, they were openly and increasingly discussed after his death. It is true that some, like Tyler, were hostile to southern power; nevertheless, the Ohioans all saw these proposals as attempts to end racial political influence completely, and they therefore rejected them as by far the greater of two evils. The next two Republican presidents offered little leadership in racial affairs. During his first term Roosevelt's Square Deal had promised equal opportunity for all, and he had fought for his southern black appointments in the face of white opposition to local black officeholding. The second term was different: Roosevelt began a complex game of working with southern black Republicans while concurrently establishing the bases for white Republican parties in the South, and he allowed black federal patronage to decrease. His dismissal of the Brownsville soldiers in 1906 without due process hardly represented fair play and justice in race relations. Perhaps the most important signs of Roosevelt's mood were the public addresses of William Howard Taft. The secretary of war called upon southern blacks to place basic education and the cultivation of middle-class values and habits before politics, and thus to make themselves worthy to receive constitutional rights at some future date. When Taft himself became president, he refused to appoint blacks to office in the South where local whites

[137] August Meier, *Negro Thought in America, 1880–1915* (Ann Arbor, 1963), p. 112.
[138] John Green to George Myers, Feb. 18, 1904, Box XII, folder 5, Myers Papers; Cleveland *Gazette*, Sept. 3, 1904.

objected, encouraging southern white Republicans even more than did his predecessor, and he allowed racial segregation to be instituted in several government office buildings at Washington. For all its earlier faults, this was hardly the Republican party of the 1870s and 1880s to which men like Myers and Brown had once looked for moral authority in race relations.[139]

In the years between Hanna's death and the emergence of Taft in 1908, the situation within the state Republican party proved too chaotic for Myers and his allies to forge alliances of the type they had once enjoyed. Because Hanna had never constructed a tightly knit political organization, his passing forced his followers to choose between Foraker and old Hanna associates, particularly Charles Dick, who succeeded Hanna in the Senate, and Myron T. Herrick of Cleveland, who served as governor in 1903 and 1904. Few looked to Foraker to replace Hanna as a patron of blacks. While he was reasonably friendly and always quick to defend the race, he was also aloof, rarely consulting Ohio black politicians, and his record on black patronage was very poor. Dick was a good friend who always had time for conversation and correspondence with black politicians, but he was not close enough to the Roosevelt administration to benefit blacks greatly, and he lacked Hanna's ability to inspire confidence and loyalty. Because Herrick had acted decisively in 1904 by sending the National Guard to Springfield in order to end racial violence, he was respected among blacks. But his unsuccessful 1905 reelection campaign ended the Ohio aspect of his career. As it was, the Democratic and reform trends were already further muddying the waters of Ohio politics.[140]

The result was a steady diminution of the influence of the state's old black political leadership as it began to retreat from active battle in confusion, disgust, despair, and exhaustion, and individuals began to go their separate ways. Out of a lingering sense of loyalty and in response to Hanna's urging, in 1903 Myers again consented to serve on the Republican state executive committee in order to stimulate black interest in electing a Republican legislature, thus helping to insure

[139] Cleveland *Gazette*, Jan. 13, 1900; Jere Brown to George Myers, Dec. 16, 1899, John Green to George Myers, Dec. 20, 1899, Box VII, folder 5, Myers Papers; Cripps, "Lily White Republicans," pp. 295–358; Cincinnati *Enquirer*, Jan. 5, 1901, Nov. 26, 1902, Mar. 12, 1909.

[140] Warner, *Progressivism in Ohio*, pp. 135, 143–144 and passim; George Myers to John Green, May 24, Box VI, folder 3, Green Papers; George Myers to Myron Herrick, Apr. 15, 1904, Box III, folder 3, and Cleveland Anti-Lynching League, "Resolutions," Mar. 28, 1904, Box II, folder 2, Myron T. Herrick Papers, OHS. Summarizing the long-standing complaints against Foraker: Ralph Tyler to George Myers, Dec. 13, 1907, and George Myers to Harry B. Alexander, Dec. 16, 1907, Box XIV, folder 2, Myers Papers.

Hanna's reelection to the Senate. But Hanna died soon after, and though Myers continued to work in politics in future years, he was less active and less aggressive. His political activities were occasional and usually local. He might become involved to help a friend obtain a position, or at the request of Booker T. Washington, or in an emergency— as in 1907, when anger among Cleveland blacks over the Brownsville affair threatened to erupt into a full-scale (and, to Myers's mind, unfair) revolt against Republicans in the fall municipal election. In addition to the death of his patrons, bitterness over the intrigues which threatened to destroy black Republican power in the South also kept him from national political activity. Myers now devoted himself almost exclusively to improving his business and feathering his own nest.[141]

Tyler befriended Washington as it became clear that Roosevelt would depend upon the Tuskegeean for advice on black affairs and patronage. Just after the turn of the century, Tyler began to desire a high federal post, but since he had refused to work for the party in 1898 and 1900, his ambitions would be frustrated. In the next years he did not work as actively in politics as he once had; however, he quietly strengthened his contacts in strategic places, particularly at Tuskegee, in the hope that something might eventually come his way. In 1907 Washington's influence with Roosevelt supplied Tyler with the opportunity he had waited for. In order to show a concern for blacks, and to embarrass Foraker by not consulting him on an important Ohio appointment in retaliation for the senator's defense of the Brownsville soldiers, Roosevelt appointed Tyler as auditor of the navy, the highest federal post ever given an Ohio Negro. Many blacks felt that he was being used. Even his friend Myers accused him of "selling his birthright" and leaked word of the appointment, which Tyler had given in confidence, to Foraker in the hope that the senator might wage a counterattack. The impression that Tyler was a tool of the administration gained ground when he emerged as one of the administration's leading black defenders in the Brownsville matter not long after taking office.[142]

Cottrill obtained an important post in the same manner. After years

141 Warner, *Progressivism in Ohio*, p. 143; George Myers to Walter L. Cohen, Sept. 18, 1902, Box XI, folder 5, and Charles Dick to George Myers, June 19, 1903, Box XII, folder 1, Myers Papers; George Myers to John Green, July 26, 1904, Box VI, folder 3, Green Papers.

142 John D. Weaver, *The Brownsville Raid* (New York, 1971), pp. 121–122; Meier, *Negro Thought*, p. 229; Ralph Tyler to George Myers, May 18, 25, 1900, Box VIII, folder 3, Mar. 22, 1904, Box VII, folder 6, Sept. 3, 1907, Box XIV, folder 2, Myers Papers; George Myers to Joseph Foraker, Jan. 23, 1907, Box 68, Joseph B. Foraker Papers, CHS.

of uneventful service as deputy recorder of Lucas County and a local Republican machine operative, he was appointed collector of internal revenue at Honolulu in 1912 on Washington's recommendation, when Taft came to fear that his poor record on race would hurt his chance for black support in a bid for reelection. Tyler and Cottrill both lost their positions during the Wilson administration, Tyler in 1913, Cottrill in 1915. Perhaps hoping to free his children from mainland black-white conflict, Cottrill decided to become a permanent resident of Hawaii.[143]

John Green lost his position much sooner—in 1906, when it was abolished. Like Parham, he spent his old age practicing law. No longer burdened by the obligation of defending Republican administrations, Green quickly began to express publicly his fears about the trend of race relations.[144] Brown, Fillmore, and Clifford experienced frustrations and setbacks in their patronage careers. Fillmore left government service in 1907 in the hope of making more money; he entered the insurance business and did not return to Ohio.[145] The elderly Brown was demoted, with a large drop in pay, when his boss in the federal service tried to push him out to make room for a friend. Compulsory retirement legislation then before Congress might have affected him anyway, but the fear that he would not be able to support his family contributed greatly to the decline of his already failing health; Brown died in 1913.[146] In 1906 Clifford lost the clerkship that Hanna had gotten for him, subsequently entering the funeral business at Washington. But he had lived off patronage for almost twenty years, and he could not imagine another means of livelihood. Moreover, he feared that business would prove an even less certain source of income than patronage. Thus, he struggled successfully to recoup his old position and sold his business at a loss in order to reenter the federal service within a year. "Fate has been unkind to me since the death of Senator Hanna," he wrote to Myers in 1907, telling of his lack of savings and the instability of his career.[147]

Arnett remained a powerful advisor to McKinley to the end. Ac-

---

[143] Cleveland *Gazette*, Dec. 24, 1910; Indianapolis *Freeman*, Nov. 8, 1913; William Crogman, *Progress of a Race* (Chicago, 1925), p. 353; George Myers to Booker T. Washington, Dec. 14, 1910, Box 430, Booker T. Washington Papers, LC.

[144] Cleveland *Gazette*, July 8, Oct. 6, Nov. 18, 1906.

[145] [Charles Fillmore], *Colored American Magazine*, XII (Apr., 1907), 306, 311–312.

[146] Cleveland *Gazette*, Apr. 5, 1913; Jere Brown to Booker T. Washington, Jan. 18, 1910, Box 402, Washington Papers.

[147] L. M. Strawn to Charles Dick, Sept. 2, 1905, Box VII, folder 2, Charles Dick Papers, OHS; William Clifford to George Myers, Mar. 3, 1907, Box XIII, folder 7, Myers Papers; Baltimore *Afro-American*, Sept. 5, 1908.

cording to Myers, the president had allegedly grown tired of the bishop's constant requests for his sons and angry that Arnett had not supported the administration publicly (let alone outspokenly, like Green) when it was criticized for its silence on lynching and disfranchisement. Yet the bishop's southern and church contacts continued to earn him the president's respect. The last months of the first term and the early weeks of the second found Arnett busily contending for positions for friends—and for a better job for Henry, a clerkship for Alonzo, and another chaplaincy for Ben Junior, who had lost his original post because of an impropriety just a few months after his appointment. But the bishop was not to enjoy influence with Roosevelt. He spent the years before his death in 1906 a sickly, aged man, hounded by his creditors.[148]

And Harry Smith slipped bitterly into middle age, never missing an issue of his *Gazette,* but never again, despite his continuing ambition, holding office after his third term as a Republican legislator ended in 1901. His bids for legislative nomination in 1901, 1912, and 1914 were frustrated in nominating conventions or primaries, largely because he lacked the endorsement of reigning Republican bosses, who saw him as a highly unreliable quantity. In 1905, when the likelihood of a Republican debacle was evident well before the campaign, Smith did obtain a nomination, but he and all other Cleveland Republicans went down to defeat. Menacing times occasionally forced Smith into temporary alliances with old adversaries like Green, whom he allowed to write an occasional column in the *Gazette.* But he denounced them bitterly when they stood in his way—as in 1911, when his successful struggle against Green in a nonpartisan race for the black delegate from Cleveland to the state constitutional convention was accompanied by weekly abuse of his opponent in the *Gazette.* Smith remained active in racial affairs, but he also remained isolated.[149]

At a time when the race needed forceful and assertive leadership, the old leaders faced the crisis of the new century in disarray—not without influence, and prestigious by age and experience, but with energies often in eclipse, basic racial premises of a lifetime under siege, and authority weakened by an erosion of its political influence. The

[148] Ralph Tyler to George Myers, Oct. 5, 1898, Box VI, folder 6, Myers Papers; George Myers to John Green, Dec. 7, 1900, Box VI, folder 1, Green Papers; B. W. Arnett to William McKinley, Feb. 8 (telegram), Mar. 11, 1901, McKinley Papers; Baltimore *Afro-American Ledger,* Oct. 14, 1906; Indianapolis *Freeman,* Oct. 9, 1909.

[149] Cleveland *Gazette,* Aug. 12, 19, 26, Sept. 23, 1911, June 1, 1912, Aug. 15, 1914. As an independent, Smith ran unsuccessfully for governor and Ohio secretary of state after 1916. Ibid., Dec. 13, 1941.

times demanded that the old leadership steel itself for further battles, more difficult than it seemed prepared to wage. Meanwhile, a new force, bred of the time, with racial ideals and goals shaped by them, was already beginning to gather force and to seek the roots of recovery.

13

The Rise and Challenge
of a New Leadership

After the turn of the century a dynamic, innovative new group, composed of a small corps of younger businessmen, lawyers, doctors, educators, and social workers who based their livelihoods largely on the black community, became prominent in racial affairs and asserted a claim to racial leadership. This group looked to the available social and intellectual trends for racial values and priorities fitted to the emerging conditions of race relations and black life. Its search revealed a growing but unorganized black urban population, rapidly expanding Negro enterprise, and a complex of inspiring racial ideals emphasizing black solidarity, self-help, and group material development, all conveniently symbolized by the life and thought of Booker T. Washington, the central racial spokesman of the first decade of the century. These social and intellectual trends, strongly reinforced by individual struggles to base personal success on the Negro market, combined to provide the foundations for a new synthesis for racial strategy, embodying new goals and suggesting new relationships between the individual and the race. Above all, the new leadership hoped to create a vital, supportive racial community and to generate unity, cooperation, and uplift.

In its formative years the new leadership had an anomalous position within black Ohio: it failed to fit neatly into existing social categories, and it posed a basic challenge to the ideological orthodoxies of the past. Educated, often successful at prestigious pursuits, and conventionally bourgeois in social and political values, lifestyles, and individual aspirations, its members were distinct from the impoverished, isolated masses and the striving yet marginal middle class. But while the group shared much with the black upper class, it was unique. The tendency of many members of the new leadership to base personal and racial aspirations upon the black community, and their commitment to group values, solidarity, and development, created perspectives and values different from those of the upper class, which had developed its economic ties with whites, sought expanded contacts with higher-status whites whenever possible, and placed primary emphasis in its racial thought upon clearing the way for individual excellence, social mobility, and acceptance. As the retreat from congregational and (in the case of some black physicians) professional bonds with whites suggests, some members of the upper class were reexamining their position and values. But such circumspection tended to be partial and tentative, constituting a questioning of a world view, not a renunciation of it. While older leaders were in flux and confused by changing times, the newer leadership was more confident in its ability to deal with the only times it knew. It lacked power and influence, and, in light of the lingering authority of the older leadership, it would have to wage a two-pronged struggle: with propaganda, and with practical daily political and racial activities.

For now we shall examine the development of the new leadership's internal and ideological solidarity and its racial ideas and priorities, and discuss the various practical and ideological challenges which it posed to older black leaders. Both generations, however, attempted to shape the race's immediate responses to its two greatest problems in early twentieth-century Ohio: the deterioration of race relations and the migration of southern blacks. The full story of these efforts will be told in the next chapter.

I

The new leaders had an internal cohesiveness which resulted not only from common interests in a racial program, but more fundamentally from common generational experiences and perspectives. It was not simply that there was a similarity in the pattern of individual lives (though there was this, too); rather, while coming of age their generation had witnessed the inception of a new epoch in the life of the race, and the young leaders could not help but be influenced by its implications. Drawing a composite portrait from individual biographies,[1] we see that most members of the new group did not

[1] Biographical information was accumulated for 89 professionals and businessmen who rose to prominence in black community affairs during and after the late 1890s. Such individuals tended to belong to the same organizations, which they themselves created for the purpose of giving voice and force to their racial ideals and attitudes, and to socialize with one another in clubs and various formal and informal social circles; this tendency aided greatly in establishing a list of names.

reach their twenties and thirties until after the turn of the century, when they became involved in racial affairs. Born between 1870 (at the earliest) and the mid-1880s, most had not experienced the high hopes and soaring expectations which those years had brought to William Parham, convincing him not to leave the United States. Nor had they, like Harry Smith, been old enough to take part in the effort to achieve the race's dramatic victories in Ohio in the 1880s. Instead, they had come of age in what was for blacks a deflationary time. As they planned their lives in a white and increasingly hostile world, contemplating their own futures in the context of the future of their people, the forces of repression and reaction gathered strength in both North and South. Gone were the old hopes for white acceptance of an early black integration into the American mainstream, which had once led Peter Clark to suggest that his children's generation might someday leave the black church for integrated worship on terms of equality. With those shattered hopes had gone optimistic speculation on a timetable for winning full equality. These younger blacks reached adulthood and began to aspire to lead their people in the midst of hundreds of headline-grabbing lynchings, the loss of the vote throughout the South, and increasing white-imposed segregation on terms of inequality and insult, all unopposed by the race's historic allies, the federal government and the Republican party. Such times offered no hope of final, dramatic victories, as an older generation had seen in school integration, or of reliable white cooperation and acceptance. Rather, there was only the possibility of small, interim gains based largely upon black strivings.

Most had not themselves experienced the worst of the changing racial situation. Few were Southerners. Approximately two-thirds of these younger people were Northerners, and over half of them were Ohioans; of the remaining third who were southern-born, most had migrated to the North as young adults. Yet even the Ohioans and Northerners had experienced migration—to the cities. While some of them became active in racial affairs in cities where they were born and

Of equal importance were surveys of new black businesses and advertisements for new businesses found in black newspapers. Major sources were the Cleveland *Gazette,* Cleveland *Journal,* Indianapolis *Freeman, Colored American Magazine,* and *Voice of the Negro,* among newspapers and magazines; Clement Richardson, editor in chief, *National Cyclopedia of the Colored Race* (Montgomery, 1919), and Thomas Yenser, ed., *Who's Who in Colored America: A Biographical Dictionary of Notable Persons of African Descent in America, 1930–31–32* (Brooklyn, 1933), among biographical dictionaries; and Russell H. Davis, *Black Americans in Cleveland from George Peake to Carl B. Stokes* (Washington, 1972); Wendell Phillips Dabney, *Cincinnati's Colored Citizens: Historical, Sociological, and Biographical* (Cincinnati, 1926).

bred, a more common experience was for talented, ambitious, and educated individuals to leave the rural areas and small towns of central
and southern Ohio and of surrounding Indiana, Michigan, and Pennsylvania, with their declining black and white populations, provincial
environments, and lack of opportunity for young blacks, to seek expanded opportunity in the cities. In Ohio the result was that, accompanying the more voluminous migration of black workers from the
towns and rural areas to the cities, there was a migration of aspiring,
often educated blacks in search of white-collar, commercial, and professional opportunities. In 1908 the Steubenville correspondent of the
Cleveland *Journal* summarized the plight of the average educated
black young adult in that town, suggesting the hard choices that they,
and others like them, faced in making careers:

> Steubenville has a number of intellectually alive, striving young people
> who have finished the high school course, and having nothing to do
> here and unwilling to strike out single-handed elsewhere, have settled
> down in the uncertain avenues which this town offers for a livelihood
> for colored youth. Among these is a young man whose parents have
> given him every opportunity offered by the schools for preparation for
> life. . . . No employment commensurate with his ability offers itself
> here. Why these young people do not venture out and undertake some-
> thing that will bring out what is best in them puzzles me. . . .[2]

The social origins of members of the new group varied considerably.
There were those like William Porter's daughter Jennie, a Cincinnati
public school teacher, and John Green's sons William and Theodore,
both attorneys; these scions of old upper-class urban families were
then searching for their own racial stance in tune with the times.[3]
Others like Samuel Huffman, an attorney setting up practice at Columbus in 1912, and Dr. Jessie Dickerson, a woman from Circleville who
began to practice medicine in Cleveland at the turn of the century,
were children of the small town–small city black elite. The Huffman
family had lived in Springfield for many years, participated in local
Republican politics, and owned a home in one of the city's better
neighborhoods. Dickerson's father was a respected A.M.E. minister
whose parishes were generally to be found in the larger black communities of southern and central Ohio throughout the late nineteenth
century.[4]

The majority, however, came from more humble and obscure black

[2] Cleveland *Journal*, Mar. 14, 1908.

[3] Davis, *Black Americans in Cleveland*, p. 173; John Green, *Fact Stranger Than Fiction: 75 Years of a Busy Life* (Cleveland, 1919), pp. 355–357.

[4] Cleveland *Gazette*, July 6, 1901; Indianapolis *Freeman*, Sept. 12, 1914.

middle-class backgrounds which encouraged their dedication to hard work, security, and a straight-and-narrow path of morality. Nahum Daniel Brascher was editor of the Cleveland *Journal,* established in 1903 to give a voice to the young professionals and entrepreneurs of that city. He was the son of a Connersville, Indiana, artisan and odd-job man, a simple, unpretentious family man, neither affluent nor poor.[5] Brascher's friend, Tom Fleming, a Cleveland attorney and politician, was reared at Meadville, Pennsylvania, in a broken home; his father, the son of a local barbershop proprietor, had deserted his wife, Lavinia, and three small children. A hard-working, pious woman dedicated to keeping what remained of her family together, Lavinia supported them for many years by doing domestic work, but she grew sickly and occasionally had to take help from more prosperous relatives.[6] Others were like Dr. Joseph Johnson, a physician who established himself in Columbus after several years of a village practice. They had been born and raised on small family farms in the North—in Johnson's case, in an area of Darke County, Ohio, which was populated mostly by black tenant farmers and owners of small holdings.[7]

Their families set education as an important goal for their children and instilled in them a strong desire for schooling and a belief in education as a means to social mobility and greater security. The younger group was, in fact, considerably better educated than the older racial leadership. While it was rare for the latter to have gone beyond elementary education, it was the rule among the younger men and women. At a time when high school was not considered necessary for a career in business, many of the entrepreneurs were high school graduates, or had had the benefit of at least some high school. While the older generation of black professionals, like its white counterpart, often was trained rather than educated for a professional career—for example, by reading law in an attorney's office or mixing practical experience with a short course in dentistry—the younger professionals fell in line with the increasingly rigorous standards governing the professions. Many pursued a more modern course of education, going from high school to college for two to four years and then to professional school. They received their educations in both white and black settings, but, perhaps because of the northern nativity of the majority, they were products less of the southern black schools than of integrated colleges and professional schools in Ohio and the Old Northwest. The southern-

[5] Cleveland *Journal,* Jan. 1, 1910.
[6] Thomas Fleming, "My Rise and Persecution" (c. 1932), typescript, WRHS.
[7] Walter Christmas, ed., *Negroes in Public Affairs and Government* (Yonkers, 1966), I, 187.

bred often attended black colleges and obtained professional degrees at Fisk or Howard; the northern-bred more frequently were graduates of local public and private institutions such as Western Reserve University, the University of Michigan, Ohio State University, and Northwestern, where they made up part of the very small but nevertheless growing group of black students.

Compared to previous black college graduates and professionals, the younger ones got through school and embarked on careers more quickly, no doubt fostering the possible impression that they were over-educated upstarts. In the past, black college graduates were typically in their late twenties at the time of commencement, and black professionals often did not finish training or professional education until into their thirties; now, however, college and professional graduates were seldom past their mid-twenties. Their rapid progress through school was partly the result of parents supporting their educations, particularly in the case of those from more affluent homes. But for those of humble origin it was more the result of the fact that their families were able, however modestly, to support themselves, leaving ambitious children not too encumbered by pressing obligations to parents, brothers, and sisters. At the same time, many, particularly among the professionals, deferred marriage until after launching their careers. They worked their way through school, of necessity often falling back on the traditional sources of black opportunity, particularly the services, to help finance their educations. While attending Western Reserve in the 1890s, young Alex Martin, later an attorney, set up a barber's chair in his dormitory and cut the hair of classmates to put himself through school.[8] Ellis Dale, who came to Cleveland from Georgia to obtain a medical education, waited on tables for the same purpose.[9] They often worked hard and long; however, extant biographies of this group lack the old-time stories of extreme sacrifice and struggle in the pursuit of education and career. Rarer than in previous decades were experiences such as Tom Fleming's. When his mother could no longer work without ruining her health, Fleming had been forced in 1885 or 1886, at about age twelve, to leave school and go to work, in spite of his mother's most heartfelt desires and bitter tears. Fleming then spent almost two decades as a barber at Meadville, Astabula, and (after 1892) Cleveland, wishing all the time to continue his education and dreaming of someday being a lawyer. In 1899, with

8 Yenser, ed., *Who's Who in Colored America*, p. 296; Davis, *Black Americans in Cleveland*, p. 173.

9 Fleming, "My Rise and Persecution," p. 26; Davis, *Black Americans in Cleveland*, p. 177.

the help of two of his white customers, he bought the barbershop at the Cleveland Chamber of Commerce building. This allowed him to earn enough money to enter law school at nearby Baldwin-Wallace College. At the same time he had to make up the studies he had missed by dropping out of school; private tutors helped him to obtain a high school education. Working, studying, and learning law, Fleming finished his legal education in 1906 at the age of thirty-two, several years behind most of his peers.[10]

As they settled in the city and began their careers, the younger professionals and businessmen established social patterns which, while not in themselves atypical, reinforced their uniqueness as a group. They usually lived in or on the fringes of the major centers of black population, rather than in the upper-class enclaves in higher-status neighborhoods. Clevelanders lived not on the city's East Side, but on the better residential streets in and around the Central Avenue district. At Cincinnati some lived in the rapidly developing black area at Walnut Hills, but few could be found in the other hilltop communities where blacks sought escape from the city; instead, most resided on the fringes of the city's West End. Daytonians invariably lived in the vicinity of West Fifth and Dunbar Avenue in the West Side black area, while those at Columbus were found in the black East Long Street section. The choice of residence indicated not only where they were most comfortable, but also a desire to be close to their work; most of the entrepreneurs and professionals had businesses and offices in the black commercial districts not far from their homes.[11]

Their associational life both mirrored and differed from that of the old upper class. Many belonged to one or several fraternal orders, but they appeared to prefer the newer Knights of Pythias and the black Elks (founded in 1898) to the more venerable Masons and Odd Fellows. They joined churches, but instead of affiliating with the Episcopalians and other higher-status white denominations, most of them belonged to either the black Baptist or A.M.E. denominations during the first decade of the century. The fact that they established their own social clubs illustrates a solidarity which reached into personal relations. Cleveland's Bachelor-Benedict Social Club, Dayton's Bachelor's

---

[10] Fleming, "My Rise and Persecution," pp. 1–20.

[11] City directories, maps found in city directories, and maps of cities obtained from the Bureau of the Census and local archives were used to trace place of residence and work. City directories: Columbus, 1901, 1910; Cleveland, 1905, 1911; Cincinnati, 1905, 1910, 1913; and Dayton, 1907. Also helpful were the Indianapolis *Freeman* surveys of black community development undertaken during 1909–15; *Freeman*, June 19, 1909, Sept. 9, 1911, Aug. 3, 1912, Sept. 12, 1914, Aug. 14, Sept. 4, 11, 1915.

Club, and Cincinnati Winona Club were all founded around the turn of the century by groups of fifteen to thirty young, as yet unmarried, businessmen and professionals who were then becoming active in racial affairs. These clubs existed largely for the purpose of fostering fellowship among men with common career interests and backgrounds; they also gave a nod to literary subjects and to the discussion of racial conditions. But the Winona Club went furthest toward capturing the entrepreneurial spirit of many of the young men: every month each member placed a fixed sum in the club's savings account, with the intention that, when the fund was large enough, the club would begin a business of its own.[12]

Thus after 1900 racial life experienced a new force of young, educated businessmen and professionals, often lacking strong ties to the old order but intimately bound up in the new urban black social and economic trends. Less reflective than activist, their interests are best approached by considering the interplay of their attitudes with their practical efforts. These efforts followed two broad paths: stimulating economic uplift and the prosperity of black commercial districts, and establishing institutional vehicles of self-help. Such concerns reflected the existence within the new leadership of two groups—urban business boosters, and educators and social workers interested in developing race educational and welfare institutions. Their broad interests often overlapped, but their activities generally remained in separate spheres.

II

The older generation of black leaders had traditionally seen economic uplift from the perspective of individual preparation and mobility. However, young businessmen, doctors, and lawyers, living and working in and around neighborhoods with growing black populations, easily came to see the question in the light of group development. A racial consumer market was then forming in the cities, and it became the basis for speculation on the rise of a black business community and on the possibility of greater intragroup economic cooperation. The simultaneous formation of race corporations in such small towns as Gallipolis has suggested a growing interest among blacks, metropolitan and otherwise, in utilizing intragroup economic coopera-

[12] Cleveland *Journal,* Jan. 28, 1905, July 18, 25, 1908; Indianapolis *Freeman,* Aug. 3, 1912, Aug. 29, 1914; Cleveland Gazette, June 29, 1907; [Winona Club], *Colored American Magazine,* IV (Mar., 1902), 316–322.

tion to deal with racial intolerance and rejection. The most promising practical basis for such cooperation lay in the cities, and within them cooperation was most fully developed.

Both social and intellectual trends served as points of departure for one of the earliest new associational activities. With the aid of a few sympathetic older businessmen, who were generally engaged in successful service and retail enterprises catering to whites, they founded black boosters organizations at Cleveland, Cincinnati, Columbus, and Dayton after 1900. The ethos of these organizations was shaped by the idea of black capitalism expounded at the time by Booker T. Washington and the National Negro Business League, which Washington had established in 1900. All four Ohio organizations were affiliated with the N.N.B.L.[13]

Washington's black capitalism was part of his larger, though informal, program for forging bonds of racial solidarity and paving the way for individual and group uplift without directly challenging the canons of white supremacy. The Tuskegeean believed that success at business was one of the most promising means for gaining white approval and ultimate entrance into the American mainstream. Thus he placed the black businessman in the vanguard of the black struggle, making success in business not simply an object of worthy individual striving, but a vital contribution to racial advancement. Blacks could succeed at business in a way which was not allowed in other fields because the immutable laws of supply and demand were thought to be colorblind: the individual who built the better mousetrap and sold it at the lower price would win the respect of the world and find all races gratefully beating a path to his door. Washington and the N.N.B.L. attempted to create a mutually supportive solidarity among black entrepreneurs and to foster a morale-boosting aura of success around existing black businesses, countering the depressing trend of race relations with the impression of a broad advance on terms honored by the white world. Paradoxically, racial patronage of race enterprise was strongly urged. Triumphs in the colorblind world of business would be won largely by disciplining a racial consumer market through appeals to race pride and solidarity.[14]

The activities of Ohio's leagues were shaped by Washington's ideas and by local conditions. All of them sought primarily to promote and

[13] Cleveland *Journal*, May 27, 1905, Aug. 24, 1907; Indianapolis *Freeman*, July 24, 1909.
[14] Louis R. Harlan, "Booker T. Washington and the National Negro Business League," in William G. Shade and Roy C. Herrenkohl, *Seven on Black* (Philadelphia, 1969), pp. 75–91; August Meier, *Negro Thought in America, 1880–1915* (Ann Arbor, 1963), pp. 124–127.

strengthen black business and the local black commercial section. They met regularly to discuss the local black and white consumer markets and business efficiency. Campaigns urged blacks in the name of solidarity and pride, both in the race and in the neighborhood with which it was associated, to eschew the often better-stocked and less expensive white shops in order to trade with their struggling brethren. Columbus boosters found that the race market was subverted by large downtown department stores which encouraged black trade; they therefore had to emphasize the convenience as well as the obligation of shopping in the black neighborhood.[15] The leagues also encouraged blacks to enter business and to make investments. This theme was particularly strong at Dayton, where the rapid physical and demographic expansion of the city after 1900 created a boom in land and housing markets. "New plats of land have been opened for miles around," said one black resident in 1912, "and different opportunities present themselves with the opening of each plat." Members of the Dayton league were said to be facing the booming real estate market "with their accustomed optimism, realizing the resources at their command in the rapid growth of the city." Leading members of the league were deeply involved in the boom (three early officers, E. T. Sherman, Edward Banks, and Thaddeus Wheeler, were realtors) and were urging others to invest in land and homes.[16]

The buoyantly optimistic spirit of all business league endeavors would have been familiar to contemporary chambers of commerce across mid-America. Typical was the ethos of the Cleveland league, the Negro Board of Trade, which was founded in 1905 by twenty-five blacks, almost exclusively young businessmen, attorneys, and doctors. New heights of business success and neighborhood commercial development were constantly projected. Said J. Walter Wills, a funeral director and insurance agent who served in 1906 as the board's second president, "We are going to make Central Avenue a credit to . . . Cleveland from a business point of view. We are going to have so complete a business community that the only reason we will have for going [downtown] will be to look it over and get a few pointers." Members were informed in advance of the appropriate mood for meetings and rallies. An early meeting was heralded with the message: "IT WILL BE A DAY FOR OPTIMISM ONLY," and speakers were urged to prepare only "an optimistic address." One of the board's first organized activities symbolized its morale-boosting function: the members

[15] Indianapolis *Freeman*, Sept. 12, 1914.
[16] Ibid., Aug. 3, 1912.

marched to a Central Avenue drugstore just opened by two of their number in order to "congratulate them on their opening." [17]

The booster mentality, the preoccupation with material development, race patronage of race enterprise, and the development of a prosperous black commercial district all represented considerable departures from both the style and strategy of the older generation. It was not surprising that the young boosters also established their own journalistic voice from developing and propagandizing their viewpoint. Where they existed at all, Ohio race papers edited by older men, such as Smith's *Gazette* and Wendell Phillips Dabney's Cincinnati *Union* (begun in 1907),[18] lacked the new vision. After 1900 weeklies began to appear to espouse the new views: the Cleveland *Journal*, the Columbus *Standard*, and (at various times between 1900 and the World War) the Dayton *Informer*, the *Record*, and the *Citizen*.

Unfortunately, a significant number of back issues exist only for the Cleveland *Journal*. But it is fortunate nonetheless that we should have it, for in a number of ways—its ethos, the ideas and ideals which informed its work, the evolution of its concerns for the development of the local black community, and the temperaments and interests of the young men behind it—the *Journal* exemplifies some of the most important tendencies defining the younger generation of racial spokesmen. Founded early in 1903, the *Journal* was the product of a collaboration between a handful of young men. The original suggestion that a paper be established to present the new trends of racial thought and the new conditions of racial life came from Nahum Daniel Brascher, who had come to Cleveland around 1901 shortly after graduating from Meredith College, a small integrated school in Zanesville. An intellectual young man fitted for no particular vocation, Brascher had worked at first as a helper in a dining room—a job secured for him by Tom Fleming, whom he had met shortly after settling in the city. Next Brascher and a friend opened a short-lived secretarial school for blacks. At this point he went to Fleming with the idea for a paper. Since neither had the money, they in turn went for advice and financial assistance to Welcome T. Blue, an aggressive young real estate man who with S. C. Green would soon establish the Mohawk Realty Company. After Blue agreed to help them raise the necessary capital, the three young men founded the Journal Printing Company. Blue was to be president, Fleming the secretary, treasurer, and (appropriately

[17] Cleveland *Journal*, May 27, 1905, Aug. 4, 1906; Nahum Brascher to Charles W. Chesnutt, Nov. 18, 1905, Charles W. Chesnutt Papers, FU.

[18] Unfortunately the only extant copies of Dabney's *Union* post-date World War I.

enough for a man with political acumen and ambition) political reporter, and Brascher the editor, a job which paid very little but provided him with a forum for his ideas. It was testimony to the ambivalence of the black capitalist movement of the time that though Blue
made his living catering to the race market, and the *Journal* would be
dedicated to fostering racial enterprise along Central Avenue, the paper made its headquarters a few doors down from Blue's downtown
office in the prestigious American Trust Building. Unique among the
new entrepreneurs, Blue kept his office where he could be surrounded
by successful white men of affairs and feel a part of the American
mainstream. From this location the paper attempted to forge a new
solidarity among Cleveland blacks.[19]

The handsome first issue of the *Journal* appeared in March, 1903,
complete with lodge, church, and women's club news and an endorsement of the Republican ticket in that spring's municipal election. Advertisements were present for Blue's various real estate endeavors and
a few white businesses. On page 4, where they would appear issue
after issue, were ads for the businesses of those black entrepreneurs
who would eventually come together along with Brascher, Fleming,
and Blue to form the Negro Board of Trade in 1905. These black businessmen and a few professionals formed the nucleus of advisors and
supporters who determined the *Journal's* course in racial affairs until
its financial collapse in 1911.[20]

Like other young Ohio racial spokesmen, the three Clevelanders accepted Booker T. Washington as the spiritual and practical leader of
black America. The *Journal* was his steadfast editorial defender, even
as his leadership came to be sharply challenged by black "Radicals"
and white racial liberals in organizations like the all-black Niagara
Movement and the integrated NAACP. Not long after the first issues
of the *Journal* had appeared, Brascher contacted Washington to suggest that the *Journal* might be an excellent advertising medium for
Tuskegee Institute. Beginning in 1903, advertisements for the school
appeared in almost every issue. In addition, the *Journal* occasionally
printed articles under Washington's name (probably ghost-written for
the busy educator) which were excellent public relations vehicles for
him. When Washington visited Cleveland early in 1905, he spent most
of his time with long-established leaders of the black community, such
as Myers and Brown, and his personal friend Charles Chesnutt. How-

[19] Cleveland *Gazette*, Oct. 19, 1901; Cleveland *Journal*, Apr. 8, 1905, Jan. 1,
1910; Fleming, "My Rise and Persecution," pp. 15–16.
[20] Cleveland *Journal*, Mar. 28, 1903, May 27, 1905; Cleveland *Gazette*, Apr. 8,
1911.

ever, by the time of his next visit in 1908, the younger men had come
to be considered important enough that Brascher and Fleming were
among his formal escorts and constant companions. The Tuskegeean
showed great interest in the activities of Cleveland's young boosters,
just as he would do in visiting members of the pro-Washington Winona
Club at their headquarters when he found himself at Cincinnati.[21]

The *Journal's* editorial policy, and particularly its specific programs
for the Cleveland black community, were heavily influenced by Washington's thought. Yet it was not generally Washington's concrete proposals which inspired them; most elements of his racial program could
not be transferred en bloc from their setting in the Jim Crow South.
No matter how much Ohio was witnessing a deterioration of race relations, it was not Washington's Alabama; discrimination was without
legal status and still often random in its application, and Ohio blacks
continued to be active members of the political community. Thus they
tended to pick and choose parts of Washington's doctrine as being
relevant or irrelevant to their needs.

The Clevelanders found few of Washington's specific programs of
direct, practical use. Particularly inappropriate was the work at which
Washington had most distinguished himself: the development and
popularizing of black industrial education. In Washington's opinion,
this training in proper work habits and basic literary and technical
skills was vital to the welfare of the southern freedmen and their children because of inept work habits bred of slavery and the misplaced
emphasis on classical education which guided post-emancipation black
schools. Some young racial leaders in southern and central Ohio
showed an interest in industrial education, but Clevelanders, with
their excellent, long-integrated public schools offering all types of curricula and their access to the colleges and universities of northern
Ohio, were unwilling to consider the applicability of special industrial
educational arrangements to the needs of most black youngsters.[22] In
addition, though Washington himself was deeply involved in politics,
he urged his followers to abjure politics and concentrate their energies
on socioeconomic uplift as a more certain means of gaining white acceptance. In the South, where whites adamantly opposed black political participation and where disfranchisement was increasingly eliminating the option of exercising political rights, the suggestion might

21 Nahum Brascher to Booker T. Washington, July 20, Aug. 25, 1903, Box 253,
May 2, 1908, Box 365, Booker T. Washington Papers, LC; Cleveland *Journal,*
May 9, Sept. 12, Dec. 26, 1903, Dec. 3, 1904, Jan. 21, 1905, July 4, 11, 1908.

22 Cleveland blacks had blocked the opening of an all-black industrial training
school in 1892, largely on the ground that the public schools adequately served
black needs; Cleveland *Gazette,* Aug. 13, 1892.

be given serious thought. But at Cleveland and in Ohio generally it was not. Blacks there had the vote and an accepted and acknowledged role in political affairs; furthermore, politics, largely through patronage, was a source of opportunity. Tom Fleming was as loyal a supporter of Washington as could be found in the state—but he was at the same time a political activist, and he betrayed no sense of contradiction. Clevelanders would even mold the concept of black capitalism to suit their own local uses and their own conception of racial needs. Indeed, in all strictly local matters the *Journal* and its supporters shaped their ideas to meet local exigencies; the same could be said for the young allies elsewhere in the state.

Instead, the larger perspectives which Washington offered and the example of his life were the major inspirations for young Ohioans. His universality lay not so much in specifics, but in two generalities. First, his thought was, even in ominous times, based on a profoundly optimistic faith that goodness, excellence, and ameliorative effort triumphed in the world. Second, while he was concerned with individual self-help and advancement, he placed strong emphasis on the group-centered values of solidarity, racial pride, and intragroup cooperation as being essential to individual and racial striving. This attitude gave added respectability and power to ideas that were functional in times which did not promise ready access to the American mainstream, but did offer a base for racial development in growing black urban populations. Washington seemed to promise that by doing the best they could as blacks united in common ties of race, history, and struggle, advancement was not merely possible but inevitable—no mean promise in the racial climate of that time. In an era when black failures and shortcomings were constantly brought up by the race's enemies, he invited blacks to measure themselves by the distance they had come, rather than by the long journey that lay ahead. Finally, they took pride in Washington's career. His dedication to and identification with the poor, untutored blacks of the rural South, his patient labors on behalf of Tuskegee, and his contacts with and recognition by the nation's most prominent whites made him a symbol of their hopes and a model for their lives.[23]

Taking its cues from the racial values espoused by Washington and mandated by the times, the *Journal* quickly dedicated itself to creating a mood of cooperation and solidarity among Cleveland blacks. "Cooperative endeavor," Brascher told his readers in an early issue, was essential to "the Journal spirit," and a motto appearing on the

[23] Cleveland *Journal*, May 9, 1903, July 4, 1908, Apr. 9, May 1, 7, 1910.

masthead of early issues asked, "Are you with us?" [24] Not long after, he stated that he was very much disturbed by the presence within the local black community of those whom he called "the drifters." These were blacks, old and new residents alike, who threatened solidarity and collective effort by allowing themselves to remain isolated from racial endeavors. "They are not a menace to society, but they have a wrong conception of life and its purpose, for they refuse to enter the great stream of life." His goal: wider interest and involvement in racial advancement by as many as possible.[25]

Solidarity and cooperation were to inspire self-help and the search for "unexplored opportunities," particularly, as the *Journal* proclaimed its earliest goal, "the material development of the Afro-American." To Brascher's mind, at the turn of the century the Cleveland black community had been in a "state of lethargy . . . akin to death." Local whites "had been alert and made great progressive strides . . . but our people did not seem to catch the spirit of the times"—a spirit of civic and neighborhood pride, boosterism, and material progress. By the summer of 1903, however, largely as the result of the rapid expansion of black enterprise around Central Avenue, Brascher sensed the start of a "New Era" for black Cleveland. The black businesses provided the foundation for a new interest in racial uplift. They would serve as the principal point of departure for the *Journal's* first concrete efforts to stimulate self-help.[26]

Two related lines were followed. From time to time, Brascher carried articles by local black businessmen which were intended to instruct aspiring entrepreneurs and new businessmen. These usually offered information on modern business methods and urged good business habits. In 1904 W. S. Doston, an older man who owned the most lucrative bicycle shop in the city and later became the first president of the Negro Board of Trade, urged other businessmen to price competitively so that high prices would not penalize black consumers for exercising race loyalty. He said that businessmen must consider their pricing policies not only from the narrow standpoint of profit, but also from the perspective of "race protection." At the same time, however, both he and the *Journal* encouraged them to compete for white patronage.[27]

More common were Brascher's attempts to educate local blacks in the importance of patronizing racially owned enterprises and aiding

[24] Ibid., Mar. 28, Dec. 26, 1903.
[25] Ibid., Nov. 21, 1903.
[26] Ibid., Mar. 28, Apr. 4, Aug. 1, Dec. 26, 1903, Apr. 8, 1905.
[27] Ibid., June 27, 1903, Dec. 24, 1904.

in the development of Central Avenue. "Out first duty is to ourselves," he editorialized, "and we should patronize Afro-American businesses where that is practical." [28] But Brascher went beyond the narrower formulation of black capitalism, which offered little to those blacks not in business, to advance greater racial economic mutuality. Though he did not advocate black withdrawal from the economic mainstream, one of his most compelling arguments for loyalty to race businesses shared with W. E. B. Du Bois's contemporary notion of "group economy"—that a self-contained, semi-autonomous black economy might be created within the larger economy [29]—the hope that black businesses might provide jobs for blacks, particularly for educated youth. On the occasion of public school graduation in 1904, the *Journal* noted that six black teenagers were about to obtain high school diplomas and would "in all probability with the exception of one or two be compelled to start their futures at the most menial employment." [30] A few years later Brascher estimated that if each of the 12,000 blacks (by his count, not that of the federal census) who lived in the city were to spend at least $200 a year in black-owned stores, some $250,000 in profits would be turned back to the race. "That amount would make Central Avenue the place where your children could find employment . . . and we could use more or all that are educated and equipped annually by the schools rather than have the educated element of the race become indolent for lack of employment." [31]

Yet Brascher was aware of the marginal nature of most race enterprises, and he knew that in the foreseeable future the overwhelming majority of blacks would continue to depend on whites for jobs. He attempted, therefore, to mobilize whatever economic power local blacks had as consumers in order to expand the scope of white-controlled opportunity. In 1904 the *Journal* began to poll Central Avenue's white shopkeepers in order to discover which ones employed blacks or desired black patronage enough to consider hiring blacks in return. The results were not encouraging. Many said that they wanted nothing to do with blacks, either as patrons or as workers, providing Brascher with an excellent opportunity to propagandize for the creation of more black businesses as an alternative. The few white businesses which promoted cooperation were given free advertising in the *Journal's* "Where to Trade" column—the existence of which, at the same time, gave reluctant white shopkeepers an incentive to change their policies.[32]

28 Ibid., Apr. 23, 1904.
29 Meier, *Negro Thought*, p. 141.
30 Cleveland *Journal*, May 21, 1904.
31 Ibid., Jan. 23, 1909.
32 Ibid., Apr. 23, 30, 1904.

Preoccupied as they were with white-collar and commercial employment, Cleveland's boosters, like their counterparts across the state, were not greatly concerned with black industrial opportunity. On one notable occasion their cooperation with white capital also involved prolonged negotiations between *Journal*-backed Tom Fleming and a white manufacturer. The result was establishment in 1910 of a Central Avenue–area dress factory which hired only black seamstresses.[33]

While the *Journal's* earliest and most abiding interest was in material uplift, it gradually became interested in correcting slum conditions around Central Avenue, in bettering the quality of life for its residents, and in meeting the needs of the growing number of black migrants settling in the neighborhood. The development of its concerns closely paralleled an evolving consciousness of social problems found within the circle of businessmen and professionals, of which Brascher, Fleming, and Blue were a part, that comprised the Negro Board of Trade. Because most of them lived and worked in the area, they were aware of its difficulties, and they knew that the emergence of a prosperous business district was not unrelated to the welfare of the people residing around it. The strong emphasis on neighborhood pride and self-help which permeated the black booster mentality also impelled them to seek improvements. From its earliest meetings the board attempted to relate to larger social problems and to search for ways of extending self-help into the social realm. One meeting discussed "the large number of strangers coming to Cleveland to make their homes," urging "that some means be adopted by which these people may become useful citizens." Other meetings spoke of obtaining the cooperation of black churches in combatting the growth of vice and crime in the Central Avenue area. At the same time, the board demonstrated a growing recognition of the need to consult with and utilize the expertise of public and semi-public agencies in such matters.[34]

Yet the business forum, with its preoccupation with market information and boosting race enterprise, did not offer the best means for dealing with social problems; interest in such problems never went beyond discussion to involve concrete action. For this reason the board reconstituted itself in 1907 as the "Cleveland Association of Colored Men." Still dominated by younger businessmen and professionals, its officers were invariably young men before 1916; Fleming, William and Theodore Green, and Dr. Ellis Dale were among the first presidents. However, its base was broadened to include a very few older men, such as Myers, Green, and Hollenden House superintendent of service

[33] Ibid., Jan. 29, Mar. 19, 1910.
[34] Ibid., July 22, Nov. 18, 1905.

William Hunley, who had established useful contacts among influential whites. The program of the C.A.C.M. attempted to combine the original goals of the Negro Board of Trade with social welfare–oriented activities, and to complement purely self-help activities with ones which sought cooperation with key white agencies offering important social services. The association consulted with Cleveland's Associated Charities, Chamber of Commerce, and Anti-Tuberculosis League in establishing programs or gaining the application of existing programs to blacks. The association itself undertook an annual "Christmas Inn," a distribution of food and clothing to the poor. In addition, it cooperated with police in efforts to rid the Central Avenue area of vice and crime, and it informally consulted with leading whites on the causes of local racial tension.[35]

The young men of the *Journal* led the way in working for neighborhood improvements. They were particularly concerned with increasing and improving municipal and public social services available to residents of the Central district, which had been neglected while services were being extended and strengthened in higher-status neighborhoods. Their proposals and achievements benefited both the neighborhood's black minority and its white majority. Tom Fleming's growing influence with the machine of Republican boss Maurice Maschke helped to yield a new park-playground complex in 1910 to fill the recreational vacuum in a section of the neighborhood with a large black concentration.[36] In addition, dear to the heart of the intellectual Brascher, a branch library opened in temporary quarters in 1909; work was begun the next year on a permanent branch building which would also contain a large auditorium for community use.[37] By 1910 the *Journal* was also attempting to raise public concern about the need for a municipal bathhouse and a public hospital in the area, but neither project excited much interest before the World War.[38]

While concerned with services and institutions open to all, the *Journal* realized that a particularly purposeful application of black self-help was necessary to confront problems resulting from the southern migration. This was felt most strongly in regard to the lack of counseling and recreational facilities for the Central Avenue area's young black men, whose leisure hours were spent on the streets and in pool

[35] Alexander Martin, "Constitution of the Cleveland Association of Colored Men," Box XIV, folder 2, George A. Myers Papers, OHS; Cleveland *Journal*, Mar. 14, May 16, 1908, Jan. 2, 9, 16, Feb. 13, Apr. 3, 1909, Jan. 1, 1910; Cleveland *Gazette*, Nov. 20, 1909, Jan. 29, 1910.
[36] Cleveland *Journal*, Nov. 13, 1909, Feb. 12, 1910.
[37] Ibid., July 17, 24, 1909, Mar. 26, 1910.
[38] Ibid., Feb. 5, 1910.

halls and saloons, with occasional conflict with the police. Existing settlement houses did not draw the color line, but their work was done largely among the white immigrant poor, and the fact that their staffs were white no doubt lessened their ability to attract blacks. At the same time, the C.A.C.M. was concerned with the desperate plight of the destitute and the sickly, rather than with the less obvious problems of growing numbers of ordinary working poor adjusting to urban life. Older black leadership had traditionally been ambivalent about the utility of separate institutions and had been loath to orient those which it controlled to confronting social problems. But in a natural extension of the ideology of self-help and solidarity and of its concern for neighborhood improvement, the *Journal* now proposed developing new activist racial institutions and innovatively manipulating existing ones to provide services for young men which would help bring them under the control of conventionally respectable influences. It called upon black churches to become more concerned with social welfare, and particularly to provide practical secular guidance and activities that might draw young people during their free time. Also, by 1906 it had joined with its wider circle of supporters in calling for the establishment of a branch YMCA in the neighborhood. While the *Journal* never said that the branch should aim its work *only* at young black men, the growing opposition of the Cleveland Y to a mixed admissions policy and the desire of the young boosters to have the proposed branch reach out especially to blacks made it clear that they were accepting a de facto segregated facility. As we shall see, because many older black Clevelanders felt that the creation of such a separate institution implied a capitulation to prejudice and violated the open racial traditions of the Western Reserve, setting a precedent for further segregation, the proposal was subject of fierce contention and was ultimately defeated. However, largely in response to similar perceptions of racial need, and often pushed by young boosters, black Y's were built at Cincinnati and Columbus, and they evolved from lyceums into social centers at Springfield and Dayton—all cities where blacks did not live with vivid memories of a lost racial Eden.[39]

Thus, within a few years the *Journal* and the men around it had constructed the bases for a new racial program for Cleveland blacks. Based upon an awareness of the problems and opportunities created by the growth of black population, and proceeding from the utilitarian and inspiring values of self-help and solidarity, their initial interest in material development had evolved into a broader program for racial

[39] Ibid., May 2, 1903, Jan. 23, 1904, June 17, July 22, Dec. 2, 1905, June 1, 1907, Jan. 23, 1909.

uplift. The immediate stimulus for broadening their concerns lay to a great extent in their own career needs and interests. Their economic base in the Central Avenue area and their strong desire for a prosperous black commercial district had contributed to their heightened concern for black social welfare. They were not alone in that concern, however; others with different perspectives and experiences, but deeply influenced by the same values, were pursuing the same course.

III

While businessmen, doctors, and lawyers comprised the nucleus of the new leadership, on its fringe were a few men and women whose different career interests allowed them to provide unique forms of racial service. They fit into two broad categories—social workers and educators—and their contribution lay in developing black institutions. While they were few in number, their influence was by no means insignificant, for their strategic positions allowed them to provide leadership in the movement for solidarity and self-help.

The establishment of urban black Y's and their evolution into social centers afforded the main opportunities for the appearance of black social workers. Earlier black Y's, the ones at Dayton and Springfield and that which was affiliated for a time with Cincinnati's Allen Temple, had been literary and debating societies offering religious and intellectual activities, but without recreational and counseling services. Leadership for them had come from ministers and interested individuals who devoted their spare time. The emergence of the black YMCA as a multi-faceted social center created employment opportunities for professional black Y workers, such as Columbus's Nimrod B. Allen, Dayton's Charles Higgins, and Springfield's Walter Burden. University-educated and specially trained in YMCA work at Y-sponsored institutes, these young social workers had expertise in the organization of athletic and leisure-time activities and counseling services which had been lacking in Ohio black communities. Their first duty was, in fact, the organization of the standardized program for a branch Y, with a comprehensiveness unequaled in the few church-related efforts in black recreation of past decades. Moreover, they began to hire and train local Y personnel, instilled with the same racial and public service ethos, to lead specific activities.[40]

While these young men were social work professionals, the same was not the case with Cleveland's Jane Edna Hunter, a black Ohioan

[40] Indianapolis *Freeman*, Sept. 9, 1911, Aug. 3, 1912; W. A. McWilliams, *Columbus Illustrated Record* (Columbus, 1919), pp. 115–116.

who pioneered in providing similar services for young black women. Her own life was not unlike the lives of those whom she served through founding and managing a home for single women. Prior to her emergence as an activist, her life had been marked by personal crisis, profound unhappiness, and racial and sexual oppression—all of which contributed to her decision to give her life to racial service. Born on a family farm in South Carolina in 1882,[41] she had an ordinary rural childhood until the age of ten, when her adored father died and her family broke up. Estranged from her mother, she was sent to do domestic work in private homes and hotels, where she experienced cruelty and sexual advances from white employers and patrons. As a teenager, she had lost the love of a young man to an older woman; at the urging of her mother she subsequently married an elderly man, only to leave him in fifteen months later. She never remarried. But through the aid and encouragement of relatives and a kindly white family, she had come to aspire to a better life, and she later obtained schooling and nurse's training.

Like many other young southern girls, she came North, in 1905, in search of a fresh start and greater opportunity. It took some years before she found either one. In the South black nurses worked closely with white doctors, but in the North she met great opposition. There was no Cleveland employment agency catering to black women skilled in anything but domestic work; until she made contacts with black doctors and a particularly sympathetic white physician, she did low-paying domestic work. She often went hungry, and for want of carfare walked miles to her jobs whatever the weather. She lived with other migrant girls in a cheap rooming house which served as a recruitment center for brothels, and again she found herself fending off sexual advances and crude propositions. She saw dozens of girls in her situation become prostitutes.

By 1911 she had been able to find better lodging and a job as a nurse, and she had established close friendships among women who had migrated from the South and survived similar hardships. Then a crucial event occurred: her mother died. The two had never been close, and after a long emotional crisis prompted (she says in her autobiography) by guilt at the knowledge that their conflicts would never be settled this side of the grave, Hunter committed herself to aiding young girls in the hope that she might give them the love and understanding she had always denied her mother.

In September, 1911, she led several friends in the creation of a Work-

[41] Biographical sketch based on Jane Hunter's autobiography, *A Nickel and a Prayer* (Cleveland, 1940), pp. 11–84.

ing Girl's Home Association; the intention was to organize a residence hall for unmarried young women. Like those involved in the concurrent effort for a black Y, they were charged with drawing the color line in a city known for its traditions of racial tolerance. Hunter and her friends were not impressed. They were partisans of self-help and racial solidarity, and, like Cleveland's young boosters, they found inspiration in the ideals and example of Booker T. Washington. As women they were twice fettered—black and female. Young black women, especially migrants, had special problems in adjusting to the city; they faced a very restricted market for their labor and a temptation of easy money to be made in the streets. Furthermore, black male leadership paid less attention to those problems than to the problems of young men. Interested in racial self-help and uplift, Hunter and her associates were thus also interested in female self-help and uplift. Through dogged determination and aggressive fund-raising, they were able in 1913 to found the Phillis Wheatley Home, named for the early American black poetess. The home offered residence, recreation, and counseling as well as an employment service to young women. Until her retirement in 1948, Jane Hunter served as its director.[42]

While Hunter and the black Y workers were founding and developing black social work institutions, other young racial spokesmen were developing black schools. They were at work in southern and central Ohio, where the idea of separate black education had never completely died; as an expression of self-help, in fact, it excited renewed interest among blacks after 1900.

Columbus's black Lincoln-Ohio Industrial Training School was founded in 1907 to provide practical training in domestic and industrial fields for poor and unskilled young black women. The institution was the work of Pearl Chavers, a man of many interests whose career encompassed concern for black enterprise and for industrial education. Born at Columbus in 1876, Chavers was a product of local public schools and a business college. In 1901 he founded the Columbus *Standard,* a race weekly dedicated to racial solidarity and self-help, which by 1906 was being distributed with local supplements at Dayton, Cincinnati, Toledo, and Springfield. Like the *Journal,* the *Standard* was a staunch defender of Booker T. Washington. The lead editorial of the first (and only extant) issue praised the Tuskegeean for "a doctrine of practical utility" which sought self-help and material accumulation, and for his dedication to the ideal of racial unity. This conception of racial priorities placed Chavers firmly in league with Cleveland's young

[42] Ibid., pp. 90–108; Cleveland *Leader,* July 24, 25, 1913.

boosters, with whom he enjoyed cordial relations. Indeed, after the collapse of the *Journal* in 1911, Brascher went to Columbus to work as the secretary of Chavers's school.[43]

Before opening his training school, Chavers's chief effort on behalf of self-help was the organization in 1906 of an "Ohio Colored Educational and Agricultural Association." He brought together a prestigious group of older men, including George Jackson, the Reverend Joshua Jones (now president of Wilberforce University), and former Columbus councilman I. D. Ross, for the purpose of staging a large exposition to advertise racial economic advancement in Ohio and boost black enterprise. The first exposition, held at Columbus in August, 1906, after months of planning, was a huge success, an acme of boosterism attracting black exhibitors from throughout the state. Speakers at rallies which accompanied the week-long activities included such dignitaries as Vice-President Charles Fairbanks, Senator Foraker, and several congressmen. Unfortunately, however, the exposition was the site of a good deal of gambling and several confidence games, for which the aging but ever-active Smoky Hobbs was partly responsible. Much to Chavers's dismay, word of these activities which leaked out later tarnished the image of the exposition. No comparable events were ever held again.[44]

Perhaps the realization that annual expositions had no future and his admiration for Washington's work at Tuskegee led Chavers to become active in industrial education. Unlike Tuskegee, however, the Lincoln-Ohio Industrial Training School did not stress basic literary and arithmetic skills, but instead concentrated on practical training for young women interested in learning dressmaking, patternmaking, cooking, and housekeeping. Food and clothing produced by students were sold commercially to help raise money for the school, and those trained as domestics had the benefit of the school's employment service. Largely because it helped alleviate the dearth of facilities aimed at aiding young migrant women in their adjustment to the city, the school attracted the support and encouragement of many prominent local whites and blacks; some of Columbus's first citizens were on its boards of trustees and advisors. Yet, as Chavers's continual quest for

[43] Columbus *Standard*, July 27, 1901; United Federation of Teachers of America, AFL-CIO, Local #2, "Pearl Chavers: Pioneer in the Banking Field," in *Lessons Plans in African-American History* (New York, n.d.), p. 150; Pearl Chavers to Booker T. Washington, Dec. 3, 1906, Box 317, Washington Papers; Fleming, "My Rise and Persecution," p. 23.

[44] Chicago *Broad Ax*, Aug. 25, 1906; Columbus *Ohio Sun*, Nov. 29, 1906; Columbus *Press Post*, Feb. 16, 1907; Pearl Chavers to Booker T. Washington, Nov. 14, 1906, Box 317, Washington Papers.

funds suggests, its good intentions did not make it a prosperous endeavor, and in 1916 it was forced to close.[45]

Modeled more self-consciously after Tuskegee, though smaller in size, was the Curry Institute, which was the life's work of the Reverend Elmer W. B. Curry, a Baptist minister and educator who was an influential proponent of separate black public education and of black industrial education. Born at Delaware, Ohio, in 1871 and educated in its public schools and at local Ohio Wesleyan University, Curry spent some years preaching before founding a black school with a program of elementary, industrial, normal, and religious training in 1897. He labored not in the city, but in the small town of Urbana, where he established himself with a handful of pupils. Curry, however, was by no means isolated from either urban developments or leaders. He frequently spoke before Baptist audiences at nearby Dayton, Springfield, Columbus, and Cincinnati, where he often gave his standard lecture, "Booker T. Washington: The Wizard of Tuskegee." In addition, his active involvement in the black Ohio State Baptist Convention brought him in contact with numerous urban ministers. His monthly newsletter, the Urbana Informer, offered a forum for his views and also advertised the work of the institute; it had a large circulation among the state's black Baptist majority. Prominent urban Baptists, including George Hayes, Poindexter (before his death in 1907), and Dr. Thomas Burton of Springfield were among the school's supporters.[46]

The Curry Institute resembled Tuskegee in many ways. Practicality was the watchward of Curry's educational program: "Nothing is taught that does not have a bearing upon actual everyday life." [47] The student body, which never numbered over fifty at any one time, was given instruction in the "three-'R's," but the heart of the institute's program was training in work. Students, including those who wished to be teachers, learned practical work skills; these were applied in making improvements in the school and sustaining its daily activities. Boys mixed cement, did masonry and carpentry, gardened and raised live-

[45] Columbus Dispatch, Jan. 19, Nov. 16, 1908, Jan. 19, 1909; Pearl Chavers to Booker T. Washington, Sept. 10, 1912, Box 831, Washington Papers; Pearl Chavers to "Dear Friend," Feb. 6, 1913 [solicitation for funds], James M. Cox Governor's Papers, OHS; Thomas Jesse Jones, Negro Education: A Study of the Private and Higher Schools for Colored People in the United States, U.S. Department of Interior, Bureau of Education, Bulletin no. 38 (Washington, 1917), II, 696.

[46] Yenser, ed., Who's Who in Colored America, p. 113; F. Alphonse McGinnis, "The Curry School, Urbana and Its Founder," Colored American Magazine, IX (Oct., 1905), 560–565; Elmer W. B. Curry to Booker T. Washington, Jan. 19, 1906, Box 299, Dec. 4, 1906, Box 317, Washington Papers.

[47] Urbana Informer, July, 1903.

stock, and operated the school's printing press, publishing monthly editions of the *Informer*. Girls cooked, cleaned, and sewed as part of their training in domestic science. Curry helped to place graduates in industrial, domestic, and teaching positions. Like Washington, he developed dependable black and white networks of support in order to routinize fund-raising. He obtained small subsidies from the Ohio State Baptist Convention and established both men's and women's alumni groups in five states. Alumni held periodic conferences to discuss black education, racial advancement, and the organization of fund drives for the institute. At the same time, the diplomatic Curry enjoyed excellent relations with Urbana's whites, and the most important local politicians, bankers, businessmen, professionals, and wealthy farmers helped to govern and support the institute. Considering that the community had witnessed a brutal lynching in the year when Curry came to Urbana, such support was a substantial accomplishment —testimony, perhaps, to his ability to provide Urbana's white upper class with a means for assuaging its discomfort about that bloody event without disturbing the racial status quo which helped to bring it about.[48]

Curry's educational concerns went beyond the advocacy of black industrial education. Indeed, more than any other racial spokesman in Ohio, he helped to revive the debate over the efficacy of separate black public education and to challenge the older leaders' conviction that integrated education was the sine qua non of racial advancement. Curry's desire for separate schools sprang from his belief that black teachers played a unique role in stimulating racial and individual uplift. His argument emphasized the special emotional and educational needs of black children, the compensations of separate development, and the contributions of the teaching profession to the social and material development of the race, differing little from that which had been offered by Ohio's previous black opponents of school desegregation. In 1905 in a characteristic address steeped in the rhetoric of self-help and racial solidarity, Curry stated:

. . . Colored persons should be preferred as teachers of colored children. There is nothing greater as a principle of self-help than an inborn, highly and carefully cultivated confidence in the members of the race, who are fully prepared in heart, head, and hand to dignify their well-chosen profession, and when given an equal chance prove a blessing to humanity in one of our greatest needs. By placing competent colored

[48] Elmer W. B. Curry, *A Story of Curry Institute* (Urbana, 1907), pp. 23–40; McGinnis, "Curry School," 557–561; Evan P. Middleton, ed., *History of Champaign County, Ohio* (Indianapolis, 1917), pp. 576–581.

teachers over colored children we cultivate this implicit confidence and can better our own possibilities. The teacher has an opportunity for professional development; the child of his own race, whose struggles for mastery have been the experience of the instructor, becomes the object for study; the teacher becomes the ideal of the pupil who is inspired with the glowing ambition to fill his teacher's place or another station of honor and trust in life.[49]

Curry buttressed older arguments for separate schools with new evidence pointing to the inadequacies, for blacks, of Ohio's integrated ones. He posited the deadening effect which instruction by white teachers in white-dominated schools had upon the ambitions and abilities of black students. In the same 1905 address he noted a survey which he had undertaken regarding the educational backgrounds of the forty-one blacks who had recently graduated from high school in Ohio's sixteen largest cities and towns. Twenty-nine (70%) came from communities employing black teachers in separate elementary and high school buildings. Xenia, with a black school system from kindergarten through high school, produced eleven (27%) of these graduates, greater than the combined total from Cincinnati, Columbus, Dayton, and Springfield, where the large majority of blacks were educated by whites. Such data, to his mind, offered conclusive proof of the superiority of black teachers and black schools. At the same time, Curry spoke of the abuse and the distractions to which black pupils were subject in integrated schools, pointing to attempts by some white parents at Springfield to institute separate seating arrangements in integrated classrooms, and to the occasional fist-fights between black and white students attending the integrated elementary schools of Cincinnati's West End.[50]

As a practical alternative, Curry did not favor legislative restitution of separate schools on a statewide basis, nor did he think that every community was fitted to have separate black public schools. Instead, he favored allowing local conditions to define the suitability of a community for the existence of a dual school system. As he said in 1905, "where the number of colored children is sufficient to maintain a school with the same course of study, same number of months for school, a good school house, playgrounds, and no inconvenience to the pupil as to location, and [where] the teachers are the equal to the best, I

[49] Elmer W. B. Curry, "Should Colored Persons Be Preferred as Teachers of Colored Children in Elementary and High Schools?" in *Addresses* (Urbana, 1911), p. 38.
[50] Ibid., p. 40.

prefer . . . separate schools for colored children with teachers of their own race." [51]

While Curry did not spell it out at the time, it was the urban community which possessed the demographic, economic, and cultural resources necessary to insure adequate numbers, equal facilities, and excellent teachers. In the next decade two other young racial educators from one such community, Cincinnati, evolved ideas similar to Curry's. Francis Russell and Jennie Porter were both in their twenties during the first decade of the century; both were educated in local public schools and at the University of Cincinnati, and both launched their local careers at the city's last remaining separate school, located in the black section of Walnut Hills. An aggressive young man of fixed opinions, Russell was appointed principal of that school in 1909. He was one of Cincinnati's most influential young racial spokesmen and perhaps its leading partisan of Booker T. Washington. At the same time, he was deeply influenced by the ideas of the contemporary progressive education movement. Thus, he favored separate schools not only for the reasons given by Curry, but also because he believed that, especially in urban neighborhoods, schools must become vital, unifying community centers. With the cooperation of the Cincinnati Board of Education, he transformed his school into just such an institution. [52]

Porter was Russell's close ally in educational affairs. She also revealed influences from both the progressive education movement and the Washingtonian camp; she was specifically interested in using modern psychological and intelligence testing as a device for shaping an educational environment especially suited to the needs of black children and for demonstrating the benefits of separate schools. She sought to test her ideas, first in a small kindergarten, which was begun with the help of white philanthropist Annie Laws in 1911 in the basement of the black church in the West End, and later, with the support of the school board, in a separate public school. [53]

Both Russell and Porter found the black community receptive to their ideas, for at Cincinnati, as at Dayton and to some extent Columbus, blacks were beginning to display growing interest in the ways in which separate schools might be used for racial advancement. Yet (as the next chapter will demonstrate) that reinterest, and the work of Porter and Russell, must be seen not in isolation, but in the larger context of efforts to find ways of dealing with the deterioration of race relations and the migration of southern blacks into Ohio cities.

51 Ibid., pp. 41–42.
52 Dabney, *Cincinnati's Colored Citizens*, pp. 243–244.
53 Ibid., pp. 235–236.

IV

The sudden appearance after 1900 of a new generation of racial spokesmen created a sharp challenge to older leaders. That challenge existed on different levels, manifesting itself sometimes as a practical struggle for racial leadership, and other times as a conflict of values, world views, and racial programs. In the former guise it often took shape as a contention for black political leadership and for patronage and influence. On the face of it, the issues defining the political conflict seem clear. Politics was a matter of power and opportunity; for those like Brown and Clifford who depended on it for a living, it was a matter of dollars and cents. In constituencies in which blacks could not claim to be the balance of power, politics tended to be a zero-sum game, with rewards limited to crumbs from the whites' table. One group might win meager rewards in patronage or influence through its ties with whites, while another might lose everything. The challenge of the younger men, therefore, posed a threat to the political power of their elders, who were already struggling to preserve their influence in a rapidly changing political environment.

But political conflict resulted not merely from the challenge to a structure of privilege. In themselves, the different political styles of the generations became sources of considerable tension. Though many of the fathers of Ohio's black politics were opportunists, the best of the older men had always conceived of racial politics not only in the narrow terms of personal and clique power, but also in terms of race protection and advancement. They viewed the vote and political activity as essential tools for safeguarding racial welfare, and they had not been loath to talk the rebellious language of political independence when the Republican party failed to live up to its historic commitment to black rights. The turn of the century found the older men deeply concerned by the party's retreat from a progressive position in racial affairs; some sought a means to change its course, and most looked for a way of understanding what had gone wrong.

In contrast, the young men were unquestioningly partisan and utterly pragmatic. Having no memories of a Republican party guided by the great egalitarian principles of Reconstruction, and tending to consider racial material and social development as the primary weapons in the struggle for advancement, they looked to the Republican party not so much as an active force in the struggle for black rights, but as a means for recognizing the talents of deserving blacks aspiring to political office, and at the very least as a political force which might be counted on not to initiate harmful action against the race. Thus, in announcing its preferences at the start of the 1903 fall campaign for state and county offices, the Cleveland *Journal* stated that it was naturally behind the Republican ticket, explaining only that "that party at least recognizes the race in relative terms." In future weeks it elaborated upon its position. Staunchly conservative on economic issues, the paper favored Republican fiscal conservatism and tariff policies. It also noted that blacks got less patronage when Democrats held control of the county than when Republicans did. Gone was the old rhetoric of gratitude for past favors, and the vision of the Republican party as the vanguard in the struggle for racial equality; in their place was a dispassionate but reasoned appraisal of black political interest. Asking little from either politics or their party, they expected little. "That party at least recognizes the race in relative terms" was the way Brascher explained his Republicanism, simply and succinctly, without any apparent sense of failed hopes or a trace of bitterness.[54]

The opportunism and partisanship of their political orientation was strongly reinforced by an appraisal of how ambitious young men might attain power. Entering politics, they found that black political influence was monopolized by a few elders; as Brascher lamented in 1905, many people were under the impression that the only black political leaders were a few older men like Green, Myers, and Smith.[55] Under the circumstances, they had to be most cautious and calculating in plotting their course; the younger men were weak yet desirous of power, ambitious yet without influence. Their strategy was to alienate no one who mattered: they stayed close to the established, unquestioned white Republican power centers, kept a low profile in intra-party conflicts regardless of the principles at stake, and always backed the probable winner. They never flirted with the Democracy or with political independents as their elders had done. This was not merely because they had nothing in common with the reformist progressives who represented the most significant alternative to the Republicans. (Brascher dismissed Tom Johnson as a demagogue and, because of his program for local tax reform, a socialist.[56]) It was also because of a sense that the black position in Ohio politics was no longer as strategic as it had been, when threats to desert the party were more meaningful to those concerned with winning elections. Instead, they sought productive alliances with powerful Republicans, offering them unquestioned loyalty and service.

The generational differences in political style were most evident in

54 Cleveland *Journal*, Aug. 29, 1903.
55 Ibid., June 24, 1905.
56 Ibid., Oct. 10, 17, 24, 1903.

reactions to the Brownsville affair and to a concurrent local political situation. In Ohio a unique drama, which provoked the decade's greatest upheaval in black politics, was being played. Early in 1907, shortly after President Roosevelt's order dismissing the black soldiers was made public and implemented by Secretary of War Taft, Foraker emerged as the leading critic of the administration's handling of the matter, greatly angering the president. Roosevelt's first reaction was to attempt to humiliate Foraker with the Tyler appointment. When this failed to silence him, Roosevelt eventually offered Foraker any position in the administration if only he would drop the matter. Yet the president underestimated Foraker's ability to commit himself to a principled course; the arch-conservative legislator, with his ties to the large trusts and his uncompromising support for laissez faire capitalism, became an even more uncompromising, if unlikely, agitator in behalf of justice for the black soldiers.[57]

At the same time political forces in Ohio were preparing for the battle for the 1908 Republican presidential nomination. There was talk in 1907 that Foraker had presidential ambitions, and the senator refused either to deny or confirm these rumors. Thus Roosevelt and Taft (who hoped to succeed to the presidency) were worried that Foraker would use his power among older, conservative and anti-Roosevelt Ohio Republican officeholders and party workers to block Taft's lining up the Ohio delegation, which was essential to either Ohioan in a campaign for the nomination. Others were more realistic about Foraker's immediate political ambitions. They believed that he was using a threat to campaign in order to force a deal by which he might save his Senate seat from an upcoming challenge by Theodore Burton, the ambitious, pro-Roosevelt congressman from Cleveland. Though he had lost that city's mayoral race to Tom Johnson in 1907, Burton remained one of the fastest-rising stars in Ohio Republican politics.[58]

The animosity between Foraker and the Taft-Roosevelt camp was largely a matter of party politics and (to some extent) a hatred of Foraker by less conservative Ohio Republicans. These complex political contentions had little to do with Brownsville, and in the end they were resolved without reference to it. An Ohio Supreme Court decision sustaining a law which created primary elections for delegates to county nominating conventions completely undercut Foraker's bid to capture the Ohio delegation, since Taft was the favorite of rank-

[57] John D. Weaver, *The Brownsville Raid* (New York, 1970), pp. 97–122; Everett Walters, *Joseph Benson Foraker: Uncompromising Republican* (Columbus, 1948), p. 247.

[58] Walters, *Foraker*, pp. 256–266.

and-file Republicans. Foraker's drive for Senate reelection was destroyed in 1908 by William Randolph Hearst's dramatic revelation of a series of letters which showed that Foraker had been a paid agent of the Standard Oil Company while serving in the Senate. Burton, whom Foraker had endorsed for mayor of Cleveland despite their rivalry, succeeded him in the Senate. This marked the end of Foraker's long political career.[59]

Yet for Harry Smith and a large number of older men, the only issues were Brownsville and the attempt they saw gathering strength to drive their champion from public life, in their eyes largely for his defense of the black soldiers. It was not a fight for power among white politicians, but a matter of racial principle which was beyond compromise. They saw the Tyler appointment as part of a calculated, cynical effort to embarrass Foraker and buy the race's loyalty, and therefore denounced the administration's motives and (at least in Smith's case) publicly criticized Tyler for allowing himself to be used.[60] In May, 1907, a full year before the presidential nomination would be decided, many older black politicians and race leaders put themselves out on a political limb by openly and aggressively taking sides in the Taft-Foraker rivalry. Under Smith's leadership, over a hundred of them met at Columbus to form an anti-administration, anti-Taft, pro-Foraker "Ohio Afro-American Political League," and to endorse Foraker for any office he desired, including the presidency. Present were many of the Old Guard: Wilberforce's Scarborough, Xenia's Maxwell, Stewart of Youngstown, Dabney of Cincinnati, J. S. Attwood of Ripley, Dr. Burton of Springfield, the Reverend J. W. Gazaway, now preaching at Zanesville—the list read like a roster of the black political conventions of the 1880s.[61] In spite of his dislike for Smith, even Myers joined the movement; shortly after the meeting he was quoted by the *Gazette* as pledging his undying loyalty to Foraker and vowing, if need be, to go down to defeat with him "with my colors flying." [62] Among the older black politicians, only the officeholders, fearing for their jobs, kept their distance.

The younger men responded quite differently. They were conspicuously absent from these early activities for Foraker; indeed, from the beginning some of them lined up with the administration. Chavers, for

59 Ibid., pp. 266–272.

60 Cleveland *Gazette*, Feb. 9, 16, 23, June 8, 15, 1907; Ralph Tyler to George Myers, Apr. 11, 1907, Box XIII, folder 6, Myers Papers; George Myers to Joseph B. Foraker, Jan. 23, 1907, Box 68, Joseph B. Foraker Papers, CHS.

61 Cleveland *Gazette*, May 18, 1907; Columbus *Press-Post*, May 14, 15, 16, 1907.

62 Cleveland *Gazette*, May 25, 1907.

example, was actively contending for the position which Tyler eventually secured; in February, 1907, he traveled to Washington to lobby on his own behalf.[63] In return for money for his school, Curry was quietly attempting to gather some support for Taft's nomination among Miami Valley blacks as early as June, 1907.[64] The *Journal*, whose stance was identical to Booker T. Washington's, probably best expressed the feelings of young men. While lamenting Roosevelt's treatment of the black soldiers and earnestly hoping that he would set the matter right, Brascher and his political expert Fleming refused to allow Brownsville to color their politics. In April, 1907, when their elders were busy plotting a pro-Foraker strategy, the young men of the *Journal* praised the Tyler appointment as a sign of good faith and an important expansion of Ohio black patronage. The *Journal* further pleaded with blacks not to become embroiled in internal (i.e., white) party squabbles.[65] Brascher spoke vaguely of the race's duty to Foraker, but at the same time he called for realism and caution, stating that the Republican party was no longer dedicated to elevated egalitarian principles and that, under the circumstances, it was best for the race to choose "the side that will bring the best results." [66] The paper explained several months later that Foraker "has not a ghost of a chance for the presidency," and thus Brascher implored the race to "forego petty grievances" and "get on the bandwagon and ride with the victors." [67]

It was opportunism of the rankest sort, dictated only by considerations of power and reward, and for a time it led to a bitter war of words between the generations, fought in the pages of the black press. But most older men eventually fell in line when it bcame clear which was the politic course. When Smith tried to unite Cleveland blacks against Burton's mayoral bid, the *Journal* said simply that the local contest had nothing to do with Foraker's future or with Brownsville— a point which Foraker himself made in endorsing Burton and warning his followers against injecting the presidential contest into the 1907 local campaigns. Myers hesitated but soon came to the same conclusion. Indeed, in spite of his friendship with Tom Johnson, he accepted an offer to run Burton's black campaign. The large majority of both younger and older black leaders joined the Burton camp, and Scarborough endorsed Burton from the Wilberforce campus over two

[63] Columbus *Press-Post*, Feb. 1, 1907.
[64] Phil H. Brown to Harry C. Smith, July 12, 1907, Box 59, Foraker Papers.
[65] Cleveland *Journal*, Apr. 20, 1907.
[66] Ibid., Apr. 6, 1907.
[67] Ibid., Sept. 14, 1907.

hundred miles away. [68] Nor did Smith's attempt to organize a protest against Taft at the polls in 1908 gain much support. Ohio's older black politicos climbed on the Taft bandwagon when it became clear that Foraker could not wage a contest for the nomination. The younger men had shown the way.[69]

It should not be thought, however, that the young men were pre-occupied with national politics, for their most intense political activities were local. This was due not only to the generally local orientation of their thought and racial programs, but also to the fact that their elders still controlled whatever political influence Ohio blacks continued to enjoy outside the local sphere. Thus, when Booker T. Washington sought advisement on black politics from Ohioans, he went not to Brascher, Curry, Chavers, or Fleming, but to Myers, Cottrill, and Tyler. Under the circumstances, municipal politics offered the only path to prominence.

The young men's gains varied around the state, depending on the configuration of black and white political forces. At Cincinnati they were prevented from gaining significant power by the continuing in-fluence of the Cox machine and its traditional black operatives and allies, such as George Jackson, William Copeland, and George Hayes, all of whom had affiliated with the Republican machine for years. At the same time, the rise of local progressivism through the Demo-cratic party undermined Republican influence generally.[70] At Colum-bus, however, after 1900 little remained of the older black leadership; its political forces were in particularly rapid decline, the product of years of control by a few aging and (like Poindexter) dying men. Of those who had risen to power in the late nineteenth century, only Wilbur King, a city councilman in the 1890s and later the long-time assistant prosecuting attorney of Franklin County, remained a potent factor in local political affairs. The rise of a strong and ambitious group of younger professionals and entrepreneurs was relatively easy;

[68] Cleveland *Gazette*, Sept. 14, 21, Oct. 5, 12, 26, 1907; Cleveland *Journal*, Sept. 14, 21, 28, Oct. 19, 26, 1907; Cleveland *Leader*, Oct. 29, 1907; Ralph Tyler to George Myers, Sept. 4, 17, 1907, Box XIV, folder 2, Myers Papers.

[69] Cleveland *Gazette*, July 4, 11, Aug. 15, 22, Sept. 12, Oct. 31, 1907; Cleveland *Journal*, Jan. 11, Feb. 1, Apr. 25, June 6, Aug. 1, Oct. 31, 1908.

[70] The generational rivalry manifested itself particularly strongly here over the attempt of the younger men to boost attorney A. Lee Beatty for the state legisla-ture, at a time when the older Cox allies were still regularly obtaining the black legislative nominations. It was not until after 1915 that Beatty was able to obtain a legislative slot on the Republican ticket. Wendell P. Dabney to Joseph B. Foraker, Oct. 5, 1908, Box 77, Foraker Papers; Dabney, *Cincinnati's Colored Citizens*, p. 344; Zane Miller, *Boss Cox's Cincinnati: Urban Politics in the Pro-gressive Era* (New York, 1968), pp. 180–214.

several elevated clerkships were obtained, and the first legislative nomination in four decades went to realtor John Logan. (Logan, however, was defeated when the Democrats swept the Franklin County elections of 1914.[71])

Black politicos had always lacked power in Dayton. The race had never had much influence or patronage, and it also lacked organization. The first decade of the century saw an effort for recognition renewed by a coalition of the generations; the movement was bolstered by an awareness of a rapidly growing local black voting population. White politicians allowed the formation of a small, informal "Black Cabinet" to advise them on black politics, but the results were still meager by the end of the decade: two deputy clerks, two policemen, and a court messenger.[72]

It was at Cleveland that the young men, through Tom Fleming, scored their greatest victory. At the very beginning of his political career in 1903, Fleming set his aim—not for a federal post or a place in the state legislature, but a seat on the Cleveland city council. Normally this would have been impossible, because no ward had enough black votes to assure his nomination and election, and he had no power base from which to stage a claim. Yet both checks on his ambition were then being erased. The legislature had recently established several at-large seats on the council, so Fleming could run not from a ward but as the candidate of Republican Cleveland. At the same time, he and a group of young black Central Avenue businessmen and professionals were establishing their own organization and forming their own political ties. Tired of unproductive alliances with Harry Smith, who did not allow them to accumulate any influence of their own, they formed the Twelfth Ward Republican Club in 1903; in 1907 the organization became the Attucks Republican Club, encompassing young black men throughout the city. Fleming then made alliances with powerful new forces, black and white, in the Republican party. He affiliated with the political machine of Boss Maurice Maschke when it emerged in 1905, and he brought "Starlight" Boyd into his camp. Fleming appreciated Boyd's influence among voters in the Central Avenue slums and white Republican ward heelers, while Boyd saw in Fleming added insurance for the safety of his vice operations.

These ties enabled Fleming to win nomination to a councilman-at-large spot at the 1907 Republican city convention, despite the chal-

[71] Indianapolis *Freeman*, Aug. 29, 1914; Richard Clyde Minor, "Negroes in Columbus" (Ph.D. dissertation, Ohio State University, 1936), pp. 172–177.
[72] Indianapolis *Freeman*, June 19, 26, 1909.

lenge of black fishmarket owner Jacob Reed, the candidate of a coalition of older men including both Myers and Smith, whose desire to block the younger man was greater than their dislike for one another. Defeated in that year's Democratic landslide, Fleming reemerged in 1909 and became the city's first black councilman. After losing a reelection bid because of the 1911 Democratic sweep, he waited several years before eventually running for Twelfth Ward councilman against several whites in the 1915 primary. The white vote split, and Fleming won with a 71-vote plurality. It was as good as election in the largely white but strongly Republican Twelfth; in 1916 Fleming took his seat as the first black councilman elected from a ward. In all of these electoral battles he received little aid from older black politicians. While attention was focused on him, other young men scored local victories. Smith was beaten in legislative primaries in 1912 and 1914, first by William Green and then by Green's brother Theodore, each of whom had machine backing. Both men lost in Democratic landslides.[73]

Fleming and other younger politicians approached black patronage from a new perspective. The Old Guard had fought largely for the more prestigious clerical and managerial posts for its upper-class friends. Smith, for example, was continually agitating for respectable clerkships in various municipal departments, while Cincinnati's black political leaders had done likewise throughout the late nineteenth century. The younger men reversed patronage priorities, focusing their efforts upon more numerous and less attractive jobs for the masses. They would spread the black payroll thin, but they would increase the race's share. In 1909 Maschke's ally, Mayor Herman C. Baehr, was elected, along with Fleming. After consultation with the black councilman, the new mayor began to turn over the city's garbage collection department to blacks. Within a few years, blacks went from 25 to 75 percent of the city's garbage collectors. Baehr also appointed seventeen black janitors, but he gave blacks very few white-collar jobs. In 1911, at the end of his term, 175 of 184 blacks on the municipal payroll were janitors and sanitation workers.[74]

A similar concentration of black patronage in lower-level municipal service jobs was then taking place at Columbus. Anxious to reward the blacks who supported him in his primary race against a candidate

[73] Fleming, "My Life and Persecution," pp. 16–47; Davis, *Black Americans in Cleveland,* pp. 144–145, 168; Cleveland *Journal,* May 2, 1903, June 29, Aug. 3, 1907, Jan. 9, May 1, 22, Sept. 11, Nov. 6, 1909; Cleveland *Gazette,* Feb. 14, Mar. 7, 28, Nov. 14, 1903, June 29, Aug. 10, Sept. 14, 28, 1907, Sept. 11, Oct. 23, Nov. 13, 1909, Sept. 2, 9, 1911, June 1, 1912, Aug. 15, 1914.

[74] Cleveland *Journal,* Nov. 20, 1909, Jan. 1, 8, Feb. 19, 26, 1910.

controlled by liquor interests, Republican Mayor George Marshall sent his leading black supporter, Everett Spurlock, a younger black politician, to Cleveland in 1910 to observe the Baehr system of black patronage at work. After obtaining a favorable appraisal, Marshall named Spurlock superintendent of the city's street cleaning department; the mayor publicly announced that he would concentrate all his appointments in the hundred-man department so that eventually blacks would control it. It was also anticipated that the seven white foremen then employed in the department would refuse to work under blacks, and that the foremanships would thus become black. In fact, all but one white foreman resigned within three days of Spurlock's appointment. Local blacks began to rejoice at the prospect of the $9,700 a month in salaries which their new opportunity might ultimately yield for the black community.[75]

From the white politicians' viewpoint, the new situation was ideal. They could appease black constituents without disturbing the racial strictures against blacks obtaining prestigious, well-paying jobs on the basis of ability or in proportion to voting strength and political loyalty. For the race, however, it was a mixed blessing. The new tendency accepted and perpetuated a castelike structure of opportunity. The fact that blacks swept Columbus's streets or collected Cleveland's garbage merely confirmed whites' suspicions that these were the jobs which blacks were best fitted to do after all. Yet it could not be denied that the situation broadened black opportunity. Fleming and Spurlock could take some pride in the fact that they had contributed significantly to the material development of their people, adding money to their pockets and security to their lives. Harry Smith did not see it that way at all. Viewing this assignment of blacks to the lowest rungs of patronage a backward-looking compromise of equality, he angrily denounced Fleming, Spurlock, and all blacks who approved of the new patronage policies as "Jim Crow Negroes"—a term he used to describe members of the race who were willing tools of prejudiced whites. At the same time, however, in the *Gazette* he made equally persistent efforts to play down Fleming's role in bringing about these patronage opportunities.[76] This strongly suggests that Smith was also troubled by the increasing influence of Fleming and his young allies, who now possessed the foundations of their own effective political machine. They now were acquiring reputations as

[75] Columbus *Dispatch*, Mar. 2, 4, 7, 8, 1910; Columbus *Ohio State Journal*, Mar. 4, 1910; Cleveland *Journal*, Mar. 19, 1910; Cleveland *Gazette*, Mar. 26, 1910.
[76] Cleveland *Gazette*, Jan. 29, Feb. 5, 12, Apr. 2, 1910.

job-finders and were at the center of new networks of aid and obligation. The situation was not only a challenge to the racial goals of
Smith and the older men; it was also a sign of the diminution of their
influence.

V

As the different attitudes concerning black patronage suggest,
there were deep sources of animosity and conflict between racial
spokesmen of both generations. Fundamental differences, products
of dissimilar experiences within racial history and of contrary readings
of the times, lay in perceptions of the race's present and future. On
the one side were Chavers, Brascher, and Fleming, seeking inspiration
from the world around them and struggling after a racial program in
tune with the times. On the other side were older men like Smith.
Though their hopes were being dashed, they continued to uphold
the priorities and values of an earlier day and found it difficult to
accept the new ideas and styles of racial leadership offered by the
younger generation. These more illusive differences of attitude manifested themselves most clearly in three broad, related areas: their
willingness to find sources for hope in the times and in existing black
strivings and accomplishments; their response to the rising tide of
racial repression throughout the nation; and their attitudes toward the
leadership and thought of the most widely acknowledged racial
spokesman of the time, Booker T. Washington.

Nahum Brascher and his *Journal* personified the mood which the
younger leaders brought to their public activities, whether as boosters
of race enterprise, developers of black institutions, or organizers of
everyday, practical activities. "Each week we endeavor to hold out new
and greater hope for those who aspire to higher and better things,"
Brascher said in 1903, characterizing what would remain the ethos of
his *Journal* editorials.[77] The young editor understood that, without
evidence that faith in the future was indeed a realistic stance, the
striving and commitment which he asked of his readers would eventually be seen as worthless and empty, and the race would appear
utterly powerless to shape its destiny. Thus, week after week,
Brascher's pen transformed marginal black enterprises into certain
signs of economic advance; only rarely did he admit to the high
attrition rate among them. In his zeal to boost race business, he
occasionally accepted the word of a promoter—only to discover that
he had given uncritical praise and offered free advertisement to crooks

[77] Cleveland *Journal*, Dec. 26, 1903.

or incompetents. Just as business failures were rarely acknowledged, so, too, were evidences of bad faith, which might give rise to cynicism and hinder the cause of solidarity. Brascher never publicly denounced or exposed those who had taken advantage of him. Once when he was chastised for promoting certain real estate "sharks," who used appeals to race solidarity to win people's patronage and then charged them exorbitant rents, he replied, "The man who sees no good in anything is far worse than the man who sees good in everything." [78]

The *Journal* hoped not only to generate faith in order to stimulate collective effort. Its constant emphasis on compensatory striving, on seizing available opportunities rather than dwelling on those which were withheld, was based on Brascher's desire to give black youth the courage to face a hostile world with individual ambition and goals of racial service intact. A young man himself, he knew how incessant harping on wrongs done to the race could undermine the aspirations of young people: "It is indeed sad to have the darker side of our life continually told to our young people. What such tales have meant in the destruction of their ambition we may never know! I believe in holding out the bright side and if there is a dark side they will find it soon enough. . . . It is their duty and mine to make the most of every opportunity." He begged parents "to let a little sunshine in" and encourage their children to aspire to the highest goals. [79]

To this end, and to help foster racial solidarity and pride, the *Journal* continued the nineteenth-century Negro press's tradition of printing biographical sketches of conventionally successful blacks who were contributing to racial welfare. But while earlier papers had concentrated on mature men, the *Journal* dwelled upon younger ones, some of whom had just finished college and were about to embark on promising careers. [80] Aware that the overwhelming majority of young blacks would have to obtain employment from whites, the paper also tried to prepare them for the competitive struggle. Occasionally it printed brief inspirational articles by successful young men; these pieces pictured the search for decent employment less as a matter of color than of the eternal struggle for the survival of the fittest. Just as the business leagues contended that consumers were colorblind in choosing stores to patronize, so these young men claimed that businessmen were colorblind in choosing their employees; the sole concern was making money, and they would gladly employ anyone

[78] Ibid., Dec. 2, 1905, July 29, Dec. 15, 1906, Sept. 25, Nov. 13, 1909; Cleveland *Gazette*, Apr. 7, May 19, 26, June 16, 1906, Mar. 7, 21, 1908.
[79] Cleveland *Journal*, Dec. 10, 1904.
[80] Ibid., e.g., May 20, 1905.

with talent and skill who could help them toward that end. But in line with the boosters' concern for material development and racial solidarity, young blacks were told to gain practical experience in white businesses, not only for their individual sakes, but, according to Robert Ray Cheeks, a young black stenographer working for the white Cleveland Machine Company and an early president of the Cleveland Association of Colored Men, so that blacks might then come to start their own businesses in larger numbers.[81]

Of course, most white businessmen were *not* colorblind in choosing their employees. But in order to be black and optimistic at the turn of the century, it was necessary for young boosters, as it was for their mentor Booker T. Washington, to address themselves only rarely to the gloomy and menacing trends around them. The *Journal* particularly avoided the rapidly deteriorating situation in the South. Few were the discussions of disfranchisement, lynching, segregation, the plight of the southern sharecropper and farm laborer, and the daily violations of the most fundamental human rights and civil liberties. When it did address itself to southern racial repression, the *Journal* accepted Booker T. Washington's guidance on the subject, just as it did in forging its local program. While it never endorsed disfranchisement (as Washington did for a time, on the condition that it might be applied equally to the poor, propertyless, and ignorant of both races), the *Journal* saw it, as well as the rising tide of southern segregation, as a fait accompli. The paper sought to replace politics with intraracial and economic development, what it broadly referred to as "the Tuskegee plan," as the basis for race protection and uplift among the black majority in the South. In effect this attitude denigrated the importance of political activity, even though the *Journal* and the men around it were deeply involved in local politics, just as Washington himself was deeply involved in national politics.[82]

Like Washington, Brascher was quick to balance any evidence of racism with still more reasons for optimism. In 1904 he published an unusual exposé of local racial proscription, a four-part series on "Discrimination in Cleveland," in which he acknowledged that discrimination in public places was on the rise. He described the daily insults to which educated, respectable blacks like himself were subjected in theaters and restaurants and, less than a year after Cheek's article, the long-standing job discrimination that barred blacks from work in most

81 Robert Ray Cheeks, "Possibilities in the Business World for Young Men of Cleveland," ibid., Dec. 26, 1903.

82 Cleveland *Journal*, Apr. 18, 1903, Jan. 4, 1908; Meier, *Negro Thought*, pp. 109–111.

factories and commercial businesses. Yet he countered by noting the small but growing number of blacks prospering in business and the professions, some of them enjoying white as well as black patronage. Thus he concluded a series on the machinations of racism and the growth of intolerance on a note far different from that which might have been expected by one uninitiated in the contours of his thought. He granted that blacks were being denied "some privileges" but found "another theme for conclusion": "It is also true that we have large, very large opportunities, and we may use them for our own if we are prepared to do so." [83] The doctrine of accentuating the positive was much less convincing when it was applied to the South, but here too Brascher struggled to find cause for optimism. During the same week when he mysteriously reached his hopeful conclusions about the situation at Cleveland, he was somehow moved to editorialize that the nation was "awakening from a passive acceptance" of lynching, disfranchisement, and segregation. He rhapsodized: "The South is awakening, and says, 'Give the Negro a chance; we are his best friends and love him the most.' . . . Everywhere there is a providential desire to be fair and just." [84]

To be sure, such reluctance to acknowledge the course of race relations was not always true of younger leaders. Ever Brascher occasionally revealed that he was at odds with himself when he confronted evidence of increasing white intolerance. Just as Washington was ultimately moved covertly to support efforts to challenge segregation and disfranchisement in the courts, so Brascher at times spoke out against or applauded action against intolerance. At times the *Journal* praised those who filed civil rights suits, and in 1906 it strongly denounced the impending speaking engagement of South Carolina Senator Ben Tillman. (The paper stated that Tillman's appearance in Cleveland, at the behest of a white teachers' organization, would exacerbate racial tensions.) While these were far from Brascher's usual concerns, a few younger spokesmen attempted to combine his interest in racial self-help and solidarity with an appreciation of the need to militantly combat discrimination. Particularly those descended from established upper-class families often displayed their strong integrationist heritage and seemed bent on bridging old and new strategic orientations. For example, Cincinnati stenographer William Stevenson and Cleveland attorneys Theodore Green and Harry E. Davis and librarian Edward C. Williams (Chesnutt's son-in-law) took part both in booster-oriented activities and in protest movements like the Niagara Movement and

[83] Cleveland *Journal*, Nov. 19, 26, Dec. 3, 10, 1904.
[84] Ibid., Dec. 10, 1904.

the NAACP. But this was by no means the case with every scion of the upper class. In contrast to Theodore Green, an early officer of the Negro Board of Trade, the Cleveland Association of Colored Men, and the militant local NAACP chapter, was his brother William. Also an early officer of the Negro Board of Trade and the C.A.C.M., and one of the most outspoken advocates of race patronage of race enterprise in the city, William was much less a fighter against color lines; he seemed more comfortable (as did Jennie Porter, another member of an old family) with a viewpoint like Brascher's. None of the younger leaders necessarily agreed with Chavers that a racial strategy such as Washington's was especially valuable because it recognized that "earning and saving money" was more important than "getting the best seats in a theater"—as if this were the choice facing black leaders as they attempted to establish goals for the race. Yet, like Brascher, in their daily public racial activities most of them favored the former over the latter in their conception of racial strategy.[85]

Despite the emergence of these young activists and the growing popularity of their racial ideology, the school of thought represented by the older leadership remained a significant theme in the life of Ohio blacks. No one better articulated this tendency than Harry Smith. Like most of the older men, Smith often disagreed with younger leaders like Brascher; the *Gazette* therefore greatly differed in both reportage and editorial policy from its chief rival, the *Journal*. The differences illustrate the varying perspectives of both generations.[86] Smith, who had come of age in the early 1880s, continued to represent the concerns of an earlier time—one of relative tolerance in race relations and of a more direct pursuit of equality. The *Gazette* carried much more news of, and protest against, anti-black violence, disfranchisement, southern segregation, and discrimination in public places in

[85] Columbus *Standard*, July 27, 1901; Cleveland *Journal*, Jan. 20, Nov. 17, 24, 1906, Mar. 26, 1910; Cleveland *Gazette*, Dec. 4, 1909, Jan. 29, Oct. 15, 1910; Green, *Fact Stranger Than Fiction*, p. 357.

[86] While we do not have the benefit of extant pre–World War I copies of Dabney's Cincinnati *Union*, a comparison of the *Union* and the *Journal* would doubtless yield the very same results. Like Smith, who was his ally in racial affairs, Dabney continued to maintain the ideological orientation of the late nineteenth century; this was reflected in the fact that Smith quoted Dabney editorials much more frequently than did the *Journal*. Indeed, between the inception of the *Union* in 1907 and the *Journal*'s demise in 1911, the *Journal* reprinted only one of Dabney's editorials; it dealt with the competitive difficulties of black barbershops. This probably reflected the fact that Brascher found little good news in the *Union*, which tended to place editorial emphasis on the deterioration of race relations. On the other hand, given Smith's interests, he found much more of use in the Cincinnati paper. Cleveland *Journal*, Mar. 5, 1910; Cleveland *Gazette*, Mar. 11, 1911, May 24, 1913, Nov. 14, 1914, Apr. 10, Sept. 11, 1915.

Cleveland and other Ohio cities. While the *Journal* denounced Till-man's appearance, the *Gazette* helped to organize the (ultimately un-successful) campaign against it; while the *Journal* only occasionally praised those who filed civil rights suits, the *Gazette* often did so, and even criticized those victims of discrimination who did *not* fight for their rights in court. After 1900 Smith's major editorial concerns were disfranchisement, segregation, and the failure of Republican leadership to deter the general erosion of southern black citizenship. He saw that disfranchisement left most of the race more powerless and isolated than at any time since slavery. And while younger men like Brascher tended to adopt a Washingtonian stance, seeing in segregation the opportunity for increased solidarity and intragroup cooperation, Smith saw segregation as a giant step toward formalizing inequality.[87]

Smith was sensitive to the need for racial self-help, solidarity, and economic uplift, and he actually showed greater concern for these issues after 1900. Like the *Journal,* the *Gazette* took pleasure at the twentieth-century expansion of black business. Smith sometimes did his own boosting of race enterprise and asked his readers, in the name of race loyalty, to buy at black shops. He endorsed the Negro Board of Trade when it was organized. He wanted existing racial institutions and organizations to deal with social problems created by the migra-tions; the *Gazette* called upon the church to respond to increasing con-flict with the law by developing greater concern for the moral training of youth. After 1900 Smith continued to give an occasional nod to racial pride and solidarity as ideals in the conduct of life by printing inspirational pieces on black history and on black genius, achievement, and courage.[88]

But these were not the *Gazette*'s major concerns, and Smith just as often took offense at the errors he believed were committed in the name of racial pride and self-help. Feeling that it was the race's right to participate fully in American life, he rejected voluntary retreat from facilities like the YMCA or from integrated schools. He felt that any distinction between black-initiated, voluntary separation and white-imposed segregation was a sham, since both capitulated to the reac-

[87] On the Springfield riot of 1904, for example, see Cleveland *Journal,* Apr. 2, 1904; and Cleveland *Gazette,* Mar. 12, 19, 26, Apr. 2, 9, 16, 30, May 7, 21, 1904. Smith's editorials on disfranchisement, segregation, and Republican racial policies are too numerous to document. For examples, see Cleveland *Gazette,* Jan. 13, June 23, 1900, Apr. 20, 27, 1901, Feb. 1, Sept. 20, 1902, Jan. 2, 1905, May 12, July 14, 21, 1906, May 11, 1907, July 11, Oct. 31, 1908, Jan. 21, 1911, Sept. 27, 1913. On Tillman, ibid., Oct. 27, Nov. 3, 10, 17, 24, Dec. 22, 1906.

[88] Cleveland *Gazette,* May 11, 1901, Mar. 22, Apr. 12, 1902, May 18, 1905, Sept. 1, 8, 1906, Jan. 23, 1909, Feb. 18, 1911, Jan. 25, Aug. 13, 1913, Dec. 19, 1914.

tionary trend of the times and both accomplished the same end—the postponement of full equality.[89]

The *Gazette* rejected pride and solidarity when Smith felt they became distortions of reality and masks for deceit. His paper criticized the *Journal* for its indiscriminate praise of black businesses which bilked the poor. Moreover, he deplored the nationwide tendency of the booster press to employ inflated rhetoric when discussing racial and individual accomplishments. In a 1909 editorial he conveyed his disgust with the way in which a competent but ordinary black doctor, lawyer, or teacher became in the booster press a "renowned surgeon," or "an eminent jurist," or "a distinguished educator and philosopher." These exaggerations revealed ". . . a race weakness for notoriety and parade which at once discredits our judgment in the eyes of our neighbors and exposes our cultural deficiency . . . [and] show[s] how little it takes to make us great *in the eyes of each other*." Establishing nearly impossible and rigidly deterministic criteria for black achievement in a hostile world, he argued, "The one standard of excellence in this country is that set by those whose opportunities, environments, achievements, and possessions—moral, mental, and material—entitle them to set it. In fine, it is the so-called 'Anglo-Saxon standard.' Measured by that our so-called 'great' . . . would in far too many cases fall far behind." [90] It was a cruel judgment, not only because it had a ring of truth, but more fundamentally because it seemed to accept the insidious logic by which blacks were found wanting for their failure to meet standards which whites made it all but impossible for them to pursue. Smith's judgment created negativism, loss of self-confidence, and crippling feelings of inferiority, and as such it was one which few younger leaders would accept. But it came more easily to his own generation, which had taken so many of its social and cultural cues from those higher-status whites who set America's "Anglo-Saxon standard."

More than race pride, self-help, and solidarity, Smith valued equality and justice, the keys which he and others of his generation felt would open the doors of American society to worthy individuals. His feeling that Washington's leadership compromised both equality and justice led Smith to join forces with the Tuskegeean's opponents, first in the Niagara Movement and then in the NAACP. To be sure, Smith knew that Washington's program was not wholly incompatible with the individualized racial goals which he and his peers honored, and occasionally the *Gazette* praised Washington's contributions in black education and in encouraging blacks to enter business—both activities

[89] Ibid., Jan. 10, 1903, July 22, 1905, Mar. 16, 1906, Mar. 9, 1910.
[90] Ibid., May 19, 26, 1906, Mar. 7, 21, 1908, Jan. 23, 1909.

which helped in the work of preparing individuals to succeed on terms America valued. But the *Gazette* was angered by Washington's refusal to speak out against the erosion of black rights. During the century's first decade the *Gazette's* criticism of Washington grew more intense, both because of his statements accommodating the white South and because of his close ties with Roosevelt and Taft. In 1912 Smith's increasing distrust of Washington led him to denounce the National Negro Business League as a tool for the consolidation of the Tuskegeean's personal power.[91]

Smith's singular personality made him more uncompromising in his views and more harsh in his criticism; not all older leaders were as set in their racial views. The challenges of the times, particularly pressing local racial needs prompted by the migrations, moved some of them to recognize the need to balance group-centered racial values (such as those posited by the *Journal*) with the traditional concern for equality, individual mobility, and integration into the American mainstream. Yet the legacy of their late nineteenth-century hopes and attitudes continued to exert a powerful influence upon them. This was most clearly manifest in their relationship to Washington, which betrayed anxieties (not unlike Smith's) about current race relations and the future of the race, and which marked the ideological gap between them and the younger generation.

While Smith was alone among older leaders in his outspoken, public criticisms of Washington, many other older men like George Jackson, Green, Dabney, and Scarborough shared his concern for the negative consequences of Washington's leadership.[92] Moreover, the cordial relations which Washington enjoyed with older blacks like Charles Chesnutt and Carrie Clifford cannot be taken as a sign that they differed substantially with Smith in anything but style. Such cordial relations in public often masked growing disenchantment. Clifford, in fact, was on a collision course with Washington almost from the start of the Tuskegeean's ascendancy. A founder of the Ohio branch of the National Association of Colored Women and the branch's president from 1901 to 1905 before departing left for Washington to join her husband, William, who was working for the government, she had led a movement which year after year demonstrated a concern for lynching, disfranchisement, and segregation. It is not surprising that she joined the

[91] Ibid., Nov. 2, Dec. 7, 1895, July 14, 1900, Feb. 17, 1906, Nov. 21, 1908, Jan. 6, 1912.
[92] Cleveland *Gazette*, July 8, 15, 22, 1905; Cleveland *Plain Dealer*, Aug. 31, 1908; Herbert Aptheker, "The Niagara Movement," in *Afro-American History: The Modern Era* (New York, 1971), p. 155.

opposition to Washington by 1908.[93] Chesnutt, who left decades of blue vein isolation in response to the crisis he saw around him after the turn of the century, and who would become increasingly involved in racial affairs,[94] liked Washington personally, and had ties with Tuskegee through his young son Edwin, who taught there for a time. But Chesnutt was greatly concerned with the conservation of black voting and civil rights, and for this reason he eventually parted company with Washington.[95]

Even those older Ohioans who refused to break with Washington often had motives which belied concern for personal interests rather than support for his program. This was the case among politicians: neither George Myers nor Ralph Tyler wished to see a northward spread of the repressive conditions against which Washington failed to speak out. As their reactions to McKinley administration policies demonstrated, both were deeply troubled by the eclipse of black citizenship in the South. But they, along with others involved in politics, were realistic enough to respect Washington's political power. As Ohioans and Northerners with no creditable black political base and no outstanding white allies after the death of Hanna, they knew that Washington provided a vital connection if they wished to retain a modicum of influence. On that basis they tended to accept his leadership as a fact of life, regardless of ideological qualms. Officeholders like Jere Brown, Cottrill, and William Clifford (the latter in contrast to his wife) simply lay low in the interests of keeping their positions; in their minds, they were no more free to criticize Washington than to criticize the racial policies of the governments they served. Tyler's desire for office took precedence over his disgust with the Republican party on the southern question. His increasing correspondence with Washington as Myers began to retreat from the active political role which he had played before Hanna's death, and his eventual elevation to a high office with Washington's support, indicate his opportunistic willingness to bend racial views to suit career needs. Myers

[93] Cleveland *Journal*, Dec. 3, 1904, Jan. 21, 1905; Carrie Clifford to Charles Chesnutt, Oct. 9, 1908, Charles W. Chesnutt Papers, FU.

[94] Cleveland *Journal*, Jan. 21, Oct. 24, Nov. 25, Dec. 2, 1905; Cleveland *Leader*, Oct. 29, 1907; Cleveland *Plain Dealer*, Feb. 1, 1911. Cf. S. P. Fullinwider, *The Mind and Mood of Black America* (Homewood, 1969), p. 82. Chesnutt's increasing involvement in racial affairs, local and national, does little to sustain that author's view that Chesnutt's identification with the race grew weaker after the turn of the century; indeed, it strongly suggests the opposite.

[95] Charles Chesnutt to Booker T. Washington, Oct. 9, Nov. 3, 1906, Box 317, Jan. 1, 1907, Box 886, Washington Papers; Charles Thwing to Harry E. Davis, Oct. 7, 1910, Charles Chesnutt to W. E. B. Du Bois, Nov. 21, 1910, W. E. B. Du Bois to Charles W. Chesnutt, Jan. 9, 1912, Chesnutt Papers.

also collaborated with Washington, primarily on federal patronage for black Ohioans and occasionally on fund-raising for Tuskegee Institute. Myers liked wielding influence and being close to the centers of power; though his contacts with Washington were not frequent, he tended to offer the same unswerving loyalty that he had brought to Mark Hanna. Yet Myers did not allow a personal need to possess influence and to be of service to powerful men to go too far in compromising his larger views. His indifference to Washington's continued entreaties that he, one of the nation's most successful black barbershop owners, become an active worker in behalf of the National Negro Business League suggests his own lack of excitement for Washington's larger program.[96] Though very few of them chose this course, the act of leaving politics could have a liberating impact on such men. When John Green's position at Washington was abolished and he decided to give up political activity for his law practice, his public expressions on racial questions subsequently displayed greater concern and eventually militance. His office had forced him to defend Republican policies and to remain silent on racial controversies. Within a few months after leaving office in 1906, Green was publishing articles on the crisis in race relations; within a few years he became one of the leading Niagara Movement figures at Cleveland.[97]

Thus in Ohio after 1900 two generations of racial leadership were manifesting different interpretations of the times and developing different ideas on how to respond to them. While these larger orientations were evolving, the Ohioans faced two immediate problems within their own communities: a serious deterioration of race relations, and a growing black urban population based on migration from the South. When facing these challenges the groups of leaders clashed, compromised, and allied in complex patterns. In the final analysis, their response was the measure of their leadership.

[96] For years Myers found excuses for not attending business league conventions. He never joined the league, and it appears that eventually Washington gave up trying to interest him in its work. George Myers to Booker T. Washington, July 29, 1901, Box 235, Feb. 10, 1904, Box 292, Emmett Scott to George Myers, July 14, 1905, Box 304, Washington Papers; Booker T. Washington to George Myers, July 11, 1907, Box XIV, folder 1, Myers Papers.

[97] Cleveland *Gazette,* Oct. 6, 1906; Cleveland *Plain Dealer,* Aug. 31, 1908.

14

Organized and Institutional Responses to the Migrations and to the Crisis in Race Relations

Ohio's black leaders responded to the migrations and to the crisis in race relations with various practical endeavors which spanned the ideological spectrum from militant protest aimed at facilitating integration, to the institutionalization of black self-help which furthered their separation from society. If larger goals were to be pursued effectively, any of these responses required the marshaling of black community energies and resources; thus, in the last years of the period blacks were recognizing the need to coalesce, formally and informally, around various programs designed to deal with pressing problems. In their most deliberate efforts to fashion vehicles for racial action, they sought both the reorientation of existing black institutions and the establishment of new ones. Before turning our attention to all of these organized efforts, it is important to emphasize that they were framed within a web of complex, sometimes conflicting, attitudes and emotions. They must be seen in light of the perspectives and motivations which both generations of racial leaders brought to their relations with the southern migrants, and to their efforts to deal with growing racial conflict, prejudice, and discrimination.

I

In attempting to interpret the origins and nature of the problems in their communities, black leaders saw the migrations and the crisis in race relations as both separate and closely related challenges. This was particularly true of older black leaders. On the one hand, they were prone to observe that the change in Ohio race relations was part of a national trend; in the words of the Reverend E. L. Gilliam, an older Methodist minister who came from Indiana to preach at Columbus in 1902, their white neighbors were being swept up in a national tidal wave of "color line hysteria." [1] Older leaders sometimes tied their situation directly to developments in the South. They were aware, for example, of the northward migration of the southern example of race proscription, and some of them believed that southern whites were more or less deliberately campaigning to win over the North to their own racial mores. When anti-intermarriage bills flooded northern legislatures, Harry Smith acknowledged the possible validity of a correspondent's view that the proposed legislation was part of a southern "conspiracy" to nationalize the southern system of comprehensive segregation. [2] Others might have scoffed at the tendency to speak of the matter as a conspiracy, but they nevertheless offered proof that southern ways were coming North and that Southerners were not altogether unhappy about it. In 1907 William Sanders Scarborough coined the term "the subsidized North," intending to conjure up the image of the South offering a willing North instruction on methods of race proscription. For Scarborough, the proliferation of the "Jim Crow" system, through means such as "White Only" signs in northern theaters and restaurants, indicated that southern ways were taking root in the North. He pointed to Tillman's inflammatory speeches in the North, and to the tendency of northbound trains to retain the signs marking their separate cars when crossing the Mason-Dixon Line, as but two ways in which northern whites were getting instruction in bigotry. [3]

On the other hand, they also tended to throw back upon the black masses the onus for increasing white prejudice and discrimination in the North. From this perspective, fault for the negative trends in race relations appeared to lie not so much with the changing attitudes of whites or with the structure of a society permeated by discrimination, but with the variant behavior and lifestyles of the most constant victims of oppression, the black lower class. Migrants often came in for a large share of the blame, not only because their difficulties of adjustment to northern urban life influenced the growth of racial tensions, but also because the migrants were poor outlanders, less acculturated to middle-class norms and urban ways, whose very difficulties of adjustment appeared to reflect upon the capacities of the race. When the migrants were viewed in this light, their mere presence was a discomforting and constant reminder of the distance that most of the race had to travel

---

[1] Cleveland *Gazette*, Apr. 29, 1911.

[2] Ibid., Mar. 29, 1913.

[3] William Sanders Scarborough, "The Subsidized North," *Voice of the Negro*, III, 1 (1907), 31–34.

in preparing to enter the American mainstream. Prior to the migrations, upper-class black Ohioans had experienced such a reminder less often. It was the sort of reminder which, along with the eclipse of white tolerance, mocked their hopes.

The argument which blamed changing conditions on the migrants in particular or on the lower class generally emerged during the first years of the new century, when the trends in population and race relations became increasingly clear. One of the argument's basic components was the contention that, by and large, the only southern blacks who came North were criminal or disreputable, indolent, stupid, and rootless. Ralph Tyler gave a bitter appraisal of the situation in his hometown, Columbus:

> Columbus is joining the list of Negro-hating towns, due largely to the influx of a lot of cheap, worthless niggers from the South. The same class is infesting. . . most all other northern cities. They make it hard for us wherever they light. The well-meaning, industrious, progressive Negroes, as a rule, remain in the South to fight out the question there. The lazy, shiftless, worthless class come to northern cities to reduce our opportunities and privileges to a minimum.[4]

Others of the Old Guard were prone to agree with Tyler. For George Myers, the growth of prejudice and discrimination was the result of the "ill-conduct of the scum of southern Negroes who have in recent years settled within them [cities] and of a few bad ones to the manor born." [5] Cincinnati's George Jackson took a similar position; though he failed to mention the migrants, his stance suggests that he had them at least partly in mind. At a meeting of the city's prestigious Dunbar Lyceum, an upper-class literary society, he responded to the question "How Can We Best Meet Conditions Which Arise from the Growth of Prejudice in Cincinnati?" by calling for the suppression of the growing numbers of "the criminal classes" and of the "socially unrespectable," whom he believed to be responsible for increasing intolerance.[6]

Because it might inflame white opinion, lead to well-publicized conflicts with the police, and fulfill stereotypes of blacks as vicious and uncivilized, black crime was an obvious, immediate danger to race relations. Black Ohioans were aware that growing numbers of urban blacks were going to jail, and they knew that the migrations helped determine the rising rates of black incarceration and set the back-

4 Ralph Tyler to George Myers, Aug. 13, 1908, Box XIV, folder 5, George A. Myers Papers, OHS.

5 George Myers to Booker T. Washington, Feb. 4, 1911, Box 403, Booker T. Washington Papers, LC.

6 Indianapolis *Freeman,* Dec. 31, 1910.

ground for the increasing vice and the growing number of saloons in black neighborhoods. That the 1904 Springfield riot was precipitated by the shooting of a policeman by a recently settled drunken black Kentuckian and by the popular association of blacks with vice and crime, and that among the transients in their communities were desperate men, were facts not lost upon Harry Smith and other commentators on the 1904 riot.[7]

But more often than not, they believed that white intolerance was increased by ordinary, daily behavior which was a product of lower-class values and lifestyles, simply unconventional or only marginally anti-social and illegal. In this view, racial stereotypes were fulfilled and respectable white opinion scandalized in several ways. First, there were the conditions and style of lower-class slum life. These were singled out by a Columbus black businessman when he was questioned about the causes of changing race relations. Pointing to the squalor of tenement life, with its filth, lack of privacy, and socializing and public drinking on front stoops and in the streets, he said, "There [is] no question that the ordinary negroes of Columbus, especially . . . the new negroes who have lately come from the South . . . merit the ill-opinion of all decent people for the manner in which they live."[8]

Then, too, loud, exuberant, and assertive behavior by blacks who were unconcerned with presenting a respectable image in public places such as theaters and streetcars, often the only places of contact between lower-class blacks and large numbers of whites, was thought to be particularly destructive of white tolerance. Harry Smith became troubled enough by the presumed effects of actions which brought attention to blacks in public places that he began to call upon the Negro clergy to exercise a "restraining influence" through moral suasion and preaching. Perhaps because he did not at first connect the migrants in particular with such behavior, or because he was wary of producing white anxieties about an invading black horde rising out of the South, Smith's early remarks did not blame the migrants. In 1905, when he reported that a drunken black woman had recently shouted encouragement to actors from the audience of a crowded, integrated theater, he singled out "the loud-mouthed lower class of our people." A year later he pointed to "the loud-mouthed, drunken Negro and the 'ragtime' singing and whistling young monkey Negro" whose con-

[7] Cleveland *Gazette*, Mar. 12, 1904; Washington *Colored American*, Mar. 26, 1904; Springfield *Press-Republic*, Mar. 11, 1904.

[8] Quoted in Frank U. Quillin, *The Color Line in Ohio* (Ann Arbor, 1913), p. 145.

spicuous conversation and buffoonery on street corners and on trolley cars were doing "incalculable harm" to local blacks.[9] But eventually Smith concluded that the southern migrants were responsible for much, if not all, of the blame for the trend of northern race relations, largely because of their rude, undignified public behavior. In 1911 he reprinted a long editorial, taken from the black Rochester (New York) *Sentinel,* which probably expressed his own feeling on the matter. The *Sentinel* claimed that northern-bred blacks were "refined, dignified, and conservative," and had traditionally enjoyed a "cordial, intimate, and confidential relationship" with whites who lived around them. But the migrants had introduced "the gregarious habits of the South" and "the loudness and boisterousness of the plantation" into the crowded streets of northern cities, and thus had created "changed sentiment and conditions in the North." Thus, the paper concluded that the race itself, not white prejudice, was responsible for the deterioration of northern race relations: "The changed condition in the North which is anti-colored came about because the colored man forced it." [10]

This bitter conclusion left much unexplained. It failed to account for the negative trend of race relations in places, such as the small towns of the Western Reserve, which had received few, if any, migrants. To be sure, the migrations did have a negative impact on race relations, but they did so in a climate of opinion and action which was decidedly anti-black. Myers, Tyler, Jackson, and especially Smith, who discerned a national trend toward prejudice and recognized the power of the southern example, probably were not unaware of the weakness of such a conclusion. Of course, theirs was an understandable reaction. They were angry as they saw their long-time privileged position eroding; they assumed that the migrants' behavior and the cruel dynamic of stereotyping were creating new criteria by which whites now found them wanting. Yet, whatever its psychological function, such a reaction did little to clarify the times, and even less to prepare black leaders to reach out with empathy to those whose destiny was irrevocably tied to their own.

Younger men like Brascher were in some ways no less myopic in their perceptions of the race's deteriorating position. While their elders were often acutely aware of the relationship between northern and southern trends, Brascher only occasionally demonstrated such a recognition. In 1906 he denounced the impending speech of Tillman at Cleveland, but his descriptions and appraisals of the "color line hysteria" sweeping white America were infrequent. Then, too, Brascher

9 Cleveland *Gazette,* Feb. 11, 1905, Oct. 13, 20, 1906, May 16, 23, 1908.
10 Ibid., May 6, 1911, quoting Rochester *Sentinel* (n.d.).

was not immune to the same emotional reaction against the migrant poor that Smith displayed. However seldom he gave vent to his feelings, he resented the fact that higher-status blacks like himself were facing increasing discrimination in the North. At first he lashed out at the most convenient targets—the migrants—just like Smith and Myers. Shortly after the *Journal's* birth in 1903, Brascher expressed bitterness and fear in an editorial, "The Vicious Element," which noted the northbound influx "of indolent Negroes locating in the large cities and by their vicious, disgraceful conduct . . . creating a baneful sentiment against the people they represent." Whites "either by ignorance or indifference" were failing to separate the good and bad of the race; as a result, "cities in which the Afro-American was once highly honored and respected are now discriminating against him in the unfairest manner." But at this time Brascher was unable to suggest any strategy for correcting the situation, other than singling out the need for "more arrests" of a "criminal element" among the migrants.[11]

In future years the *Journal* went no further in analyzing the larger causes of increasing racial discrimination and white intolerance, less because it dwelled on the migrant's role than because it sought to avoid bad news. Only occasionally did the editor allow his concern about changing racial conditions to dampen the paper's spirit of hope, enthusiasm, and progress. At the same time, however, younger racial spokesmen were coming to terms with the trends in Ohio race relations in their own way, developing a group-oriented racial program which, to their minds, suited an age of reaction which seemed to demand that blacks fall back on their own resources, rather than devoting their energies to seeking an early entrance into the American mainstream. Thus the *Journal* eventually outgrew its emotional response to the migrants. It continued to call for a crackdown on the criminal element, because Negro crime posed a threat to racial tolerance and to the development of a prosperous black commercial district along Central Avenue,[12] but never again did it blame the migrants specifically for the worsening of race relations or the growth of black crime. Gradually the paper evolved a more positive stand which mixed sympathy for the migrants' plight with a view of the integral role they might play in furthering the cause of racial solidarity, self-help, and economic and neighborhood development. By 1904 Brascher had already begun to reappraise his position. He pointed out the numerous difficulties facing the migrants, arguing persuasively that intragroup cooperation and innovative activities would be needed to aid them. In

[11] Cleveland *Journal*, May 2, 1903.
[12] Ibid., July 18, 25, 1908.

the next several years this desire to aid the migrants emerged as a major theme of the *Journal's* local program, intimately bound up with its interest in creating vital, supportive racial communities in northern cities and its ideological commitment to group-oriented values and priorities. By 1906 Brascher had not only stopped stressing the dangers posed by the migrations, but he had also begun to see the migrations' dynamic possibilities for racial progress. In fact, he had almost come full circle. He now noted that if "the noticeable inflow of colored people during recent years" were to continue at the same rate, in a decade Cleveland would have perhaps 20,000 blacks, giving it one of the North's largest black populations. Because of the social and individual dislocations caused by migration and resettlement, he shrank from espousing a massive influx. Instead, he encouraged the urban migration of "the young and valiant," hopefully with a source of employment prearranged.[13] Still, it was a more certain sign of welcome than the migrants would receive from Smith's *Gazette*—and it was not forced or feigned; it flowed naturally from the interests and ideas of Brascher and other young men and women who shared his concerns.

Thus, the different bases for collective action were taking shape. They implied the possibility of consensus as well as conflict, for though their larger strategic orientations and perspectives were different, the immediate concerns of both leadership groups were similar. To the extent that both were concerned with keeping interracial peace, and the young boosters were particularly interested in having an orderly setting for the development of a black commercial district, both saw the need to check the increase in black crime and to assert the rule of law and order in black neighborhoods. Both saw the need to offer migrants conventional restraining and guiding influences in order to speed their adjustment to northern urban life and to lessen the tensions which their presence created in the cities. Older spokesmen often saw the matter in terms of restraint, while younger ones spoke in terms of guidance. But, practically speaking, both restraint and guidance implied attempts to inculcate the bourgeois values, standards, and lifestyles shared by young and old alike. Finally, both groups acknowledged that in order to check the spread of prejudice and discrimination they would have to find a method for confronting the hostile attitudes and actions of their white neighbors.

Of course, differences between them would exist. They might simply be differences in the way of reaching similar conclusions. But more serious, acrimonious sources of division were differences over the par-

13 Ibid., Jan. 23, 1904, Feb. 2, 1906.

ticular means needed to deal with pressing problems, such as the
growing discrimination in public accommodations or the social welfare needs of migrants. Differing racial ideologies helped create and
exacerbate such differences. So, too, would regional and local traditions and current conditions, ties of loyalty and friendship, and individual self-interest; but even though the latter might create division,
they might also be unifying forces.

II

After 1900 the growth of vice, crime, and "anti-social behavior," and the widely held belief that these hampered race relations
and black community development, led a wide spectrum of black leadership to become interested in various types of black self-policing activities and in improving relations between blacks and police. At first
these efforts were random and informal. Harry Smith, Wendell Phillips Dabney, and others took an interest in bettering black relations
with local law enforcement agencies, while Cleveland's Negro Board
of Trade, the Cleveland Association of Colored Men, and Columbus's
recently founded Colored Ministers' Association consulted with police
and officials on the need to combat vice and crime in black sections of
both cities.[14] Eventually, however, they all recognized a need to extend self-help into the realm of social control on a routinized basis
through special organizations. The stated aims of Cincinnati's National
Negro Reform League and Criminal Elimination Society, founded in
September, 1914, reflected the basic goals of other organizations like
Columbus's Civic Betterment and Protective League (established
around 1910 by a coalition of young boosters and some older men)
and Cleveland's Law and Order League (founded in 1911 by Harry
Smith).[15] Demonstrating a belief in the causal relationship between
"the great influx of undesirables" and "a keenly felt change in favorable sentiment and desirable conditions" (in the words of the Columbus organization), the Cincinnati society was dedicated "to assist in
the protection of the commonwealth from the criminal class of Negroes; to help the better class of Negroes distinguish itself from the

[14] Cleveland *Gazette,* July 15, 1905, Aug. 22, 1908, Aug. 6, 1910; Cleveland
Journal, Nov. 18, 1905, Jan. 16, 1909; Columbus *Dispatch,* Oct. 6, 1907; George
Jones et al., compilers, *The Cleveland Association of Colored Men* (pamphlet
dated Feb., 1914), p. 2, Box XI, John P. Green Papers, WRHS; Wendell Phillips
Dabney, *Cincinnati's Colored Citizens: Historical, Sociological, and Biographical*
(Cincinnati, 1926), p. 166.
[15] Cleveland *Gazette,* July 8, 15, 1911; Indianapolis *Freeman,* Aug. 23, Oct. 3,
1914.

bad citizens; to secure the arrest and conviction of lawbreakers and assist the innocent; and to protect young colored women." (This last goal referred to a proposed campaign against brothels and procurers.) [16]

Whether racial efforts were informal or organized, the goal of assisting the police and establishing firm ties with local police chiefs was always considered essential, both for checking the spread of crime and for protecting the innocent and respectable from harassment by white policemen, who often failed to distinguish between black law-abiders and black felons. In 1910 a Cincinnati correspondent of the Indianapolis *Freeman* cogently described the importance of cordial relations with urban police chiefs:

> The chief of police of any large city is always of interest to colored people . . . because they are more likely to suffer at the hands of the police department than any other race of people, owing to the large number of ignorant, uncouth Negroes who flock to large cities. The better element are usually insulted and humiliated through the lack of intelligence of some member of the force because his first thought is that all niggers look alike. The temperament of the heads of a Police Department has more to do with regulating this one fault than anything else. The better element of Negroes of this city can do more and should do more than anyone else to assist our new chief in regulating the bad element that is getting into our city by furnishing information to the chief or his subordinates on all known criminals hiding in our city. . . .[17]

Self-policing activities and attempts to gain the cooperation of local authorities were not limited to the major metropolitan areas. Smaller communities, such as Lima and Oberlin, where the same disorganizing effects of migration were likely to be seen immediately, even if the extent of the migration was very small or limited to the comings and goings of groups of transients, also witnessed similar efforts geared to their particular conditions. The experience of tiny Oberlin was representative. In late August, 1908, a local newspaper reported a disorder on an inter-urban trolley between Oberlin and nearby Elyria which had resulted when two blacks, for no apparent reason except drunkenness, fought with the conductor until they were overpowered by other train employees. Both assailants were migrants to Ohio (though from Indiana and Pennsylvania, rather than the South); the paper noted that Oberlin had lately been receiving blacks from everywhere "at frequent intervals [because] work elsewhere for colored people has not been plentiful this year while they have been kept busy here nearly

16 Indianapolis *Freeman,* Oct. 3, 1914.
17 Ibid., Oct. 22, 1910.

all the time." Several similar incidents involving black transients had apparently occurred in the town in the recent past; a number of established local blacks perceived a threat to the relatively benign ordering of race relations and reacted angrily and immediately. At a meeting several days later the town's most influential blacks, all artisans and shopkeepers who had lived there for many years and in several cases were graduates of the college, formed a "Citizen's Law and Order League," dedicated to the protection of "the purity of private life, sanctity of home, honesty of purpose, and strictest morality and character." Their meeting debated a number of anti-crime strategies to which their league might be dedicated. While they quickly decided to aid the local police in apprehending criminals, this was not their major concern. The small-town environment lent itself to monitoring of individual behavior and to striking directly and peremptorily at potential lawbreakers. They chose, therefore, to attempt to rid Oberlin of likely troublemakers by making it impossible for them to find or keep jobs. Oberlin whites were asked not "to employ men who loaf on corners, use vile language, patronize . . . saloons, and make Saturday night hideous in Oberlin and travel on the street cars dangerous." White women were asked to cease "to employ cooks they know use intoxicating liquors to excess."[18]

Though we lack information on the results of the Oberlin anti-crime campaign, perhaps black initiatives were successful in small towns where black crime and vice were not major problems and where those responsible for both were more easily isolated. But in large cities few benefits were achieved. The last years of the period found urban black leaders even more conscious of the need to enlist police and government cooperation against increasing crime and vice in black neighborhoods, and even more organized to help wage that struggle. Yet public officials seldom had the will to initiate comprehensive clean-up campaigns in neighborhoods which had long been officially accepted as centers of vice—and the fact that vice operators often had political influence also worked against reform. Furthermore, black communities experienced strained relations with the very police with whom black leaders sought to ally. The tactics and racial attitudes of police, and their conscientious enforcement of laws which saw "loitering" and "disturbing the peace" in such activities as hanging out on street corners and loud talking, often angered the black poor. While struggles for law and order helped to unify black leadership, they did not nar-

18 Oberlin *News*, Sept. 23, 26, 1908. On Lima, see Cleveland *Gazette*, June 5, 1909.

row the gulf between the migrant poor and established, higher-status residents. To the extent that such struggles added tensions to black-police relations, they created a double bind: pursuit of goals deemed vital to black welfare produced problems detrimental to it.

Levels of black incarceration suggest the magnitude of the problem, mirroring not only the actual commission of crime, but also conflict between lower-class culture and the respectable values which the police defended, as well as the victimization of blacks by agents of the law. In all seven major metropolitan counties save Clark (Springfield), where the peak of black in-migration and population growth came before 1900 and where the 1906 riot led to a crusade against vice operations, blacks constituted ever-increasing percentages of county jail populations during 1900–1909. During the decade their rate of increase as county jail prisoners was also considerably greater than the general rate of black population increase. During 1910–15 in most metropolitan counties the number of black prisoners was growing more quickly than the number of white prisoners; indeed, by 1915 the five-year total had already surpassed that of the entire previous decade.[19]

Conditions were worst in the three major cities. At Cincinnati an interracial struggle against vice in the city's nationally known red light district, located on George Street in the heart of the black West End, had intensified at the turn of the century. But it resulted only in greater regulation of brothels, especially the once-thriving interracial ones, because the police and politicians continued to accept containment as the solution to the vice problem. The Cox machine had always tolerated prostitution as long as it was restricted to a lower-status neighborhood; although the anti-machine Democratic reformers were interested in reducing crime in the slums, they subscribed to the same view. By 1915, therefore, the city's brothels and its criminal demimonde were entrenched on George Street. Relations with the police were poor. Police continued to be disturbed, occasionally violently so, by interracial sexual relations. The press occasionally reported violent confrontations between officers and groups of poor blacks, prompted by the suppression of crime and by such symbolic confrontations as the attempt of police to arrest a black man for sleeping on a park bench.[20]

[19] Based on annual reports of county sheriffs found in Ohio *Statistics*. See above, ch. 10, esp. note 39.

[20] Dabney, *Cincinnati's Colored Citizens*, pp. 166–170; Cincinnati *Enquirer*, June 28, 29, 1911; Zane Miller, *Boss Cox's Cincinnati: Urban Politics in the Progressive Era* (New York, 1968), p. 214.

Columbus blacks were waging an increasing struggle against conditions in the "Bad Lands," the black area of downtown East Long Street. Though most of them lived in the more fashionable sections of the East Side, many black ministers and booster organization activists were disturbed with the growing white association of the race with crime and vice; they blamed the thriving Bad Lands, with its large migrant population and its brothels, gambling dens, saloons, and Smoky Hobbs's opium den for the deteriorating image of Columbus blacks. During the 1907 and 1909 municipal elections they campaigned for anti-vice candidates who promised what a growing number of whites also demanded: a crackdown on all vice operators and saloon-keepers who did not obey closing laws. In 1907, after backing an unsuccessful anti-vice Republican in the primaries, some of them crossed party lines to come out for the election of the Democratic mayoral candidate because of his call for moral reform. Several black "law and order rallies" attempted to influence the black vote. In addition, in spite of their usual desire to avoid the appearance of partisanship, under the Reverend Gilliam's lead the Colored Ministers' Association all but endorsed the Democrat, publicly applauding his principles though not backing him by name. Yet the 1907 anti-vice campaign did not evoke much enthusiasm among blacks. The poor who resided in and around the Bad Lands often had ties with saloon and vice operator politicians like Hobbs, and the area's saloons were the nearest approximation of social centers. In addition, the anti-vice candidate's Democratic affiliation did not help his cause among blacks, even those who agreed with his stand. Most blacks backed the victorious Republican candidate C. A. Bond, an ally of the local liquor interests and of Hobbs, who campaigned actively for him.[21]

The next battle of the black anti-vice advocates was fought in the 1909 Republican primaries. With their numbers swelled by other black respectables who were concerned about vice but had been loath to vote Democratic, they backed law-and-order candidate George Marshall for the mayoral nomination. Marshall, who pledged to clean up the Bad Lands, won both nomination and election. The long-desired clean-up was only partially successful, however. A few brothels were shut down, and the saloon closing laws were enforced for a time, but, whether because of the political influence of vice operators or their skill at escaping detection, much was left untouched. Furthermore, the

[21] Columbus *Dispatch*, Sept. 9, 11, Oct. 6, 9, Nov. 5, 1907; Columbus *Ohio State Journal*, Nov. 2, 1907; Richard Clyde Minor, "Negroes in Columbus" (Ph.D. dissertation, Ohio State University, 1936), pp. 116–118; Mary Louise Mark, *Negroes in Columbus* (Columbus, 1928), pp. 18.

southeast brothel district in the black area around Seventh and Main was not disturbed.[22]

Relations between blacks and police were poor at Columbus in the closing years of the period. In 1910 there were incidents of street fighting between police and the black poor of the downtown fringe slums; blacks, rich and poor alike, increasingly complained that the police showed little concern for legal procedure when dealing with them and failed repeatedly to differentiate between lawbreakers and innocent citizens. For all the efforts of Columbus's Civic Betterment and Protective Association to create good relations with the police, there were three closely spaced, alarming incidents of police abuse in 1915 alone. Twice blacks were subject to unwarranted arrests and then detained for hours without cause, as were Ralph Tyler's two college-age sons in August; in the third case two black women were shot at indiscriminately, and one of them was wounded by the police.[23]

Cleveland blacks were no more successful in dealing with vice and crime and in improving black-police relations. Indeed, Cleveland's black community suffered most from crime and conflict with the law, and periodic clean-up campaigns merely strained black-police relations. After 1900 many vice operations were established along Central Avenue; these complemented the existing brothels, gambling dens, and saloons, at the same time pushing the area of vice further and further east into once quiet, if poor, residential neighborhoods. For years, however, the police were lax about law enforcement, and the area earned a reputation throughout the East and Midwest as a particularly hospitable haven for criminals. This notoriety, in combination with the migrations from the South, caused a particularly large population of hold-up men, thieves, prostitutes, gamblers, and con men to take root in the Central area.[24]

While there was growing discontent with the ascendance of this criminal demimonde, and various black leaders and organizations discussed the subject with police during the first years of the century, it was not until 1908 that local black leadership began actively seeking police cooperation in a deliberate campaign against vice and crime. The immediate inspiration for the 1908 campaign came from the circle of young boosters surrounding the Cleveland *Journal;* they feared that "further encroachments of vice and immorality" would lead to an

22 Minor, "Negroes in Columbus," p. 118; Mark, *Negroes in Columbus,* p. 20.

23 Columbus *Dispatch,* July 8, 1910; Cleveland *Gazette,* Feb. 10, 1912, Sept. 4, 1915; Columbus *Ohio State Journal,* Aug. 31, 1915; *Crisis,* X (Aug., 1915), 244.

24 Cleveland *Gazette,* Mar. 6, 1909, Aug. 6, 1910; Cleveland *Plain Dealer,* Mar. 1, 1909; Cleveland *Leader,* Feb. 19, 1912.

exodus of black shoppers and respectable residents from the area. In July the *Journal* called for an immediate investigation of brothels, gambling houses, and all questionable saloons. Shortly thereafter a committee of Central Avenue boosters conferred with police chief Fred Kohler, who gave his support to a crackdown. This was only one of several campaigns initiated in the years before the war as the complaints of blacks, Harry Smith and eventually his Law and Order League among them, grew louder and louder. Yet despite pledges of cooperation from local officials, all the campaigns were perfunctory. Their successes were at best minimal, and at worst simply another factor contributing to tense relations between blacks and police.[25]

There were several reasons for the continual failure of these efforts. While Kohler and his successors were sympathetic, their department was badly understaffed and could hardly afford to devote a large number of patrolmen to any one area of Cleveland.[26] In addition, the police lacked the confidence among Central Avenue blacks that would have been essential to an effective war against vice and crime. In fact, as blacks and police came in increasing and unfriendly contact after 1900, their relations rapidly deteriorated. One reason for this involved the increasing zeal with which police were arresting blacks, and with which public prosecutors were getting them convicted to terms in local penal institutions. No metropolitan county in Ohio had as sharp an increase in the number of black incarcerations in the county jail as did Cuyahoga County between 1890 to 1910; the figure more than quadrupled, rising from 768 in 1890–99 to 3,148 in 1900–1909, and the black percentage of the total local county jail population jumped from 6 to 13. But the tension in black-police relations was also reflected in on-the-street conflicts which were prompted by conflicting standards of public behavior. Fighting between groups of Central Avenue blacks and the police was reported in 1907, when officers tried to arrest large numbers of men hanging out on the corners on charges of loitering. The next few years saw more such incidents, and police were increasingly charged with using excessive force against blacks and showing contempt for their civil rights.[27]

[25] Cleveland *Journal*, July 18, 25, 1908; Cleveland *Gazette*, Jan. 16, 1909, Feb. 17, 24, Mar. 9, May 11, 1912; Cleveland *Leader*, Feb. 19, 20, 1912; Cleveland *Journal*, July 18, 1908.

[26] Cleveland *Gazette*, Aug. 6, 1910; Cleveland *Leader*, June 3, 1914. In 1915 Cleveland had the fewest patrolmen of any American city with a population of 500,000 or more. See Bureau of the Census, *General Statistics of Cities, 1915, Statistics of Governmental Organization* (Washington, 1916), p. 60.

[27] Ohio *Statistics*, 1890–1910; Cleveland *Gazette*, July 20, 27, 1907.

Also hindering cooperation between blacks and police was the lack of support of a number of influential blacks. Starlight Boyd and others stood to suffer from a wholesale assault on vice; along with white vice operators, they had the political power and connections to defend their own interests. Several months into the 1908 campaign, while the police were investigating gambling operations in the Central district, Chief Kohler announced that "some men high up in the councils of Cleveland's Negro citizens" were deeply involved in gambling. A few, including an attorney and physician, were arrested, but the majority, including Boyd, remained undisturbed. As for the young men of the *Journal:* however sincere their demand for police action, neither the paper nor Tom Fleming ever renounced ties with Boyd, despite his widely reputed vice activities. Brascher's public defense of Boyd as a legitimate businessman was testimony either to his refusal to see bad in anyone or to his unwillingness to give up an alliance which was profitable to his friend Fleming. Whatever its basis, the stance compromised the paper's demand for a clean-up.[28]

If a crackdown on vice proved frustrating, an effort to combat thieves and hold-up men brought relations with the police to the breaking point. Police refused to distinguish between black law-abiders and felons—a fact which became evident during 1914. For several weeks prior to his arrest on June 2, a black man had been attacking and robbing women in the poorly lit parks of eastern Cleveland. Fear spread through the city, deepened by considerable coverage of the attacks in the local press, and by newspaper charges that the understaffed police department lacked the resources to guarantee public safety. Clevelanders became so aroused that a mass vigilance committee to aid police was suggested, and the police themselves actually began to register the names of volunteers at neighborhood stationhouses.[29] In the midst of the panic, the entire police force was mobilized to search for the assailant and other thieves with the same modus operandi. Sensitive to growing public criticism and frustrated by failure, the department adopted desperate tactics. On the evening of May 25 police invaded the Central Avenue area and arrested all blacks walking the streets and doing business in the shops. Black shopkeepers as well as their patrons were taken out of stores, placed in police vans, and arrested. A few days later, shortly before the felon was caught,

[28] Cleveland *Gazette*, Jan. 16, June 12, Nov. 27, 1909, Jan. 8, 22, 1910; Cleveland *Journal*, Jan. 15, 22, 1910.
[29] Cleveland *Leader*, June 3, 1914. For complaints about the treatment of black crime in the daily press, see Cleveland *Gazette*, Jan. 2, 9, 1909.

police employed a modified version of the same tactic, arresting black men found in the parks during evening hours.[30]

The mass arrests placed black law-and-order spokesmen in a difficult position. While they were furious over the violation of basic civil rights, Smith feared that too many protests would, in his words, "discourage the praiseworthy efforts of the police to drive from the city the many undesirable characters who are bringing into disrepute particularly our people." The mass arrests were seen as a means not only for finding the one felon guilty of the attacks on women, but also for ridding the Central area of its criminal demimonde. Thus, while some blacks criticized the arrests, for Smith at least there was also the feeling that conditions were "so bad as to justify wisely directed drastic action." He warned blacks to prepare for the possibility of more mass arrests, urging them ". . . to refrain from allowing their curiosity to draw them into crowds and to refuse to permit Central Avenue loiterers to engage them in conversation. . . ."[31]

The next year the same tensions between order and liberty were again created, now because of a tougher police policy on loitering. The individuals and organizations that had protested the mass arrests were unwilling to discourage police by monitoring the daily activities of patrolmen in the neighborhood, and Smith again urged Central Avenue blacks to cooperate with the police because "conditions have grown so very bad again on the avenue and in its immediate vicinity." Yet ordinary blacks who suffered the most from police tactics shared none of Smith's doubts about the wisdom of reacting sharply to what they saw as harassment and insensitivity to their rights. Not only was there little cooperation with the police, but the police grew less and less welcome among them. In May, 1915, a patrolman was badly beaten by an angry crowd when he tried to arrest the leader of a group of streetcorner idlers whom he charged with creating a disturbance. A short time later a black man was severely beaten by officers, who claimed that he was resisting arrest; the ensuing charges of police brutality which swept Central Avenue created ominous tension and, for Harry Smith, fear of riot.[32]

Thus the period ended at Cleveland with one group of blacks, generally of high status, calling for greater police activity, even if they themselves were occasionally the victims of police tactics; another group, generally poor, despised, and profoundly alienated from the police, felt that police activity was usually undertaken at its expense.

[30] Cleveland *Leader*, June 2, 1914; Cleveland *Gazette*, May 30, June 6, 1914.
[31] Cleveland *Gazette*, June 6, 13, 1914.
[32] Ibid., May 22, 29, 1914.

For the former, the police still stood for law, order, and the reign of morality regardless of the occasional errors; for the latter, the police symbolized violence and repression. Such ambivalent ties were more typical than not of black-police relations in Ohio's major cities when they were about to receive, beginning in 1916, the largest sudden influx of southern blacks since the Civil War. The difficulties of pre-war black-police relations established an ominous background for the reception of those southern blacks.

III

While black leaders saw the struggle for law and order as an essential element of any effective response to the times, many of them also recognized the necessity of establishing various types of self-help projects to ease the transition of the migrant poor to productive, self-sufficient lives in northern cities. Though it was partly a response to the desire for social control of the lower class which informed the campaign against crime, vice, and anti-social behavior, the desire to offer assistance was also prompted by feelings of charity and racial solidarity. Often it was closely bound up with the larger, group-oriented response of blacks to an age of intolerance and rejection.

Blacks organized self-help projects in a transitional context. The changing thrust and utility of past alliances with whites, as well as the substantial limitations of traditional black attitudes, organizations, and institutions, were becoming increasingly apparent. Those whites who were interested in the race's welfare were growing more willing to stimulate the institutionalization of black self-help, and thus to foster racial separateness, than to take action against the color line as they and their ancestors had sometimes before. Thus, whites often made generous offers of money and moral support for black efforts to aid the race's urban poor; they were seldom active, however, in the day-to-day work of black social welfare projects. Nahum Brascher asserted that the majority of even the most well-meaning civic-conscious whites were too busy stimulating local economic development, campaigning for good government, and meeting the vast welfare needs of tens of thousands of white urban immigrants to pay attention to the relatively small influx of blacks.[33] As a result, the task fell largely to the race itself.

Yet at the turn of the century urban black communities were sorely unprepared to confront the human consequences of the migrations, and

[33] Cleveland *Journal*, May 16, 1908.

they lacked models for effective black urban welfare work. No black social welfare agencies existed in the cities. No existing black organization or institution—including the black church, which was the most prestigious, widely proliferated, and securely established of black institutions and the most universalistic in its claims—appeared prepared to gear itself to act as such an agency on an ongoing, routine basis. Doubtless the church's limitations became increasingly evident to Harry Smith; his periodic, urgent pleas for Cleveland's black clergymen to assert their "restraining influence" upon those who were prone to misbehave continually failed to produce any results.[34] Smith and others slowly came to see that the denominations, churches, and ministers lacked the resources, experience, and indeed the will to become actively involved in such a non-traditional sphere. To expect them to systematically take up the burden of providing practical assistance to the migrants would be to misjudge the character and function of the urban church at the time, and in doing so fail to comprehend the response which it did make to the migrations.

After 1900 the broad outlines of church development closely paralleled those of previous decades. The churches continued to be primarily concerned with saving souls, inculcating morality among congregants, organizing formal religious practice, adding members, improving facilities, and relieving debts incurred in such improvement. Yet while the outlines were the same, the migrations did succeed in accelerating the growth of formal church affiliation, and hence in stimulating the expansion of existing congregations and the organization of new ones. It remained the case that many blacks were not church members, and that women continued to constitute two-thirds of church members; however, the influx of southern blacks, whose cultural and social experience in the rural South had been so closely centered around the church, led to increases in church membership to a much greater extent than had the intrastate migrations of the late nineteenth century. While in 1900 approximately 40 percent (28,000) and in 1906 approximately 43 percent (33,719) of the Ohio black population 15 and over was formally affiliated with a church congregation, the 1916 federal census of religious bodies found that slightly over 53 percent (49,921) were thus affiliated. Ohio black affiliation still did not compare favorably with national figures; largely reflecting the southern experience, some 70 percent of the total black population 15 and over was formally affiliated with a church in 1916. Nor did black affiliation compare favorably with white affiliation in Ohio: in 1916 almost 63

[34] Cleveland *Gazette*, Oct. 13, 20, 1906, May 16, 1908, Mar. 6, 1909.

percent of the white population was church-affiliated. But when compared to black population growth, the increase in church membership is much more impressive. While Ohio's black population 15 and over increased by 21 percent in 1900–1910, the number of black Ohioans who were church members increased by 78 percent.[35]

The growth of church membership was particularly evident in the large cities. As in the late nineteenth century, urban blacks were less often affiliated than blacks in the state at large. But the rate of increase of affiliation in the cities was significant. At Cincinnati, 3,925 blacks (just under 31 percent of the black population) belonged to churches in 1902–3; at the time of the 1916 census, however, 8,481 blacks (45%) were church affiliated. The growth of affiliation at Columbus was of similar magnitude; 2,344 blacks (31%) belonged to churches in 1902–3, compared with 6,201 (48%) in 1916. Though we lack data for Cleveland prior to 1906, that city also appears to have witnessed increases. While 2,106 blacks (approximately 37%) were formally affiliated in 1906, by 1916 the figure had risen to to 5,055, a very high (for Ohio) 61 percent of those 15 and over.[36]

The growth of urban church membership was reflected in the development of individual congregations. The migrations brought about the appearance of churches representing denominations which were usually associated with the South and which had had little or no presence in Ohio during the late nineteenth century. Thus, while the vast majority of black Ohio church members after 1900 remained Baptists (60%) or African Methodist Episcopalians (25%), small congregations composed largely of migrants of the African Methodist Episcopal Zion and Colored Methodist Episcopal faiths were founded at Columbus, Cincinnati, Cleveland, and Springfield.[37]

But the most pronounced effect of the migrations was on the Baptists. Reflecting the fact that almost two-thirds of southern black church members were Baptists, Ohio's urban Baptists experienced large gains as migrants affiliated with their northern co-religionists. The number of Baptists doubled or nearly doubled at Cincinnati,

[35] R. R. Wright, Jr., "The Middle West, Ohio," in W. E. B. Du Bois, ed., *The Negro Church* (Atlanta, 1903), p. 92; Bureau of the Census, *Religious Bodies, 1906*, pt. 1, *Summary and General Tables* (Washington, 1910), pp. 345, 556–557, and *Religious Bodies, 1916*, pt. 1, *Summary and General Tables* (Washington, 1919), pp. 570–571.

[36] Bureau of the Census, *Religious Bodies, 1906*, pt. 1, pp. 426–429, and *Religious Bodies, 1916*, pt. 1, pp. 380–382, 570–571. For methodology used to calculate church affiliation see above, ch. 6, note 14.

[37] Bureau of the Census, *Religious Bodies, 1916*, pt. 1, pp. 380–390, 502–503, 524–525; Cleveland *Journal*, Mar. 28, 1903, Apr. 9, 1910; Cleveland *Gazette*, May 23, 1914.

Cleveland, Columbus, and Dayton between 1906 and 1916. Some established Baptist congregations experienced large increases in membership: between 1903 and 1911 Cincinnati's Antioch and Zion Baptist
church memberships increased from 450 to 1,005 and 307 to 1,000 respectively, while members of Dayton's Bethel Baptist Church increased
from 269 to 620. At Columbus between 1903 and 1914 the Second,
Shiloh, and Union Grove Baptist congregations increased from 339 to
804, 338 to 623, and 177 to 405 respectively.[38]

At the same time, the migrations helped to spur an increase in the
number of urban churches. This was particularly true among the Baptists, who did not have the benefit of powerful, parsimonious bishops
to pass judgment on the likelihood of a proposed congregation becoming self-sustaining before new congregations could be warranted.
A.M.E. expansion followed past lines; bishops limited expansion to
suburban areas or newly annexed parts of cities into which blacks were
moving, but they would not allow a proliferation of churches within
cities. In contrast, Baptist city churches proliferated. Dayton had only
two Baptist congregations in 1900, but five in 1916; Columbus, with
seven in 1903, had twelve in 1916; Cleveland's two in 1900 had become
six by 1916.[39]

The single most obvious consequence of this rapid expansion was a
round of church building, improvement, and enlargement similar to
that which had taken place after the Civil War migrations.[40] Between
1906 and 1916, the value of church property among the Baptists of

[38] Bureau of the Census, *Religious Bodies, 1906*, pt. 1, pp. 426–429, and
Religious Bodies, 1916, pt. 1, pp. 380–382, 570–571; Eastern Union Baptist
Association, *Minutes of the 29th Annual Meeting . . . 1903* (Urbana, 1903),
p. 32; Western Union Baptist Association, *Proceedings of the 31st Annual Session
. . . 1903* (n.p., 1903), p. 41; Ohio State Baptist Convention, *16th Annual
Session . . . 1911* (n.p., 1911), p. 39; Eastern Union Baptist Association,
Minutes of the 42nd Annual Meeting . . . 1914 (n.p., 1914), "Membership
Statistics for Year Ending August 1, 1914."

[39] Bureau of the Census, *Religious Bodies, 1916*, pt. 1, pp. 380–390, 502–503,
524–525; Western Union Baptist Sunday School Convention, *Minutes of the 27th
Annual Session . . . 1900* (Columbus, 1900), "Statistical Report"; Eastern Union
Baptist Association, *Minutes . . . 1903*, p. 32; Western Union Baptist Association,
Proceedings . . . 1903, p. 41; A.M.E. Church, North Ohio Conference, *Minutes
of the 23rd Session . . . Annual Conference, 1903* (n.p., 1904), "Statistical
Table A," and *Minutes of the 34th Session . . . Annual Conference, 1915*
(n.p., 1916), "Springfield District," and "Cleveland District" [statistical tables];
A.M.E. Church, Ohio Conference, *Minutes of the 84th Session . . . Annual Con-
ference, 1914* (n.p., 1915), "Statistical Table—Numerical and Financial."

[40] The Indianapolis *Freeman's* informative post-1900 survey of black economic
and institutional development in various large Ohio cities found the different
stages of building and improvement everywhere, among all denominations. See
ibid., June 19, 1909, Sept. 9, 1911, Aug. 3, 1912, Sept. 12, 1914, Aug. 14, Sept. 4,
11, 1915.

Cincinnati rose by 75 percent, from $127,376 to $222,400; at Columbus the increase was 40 percent, from $76,000 to $106,700. Large increases were also to be found among the urban A.M.E. congregations: Columbus's Mt. Vernon church grew in value from $9,000 to $20,000 after the turn of the century, while Springfield's Trinity grew from $3,000 to $15,000. The increase of Cleveland's St. John's from $72,000 to $105,000 ranked it as perhaps the wealthiest black congregation in Ohio.[41]

Accompanying building and improvement was the growth of debt, which brought into the new century the fiscal preoccupations of previous decades. There were, however, two important innovations in fundraising, and these ranked among the most prominent adaptations to which the growth of membership, and hence the migrations, led congregations. Largely in response to the proliferation of small, financially weak Baptist congregations after 1900, the State Baptist Convention established a Committee on Feeble Churches, which was charged with gathering facts on financially weak congregations and helping them to obtain aid from more secure ones.[42] At the same time, the large urban congregations developed a more business-minded approach to fund-raising. Though Cleveland's St. John's Church constructed a new building in 1908, the church ended the period with a mere $3,000 debt—about $3 per each congregant. The church avoided a large debt by making wise real estate investments with funds received from the sale of its old building. Income from these investments allowed the congregation not only to construct and equip a large new building, but also to provide some freedom from future dependence upon voluntary offerings.[43]

But while they were intensely active in building and improvement and innovative in financing, the churches were less willing to test new modes of action in non-religious and non-congregational endeavors. At a time when a reform gospel was spreading among white Protestants the belief that social welfare and service were proper and vital obliga-

[41] Bureau of the Census, *Religious Bodies, 1906*, pt. 1, pp. 426–427, and *Religious Bodies, 1916*, pt. 1, pp. 380–391; A.M.E. Church, Ohio Conference, *Minutes of the 72nd Session . . . Annual Conference, 1902* (Hamilton, 1902), "Table D," and *Minutes . . . 84th Session . . . 1914*, "Statistical Table—Numerical and Financial"; A.M.E. Church, North Ohio Conference, *Minutes of the 27th Session . . . Annual Conference, 1907* (n.p., 1907), "Table D," and *Minutes . . . 34th Session . . . 1915*, "Springfield District" [statistical table].
[42] Ohio State Baptist Convention, *Fifteenth Annual Session . . . 1910* (n.p., 1910), p. 21, and *Sixteenth Annual Session . . . 1911* (n.p., 1911), p. 14.
[43] Cleveland *Plain Dealer*, Nov. 3, 1908; A.M.E. Church, North Ohio Conference, *Minutes . . . 34th Session . . . 1915*, "Cleveland District" [statistical table].

tions of organized Christianity, Ohio's black churches had difficulty breaking out of traditional molds and relating to the needs of those who remained outside the scope of regular church activities.[44] In fact, the only sustained efforts in the field of social welfare were undertaken by some black Catholics and Episcopalians, who were aided and encouraged by the white hierarchy of their denominations. At Cincinnati around 1908 Negro Catholics, with the aid of their bishop, established an institutional church which offered social and recreational services, as well as religious ones, to the West End black community where it was located.[45] Two years later Columbus Episcopalians of both races began to raise funds to build a social settlement house, with its daily operations heavily subsidized by the Episcopal bishop of southern Ohio. While it was located on the grounds of St. Phillip's Episcopal Church, situated midway between affluent sections of the black East Side and the downtown East Long Street area, the settlement was a response to the lack of recreation for all Columbus blacks and was open to them regardless of religious affiliation.[46] A few years later, a similar settlement for blacks was established by Episcopalians at Dayton.[47]

However, the churches and ministers of the major black denominations moved only haltingly toward active social concern. At Cleveland, Columbus, and Dayton black ministers, usually older men of the more venerable churches, joined together across denominational lines to form ministers' alliances for the sake of more effectively relating to community issues. Most such alliances defined their secular concerns narrowly. As the activities of Columbus's ministers suggest, their major extra-religious interest was in the struggle for law and order in black neighborhoods. This concern led them to take some interest in proposing recreational alternatives for blacks to keep them off the streets and out of saloons. But there were limits on how active ministers' groups (as opposed to individual ministers) could become in secular matters. Their desire to serve the community as a unifying moral force often led them to be wary of venturing too far in front of black opin-

---

[44] R. R. Wright, Jr., drew the same conclusion from his survey of the social welfare activities of the black church throughout the nation. See "Social Work and the Influence of the Negro Church," *Annals*, XXX (July–Dec., 1907), 509–521. So has a contemporary scholar who has examined the churches in the early twentieth-century northern urban context; see Seth M. Scheiner, "The Negro Church and the Northern City, 1890–1930," in William G. Shade and Roy C. Herrenkohl, eds., *Seven on Black* (Philadelphia, 1969), pp. 99–117.

[45] John H. Lamott, *History of the Archdiocese of Cincinnati, 1821–1921* (New York and Cincinnati, 1921), pp. 144; Miller, *Boss Cox's Cincinnati*, p. 139.

[46] Columbus *Dispatch*, Mar. 1, 1910; Cleveland *Journal*, Mar. 12, 1910.

[47] Indianapolis *Freeman*, Aug. 3, 1912.

ion, especially on issues upon which there was no consensus among black leaders. Thus the Ministers' Association of Columbus took an active, if only quasi-partisan, stand on the vice issue during the 1907 mayoral campaign in the midst of a growing revulsion among many local blacks against vice. But though in Cleveland the Ministers' Union at first supported the creation of an all-black social center, when the issue became a matter of serious controversy among blacks the union quickly stopped campaigning for it.[48]

Some urban congregations were also struggling to expand their spheres of action, though they often limited themselves to efforts largely on behalf of their own membership. The larger, wealthier congregations then in the process of building or improving their facilities were increasing the amount of space available for activities other than Sunday services and prayer meetings, suggesting a growing concern for the social and recreational needs of congregants. Cleveland's St. John's made sure that a basement dining hall, "entertainment room," and furnished parlors suitable for casual conversation and meetings were included in its new building. Springfield's Second Baptist Church included a large library in the plans for its new building. At the same time, there was some movement toward various forms of social and recreational service. Both the Second Baptist and Youngstown's Oak Hill A.M.E. developed a number of clubs for young people, and the Springfield church began a day nursery for children of working congregant mothers. But few churches were systematically reaching outside their own congregations; an exception was Cleveland's Antioch Baptist, which aided orphans and helped to reform and guide juvenile offenders.[49]

Yet many contemporaries were coming to desire more than isolated, piecemeal action, and they grew increasingly impatient with the inability of the churches to play more vital social roles in their communities. This was something on which the *Journal* and the *Gazette* could agree. The former, interested in recreation and counseling, urged the churches to become social centers; the latter, interested in social control and behavior in public places, urged them to become more methodically involved in influencing the conduct of the lower class. Even those who perceived a change in church interests often found the pace of change too slow. In response to the question, "What is the church

[48] Columbus *Dispatch,* Oct. 9, 1907; Cleveland *Journal,* Oct. 6, 13, 1906; Indianapolis *Freeman,* Aug. 3, 1912; Cleveland *Gazette,* Feb. 17, 1912, Jan. 24, Feb. 7, 14, 1914; Jere Brown to George Myers, June 16, 1902, Box XI, folder 3, Myers Papers.
[49] Cleveland *Plain Dealer,* May 18, 1902, Nov. 3, 1908; Indianapolis *Freeman,* Sept. 9, 1911, Sept. 15, 1915.

doing about social uplift?" posed by the 1913 Atlanta University study on *Manners and Morals among Negro Americans,* one of the two Ohio respondents replied that the church was only "gradually awakening to the real sense of its real duty." Those who sought reasons for the church's inflexibility tended to blame the cycle of debt-improvement-debt, which played a large role in determining daily church affairs and was thought to sap black energies and resources. Ohio's other respondent for the 1913 study answered "not much" to the same question, and explained that "current expenses and keeping out of debt" kept the churches from an active social role. "There ought to be fewer churches and larger congregations," he said. "We need to study Church Economy." George Myers agreed; in 1915 he began to prepare an extensive article which called for "the centralization of churches" in order to more wisely distribute the race's money and to free the church from a preoccupation with narrow, fiscal concerns.[50]

Fiscal imperatives, as well as a traditional reluctance to mingle religious and secular concerns, help to explain the church's inability to relate systematically and deliberately to the period's major black social problems. But in those large, affluent, and prestigious congregations which were best able to respond, such inflexibility also mirrored larger contradictions in the life of the black upper class, which had shaped the development of those congregations. Upper-class leaders had long felt an obligation to aid the masses, and they were acutely aware that the behavior, social status, and position of the masses had much to do with the way in which they themselves would be judged by whites. Yet they lacked the ability to directly influence the uplift of the masses. They did not have firm cultural and socioeconomic ties with them, and their attitudes toward racial advancement had done little to strengthen or expand those ties that did exist. Older leaders had been committed to individual moral uplift, social mobility, and the social acceptance of worthy individuals. They had sought to motivate and inspire individuals by holding up before them the moral example and the trials and triumphs of the race's "representative" men and women. They had tried to clear the way for aspiring individuals by winning the removal of inequities in education, social intercourse, and law so that they might enter and compete effectively within the American mainstream. Yet the conditions of life of members of the lower class—poverty, lack of opportunity, lack of skills, and social and cultural isolation—made it

[50] Cleveland *Gazette,* Oct. 13, 20, 1905, May 16, 1908, Mar. 6, 1909, May 1, 1915; Cleveland *Journal,* May 16, 1908; W. E. B. Du Bois, ed., *Manners and Morals among Negro Americans* (Atlanta, 1913), p. 114; George Myers to Booker T. Washington, June 12, 1915, Box 941, Washington Papers.

extremely difficult for them to conceive of success and mobility, and hence to develop the values and motivations necessary to reach out for those goals. Nor could upper-class leaders be of much practical assistance in guiding the lower class into the mainstream. The former lacked both the will and the economic power to create new opportunities which might have encouraged the masses to take on the bourgeois values of the upper class and sped their socioeconomic mobility. Moreover, the social conservatism of the upper class prevented its leadership from intervening with practical assistance in the ordinary, daily struggles of the individual, for those struggles were seen as part of the larger ennobling effort for self-improvement and social recognition that gave dignity and meaning to life. At the same time, the attitudes of upper-class leaders toward separate institutions had reinforced their unwillingness to engage in systematized racial social work. To the extent they had desired and believed in the possibility of an imminent entrance into the American mainstream, they had had doubts about the wisdom of voluntary separation and hence about the function and future of racial institutions. As a result, they had been loath to create institutions which might have offered that practical assistance, and they had not allowed existing institutions to develop beyond their original goals and purposes. In the specific case of the church, it remained within traditional molds, even as a movement which conceived of new social functions for organized religion gathered force among white Protestant churches. To the extent that the black church was acknowledged to have a secular function, that function was not as an evolving multifaceted social agency, but as a shining moral example to spur individual uplift and reinforce individual morality.

As long as the future of race relations seemed promising and the burden of the masses had not been too heavily thrust upon them, upper-class leaders had not been required to confront the profound problems inherent in their relations with the masses. But after 1900 there was no choice, especially for those who saw a relationship between the migrations, the lifestyle of the lower class, and the deterioration of race relations. The limitations implicit in the commitment of upper-class leadership to individualized means and goals, its lack of contact and connection with the masses, and its inability to forge and institutionalize programs seeking racial solidarity and cooperation—all of these factors now combined to hamper its efforts to utilize traditional perspectives in relating to social problems within the race.

Nowhere was this more evident than in the attempts of the more socially conscious, post-1900 women's club movement to define its obligation to uplift the lower class. In some ways, the women's clubs were particularly suited for assisting the migrant poor. They were well established and widely proliferated; while their members were especially concerned with southern repression and with the conservation of black rights and existing opportunities, they also seemed eager to serve their less fortunate sisters. The club women generally were not employed, so they had time to do voluntary social welfare work that would not make demands upon the race's scarce resources. Yet the club women were less concerned with solidifying their contacts and with providing less fortunate women with practical assistance than with clarifying and consolidating their role as "representative" women —influential moral teachers, models of respectable womanhood, and upholders of conventional culture. Suggestive of their distance from those outside their ranks was the presentation at their meetings of papers like Hallie Quinn Brown's "What to Do with the Children While Mother Is at the Club," which were sandwiched between discussions of the need for racial unity and the uplift of the lower class.[51]

The first convention of the Ohio branch of the National Association of Colored Women in 1901 set the tone which would generally govern the response of the women's clubs to the migrations and the plight of the lower class. Those in attendance discussed the need to awaken the young women with whom they came into contact to the responsibilities of motherhood and homemaking, and to the importance of home life in racial uplift. At the same time, they realized that many less affluent women would have to work, particularly in service and domestic fields. For that reason club women were deeply troubled by the evidence around them of deep resentment of service work among many young women; they felt that it was their duty to emphasize the value and dignity of all work, no matter how menial, and the need to take advantage of all available opportunities. Mrs. Hattie Fairfax, one of Cleveland's leading club women who had for some years run an employment service placing young women in domestic jobs, was appropriately elected director of the "Industrial Section" of the Ohio branch that year. In her acceptance speech she outlined the future stand of the clubs as proponents of service work. "It is no disgrace to cook, wash, iron, and sew. . . . We as a poor race must not despise service work. . . . We can never be a thrifty race and compete with other races if we neglect to do what we can find to do." At the same time, she was

[51] "Third Annual Meeting of the Ohio Federation of Women's Clubs (Afro American)," in Xenia *Gazette*, July 21, 1903. A collective social profile of the members of the Ohio State Federation of the National Association of Colored Women's Clubs is found in W. E. B. Du Bois, ed., *Efforts for Social Betterment among Negro Americans* (Atlanta, 1909), p. 53.

aware that upper-class women did not always maintain such a view in their daily lives, and she warned them that they must not look down upon less affluent women for their humble, servile labors. "We cannot afford above all else to show a haughty spirit to our sister because we have been more fortunate than she who had to resort to domestic science for a living." To encourage work in domestic fields and better prepare young women for both homemaking and service work, Fairfax called upon them to take advantage of existing public school programs offering domestic training.[52]

If the resentment of service work among lower-status women troubled the club women, another element of lower-class culture was even more disturbing to them. The popularity of ragtime music led to their first organized statewide campaign in behalf of moral uplift. The 1901 convention discussed and then endorsed an effort against ragtime, electing a state superintendent of music to spearhead the battle. The women were by no means ashamed of the contributions of black artists who worked within accepted Western idioms, however—witness the fact that they later invited Paul Laurence Dunbar to read his poetry before one of their annual meetings. Indeed, their literary societies had for years been named for black artists such as Dunbar and Phillis Wheatley. But ragtime was not within conventional Western musical traditions, and it was thought to undermine morality by exerting "an evil influence and a degenerating one." Of course, it was not simply the hypnotic quality of the elaborately syncopated ragtime rhythms which disturbed the club women, but also the connection of ragtime with the brothels, saloons, and dance halls where it was played. In defense of the federation's campaign "to push ragtime back behind the compositions of the great masters," Carrie Clifford made it clear that the effort was essential to the work of moral uplift to which the club women were dedicated:

We are organized for culture. We intend to band together the good women of our race to uplift wherever there is need for betterment. We want our men and women to come to the front, to become powers for good and the only way that they can place themselves upon and above the level of the Caucasian race is to develop their entire energies to those things which develop the best qualities of manhood and womanhood.[53]

The concerns outlined at the first convention remained vital as the state federation and local clubs sought to reach out to the masses dur-

52 Cleveland *Leader,* Dec. 29, 1901.
53 Cleveland *Plain Dealer,* Dec. 28, 29, 1901.

ing the next fifteen years. The club women continued their commitment to encouraging black working women to find dignity in humble service, and to advocating respect for the values which sustained temperance, chastity, and family life. In addition, the campaign against ragtime was brought into the churches and other contexts where blacks might be educated about the evils of popular music; the fact that the campaign did not enter those places where the music was played, however, doubtless limited its effectiveness. Eventually some social work was encouraged, but generally the women's clubs neglected to create programs which offered sustained, practical assistance to the migrant poor.[54] Too distant from lower-class women to understand either their daily struggles or their frames of reference, many club women could not imagine what practical assistance might be. Moreover, their ability to frame group-oriented self-help programs was limited by their own somewhat contradictory conception of contemporary race relations and opportunities. Although they saw the need for united opposition to the increasingly rigid and repressive color line, they still wanted to believe that individual moral uplift, hard work, and conventional preparation in the public schools could equalize the terms of competition between black and white. In one of the closing addresses at the 1901 convention, a Cleveland public school teacher revealed the lingering influence of past attitudes toward racial advancement when she stated that the club woman's most important duty was

> to see to it that the coming generation is so trained that there can be no question of inferiority in mental or moral qualities raised against it. . . . Let there be training against loud talking, let modesty in all things be cultivated, and the vices eliminated. . . . All we need is a fair field and the color problem will solve itself on the broad basis of equality.[55]

To the extent that they still struggled to believe in the inevitable acceptance of worthy, respectable individuals who deferred to conventional rules and values, it was no wonder that the club women could not go beyond simply propagating those rules and values to search for special means for helping the poor and ostracized. While they might have offered proposals for creating interim communities which would help find work, lodging, and supportive advice, with great sincerity and honesty of purpose the women's clubs instead responded with homilies encouraging diligent labor and straight-and-narrow path morality. As

[54] Remarks based on reportage of annual stage conventions of Ohio Federation; see, Xenia *Gazette*, July 21, 1903, Aug. 5, 6, 7, 8, 9, 10, 1914; Cleveland *Gazette*, Aug. 1, 1903, July 22, 1905; Cleveland *Plain Dealer*, July 3, 4, 5, 6, 1912; and the special women's club issue of the Cleveland *Journal*, Feb. 25, 1905.
[55] Cleveland *Plain Dealer*, Dec. 29, 1901.

a result, as we shall now see, while some black club women would become involved individually, most attempts to assist young migrant and other poor women were generally made outside of or (as at Cleveland) against the will of the clubs.[56]

IV

Given the limitations of established institutions and traditional attitudes, the response which proved the most productive was the one associated with the younger racial spokesmen, who advocated innovative, group-oriented self-help for the sake of mutually reinforcing individual and racial uplift. But, depending on local circumstance and traditions, this stance also received the backing of shifting numbers of older leaders. It entailed the creation of black institutions dedicated to providing practical services. There remained the problem of effective communication with the lower class; it could not be fully resolved as long as racial leadership was separated from those it was supposed to lead by a chasm of culture and experience. But while the new institutions were formed by those apart from the masses, they were still framed in a spirit of race solidarity, attempting to respond to problems of the poor and of the black communities in which they lived. As such, the new institutions stood a better chance of bridging that chasm than anything which had come before.

The most intense and comprehensive efforts to institutionalize racial social work occurred in the cities of southern and central Ohio. There such efforts were often a part of a more generalized response to an era which encouraged racial separateness, involving calls for both welfare institutions and separate schools. The more intolerant racial environments of Springfield, Dayton, Cincinnati, and Columbus encouraged the realization, regardless of possible ideological qualms, of the urgent need to marshal black resources to deal with the combined effects of migrations, growing local black populations, and bitter racial hostility. As a consequence, in these cities, unlike Cleveland, there tended to be some consensus among the generations of racial leadership as to the institutionalization of self-help. A number of older residents not only aided the newcomers and worked alongside younger activists, but

[56] Cf. Gerda Lerner, ed., *Black Women in White America: A Documentary History* (New York, 1972), pp. 450–458, and Lerner, "Early Community Work of Black Club Women," *Journal of Negro History*, LIX (Apr., 1974), 162–165. Lerner contends that the women's clubs were deeply involved in social work, but the evidence she presents is largely based upon the experience of southern and border cities. More work on northern cities would be helpful in guiding us toward some generalization about the northern black experience.

sometimes even organized and led them. Even where old-timers did not cooperate, conflicts over the institutionalization of self-help and voluntary separation were muted, with opposition not overtly manifest or even necessarily articulated. Instead, disagreement was expressed by what was *not* said and done. Those whose views prevented them from participating generally seem to have been aware, against their hopes and fears for the future, of the necessity for racial action, and they remained silent.

In each of the four cities, black YMCAs were strengthened or established in response to the need for social centers offering recreation and counseling. At Dayton and Springfield there were black Y's which had been established as literary societies existing at the turn of the century. While Dayton's Y did not have its own building at first, Springfield's did—but the small frame structure allowed little program development and limited the expansion of membership. In 1908 blacks in both cities began to transform their Y's into social centers in response to the growing demand for social services; efforts were also made to improve their quarters. At Springfield a campaign was mounted to pay off the debt on the old building and to erect a larger structure, with classrooms, gymnasium, swimming pool, showers, and game room. The successful drive profited from wide local support among both races. By 1911, when a professional YMCA worker, Walter Burden, was hired to supervise its work, the black Y was housed in its own well-equipped building on Center Street, convenient to many of the city's blacks; it had 160 formal members and many times that number of frequent visitors. At Dayton a young real estate salesman and business league member named Edward Banks, who served for several years as the secretary of the black Y, led a campaign to raise funds for the construction of a YMCA social center on West Fifth, in the heart of the black section of the West Side. By the fall of 1912 there was enough money to purchase a lot and begin construction; in that year Charles D. Higgins, a professional Y worker, was brought to Dayton to begin a systematic program organization.[57]

Both Columbus and Cincinnati would act several years later in response to the announcement by Chicago philanthropist Julius Rosenwald in late December, 1910, that he would offer blacks in any city in the nation $25,000 toward the construction of a separate Y, if they were

[57] Cleveland *Gazette*, Jan. 18, Feb. 29, 1896, Feb. 19, 1910; Indianapolis *Freeman*, June 12, 1909, Sept. 9, 1911, Aug. 3, 1912; T. C. McMillen, *The Springfield, Ohio YMCA, 1854–1954* (Springfield, 1954), pp. 115–118; G. Jackson (Springfield) to Booker T. Washington, Nov. 5, 1908, Box 817, Washington Papers.

able to raise $75,000 within five years for the same purpose.[58] Columbus blacks had not been very successful in the past in generating their own self-help projects. They had only been able to raise $1,300 for an old people's home between 1888 and 1903, the year when Pearl Chavers took over the campaign; under Chavers a small home eventually opened, after several more years of fund-raising. But the response to the Rosenwald proposal was immediate. A small committee composed almost exclusively of the most respected young professionals and entrepreneurs, like attorney Robert Barcus and Dr. W. J. Woodlin, began the work of fund-raising. The committee enjoyed the cooperation of J. A. Metcalf, a white haberdasher whose store had a reputation for its excellent treatment of black shoppers. Spurred on by his discovery, based on an informal poll, that about three-quarters of Columbus's young black men were not churchgoers, the pious Metcalf went on to make appeals before local white audiences. He also served as an important liaison to the business community. Enough money was collected by late 1911 to open temporary headquarters at Fifth Street and East Spring; the rented building was on the eastern fringe of the downtown East Long Street section, not far from the slums. Here some educational classes and recreational work went on while fund-raising efforts continued. In December, with the goal of $75,000 in sight, Y worker Nimrod B. Allen was hired to begin a comprehensive program of activities, and early the next year construction began on a permanent building.[59]

Cincinnatians had recognized for some years that a social center catering to blacks in the downtown fringe slums was desperately needed. In 1904 Wendell Phillips Dabney had stated that he saw among the city's blacks a tendency toward ill health "produced by deficiency of hygienic knowledge and a lack of systematic exercise, bathing facilities, and suitable resorts of recreation." Dabney attributed the situation to a denial of access to municipal bathhouses and the Y's as much as to ignorance and poverty; he and several ministers and

[58] C. Howard Hopkins, *History of the YMCA of North America* (New York, 1951), p. 458; Julius Rosenwald to "Gentlemen," Dec. 30, 1910; "Rosenwald Aid to Negro YMCAs" (undated typescript), Julius Rosenwald Papers, UC.

[59] Indianapolis *Freeman*, Oct. 4, 1913, Aug. 29, 1914; Cleveland *Gazette*, Jan. 16, 1915; J. A. Metcalf to Booker T. Washington, May 12, 1913, Box 835, and John J. Jackson to Booker T. Washington, Box 841, Washington Papers; unsigned to John W. Pontius, June 15, 1916, and Jesse Moreland to William C. Graves, No. 13, 1916, Rosenwald Papers; W. A. McWilliams, *Columbus Illustrated Record* (Columbus, 1919), pp. 115–116. On the long struggle at Columbus to establish a home for the aged, see Columbus *Press*, Sept. 23, 1903; Du Bois, ed., *Efforts for Social Betterment*, p. 122.

doctors attempted to rectify the situation by opening a black gymnasium and bathhouse in the east side in the old Bucktown area, in a building which Dabney owned. But the black population there was rapidly declining, and the facility soon closed for want of public support.[60] The Rosenwald proposal revived interest in a social center. Though not as quick to respond as Columbus blacks, the Cincinnatians were considerably more effective, not only because of the tremendous enthusiasm for the project among local blacks, but also perhaps because of their greater experience in raising large sums of money. After all, they had been managing their orphanage since ante-bellum times and, more recently, two small homes for old people. In addition, there was a well-established local tradition of white philanthropic support for these black charitable institutions. The black fund-raising committee organized early in 1913 was an amalgam of all groups. Younger men like Francis Russell mixed with older ones like George Hayes and caterer Washington Simms; despite the long association between the Y movement and evangelical Protestantism, black Catholics who were desirous of a large racial social center also took part. It was the Catholics who chose to bring the campaign into several factories where blacks worked, in order to solicit funds from them and to educate them in the purposes of the proposed Y. The unity of the blacks, commented upon by whites working along with them, was evident in the large sum ($15,300) collected exclusively from within the race during the next three years. While not much compared to the nearly $60,000 contributed by local whites, it was a great deal from a relatively poor people—and the more marginal were said to have been prominent among the contributors. By April, 1915, enough had been collected to begin construction at a site on West Ninth in the West End.[61]

Similar efforts on behalf of black women were often not as effective. At Columbus a black women's club eventually was given control of a day nursery which had been opened in 1902 by a white women's group after it had heard a school principal complain that many of his poor black students were staying home from school to care for infants while their mothers worked. However, no social center or YWCA was cre-

[60] Dabney, *Cincinnati's Colored Citizens*, pp. 135, 138–139; [invitation to opening of National Gymnasium, dated Oct. 15, 1904], Wendell Phillips Dabney Collection, folder 2, CHS.

[61] Dabney, *Cincinnati's Colored Citizens*, p. 211; *Crisis*, X (June, 1915), 60, and XI (Dec., 1915), 61; D. B. Meachem to Julius Rosenwald, May 31, 1913, Jesse Moorland to Julius Rosenwald, May 14, 1914, "Report of the Ninth Street Branch YMCA for Week Closing January 31, 1915," and "Report of Progress on the Ninth Street Branch YMCA, August 4, 1915," Rosenwald Papers.

ated, and no systematic attempts were made to aid black migrant women, though Chavers's combination vocational school, factory, and employment service no doubt found jobs for some.[62] The only efforts at Springfield were those of Mrs. Harry Linden, a black club woman with strong ties to white counterparts. (She was elected president of the local Women's Christian Temperance Union in 1909 when its membership was composed of 900 whites and 15 blacks.) In 1907 Mrs. Linden was the leading force behind the call for organization of a black YWCA, but the effort failed to win support among higher-status blacks. She then turned her attention to establishing on her own initiative a small "Golden Rule Cottage," a home for young women "without homes and friends" which would help them until they could become self-sufficient.[63]

Efforts at Dayton and Cincinnati were more comprehensive. At Dayton older club women and the wives of young booster organization activists united to form a Colored Women's League; the new coalition opened a day nursery and a home for working girls, and then began a campaign to transform the local black YWCA from a social club to a community center with its own building. In addition, the group formed a Colored Women's Industrial Union, located conveniently on Dunbar Avenue and equipped with sewing machines and weaving, upholstering, and laundering facilities, where jobless women might come to find work.[64] Aid to women at Cincinnati was the product of cooperation between some upper-class women, prominent black men (particularly Hayes and Dabney), and several white philanthropists, such as James N. Gamble (of Cincinnati-based Procter and Gamble), Sarah Emery (whose family had long supported the black orphanage), and Jacob Schmidlapp (a businessman whose growing interest in local blacks led to pioneering efforts to plan and finance low-cost housing for blacks in 1911). The result of this cooperation was impressive. In 1911 a building on West Ninth opened; it housed a home for dependent children of working mothers, lodging quarters for young women, a day nursery, and an employment bureau. This "Home for Colored Girls" used depot employees and volunteer greeters in its special efforts

62 Du Bois, ed., *Efforts for Social Betterment,* p. 12. At Columbus, the period ended with a recognition among some local blacks that although the needs of young black working women were very pressing, nothing had been done to assist them. See J. H. Pursley to Editor, Columbus *Ohio State Journal,* Aug. 28, 1915.

63 Cleveland *Gazette,* Nov. 30, 1907; Indianapolis *Freeman,* Sept. 9, 1911; Charles D. Swayne, *Facts and Figures about the Negro in Springfield and Clark County, Ohio, as They Stood December 31st, 1907* (Urbana, 1908), p. 11.

64 Indianapolis *Freeman,* June 12, Aug. 21, 1909, Aug. 3, 1912; *Crisis,* IV (May, 1912), 9.

to reach migrant girls as soon as they arrived on in-coming trains. The girls were then provided with temporary room and board, and help in finding jobs and permanent lodging. In 1912 the same coalition was responsible for the opening of a home for unwed mothers and their children.[65]

While blacks at Dayton, Columbus, and Cincinnati were creating networks of supportive institutions, they were also (with varying degrees of unity, intensity, and success) engaged in efforts to reestablish or revitalize separate black schools which had been abolished or weakened at the time of school desegregation. The motives and influences defining these interests were similar: each resulted from the desire to extend self-help and solidarity into broader realms in the name of race protection and welfare, and each was deeply influenced by the migrations. Similar to E. W. B. Curry's desire for a setting which would provide black education free from race prejudice, as well as employment for empathetic black teachers, the call for separate schools recognized the special role which the race had to play in caring for its children and preparing them to bear the burden of being black in a competitive and increasingly hostile white world. While the migrations did not directly stimulate renewed interest in separate schools, they formed a dynamic background for that interest. Located in increasingly black neighborhoods, the new schools could easily be part of that vision, which the migrations had made possible, of a semi-autonomous black urban community with its own businesses and institutions, rooted in a specific section of the city.

Because it renounced the most significant achievement of late nineteenth-century black leadership, the call for separate schools was not as popular as the one for the institutionalization of racial social work. Dissent, especially from older leaders, was manifest, but the extent of opposition varied according to local circumstances. At Cincinnati and Dayton, the initiative in the movement for new or revitalized black schools came from within the black community; there opposition tended to be muted. At Columbus, action by a hostile Board of Education made opponents more vociferous.

Cincinnati experienced a significant degree of unity in support of black schools. The situation there was somewhat different, because

[65] Dabney, *Cincinnati's Colored Citizens*, pp. 216–219; *Crisis*, I (Jan., 1911), 6; Cincinnati Protective and Industrial Association for Colored Women and Children, *Home for Colored Girls* (Cincinnati, n.d.). On the work of Jacob Schmidlapp, see Dabney, *Cincinnati's Colored Citizens*, pp. 385–390, and Jacob Schmidlapp, "Cincinnati's Answer: Philanthropy at 5%," *World Outlook*, V (Oct., 1919), 15. While the first housing units sponsored by Schmidlapp opened in 1911, it was not until after 1915 that his efforts assumed significant proportions.

black schools had never been completely eliminated (as they had been at Dayton and Columbus). As already noted, one separate school, which was located in the heart of the black section of Walnut Hills and black by virtue of its teaching staff as well as residential patterns, remained after the turn of the century. Black residents of Walnut Hills were far from bitter about the situation. Indeed, the school was a source of racial pride and community concern, both of which were evident in a successful drive to change its name to the Frederick Douglass School, and in the long campaign to acquire new educational programs and repairs for the aging building. By March, 1908, as illustrated by a 2,017-signature petition to the school board, black parents were uniting around the desire to have a fully equipped, modern building constructed at the same site. The board decided to build a sixteen-classroom school, complete with inside playrooms, kindergarten, vocational training facilities, auditorium, gymnasium, and teachers' lounge; later a lunchroom and special accommodations for tubercular children were added. A budget of $160,000 was allocated to build and equip the new Douglass School, which opened in 1911. Francis Russell had been teaching across the river in the black schools in Newport, Kentucky, before becoming principal of the Douglass School in 1909; he found that the large, well-appointed building provided an excellent opportunity to actuate the values of solidarity and self-help in which he deeply believed. Russell hired a number of young teachers who shared his views, and the school quickly became Cincinnati's leading center for the advocacy of self-help and solidarity. Moreover, under his direction and with the enthusiastic support of neighborhood black parents, the new Douglass School became a community center. A branch public library was located there; a parents' club was formed; and the auditorium was regularly used for community meetings and public entertainments.[66]

While the improvement of Douglass School did not involve a departure from the board's commitment to integration, the creation of an all-black school on West Fifth in the West End in 1914 certainly did. The Harriet Beecher Stowe School (as it later became known) was a

[66] Cincinnati *Enquirer*, June 1, 1900, Mar. 5, June 22, Aug. 20, 1911; Indianapolis *Freeman*, Aug. 8, Dec. 3, 1910; Dabney, *Cincinnati's Colored Citizens*, pp. 243–244; Works Progress Administration, Writers' Program, *Cincinnati: A Guide to the Queen City and Its Neighbors* (Cincinnati, 1943), p. 293; Cincinnati, Board of Education, *Minutes*, v. 25, Feb. 5, 1906, p. 585; v. 26, May 28, 1906, pp. 51, 58, June ?, 1906, p. 81, May 27, 1907, p. 444; v. 27, Mar. 30, 1908, p. 133, June 2, 1908, p. 222, Mar. 16, 1909, p. 585; v. 28, Aug. 2, 1909, p. 96, July 17, 1911, p. 639, Nov. 6, 1911, p. 726, May 20, 1912, p. 868, July 15, 1912, p. 938; v. 29, May 11, 1914, p. 475; v. 30, July 2, 1915, p. 230, Mar. 27, 1916, p. 461,

result of many West End parents' desire for black teachers and separate schools. Proposing to utilize a recently abandoned school building next door to an integrated school as the site for instruction of about 350 black children who wanted black teachers, school superintendent R. J. Condon explained at a board meeting in September, 1914, that he himself was against separate schools unless blacks desired them. He pointed to two influences which were leading West End blacks in the direction of separate education. First, they had been pleased with the work which black part-time teachers had done with their children in a neighborhood summer school. Also, they were very much impressed with the new Douglass School. Aware of the danger that separate schools might become second-rate ones, Condon asked the board for a pledge of full equality of facilities and a commitment to an excellent professional staff. Approving his proposal, the board heeded his warning. The new school was placed on a temporary basis to insure that it would enjoy enough support to maintain the excellence. Jennie Porter was then teaching at Douglass but was well known to West End blacks for her part in creating a private black kindergarten in the neighborhood in 1911; she was appointed principal at Condon's suggestion. During 1915 she and Russell recruited a corps of black teachers and set the school on a proper footing. Impressed with the results and with the degree of neighborhood support, the board decided to construct a new home for Stowe School a year later.[67]

Though the creation of Stowe School was a reversal of board policy, there was surprisingly little public opposition to the 1914 decision. Indeed, the sole voice which was critical of the resurgence of separate education belonged to Wendell Phillips Dabney. He saw the new school as a step backward: "The 'Colored' school on Fifth Street is next-door to a 'white' school in which the same grades are taught, and the population of that section is a mixture of all races and possesses the smallest amount of race prejudice. There is no excuse for its establishment that is worthy of acceptance. . . ."[68] But, as Dabney knew, many black West Enders disagreed; they found adequate excuse in the school board's refusal to hire black teachers in integrated schools during the

[67] Dabney, *Cincinnati's Colored Citizens*, pp. 235–236; G. Gwendolyn Brown, "The Influences Surrounding the Establishment of the Present Segregated Schools in Selected Cities of Ohio" (M.A. thesis, Howard University, 1947), p. 94; Mame Charlotte Mason, "The Policy of the Segregation of the Negro in the Public Schools of Ohio, Indiana, and Illinois" (Master's thesis, University of Chicago, 1917), pp. 50–52; Cincinnati, Board of Education, *Minutes*, v. 29, Sept. 14, 1914, pp. 563–564, Oct. 26, 1914, pp. 593–594; v. 30, Apr. 26, 1915, p. 167.

[68] Cincinnati *Union*, n.d., quoted in Cleveland *Gazette*, Sept. 11, 1915. Dabney had actually begun to criticize the growing desire among local blacks for separate schools several years before; see Cleveland *Gazette*, Mar. 11, May 24, 1913, Nov. 14, 1914.

regular school year. No doubt it was the strength of neighborhood opinion which kept Dabney from pressing the matter before the board or in the courts. Yet at the same time, his own ideas seem to have been in flux. To be sure, Dabney was strongly opposed to color lines drawn by powerful, white-controlled institutions—especially when the law was on the side of integration, as was the case with the schools. But he was not necessarily against separate education per se. When local white philanthropist Sallie Peters McCall willed $400,000 to the Cincinnati black community for the creation of a black industrial training school, Dabney gladly served with older and younger leaders, including Porter and Russell, on the board of trustees of the school, which opened to 85 pupils in 1914.[69] Of course, public education presented different problems, but Dabney was gradually adopting a pragmatic "Show me what you can do" attitude toward separate education. Within the next decade he emerged as an admirer of Jennie Porter because he felt that she had created an excellent learning environment at Stowe School.[70]

In contrast, at Dayton a campaign for a black school, largely prompted by a desire for black teachers, was unsuccessful. The situation here had its origin in the abolition of special educational arrangements which had been made between West Side blacks and the school board in the early 1890s. As already noted, the desire for black teachers had not died among black Daytonians in the years just after desegregation, and it had led them to agree to the creation of a separate classroom, staffed by a black teacher, at the West Side Garfield School. When the school board allowed this arrangement to lapse in 1909, Edward Banks and a young doctor attempted to interest the board in hiring black teachers. But when the board did not act (doubtless largely because that suggested the impossibility of obtaining black teachers for integrated schools), the Dayton *Citizen* led young boosters in a campaign for separate schools. They met with some black opposition (the evidence does not make clear from whom), but this factor was less decisive than the board's reluctance to establish a separate school in the face of Ohio's school integration law. The board was willing to reinstitute the separate classroom at Garfield School, and when the period closed board members were engaged in serious discussions about creating black schools; however, they did not create any separate schools before 1916.[71]

[69] George W. Hayes to Booker T. Washington, Apr. 30, 1912, Box 831, Washington Papers; Dabney, *Cincinnati's Colored Citizens*, p. 355.

[70] Dabney, *Cincinnati's Colored Citizens*, pp. 235–236, for laudatory comments, made in about 1925–26, on Porter's educational work.

[71] Richmond *Planet*, Mar. 7, 1896; Cleveland *Gazette*, Feb. 19, 26, Apr. 2, Oct. 1, 1910, Feb. 3, 1911; Dayton *Journal*, Sept. 16, 1910; Dayton Board of

At Columbus, intraracial debate on the school question was complicated by resentment over the school board's foisting of a separate
junior high school on East Side blacks. The controversy tended to
cross ideological and generational lines. The opposition, composed of
a small, dedicated circle of older men and a few young professionals,
pressed its case in the courts between 1908 and 1913, only to lose at
both common pleas and circuit levels when judges ruled that the
board's gerrymandering of school districts was legal. But black
opinion was deeply divided at Columbus, and the opposition was
weakened by the fact that little remained of the city's late nineteenth-
century black leadership. It was suggestive of its weakness that it
depended on the active participation of several older outsiders,
Cleveland's Harry Smith, Chillicothe's Charles Doll, and Xenia's
Campbell Maxwell, who appeared at rallies and helped to plan legal
strategy. As Smith observed, Columbus blacks seemed unconcerned
with resisting the board. Most prominent young boosters provided
no opposition, and observers noted a groundswell of opinion for the
school among neighborhood blacks, who were said to be pleased at
the prospect of a large modern school staffed by black teachers. Perhaps fearful of being accused of accommodating white prejudice, no
local racial spokesman seems to have spoken out in favor of the new
school.[72]

While southern and central Ohio communities were creating new
educational and welfare institutions, and older men like Dabney
within them were being forced to change their views on the utility
of separate institutions and group-oriented self-help, there was no
counterpart of either trend in the cities of northern Ohio. The school
question was not raised at all—this was not surprising, since northern
Ohio schools had long been integrated, and there neither race had a
tradition of interest in separate schools. Migrations on various scales
occurred, but there was little or no attempt to deal with their consequences. Toledo and Youngstown black populations were growing, but
each still remained small (under 2,000, according to the 1910 census)
and failed to present the type of challenge found in larger cities. At

Education, Minutes, v. 1908–9, p. 36, v. 1909–11, p. 260; Crisis, XI (Dec., 1915),
61. (The Crisis article is wrong, however, in stating that a separate school existed
at Dayton.)
    [72] Columbus Ohio State Journal, May 15, 26, 1908, Aug. 23, 1910; Columbus
Dispatch, Aug. 5, 1910, Mar. 15, 1911; Cleveland Gazette, May 30, 1908, July 2,
Aug. 13, Oct. 1, 1910, Apr. 29, 1911; Cleveland Journal, Feb. 19, 1910; Columbus
Board of Education, Minutes, May 11, June 8, 1908, Aug. 29, 1910, Mar. 21,
1911, Jan. 13, 1913; Minor, "Negroes in Columbus," pp. 152–154; Brown, "Influences Surrounding the Establishment," p. 66,

the same time, the lack of significant growth hampered the development of group-oriented young boosters. Only after 1910 did the race market grow large enough that new groups began to develop. Since there was no corps of activists at either city to propose new institutional arrangements, the older leadership remained supreme, and it did little to institutionalize race social work.[73]

At Cleveland, however, where the migrations were of a much larger scale, the question of response became a major black community issue, and it led to bitter confrontations between the two groups of racial leaders. Nostalgia for the open race relations of an earlier era made it impossible for older men and women to support the creation of new black institutions, which they saw as capitulations to white prejudice and likely precedents for white-imposed segregation. Thus they opposed the young activists' proposals that all-black social centers be established to deal with the needs of the migrant poor. Coming at a time when the local YMCA and YWCA were both limiting black participation, the proposals were seen not as realistic alternatives to a dependence upon whites, but as accommodations to a hated change in race relations. Lacking the leverage to change the policies of private white institutions, and without white support for assaults on the color line, the older leadership refused to crusade against discriminatory policies. But it did attempt (with some success) to block attempts to create black alternatives which might play into the hands of prejudiced whites.

The most bitter and prolonged controversy, lasting from 1906 to the end of the period, concerned the call for the creation of a black YMCA branch in the Central Avenue area. The battle lines were largely generational: on one side, with the exception of two more militant young men (Harry E. Davis and Theodore Green, who sided with the elders), were the young boosters of the Cleveland Association of Colored Men and of the Central Avenue business community; they made their case through the *Journal*. On the other were the elders of black Cleveland, brought together in an unusual display of unity. As the conflict intensified, Harry Smith, the original member of the opposition, was joined by George Myers and other long-time residents such as Chesnutt, Walter Wright, and William Hunley. Of established

---

[73] The Indianapolis *Freeman*'s surveys of black community development at Toledo and Youngstown make it clear that many of the new enterprises were begun after 1910; ibid., Aug. 14, Sept. 11, 1915. The extent of institutionalized social work among Youngstown blacks was a rescue mission begun in 1905; Cleveland *Gazette*, Mar. 11, 1905. At Toledo in 1914, a number of working girls formed a recreational and educational club which met in private homes and rented a gymnasium for weekly exercise sessions; *Crisis*, XII (June, 1914), 61.

older leaders, only Carrie Clifford (for a short time before she moved to Washington) and John Green espoused the creation of the black Y branch; both explained their positions in terms of the need to provide forms of recreation as alternatives to streetcorner loitering. Prestigious older ministers of the Colored Minister's Union joined in the earliest calls for the establishment of a branch Y; however, all of them later sided with the opposition (as did Ira Collins) or simply refused to become involved in what soon became a heated controversy. For years both sides sniped at each other. Calling for a response to "real conditions and practical needs," the *Journal* accused older residents of lacking concern for the problems of the migrant poor. The *Gazette* dwelled on the dangerous precedent of self-imposed color lines, warning that school segregation would inevitably follow a separate Y. After it was discovered that several young boosters had met with Y officials early in 1907 in order to begin discussions on the creation of a branch, the *Gazette* inveighed bitterly against "Jim Crow Negroes" (who allied with prejudiced whites to segregate their own people) and against "yesterday Negroes" (more recently settled black Clevelanders, like Brascher, who presumed to know what was best for established residents).[74]

Matters did not come to a head until after the 1910 Rosenwald proposal provided blacks who favored the branch with a practical basis on which to organize a fund drive. The prospect of the young boosters going before wealthy white Cleveland as race leaders in order to solicit large sums of money for a "Jim Crow" project led Smith, Myers, and a dozen of their allies to take steps to check the proposal in 1911 once and for all. Their strategy was to destroy the possibility of a successful fund drive by influencing whites. Myers used his ties with the editor of the Cleveland *Plain Dealer* to obtain sympathetic coverage of the opposition's views, and he countered Brascher's effort to enlist Booker T. Washington's support in contacting white philanthropists. Myers informed Washington that the project was neither desired nor needed; doubtless because he was unwilling to become embroiled unnecessarily in a local dispute, and because Myers's prestige outweighed the ideological ties with Brascher, Washington did not allow his name to lend prestige to the project. As if the opposition's vast influence was not enough, in April, 1911, the *Journal* collapsed after prolonged financial agony, and Brascher was sent job-hunting,

[74] Cleveland *Journal*, Aug. 11, Oct. 6, 13, 20, 1906, Mar. 23, June 1, 1907, Jan. 23, 30, 1909, Jan. 15, Feb. 26, Mar. 5, 1910; Cleveland *Gazette*, Dec. 2, 1905, Aug. 18, Oct. 13, 1906, Mar. 3, 16, Apr. 20, June 15, 1907, Feb. 26, Mar. 9, 1910; Cleveland *Plain Dealer*, Feb. 1, 1911.

removing at once the major spokesman and institutional voice of the pro-branch forces. There was some further discussion of the need for a black Y, but the proposal did not recover from these setbacks before 1916.[75]

Older residents also attempted, without success, to block the efforts of Jane Hunter and her friends to develop a women's settlement house. Late in 1911 at an open meeting of the Working Girl's Home Association, black club women accused Hunter and other association members of attempting to bring segregation to the city; the club women urged that efforts be made to increase black use of the YWCA instead. But in a subsequent conference with Mrs. Levi T. Scofield, the chairwoman of the Y board of trustees, Hunter was told that black participation might drive whites away. Though sympathetic, Scofield frankly suggested that the black community take care of its own. A definite statement of policy did not help Hunter win the aid of established residents. Though John Green and several ministers encouraged her, most club women remained unsympathetic, and Smith's *Gazette* criticized her bitterly. Myers blocked her attempts to gain Washington's support. When Hunter, like Brascher before her, wrote to ask Washington's aid, the Tuskegeean requested particulars from Myers, who replied that Hunter was driven by a desire for notoriety and lacked "standing among the better class of our women." Because Myers stated that the proposed home was not needed, Washington did not help Hunter raise funds.[76]

Jane Hunter persevered. She went directly to wealthy whites, whose interest was quickened not only by her effective speeches but also by the support she received from Scofield and the philanthropic Henry Sherwin of the Sherwin-Williams Paint Company. Ultimately, however, her success was due as much to the modesty of her requests as

[75] Cleveland *Plain Dealer*, Feb. 1, 1911; Cleveland *Gazette*, Feb. 4, Mar. 16, Aug. 18, Oct. 13, 1911, July 2, 1912; Nahum Brascher to Booker T. Washington, Jan. 20 and Feb. 1, 1911, Emmett Scott to Nahum Brascher, Feb. 4, 1911, Box 418, George Myers to Booker T. Washington, Feb. 11, 1911, Booker T. Washington to George Myers, Feb. 17, 1911, Box 430, Washington Papers. A brief attempt to revive active interest in the YMCA project was made in 1914 when the ministers' alliance against discussed the matter, but again quickly backed off from involvement and confrontation. See Cleveland *Gazette*, Feb. 7, 14, 1914; Harry C. Smith to George Myers, Feb. 3, 1914, Box XVI, folder 4, Myers Papers.

[76] Jane Edna Hunter, *A Nickel and a Prayer* (Cleveland, 1940), pp. 90–94; Cleveland *Gazette*, Feb. 1, Mar. 15, 22, June 7, 1913, Jan. 17, 24, 1914; Jane Hunter to Booker T. Washington, June 17, 1914, and George Myers to Booker T. Washington, July 20, 1914, Box 841, and George Myers to Booker T. Washington, July 20, 1914, Box 509, Washington Papers; Harry Smith to George Myers, Apr. 10, 1914, and Booker T. Washington to George Myers, July 15, Aug. 4, 1914, Box XVI, folder 5, Myers Papers.

to white interest. The first annual budget of the Phillis Wheatley Home was only $1,500; in contrast to the $100,000 YMCA branches going up around Ohio, the home opened in 1913 in an old, though large, Central Avenue house which had been leased for its use. Despite its humble beginnings and the criticism which Smith continued to heap upon it, the home soon proved its usefuless. It provided lodging to the relatively few women whom it could accommodate; in addition, it made available its recreational facilities and counseling and employment services to much greater numbers. In the next decade, amidst massive migrations from the South, it emerged as a major force in the Cleveland black community.[77]

The Phillis Wheatley Home was the most significant self-help project undertaken at Cleveland before 1916, not only because of the importance of its work, but because, with the exception of the Cleveland Association of Colored Men's efforts in behalf of the indigent and sickly, little else was done by local blacks. Various minor efforts at creating small neighborhood centers, such as the one undertaken in 1912 by a few teenage parishioners of black St. Andrew's Episcopal Church, or that same year by some women's clubs, quickly failed for lack of method, support, and resources.[78] Yet the needs of the black community continued to grow. Worried by rising crime, conflicts between blacks and police, and growing disorder in the Central Avenue area, older residents responded as best they could, given the limitations which their larger views imposed. In 1915 Smith, Chesnutt, and others supported the establishment of a small, integrated settlement house at East 38th and Central. The effort was sponsored by the wealthy white Second Presbyterian Church. The two dedicated, young white social workers who supervised it, Russell and Rowena Jelliffe, were recent graduates of Oberlin. Their work resulted eventually in the founding of Karamu House, which much later distinguished itself nationally for its work among the poor and for its pioneering development of neighborhood theater.[79]

V

At the same time that blacks were debating to what extent they should voluntarily separate themselves from whites and estab-

[77] Hunter, *A Nickel and a Prayer*, pp. 95–108; Cleveland *Leader*, July 24, 25, 1913; Cleveland *Gazette*, June 26, 1915; Phillis Wheatley Association, *Annual Report, 1923* (Cleveland, 1924), p. 4; Russell H. Davis, *Black Americans in Cleveland from George Peake to Carl B. Stokes* (Washington, 1972), pp. 195–197.

[78] Davis, *Black Americans in Cleveland*, pp. 194–195; Cleveland *Gazette*, Aug. 31, Dec. 28, 1912.

[79] Cleveland *Gazette*, Feb. 7, 28, 1914, July 3, 1915; John Selby, *Beyond Civil Rights* (Cleveland, 1966), secs. I and II.

lish separate institutions, some of them were also involved in protesting the growing white-imposed segregation and general racial abuse found in their communities. As responses to individual insults in public places, such actions were not exclusively the province of older men; younger ones might also occasionally press suit when discriminated against in restaurants, theaters, and the like. This was particularly the case at Cleveland; since civil rights suits fared better in the courts there than elsewhere in Ohio, blacks, young and old, felt encouraged to file suit. Some of the approximately two dozen civil rights suits filed at Cleveland between 1900 and 1916 and reported in the Negro press were filed by young men and women. Attorney Theodore Green established his reputation for militance partly by handling such suits, both on behalf of himself and for other offended parties, usually his peers.[80] Elsewhere in Ohio these suits were almost always unsuccessful, but older men still chose occasionally to tilt at windmills in the courts. In 1911 the first civil rights suit to be pursued in many years, according to a local commentator, was filed by attorney Graham Dewell (counsel for Eva Gazaway in the 1882 Springfield school segregation case) against the proprietor of a Columbus establishment who refused to sell him a glass of soda. Few central and southern Ohio blacks of any age, however, cared to press a lawsuit, if it meant the time, effort, and meager reward it did for Dewell: he lost in a lower court but successfully took the matter through appeal, for the sake of principle. For his two years of effort, he ultimately received fifty dollars in damages.[81]

Protest activity resulting not from personal grievance but from a larger concern for the race's status was undertaken exclusively by those older men who were especially disturbed by deteriorating conditions. Only a few of the elders took part; age, apathy, and hopelessness were all taking their toll upon the militance which had, in the 1880s, led them to establish equal rights leagues in direct pursuit of racial justice. Then too, they had always been loath to act against discrimination in semi-public contexts where local white opinion was particularly set against race mixing. Thus the existing protest was always a product of individual or small group action among a handful of men. It was further limited by its ad hoc and random nature, its inconsistent and irregular efforts, and its cautious tactics.

[80] On Theodore Green's activities: Cleveland *Gazette*, July 29, 1899, Apr. 18, 1908; Cleveland *Journal*, Jan. 20, 1906. For other Cleveland civil rights suits see Cleveland *Gazette*, May 26, 1900, Feb. 1, May 24, 1902, Feb. 14, Mar. 21, 1903, July 16, 1904, Mar. 25, Apr. 29, May 27, July 1, 1905, Aug. 18, 1906, Jan. 30, 1909, Apr. 2, 1910, Mar. 11, 1911, Oct. 12, 1912, Jan. 31, 1914.

[81] Cleveland *Gazette*, Feb. 15, Aug. 23, 1913, Apr. 10, 1915; *Crisis*, III (Dec., 1911), 56, and VI (Aug., 1913), 168.

A few examples suggest the range and method of these activities. In a largely symbolic attempt to impede the northward progress of the southern example, Dabney, Smith, and Scarborough, alone or in combination, frequently undertook letter-writing campaigns and lobbied before the governor and state railroad commissioner, demanding that trains entering Ohio from the South be forced to take down signs marking segregated cars.[82] They also urged blacks to file suit against proprietors guilty of discrimination; in addition, Smith often wrote angry letters (always reprinted in the *Gazette* as morale-boosting examples of militance) demanding, for example, that a store owner remove an offensive sign, or that a theater or the restaurants in both the Bailey and the May companies' departments stores stop mistreating blacks. Accompanied at times by threats to mobilize a boycott, this barrage of letters and propagandizing via the *Gazette* occasionally won promises of changes in policy.[83] However, when Smith in 1904 began a long, emotional campaign against the defamatory treatment of blacks in the Cleveland daily press, particularly the *News* and the once-tolerant *Leader* (now under new ownership), his efforts produced little besides greater concern among blacks.[84] Back at Columbus after leaving government service, Ralph Tyler engaged in similar activities. While theater segregation was too well entrenched to be uprooted by one angry individual, Tyler campaigned through sometimes heated discussions with police and movie house owners against the "Jim Crow" signs publicly displayed in front of theaters.[85] For years George Myers constituted a successful, virtually one-man lobby against union-sponsored bills to regulate barbering because he felt that they would be injurious to black barbers; too, in 1906 he and Smith persuaded Cleveland school board officials not to allow Tillman to give his scheduled address before a local teachers' group.[86]

Thus methods were moderate and goals were often limited and defensive. But to the extent that these activities involved public confrontation, they were by no means mild at the time. There were few contemporary models for more militant protest, and accommodation was practiced and preached by many blacks and expected by the

[82] Cleveland *Gazette*, June 1, 15, 29, Aug. 17, 1901, Sept. 24, 1904, Aug. 12, Sept. 23, 1905, Jan. 13, May 4, 1912.
[83] Cleveland *Gazette*, Oct. 15, 1904, Mar. 25, 1905, June 20, 1908, July 26, 1913, Apr. 3, 10, 17, May 1, 1915.
[84] Ibid., Nov. 18, 1905, Jan. 13, 20, Mar. 17, Aug. 4, 11, 18, 1906, Jan. 5, 26, June 15, 1907, Jan. 2, 9, 23, Apr. 24, 1909; *Crisis*, VII (Jan., 1914), 126–127.
[85] Cleveland *Gazette*, Mar. 27, 1915.
[86] Ibid., Nov. 24, 1906, and above, ch. 12, note 44.

overwhelming majority of whites. The last point was crucial: few indeed were the whites who would support an organized assault on the color line at the expense of social order and widely held views sanctioning racial separation. Under the circumstances, and given the delicate balance upon which racial peace rested in Ohio, such tactics and limited goals were not unrealistic for a handful of men within a small black minority, governed and policed by whites and dependent upon them, as was Myers, for their livelihood.

Moreover, the methods of these older men were certainly more direct and purposeful than those of young boosters. On the occasions when the new generation chose to deal with discrimination, its approach was not one of active, vocal protest or confrontation, but of quiet efforts to influence the general racial climate in the direction of tolerance through contacts with influential whites and education of the white community. Though it was primarily concerned with fighting crime and vice and improving relations with police, Columbus's booster-controlled Civic Betterment and Protective League also attempted to check "the depressing spread of colorphobia" by seeking alliance "with the best-thinking white people . . . generous in their thoughts and ways of justice and fair play"; it tried to combat "the doctrine of hate" with "gentle reminders" to local whites of the need for tolerance.[87]

The same method was used by the Cleveland Association of Colored Men. However, Theodore Green [88] and a few other more militant members eventually caused the C.A.C.M. to take a more direct interest in discrimination. Its militance seemed to vary directly with the distance of its targets from Cleveland: while it sent lobbyists to Columbus in 1913 to join the ad hoc black committees fighting the anti-intermarriage bill, it took no independent initiatives challenging local discrimination. Instead, the association awaited occasional complaints voiced by individuals who had encountered abuse in some public accommodation. While Smith might have tried to persuade the offended party to go to court, the C.A.C.M. instead chose an informal committee of members to investigate the affair. Working quietly and without publicity, the committee talked with proprietors, urging them to reverse or modify their policies.[89]

It is not clear what, if any, practical results were derived from

[87] Indianapolis *Freeman*, Aug. 29, 1914.

[88] Cleveland *Gazette*, Dec. 4, 1909, notes Green's active dissent from the association's moderation on racial discrimination, and his urging of greater militance.

[89] Cleveland *Journal*, Sept. 5, 1908, Jan. 16, 1909; Jones et al., *The Cleveland Association of Colored Men*, p. 2.

such an unaggressive approach. But while members of the C.A.C.M. were engaged in consultations with proprietors, they cast doubt upon their commitment to opposing the color line by temporizing with discrimination when it was convenient to do so. Though Smith urged blacks to boycott Cleveland's leading amusement park, Luna Park, because of its mistreatment of blacks, the association held its popular public fund-raising outing there year after year. Even on the day of the outing, a number of facilities were either closed to blacks or available to them only at special times.[90] Nor would the association censure one of its number, S. C. Green, for closing his roller skating rink to blacks during several nights of the week in order to attract white patronage. Smith's friend Walter Brown, a streetcar conductor, challenged Green with a successful lawsuit, and it was the *Gazette*, rather than the association's voice, the *Journal*, which exposed him.[91] Nor would the association and the *Journal* cooperate with Smith's campaign against those Cleveland dailies which regularly mocked the race. In the face of Smith's criticism for its acceptance of advertising from the Cleveland *News*, the *Journal* at first praised the *News* for its community service and spoke of the need for good relations with powerful white institutions. Eventually Brascher admitted that the *News* was hurting the image of blacks, but he stated frankly that the race was not influential enough to successfully oppose the policies of the white press, and that the *Journal* needed all the advertising revenues it could obtain.[92]

Emerging national protest movements offered black Ohioans the chance to act upon the realization that the decline of northern race relations was tied to events in the South. However, their response evolved within this framework of hesitancy, accommodation, conflicting interests, and militance. The all-black Niagara Movement, established in 1905 to propagandize for the conservation of black rights and to oppose the accommodationist leadership of Booker T. Washington, found its greatest strength in Ohio in older racial leaders like Smith, Green, Chesnutt, Scarborough, Jackson, and Carrie Clifford.[93] Loyalty to Washington and to the Republican party, which the

[90] Cleveland *Journal*, July 17, 24, Aug. 7, 1909; Cleveland *Gazette*, July 6, 20, 27, Aug. 3, 10, 24, 1912, July 26, Aug. 9, 23, Oct. 4, 1913, June 27, 1914, July 17, 1915.

[91] Cleveland *Gazette*, Jan. 16, 23, 30, Mar. 6, 1909.

[92] Cleveland *Journal*, July 28, Aug. 11, Sept. 8, 1906, Jan. 5, Feb. 2, 1907.

[93] Carrie Clifford to Charles Chesnutt, Oct. 9, 1909, Charles W. Chesnutt Papers, FU; D. C. Fisher to W. E. B. Du Bois, June 6, 1905, Robert Barcus to W. E. B. Du Bois, Sept. 9, 1908, E. C. Williams to W. E. B. Du Bois, Jan. 20, 1909, W. E. B. Du Bois Papers (in the custody of Herbert Aptheker).

nonpartisan Niagara Movement frequently criticized, still led others of their generation to fight the movement. Out of such loyalties, Myers and Tyler conspired successfully to convince the Associated Press to institute a news blackout of the movement's 1908 convention, held at Oberlin College.[94] The few younger men who were attracted to the movement, like Cincinnati's William Stevenson and Chesnutt's son-in-law Edward C. Williams, tended to be from older families.[95] Most younger professionals and businessmen kept their distance. When Frederick L. McGee, an officer of the Niagara Movement, came before Cleveland's most prominent young boosters at a dinner in January, 1908, to explain its purposes, he was given a courteous hearing but made few converts. Brascher explained a short time later, after reviewing the evening's events, that the movement stood for "war," while Washington's "Tuskegee Plan" stood for "arbitration." "We believe," said Brascher with unusual vigor, "in arbitration as long as it can be carried on successfully without equivocation and deceit. Where there can be no arbitration let us fight. . . ." Hopeful, conciliatory, and cautious as Brascher and his allies were, they nevertheless continued to consider arbitration possible and fighting unnecessary, if not dangerous. Before long Brascher was engaged in bitter criticism of the Niagara Movement. At the time of its 1908 convention he branded its members "intellectual agitators"; their activities were as dangerous to the race, he said, as those of the white hoodlums responsible for several days of recent anti-Negro rioting at Springfield, Illinois.[96]

The integrated NAACP, dedicated from its founding (in 1909) to aggressive interracial protest against all color lines and to opposition to Washingtonian accommodation, also faced formidable obstacles in taking root in Ohio. Though a few influential blacks (like Smith, Dabney, Scarborough, and Chesnutt) and whites (like Oberlin President H. C. King, Western Reserve University President Charles F. Thwing, and Toledo's progressive Mayor Brand Whitlock) [97] had frequent contact with the national office, at the local level the NAACP experienced difficulties in interesting both races and in creating

[94] Oberlin *News*, Aug. 26, Sept. 2, 9, 1908; George Myers to Charles Otis, Sept. 3, 1908, Ralph Tyler to George Myers, Sept. 9, 1908, Box XIV, folder 5, Myers Papers; Ralph Tyler to Booker T. Washington, Sept. 4, 1908, Box 8, Washington Papers.

[95] Du Bois correspondence, cited above, note 93.

[96] Cleveland *Journal*, Jan. 4, Sept. 12, 1908.

[97] Charles Flint Kellogg, *NAACP: The National Association for the Advancement of Colored People, v. I, 1909–1920* (Baltimore, 1967), p. 48, note 7, and pp. 298–301.

branches. It was not easy to find whites who would commit themselves to the association's militant methods and integrationist goals. In 1910 Chesnutt wrote to William English Walling, a white socialist who was one of the NAACP's founders, stating that he could not think of a "half-dozen white people who would take an active, not to say aggressive part, in the movement" at Cleveland. In fact, early efforts to involve whites yielded only a few clergymen and public officials, dedicated enough, yet isolated from white opinion.[98] At Springfield the attempt to enlist whites through the good offices of a sympathetic ex-state senator failed utterly.[99] Among blacks, personal and ideological loyalty to Washington vied with apathy and the demoralizing effect of finding few whites interested in shaping responses. At Cleveland in 1910 Myers worked successfully to have rescinded a motion, which had been passed by the C.A.C.M. at the request of Chesnutt and Walling, mildly supporting the association. Myers claimed before the C.A.C.M. that the NAACP sought to discredit Washington.[100] At Columbus, where young boosters were almost unchallenged as the most powerful element of race leadership, little interest was shown during the association's first years. Indeed, a local *Gazette* correspondent, commenting in 1915 on the years of local indifference to the association, said the city had been "long-regarded as a Washington stronghold." [101] While interest was taken by younger leaders at Cincinnati, that interest was indeed suspicious. One leading early local NAACP activist was Francis Russell; his defense of separate public schools directly contradicted the spirit of the association, and his larger racial views were purely Washingtonian. Russell brought some like-minded young teachers from Douglass School into the association with him. It is not likely that Russell or his allies had come into the NAACP ignorant of its militance. Instead, as Dabney contended, they probably sought to take over the local organization, intending to gear it toward a Washingtonian view of racial advancement. Therefore it was not surprising that while Russell was actively engaged in organizing NAACP rallies, he was also known to be speaking publicly against the association's journal, the *Crisis*, for its emphasis on the depressing trends of contemporary race relations.[102]

[98] Ibid., pp. 54–55; Cleveland *Gazette*, Jan. 31, 1914.

[99] "Spingarn Trip-Committees and Supplementary Data," note dated 1914, Box C-75, NAACP Papers, LC.

[100] George Myers to Booker T. Washington, Oct. 31, 1910, Box 909, and Dec. 14, 1910, Box 430, Washington Papers; Cleveland *Gazette*, Dec. 3, 1910.

[101] Cleveland *Gazette*, Feb. 27, 1915.

[102] Wendell Phillips Dabney to May Childs Nerney, Feb. 19, 1915, Box G-155, NAACP Papers, LC.

In spite of these difficulties, local branches slowly emerged. By 1916 every major city (save Youngstown), as well as tiny Oberlin, had the benefit of the NAACP's formal presence.[103] Information on the personnel of the early branches is sketchy, but two generalizations are possible. First, both leaders and followers were mainly black, with a few whites (generally clergymen and public officials) participating on the ancillary advisory committees. Second, leadership among blacks was derived from the ranks of both older and younger men, though in varying numbers and complex patterns according to locality.

At Cleveland, the affiliation of a number of young men reflected their hope as members of a special interest group of using the association for their own limited though legitimate purposes. Though Smith and Chesnutt were active in the association from the beginning, a Cleveland branch was not formally established until 1913, when a number of postal clerks and their allies—most without experience in racial affairs, let alone in leadership roles—started a branch in order that they might have a vehicle for combatting white postal employees' demands for segregation at local post offices. The black clerks had heard that the association was fighting segregation in government offices at Washington, D.C., and this led them into the NAACP. Subsequently Chesnutt and a few older men, and some of the more militant younger ones (generally men like Harry E. Davis and Theodore Green, from older families) entered the local branch and took the highest leadership positions away from the more obscure founders. But the large majority of booster organization activists and pro-Washington advocates of group self-help and solidarity, including most members of the C.A.C.M., avoided the association, as did George Myers, Washington's most loyal older ally at Cleveland.[104]

Patterns of early NAACP leadership at Cincinnati and Columbus were both similar to and different from those found at Cleveland. At Cincinnati, the organization of a local branch in 1915 was accomplished without the leading young pro-Washingtonians, Russell and

---

[103] NAACP, *Completing the Work of the Emancipator: Six Years of Struggle toward Democracy in Race Relations* (New York, 1916), pp. 15–21; undated clipping (Dec., 1915), Oberlin *News*, Box G-167, NAACP Papers, LC. There was interest in forming a branch at Youngstown, but the association's national office encouraged blacks there to wait until they had a larger number of prospective members; May Childs Nerney to H. Skator, Feb. 20, 1915, and to J. Maynard Dickerson, Sept. 16, 1915, Box G-170, NAACP Papers, LC.

[104] "Charter Members of the Cleveland NAACP," typescript, Black History Archives, WRHS; Russell Jelliffe to author, Nov. 27, 1972; Russell H. Davis to author, Nov. 13, 1973; Cleveland *Gazette*, Jan. 10, 1914; NAACP, *Fourth Annual Report* (New York, 1914), p. 50, and *Fifth Annual Report* (New York, 1915), p. 18.

his teachers. They ultimately lost the struggle for control of local NAACP affairs to a few young men like William Stevenson and the West Indies–bred Reverend E. H. Oxley, and older ones like Dabney and C. R. Davis, a real estate agent and contractor.[105] But a Columbus branch was formed in that same year by the city's most influential young boosters (with the exception of Washington's most loyal local ally, Pearl Chavers). These young men experienced a sudden conversion to the NAACP. According to the *Gazette's* local correspondent, their transition from "the Washington policy of emphasizing farm labor and soft-peddling freedmen's rights [to the] preaching of equality before the law" was brought about by the "splendid impression" made by Joel Spingarn, the white chairman of the board of the national organization, in a speech made at Columbus in February. A local organization had arisen almost immediately after Spingarn's appearance; the *Gazette's* correspondent saw this as a "marvel," in light of the many "converts" who had past commitments to Washington.[106]

One might question the depth of conversions so hastily made; too, there was reason to wonder about the ideological consistency of some prime movers of the NAACP at Columbus and Cincinnati. While they felt the need to join in a national movement against color lines, some were also involved in local activities which responded to other racial needs at the expense of integration. At Cincinnati and (as the *Gazette's* correspondent noted, with full knowledge of the situation's irony) at Columbus, a number of those who established early branches were concurrently involved in separate welfare institutions. This was true for older men like Dabney and Davis, and for younger ones like Columbus attorney Robert Barcus, a leading figure in the fundraising drive on behalf of a black YMCA.[107] Thus, the complex practical and psychological demands of the time combined with the racial environments of southern and central Ohio to produce a strange alchemy of principle, expediency, and inconsistency in black responses.

Because of the delay in establishing branches and the varying degrees of commitment to the ethos and larger goals of the organiza-

[105] John T. Taylor to W. E. B. Du Bois, Feb. 22, 1915, Box C-155, NAACP Papers, LC.

[106] Cleveland *Gazette*, Feb. 27, 1915.

[107] It is interesting to note the appearance of the same names of the lists of early NAACP officers and on lists on leaders of fund-raising campaigns for the black YMCAs. Cf., for Columbus, Cleveland *Gazette*, Feb. 27, 1915; "Spingarn Trip-Committees and Supplementary Data" (list of officers), Box C-75, NAACP Papers, and Jesse Moorland to William C. Graves, Nov. 13, 1916, Rosenwald Papers; and for Cincinnati, John T. Taylor to W. E. B. Du Bois, Feb. 22, 1915, Box C-155, NAACP Papers, and Jesse Moorland to Julius Rosenwald, May 31, 1913, Rosenwald Papers.

tion, the Ohio branches could not accomplish much of practical value before 1916. Indeed, even then local branches were without systematic approaches and programs. None had been able to seize an initiative against local discrimination; their early activities were largely defensive reactions against individual problems. Yet when they did act, the NAACP branches showed skill and energy. Throughout Ohio they responded forcefully in opposing a spate of racially offensive films, particularly "The Birth of a Nation," and they often succeeded in having them banned or edited to remove offensive scenes.[108] In addition, the Columbus branch protested police brutality.[109] The Cleveland branch also protested police abuses, and it successfully obtained the removal of several "Jim Crow" signs and the firing of a public school teacher who mistreated her black students.[110] To be sure, such activities merely skimmed the surface of racial discrimination. Yet the organization of local NAACP branches and these early branch efforts were important steps toward reestablishing an organized, direct effort in behalf of racial equality of the sort which had not existed in Ohio since the long-gone 1880s. They marked the possibility that blacks might again take the offensive in a campaign for a fuller, freer citizenship.

108 Cleveland *Gazette*, Apr. 10, June 19, 1915; May Childs Nerney to Della Fields, Apr. 5, 1915, Box 33, S. B. Keeble to May Childs Nerney, Apr. 7, 1915, Box C-303, unsigned to NAACP, Nov. 1, 1915, Box C-301, NAACP Papers.

109 *Crisis*, XI (Nov., 1915), 34.

110 NAACP, *Completing the Work of the Emancipator*, p. 17. The branch was unsuccessful in its attempts to raise a legal defense fund in order to facilitate the prosecution of civil rights cases; "Report of the Cleveland Branch," Apr. 25, 1914, Box G-157, NAACP Papers.

Epilogue

Motivated by contradictory and contending emotions and attitudes, Ohio blacks had begun to meet the challenges of a new period in the race's history. Poised between fear and hope, between charity and misanthropy, between a longing after a once-promising past and a willingness to face a distressing present, they had begun to reach out to the migrant poor—to guide and assist on one hand, and to coerce and repress on the other. The latter response, seen most clearly in the call for law and order, drove apart the various elements of the race; the former, involving the further institutionalization of group-oriented self-help, attempted to bring them together in new bonds of solidarity and obligation. At the same time, in affiliating with a national movement dedicated to racial justice and an open society, Ohio blacks had begun to challenge the consequences of white America's change in racial attitudes.

To be sure, the steps they had taken were tentative. The revival of the protest tradition as demonstrated by their acceptance of the NAACP was at best merely incipient. It success would depend on the ability of blacks to conquer their great reluctance to openly challenge white racial views and discrimination and to resolve their own disagreement, seen most constantly after 1870 in the school issue, on whether the race should be willing to postpone full entrance into the American mainstream in favor of the construction of a vital, supportive racial community. The inability to resolve this last problem helps to account for the paucity and insufficiency of black welfare efforts. Though the situation varied from place to place, nowhere were these efforts confident, systematic, or comprehensive. The aged and the young, the unemployed and the destitute, the stranger, and the person in trouble with the law—all these needed more diverse assistance than existing black agencies could give or white agencies seemed willing to provide. Nowhere had the few existing black agencies coordinated their work for the sake of greater efficiency and hence better service to the race; nowhere did the new black endeavors have firm and routinized commitments of moral and financial support from their much wealthier and more experienced white counterparts.

The irresolute black response reflected the hesitancy of a leadership divided against itself by history, experience, ideology, and self-interest. The older generation had known years of relative progress in race relations and a hope for imminent social acceptance; distant from the masses, and individualistic in their attitudes toward racial advancement, the older leaders had not found it easy to effect separate arrangements to reach out to the migrant poor. The Old Guard's failure in northern Ohio was reinforced by a particularly intense longing for a uniquely tolerant but rapidly disappearing racial milieu. Yet the older leadership's reluctance to draw color lines, and its desire for racial equality and full participation in society, had tended to make it more willing to challenge the reactionary trend in race relations. In contrast, younger black Ohioans were born of more recent, menacing times; they had less difficulty embracing the race's need to turn inward and care for its own. Yet their very concern for intraracial development reinforced an unwillingness, bred of a lack of faith in the possibility of attaining full equality, to challenge the hostility of white America. Occasionally individuals in one camp had been able to build bridges to the other and cast off the limitations of each viewpoint, but large differences still remained. A synthesis of the best of both views was needed, for the race had to continue to take special responsibility for its own, and at the same time to insist upon equal opportunity and civil status if its citizenship was to be fulfilled.

Between 1915 and 1920 the need for this synthesis became especially clear. The problems which had become manifest after the turn of the century grew even more prominent. Migration from the South reached unprecedented proportions; new wartime opportunities beckoned from burgeoning northern foundries, factories, and mines. At a time when agricultural depression, floods, and the boll weevil were undermining the southern cotton economy and war in Europe was cutting off the flow of cheap immigrant labor, tens of thousands of southern blacks found their way to Ohio. Largely on the basis of wartime migration, Ohio's black population rose by 70 percent between 1910 and 1920, from 111,452 to 186,187. Like their predecessors, the new migrants were bound for the cities. Cleveland experienced a quadrupling of black population—after Detroit's, the largest such rate of increase in any major city at the time. By 1920 there were 34,454 blacks in Cleveland, over 26,000 more than in 1910. Some other cities had experienced very little pre-war migration; though their increases were not necessarily as large, they were no less dramatic. Cincinnati's black population increased by a third, while Columbus's and Dayton's doubled, Toledo's and Youngstown's tripled, and Akron's increased almost tenfold. Nor would the migration stop. Long after the wartime boom had ended, blacks continued to leave the South in search of opportunity and dignity.[1]

The consequences of this epic migration were many and varied, but the chief result was an acceleration of trends already underway.[2] Huddled together in increasingly large concentrations in decaying, congested neighborhoods, suffering from disease, low wages, periodic or chronic unemployment, discrimination, and the dislocations of re-settlement, the black newcomers needed practical assistance just as had those who came before them. Black institutions and leaders could no longer easily evade their responsibility to recognize the need and to respond vigorously to it. At the same time, the growing presence of these southern migrants severely strained the limits of an already weakened white tolerance. Ohio cities avoided the bloody race riots which swept the nation in 1919, but that hardly implies that whites greeted black newcomers with open arms. In relations with police, in the on-going development of segregation and discrimination, and in less evident indicators of racial tension, the strain became evident. As a consequence, it became more difficult for racial leadership to avoid taking a more public role and adopting more militant tactics in the struggle against discrimination. The alternative was to be swept up helplessly in the approaching wave of repression and proscription.

While these massive migrations exacerbated existing problems, they also provided a demographic foundation for unprecedented black community development and for the emergence of greater solidarity among urban blacks. Now more than ever the vision of a semi-autonomous black community within the city (an idea which had earlier excited the booster) had meaning; growing residential segre-gation and constant black population increases expanded the area of

[1] Bureau of the Census, *Negroes in the United States, 1920–1932* (Washington, 1935), pp. 9, 12, 32, 62–63; Emmett J. Scott, *Negro Migration during the War* (New York, 1920), pp. 14–16, 17–58.

[2] Remarks based on William Giffin, "The Negro in Ohio, 1914–1939" (Ph.D. dissertation, Ohio State University, 1968); Kenneth Kusmer, "Black Cleveland: The Origins and Development of a Ghetto, 1890–1930" (Master's thesis, Kent State University, 1970); Louise Venable Kennedy, *The Negro Peasant Turns Cityward: Effects of Recent Migration to Northern Centers* (New York, 1930); and Scott, *Negro Migration during the War*, pp. 126–129.

the city which was associated exclusively with blacks and deepened the strength of that association. One result, along with the steady decline of late nineteenth-century upper-class leadership, was the ascendance to power of the generation which had come of age after the turn of the century. The migrations produced a more solid base for black business and black professionals, giving boosterism and the business ethos more fertile soil in which to develop; in addition, they supplied the basis for a resurgence of black political influence at the urban ward level. The new style of urban leadership, taking its cues from the social potential which it saw in the black neighborhood, was now based on firmer economic and political grounds. Thus, for all its frustrations, the vision of the boosters and their allies grew more attainable with the passage of the decades.

Yet time would reveal the profound limitations of that vision as a chart for racial advancement. Northern blacks would not think it enough to develop their own separate communities within the city; they would also come to insist upon a full recognition of their humanity and equality. The wretched lives of the black poor in the North's industrial cities, and the expectations and energies unleashed by the migration to these cities, would ultimately place the masses of northern blacks firmly behind efforts to destroy a time-honored national structure of racial privilege. In this way the vision that had inspired the efforts of the 1880s also gained relevance with the passage of the decades, and the synthesis of responses which had eluded black leadership at the turn of the century would come closer to realization.

A Note on Sources

Manuscript Collections

Researchers, especially those working on regional or local black social and political history, have often noted the paucity of manuscript collections of major racial spokesmen. I was particularly fortunate to have had access to two very rich but generally underutilized collections—those of Clevelanders John Green and George A. Myers. Students of late nineteenth and early twentieth century Afro-America may profit greatly from both collections, for their materials provide great insight into black politics and leadership, nationally as well as locally and regionally. While lacking information on Myers's pre-1890 years, the George A. Myers Papers at the Manuscripts Division of the Ohio Historical Society in Columbus contains a wealth of correspondence on black political life at all levels of politics—particularly for the 1890s and first years of the twentieth century, when Myers was deeply involved in politics because of his close ties with the then ascendant Hanna-McKinley forces. The large majority of the collection consists of correspondence between Myers and his black Ohio allies concerning routine matters of patronage, political strategy, and electioneering; there are also some letters from powerful white politicians like Mark Hanna. The collection provides an excellent view of the workings of a contemporary black political "machine": its perceptions of power, its methods, its hopes, anxieties, failures, and triumphs. There are a few letters from blacks outside the state, including Booker T. Washington and various black political leaders and officeholders. Some interesting letters can also be found on social and lodge matters, and there are others which give an important insight into the running of Myers's Hollenden House barbershop, one of the most successful black enterprises of the day. The collection is comprised of seventeen boxes of correspondence and one box of clippings and miscellaneous printed materials, including several biographical sketches of Myers. In *The Barber and the Historian: The Correspondence of George A. Myers and James Ford Rhodes, 1910–1923* (Columbus, 1956), John A. Garraty has brought together the small number of letters exchanged by Myers and one of the leading American scholars of the day who frequented Myers's shop when a resident of Cleveland. These letters are deposited at the Massachusetts Historical Society; together with Garraty's useful introduction, they provide an interesting overview of Myers's life and thought.

Larger than the Myers collection, the John P. Green Papers at the Western Reserve Historical Society provide a more diversified assortment of correspondence. In addition to letters on political affairs which relate to Green's numerous candidacies for elective and appointive office, there is a large amount of correspondence concerning his long legal career in Cleveland, the battles against racial discrimination, leadership struggles in Cleveland and nationally, and social matters, including membership in the Cleveland Social Circle; there are also letters relating to Green's years as a state legislator, and to his tenure as U.S. postage stamp agent. In addition to the Green collection, the Western Reserve Historical Society has gathered other collections which shed light on the history of Cleveland blacks. These are generally oriented to the post–World War I era, but I was able to make use of materials which have been collected on the Cleveland NAACP and the Phillis Wheatley Home.

Three considerably smaller collections were of some use to me. The Charles W. Chesnutt Papers at Fisk University contain some material on racial affairs in Cleveland, though most items concern Chesnutt's literary career. The William Sanders Scarborough Papers at the Carnegie Library of Wilberforce University contain some items relevant to black political life and to the Wilberforce administration, including the relationship of the university to the state of Ohio. The Wendell Phillips Dabney Papers at the Cincinnati Historical Society contain little correspondence but some interesting printed materials, including pamphlet-size works by Dabney.

Of major importance to any student of black history in these years is the mammoth collection of Booker T. Washington Papers at the Manuscripts Division of the Library of Congress. The broad range of Washington's correspondence with blacks and whites throughout the nation gives one a full appreciation of the meaning of the term "Tuskegee Machine"—used to describe the informal network of power (black and white contacts, employees, and paid agents) through which Washington influenced, if not commanded, black affairs in his day. There is a great deal of correspondence on local politics and leadership struggles in the first decade of the twentieth century.

Collections of the major figures in Ohio and national politics were very useful in dealing with the relationship of Ohio blacks to the Republican and Democratic parties. At the Manuscripts Division of the Library of Congress, the collections of Presidents James Garfield, Grover Cleveland, Benjamin Harrison, William McKinley, Theodore Roosevelt, and William Howard Taft were consulted, as were those of Senators John Sherman and Joseph Benson Foraker. Larger and more significant, especially in regard to the senator's role in the Brownsville affair, is the collection of Foraker papers found at the Cincinnati Historical Society. The Hayes Library at Speigel Grove in Fremont, Ohio, has some items relating to black politics during Hayes's presidency and to the reception of Hayes's southern policy by blacks. Useful for the light they shed on black participation in state and local politics are several collections at the Manuscripts Division of the Ohio Historical Society. These include the papers of Governors Edward Noyes, George Hoadley, Asa Bushnell, George K. Nash, Myron Herrick, Andrew Harris, Judson Harmon, and James M. Cox, and of Republican party leaders Charles Kurtz and Arthur Garford, and Senator Charles Dick.

Finally, several collections were helpful in dealing with specific aspects of the past. The Albion Winegar Tourgee Papers at the Chautauqua County Historical Society at Westfield, New York, were of use in tracing anti-lynching efforts in Ohio. (These materials are now available on microfilm.) The Julius Rosenwald Papers at the Joseph Regenstein Library of the University of Chicago are an important source for the study of the origins of the black YMCA movement in the early twentieth century. Finally, the papers of the National Association for the Advancement of Colored People at the Manuscripts Division of the Library of Congress are weak in information on the association's first decade, but they still serve as an indispensable source for understanding the formation of major NAACP branches.

Newspapers and Magazines

The research for this study has been largely based on newspapers, black and white. The most important of these is the quite remarkable Cleveland *Gazette*, published weekly between 1883 and 1941 under the supervision of its indefatigable editor, Harry C. Smith. Available on microfilm, the *Gazette* represents a singular example of continuity in black journalism, spanning eras of race relations. Also helpful were other Ohio black newspapers, particularly the Cleveland *Journal* (1903–10). Scattered issues also exist for the Cleveland *Aliened American* (1853), the Cincinnati *Colored Citizen* (1863–68), the Cincinnati *Colored Patriot* (1883), the Cincinnati *Afro-American* (1885), the Columbus *Free American* (1887), the Dayton *Tattler* (1890, microfilm), the Xenia *Standard and Observer* (1901), and the Columbus *Standard* (1901). There are also scattered issues of E. W. B. Curry's monthly newspaper the *Urbana Informer* (1902–3). I was unable, however, to locate any pre–World War I issues of Wendell Phillips Dabney's Cincinnati *Union*, founded in 1907.

Some black newspapers from other cities are useful for their coverage of Ohio black politics, and for their letters from various Ohio cities and towns. Among these are the Harrisburg (Pa.) *State Journal* (1884), Martinsburg (W.Va.) *Pioneer Press* (1887–1912), New York *Globe* (1883–84), New York *Freeman* (1884–86), New York *Age* (1889–91), Richmond *Planet* (1896–97), Indianapolis *Freeman* (1897–1915), Washington *Bee* (1897–1906), Washington *Colored American* (1897–1904), Chicago *Broad Ax* (1906–7), and Baltimore *Afro-American Ledger* (1906–8).

Considering the small size of most Ohio black communities, one might have expected white newspapers to have relatively little coverage of black community matters. Surprisingly, however, much information can be found in the regular press. The following newspapers proved especially helpful, offering much information on black political and social life and local race relations, and were consulted generally throughout research on the late nineteenth and early twentieth centuries: the Akron *Beacon Journal*, Athens *Messenger*, Batavia *Clermont Sun*, Cincinnati *Commercial* (later, *Commercial Gazette* and *Commercial Tribune*), Cincinnati *Enquirer*, Cincinnati *Times-Star*, Circleville *Democrat*, Cleveland *Leader*, Cleveland *Plain Dealer*, Columbus *Dispatch*, Columbus *Ohio State Journal*, Columbus *Press-Post*, Dayton *Journal*, Gallipolis *Journal*, Ironton *Register*, Portsmouth *Tribune*, Springfield *Republic*, Steubenville *Herald*, Xenia *Gazette*, and Xenia *Torchlight*. Of particular note among the thousands of newspaper articles which I came across is George Myers's "Cleveland's Colored People," which appears in the Sunday magazine section of the Cleveland *Plain Dealer* for May 18, 1902, and contains information on many facets of black community life in the city at that time.

Also of use in charting the history of blacks in the coal mines of southern Ohio and in the United Mine Workers Union is the *United Mine Workers Journal* (1891–1915).

Of magazines, it should be noted that the following often carried brief, untitled articles, editorials, and random paragraphs of interest: the *Colored American Magazine* (1901–9); the NAACP organ, the *Crisis* (1910–15); and the *Voice of the Negro* (1904–7). Only one issue of the Cleveland blue vein *Social Circle Journal* (November, 1886) is known to exist, located in the Charles Chesnutt Papers at Fisk University.

Unpublished Theses and Doctoral Dissertations

The following theses and dissertations proved useful in varying degrees. On race and public education, the most helpful work was Leonard Erickson, "The Color Line in Ohio Public Schools, 1829–90" (Ph.D. dissertation, Ohio State University, 1959), which has a great deal of information about the origins of black public education in Ohio but is less comprehensive in its treatment of public school desegregation in 1887. Of use in understanding de facto segregation in Ohio after 1887 are G. Gwendolyn Brown, "The Influences Surrounding the Establishment of the Present Segregated Schools in Selected Cities of Ohio" (Master's thesis, Howard University, 1947); Mame Charlotte Mason, "The Policy of the Segregation of the Negro in the Public Schools of Ohio, Indiana, and Illinois" (Master's thesis, University of Chicago, 1917); and Thomas Paul Kessen, "Segregation in Cincinnati Public Education: The Nineteenth-Century Black Experience" (Ed.D. dissertation, University of Cincinnati, 1973). Some light is shed on blacks in the mines, in industry, and in the labor movement by John W. Lozier, "The Hocking Valley Miners' Strike, 1884–85" (Master's thesis, Ohio State University,

1963); Mahavira Prasada Shreevastva, "The Industrial Development of Springfield, Ohio: A Study of Economic Geography" (Ph.D. dissertation, Ohio State University, 1956); and John Delmer Truster, "Unionism among Ohio Miners in the Nineteenth Century" (Master's thesis, Ohio State University, 1947). Of use in understanding the development of local black communities are Jennie Braddock, "The Colored People and Greene County, Ohio, 1880–1865" (Senior thesis, Antioch College, 1953 [rev., 1962]); Thomas Goliber, "Cuyahoga Blacks: A Social and Demographic Study, 1850–80" (Master's thesis, Kent State University, 1972); Kenneth Kusmer, "Black Cleveland: The Origins and Development of a Ghetto, 1890–1930" (Master's thesis, Kent State University, 1970), published as *A Ghetto Takes Shape: Black Cleveland, 1870–1930* (Urbana, Ill., 1976); Leonard Harding, "The Negro in Cincinnati, 1860–70: A Demographic Study of a Transitional Decade" (Master's thesis, University of Cincinnati, 1967); Alma May, "The Negro and Mercer County" (Master's thesis, University of Dayton, 1968); Richard Clyde Minor, "Negroes in Columbus" (Ph.D. dissertation, Ohio State University, 1936); Ivan Tribe, "The Development of a Rural Community: Albany, Ohio, 1840–80" (Master's thesis, Ohio University, 1967); Shirla R. McClain, "The Contributions of Blacks in Akron, 1825–1975" (Ph.D. dissertation, University of Akron, 1975). On the treatment of blacks in the reportage of one of the state's most important daily newspapers: Sebron B. Billingslea, "The Negro, 1901–1920, As Portrayed in the Cincinnati *Enquirer*" (Master's thesis, Howard University, 1950), and Shirley M. Smith, "The Negro, 1877–98, as Portrayed in the Cincinnati *Enquirer*" (Master's thesis, Howard University, 1948). Of general use in the study of black association life are Monroe Fordham, "Major Themes in Northern Black Religious Thought, 1800–1860" (Ph.D. dissertation, State University of New York at Buffalo, 1973); A. E. Hardy, "A Study of the Organization and Operation of Rosenwald YMCAs for the period 1917–27" (Master's thesis, Ohio State University, 1928); and William Muraskin, "Black Masons: The Role of Fraternal Orders in the Creation of a Middle-Class Black Community" (Ph.D. dissertation, University of California at Berkeley, 1970), published as *Middle Class Blacks in a White World: Prince Hall Masonry in America* (Berkeley, 1975). Used in tracing the development of black politics were Thomas Cripps, "The Lily White Republicans: The Negro, the Party, and the South in the Progressive Era" (Ph.D. dissertation, University of Maryland, 1967); Thomas Felt, "The Rise of Mark Hanna" (Ph.D. dissertation, Michigan State University, 1960); Henry Siebert, "George Myers: Ohio Negro Leader and Political Ally of Mark Hanna" (Senior thesis, Princeton University, 1965); and Phillip Warken, "The First Election of Mark Hanna to the United States Senate" (Master's thesis, Ohio State University, 1960). Of interest for the study of race relations in Ohio and the North: Betty Culpepper, "The Negro and the Black Laws of Ohio, 1803–1860" (Master's thesis, Kent State University, 1965); Leslie Fishel, Jr., "The North and the Negro, 1865–1900: A Study in Race Discrimination" (Ph.D.

dissertation, Harvard University, 1954); David Fowler, "Northern Attitudes toward Interracial Marriage: A Study of Legislation and Public Opinion in the Middle Atlantic and the States of the Old Northwest" (Ph.D. dissertation, Yale University, 1963); Sarah Grace Rider, "The Negro in Ohio with Special Reference to the Influence of the Civil War" (Master's thesis, Ohio State University, 1931); Richard A. Folk, "Black Man's Burden in Ohio, 1849–1863" (Ph.D. dissertation, University of Toledo, 1972); William Griffin, "The Negro in Ohio, 1914–1939" (Ph.D. dissertation, Ohio State University, 1968). The following are biographies of black Ohioans: Gail Berry, "Wendell Phillips Dabney: Leader of Negro Protest" (Master's thesis, University of Cincinnati, 1965); Gossie Harold Hudson, "A Biography of Paul Laurence Dunbar" (Ph.D. dissertation, Ohio State University, 1970); Francis Richardson Keller, "Toward Human Understanding: The Life and Times of Charles W. Chesnutt" (Ph. D. dissertation, University of Chicago, 1974).

State and Local Studies

The best history of the state of Ohio is a multi-volume *History of the State of Ohio*. Edited by Carl Wittke and published during the 1930s and 1940s, the five-volume series covers the years before 1900, but there is work underway on a volume on the twentieth century. While these volumes trace the development of the state's internal regionalism, other useful works are J. D. Barnhart, "The Southern Influence in the Formation of Ohio," *Journal of Southern History*, III (Feb., 1937), 28–42; Robert E. Chaddock, *Ohio before 1850: A Study of the Early Influence of Pennsylvania and Southern Populations in Ohio* (New York, 1908); and David Carl Shilling, "Relations of Southern Ohio to the South during the Decade Preceding the Civil War," *Historical and Philosophical Society of Ohio Quarterly*, VIII, 1 (1913), 3–62. The published *Tracts and Manuscripts* series of the Western Reserve Historical Society contains many useful articles on the history of the Western Reserve.

On the history of blacks in the state, Charles T. Hickok's *The Negro in Ohio, 1802–1870* (Cleveland, 1896) is still a useful survey, though it is becoming antiquated in light of a growing monographic literature, much of which appears in the pages of *Ohio History*, the historical journal of the Ohio Historical Society. Frank U. Quillin's *The Color Line in Ohio* (Ann Arbor, 1913) contains some useful information based on the author's observations of race relations throughout the state around 1910, but it is severely compromised by Quillin's inability to transcend the racial attitudes of his era. Also of interest are William A. Joiner, ed., *A Half Century of Negro Freedom in Ohio* (Xenia, 1915); James H. Rodabaugh, "The Negro in Ohio," *Journal of Negro History*, XXXI (Jan., 1946), 9–29; Reuben Sheeler, "The Struggle of the Negro in Ohio for Freedom," *Journal of Negro History*, XXXI (Apr., 1946), 208–226; and Charles Wesley, *Ohio Negroes in the Civil War* (Columbus, 1962).

In addition to many published county histories, a number of works illuminate the history of blacks in various areas and communities. For Cincinnati there is the very useful and comprehensive volume of facts, biographical sketches, and short institutional histories by Wendell Phillips Dabney, *Cincinnati's Colored Citizens: Historical, Sociological, and Biographical* (Cincinnati, 1926). Historians have tended to concentrate on the antebellum history of the Cincinnati black community; see Richard W. Pih, "Negro Self-Improvement Efforts in Ante-Bellum Cincinnati, 1836–1850," *Ohio History*, LXXVIII (Summer, 1969), 179–187; Richard C. Wade, "The Negro in Cincinnati, 1800–1830," *Journal of Negro History*, XXXIX (Jan., 1954), 43–57; and Carter Woodson, "The Negroes of Cincinnati prior to the Civil War," *Journal of Negro History*, I (Jan., 1916), 1–22. These articles are of particular importance because they trace the unusually early development (for a midwestern black community) of traditions of self-help and racial social institutions, important to the later history of Cincinnati's blacks.

For Cleveland, Russell H. Davis, *Black Americans in Cleveland from George Peake to Carl B. Stokes, 1796–1969* (Washington, 1972), offers an impressive array of biographical and institutional information, but lacks a general interpretive framework. The history of Columbus's black community is told impressionistically in Columbus *Citizen-Journal* reporter Ben Hayes's ten-part series of newspaper articles (undated and on file at the Ohio Historical Society). Mary Louise Mark, *Negroes in Columbus* (Columbus, 1928), is an important history of the development of black residential neighborhoods in Columbus. Also useful is J. S. Himes, "Forty Years of Negro Life in Columbus, Ohio," *Journal of Negro History*, XXVII (Apr., 1942), 133–154, dealing with the first decades of the twentieth century; and Nimrod B. Allen, "East Long Street," *Crisis*, XXV (Nov., 1922), 12–16, which traces the development of the leading black residential section of Columbus during this century.

Aspects of black community life in the various towns of Greene County are illuminated by Wilhelmina Robinson, "The Negro in the Village of Yellow Springs, Ohio," *Negro History Bulletin*, XXIX (Feb., 1966), 103–104, 110–112; Helen Hooven Santemyer, *Ohio Town* (Columbus, 1962), a sensitive, evocative book on life in Xenia in the late nineteenth and early twentieth centuries, with many astute observations on race; Booker T. Washington, "A Negro College Town: The Uplifting Influence of Fifty Years' Growth of Wilberforce, Ohio," *World's Week*, XIV (Sept., 1907), 9361–67; and Richard R. Wright, Jr., "The Negroes of Xenia, Ohio: A Social Study," U.S. Department of Labor *Bulletin* no. 48 (Sept., 1903), 1006–43, an excellent survey of the socioeconomic status and institutional life of a turn-of-the-century black community.

Also useful were, for Springfield, Charles D. Swayne, *Facts and Figures about the Negro in Springfield and Clark County, Ohio . . . 1907* (Urbana, 1908), and Edwin S. Todd, *A Social Study of Springfield and Clark County, Ohio* (Springfield, 1904); and, on Oberlin, Alfred Vance Churchill, "Midwestern: The Colored People," *Northwestern Ohio Quarterly,* XXV (Autumn, 1953), 165–180, which, despite the author's paternalistic attitudes on race, offers some insight into race relations and the socioeconomic status of blacks in that community at the turn of the century.

Biographical Information

The following compilations of biographical sketches or general works containing biographical sketches were used: Hallie Q. Brown, *Homespun Heroines and Other Women of Distinction* (Xenia, 1926), and *Pen Pictures of Pioneers of Wilberforce* (Xenia, 1937); William Crogman, *Progress of a Race* (Naperville, Ill., 1902), and *New Progress of a Race* (Naperville, Ill., 1920); Russell H. Davis, *Memorable Negroes of Cleveland's Past* (Cleveland, 1969); M. A. Major, *Noted Negro Women* (Chicago, 1893); Irvine Garland Penn, *The Afro-American Press and Its Editors* (Springfield, Mass., 1891); Clement Richardson, ed., *National Encyclopedia of the Colored Race* (Montgomery, 1919); G. F. Richings, *Evidence of Progress among Colored People* (Philadelphia, 1903); W. H. Rogers, *Senator John P. Green and Sketches of Prominent Men of Ohio* (Washington and Cleveland, 1893); William B. Simmons, *Men of Mark: Eminent, Progressive, and Rising* (Cleveland, 1887); Susan M. Steward, *Women in Medicine* (Wilberforce, 1915); and Thomas Yenser, ed., *Who's Who in Colored America: A Biographical Dictionary of Notable Living Persons of African Descent in America* (Brooklyn, 1919, 1932).

Biographies and biographical articles used were Helen M. Chesnutt, *Charles W. Chesnutt: Pioneer of the Color Line* (Chapel Hill, 1952); Josephus R. Coan, *Daniel Payne—Christian Educator* (Philadelphia, 1935); Lucretia H. Coleman, *Poor Ben: A Story of Life* (Nashville, 1890), which tells of the progress of Benjamin Arnett from a poverty-stricken, accident-scarred boyhood to leadership in the A.M.E. Church; John Hope Franklin, "George Washington Williams, Historian," *Journal of Negro History,* XXXI (Jan., 1946), 60–90; E. L. Josey, "Edward Christopher Williams: Librarian's Librarian," *Negro History Bulletin,* XXXIII (Mar., 1970), 70–77; Richard Clyde Minor, "James Preston Poindexter: Elder Statesman of Columbus," *Ohio State Historical Quarterly,* LVI (Oct., 1947), 266–286; Dorothy Porter, "Phylon Profile XIV: Edward Christopher Williams," *Phylon,* VIII, 4 (1947), 315–321; and Francis Weisenburger, "William Sanders Scarborough: Early Life and Years at Wilberforce," *Ohio History,* LXXI (Jan., 1963), 25–50.

Autobiographies and memoirs which might prove useful to the researcher are Thomas Burton, *What Experience Has Taught Me* (Springfield, 1910); John P. Green, *Fact Stranger Than Fiction: 75 Years of a Busy Life* (Cleveland, 1920); Thomas Fleming, "My Rise and Persecution," a typescript in the possession of the Western Reserve Historical Society, the title of which refers to Fleming's struggle from poverty to election to the Cleveland city council, and his indictment and conviction in 1929 on charges of taking a bribe, which brought about a three-year prison term; Jane Edna Hunter, *A Nickel and a Prayer* (Cleveland, 1940); Reverdy Ransom, *The Pilgrimage of Harriet Ransom's Son* (Nashville, n.d.); and Sarah C. B. Scarborough and Bernice Sanders, eds., "Autobiography of the Life of William Sanders Scarborough," a typescript in the possession of T. K. Gibson of Chicago.

Occupations, places of business, and places of residence may be traced through city directories. These are generally available for major Ohio cities and towns for the years 1860–1915, although there are considerable gaps for some locations. The Ohio Historical Society and the Library of Congress have excellent collections of Ohio directories for major population centers, while local public libraries and historical societies usually have the directories for smaller ones. Numerous, often untitled, biographical sketches were found in the pages of the *Colored American Magazine* (1901–9). Finally, Carter Woodson, *Free Negro Heads of Families in the United States in 1830* (Washington, 1925), provided convenient data, taken from the pages of the manuscript federal census, on the pioneering black Ohio families.

Institutions, Organizations, and Self-Help

The most helpful sources for tracing the development of the major black social institution were church conference records, histories of individual congregations, and black newspapers. Published annually and containing statistical data on membership, expenses, and debts, as well as reports on national, racial denominational, and congregational matters, church conference records are an especially rich but often neglected source of information for historians. For Ohio's black churches, these published records are to be found conveniently in three major repositories. African Methodist Episcopal Church reports for both Ohio conferences (the Ohio and North Ohio episcopal districts) may be found in the very complete Benjamin Arnett Collection at the Carnegie Library of Wilberforce University. Composed almost solely of published church records, the Arnett Collection has conference records for episcopal districts outside Ohio, as well as an almost complete set of late nineteenth and early twentieth century Ohio conferences. Lacking carefully defined episcopal districts and centralized administration, the Baptists were less diligent in keeping records. Yet the American Baptist Historical Association at Rochester, New York, has a fairly complete collection of the published reports of the various Baptist state and regional organizations after the Civil War. Finally, the Ohio Historical Society has a number of A.M.E. and Baptist conference records in its pamphlet collection, while the society's Manuscripts Division has acquired a major collection, largely for the twentieth century, of the published records of the Ohio State Baptist Association. Church congregational histories are everywhere, but locating them requires patient digging in local archives and inquiring among congregations; those which I found are cited in the footnotes. Black newspapers regularly reported on church matters, as well as on the activities of black fraternal and sororal organizations. Also of use in viewing the development of the A.M.E. Church in Ohio in light of its development elsewhere were the annual *Budgets,* for many years edited by Bishop Arnett, and the mammoth *Centennial Budget* of 1887, which he also edited. Containing great quantities of statistical data on the church and its educational and missionary endeavors, these volumes are located in the Arnett Collection at Wilberforce.

Of more general use on black churches and black religion, in Ohio and the nation at large, are Benjamin Arnett, ed., *Proceedings of the Semi-Centenary Celebration of the African Methodist Episcopal Church of Cincinnati* (Cincinnati, 1874); George Bragg, *History of the Afro-American Group of the Episcopal Church* (Baltimore, 1922); G. Lincoln Caddell, "Brief History of the North Ohio Annual Conference of the A.M.E. Church" (n.p., 1948); W. E. B. Du Bois, *The Negro Church* (Atlanta, 1903); E. Franklin Frazier, *The Negro Church in America* (New York, 1964); Lewis G. Jordan, *Negro Baptist History* (Nashville, 1930); John H. Lamott, *History of the Archdiocese of Cincinnati, 1821–1921* (New York and Cincinnati, 1921); Daniel Payne, *History of the A.M.E. Church,* ed. C. S. Smith (Nashville, 1891), an indispensable volume with a great deal of information on the early development of the A.M.E. Church; A. W. Pegues, *Our Baptist Ministers and Our Schools* (Springfield, Mass., 1892); and Carter Woodson, *The History of the Negro Church* (Washington, 1921), the most complete history of black church life at present.

On fraternal and sororal organizations and other associational activities: Benjamin Arnett, *Biennial Oration before the Second B.M.C. of the Grand United Order of Odd Fellows . . . 1884* (Dayton, 1884); Harry E. Davis, *A History of Free Masonry among Negroes in America* (Cleveland, 1946); S. W. Green, Joseph L. Jones, and E. A. Williams, *History and Manual of the Colored Knights of Pythias* (Nashville, 1913); Howard C. Hopkins, *History of the YMCA in North America* (New York, 1951); and Charles Wesley, *The History of the Prince Hall Grand Lodge of Free and Accepted Masons of the State of Ohio, 1849–1960: An Epoch in American Fraternalism* (Wilberforce, 1961). Three of W. E. B. Du Bois's Atlanta University Studies (nos. 1, 10, and 12) survey black self-help and associational activities at the turn of the century and beyond: *Some Efforts of American Negroes for Their Own Social Betterment* (Atlanta, 1898); *Economic Cooperation among Negro Americans* (Atlanta, 1907); and *Efforts for Social Betterment among Negro Americans* (Atlanta, 1909).

On black initiatives in education in Ohio: Florence Brown and Jane Daily, "Enterprise Academy," typescript at Ohio University Library; E. W. B. Curry, *A Story of Curry Institute* (Urbana, 1907); F. Alphonse McGinnis, "The Curry School, Urbana and Its Founder," *Colored American Magazine,* IX (Oct., 1905), 555–565; Frederick A. McGinnis, *A History and Interpretation of Wilberforce University* (Blanchester, Ohio, 1941), a well-documented official history of Wilberforce which, while thorough in the subjects it chooses to treat, is limited by its refusal to deal with controversies in the school's past. Thomas Jesse Jones, *Negro Education: A Study of the Private and Higher Schools for Colored People in the United States*, U.S. Department of Interior, Bureau of Education, *Bulletin* no. 38 (Washington, 1917), II, 683–690, lists and describes all of the private black educational activities in the state in the years immediately before World War I, and also notes the development of the state-financed department on the Wilberforce campus.

Public Education

The manuscript *Minutes* of the Cincinnati, Columbus, and Dayton boards of education were consulted in tracing the creation of dual school systems, desegregation, and the movement toward separate schools after the turn of the century. The published *Annual Reports* of various school systems, including (for the years 1864–72) those of the black schools of Cincinnati, also proved useful. All nineteenth-century Ohio public school laws, including those relevant to the study of race and education, are conveniently summarized in E. A. Miller, "History of Educational Legislation in Ohio from 1803 to 1850," *Ohio State Archeological and Historical Quarterly*, XXVII (1918), 7–142, and Nelson Bossing, "The History of Educational Legislation in Ohio from 1851 to 1900," *Ohio Archeological and Historical Quarterly*, XXXIX, 1, 2 (1930), 78–219, 223–399. Also shedding light on race and public education in the state are George David, *The Effect of School Segregation in Xenia, Ohio* (Wilberforce, 1939); Leonard Erickson, "Toledo Desegregates," *Northwest Ohio Quarterly*, XXXXI (Winter, 1968–69), 5–12; John P. Foote, *The Schools of Cincinnati and Its Vicinity* (Cincinnati, 1855); Frederick A. McGinnis, *The Education of Negroes in Ohio* (Blanchester, Ohio, 1962); John B. Shotwell, *History of the Schools of Cincinnati* (Cincinnati, 1902); and Carter Woodson, *The Education of the Negro prior to 1861* (New York and London, 1915).

Politics and Civil Status

Several sources trace the history of legislation defining the civil status of Ohio blacks in the ante-bellum period. Helen M. Thurston, "The 1802 Ohio Constitutional Convention and the Status of the Negro," *Ohio History*, LXXXI (Winter, 1971), 15–37, deals with the origins of the state's Black Laws, while Leonard Erickson, "Politics and the Repeal of Ohio's Black Laws, 1837–49," *Ohio History*, LXXXII (Summer-Autumn, 1973), 154–175, deals with the first, and only partly successful, attempt to repeal them. Changes in the civil status of Ohio blacks during Reconstruction are developed in Felice A. Bonadio, *North of Reconstruction* (New York, 1970); George H. Porter, *Ohio Politics in the Civil War Era* (New York, 1911); and Edgar A. Toppin, "Negro Emancipation in Historic Retrospect, Ohio: The Negro Suffrage Issue in Post-Bellum Ohio Politics," *Journal of Human Relations*, XI (1962–63), 232–246. Placing black enfranchisement in Ohio in the context of the issue in other northern states and of national Republican politics is Leslie Fishel, Jr., "Northern Prejudice and Negro Suffrage, 1865–70," *Journal of Negro History*, XXXIX (Jan., 1954), 8–26. Gilbert T. Stephenson, *Race Distinctions in American Law* (New York and London, 1910), provides a convenient compilation of the laws advancing and proscribing black citizenship in all states during the late nineteenth and early twentieth centuries.

The best source for the study of black participation in state and local politics during the period is the press, black and white. Indeed, in an era of intensive political contention, virtually the only interest of many white dailies in local black communities concerned the size and direction of the black vote; the larger that vote and more independent-minded it threatened to become, the more active the interest. Supplementing the press, the state's *Ohio Statistics* provides annual data on the results of all major elections, state and national, with tallies for county, legislative, and congressional subdivisions. W. A. Taylor, *Ohio Statesman and Hundred Year Book* (Columbus, 1892), provides convenient lists of all black legislators and major appointees up to 1892.

Of interest in understanding politics in Ohio between 1870 and 1916 are Herbert Croly, *Marcus Alonzo Hanna: His Life and Work* (New York, 1923); Margaret Leech, *In the Days of McKinley* (New York, 1959); Thomas Powell, ed., *The Democratic Party of the State of Ohio* (n.p., 1913); Everett Walters, *Joseph Benson Foraker: Uncompromising Republican* (Columbus, 1948); Hoyt Landon Warner, *Progressivism in Ohio, 1897–1917* (Columbus, 1964), a most thorough history of political progressivism on the state and local levels; and Henry C. Wright, *Bossism in Cincinnati* (Cincinnati, 1905), a view of urban politics from a contemporary reformer's standpoint with some insight into the relationship between the black poor and the ward-heeler. Zane Miller, *Boss Cox's Cincinnati: Urban Politics in the Progressive Era* (New York, 1968), offers an interpretation of several decades of politics in the Ohio city with the largest black vote, and recognizes the role of complex class and interest factors in determining local black political allegiances.

Relevant for an understanding of the general position of blacks in northern politics and their evolving discontent with the party of Lincoln are Lawrence Grossman, *The Democratic Party and the Negro: Northern and National Politics, 1868–92* (Urbana, Ill., 1976); Vincent P. DeSantis, "Negro Dissatisfaction with Republican Policy in the South, 1882–84," *Journal of Negro History*, XXXVI (Apr., 1951), 148–159; Leslie Fishel, Jr., "The Negro in Northern Politics, 1870–1900," *Mississippi Valley Historical Review*, XXXXII (Dec., 1955), 466–489; Herbert Gutman, "Peter H. Clark: Pioneer Negro Socialist, 1877," *Journal of Negro Education*, XXXIV, 4 (1965), 413–418; and August Meier, "The Negro and the Democratic Party, 1875–1915," *Phylon*, XVII, 2 (1956), 172–191.

Index